D1595291

Knowledge Discovery in Databases

Knowledge Discovery in Databases

Gregory Piatetsky-Shapiro & William J. Frawley, editors

AAAI Press / The MIT Press

Menlo Park, California
Cambridge, Massachusetts
London, England

445 Burgess Drive
Menlo Park, California 94025

Copublished and distributed by The MIT Press, Massachusetts Institute of Technology, Cambridge, Massachusetts, and London, England.

ISBN 0-262-66070-9

First printed, February, 1991
Second printing, March, 1992
Third printing, May, 1993

Manufactured in the United States of America

Contents

Preface

The growth in the size and number of existing databases far exceeds human abilities to analyze this data. To cope with the data deluge, tools for intelligent data analysis have been developed by specialists in different areas, including machine learning, statistics, expert databases, and knowledge acquisition for expert systems. Growing research interest in discovery in databases, coupled with the realization that the specialists in these areas were not always aware of the state of the art in other areas, led us to organize a workshop on knowledge discovery in databases at the Eleventh International Joint Conference on Artificial Intelligence, held in Detroit, Michigan.

The workshop generated a tremendous international response, with 69 submissions from 12 countries on 4 continents. Many leading researchers in machine learning and other areas attended, along with government and industry representatives. A day of lively discussions (see *AI Magazine,* Volume 11, Number 5 for a workshop report) illuminated many issues important for discovery in databases.

This collection is composed of the best papers from the workshop, with a few additions, all rewritten to provide a uniform treatment of certain key issues, such as the use of domain knowledge in discovery, algorithmic complexity, and the treatment of uncertainty. Along with the introductory chapter, the collection gives a broad overview of the state of the art in research in knowledge discovery in databases.

This collection is the result of an outstanding cooperation of almost a hundred people on several continents. It is impossible to mention everyone by name, but we will mention a few. First, we thank our managers at GTE Laboratories, Shri Goyal, John Vittal, and Bill Griffin, for encouraging this effort throughout the last two years. Jaime Carbonell, Kamran Parsaye, Ross Quinlan, Michael Siegel, and Samy Uthurusamy were instrumental as the workshop program committee members. Their help, advice, and encouragement are much appreciated. Chris Matheus provided many excellent ideas and co-wrote the introductory chapter.

We received a lot of support from AAAI Press, especially from Sunny Ludvik, who did an excellent job of editing all the chapters, and Mike Hamilton, who ably coordinated the production and typesetting.

Finally, and most importantly, we thank Marina and Shirley for their wonderful patience and help.

– *Gregory Piatetsky-Shapiro and William J. Frawley.*

Foreword

John Ross Quinlan
University of Sydney, Australia

Knowledge Discovery in Databases is a pretty ambitious title for a workshop. After attending the event, I still regard it as ambitious but in the best sense of capturing the essence of something that is both achievable and worth attaining. To explain my reaction, let me dwell on the key words of the title.

Knowledge: In one of several illuminating essays on different facets of knowledge, Donald Michie (1986) identifies *concept expressions* as those correct and effectively computable descriptions that can also be assimilated and used by a human being. As a counterexample, he cites a case in which ID3 derived a decision tree for a chess end game from a complete set of positions. The tree was absolutely correct and computationally efficient but, alas, completely incomprehensible to human chess experts. As he put it, "It was not a question of a few glimmers of sense here and there scattered through a large obscure structure, but just a total blackout." In Michie's view, which I share, such a structure does not qualify as knowledge.

What, then, does qualify? Let me illustrate with reference to two historical successes. In the early 1970s, Edward Feigenbaum and his co-workers were demonstrating, via the Dendral project (Feigenbaum, Buchanan, and Lederberg 1971), that knowledge-based systems could attain high levels of proficiency. The domain for this pioneering achievement was the interpretation of mass spectrograms to reveal the structure of complex molecules. Heuristic Dendral contained explicit representations of large bodies of chemical knowledge, so a natural follow-on was to see whether some of this knowledge could be extracted from data. Bruce Buchanan, Edward Feigenbaum, Tom Mitchell, and others built Meta-Dendral to show that this was feasible. To quote Buchanan and Mitchell (1978),

> The Meta-Dendral program has successfully rediscovered known, published rules of mass spectrometry for two classes of molecules. More importantly, it has discovered rules for three closely related families of structures for which rules had not previously been reported. Meta-Dendral's rules for these classes have been published in the Chemistry literature.

Proof indeed: If chemists can use rules learned by the program, then these rules must be knowledge in Michie's sense.

Meta-Dendral is a special-purpose learning program, although it subsequently found rules for a quite different spectroscopic technique. Ryszard Michalski and his co-workers at the University of Illinois have been studying general learning techniques for some time, and in the late 1970s, they applied one of them, called AQ, to the problem of diagnosing soybean diseases (Michalski and Chilausky 1980). Not only did AQ find rules that outperformed those of their expert collaborator, but the same expert was so impressed that he adopted the discovered rules in place of his own!

Databases: As computers come to affect more and more aspects of modern society, one by-product is the growing amount of information that is captured in machine-readable form. Almost every transaction from a bank withdrawal to a car rental is recorded and archived somewhere. These days, a collection of data hardly qualifies as a database unless it contains many thousands of records. Such collections are potential lodes of valuable knowledge, but in order to extract the ore, we must have efficient mining tools. Although there is no universally agreed definition of "efficient," a useful benchmark is "of the same order as sorting," or $0(n \ log \ n)$ for an n-record database. Algorithms whose computational requirements grow substantially faster than $0(n^2)$ are unlikely to scale up well enough to tackle large applications.

Another important consideration is the form of the data. Most research commonly labeled as empirical learning has concentrated on the simple attribute-value format in which a record has a fixed number of constant-valued fields or properties. On the other hand, databases are often expressed as a set of *relations*, with multiple records for a single entity and fields that reference other records or relations. It is interesting that several projects are under way to port techniques from attribute-value data formats to these more structured formalisms, the one described in chapter 17 by Manago and Kodratoff being an excellent example.

Unfortunately, most live data is imperfect; some information is garbled, some missing. Anything we discover in such data will be inexact, in that there will be exceptions to every rule and cases not covered by any rule. Algorithms need to be robust enough to cope with imperfect data and to find in it regularities that are inexact but useful.

Finally, databases are characterized by growth. An ideal knowledge discovery method would be *incremental*, able to modify what has already been learned in the light of new information at hand. The last few years have seen an emphasis on incremental learning algorithms, such as those proposed by Schlimmer and Fisher (1986), Utgoff (1989), and others.

Discovery: Underlying all machine learning is the idea of *bias*, first enunciated by Tom Mitchell (1980). Any incomplete collection of data can be explained to the same degree by a (usually enormous) number of different theories. Settling on any one of them requires some criterion other than goodness of fit. Occam's razor is one such criterion, which suggests we should choose the simplest satisfactory theory.

This topic came up during a lively panel discussion at the conclusion of the workshop. The specific subject was the extent to which discovery programs should employ specialist knowledge of the domain in which they are attempting to learn. Clearly, information about the data itself and how it was assembled can only assist the knowledge discovery process. But providing knowledge about the domain may limit objectivity; we see what we expect to see, a very subtle bias. On the other hand, many argued that algorithms need to exploit what is already known about a domain if they are to make significant discoveries. Whether background knowledge is an asset or a liability is unclear as yet, at least to me.

As Feigenbaum, McCorduck, and Nii (1988) express it, "The history of technology shows us that we overestimate what a technology can do for us in a few years and underestimate what it can do in a decade or two." After a decade of fundamental interdisciplinary research in machine learning, the spadework has been done; the 1990s should see the widespread exploitation of knowledge discovery as an aid to assembling knowledge bases. Participants at the workshop were excited at the potential benefits of this research, and I hope that some of this excitement will communicate itself to readers of this volume.

References

Buchanan, B. G., and Mitchell, T. M. 1978. Model-Directed Learning of Production Rules. In *Pattern-Directed Inference Systems*, eds. D. A. Waterman and F. Hayes-Roth, 297–312. New York: Academic Press.

Feigenbaum, E. A.; Buchanan, B. G.; and Lederberg, J. 1971. On Generality and Problem-Solving: a Case Study Using the Dendral Program. In *Machine Intelligence*, volume 6, eds. B. Meltzer and D. Michie, 165–190. New York: American Elsevier.

Feigenbaum, E., McCorduck, P., and Nii, H. 1988. *The Rise of the Expert Company: How Visionary Companies Are Using Computers to Make Huge Profits.* New York: Random House.

Michalski, R. S., and Chilausky, R. L. 1980. Learning by Being Told and Learning from Examples: An Experimental Comparison of the Two Methods of Knowledge Acquisition in the Context of Developing an Expert system for Soybean Disease Diagnosis. *International Journal of Policy Analysis and Information Systems* 4(2): 125–161.

Michie, D. 1986. *On Machine Intelligence*, 2d ed. Chichester, England: Ellis Horwood.

Mitchell, T. M. 1990. The Need for Biases in Learning Generalizations. In *Readings in Machine Learning*, eds. J. W. Shavlik and T. G. Dietterich, 184–191. San Mateo, Calif.: Morgan Kaufmann.

Schlimmer, J. C., and Fisher, D. 1986. A Case Study of Incremental Concept Induction. In Proceedings of the Fifth National Conference on Artificial Intelligence, 496–501. Menlo Park, Calif.: American Association for Artificial Intelligence.

Utgoff, P. E. 1989. Incremental Induction of Decision Trees. *Machine Learning* 4(2): 161–186.

1 Knowledge Discovery in Databases: An Overview

William J. Frawley, Gregory Piatetsky-Shapiro, and Christopher J. Matheus
GTE Laboratories Incorporated

Computers have promised us a fountain of wisdom
but delivered a flood of data
– *A frustrated MIS executive*

Abstract

This chapter presents an overview of the state of the art in research on knowledge discovery in databases. We analyze *Knowledge Discovery* and define it as the nontrivial extraction of implicit, previously unknown, and potentially useful information from data. We then compare and contrast database, machine learning, and other approaches to discovery in data. We present a framework for knowledge discovery and examine problems in dealing with large, noisy databases, the use of domain knowledge, the role of the user in the discovery process, discovery methods, and the form and uses of discovered knowledge.

We also discuss application issues, including the variety of existing applications and propriety of discovery in social databases. We present criteria for selecting an application in a corporate environment. In conclusion, we argue that discovery in databases is both feasible and practical and outline directions for future research, which include better use of domain knowledge, efficient and incremental algorithms, interactive systems, and integration on multiple levels.

1.1 Introduction

It has been estimated that the amount of information in the world doubles every 20 months. The size and number of databases probably increases even faster. In 1989, the total number of databases in the world was estimated at five million, although most of them are small dbaseIII databases. The automation of business activities produces an ever-increasing stream of data because even simple transactions, such as a telephone call, the use of a credit card, or a medical test, are typically recorded in a computer.

Scientific and government databases are also rapidly growing. The National Aeronautics and Space Administration already has much more data than it can analyze. Earth observation satellites, planned for the 1990s, are expected to generate one terabyte (10^{15} bytes) of data every day—more than all previous missions combined. At a rate of one picture each second, it would take a person several years (working nights and weekends) just to look at the pictures generated in one day. In biology, the federally funded Human Genome project will store thousands of bytes for each of the several billion genetic bases. Closer to everyday lives, the 1990 U.S. census data of a million million bytes encode patterns that in hidden ways describe the lifestyles and subcultures of today's United States.

What are we supposed to do with this flood of raw data? Clearly, little of it will ever be seen by human eyes. If it will be understood at all, it will have to be analyzed by computers. Although simple statistical techniques for data analysis were developed long ago, advanced techniques for intelligent data analysis are not yet mature. As a result, there is a growing gap between data generation and data understanding. At the same time, there is a growing realization and expectation that data, intelligently analyzed and presented, will be a valuable resource to be used for a competitive advantage.

The computer science community is responding to both the scientific and practical challenges presented by the need to find the knowledge adrift in the flood of data. In assessing the potential of AI technologies, Michie (1990), a leading European expert on machine learning, predicted that "the next area that is going to explode is the use of machine learning tools as a component of large-scale data analysis." A recent National Science Foundation workshop on the future of database research ranked data mining among the most promising research topics for the 1990s (Silberschatz, Stonebraker, and Ullman 1990). Some research methods are already well enough developed to have been made part of commercially available software. Several expert system shells use variations of ID3 for inducing rules from examples. Other systems use inductive, neural net, or genetic learning approaches to discover patterns in personal computer databases.

Many forward-looking companies are using these and other tools to analyze their databases for interesting and useful patterns. American Airlines searches its frequent flyer database to find its better customers, targeting them for specific marketing promotions. *Farm Journal* analyzes its subscriber database and uses advanced printing technology to custom-build hundreds of editions tailored to particular groups. Several banks, using patterns discovered in loan and credit histories, have derived better loan approval and bankruptcy prediction methods. General Motors is using a database of automobile trouble reports to derive diagnostic expert systems for various models. Packaged-goods manufacturers are searching the supermarket scanner data to measure the effects of their promotions and to look for shopping patterns.

A combination of business and research interests has produced increasing demands for, as well as increased activity to provide, tools and techniques for discovery in databases. This book is the first to bring together leading-edge research from around the world on this topic. It spans many different approaches to discovery, including inductive learning, Bayesian statistics, semantic query optimization, knowledge acquisition for expert systems, information theory, and fuzzy sets. The book is aimed at those interested or involved in computer science and the management of data, to both inform and inspire further research and applications. It will be of particular interest to professionals working with databases and management information systems and to those applying machine learning to real-world problems.

1.2 What Is Knowledge Discovery?

The chapters in this collection vary widely in their focus and content, reflecting the immense diversity of current research on knowledge discovery in databases. To provide a point of reference for these works, we begin here by defining and explaining relevant terms.

1.2.1 Definition of Knowledge Discovery

Knowledge discovery is the nontrivial extraction of implicit, previously unknown, and potentially useful information from data. Given a set of facts (data) F, a language L, and some measure of certainty C, we define a *pattern* as a statement S in L that describes relationships among a subset F_S of F with a certainty c, such that S is simpler (in some sense) than the enumeration of all facts in F_S. A pattern that is interesting (according to a user-imposed interest measure) and certain enough (again according to the user's criteria) is called *knowledge.* The output of a program that monitors the set of facts in a database and produces patterns in this sense is *discovered knowledge.*

These definitions about the language, the certainty, and the simplicity and interestingness measures are intentionally vague to cover a wide variety of approaches. Collectively, these terms capture our view of the fundamental characteristics of discovery in databases. In the following paragraphs, we summarize the connotations of these terms and suggest their relevance to the problem of knowledge discovery in databases.

Patterns and languages: Although many different types of information can be discovered in data, this book focuses on patterns that are expressed in a high-level language, such as

> If Age < 25 and Driver-Education-Course = No
> Then At-fault-accident = Yes
> With Likelihood = 0.2 to 0.3.

Such patterns can be understood and used directly by people, or they can be the input to another program, for example, an expert system or a semantic query optimizer. We do not consider low-level patterns, such as those generated by neural networks.

Certainty: Seldom is a piece of discovered knowledge true across all the data. Representing and conveying the degree of certainty is essential to determining how much faith the system or user should put into a discovery. As we examine later, certainty involves several factors, including the integrity of the data; the size of the sample on which the discovery was performed; and, possibly, the degree of support from available domain knowledge. Without sufficient certainty, patterns become unjustified and, thus, fail to be knowledge.

Interesting: Although numerous patterns can be extracted from any database, only those deemed to be interesting in some way are considered knowledge. Patterns are interesting when they are novel, useful, and nontrivial to compute. Whether a pattern is novel depends on the assumed frame of reference, which can be either the scope of the system's knowledge or the scope of the user's knowledge. For example, a system might discover the following: If At-fault- accident = yes Then Age > 16. To the system, this piece of knowledge might be previously unknown and potentially useful; to a user trying to analyze insurance claims records, this pattern would be tautological and uninteresting and would not represent discovered knowledge. This example also suggests the notion of utility. Knowledge is useful when it can help achieve a goal of the system or the user. Patterns completely unrelated to current goals are of little use and do not constitute knowledge within the given situation. For example, a pattern relating at-fault-accident to a driver's age, discovered while the user's intent was to analyze sales figures, would not be useful to the user.

Novelty and utility alone, however, are not enough to qualify a pattern as discovered knowledge. Most databases contain numerous novel and useful patterns, such as the total sales for 1990, the average cost of an insurance claim, and the maximum intensity of a spectral line. These types of patterns would not typically be considered knowledge because they are trivial to compute. To be nontrivial, a system must do more than blindly compute statistics; the results of the directed calculation of straightforward statistics are, to our way of thinking, readily available to the database user. A discovery system must be capable of deciding which calculations to perform and whether the results are interesting enough to constitute knowledge in the current context. Another way of viewing this notion of nontriviality is that a discovery system must possess some degree of autonomy in processing the data and evaluating its results.

Efficiency: Finally, we are interested in discovery processes that can be efficiently implemented on a computer. An algorithm is considered efficient [1] if the run time and space used are a polynomial function of low degree of the input length. The problem of discovery of interesting sentences (concepts) that satisfy given facts is inherently hard.

[1] One of the earliest discovery processes was encountered by Jonathan Swift's Gulliver in his visit to the Academy of Labado. The "Project for improving speculative Knowledge by practical and mechanical operations" was generating sequences of words by random permutations and "where they found three or four Words that might make Part of a Sentence, they dictated them to . . . Scribes." This process, although promising to produce many interesting sentences in the (very) long run, is rather inefficient and was recently proved to be NP-hard.

Recent advances in computational learning theory (Valiant 1984; Haussler 1988) have shown that it is not possible to efficiently learn an arbitrary Boolean concept; the problem is NP-hard. However, these results are generally related to the worst-case performance of algorithms and do not eliminate the possibility that, on the average, we can find complex concepts fast. Efficient algorithms do exist for restricted concept classes, such as purely conjunctive concepts (for example, $A \wedge B \wedge C$), or the conjunction of clauses made up of disjunctions of no more than k literals (for example, $(A \vee B) \wedge (C \vee D) \wedge (E \vee F)$, for $k = 2$). Another possibility for efficiently finding concepts is to abandon the demand that the algorithm learn a desired concept with some guarantee and instead accept heuristic or approximate algorithms.

To summarize, knowledge discovery in databases exhibits four main characteristics:

- High-Level Language—Discovered knowledge is represented in a high-level language. It need not be directly used by humans, but its expression should be understandable by human users.
- Accuracy—Discoveries accurately portray the contents of the database. The extent to which this portrayal is imperfect is expressed by measures of certainty.
- Interesting Results—Discovered knowledge is interesting according to user-defined biases. In particular, being interesting implies that patterns are novel and potentially useful, and the discovery process is nontrivial.
- Efficiency—The discovery process is efficient. Running times for large-sized databases are predictable and acceptable.

The systems and techniques described in the chapters of this book generally strive to satisfy these characteristics. The approaches taken, however, are quite diverse. Most are based on machine learning methods that have been enhanced to better deal with issues particular to discovery in databases. Next, we briefly define database concepts and terminology and relate them to terms common to machine learning.

1.2.2 Databases and Machine Learning

In database management, a *database* is a logically integrated collection of data maintained in one or more files and organized to facilitate the efficient storage, modification, and retrieval of related information. In a relational database, for example, data are organized into files or tables of fixed-length records. Each record is an ordered list of values, one value for each field. Information about each field's name and potential values is maintained in a separate file called a *data dictionary*. A *database management system* is a collection of procedures for retrieving, storing, and manipulating data within databases.

Table 1.1
Translations between Database Management and Machine Learning Terms.

Database Management	Machine Learning
database: a logically integrated collection of dynamic files	a fixed set of examples
file	database, data set, set of instances
tuple, record	instance, example, feature vector
field, attribute	feature, attribute
field domain	possible field values
data dictionary	field type and domain information
relational data	a set of instances
object-oriented, structured data	relational data
logical condition	concept description

In machine learning, the term database typically refers to a collection of instances or examples maintained in a single file.[2] *Instances* are usually fixed-length feature vectors. Information is sometimes also provided about the feature names and value ranges, as in a data dictionary. A learning algorithm takes the data set and its accompanying information as input and returns a statement (for example, a concept) representing the results of the learning as output.

Table 1.1 informally compares the terminology in database management with that of machine learning. With the appropriate translation of terms, it seems that machine learning could be readily applied to databases: Rather than learning on a set of instances, learning is done on a file of records from a database. Knowledge discovery in databases, however, raises additional concerns that extend beyond those typically encountered in machine learning. In the real world, databases are often dynamic, incomplete, noisy, and much larger than typical machine learning data sets (table 1.2). These factors render most learning algorithms ineffective in the general case. Not surprisingly, much of the work on discovery in databases focuses on overcoming these complications.

1.2.3 Related Approaches

Although machine learning is the foundation for much of the work in this area, knowledge discovery in databases deals with issues relevant to several other fields, including database management, expert systems, statistical analysis, and scientific discovery.

[2] We are assuming a rather narrow view of machine learning—that is, supervised and unsupervised inductive learning from examples. See Carbonell, Michalski, and Mitchell (1983) for a broader and more detailed view.

Table 1.2
Conflicting Viewpoints between Database Management and Machine Learning.

Database Management	Machine Learning
Database is an active, evolving entity	Database is just a static collection of data
Records may contain missing or erroneous information	Instances are usually complete and noise-free
A typical field is numeric	A typical feature is binary
A database typically contains millions of records	Data sets typically contain several hundred instances
AI should get down to reality	"Databases" is a solved problem and is therefore uninteresting

Database management: A *database management* system provides procedures for storing, accessing, and modifying the data. Typical operations include retrieval, update, or deletion of all tuples satisfying a specific condition, and maintaining user-specified integrity constraints. The ability to extract tuples satisfying a common condition is like discovery in its ability to produce interesting and useful statements (for example, "Bob and Dave sold fewer widgets this year than last"). These techniques, however, cannot by themselves determine what computations are worth trying, nor do they evaluate the quality of the derived patterns. Interesting discoveries uncovered by these data-manipulation tools result from the guidance of the user. However, the new generation of deductive and object-oriented database systems (Kim, Nicolas, and Nishio 1990) will provide improved capabilities for intelligent data analysis and discovery.

Expert systems: *Expert systems* attempt to capture knowledge pertinent to a specific problem. Techniques exist for helping to extract knowledge from experts. One such method is the induction of rules from expert-generated examples of problem solutions. This method differs from discovery in databases in that the expert examples are usually of much higher quality than the data in databases, and they usually cover only the important cases (see also Gaines, chapter 29, for a comparison between knowledge acquisition from an expert and induction from data). Furthermore, experts are available to confirm the validity and usefulness of the discovered patterns. As with database-management tools, the autonomy of discovery is lacking in these methods.

Statistics: Although statistics provide a solid theoretical foundation for the problem of data analysis, a purely statistical approach is not enough. First, standard statistical methods are ill suited for the nominal and structured data types found in many databases (figure 1.2). Second, statistics are totally data driven, precluding the use of available domain knowledge, an important issue that we discuss later. Third, the results of statistical analysis can be overwhelming and difficult to interpret. Finally, statistical methods require the guidance of the user to specify where and how to analyze the data. However, some recent statistics-based techniques such as projection pursuit (Huber 1985) and discovery of causal structure from data (Glymour et al. 1987; Geiger, Paz, and Pearl 1990) address some of these problems and are much closer to intelligent data analysis. We expect that methods using domain knowledge will be developed by the statistical community. We also believe that statistics should have a vital role in all discovery systems dealing with large amounts of data.

Scientific discovery: Discovery in databases is significantly different from scientific discovery (see also Żytkow and Baker, chapter 2) in that the former is less purposeful and less controlled. Scientific data come from experiments designed to eliminate the effects of all but a few parameters and to emphasize the variation of one or a few target parameters to be explained. However, typical business databases record a plethora of information about their subjects to meet a number of organizational goals. This richness (or confusion) both captures and hides from view underlying relationships in the data. Moreover, scientists can reformulate and rerun their experiments should they find that the initial design was inadequate. Database managers rarely have the luxury of redesigning their data fields and recollecting the data.

1.2.4 A Framework for Knowledge Discovery

We have referred to discovery systems several times without specifying what a discovery system is. Although discovery systems vary considerably in their design, it is possible to describe a prototypical discovery system. Figure 1.1 depicts the basic components of our prototypical system for knowledge discovery in databases. At the core of the system is the discovery method, which computes and evaluates patterns on their way to becoming knowledge. The inputs to the discovery method include raw data from the database, information from the data dictionary, additional domain knowledge, and a set of user-defined biases that provide high-level focus. The output is discovered knowledge that can be directed to the user or back into the system as new domain knowledge. Because this model represents a prototypical system, a discovery system need not include all these aspects. The feedback of discovered knowledge into the store of domain knowledge, for example, is present in few existing systems (see Future Directions).

In the remainder of this chapter, we explore each aspect of this framework in detail. Specifically, we consider (1) the peculiarities of databases, (2) the use of domain knowledge, (3) the role of the user in the discovery process, (4) methods of knowledge discovery, and (5) the form and uses of discovered knowledge.

1.3 Database Issues

The fundamental input to a discovery system is the raw data present in a database. We previously mentioned that databases pose unique problems to discovery not typically confronted in machine learning. In particular, these problems arise from the fact that real-world databases are dynamic, incomplete, noisy, and large. Other concerns include whether the database contains adequate information for interesting discovery and how to deal with the overabundance of irrelevant information.

Dynamic data: A fundamental characteristic of most databases is that their contents are ever changing. Data can be time sensitive, and discovery is affected by the timeliness of data observations. Some data values, such as a patient's social security number, are constant over time; some vary more or less gradually over time (for example, weight and height); and some are so situation dependent that only a recently observed value will suffice (for example, pulse rate).

Irrelevant fields: Another key characteristic is the relevance of data, that is, whether an item of data is relevant to the current focus of discovery. When a patient database is being explored for interesting patterns of symptoms and diagnoses, nonmedical data, such as patient name or zip code, are irrelevant, and errors there are unimportant. On the other hand, pulse rate, a simple and typically recorded medical observation, is relevant, and errors here can affect what is discovered. If, however, we are looking for a geographic concentration of a particular disease, then a correct zip code becomes crucial. If the zip code is thought to be faulty, it can sometimes be inferred from related information, such as the patient's address.

An aspect somewhat related to relevance is the applicability of an attribute to a subset of the database; for example, a patient's pregnant field is not applicable to men (the class of patients with sex equal to male), but it is essential to know for female patients of child-bearing age.

Missing values: The presence or absence of values for relevant data attributes can affect discovery. Whether a patient was comatose at the time of diagnosis can be so important that it does not allow the substitution of a default value; less important missing data can be defaulted. In an interactive system, the absence of an important datum can spawn a request for its value or a test to determine it. Alternatively, the absence of data can be dealt with as if it were a condition in itself, and the missing attribute can be assigned a neutral value, such as unknown. For example, the absence of some patient measurements might be found to imply that the patient was formerly in excellent health.

Noise and uncertainty: For relevant attributes, the severity of error can depend on the data type of the allowed values. Values of different attributes can be real numbers

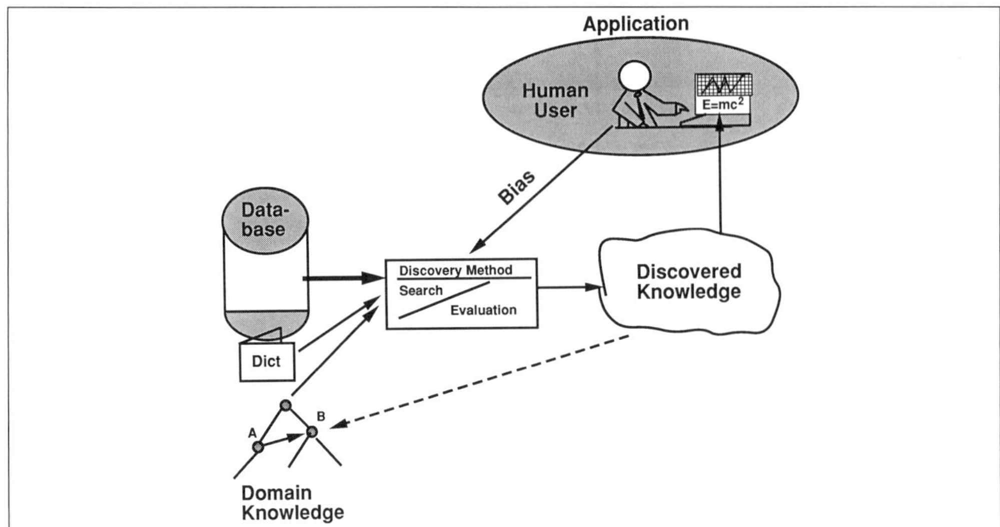

Figure 1.1
A Framework for Knowledge Discovery in Databases.

(charge), integer numbers (age), or strings (name), or can belong to a set of nominal values (patient type). Nominal values can be partially or completely ordered and can also have a semantic structure (figure 1.2).

Another aspect of uncertainty is the inherent or expected exactitude of data, that is the degree of noise in the data. Repeated measurements cluster around an average; based on a priori analysis or computations on the measurements themselves, a statistical model describing randomness is formulated and used to define expected and tolerable deviations in the data. Subjective input, such as whether a patient's condition is severe or moderate, can vary considerably about one or more cluster points. Often, statistical models are applied in an ad hoc manner to subjectively determined attributes to obtain gross statistics and judge the acceptability of (combinations of) attribute values.

Especially with regard to numeric data types, data precision can be a factor in discovery. For example, it is regarded as adequate to record body temperature to a precision of 0.1 degree. A sensitive trend analysis of body temperature would require even greater precision in the data. To a discovery system able to relate such trends to diagnosis, this imprecision would appear to be noise in the input.

Missing fields: An inadequate view of the database can make valid data appear to be in error. The database view is the totality of usable attributes or accessors that the discovery system can apply to a problem. It is assumed that the attributes differentiate cases of interest. When they don't, there appears to be some error. Suppose, for example, that a system is tasked to learn to diagnose malaria from a patient database that does not include the red blood cell count. Patients whose records are correct and who are medically identical with respect to this given view might have different diagnoses, which, in turn, might be incorrectly blamed on data error.

1.4 Databases and Knowledge

Ignorance is the curse of God
Knowledge the wing wherewith we fly to heaven.
– *William Shakespeare.*

A database is a logically integrated collection of files. Associated with a database is a data dictionary, which defines field names, the allowable data types for field values, various constraints on field values, and other related information. For example, the field *age* is a positive integer and the field *date-of-birth* has the form *MMDDYY*. Types of constraints include ranges of possible values for numeric fields, lists of possible values for nominal fields, or more complex conditions such as a department must always have exactly one manager. In a sense, the data dictionary defines the syntax of database use.

The database contains the raw data to be processed by the discovery system. In practice, the discovery system must also use the additional information about the form of data and constraints on it. Some of this information can be stored in the data dictionary, but other information might exist in manuals or experts' heads. For example, a discovery system for a hospital database needs to know which diagnosis codes (DX) are grouped into which diagnostic-related groups (DRG), which, in turn, are grouped into major diagnostic categories (MDC) (figure 1.2). Then, if a patient's DX does not match his or her DRG, an unusual side effect or an error in record keeping is indicated.

Because discovery is computationally expensive, additional knowledge regarding the form and content of data, the domain(s) described by the database, the context of a particular discovery episode, and the purposes being served by discovery are often used to guide and constrain the search for interesting knowledge. We refer to this form of information as *domain knowledge* or *background knowledge.* Domain knowledge assists discovery by focusing search. However, its use is controversial because by telling a system what to look for and where to look for it, domain knowledge restricts search and can deliberately rule out valuable discovery. An example discussed at the IJCAI-89 Knowledge Discovery Workshop illustrates the trade-off between quickly finding conventional solutions and discarding unusual ones. In logistics planning, the search space is so large that it is impossible to find solutions without using constraints such as "trucks don't drive over water." This constraint, however, eliminates potentially interesting solutions, such as those in which trucks drive over frozen lakes in winter. Of equal importance to

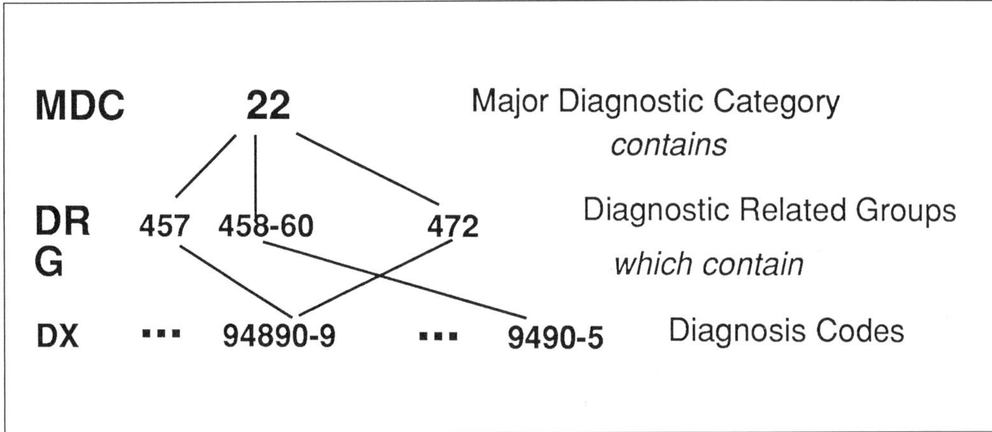

Figure 1.2
Data Dictionary: Relationships Between Fields and Values

this debate is the accuracy and timeliness of domain knowledge.

Background knowledge can take on a number of different forms. Data dictionary knowledge is the most basic and least controversial form of domain knowledge. Interfield knowledge, such as weight and height being positively correlated, and inter-instance knowledge, such as knowing that federal regulation requires the largest charge for handicapped customers be no more than the average charge for regular customers, are closely related to the data but move toward the semantics of the domain. According to data dictionary knowledge, one shouldn't add age to hair-color, but it's a matter of domain knowledge that taking the sum of age and seniority makes sense, but adding age to weight does not.

Knowledge about the content of the database can also help make the discovered knowledge more meaningful to the end user. Domain knowledge is usually provided by a domain expert, although it is possible for domain knowledge to be discovered, suggesting a bootstrapping approach.

1.5 Discovered Knowledge

This section examines three important facets of discovered knowledge: its form, its representation, and its degree of certainty.

1.5.1 Form

The form of a discovered knowledge can be categorized by the type of data pattern it describes. *Interfield patterns* relate values of fields in the same record (for example procedure = surgery implies days-in-hospital > 5). *Inter-record patterns* relate values aggregated over groups of records (for example, diabetic patients have twice as many complications as nondiabetics) or identify useful clusters, such as the group of profit-making companies. Discovery of inter-record patterns is a form of data summarization (part 4). In time-dependent data, inter-record relationships can also identify interesting trends (for example, produce-sales are up 20 percent over last year's sales).

We can also categorize the form of a discovery by its descriptive capacity. A quantitative discovery relates numeric field values using mathematical equations (see part 1). A qualitative discovery (see parts 2 and 3) finds a logical relationship among fields. We distinguish these two forms because different discovery techniques are often used in each case. For example, linear quantitative relationships are conveniently found using linear regression methods that are inappropriate for qualitative discoveries.

Qualitative and quantitative discoveries are often expressed as simple rules, such as $X > Y$, or A implies B. Discoveries, however, can take on more complex forms. Putting several simple implications together forms a causal chain or network. The discovery of relationships among simpler rules can lead to semantic models or domain theories. Models and theories of this sort imply complex relationships that can require applying of the discovery process to previous, simpler discoveries. We might refer to this discovery form as an interdiscovery discovery (see Future Directions).

1.5.2 Representation

Discoveries must be represented in a form appropriate for the intended user. For human end users, appropriate representations include natural language, formal logics, and visual depictions of information. Discoveries are sometimes intended for other computer programs, such as expert system shells; in this case, appropriate representations include programming languages and declarative formalisms. A third case arises when the intended user of the discovered knowledge is the discovery system itself. In these situations where discoveries are fed back into the system as domain knowledge, domain knowledge and discovered knowledge must share a common representation.

Natural language is often desirable from a human perspective, but it is not convenient for manipulation by discovery algorithms. Logical representations are more natural for computation and, if necessary, can be translated into a natural language form. Common logic representations include formalisms such as production rules (for example, if X, then Y), relational patterns ($X > Y$), decision trees (equivalent to ordered lists of rules), and semantic or causal networks. These representational forms offer different advantages and limitations. An appropriate choice for a discovery system depends on the expected knowledge complexity and the need for human comprehension.

For humans, some information is best presented visually (Tufte 1990). The relationships among the branches of a decision tree, for example, are more evident in a graphic presentation than as a logical representation of nested conditional statements. The same is usually true for semantic and causal networks in which the global structure of the network relationships is more clearly depicted in a diagram. Information about the shape and density of clusters of records is another type of knowledge that is best presented visually. In this case, two- or three-dimensional plots can convey certain information more concisely and clearly than any logical representation.

1.5.3 Uncertainty

Patterns in data are often probabilistic rather than certain. This situation can result from missing or erroneous data, or it can reflect the inherent indeterminism of the underlying real-world causes. Capturing this sort of probabilistic information requires a method for representing uncertainty. One common technique is to augment logical representations with probabilistic weights that indicate probabilities of success, belief measures, or standard deviations (see chapters 6, 7, and 8). Alternatively, linguistic uncertainty measures, such as fuzzy sets, are sometimes used (see Yager, chapter 20). In visual presentations, probabilistic information can be readily conveyed by size, density, and shading.

The easiest way to deal with error and uncertainty is not to have any. For example, the occurrence of noisy, missing, and inapplicable data can be minimized by rigidly applying standardized protocols in data entry. Another approach is to assume that the data are absolutely correct and terminate any calculation that encounters error (see Ziarko, chapter 11). Presuming that erroneous data cannot lead to a valid result, the remaining discoveries are regarded as highly reliable. Of course, this presumption eliminates the possibility of discovering nearly certain or probable knowledge.

Uncertainty cannot be ignored when the patterns of interest are inherently probabilistic; for example, "there's a 50 percent chance of rain tomorrow." Fortunately, databases are typically large enough for statistical analysis to determine these probabilities. In some situations, data values can be modeled as representing true information corrupted by random noise. The uncertainty in discovered knowledge can then be represented in terms of a derived probability distribution. For example, for a discovered rule, a product distribution is derived from the conjuncts making up its left-hand side and the correlation to the success of the right-hand side. More simply, a discovered rule can be matched against all entries in the database to accrue an overall success rate. The same approach applies to more complex structures, such as decision trees or classification hierarchies: Match each entry to the ordered nodes, and count the successes and failures.

When databases are very large, with records in the millions, complete analysis of all the data is infeasible. Discovery algorithms must then rely on some form of sampling, whereby only a portion of the data is considered. The resulting discoveries in these cases are necessarily uncertain. Statistical techniques, however, can measure the degree of uncertainty (see Piatetsky-Shapiro, chapter 13, for one approach toward estimating the accuracy of rules discovered from a sample). They can also be used to determine how much additional sampling would be required to achieve a desired level of confidence in the results.

1.6 Discovery Algorithms

Discovery algorithms are procedures designed to extract knowledge from data. This activity involves two processes: identifying interesting patterns and describing them in a concise and meaningful manner. The identification process categorizes or clusters records into subclasses that reflect patterns inherent in the data. The descriptive process, in turn, summarizes relevant qualities of the identified classes. In machine learning, these two processes are sometimes referred to as unsupervised and supervised learning respectively. In discovery systems, user supervision can occur in either process or, in the ideal case, can be completely absent.

1.6.1 Pattern Identification

One way to look at a pattern is as a collection or class of records sharing something in common: customers with incomes over $25,000, patients between 20 and 30 years old, or questionable insurance claims. Discovering pattern classes is a problem of pattern identification or clustering. There are two basic approaches to this problem: traditional numeric methods and conceptual clustering.

Traditional methods of clustering come from cluster analysis and mathematical taxonomy (Dunn and Everitt 1982). These algorithms produce classes that maximize similarity within classes but minimize similarity between classes. Various measures of similarity have been proposed, most based on Euclidean measures of distance between numeric attributes. Consequently, these algorithms only work well on numeric data. An additional drawback is their inability to use background information, such as knowledge about likely cluster shapes.

Conceptual clustering attempts to overcome these problems. These methods work with nominal and structured data and determine clusters not only by attribute similarity but also by conceptual cohesiveness, as defined by background information. Recent examples of this approach include AutoClass (Cheeseman et al. 1988), the Bayesian Categorizer (Anderson and Matessa 1990), Cluster, and Cobweb (Fisher 1987).

Although useful under the right conditions, these methods do not always equal the human ability to identify useful clusters, especially when dimensionality is low and visualization is possible. This situation has prompted the development of *interactive clus-*

tering algorithms that combine the computer's computational powers with the human user's knowledge and visual skills.

1.6.2 Concept Description

Once identified, useful pattern classes usually need to be described rather than simply enumerated. In machine learning, this process is known as supervised concept learning from examples: Given a set of objects labeled by class, derive an intensional description of the classes. Empirical learning algorithms, the most common approach to this problem, work by identifying commonalities or differences among class members. Well-known examples of this approach include decision tree inducers (Quinlan 1986), neural networks (Rummelhart and McClelland 1986), and genetic algorithms (Holland et al. 1986).

The main drawback to empirical methods is their inability to use available domain knowledge. This failing can result in descriptions that encode obvious or trivial relationships among class members. For example, a description of the class of pregnant patients that includes the term *sex=female* would be empirically accurate but would not provide any new information to a hospital administrator. Some learning approaches, such as explanation-based learning (Mitchell, Keller, and Kedar-Cabelli 1986), require a set of domain knowledge (called a domain theory) for use in explaining why an object falls into a particular class. Other approaches combine empirical and knowledge-based methods. Discovery in large, complex databases clearly requires both empirical methods to detect the statistical regularity of patterns and knowledge-based approaches to incorporate available domain knowledge.

1.6.3 Discovery Tasks

Discovery is performed for various reasons. The appropriateness of a specific discovery algorithm depends on the discovery task. One task we've already mentioned is class identification or clustering. For the process of concept description, we can identify at least three additional tasks:

- Summarization: Summarize class records by describing their common or characteristic features. Example: A summary of sales representatives with increased earnings last quarter might include that they are all from the Midwest and drive blue cars.
- Discrimination: Describe qualities sufficient to discriminate records of one class from another. Example: To determine whether a salesperson is from the Midwest it might be sufficient to look at the color or his or her car: if the color is blue, the salesperson is from the Midwest; otherwise the salesperson is from the East or West Coast.

- Comparison: Describe the class in a way that facilitates comparison and analysis with other records. Example: A prototypical Midwest salesperson might own a blue car, have increased sales, and average 100 phone calls a week. This description might serve as the basis against which individual salespeople are judged.

Because these different tasks require different forms and amounts of information, they often influence discovery algorithm selection or design. For example, a decision tree algorithm produces a description intended for discriminating between class instances that might exclude characteristic class qualities.

1.6.4 Complexity

Discovery algorithms for large databases must deal with the issue of computational complexity. Algorithms with computational requirements that grow faster than a small polynomial in the number of records and fields are too inefficient for large databases. Empirical methods are often overwhelmed by large quantities of data and potential patterns. The incorporation of domain knowledge can improve efficiency by narrowing the focus of the discovery process but at the risk of precluding unexpected but useful discovery. Data sampling is another way of attacking the problem of scale; it trades a degree of certainty for greater efficiency by limiting discovery to a subset of the database (see previous section on uncertainty).

1.7 Application Issues

This section starts by listing areas where discovery in databases has been applied, then discusses the key features that characterize a suitable application in a corporate environment, and ends with a cautionary note regarding the ethics of uncovering hidden knowledge in data about people.

1.7.1 Applications of Discovery in Databases

A decade ago, there were only a few examples of discovery in real data. The notable ones include discovery of mass spectrometry rules by MetaDendral (Buchanan and Mitchell 1978), new diagnostic rules for soybean disease (Michalski and Chilausky 1980), and drug side effects in a rheumatism patient database (Blum 1982).

Since this time, the discovery approach has been tried in many more domains, including those given in the following list. This list is by no means exhaustive and is meant to give representative examples for the kinds of applications where discovery in databases is possible. The largest databases used for discovery had several millions of records, and larger ones are being considered.

- Medicine: biomedicine, drug side effects, hospital cost containment, genetic sequence analysis, and prediction
- Finance: credit approval, bankruptcy prediction, stock market prediction, securities fraud detection, detection of unauthorized access to credit data, mutual fund selection
- Agriculture: soybean and tomato disease classification
- Social: demographic data, voting trends, election results
- Marketing and Sales: identification of socio-economic subgroups showing unusual behavior, retail shopping patterns, product analysis, frequent flying patterns, sales prediction
- Insurance: detection of fraudulent and excessive claims, claims "unbundling." Of course, all insurance data analysis can be considered a form of knowledge discovery in databases.
- Engineering: automotive diagnostic expert systems, Hubble space telescope, computer-aided design (CAD) databases, job estimates
- Physics and Chemistry: electrochemistry, superconductivity research
- Military: intelligence analysis, data fusion, and . . . (the rest is classified)
- Law Enforcement: tax and welfare fraud, fingerprint matching, recovery of stolen cars
- Space Science: astronomy, search for extraterrestrial intelligence, space data analysis (this will become more important as huge amounts of data are gathered in future space missions)
- Publishing: custom editions of journals.

1.7.2 Selecting an Application in a Corporate Environment

As with any emerging technology, it is important to carefully select the initial applications for discovery in databases. We developed a list of criteria for selecting an application in a corporate environment. The criteria will be different for a university or a government project, but many important considerations will be the same. The knowledge tree in figure 1.3 illustrates our criteria.

The fruits of knowledge growing on the tree of data are not easy to pick. To get there, we need to climb a multistep ladder. The first step is the business need for discovery. The discovered knowledge should have the potential for significant and measurable financial benefit. There should be many unknown patterns in data that cannot be found easily by conventional statistical methods. It is helpful if the problem is typical, but the need to solve unique problems with high payoff also exists (for example, location of human gene activators).

The second step is having sufficient and reliable data. Having at least 1,000 examples is desirable. The portion of the data that is incomplete or noisy should be relatively small. Most fields relevant to the discovery focus should be stored in the database. For example, it is hard to find likely potential customers for a mobile phone without information about a customer's car.

The next step is having the organizational support for the project. There should be an enthusiastic and influential supporter in the organization and the commitment for (potentially) long-term research.

The final step is to have significant but incomplete domain knowledge. The best chance for discovery is with things we almost but not quite know already. It is desirable to have user-specified hierarchies of field-value codes and rules relating possible field values. Domain knowledge should be codified and computer readable.

After climbing these steps, we can discover some useful knowledge (possibly, including something controversial) and receive the desired business payoff. We might also reach the research value cloud. The research value is high for complex applications where existing methods are insufficient. Such applications are characterized by a variety of data types, including numeric, nominal, and structured fields; a very large database (millions of records); noisy, incomplete, and contradictory data; and complex domain knowledge. Research value is high for difficult problems and, thus, is frequently in conflict with the business need to have quick results.

1.7.3 Will Discovery Open a Pandora's Box?

An important issue to consider in analyzing social or demographic databases is the appropriateness of discovery. A careless approach to discovery can open a Pandora's box of unpleasant surprises. Some kinds of discovery are actually illegal: Federal and state privacy laws limit what can be discovered about individuals. The use of drug traffickers' profiles by law enforcement agencies has been controversial, and use of some parts of the profile, such as race, have been ruled illegal. Political, ethical, and moral considerations can affect other discoveries. A Federal Bureau of Investigation proposal to establish a nationwide database of criminal suspects was dropped after congressional objections about possible invasion of privacy. Advanced algorithms for discovery in databases might also become a threat to database security (see O'Leary, chapter 30).

A pattern that involves racial or ethnic characteristics is likely to be controversial. The plans to market the Uptown cigarette, a campaign that was directed at young, black males (devised, possibly, after market research identified this group as smoking more

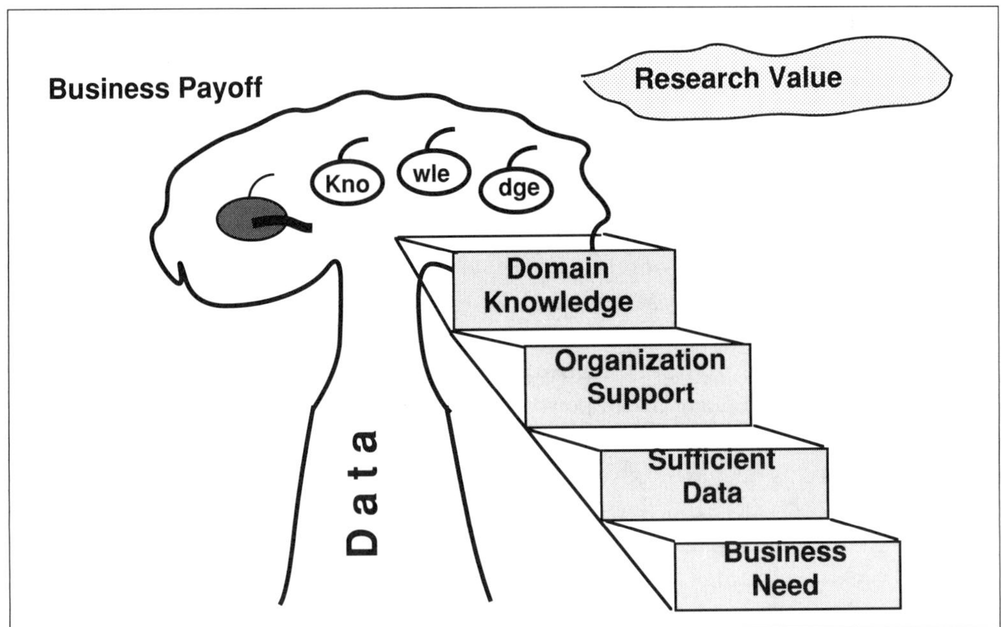

Figure 1.3
Selecting Application for Discovery in Databases in a Corporate Environment.

than average) was shelved after many protests (Wildavsky 1990). Another example is the Food and Drug Administration ban on blood donations by people from Haiti and Sub-Saharan Africa. The discovered pattern of the high incidence of AIDS in these groups was protested as being racially motivated because there was also a high incidence of AIDS in another geographically defined group, that is men from New York and San Francisco, whose members were not forbidden to donate blood. However, reports on this controversy did not make clear what the strength or coverage of these patterns was and what additional factors were considered. In such cases, it is desirable to give more detailed information, such as "Based on a sample of size S, people in group Z have 33 to 41 percent likelihood of developing the disease X. The nationwide risk of developing X is 10 to 12 percent." The public then has a clearer notion of the nature of discovered assertions and is better able to make an informed decision about them, even if they still remain controversial.

1.8 Future Directions

Although some aspects of discovery in databases, such as finding simple formulas to fit scientific data or inducing decision trees for classification, are relatively well understood, many more aspects are in need of research. This research will not only be driven by academic considerations but also by the practical need to analyze more data that are more complex than ever before, including object-oriented, CAD-CAM, textual, and multimedia databases. Data complexity will make it necessary to use more domain knowledge. Much larger databases will require more efficient algorithms. Dealing with a fast-changing environment will demand much more incremental methods. Complex problems such as network control might require the integration of multiple approaches to discovery. The results should be presented to users in more understandable ways, using interactive approaches. Finally, discovery in social, business, and demographic databases requires caution about findings that may be illegal or unethical. The following paragraphs examine these directions in detail.

Domain knowledge can be used in all aspects of automated discovery, from data representation to selecting interesting features to making the discovered results more understandable. Using domain knowledge constraints to reduce search, however, is controversial, as illustrated by the "trucks don't drive over water" example mentioned earlier. The challenge is to use domain knowledge in such a way that we don't block the discovery of unexpected solutions. The use of domain knowledge taken to the extreme will produce a specialized learning algorithm (see Part 5, Domain-Specific Discovery Methods) that will outperform any general method in its domain but will not be useful outside it. A desirable compromise is to develop a framework for augmenting the general method with the specific domain knowledge. Some recent attempts are described in Quinlan (1990).

Efficient algorithms will be crucial. Exponential and even high-order polynomial algorithms will not scale up for dealing with large volumes of data. Although the efficient discovery of arbitrary rules is not possible in general (assuming $P \neq NP$), this problem can be sidestepped by using restricted rule types, heuristic and approximate algorithms, and careful use of sampling. Discovery algorithms should also use the latest advances in hardware and software. Parallel computers, large memories, and object-oriented and deductive databases not only can speed up existing methods but also present opportunities for new, faster algorithms.

Incremental methods are needed to efficiently keep pace with changes in data. More importantly, incremental discovery systems that can reuse their discoveries can bootstrap themselves and make more complex discoveries possible.

Interactive systems will provide, perhaps, the best opportunity for discovery in the near term. In such systems, a knowledge analyst is included in the discovery loop. This approach combines the best features of human and machine: Use human judgment but rely on the machine to do search and to crunch numbers. The interactive approach requires the discovered knowledge to be presented in a human-oriented form, whether as written reports (Schmitz, Armstrong, and Little 1990) or visual and sound patterns

(Smith, Bergeron, and Grinstein 1990). Such novel output presentations might allow the use of the phenomenal perceptual capabilities of humans. Tools need to be built to support effective interaction between the user and the discovery system. Also, algorithms need to be reexamined from the viewpoint of human-oriented presentation. A neural network, for example, might have to generate explanations from its weights (Gallant 1988).

Integration on many levels will be required for future systems. Accessing existing databases and data dictionaries, they will combine different types of learning and discovery. The results of discovery will not stand alone but feed back for more discoveries or feed forward to other systems. Recent examples of integrated learning systems are Silver et al. (1990) and Part 6, Integrated and Multiparadigm Systems. The incremental, knowledge-based, and interactive discovery methods may transform the static databases of today into evolving information systems of tomorrow.

1.9 Organization of the Book

A number of candidate themes and issues could be used to organize the following chapters. One is the nature of what is discovered and how it is expressed. Another is the treatment of data uncertainty. Also crucial is the user-supplied bias that determines what is interesting and novel during the discovery. There is also the controversial issue of whether and how to use domain knowledge. None of these issues provides a neat, linear progression describing ongoing research. For the following twenty-nine chapters, grouped into seven parts, we chose the path that leads from the general to the specific: from less reliance on domain knowledge to more, from less restricted forms of discovered knowledge to more specialized, from general methods to domain-specific techniques. Here is a quick overview.

1.9.1 Discovery of Quantitative Laws—Part 1

Four chapters explore domain-independent function-finding discovery programs whose purpose is to automate the discovery of numeric laws of the type commonly found in physics and chemistry. Here, the domain knowledge is used only indirectly by restricting results to a class of allowable functional forms.

Chapter 2, by J. M. Żytkow and J. Baker, describes how a numeric function-finding system Fahrenheit, designed for scientific discovery, was adapted to database exploration.

The next chapter, by Y.-H. Wu and S. Wang, uses the Reduction algorithm, which discovers a multivariate formula by finding its components from a predefined set of primitive functions.

Chapter 4, by E. P. D. Pednault, presents an approach to inferring probabilistic theories from low-dimensional data by using the minimum description length principle and shows a successful application to computer vision.

C. Schaffer, in chapter 5, outlines a framework for evaluating the systems that discover functional relationships in scientific data.

1.9.2 Data-Driven Discovery of Qualitative Laws—Part 2

These six chapters focus on the discovery of qualitative laws using techniques with little or no domain knowledge. These laws are represented as rules, decision trees, patterns, or dependency tables.

In chapter 6, K. C. C. Chan and A. K. C. Wong describe a statistical approach to extracting classificatory knowledge from data, capable of handling noisy data with mixed continuous- and discrete-valued fields.

Chapter 7, by D. K. Y. Chiu, A. K. C. Wong, and B. Cheung, presents an information-based method for the discovery of patterns using a hierarchical, maximum-entropy scheme that iteratively partitions the event space by minimizing the loss of information.

In chapter 8, R. Uthurusamy, U. M. Fayyad, and S. Spangler address the difficult problem of deciding when to stop specialization during top-down decision tree generation and present an algorithm that produced good results on a real-world diagnostic database.

In chapter 9, P. Smyth and R. M. Goodman present an information-based method for finding the best probabilistic rules relating a given set of discrete-valued domain variables.

J. Hong and C. Mao (chapter 10) present a method for incremental discovery of rules and structure through hierarchical and parallel clustering.

W. Ziarko, in chapter 11, describes how to find exact dependencies in databases, represented as the minimal subsets of data sufficient for uniquely predicting the target attribute.

1.9.3 Using Knowledge in Discovery—Part 3

In this part, six chapters explore the mechanisms by which the user can provide discovery-directing knowledge, including hierarchical structures, rule-interest measures, Horn clauses, and functions.

Y. Cai, N. Cercone, and J. Han (chapter 12) use attribute-oriented induction to extract characteristic rules and classification rules from relational databases. Their method performs generalization of field values guided by a concept tree and integrates database operations with the learning process.

In addressing the discovery of strong rules in databases, G. Piatetsky-Shapiro (chapter

13) discusses principles applicable to rule-interest functions, presents a fast algorithm for rule discovery, and analyzes the expected accuracy of discovered rules.

To overcome the practical limitations of conventional statistical classification methods, Q. Wu, P. Suetens, and A. Oosterlinck (chapter 14) examine the use of domain hierarchical classification structure to guide search and Bayesian classification; they show positive results in a biomedical domain.

In chapter 15, W. J. Frawley encodes both domain knowledge and contextual information as functions to be used as the building blocks of decision trees. This representation allows disjunctive concepts discovered in one pass over a database to be used in building subsequent trees.

F. Bergadano, A. Giordana, L. Saitta, F. Brancadori, and D. De Marchi (chapter 16) discuss their system to learn structured knowledge using both induction from examples and deduction from a logically specified domain theory.

In chapter 17, M. Manago and Y. Kodratoff show how the use of frames to represent examples extends the applicability of traditional machine learning induction to discovery in object-oriented databases.

1.9.4 Data Summarization—Part 4

Unlike the previous parts, which deal mostly with finding patterns that apply to an individual instance (interfield dependencies), these three chapters describe methods for finding patterns relating groups of instances (inter-record dependencies).

Chapter 18, by M. C. Chen and L. McNamee, shows how to adapt a decision tree algorithm for estimating the value of a summarized attribute and the cardinality of the queried category.

Chapter 19, by P. Hoschka and W. Klöesgen, describes a system for searching for high-level, interesting statements that summarize subsets of data, with applications to marketing and vote analysis.

Finally, in chapter 20, R. Yager introduces an approach to linguistic data summarization using fuzzy set theory.

1.9.5 Domain-Specific Discovery Methods—Part 5

At one extreme of the knowledge versus data spectrum are methods whose domain models and representations determine and direct the discovery process. Each of the domains addressed by these four chapters is general enough to encompass a broad range of practical problems.

In the future, discovery methods will be used on a wealth of information now stored as text and in specialized databases. C.-S. Ai, P. E. Blower, and R. A. Ledwith (chapter

21) extract chemical reaction information from a full-text database and create a new database, understandable to humans and readable by computer, whose structured data objects represent chemical reactions described in the text.

A. J. Gonzalez, H. R. Myler, M. Towhidnejad, F. D. McKenzie, and R. R. Kladke (chapter 22) are working to create a complete knowledge base directly and automatically from computer-resident data sources. Their prototype system deals with CAD database files and produces a frame-based knowledge base.

In chapter 23, the experimental domain of the research of J. C, Schlimmer, T. M. Mitchell, and J. McDermott is the maintenance of large knowledge bases. They describe an approach and a prototype computer program that accepts rules from a knowledge base developer, attempts to justify the behavior of each rule, and then utilizes these justifications to suggest refinements to the rules.

In chapter 24, M. Siegel, E. Sciore, and S. Salveter, experimenting with a shipping database provided by Lloyd's of London, define a method for deriving and maintaining a set of rules for semantic query optimization by using intermediate results from the optimization process to direct the search for new rules.

1.9.6 Integrated and Multiparadigm Systems—Part 6

In the near future, we expect increased interest in multiparadigmatic discovery systems. Here, two chapters focus on the integration of techniques and the use of a number of modes of knowledge representation within a single system.

In chapter 25, B. Silverman, M. R. Hieb, and T. M. Mezher present an approach to discovery in the absence of human experts or trainers for domains for which large simulators exist.

K. A. Kaufman, R. S. Michalski, and L. Kerschberg (chapter 26) describe a system that combines database, knowledge base, and machine learning techniques to provide a user with an integrated set of tools for conceptually analyzing data and searching it for interesting relationships.

1.9.7 Methodology and Application Issues—Part 7

The final four chapters compare knowledge discovery methods, analyze the role of knowledge discovery in developing knowledge bases, and address the issue of database security.

J. W. Long, E. H. Irani, and J. R. Slagle are part of a data analysis effort associated with a major multiclinic clinical trial. As seen in chapter 27, their attempts to discover structural relationships in data are appropriate to databases in which it is unlikely for data to be missing or incorrect.

In chapter 28, M. McLeish, P. Yao, M. Garg, and T. Stirtzinger report on the application of a number of machine learning and statistical methods to veterinary medicine databases, showing that diagnostic systems based on these methods can outperform domain experts.

Chapter 29, by B. R. Gaines, provides a quantitative framework for knowledge acquisition that encompasses machine learning and expertise transfer as related paradigms within a single spectrum and shows that techniques supporting the development of practical knowledge-based systems generally lie between these extremes.

In the concluding chapter, D. E. O'Leary addresses the database security aspects of knowledge discovery, in particular, unauthorized discovery from databases and the need to develop new database security controls. New controls can arise from the technology of knowledge discovery itself.

References

Anderson, J. R. and Matessa, M. 1990. A Rational Analysis of Categorization. In Proceedings of the Seventh International Machine Learning Conference, 76–84.

Blum, R. 1982. Discovery and Representation of Causal Relationships from a Large Time-Oriented Clinical Database: The RX Project. In *Lecture Notes in Medical Informatics*, no. 19. New York: Springer-Verlag.

Buchanan, B., and Mitchell, T. 1978. Model-Directed Learning of Production Rules. In *Pattern-Directed Inference Systems*, eds. D. A. Waterman and F. Hayes-Roth, 297–312. New York: Academic Press.

Carbonell, J. G.; Michalski, R. S.; and Mitchell, T. M. 1983. An Overview of Machine Learning. In *Machine Learning: An Artificial Intelligence Approach*, volume 1, eds. R. S. Michalski, J. G. Carbonell, and T. M. Mitchell, 3–23. San Mateo, Calif.: Morgan Kaufmann.

Cheeseman, P.; Kelly, J.; Self, M.; Sutz, J.; Taylor, W.; and Freeman, D. 1988. AutoClass: a Bayesian Classification System. In Proceedings of the Fifth International Conference on Machine Learning. 54–64. San Mateo, Calif.: Morgan Kaufmann.

Dunn, G., and Everitt, B. S. 1982. *An Introduction to Mathematical Taxonomy.* Cambridge, Mass.: Cambridge University Press.

Fisher, D. H. 1987. Knowledge Acquisition Via Incremental Conceptual Clustering. *Machine Learning* 2(2): 139–172.

Gallant, S. I. 1988. Connectionist Expert Systems. *Communications of the ACM* 31(2): 153–168.

Geiger, D.; Paz, A.; and Pearl, J. 1990. Learning Causal Trees from Dependence Information. In Proceedings of the Eighth National Conference on Artificial Intelligence, 771–776. Menlo Park, Calif.: AAAI.

Glymour, C.; Scheines, R.; Spirtes, P.; and Kelly, K. 1987. *Discovering Causal Structure.* San Diego, Calif.: Academic Press.

Haussler, D. 1988. Quantifying Inductive Bias: AI Learning Algorithms and Valiant's Learning Framework. *Artificial Intelligence* 36(2): 177–221.

Holland, J. H.; Holyoak, K. J.; Nisbett, R. E.; and Thagard, P. R. 1986. *Induction: Processes of Inference, Learning, and Discovery.* Cambridge, Mass: MIT Press.

Huber, P. J. 1985. Projection Pursuit. In *The Annals of Statistics* 13(2): 435–474.

Kim, W.; Nicolas, J.-M.; and Nishio, S. 1990. *Deductive and Object-Oriented Databases.* Amsterdam: Elsevier.

Michalski, R. S.; and Chilausky, R. L. 1980. Learning by Being Told and Learning from Examples: An Experimental Comparison of the Two Methods of Knowledge Acquisition in the Context of Developing an Expert System for Soybean Disease Diagnosis. *International Journal of Policy Analysis and Information Systems* 4(2): 125–161.

Michie, D., 1990. March 15 Interview. *AI Week* 7(6): 7–12.

Mitchell, T. M.; Keller, R. M.; and Kedar-Cabelli; S. T. 1986. Explanation-Based Generalization: A Unifying View. *Machine Learning,* 1(1), 47–80.

Nordhausen, B., and Langley, P. 1990. An Integrated Approach to Empirical Discovery. In *Computational Models of Discovery and Theory Formation,* eds. J. Shrager and P. Langley, 97–128. San Mateo, Calif.: Morgan Kaufmann.

Quinlan, J. R. 1990. Learning Logical Definitions from Relations. *Machine Learning* 5(3): 239–266.

Quinlan J. R. 1986. Induction of Decision Trees. *Machine Learning,* 1(1): 81–106.

Rummelhart, D. E., and McClelland, J. L. 1986. *Parallel Distributed Processing, Volume 1.* Cambridge, Mass: MIT Press.

Schmitz, J.; Armstrong, G.; and Little, J. D. C. 1990. CoverStory—Automated News Finding in Marketing. In *DSS Transactions,* ed. L. Volino, 46–54. Providence, R.I.: Institute of Management Sciences.

Silberschatz, A.; Stonebraker, M.; and Ullman, J., 1990. Database Systems: Achievements and Opportunities, The "Lagunita" Report of the NSF Invitational Workshop, TR-90-22, Dept. of Computer Science, Univ. of Texas at Austin.

Silver, B.; Frawley, W.; Iba, G.; Vittal, J.; and Bradford, K. 1990. ILS: A Framework for Multi-Paradigmatic Learning", In Proceedings of the Seventh International Conference on Machine Learning, 348–356. San Mateo, Calif.: Morgan Kaufmann.

Smith, S.; Bergeron, D.; and Grinstein, G. 1990. Stereophonic and Surface Sound Generation for Exploratory Data Analysis. In Proceedings of the Conference of the Special Interest Group in Computer and Human Interaction (SIGCHI), 125–131. Reading, Mass.: Addison-Wesley.

Tufte, E. R. 1990. *Envisioning Information,* Cheshire Conn.: Graphics Press.

Valiant, L. G. 1984. A Theory of the Learnable, *Communications of the ACM* 27(11): 1134–42.

Wildavsky, B. 1990. Tilting at Billboards. *New Republic* August 20 and 27, 19–20.

I DISCOVERY OF QUANTITATIVE LAWS

2 Interactive Mining of Regularities in Databases

Jan M. Żytkow
Wichita State University

John Baker
George Mason University

Abstract

In this chapter, we discuss the theory and practice of database exploration in search of useful regularities. We point out that database miners cannot count on the same quality of data as scientists can. Database miners must be content with sparse, static data because they cannot count on experiments and data refinement that are available in scientific data collection. Consequently, database miners cannot be expected to produce glamorous, deterministic regularities similar to those discovered in the physical sciences; they should be happy with comparatively weak statistical regularities. These regularities, however, can still be significant compared to the null distribution hypothesis. A *regularity* is understood as a limitation on the set of all possible facts. We review the basic mechanisms by which machine discovery systems BACON and FAHRENHEIT make their discoveries, and we present FORTY-NINER, a system that discovers regularities in databases. FORTY-NINER borrows solutions from BACON and FAHRENHEIT, adjusting them to the specific needs of database exploration. We discuss basic operations on the space of data that determine the scope of FORTY-NINER's search and help the system to deal with sparse data. We discuss FORTY-NINER's architecture, which allows human inspection and guidance at intermediate stages, and we review the system's performance.

2.1 Introduction

A *database* is traditionally viewed as a large collection of data from which different facts can be retrieved efficiently in response to specific queries. In a large amount of data, however, a potential exists for discovering useful regularities. Many people believe that significant knowledge is hidden in databases, and there has been considerable interest in recent years in automated methods of mining databases for useful knowledge (Piatetsky-Shapiro and Frawley 1989). Judging by the number of papers on knowledge discovery in databases, we are experiencing a gold rush; whether it leaves ghost towns or a prosperous industry remains to be seen.

Database mining is attractive for many reasons. There are many available databases, they are simple and uniform in structure, and a considerable amount of effort has already been spent in designing them and collecting useful data. Many historical records are available in the form of databases, such as stock market prices and indexes, corporate records, census results, and weather records. The search for regularities is relatively inexpensive, and search algorithms can be reused because of the similarity in structure of all relational databases.

Database exploration is attractive also from the technical perspective of testing the discovery systems. Databases offer a solution to the input bottleneck that has been experienced in research on discovery. Typically, discovery systems have relied either on user input or on simulation. In the former case, the data are severely limited in number; in the latter, they are idealized, lacking many real-world characteristics. Databases can solve these problems by providing large quantities of real data.

A database search for regularities can be automated to various degrees. In a limited form of automation, the user is charged with hypotheses generation, and verification is automatically conducted (Naqvi and Tsur 1989). This approach, called *data dredging* (Chimenti et al. 1990) does not go beyond the traditional database management mode of answering user-generated queries. In contrast, Cai, Cercone, and Han (chapter 12, this volume) propose an inductive, partially automated process of generation and generalization of hypotheses. Their search is guided by concept hierarchies for the database attributes and the user-specified relevance relation. The progress is evaluated based on the user-specified thresholds.

Researchers in the area of machine discovery explore an even more extensive automation, yet only recently did they turn to databases. The preponderance of work on machine discovery takes inspiration from science (Langley et al. 1987; Shrager and Langley 1990). Many discovery systems incorporate elements of scientific method and are tested on scientific data. Some of them are large-scale search systems (BACON: Langley et al. 1987; FAHRENHEIT: Żytkow 1987; and IDS: Nordhausen and Langley 1990). Can we apply methods used in scientific discovery systems to database exploration? Our experience justified a positive answer, but we found that a nontrivial adaptation is needed.

In this chapter, we describe a computer system for automated database mining that we call FORTY-NINER, a name that emphasizes that the current rush to dig chunks of knowledge in databases resembles the California gold rush of 1849. FORTY-NINER is a mutated descendant of FAHRENHEIT and BACON. It can explore large relational databases in search of regularities. FORTY-NINER's search parameters can be adjusted to satisfy various requirements, such as the admissible duration of search, the level of statistical significance of regularities, and the type of regularities searched for. We explain why FAHRENHEIT's techniques have been adjusted to operate on databases. We also introduce the basic theoretical framework for the search for regularities in relational databases.

Are systems such as FORTY-NINER able to discover significant regularities in databases, regularities that have practical applications? More research must be conducted before we can answer this question, and the answer can be different for different databases. No matter what the answer, databases are an exciting new application of machine discovery.

2.2 Scientific Data and Data in Databases Are Different

When we sift through megabytes of data, approaching the same data many times from different angles, we might get the impression that the data are abundant rather than sparse. However, the situation is really the opposite. Unlike an experimental scientist, a database explorer must be prepared to deal with sparse data of low quality.

2.2.1 Experimental Science Provides an Abundance of Data

The distinguishing characteristic of science in modern times is its emphasis on experimentation. Experimental scientists actively create new physical situations to collect data that is fitted to their research tasks. Experimentation carries a number of advantages. First, it provides us with an abundance of data. Even in a seemingly narrow physical situation, several parameters can usually be varied over many values, so we can still collect a great deal of data. Second, the data can be changed and improved. Experimental scientists can reduce error, enhance repeatability, and switch to more diagnostic measurements. They recognize new relevant variables and learn to control them; they design and modify their measuring instruments. As a result, the magnitudes that they are measuring at the end can vary considerably from the magnitudes used at the outset. The new data are more conducive to the discovery task at hand. Third, an experimenter can create special situations that are otherwise not available. For example, he or she can study a phase change of a newly synthesized superconductor near the temperature of absolute zero. Fourth, the experimenter can create simple experimental situations, so that empirical regularities are easy to discover, and they can be decomposed into basic laws. *Basic laws* are expressions that describe elementary processes and situations (Żytkow 1990). Basic laws are essential in model construction when they are recombined into descriptions of complex processes and situations (Żytkow and Lewenstam 1990). If a complex process P can be viewed as a combination of several simple processes p_1, p_2, . . . , p_n, then the expressions that describe p_1, p_2, . . . , p_n can be combined into a description of P. Recombination of basic laws into descriptions of new complex processes allows knowledge transfer and generalization, which are common in domains such as physics and chemistry.

None of the benefits created by data abundance and refinement and by access to situations that are novel and simple is available to a database explorer. In a database, the data are fixed and sparse. The number of records is fixed, and no other observational attributes can be introduced. Even if there is a regularity in the data, it might be too crude to be decomposed into elementary units suitable for knowledge transfer. As a result, the analysis of a database that contains facts about domain D might not yield regularities, even when there are regularities in D, that scientists could discover.

2.2.2 Observational Science Is Still Better Off than Database Exploration

In some domains of science, experimentation is not possible, and scientific data collection is limited to observations. In observational science, scientists cannot create new situations or vary the properties of investigated objects, but they can select which observations they make. Although an experimenter can actively change the temperature of a sample, an observer can only select the time and location in which he or she measures the temperature. Even though the observers cannot create new situations, they are still free to measure any observable properties of any available objects. They can define new concepts and can develop or refine their methods of measurement to reduce error. None of these freedoms is available to a database explorer.

2.2.3 Database Exploration Must Use the Archival Mode

In some domains, even observations are not possible, especially when we study history. Historical data are only available as records of past events, and we can neither increase their number nor improve their accuracy. This mode of accessing data, which we call *archival*, is equivalent to the exploration of databases. Measuring the actual temperature at any location on earth belongs to the *observational mode*, but using nineteenth-century records of temperature is an example of archival mode.

The experimental mode provides the most freedom in obtaining data. Observational mode provides less control because it does not allow desired situations to be actively created. However, it can yield an unlimited number of data points and allows us to refine the data. The archival mode is the most constraining because it limits the data to those available in existing records. There is no possibility of defining new observational attributes or refining the data. Data transformation is possible, but it is limited to pencil-and-paper operations on the existing records that cannot improve the accuracy of data. As a result, databases can hardly offer the data quality available to an experimental scientist. Scientific facts are usually highly repeatable, leading to regularities described by deterministic mathematical formulas. We cannot expect the same quality regularities in databases. For this reason, we concentrate on a search for weaker, statistical regularities.

2.3 What Is a Regularity?

In a domain in which everything is possible, and each possibility is equally probable, there are no regularities. A *regularity* can be defined as a limitation in a space of all possible situations. A regularity exists if some events are either impossible or less probable than others. This characteristic is perhaps the most general. Regularities can be expressed in many forms. A deterministic scientific regularity is typically expressed as an equation.

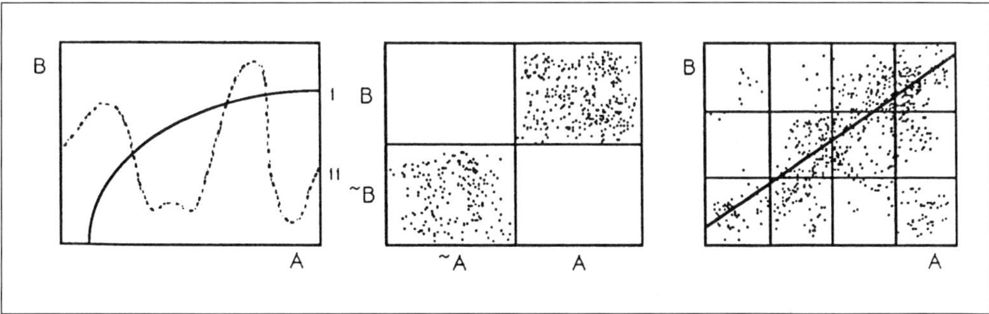

Figure 2.1
Types of Regularities.

In simple cases, this expression is an algebraic equation, such as $PV = nRT$. Equations (figure 2.1a) are parsimonious, easy to manipulate, and useful for making predictions and explanations. Another formalism, the language of first-order logic, is particularly useful on symbolic data for which numeric equations cannot directly be used. First-order language provides a concise representation of many relational regularities (figure 2.1b).

Not all regularities can be expressed by simple equations or concise first-order sentences. Even if we cannot find an equation, the data plotted on a diagram can also be viewed as a regularity (figure 2.1a), but an equation extrapolates a limited number of data points to all combinations of values that satisfy the equation. In a two-dimensional diagram, each pair of values of both variables is either occupied by a data point or is not. A diagram can describe either a unique-valued function or a multivalued relation. If all combinations of values of two variables are possible but occur with actual probabilities different than expected a priori, then the basic way of expressing them is a contingency table (figure 2.1c) (Bhattacharyya and Johnson 1986).

Given a relational database, the space of all possible events is determined by all possible combinations of values of the attributes. The language in which the regularities can be expressed is also determined by the attributes. Consider a language defined by the attributes A_1, A_2, . . . , A_n. Let V_1, V_2, . . ., V_n be the corresponding sets of values. The Cartesian product $W = V_1 \times V_2 \times ... \times V_n$ represents the set of all possible events. A black-and-white regularity exists if some events can never occur in W. If all events can occur but with unequal probabilities, then we have a statistical gray-level regularity. Let us consider an example.

Take a database of 40 high school basketball players, where each record consists of two attributes: age and height. The ages range from 15 to 17, and the heights range from 5'10" to 6'2", measured to the nearest inch. A total of three possible ages and five possible heights makes a total of $3 \times 5 = 15$ possible events, or categories. If all the players under age 17 are less than 6' tall, then we have a black-and-white regularity. However, we might find that at least one player falls into each category. In this case, the regularity would consist of a table of probabilities, such as 25 percent of the players are of age 17 and height 6'1".

A probabilistic regularity can be represented by a probability distribution on W. Actual probability distribution must be compared with the expected distribution based on the null hypothesis of variables independence. When the Cartesian product is finite, the regularity can take on the form of a contingency table, defined by $(A_i - E_i)/E_i$, where A_i is the actual number of records in cell i, and E_i is the value based on the null hypothesis of independence applied to the histograms of the variables used in the table. A black-and-white regularity can be represented by a subset R of W. It can be viewed as a special case of probabilistic distribution, namely, the characteristic function of the set R in W (equal to 1 on the elements in R and equal to $\emptyset$ on the elements in $W-R$), normalized to the measure of R in W. Black-and-white regularities can be expressed in first-order logic. Some can be expressed by equations.

Our definition of a regularity is compatible with other approaches. In first-order logic, every contingent formula (neither a tautology nor its negations) is a candidate for a regularity. A contingent formula describes a limitation in the set of all possibilities because it is true in some possible worlds and false in others. Our definition fits the "falsificationist" view of science because each formula that claims that some possibilities never occur is falsified if they are shown to exist. It also satisfies the information measure approach. The less likely it is that the empirical distribution would have been randomly generated as the null hypothesis distribution, the more information it contains, and the stronger a regularity it is.

2.4 Machine Discovery Research: Can We Transfer the Solutions?

Scientific discovery systems were not developed with the focus on knowledge discovery in databases. However, with some changes, they can be used for database mining. BLIP (Morik 1987), GLAUBER, and STAHL (Langley et al. 1987; Rose and Langley 1986) work on lists of qualitative facts that can occur in relational databases. Systems such as BACON (Langley et al. 1987) and FAHRENHEIT (Koehn and Żytkow 1986; Żytkow 1987) can work on quantitative attributes and can also introduce intrinsic numeric variables for each qualitative attribute. Because BACON and FAHRENHEIT are among the strongest discovery systems to date, they are of special interest when we attempt knowledge discovery in databases.

Our previous discussion pointed out the inherent limitations of the archival approach to data. It follows that we should direct our attention toward weak and statistical, rather than functional, regularities. We turn now to the second problem—the sparsity of data in databases.

2.4.1 Data in Databases Are Sparse

With the assumption that a given database has 40 attributes and that each attribute has on average, four values, the set W of all possible value combinations consists of 4^{40} possible records or, approximately, 10^{25}. A large database can consist of some 10^6 or 10^7 records. Comparison of the number of possible and actual events makes it clear that most of the cells in W cannot be occupied. In this situation, we cannot be sure whether a particular cell is empty because the corresponding combination of values never occurs or because the number of records is so small that most empirically admissible events have not been recorded in the database. In FORTY-NINER, we solve this problem by using a combination of two operations. We aggregate values of each attribute into a small number of classes of abstraction so that each contains a significant number of records. We also project some attributes, making the distribution denser in the Cartesian product of the remaining attributes (figure 2.3).

Both BACON and FAHRENHEIT perform experiments to collect data. A seemingly simple solution in database applications would be to replace the experimentation with database queries. However, because the data are sparse, most of the queries would be unanswered.

Now that we have examined problems specific to search for regularities in databases, we will briefly review BACON and FAHRENHEIT and discuss how they can be adapted to database discovery.

2.4.2 BACON Collects Experimental Data and Discovers Regularities

The BACON discovery system, developed at the beginning of the 1980s, couples two searches. One search, which we call BACON3, controls the design of experiments and summarizes the experiment results by calling the second search, BACON1, which is a curve fitter. When supplied with high-quality, clean data, BACON can discover a wide range of scientific laws (Langley et al. 1987).

BACON3 builds a tree similar to the tree in figure 2.5, selecting values of one independent variable at each level. At the leaves, when all values of independent variables have been selected, the experiments are performed. After a sequence of experiments has been conducted in which the independent variable has been varied at the lowest level, the curve-fitting mechanism (BACON1) is called to find a regularity. As the BACON3 search unwinds to higher levels, the regularity is generalized at each level, including the independent variable that was varied at this level.

A straightforward database application of BACON3 is not possible because the system applies a rigid mechanism of experimental data collection. For each attribute, BACON3 collects a fixed number of N values, and it experimentally explores the full Cartesian product of all independent value combinations, building a tree with the branching factor of N. Because data are sparse in databases—that is, most of the cells in the Cartesian product will contain no records—the curve fitter will not receive enough data to find a regularity. The mechanism used by BACON3 for building a tree of data must be made more flexible. It is important that the curve fitter obtains sufficient data at each level, but the data can be flexibly selected according to what is available in the database. When the rigid mechanism fails, a flexible mechanism can still provide sufficient data.

2.4.3 FAHRENHEIT Extends BACON in a Number of Ways

FAHRENHEIT extends BACON in several directions. First, it finds the range of the law it has discovered by determining the boundary that separates events that obey the law from events that do not. Phase boundaries are a good example. FAHRENHEIT applies the boundary search to collect the points that best approximate the boundaries and calls its own version of BACON1 to find regularities for boundaries. In general, the range can be described by a set of inequalities expressed in terms of independent variables. The description of the range of a law is the antecedent A of the conditional $A \rightarrow B$, and the mathematical formula B of the law becomes the consequent. Testing for A's satisfaction is critical for the proper use of the law.

Because we can hardly expect universal regularities in databases, the idea of a limited range of application is useful. However, although FAHRENHEIT detects a regularity and then searches for the range, this strategy might not work in databases because it is based on the difference between the predicted value and the one actually measured, compared against the measurement error. Although the equations discovered by FAHRENHEIT can be naturally expanded, it is hard to extrapolate a weak statistical regularity expressed as a contingency table.

Second, FAHRENHEIT can find a number of regularities separated by their boundaries, whereas BACON fails when data cannot be summarized by a single regularity. FAHRENHEIT's curve fitter is used in combination with a partitioning search that allows for the decomposition of a sequence of data into parts and for the finding of equations that separately fit different parts. If a number of regularities have been detected for different portions of data, FAHRENHEIT tries to generalize each as far as possible. As we discussed earlier, however, the boundaries are not well defined for statistical regularities, so that a straightforward application of FAHRENHEIT would not work. This dictates the reverse approach, in which a space of possible ranges is searched, and for each candidate range, the search for regularities is used.

Third, FAHRENHEIT is able to find areas in which no regularity has yet been detected. It finds regularities in these areas and continues until the whole space spanned by the values of independent variables is covered with regularities. Extending our terminology, we can call that space W_I. W_I is a subspace of W. In databases, we would also like to consider all areas of W_I, but because range selection comes before the regularity detection, the search in the space of possible ranges should be exhaustive.

Fourth, FAHRENHEIT dynamically controls data acquisition in response to earlier findings and new goals. Dynamic data acquisition requires unrestricted freedom in choosing the values of the independent variables in W_I. Full control over experiment generation cannot be assumed in database exploration because of the sparsity of data. We must use data selection strategies that are driven by the available data.

FAHRENHEIT combines a number of searches and builds a network of knowledge states. BACON3 selects values of independent variables, makes experiments, and collects experimental results. Another search manages the partitioning of data, and BACON1 attempts to find numeric regularities. The fourth search uses the discovered regularity on additional values of the independent variable and finds the boundaries of the regularity. The fifth search tries to generalize the regularity by adding new independent variables. The sixth search looks for new areas in which the regularity search hasn't been performed yet. Two other searches try to resolve conflicts and design crucial experiments in case of overlapping ranges. Each search is implemented as a separate search template, following the same generic structure. The whole multisearch system is automatically propelled by a common driving mechanism called the search interpreter (Żytkow and Jankowski 1988).

2.5 FORTY-NINER's Approach to Database Exploration

FORTY-NINER combines most of the features of BACON and FAHRENHEIT, but is organized differently. First, we briefly outline the system, and then we discuss the reasons for this particular design.

2.5.1 System Overview

The architecture of FORTY-NINER is illustrated in figure 2.2. The system operates in two phases. In the first phase, FORTY-NINER performs a search for two-dimensional regularities in a large space determined by subsets of data and combinations of independent and dependent variables. In the second phase, the regularities are generalized from two to more dimensions. Either phase can be repeated many times; at each cycle, the user can change search parameters and continue the exploration. This architecture links large-

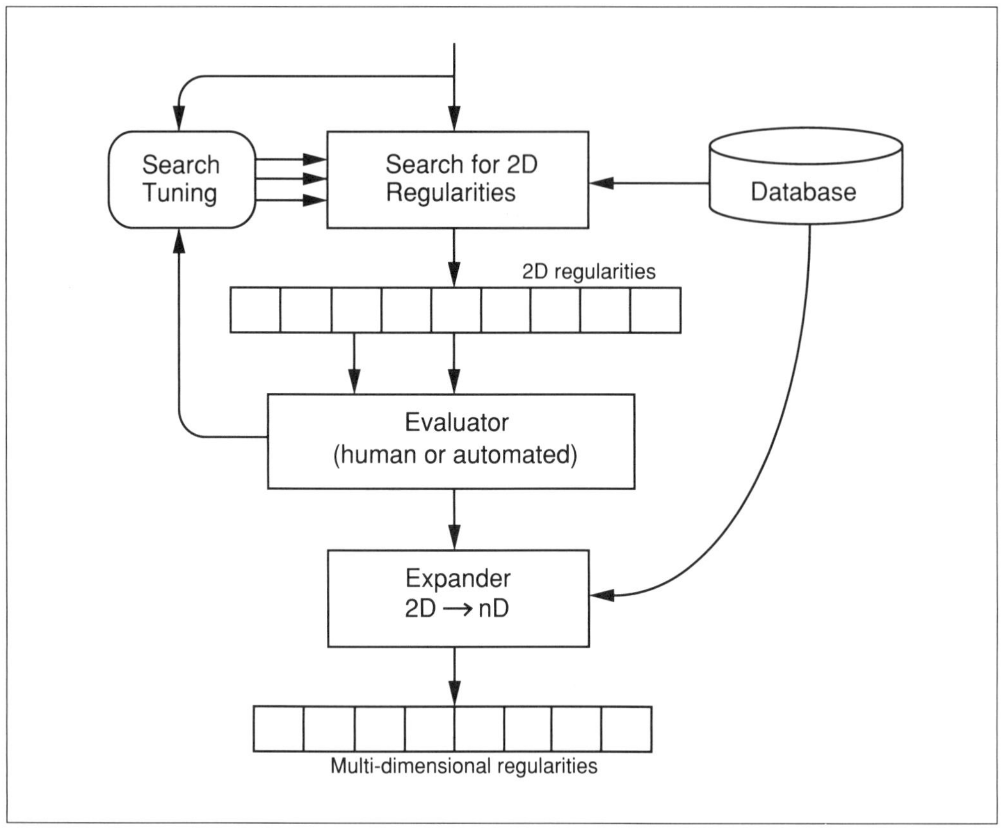

Figure 2.2
Overview of DB–49er.

scale automation with intervention by a human operator, combining the advantages of both approaches.

2.5.2 FORTY-NINER Adapts BACON and FAHRENHEIT to Database Mining

BACON and FAHRENHEIT belong to the research program that aims at the cognitive autonomy by expanding automation and limiting human intervention in the discovery process. In building FORTY-NINER, we followed the automation paradigm, but we also required the user to examine the results and decide which of them should be further refined and generalized. The space of possible regularities that can occur in various types of databases is far too large and complex to be efficiently implemented and searched. BACON was designed to detect functional regularities that are characteristic of the physical sciences. FAHRENHEIT's find-regularity search is more powerful, but it is also designed to succeed on functional applications. The data in many databases, however, follow statistical patterns that can take on an enormous number of forms. Because so many types of regularities are possible, we decided to use a simple formalism that visualizes the statistical information for the user. With the help of visual inspection, the user can decide in each case whether a focused search for regularities is useful. For each database and each intended application of the results, a different direction of search for regularity refinement might be appropriate. Although we could include many curve-fitting capabilities in one automated system, such a system would spend much effort on a single data set with little probability of useful findings, whereas FORTY-NINER can examine hundreds of sets of data and present many regularities for the user's screening.

FAHRENHEIT tries to find a regularity in the data, and after it succeeds, it tries to determine the range of validity. FORTY-NINER follows the opposite strategy. It systematically searches a large class of possible ranges and tries to detect regularities within each range.

In the second phase, generalizing regularities to more dimensions, FORTY-NINER uses the idea of BACON3 and BACON1 but arranges them differently. Because of the sparsity of data, both searches are separated. First, the entire BACON3 tree is constructed; it must have enough data in it so that the following search for a regularity might have a chance to succeed. In the second stage, the tree is unwound as the curve fitter works recursively from the leaves to the root of the tree, at each step generalizing the regularity to the new dimension.

2.5.3 Human Intervention Helps in Regularity Refinement

Several reasons justify human intervention. In the first phase, FORTY-NINER can efficiently find a large number of two-dimensional regularities. We want the user to examine them because given an effective visualization, the eyes are able to quickly capture the specificity of regularities. Initially, FORTY-NINER looks for simple statistical regularities, but realizing that the data follow specific patterns, the user might apply more subtle curve-fitting mechanisms. Like BACON and FAHRENHEIT, FORTY-NINER is designed in a modular way, and one search mechanism can be replaced by another that performs an analogous function. The evaluation of regularities requires statistical tests and the selection of a threshold of acceptance for each test. Threshold selection can be either an arbitrary choice or a decision motivated by the domain knowledge and user goals. Humans can focus on the particularly interesting regularities and push the search in the direction of the most promising generalizations. Although FORTY-NINER lacks domain knowledge and does not understand the external meaning of regularities and data, the user can select particularly promising regularities and guide their refinement, for example, relevant variables for generalization.

2.6 Search for Two-Dimensional Regularities

The first phase of FORTY-NINER's operation uses two searches: partitioning and find-regularity. Before we analyze these searches, let us describe the input, output, and the repertoire of basic operations on attributes.

2.6.1 Input

FORTY-NINER can be used on relational databases. The database must consist of records of equal length, each record being a list of attribute values for the same sequence of attributes. Each value must be a number. Any missing values, such as the value of the fourth attribute in the third record in the following example, are disregarded in the formation of regularities that depend on this attribute:

```
record 1:    (12   0   121   1    33)
record 2:    (15   0   151   1    33)
record 3:    (15   0   185   nil  30)
```

If a relational database consists of more than one relational table, FORTY-NINER must be separately applied to each.

2.6.2 Output

In this phase, FORTY-NINER creates a list of two-dimensional regularities. Each regularity has been found in a particular subset of data and is returned in the form of a list **(size attr-list range reg-list)**, where **size** is the number of elements in the set of data (the sample size) in which this regularity was found. Other things being equal, the larger the size is, the more significant the regularity. Regularities that are supported by a small amount of data can be statistical fluctuations. The minimum size of the data set is a search parameter available to the user. **attr-list** is a list $(A_i A_j)$ of two attributes that have been compared to produce this regularity. **range** is the list of restrictions on the original data set that were used to form the data subset in which this regularity was found. Each restriction takes on the form $(A\ min\ max)$, which means that those values v of the attribute A are included, for which $min \leq v \leq max$. **reg-list** is a list of regularities on the data in the specified range. Each regularity captures a different aspect of data. Currently, three regularity patterns are used: two statistical contingency tables, called Stat-2 and Stat-All, and the best linear fit, Lin. To be recorded, each regularity must exceed a user-controlled threshold of significance.

2.6.3 Operations on Variables

FORTY-NINER performs three basic operations on each attribute: aggregation, slicing, and projection. *Aggregation* combines values of an attribute into classes of abstraction. By reducing the number of values, we increase the relative density of data, allowing for efficient screening of large ranges of data by the fast computation of simple statistical regularities. Typically, FORTY-NINER aggregates all values of an attribute into two classes: lower and higher. The system tries to ensure that the sets of records corresponding to both aggregates are of equal size, making the best possible approximation. However, other aggregation methods can also be used. For example, the data could be divided into more than two subsets, or the dividing point could be chosen by a different method.

We call the next operation *slicing*, or data partitioning. Taking a slice of a data set using the value v_i of attribute A_i means selecting all elements of the data set that have value v_i. Slicing reduces the amount and narrows the range of data. If a regularity is weak when we consider all values of the attribute A_i, it is possible that stronger regularities exist in one or more slices of A_i. When slicing works on the results of aggregation, and v_i is an aggregate of values, all elements with a value of A_i in v_i are included in the slice. Because of the search complexity caused by slicing in our system, slicing is restricted to the aggregated attributes.

Projecting the attribute A_i is equivalent to ignoring this attribute; all records are included regardless of the value of A_i. In the multidimensional space W introduced in section 2.3, "What is a Regularity?," where each attribute represents one dimension, slicing and projecting reduce the number of dimensions. Projection and aggregation are useful in reducing the sparsity of data in W.

In figure 2.3, we show examples of slicing and projecting a three-dimensional space. The data in this space follow a strong regularity: $A_3 = (A_1 + A_2)/2$. If the space is sliced using a particular value of A_1, then a similarly strong linear regularity is found between A_2 and A_3. However, if it is projected along A_1 instead, only a weak linear relationship can be detected. If we first aggregated values of A_1 and then took a slice using one of the aggregates, we could find a moderately strong linear relationship between A_2 and A_3. Note that if the variable A_3 is used for projection, the regularity is virtually lost as a result.

2.6.4 Partitioning Search

The partitioning search is used to produce subsets of the database to be searched for two-dimensional regularities. Partitioning generates all combinations of the given independent and dependent variables (figure 2.4). It also considers all slices of data unless they contain too few data points. The find-regularity search for two-dimensional regu-

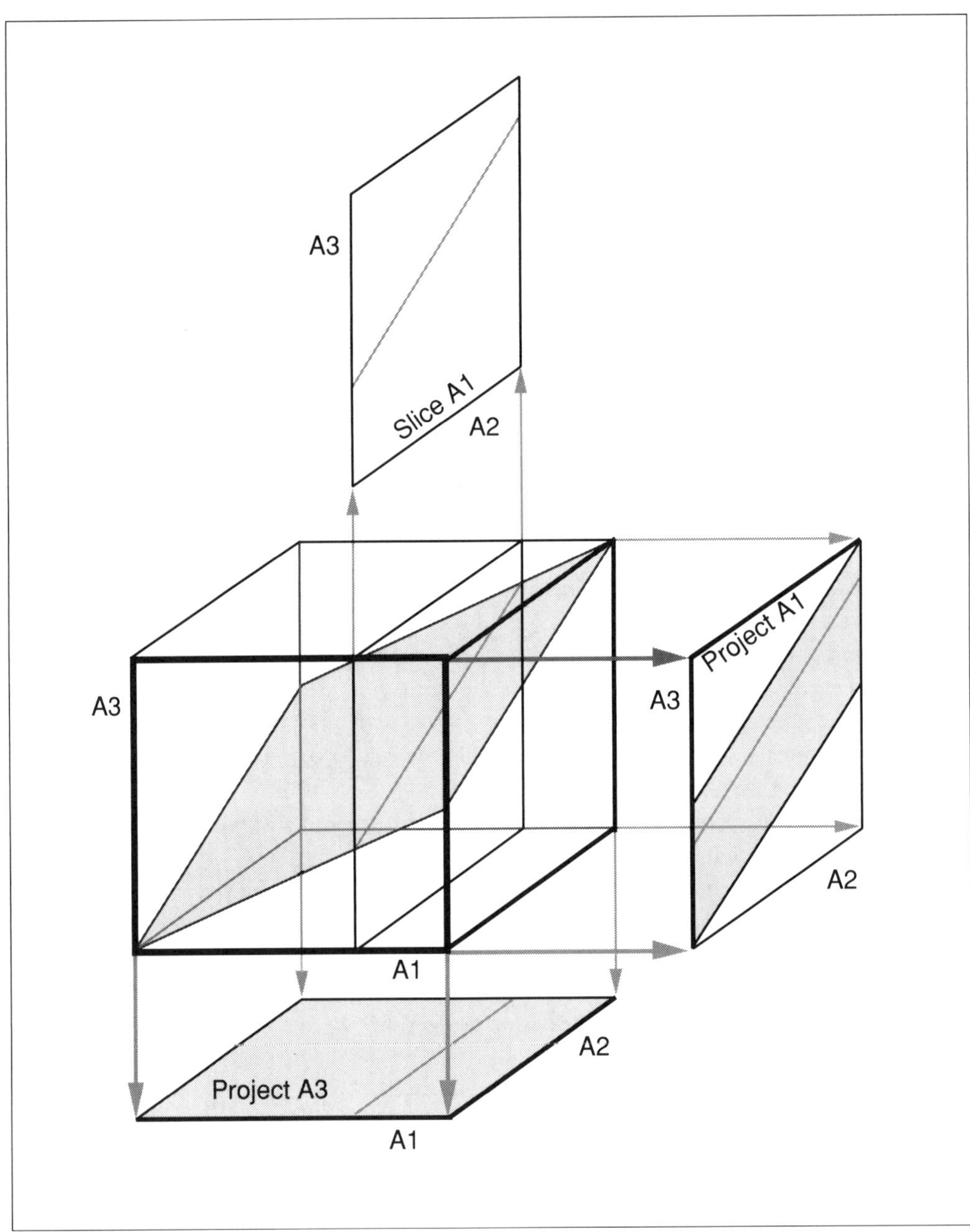

Figure 2.3
Slicing and Projecting.

larities is called at each leaf of the partitioning search tree. It is passed onto the set of data available at a given leaf.

Search control: Partitioning can be controlled by the selection of the sets of independent and dependent variables and by the minimum size of a data set that will not be further sliced. The effect of the minimum slice size on the depth of the partitioning search is depicted as the boundary on the minimum number of records in figure 2.4. The data set is either sliced or projected for each independent attribute.

For the sake of a meaningful and efficient search, FORTY-NINER should be told which attributes are independent and which are dependent. Whether a variable is dependent or independent is really a decision made outside the working of FORTY-NINER. The useful regularities hold between the independent or control variables, whose values can be set by user actions, and the dependent variables, those that the user wants to change indirectly and whose values are determined by the values of independent variables. If it is not known which variables are independent and which are dependent, all attribute pairs can be compared in an exhaustive search.

Search complexity: For N independent variables and M dependent variables, the number of combinations that can lead to two-dimensional regularities is $M \times N$. For $N = 30$ and $M = 5$, the number is 150. The partitioning search produces far more nodes, however, because in addition to situations in which all data are considered, there are many situations in which the data are sliced across one or more independent attribute. When FORTY-NINER considers two slices (based on two aggregates) for each independent attribute, plus the projection, a crude estimate of the total number of combinations seems to be on the order of 3^{N-1}. Fortunately, the search can be reduced by the use of two mechanisms: first, for each dependent variable, by limiting N to relevant independent variables and, second, by increasing the minimum slice size. Limiting data partition to K steps reduces the number of search leaves to 3^K. If $N = 30$ and $K = 5$, this number is a reduction from 3^{29} to 3^5 or a factor of 3^{24}. Dividing the minimum slice size by two, we add one more level to the search. The depth at which the search no longer branches is varied (figure 2.4) depending on the number of independent attributes and the minimum slice size.

2.6.5 Search for Regularities

The find-regularity search is applied to each data subset after all independent attributes have been sliced or projected. Find-regularity tries to find relationships between a dependent attribute D and an independent attribute I. Each sufficiently strong regularity is saved.

The use of numeric curve fitters was described in Langley et al. (1987). Each curve fitter can be viewed as a specialized tool. A collection of curve fitters can be viewed

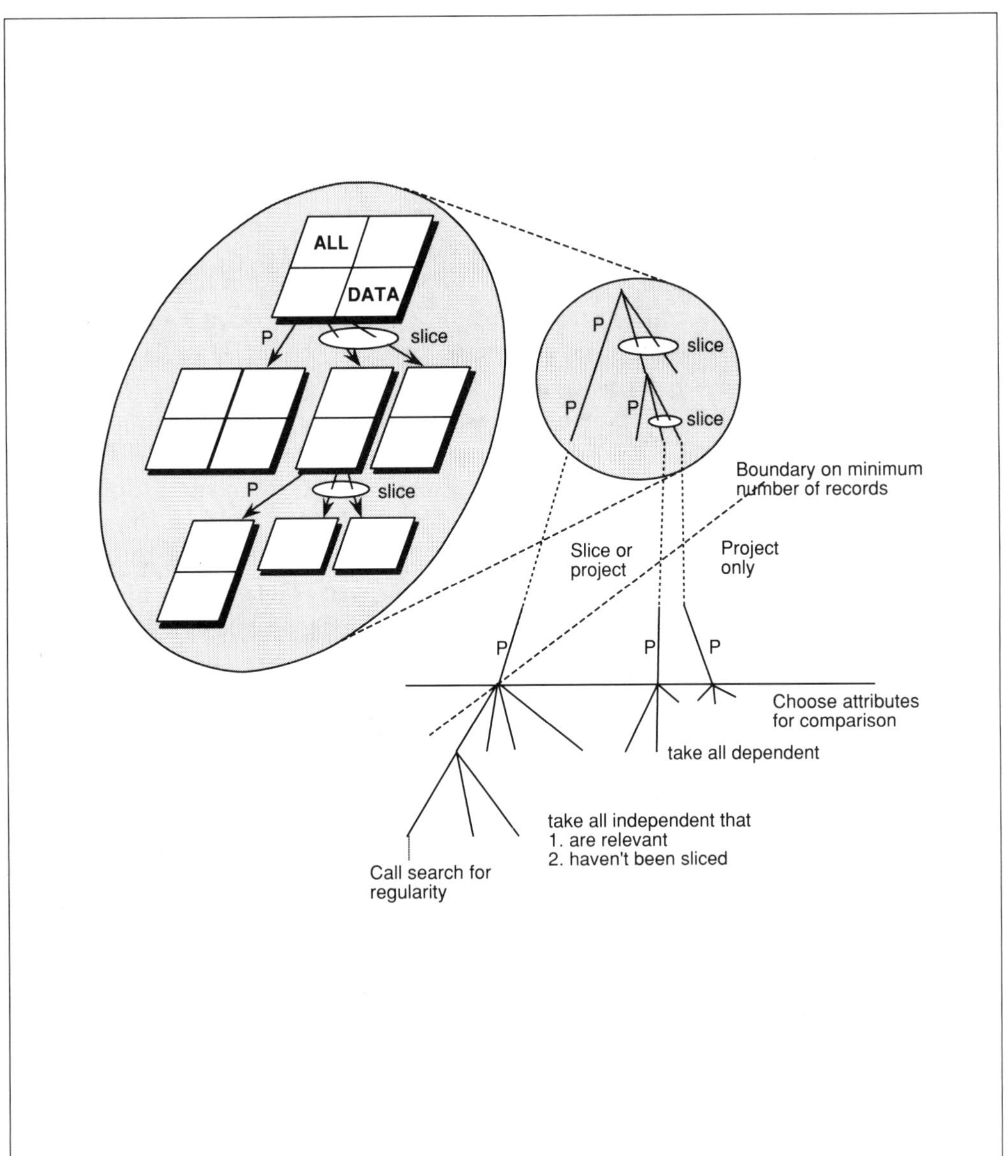

Figure 2.4
Data-Partitioning Search Tree.

as a collection of wrenches, among which we select those that can best do the job. FORTY-NINER uses an alternative to traditional curve fitters that is particularly useful for databases when only statistical regularities occur or when we want the user to visually inspect the regularities to decide on further refinements. We implemented two types of regularities, Stat-2 and Stat-All, represented in the form of contingency tables, and the best linear fit, Lin. The contingency tables Stat-2 and Stat-All occupy the opposite extremes in the spectrum of all contingency tables. In Stat-2, the values of each variable are aggregated into two classes, lower and higher. Thus, the contingency table consists of four fields. In Stat-All, we use the set $V(I)$ of all values of independent variables and the set $V(D)$ of all values of dependent variables. The Stat-All table consists of $|V(I)| \times |V(D)|$ fields. There is a separate field for every possible pair (i,d) of attribute values of the attributes I and D.

Each of these types of regularities is useful for different purposes. The simplest and most efficient—although crude—way to summarize a regularity in data is to use Stat-2. FORTY-NINER computes Stat-2 each time the partitioning search selects a range. The computation of Stat-All is much more costly if the product of the numbers of values of both attributes is large, but as a result, we obtain a table that can be displayed in a readable form and visually inspected. For large numbers of values of both attributes, Stat-All can be turned off or an aggregation can be applied to reduce the number of values.

Both Stat-2 and Stat-All regularities are expressed in the form **(reg-grid max-dif χ^2 expected actual)**, where **reg-grid** is a two-dimensional grid of values r_{jk} , $r_{jk} = (a_{jk} - e_{jk})/e_{jk}$, where a_{jk} is the actual number of records in which the value of the independent variable I is j, and the value of the dependent variable D is k. e_{jk} is the expected number of records. **max-dif** is the maximum percent difference between the observed and expected frequency of elements for one quadrant. A big deviation in one square is suspicious; so, we want the user to view such a regularity. χ^2 is the statistical measure of the significance of the given regularity. The higher this value, the more the observed data differ from the data expected in the absence of any regularity between I and D. **expected** is the grid of expected values e_{jk} calculated from the histograms of each attribute. Expected values are computed based on the null hypothesis assumption that both variables I and D are fully independent. If $|V(j)|$ is the number of records in which the value of I is j, $|V(k)|$ is the corresponding number of records for the value k of D, and N is the total number of records, then $e_{jk} = |V(j)| \times |V(k)|/N$. The expected values can be computed in two ways: (1) using the histograms made for the whole data set or (2) using histograms generated separately for each given subset of data considered by the search for regularities. The first method uses a larger sample size and can lead to a more legitimate model, provided that the independence of values holds for the partition.

However, if partitioning introduces an important distinction, so that the independence of values (null hypothesis) no longer holds, we would rather use the histogram that is separately generated for each data set. **actual** is the actual number of elements a_{jk} in each section of the grid.

Typically, FORTY-NINER detects plenty of regularities that are weak in comparison with regularities common in science but, nevertheless, are statistically significant according to χ^2 and max-dif measures.

Lin is obtained by using the least squares method, which returns the best linear fit for two variables, I and D, in a given data set. Lin can be represented in the form (**linear deviation** r^2), where **linear** is a linear regularity $D = mI + b$, m is the slope, and b is the intercept. **deviation** is the standard deviation of the line $D = mI + b$ against all data points used in the derivation of this equation. r^2 measures the proportion of variation explained by the proposed model. We use it as a measure of significance of linear regularities. r^2 is a value between 0 and 1, where 0 means no linear relationship, and 1 means that the data form a perfect line. The higher the value of r^2 is, the stronger the support of the given linear regularity. r^2 is calculated using the following formula:

$$r^2 = 1 - \frac{\sum_{i=1}^{n}(Y_i - \hat{Y}_i)^2}{\sqrt{\sum_{i=1}^{n}(Y_i - \overline{Y})^2}}$$

over all data points (X_i, Y_i), $n = 1, ..., n$, where $\overline{Y}$ is the average value of Y over the n data points, and $\hat{Y}_i$ is the value of Y predicted by the linear regularity.

Search control: Find-regularity can be controlled by a number of variables. Each of the three types of regularities has its own acceptance threshold, allowing us to introduce our own measure of weakness. All regularities that do not reach the thresholds are discarded. If all thresholds are set to Ø, FORTY-NINER will store all results, no matter how weak they are. We advise beginning the exploration with relatively high threshold values and adjusting them depending on the number of regularities reported.

Manipulations on the thresholds affect the required amount of storage but do not affect the temporal efficiency. To increase the speed of the search, we can turn off the costly computation of Stat-All and Lin regularities or trigger these computations only for strong regularities in Stat-2. Other factors can also be used to determine the usefulness of a regularity, such as the number of data points for which the regularity holds or the simplicity of the regularity.

Two variables allow alternating between different strategies of aggregation and histogram computation. FORTY-NINER can aggregate the attribute values into abstraction classes and compute the histograms at the beginning of search, or it can repeat the computations for each new range selected by partitioning. The first strategy saves time because the computation is only done once for each attribute, and the second allows flexibility of concepts and can lead to more incisive results.

Search complexity: Search complexity is low for a single call to find regularities unless the number of values of each variable is large. Complexity depends on the number of data in the range, the number of distinct values of both attributes, and the regularities that the system looks for. Even if a single invocation of find-regularity takes little time, however, this search is repeated at each leaf of the partitioning tree; so, it consumes a large fraction of time.

2.7 From Two-Dimensional to Many-Dimensional Regularities

Expanding a regularity to include new variables offers several advantages. Regularities that include more variables are more general, fitting a larger class of situations. A multidimensional regularity allows us to better understand the interdependence between variables and the processes it describes. One n dimensional regularity can replace several $n-1$ dimensional regularities. For example, if a family of slices of a data set contains gradually changing linear regularities, then we might be able to combine these regularities into one regularity that fits the entire data set by adding a new dimension corresponding to the sliced attribute.

The regularity expansion module is used to extend regularities to more dimensions, working on one regularity at a time. The regularity expander requires a data set and a list of attributes to use. The attributes consist of one dependent attribute and several independent attributes. The desired form of the new regularity can also be supplied.

The regularity expander can be recursively applied, adding one dimension at a time.

2.7.1 Choosing Parameters for the Regularity Expander

Given the list of two-dimensional regularities produced in the first phase, it is up to the user to determine the promising candidates for generalization to many dimensions. One method might be to try to extend each two-dimensional regularity to include every other attribute, one at a time. Another approach would be to look for several related regularities and attempt to find a new regularity that combines them.

The system could have been designed to apply a regularity search to all possible multidimensional combinations of attributes; however, this search size would be exponential. User intervention allows multidimensional regularities to be sought based on the hints provided by the two-dimensional regularities. A human analyzer must look at the two-

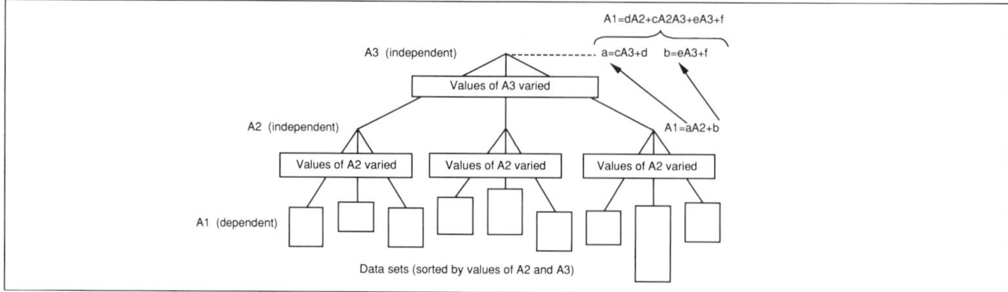

Figure 2.5
Generalizing Regularities to More Dimensions.

dimensional regularities and determine where the expander should focus. Particularly interesting regularities can be expanded first and some weaker regularities discarded.

2.7.2 Building a Data Tree

The regularity expander first uses the data set to form a BACON3 tree, the structure that includes enough data to enable a successful generalization. The number of levels in this tree equals the number of dimensions in the regularity being formed. A recursive algorithm is used to form the tree, which is completed if there is enough data in the supplied data set to achieve the required branching. Each iteration separates the data by the values of one of the attributes.

2.7.3 Backtracking the BACON3 Tree

Once the BACON3 tree has been created, it contains enough data to form the regularity. In the regularity generalization process, the BACON3 tree is backtracked from the leaves. At each level, one dimension is added to the regularities, which are gradually combined until there is one complete regularity when the root node is reached (figure 2.5).

2.8 Performance

FORTY-NINER has been applied on several databases. Typically, it finds a large number of statistically significant regularities. On closer scrutiny, many of these regularities are new and interesting, but many others are obvious to the database owner. For example, if after 1980 a job requires a high school diploma, then FORTY-NINER will find a much higher than expected percentage of employees with a high-school diploma among the post-1980 new hires, but it will find a percentage much lower than expected among employees hired prior to 1980.

Table 2.1
Search for Stat-2 Regularities in a Database of 6224 Records and Six Attributes. The same tree was traversed each time so that the difference in run time indicates the time spent on output delays and the waits associated with storing the regularities. Max-dif measures the significance of regularities as the maximum percentage difference between the actual and expected number of records in one cell. Time is in minutes on a Sun 3/60 workstation.

max-dif	0.01	0.05	0.10	0.20	0.30	1.0
Time	5:26	4:45	4:06	3:01	2:35	2:06
Number of regularities	199	166	126	64	35	0

The computational complexity of FORTY-NINER depends on many factors. We concentrate on a few. In the first phase, the partitioning search is affected by the number of independent and dependent attributes being examined as well as the minimum data set allowed. The search for regularities is mainly affected by the choice of regularities searched for and somewhat by the minimum strength required to accept regularities. Our tests confirmed that increasing the number of independent attributes exponentially increased the computation time, and increasing the number of dependent attributes linearly increased the computation time. Increasing the minimum range size decreased both the computation time and the number of regularities found. The exponential increase in complexity caused by the number of independent variables is bounded by the minimum range size. The exponent is equal to $min(I-1, \log_2(R/M))$, where I is the number of independent variables, R is the number of records, and M is the minimum range size. Increasing the minimum acceptable strength of regularity significantly reduced the number of regularities found, as shown in table 2.1.

To give an example of FORTY-NINER's performance, we have conducted several runs of the system on a database containing 6224 records of 36 attributes, from which we selected up to 6 attributes at a time. The time to complete the two-dimensional regularity search varied from a few seconds to more than five minutes on a Sun 3/60. The number of two-dimensional regularities found ranged from a few to a few hundred. Building a BACON3 search tree took from a few seconds to several minutes. The unwinding search for the regularities never exceeded 3 seconds.

The performance in the second phase depends to a larger degree on the type of data. Failure in building a BACON3 tree is possible because of the sparsity of data.

2.9 Summary

FORTY-NINER can efficiently search large databases. It generates three types of two-dimensional regularities and allows the user to guide the generalization of the selected regularities. Global variables allow the user to adjust the search process to specific requirements of time and space, and to specify the significance level at which the user wants to retain regularities for further perusal. Experience in setting the level of significance at which regularities are retained is important because running the search on a large database can take a long time, during which FORTY-NINER examines thousands of regularities.

Acknowledgments

This work was supported by the Office of Naval Research under grant N00014-90-J-1603 and a Naval Personnel Research Development Center contract (Battelle 1653). The authors would like to thank Dr. Steven Sorensen for his stimulating ideas on database mining; Dr. Clifton Sutton for his advice on the application of statistical methods; and Sunny Ludvik, Barbara Mason, and Lance Petrie for their help in copyediting and proofing this chapter.

References

Bhattacharyya, G. K. and Johnson R. A. 1986. *Statistical Concepts and Methods*. New York: Wiley.

Chimenti, D.; Gamboa, R.; Krishnamurthy, R.; Naqvi, S.; Tsur, S.; and Zaniolo, C. 1990. The LDL System Prototype. *IEEE Transactions on Knowledge and Data Engineering* 2: 76–90.

Koehn, B., and Żytkow, J. M. 1986. Experimenting and Theorizing in Theory Formation. In Proceedings of the International Symposium on Methodologies for Intelligent Systems, 296-307. New York: Association for Computing Machinery.

Langley, P.; Simon, H. A.; Bradshaw, G.; and Żytkow, J. M. 1987. *Scientific Discovery: An Account of the Creative Processes*. Cambridge, Mass.: MIT Press.

Morik, K. 1987. Acquiring Domain Models. *International Journal of Man-Machine Studies* 26: 93–104.

Naqvi, S., and Tsur, S. 1989. *Logical Language for Data and Knowledge Bases*. New York: Computer Science Press.

Nordhausen, B., and Langley, P. 1990. An Integrated Approach to Empirical Discovery. In *Computational Models of Scientific Discovery and Theory Formation*, eds. J. Shrager and P. Langley, 97–128. San Mateo, Calif.: Morgan Kaufmann.

Piatetsky-Shapiro, G., and Frawley, W. eds. 1989. Proceedings of the IJCAI-89 Workshop on Knowledge Discovery in Databases. Waltham, Mass.: GTE Laboratories.

Rose, D., and Langley, P. 1986. Chemical Discovery as Belief Revision. *Machine Learning* 1: 423–451.

Shrager, J., and Langley, P. eds. 1990. *Computational Models of Scientific Discovery and Theory Formation*. San Mateo, Calif.: Morgan Kaufmann.

Żytkow, J. M. 1990. Deriving Laws through Analysis of Processes and Equations. In *Computational Models of Scientific Discovery and Theory Formation*, eds. J. Shrager and P. Langley, 129–156. San Mateo, Calif.: Morgan Kaufmann.

Żytkow, J. M. 1987. Combining Many Searches in the FAHRENHEIT Discovery System. In *Proceedings of the Fourth International Workshop on Machine Learning*, 281–287. San Mateo, Calif.: Morgan Kaufmann.

Żytkow, J. M., and Jankowski, A. 1988. Hierarchical Control and Heuristics in Multisearch Systems, In *Methodologies for Intelligent Systems*, volume 4, ed. Z. Ras, 86–93. New York: Elsevier.

Żytkow, J. M., and Lewenstam, A. 1990. Analytical Chemistry: The Science of Many Models. *Fresenius Journal of Analytical Chemistry* 338: 225-233.

3 Discovering Functional Relationships from Observational Data

Yi-Hua Wu and Shulin Wang
Academia Sinica

Abstract

This chapter outlines the Reduction algorithm for discovery of functional relationships from observational data and its implementation in the KEPLER system. The Reduction algorithm decomposes a multivariate formula into binary formulas and finds the appropriate binary formula by varying two variables at a time and matching data to a set of prototype functions. We prove that under certain assumptions, Reduction has polynomial run time. The main features of the KEPLER system include the discovery of multiple equations; the ability to check data correctness; the discovery of partial relations; and a user-friendly, interactive environment. We also report several interesting results, including discoveries and rediscoveries of numeric laws, mainly in physics. Finally, we compare our approach to BACON, ABACUS, and COPER.

3.1 Introduction

With the rapid growth of the amount of accessible data, there is a growing need for the discovery of knowledge hidden in data. Traditional data analysis emphasizes the statistical aspects of data and ignores the domain knowledge. As a result, it frequently fails to reveal the physical nature that the data imply. Recent advances in machine learning open the possibility of automated discovery. In this chapter, we focus on the discovery of functional relationships, such as physical laws, from observational data. This problem can be stated as follows:

Problem: Given n variables (also called terms) $x_1, x_2, \ldots, x_n$ and k groups of observational data $d_1, d_2, \ldots, d_k$ (where each d_i is a set of n values—one for each variable), find a formula $f(x_1, \ldots, x_n)$ that best fits the data and symbolically reveals the physical relationship among the variables.

The search space for this problem is a function of the number of data points, the number of variables, and the number and types of operators that connect the variables. Except for very small values of these parameters, the search space for the problem—the number of possible formulas that fit the data—is extremely large. To make the search feasible, we adopt three simplifying assumptions: (1) each variable appears in the formula just once, (2) each operator takes at most two variables as its arguments, and (3) two functions that differ only by a constant (for example, $x^2 + 3$ and $x^2 + 7$) are considered equivalent.

Because too many formulas might still fit the data, we need to use additional domain knowledge to provide the bias toward the formulas that are appropriate for the domain. This approach was pioneered by Langley with the BACON system (Langley, Bradshaw, and Simon 1983; Langley et al. 1987) and was extended by Falkenhainer and Michalski (1986) with the ABACUS system. The common problem of these systems is that user hints are required to handle nonlinear or nonhyperbolic relations. Wu (1988a, 1988b, 1988c, 1989) introduced and implemented the Reduction algorithm for searching for regularities, which can better handle more complex functional forms.

This chapter describes Rreduction and its implementation and compares Reduction with BACON, ABACUS, and COPER (Kokar 1986). Some interesting experimental results are presented.

3.2 The Reduction Method

The main purpose of Reduction is to search for regularities implied in data. Given a set of relevant and complete variables and their corresponding observational data, Reduction efficiently finds the underlying numeric relation among the variables. The relation is supposed to reveal the physical nature in the domain. Here, we simply present an outline with no theoretical details. For a strict definition and proof, refer to Wu (1988c) (an English version is being prepared).

Considering the difficulty of discovering a complex law with multiple variables, Reduction decomposes a multivariate law into binary laws. Discovering a binary law is much simpler because the possible forms of binary formulas are greatly limited. The following figure presents the algorithm of Reduction R(n,2) in a Pascal–like language (Wu 1988a). Here, n is the number of variables, and 2 is the number of terms considered on each cycle. In the following discussion, we sometimes refer to data groups as data points; each group is a point in n–dimensional space.

3.2.1 Primitive Functions and Prototypes

The primitive function (Wu 1988b, 1988c) is the key concept underlying Reduction, as shown in figure 3.1. Conceptually, the *primitive function* is the nondivisible part of a formula. Dividing a formula means putting the formula into different parts, with each variable appearing in only one part. You discover a formula by discovering its parts. This discovery is possible because parts are independent of each other. Therefore, with Reduction, discovering a complex multivariate formula is accomplished by finding its primitive functions.

In most cases, a primitive is simply considered a binary function that appears in the

```
success = TRUE
for k = n downto 2 do
 if success then
   begin
    success = FALSE
    for i = 1 to k do
     for j = i + 1 to k do
      if not success then
        begin
         Obtain data points where x_i and x_j vary,
         while other variables are constant;
         if there is a primitive function p(x_i, x_j) then
           begin
            Define x_ij = p(x_i, x_j);
            Replace x_i and x_j with x_ij in input data;
            success = TRUE
           end
        end
   end
output results.
```

Figure 3.1
An Outline of the Reduction R(n,2) Algorithm.

formula. Given the example $x^2 - yz = 1$, Reduction first considers x and y but fails to find a primitive function between x and y. It then considers x and z. This process is repeated until it finds a primitive function $p(y, z) = yz$. After defining a new term (also called a theoretical term) $T = yz$ and removing y and z, Reduction tries to match the data with x and T. In the second cycle, it finds another primitive function $p(x, T) = x^2 - T$. The process is stopped when success is achieved.

Obviously, successful discovery heavily depends on having appropriate primitive functions, which is typical for the generate-and-test approach. First, we generate a function whose value is invariant under changes in two variables (also called a *constant function*), and then we check if it is a primitive function. Generation is accomplished by matching data with a set of prototypes. The prototype is an undetermined binary function, such as

1. $p(x, y) = x^{r_1} + c * y^{r_2}$
2. $p(x, y) = x^{r_1} * y^{r_2}$
3. $p(x, y) = (x^{r_1} + c_1)^{r_2} * (y^{r_3} + c_2)$

Let us consider this example: Data satisfy the unknown to us formula $x^2 - yz = 1$. When z is held constant to 1, we have a set of varying x and y values:

$x =$	2	3	4	6
$y =$	3	8	15	35

We match the data with each prototype p to see if we can set the parameters of the prototype to satisfy the equations: $p(2,3) = p(3,8) = p(4,15) = p(6,35)$. Setting the parameters is done by solving a system of nonlinear equations. For the first prototype, $p(x,y) = x^{r_1} + c * y^{r_2}$, the equations are:

$$2^{r_1} + c * 3^{r_2} = 3^{r_1} + c * 8^{r_2} = 4^{r_1} + c * 15^{r_2} = 6^{r_1} + c * 35^{r_2}. \tag{3.1}$$

We use three methods to solve such equations for values of parameters r_1, c, and r_2. The simplest one is to enumerate possible integer or rational values. This method is useful when the number of possible values is small and is typically used for values of powers, such as r_1 and r_2. The second method is to obtain in advance an analytic solution for values of each parameter in the prototype. Unfortunately, this method is applicable only to simple prototypes. In our case, we can apply this method for getting the value of c, while enumerating the values of r_1 and r_2. When the first two methods fail, we resort to universal methods for numeric solutions of nonlinear equations, such as the B-F-S algorithm (Ortega and Rheinboldt 1970).

The final result is that equation 3.1 is solvable by $r_1 = 2$, $c = -1$, $r_2 = 1$. This means that when $z = 1$, x and y match the prototype 1, giving us a constant function $p(x,y) = x^2 - y$.

The next, most creative step of Reduction method is verification. Here, we present an outline and refer an interested reader to Wu (1988b, 1988c) for more details. We illustrate verification using the previous example $x^2 - yz = 1$. However, the same steps can be applied to other formulas.

Step 1. Change z to a new value $z = 2$, and get two data points, where $x = 2, y = 1.5$ and $x = 3, y = 4$.

Step 2. Compute $p(2, 1.5)$ and $p(3, 4)$.

Step 3. If $p(2, 1.5) = p(3, 4)$, then $p(x, y)$ is considered to be constant for z, and we need to change other variables and make a new comparison, as previously described. Otherwise, $p(x, y)$ is not a primitive function.

Step 4. If $p(x, y)$ is constant for all other variables, then it is a primitive function.

In our example, the verification step will not find a primitive function for x and y or for x and z. However, when this procedure is applied to y and z, it will find a primitive function, $p(y, z) = yz$.

Clearly, the prototypes play an important role in discovery. Any complex formula to be discovered is an iterative combination of simple prototypes, with their parameters assigned to specific values. Thus, the set of prototypes determines the formula search space.

3.2.2 Theoretical Analysis

We do not go into theoretical details, but some analysis is necessary. Please refer to Wu (1988c) for a complete description.

First, we analyze the run-time complexity. For n variables, the Reduction algorithm has at most $n-1$ cycles. In cycle k, there are $n-k+1$ variables left. In the worst case, all C_2^{n-k+1} pairs of variables will have to be examined, where $C_J^I = \frac{I!}{J!(I-J)!}$. Let T_{GF} be the time for generating and verifying a primitive function for a pair of variables. Generation of test data and solution of nonlinear equation system require a constant time. Verification requires $n-2$ computations and comparisons. Thus, the worst-case run time is

$$WORST(R(n,2)) = T_{GF} * (C_2^n + C_2^{n-1} + \ldots + C_2^2) \approx O(n^4). \tag{3.2}$$

In the average case, we can expect that half of all variable pairs will be examined; the average run time will be about half of the worst-case run time. In both cases, run time is a polynomial in n—the number of variables.

By studying R(n,2) in figure 3.1, we can easily see that Reduction adopts a depth-first search without backtracking. This search strategy is successful in limiting the run-time complexity, but what about its validity? In regular search, backtracking is necessary because it leads to an alternative when a failure node is reached. Fortunately, we found one of the most interesting theorems (Wu 1988c) of Reduction, called the *backtracking elimination principle*, which says that any alternative originating from backtracking does not help to find a successful solution.

Theorem 1 (backtracking elimination principle): Given a prototype base, m primitive functions that have been found, and m terms $T_1, \ldots, T_m$ that have been defined during Reduction, if a new primitive function cannot be found among $T_1, \ldots, T_m$ and the remaining variables under the *normal condition*, then there is no need to backtrack to redefine $T_1, \ldots, T_m$ to consider other search paths, because any new path will also lead to a failure node where no primitive function can be found with the same prototype base.

The precise specification of the *normal condition* is too mathematical to describe here, but we can give an intuitive description. For a system of n equations with n unknowns, the normal condition means that the system has only one solution. Thus, the normal condition is a common case that most common formulas satisfy.

After generating a constant function $h(x_1, x_2)$, it is necessary to verify if it remains constant when other variables change. This property is satisfied by a primitive function but can be violated by nonprimitive constant functions. The key point is that a primitive function must be a non-divisible part of the entire formula. Thus, the central criterion of verification is to see whether the generated constant function is a nondivisible part of the formula. The previous section gave a step-by-step procedure for fast verification. The validity of this procedure is guaranteed by following theorem 2. The intuition behind this theorem is that $h(x_1, x_2)$ will be a nondivisible part of the formula if changing $x_3, \ldots, x_n$ to new values will lead to the same constant function $h(x_1, x_2)$. The idea of the fast verification method is that there is no need to generate other constant functions of x_1 and x_2 when changing $x_3, \ldots, x_n$. Instead, only a simple computation is done, as described in the previous section.

Theorem 2 (verification principle): Given a formula $f(x_1, x_2, \ldots, x_n) = C$, let $h(x_1, x_2)$ be a constant function generated from a set of data where x_1 and x_2 vary, and values of $x_3, \ldots, x_n$ are fixed at $d_3, \ldots, d_n$. With x_3 changed to d'_3, let us examine two data points $(x_1 = a_1, x_2 = a_2, x_3 = d'_3, \ldots)$ and $(x_1 = b_1, x_2 = b_2, x_3 = d'_3, \ldots)$. If $h(a_1, a_2) = h(b_1, b_2)$, then x_3 does not appear in $h(x_1, x_2)$ under the normal condition.

From this theorem, we immediately get a simple method for verification: Alternatively change other variables, and verify whether the constant function keeps the same value. This method is much faster than generating all other constant functions.

3.2.3 Data Model

Reduction places a special requirement on input data, which consist of two parts: data for the generation of constant functions, and data for their verification. There are C_2^n pairs of n terms. For each pair x_i, x_j, we need m generation data points (that is, groups of data) and $2(n-2)$ verification data points—a pair of points for each remaining variable $x_k, k \neq i, j$. Therefore, the number of data points needed is

$$C_2^n * (m + 2 * (n - 2)) = \frac{1}{2} n(n-1)(m + 2n - 4). \tag{3.3}$$

When a new term $x_{ij} = h(x_i, x_j)$ is introduced, the input data are reorganized by replacing values of x_i with $h(x_i, x_j)$ and deleting x_j. No extra data are needed.

3.2.4 Implementation Issues

The Reduction method is implemented in the KEPLER system (Wu 1988a, 1988c). Here, we describe the main characteristics of KEPLER.

Generality: KEPLER is a domain-independent discovery system. The domain knowledge is mainly contained in the functional prototypes. The selection of prototypes and their priority is domain dependent. KEPLER provides users with a user-friendly prototype editor to facilitate building and modifying its prototype base.

Table 3.1
Different Cases of Imperfect Data and Corresponding Solutions. $h(x_i, x_j)$ represents the primitive function of x_i and x_j.

Data	*Description*	*Solution*
Incomplete Data	Both generation and verification data points are unavailable	No primitive function between x_i and x_j
	Some generation data points are unavailable	Lessen the credit of $h(x_i, x_j)$
	Some verification data points are unavailable	same as above
Incorrect Data	Some generation data points violate the constancy	Lessen the credit of $h(x_i, x_j)$, and suggest to check the data
Imprecise Data	A small deviation from exact constancy	Adjusting ϵ (see next section)

Flexibility: KEPLER works interactively. Users can affect its behavior by adjusting parameters and control settings.

Utility: KEPLER does not ignore the real complexity of the scientific discovery. It can appropriately deal with imperfect data (table 3.1). Utility is further demonstrated in the subsequent sections.

If the input data are taken from real experiments, they are always imprecise because of imprecise instruments and observers, simplified models in designing experiments, and other unavoidable complex factors from the real world. In developing a practical data analyzer, these factors cannot be ignored. The methodology adopted in KEPLER is based on distinguishing unreliable and incomplete data.

The unreliable data deviate from the theoretical (or exact) values of terms. According to the degree of deviation, it can be classified into *imprecise data* (a small deviation) and *incorrect data* (a large deviation). The incomplete data are data that are not available for various reasons. The different cases of imperfect data are listed in table 3.1, along with corresponding solutions.

To deal with situations where there is no primitive function that exactly fits the data, we introduce a measure of uncertainty called *credit*. The credit is an integer between 1 (poor fit) and 100 (exact fit). The credit is an important piece of information to aid users in choosing the best primitive function to fit the data. Exact primitive functions can be generated only on the basis of complete and correct data.

3.3 Discovering Numeric Laws

Table 3.2 presents some examples of KEPLER's discoveries of numeric laws grouped by input data. The first group of artificial data is generated according to a previously known formula, which KEPLER successfully rediscovers. As long as the prototype base stores the corresponding prototype, KEPLER will quickly find the original law. In fact, most discoveries take only a few minutes on a Compaq Deskpro 386/15 without co-processor. The run time mainly depends on the number of active prototypes.

The real data are acquired from the actual experiments or observations. Here, KEPLER discovered previously unknown laws that satisfy the data. The main difficulty is that we do not know how to build a proper prototype base that determines the possible forms of the laws. It helps if the user has some understanding of the likely primitive functions. In discovering law 7 in table 3.2, a geologist suggested that a logarithm might be appropriate to describe the relation. We set up a prototype with a high priority for matching:

$$p(x, y) = (c_1 * \ln x + c_2)^{r_1} / y^{r_2} \tag{3.4}$$

However, the problem arises when the user does not have a sufficient understanding of the domain. In this case, we suggest making the prototype base as complete as possible. Although the number of all prototype functions is unlimited, we believe that only a limited number of reasonable ones are sufficient because they can be combined in many ways to cover numerous complicated laws. In fact, our experiments used only 20 prototypes (see section 3.10, "A Prototype List" near the end of this chapter).

To handle the imprecision of real data, we consider two real numbers x and y to be equal if $\text{abs}(x - y)/x < \epsilon$, where $\text{abs}(z)$ is the absolute value of z. We found that the value of ϵ significantly affects the number of the different laws found for the same data. For example, in discovering law 1, the first run with $\epsilon = 0.12$ led to the discovery of another formula:

$$x_1^{1/2} + 0.69 * x_2^{1/2} * x_3^{1/3} = 2.665. \tag{3.5}$$

After dynamically adjusting ϵ to 0.01, only the original formula was discovered. We prefer to treat this problem as a positive phenomenon. It is the user's obligation to choose the most reasonable formula among all that satisfy the data. An appropriate setting of ϵ allows the user either to get more accurate formulas at the cost of more computation or to get fast answers at the cost of decreased accuracy.

Can KEPLER or its improved version make any significant discovery? We believe that the answer is yes but with a few conditions. First, there must be some active research in the domain of discovery with a primary theoretical foundation and many well-defined

Table 3.2
A List of Selected Laws Discovered by KEPLER 1.0.

Group 1.	Common Laws from Artificial Data.
No.	*Law*
1	$1.5 * \ln x_1 + x_2^{1/2} * x_3^{1/3} = 3$
2	$\sin i / \sin r = N_1/N_2$, Snell's Law of Refraction
3	$\frac{1}{2} d * v^2 + d * g * z + p = K$, Bernoulli's Theorem

Group 2.	Segmented Laws from Artificial Data.
No.	*Law*
4	$x_1^3 + 2.5 * (\sin x_2)^2 / \sin x_3 = 1$, when $x_4 = 3n + 1$ $x_1^3 + 2.5 * (\sin x_2)^2 / \sin x_3 = 10$, when $x_4 = 3n + 2$ $x_1^3 + 2.5 * (\sin x_2)^2 / \sin x_3 = 20$, when $x_4 = 3n$
5	$x_1^3 + 2.5 * (\sin x_2)^2 / \sin x_3 = 1$, when x_4 in [aa11,aa22,aa33,aa88]
	$x_1^3 + 2.5 * (\sin x_2)^2 / \sin x_3 = 10$, when x_4 in [bb11,bb22,bb33]
	$x_1^3 + 2.5 * (\sin x_2)^2 / \sin x_3 = 20$, when x_4 in [cc11,cc22,cc33]
6	$y = (\sin x)^{1/3} + 10$, when $z = n^2$ $y = (\sin x)^{1/3} + 20$, when $z \neq n^2$

Group 3.	Real Experimental Data That Obey an Unknown Law
No.	*Law*
7	$(2 * \ln x_1 + 30.545)^3 / (x_2^{1/3} + 92.248 * x_3^{1/4}) = 7.6^3$, it is derived from a set of data which obey an unknown relationship. The problem is to form a response equation in well-logging, which is commonly used in oil exploration. The traditional approach is to use a two-dimensional interpolation.
8	$k = t^3$, where t is the temperature and k is the thermal conductivity of ZnO ceramic

and unsolved problems. Second, the problems must be quantitative. A large amount of experimental or observational data must be available and accessible. Third, there should be numeric laws that are neither too complicated nor too simple. Complicated laws are usually considered meaningless by specialists and simple laws have been discovered already. Fourth, domain scientists must cooperate by supplying the required data and hints or instructions and paying attention to the partial findings that KEPLER has made. Any significant discoveries are likely to occur only through interaction between a human and the computer.

Unfortunately, to date, KEPLER has failed to find any significant law that helps to understand the nature of the domain. The two laws of group 3 discovered by KEPLER are not used to reveal the physical relationship among the variables. This outcome is somewhat disappointing, but the discovery of any significant law is extremely difficult even to scientists, let alone computers.

3.4 Discovering Multiple Equations

Sometimes, no prototypes match the entire data set. Then, we try to segment the data into different parts satisfying different preconditions and match each part with the prototypes. For example, a data set DS of (x, y) values that does not fit any single function h can fit $h_1(x, y) = C_1$ when condition $pre1(x, y)$ is true and $h_2(x, y) = C_2$ when $pre2(x, y)$ is true. Group 2 in table 3.2 shows some examples of multiple equations discovered by KEPLER from artificial data. KEPLER's approach to the discovery of multiple equations is similar to that of ABACUS. The types of preconditions handled by KEPLER include the following:

- Segmenting by disjoint ranges of a real or integer variable; for example,

  $DS = (1, 2), (3, 6), (4, 8), (-2, -4), (5, 6), (6, 7), (8, 9), (10, 11)$.

  After segmenting by $x \leq 4$, we have

  $$h(x, y) = \begin{cases} y - 2x = 0 & \text{if } x \leq 4 \\ y - x = 1 & \text{otherwise} \end{cases}$$

- Segmenting by remainder after division of an integer variable by some constant m divides the data into m disjoint sets, corresponding to remainders $0, 1, \ldots, m - 1$; for example,

  $DS = (1, 3), (3, 5), (7, 9), (9, 11), (2, 2), (4, 3), (6, 4), (8, 5)$.

  Segmenting by division of x by $m = 2$, we have

$$h(x,y) = \begin{cases} y - x = 2 & \text{if } x = 2n+1 \\ 2y - x = 2 & \text{if } x = 2n \end{cases}$$

- Segmenting by distinct values or subsets of values of a nominal variable: This approach is useful for discovering intrinsic properties, as done in BACON. If there is a generalization hierarchy on the values of the nominal variable, it can guide the segmentation.

3.5 Other Uses of KEPLER

One by-product of KEPLER is its ability to identify possibly incorrect data, which happens when most data match a prototype with only a few exceptions. These exceptions are suspicious as possibly incorrect data. We performed an experiment by altering a correct value and running KEPLER. It was able to successfully identify this value. We have not done extensive experiments, and no statistical results are reported here.

Another use of Reduction is its contribution to the analysis of the variable dependencies. If given n variables, KEPLER finds two laws $f(x_1, \ldots, x_m)$ and $f(x_{m+1}, \ldots, x_n)$ and no other dependencies between the variables, then it can deduce that the first m variables are independent of the remaining variables. To date, we have not found such a case in our experiments.

When KEPLER fails to discover a complete law, it displays a partial solution found, the plausible solutions, the possible source of the failure or inefficiency, and suggestions for the next step. Based on this information, users have several choices, including modifying prototypes, adjusting parameters, choosing a plausible solution, or letting KEPLER make the choice. Users can also decide to redesign experiments based on KEPLER's feedback.

3.6 Transforming the Data into Reduction Format

The Reduction algorithm requires that the input data have points where two variables vary, and others are held constant. This requirement is relatively easy to satisfy when the data come from a controllable experiment. Transformation of the uncontrolled, randomly obtained data into the format needed by Reduction is difficult, however. One possibility is to use linear interpolation to compute the missing values. This approach does not work well because the missing data are highly localized. We usually want to vary the values of two variables, and these points are centered in a region where other variables are fixed to constants. As a result, only a few sample data are used for computation, which inevitably leads to imprecise results. It is unlikely that an appropriate law can be constructed based on such data.

Another method is to fit the data to a predefined formula, such as a polynomial, as done by COPER (Kokar 1986). We use COPER's output as a method for acquiring the regular data that Reduction needs. By computing the formula, any required data are obtainable. This method is also the one currently used in KEPLER. However, in the case of multiple variables, it is computationally difficult to obtain a precise formula by curve fitting. Thus, the actual data usually deviate greatly from the predicted values, making a successful discovery difficult. To date, we have not found a good method of transforming the random data into the Reduction format.

3.7 Using Qualitative Knowledge

It is desirable to integrate quantitative and qualitative discovery. An example of such an integrated system is IDS (Nordhausen and Langley 1987).

In our context, the qualitative knowledge includes both domain-dependent and domain-independent knowledge. The former is useful in building the prototype base, selecting a prototype for matching, selecting a proper primitive function when multiple functions are found, and so on. The user typically has a lot of domain-dependent knowledge. However, it is difficult to formalize and extract this knowledge.

The domain-independent knowledge in the current version of KEPLER is stored as a set of rules that suggest which prototype should be matched first. A *rule condition* is mainly a geometric description of the shape of curves that a prototype takes on, and a *rule action* is an adjusted priority of matching a prototype. After obtaining a set of data points with varying x and y values, KEPLER computes the geometric shape of the curve of x and y and then fits the shape to the descriptions of the prototypes. The geometric shape is expressed in terms of the tendencies of the curve and its derivatives: increasing or decreasing. The prototype with a better fit is assigned a greater priority to be matched.

3.8 Discussion: BACON, ABACUS, COPER and KEPLER

In this section, we compare KEPLER with other systems for quantitative discovery, namely, BACON (Langley, Bradshaw, and Simon 1987), ABACUS (Falkenhainer and Michalski 1986), and COPER (Kokar 1986). We compare the discovery task, search mechanism, and overall performance.

3.8.1 The Discovery Task

The main goals of these four systems are basically the same—to derive a quantitative law from a set of data as stated in the problem; however, their focuses are somewhat different. BACON seems to be more oriented toward modeling the early history of physics and chemistry and cognitive process of scientific discovery rather than applications to current data. ABACUS, COPER, and KEPLER focus on creating efficient discovery techniques and trying to apply them in a real context. Another difference is the scope of functions they can discover. BACON can rediscover the simple laws as well as the intrinsic properties of objects. To discover complicated laws, BACON needs guidance from the user.

ABACUS improved on BACON by discovering multiple equations and their corresponding preconditions and using physical dimensions of variables, such as acceleration = length/time^2. COPER analyzes the relevance of variables by extensively using physical dimensions to determine the missing and unrelated arguments and verifying the completeness of a set of arguments. It also matches the data to a polynomial to discover a formula. KEPLER is totally devoted to automatically discovering the complicated laws involving multiple variables and multiple equations in a scope defined by its prototype base.

COPER and ABACUS can input data in any order, whereas the input of the other systems must be arranged in a regular way: Two variables vary, and the others are held constant. Although KEPLER makes an effort to transform randomly obtained data into the regular data (see Transforming the Data into Reduction Format), it works much better if the input data are ordered in a regular way. Imperfect data (see Discovering Numeric Laws) are extensively investigated and appropriately dealt with in KEPLER, whereas the other systems pay less attention to it.

3.8.2 Search Mechanism

In combining variables into a new term, BACON first considers a linear relation, then multiplication and division, depending on whether the new term changes monotonously. The greatest drawback of this approach is the combinatorial explosion that happens when looking for complex laws. It becomes impossible to enumerate all the cases one by one. The new term might also lead to a dead node and result in a lot of backtracking.

ABACUS incorporates more heuristic information in defining the new terms but essentially suffers from the same problems. Both ABACUS and BACON ask for hints from users to deal with complicated laws. The hints, in fact, limit the formulas to an enumerable set of candidates that can then be tested one by one.

KEPLER handles the problem of new terms much better by using the Reduction algorithm, whose run time is polynomial in the number of variables. KEPLER enumerates one class of possible candidates (prototype) each time and ensures that a new term is just one part of the final law (see theorem 2). If the normal condition holds, then no backtracking is necessary, and the depth-first search will find the hidden law (see theorem 1).

COPER uses a limited class of polynomial functions, which are sound from the perspective of physical dimensions, and uses data to instantiate the best element in each class.

3.8.3 Overall Performance

BACON is powerful early system that has made some interesting rediscoveries in classical physics and chemistry. BACON can find complex multidimensional laws, which are decomposable in each dimension, into combinations of simple two-dimensional laws. ABACUS improves on BACON in discovering multiple laws and their logical preconditions. COPER is good at analyzing the relevance of variables, but its ability to discover the physical laws is limited to those cases where the law can be modeled by a polynomial function. KEPLER, however, shows a better ability to discover unknown laws, which can be quite complex and involve multiple variables (table 3.2). KEPLER has also failed to make any significant discovery, but we are proceeding with additional experiments.

3.9 Concluding Remarks

We proved that under certain assumptions, Reduction is a valid algorithm (Wu 1988c) for quantitative discovery. We argued that KEPLER improves on other quantitative discovery systems in several aspects. The main drawback of KEPLER is that it usually needs a large amount of input data in a regular form, although it tries to cope with incomplete data.

KEPLER needs to use better methods for integrating domain-specific knowledge into the discovery process. This type of knowledge is important in the human discovery process.

For efficient data access, a discovery system should have a good interface to databases. It should also take advantage of the many existing statistical and numeric analysis packages. This point is especially true for KEPLER, which needs to solve nonlinear equations and perform polynomial curve fitting.

KEPLER's prototype base should be enhanced to cover a wide variety of mathematical formulas, such as differential equations. The addition of a new prototype only requires an extension of KEPLER's matching module and no modification to the Reduction algorithm. Also, the transformation of randomly obtained data into regular form needed for Reduction is unsatisfactory.

With the outlined improvements, the KEPLER system can serve as an intelligent data analyzer, aiding scientific research and engineering design. Further development of KE-

PLER and other quantitative discovery systems depends on the use of real experimental data, which is the only way to prove the feasibility of automated discovery. More importantly, the systems and discovery methods have to be improved to handle real data.

The final conclusion is that more experiments are required!

3.10 A Prototype List

No.	Prototype
1	$x^{r_1} * y^{r_2}$
2	x^{r_1}/y^{r_2}
3	$x^{r_1} + a_1 * y^{r_2}$
4	$(a_2 * \ln x + a_1)/y^{r_1}$
5	$(a_2 * \ln x + a_1) * y^{r_1}$
6	$(\sin x)^{r_1}/(\sin y)^{r_2}$
7	$(\sin x)^{r_1} * (\sin y)^{r_2}$
8	$a_1 * x^{r_1} + e^y$
9	$a_1 * e^x + y^{r_1}$
10	$(\ln x)^{r_1} + a_1 * (\ln y)^{r_2}$
11	$y^{r_1} + a_1 * \ln x$
12	$\sin a_1 * x + a_2 + a_3 * y^{r_1}$
13	$\sin a_1 * x + a_2/a_3 * y^{r_1}$
14	$\sin a_1 * x + a_2 * a_3 * y^{r_1}$
15	$(\sin x + a_1)^{r_1} * (\sin x + a_2)^{r_2}$
16	$(\sin x + a_1)^{r_1}/(\sin y + a_2)^{r_2}$
17	$(\sin x)^{r_1} + a_1 * (\sin y)^{r_2}$
18	$(\sin x)^{r_1} + a_1 * (\cos y)^{r_2}$
19	$(\cos x)^{r_1} + a_1 * (\cos y)^{r_2}$
20	$(\cos x)^{r_1} + a_1 * (\sin y)^{r_2}$

Acknowledgments

Special gratitude from Yi-Hua Wu goes to Gregory Piatetsky-Shapiro and Qing Zhou for their valuable help. Dr. Piatetsky-Shapiro made valuable comments on the draft of this chapter. This research is partly supported by the Chinese National Natural Science Foundation under contract 68905004.

References

Falkenhainer, B. C., and Michalski, R. S. 1986. Integrating Quantitative and Qualitative Discovery: The ABACUS System. *Machine Learning* 1(4): 367–401.

Kokar, M. M. 1986. Determining Arguments of Invariant Functional Description. *Machine Learning* 1(4): 403–422.

Langley, P.; Bradshaw, G. L.; and Simon, H. A. 1983. Rediscovering Chemistry with the BACON System. In *Machine Learning: An Artificial Intelligence Approach*, volume 1, eds. R. S. Michalski, J. G. Carbonell, and T. M. Mitchell, 307–329. San Mateo, Calif.: Morgan Kaufmann.

Langley, P.; Simon, H. A.; Bradshaw, G.; and Żytkow J. M. 1987. *Scientific Discovery: An Account of the Creative Processes.* Cambridge, Mass: The MIT Press.

Nordhausen, B., and Langley, P. 1987. Towards an Integrated Discovery System. In Proceedings of the Tenth International Joint Conference on Artificial Intelligence, 198–200. Menlo Park, Calif.: International Joint Conferences on Artificial Intelligence, Inc.

Ortega, J., and Rheinboldt, W. 1970. *Iterative Solution of Nonlinear Equations in Several Variables.* New York: Academic Press.

Wu, Y.-H. 1989. Discovering Natural Laws by Reduction. *Journal of Computer Science and Technology* 4(1): 35–51.

Wu, Y.-H. 1988a. Discovering Natural Laws by Machine. In Proceedings of the 1988 IEEE International Conference on Systems, Man and Cybernetics, 538–543. Washington, D.C.: IEEE Computer Society.

Wu, Y.-H. 1988b. Reduction: A Practical Mechanism of Searching for Regularity in Data. In Proceedings of Fifth International Conference on Machine Learning, 374–380. San Mateo, Calif.: Morgan Kaufmann.

Wu, Y. H. 1988c. Towards Automated Discovery of Empirical Laws. Ph.D. diss., Institute of Computing Technology, Academia Sinica, Beijing, China.

4 Minimal-Length Encoding and Inductive Inference

Edwin P. D. Pednault
AT&T Bell Laboratories

Abstract

The minimum description length (MDL) principle is an inductive inference rule suitable for inferring probabilistic theories from data. A number of results regarding the convergence properties of the MDL principle are summarized and discussed in this chapter. These properties are illustrated by applying the principle to the surface reconstruction problem in computer vision. The relationship between the MDL principle and Bayesian inference is also discussed. It is shown how the MDL principle can converge to a correct hypothesis in cases where one-step Bayesian inference does not.

4.1 Introduction

According to the minimum description length (MDL) principle (Wallace and Boulton 1968; Wallace and Freeman 1987; Rissanen 1978, 1983; Segen 1979, 1985; Barron and Cover 1983, 1990; Barron 1985; Sorkin 1983; Cover 1985; Pednault 1988), the theory that best accounts for a collection of observations is the one that yields the most compact encoding of the theory and the observations combined. Expressed mathematically, the best theory T is the one that minimizes

$$l(T) + l(z_1, \ldots, z_n|T), \tag{4.1}$$

where $l(T)$ is the length in bits of a machine-readable representation of T, $z_1, \ldots, z_n$ are the observations, and $l(z_1, \ldots, z_n|T)$ is the number of bits needed to encode the observations with respect to T. The quantity $l(T)$ effectively measures the complexity of T, and $l(z_1, \ldots, z_n|T)$ measures the degree to which T accounts for the observations, with fewer bits indicating a better fit. The sum of these two quantities defines the number of bits needed to exactly represent the observations.

One aspect of my work has been to explore the convergence properties of the MDL principle. Because the goal of induction is to infer general principles from individual observations, any means of automating this process should (in theory) be guaranteed to discover the correct principles given a sufficient number and variety of observations. Specifically, if we arrange the observations so that they are presented one at a time, then there should be a point at which a sufficient number of them have been seen for the correct theory to be identified. Any additional observations should merely serve to confirm this theory. Therefore, one would like to show that the MDL principle converges to the correct theory in this sense, at least for applications of interest.

One such application is the inference of probabilistic models from noisy data. The number of bits needed to encode observations $z_1, \ldots, z_n$ with respect to a probabilistic theory T is given by

$$l(z_1, \ldots, z_n|T) = -\log_2 p(z_1, \ldots, z_n), \qquad (4.2)$$

where p is the probability measure defined by T. The quantity $-\log_2 p(z_1, \ldots, z_n)$ is the length of the Shannon code for the observations (for example, Gallager 1968). Shannon coding minimizes the expected code length of the observations with respect to p.

Barron (1985) shows that the inferences made by the MDL principle will asymptotically converge to the correct probability measure if the observations form a stationary ergodic random process. Convergence in the general case, however, remains an open problem. The first part of this chapter outlines some of the results I obtained in attempting to prove general convergence. These results include a definition of what it means for a probabilistic theory to be correct as well as a modified version of the MDL principle that can be shown to converge in the general case.

The second part of the chapter illustrates how the MDL principle can be used in practice by applying it to the surface reconstruction problem in computer vision. Surface reconstruction seeks to recover the mathematical functions that describe a surface given a set of points on or near the surface (for example, Barrow and Tenenbaum 1979; Grimson 1983; Terzopoulos 1988). The problem is compounded when dealing with real data because the points will be randomly displaced away from the true surface due to measurement errors.

Surface reconstruction can be treated as an inductive inference problem by viewing surfaces as properties to be inferred and data points as observations. The MDL principle is especially well suited to this problem because it guarantees convergence of the inferences for any amount of noise in the measurements (Barron 1985; Pednault 1988; Barron and Cover 1990). As the number of available data points increases, the reconstructions obtained asymptotically converge to the true surface. This property is demonstrated in the examples presented in section 4.5, Experimental Results.

The third and final part of the chapter examines the relationship between the MDL principle and Bayesian inference. The MDL principle is closely related to Bayesian inference, the main difference being that the MDL principle requires both the set of hypotheses and the sets of possible values for the observations to be discrete. As discussed in section 4.6, The MDL Principle and Bayesian Inference, this requirement enables the MDL principle to converge to correct hypotheses in cases where straightforward applications of Bayesian inference do not.

4.2 Judging Probabilistic Theories

To prove that an inductive inference rule such as the MDL principle will eventually discover the correct theory, one must first have a general criterion for judging the success of the inferences that are made. In the deterministic case, any theory that does not absolutely agree with the observations can be ruled out. A successful theory, therefore, is one that agrees with all observations, including those yet to be made. In the nondeterministic case, however, the presence of uncertainty makes exact agreement impossible. One must, therefore, consider the degree to which a theory accounts for the observations.

The inference problem is further complicated by the fact that one cannot simply choose the nondeterministic theory that best fits the data. For a finite set of data, it is possible to select a theory that fits too well. An example would be selecting a polynomial of sufficient degree so that it passes through every point in a set of data points. This choice amounts to fitting the theory to the noise rather than the underlying curve, thereby producing a poor model of the data (for example, Tukey 1977). If we extend the theory-selection problem to an infinite set of observations, an exact fit is impossible except in the deterministic case. In the nondeterministic case, no matter what theory we might propose, another exists that more closely agrees with the observations. The problem is to judge when the fit is good enough, and an appropriate theory has been obtained.

I previously (Pednault 1988) proposed a criterion for judging whether a probabilistic theory is an appropriate model for a set of observations. The analysis assumes that one is dealing with theories for predicting future events based on past observations and that the best theory is the one with the greatest predictive power.

A gambling scenario is used to measure predictive power. Given a predictive theory, one can imagine using it to place bets on future events. If the predictions are accurate, the bets will be won, and money will be made. The more accurate the predictions are, the greater the return. The relative predictive power of two or more theories, therefore, can be assessed by comparing the amounts that each wins.

The theory that wins the most money in the long run, to within a constant factor, is deemed to have a suitable level of predictive power and, hence, is an appropriate model for the observations. The qualification of considering the long term is important because greater predictive power implies less hedging of bets. By comparing the long-term winnings, we avoid the possibility of highly unlikely events from eliminating a theory with greater predictive power because of short-term losses. Predictive power, therefore, is treated as an asymptotic property (that is, it is measured with respect to an infinite set of observations). The constant factor takes into account the ability to find increasingly better fits to an infinite set of observations.

When expressed in terms of probabilities, the gambling criterion says that a theory T is an appropriate model for an infinite sequence of observations $\{z_n\}_{n=1}^{\infty} = z_1 z_2 z_3 \cdots$ if and only if the probability measure p defined by T satisfies the condition

$$\forall q\, \exists C_q > 0\, \forall n \geq 1\; p(z_1, \ldots, z_n) \geq C_q \cdot q(z_1 \ldots, z_n). \tag{4.3}$$

That is, for any other probability measure q, there exists a constant C_q greater than zero, such that p predicts the observation sequence at least C_q times as well as q. Note that many probability measures p can satisfy this criterion. Thus, the criterion defines an equivalence class of probability measures that are equally good with respect to the accuracy of their asymptotic predictions.

This definition of adequate predictive power incorporates several considerations. The first is that if we are able to exactly predict the observations by some deterministic means, we would ideally like p to assign a probability of one to the observations. The second consideration is that if a deterministic model is inappropriate, we would ideally like p to predict the observations at least as well as any other probability measure q.

With regard to this second consideration, we cannot simply require that $p(z_1, \ldots, z_n)$ be greater than or equal to $q(z_1, \ldots, z_n)$ for any q. No matter which p we choose, we can always find a q that more closely agrees with the observations when p does not exactly predict the observations. Specifically, suppose that p assigns a probability other than one to the observations. There will then be a value of k for which

$$p(z_1, \ldots, z_k) < 1. \tag{4.4}$$

Now choose q such that

$$q(z_1, \ldots, z_k) = 1 \tag{4.5}$$

and

$$q(z_{k+m} | z_1, \ldots, z_{k+m-1}) = p(z_{k+m} | z_1, \ldots, z_{k+m-1}). \tag{4.6}$$

From equations 4.4, 4.5, and 4.6 it follows that $p(z_1, \ldots, z_n) \leq q(z_1, \ldots, z_n)$ for $n < k$, and $p(z_1, \ldots, z_n) < q(z_1, \ldots, z_n)$ for $n \geq k$. Thus, unless p exactly predicts the observations, we can always find a q whose predictions are strictly better than p's.

In defining adequate predictive power, the best we can do is require that p predict the observations at least as well as any other probability measure q, within a constant factor. This observation leads to the introduction of the constant C_q in equation 4.3. C_q must depend on q because in many cases, it is possible to make the ratio of $q(z_1, \ldots, z_n)$ to $p(z_1, \ldots, z_n)$ arbitrarily large through an appropriate choice of q.

In terms of the gambling scenario, C_q can be interpreted as a handicap placed on q. If we imagine that p is initially given one unit of starting capital, then q would only be given an amount C_q. Equation 4.3 would then require that p maintain its capital advantage over q at each and every point in the (infinite) gambling process. To maintain this advantage, p's rate of return in the long run must be at least as good as q's.

By introducing the constant factor C_q, we also end up in the deterministic case of allowing p to assign a probability other than one to the observations (that is, C_q can be less than 1). Although $p(z_1, \ldots, z_n) \leq 1$ is not exactly what we desire, we do get the property that $p(z_1, \ldots, z_n)$ must converge to a nonzero value in the limit as n tends toward infinity, of which $p(z_1, \ldots, z_n) = 1$ is only a special case. Notice, however, that this property implies that the conditional probabilities $p(z_n|z_1, \ldots, z_{n-1})$ must converge to one in the limit as n tends toward infinity because, by definition, the product of these conditional probabilities must equal $p(z_1, \ldots, z_n)$. Therefore, although we lose strict determinacy, we do get a form of asymptotic determinacy with respect to the conditional probabilities.

The third and final consideration incorporated into equation 4.3 is perhaps most important of all: The quantification over q must be restricted to computable probability measures only. This restriction is fairly natural given that we are interested in machine learning. However, it also has important mathematical and philosophical repercussions.

Every infinite sequence of observations has a well-defined generating function and, hence, a well-defined probability measure that exactly predicts the sequence. Thus, without restricting q, p would either have to be this measure or one of the asymptotically deterministic measures. The crucial point, however, is that these deterministic probability measures are not always computable. There are only countably many computer programs (that is, they can be placed in one-to-one correspondence with the natural numbers), but there are uncountably many infinite observation sequences (that is, they can be placed in one-to-one correspondence with the real numbers). Therefore, it is impossible to associate each observation sequence with a computable probability measure that predicts the sequence exactly or even asymptotically. In such cases, one has no choice but to resort to nondeterministic computational models.

In general, one of three possibilities exists for any given observation sequence: (1) The sequence has a computable generating function and, hence, can be predicted exactly. (2) A computable generating function does not exist; however, a computable probabilistic model can be constructed that predicts the sequence as well as any other computational model. (3) A computable generating function does not exist, and for every computable probabilistic model, another exists that is asymptotically more accurate in its predictions.

An example of the third possibility would be a sequence best modeled as a Bernoulli(p) random process (for example, coin flipping with p being the probability of heads) in which p is a real number that cannot be computationally represented (that is, it cannot be generated to arbitrary precision by a computer program). The best we can do is determine more accurate estimates of p, but its exact value will never be known because it simply cannot be represented.

A consequence of this analysis is that the need for probabilistic models arises only because some observation sequences do not have computable generating functions. This fact raises an intriguing philosophical question: If a sequence does not have a computable generating function, was the sequence generated by a random process? From a mathematical standpoint, the sequence exists as an entity in an abstract space. Also, a well-defined generating function exists that exactly predicts the sequence, it is just that this function is not computable. Does the fact that it is not computable necessarily imply that the sequence arose from a random process? Could it not have been predetermined in some sense? Is the apparent randomness a property of the thing being observed (that is, ontological) or does the appearance of randomness reflect a fundamental limit on the kind of knowledge one can possess of this thing (that is, epistemological)? Do random processes truly exist in the universe, as some proponents of quantum mechanics would have us believe, or is quantum mechanics merely the best theory we can come up with given the limitations of mind and machine?

Although this analysis does not purport to resolve these issues, it does contribute an interesting perspective. The final resolution would depend on just what one means by a theory in the scientific sense and on the relationship of such theories to our ability to predict events with the aid of computers.

4.3 Inductive Inference

Although equation 4.3 provides us with a definition of what it means for a computable probability measure to be a suitable model for an infinite sequence of observations, it does not provide much guidance on how to select a probability measure based only on a finite collection of data. For the latter, we need to develop separate rules of inference. Equation 4.3, however, does enable us to determine whether a proposed rule is able to make suitable inferences.

A rule of inductive inference should enable us to converge on an appropriate probability measure p in the following sense: As each observation is revealed, the rule effectively makes a guess about what p should be. If p_k is the guess made after acquiring the first k observations, this process results in a sequence of probability measures $\{p_k\}_{k=1}^{\infty}$. To eventually converge on an appropriate p (or a set of appropriate p's) is to produce a sequence for which all guesses beyond a certain point satisfy equation 4.3. This definition of convergence is analogous to identification in the limit and behaviorally correct identification in the case of deterministic theories (for example, Angluin and Smith 1983).

The MDL principle has been proposed as one criterion for selecting probability measures based on a finite number of observations. In this context, the MDL principle calls for p_k to be chosen to minimize

$$l(p_k) - \log_2 p_k(z_1, \ldots, z_k), \tag{4.7}$$

where $l(p_k)$ is the length of the program for computing p_k. It can be shown (Pednault 1988) that this criterion enables one to converge on a probability measure satisfying equation 4.3 whenever the sequence of guesses $\{p_k\}_{k=1}^{\infty}$ contains only finitely many distinct probability measures. For example, one can show using Barron's (1985) analysis that $\{p_k\}_{k=1}^{\infty}$ will contain only finitely many distinct probability measures if the appropriate model is a stationary ergodic random process. A general proof in which the number of distinct p_k's is allowed to be infinite, however, has not yet been obtained.

I previously (Pednault 1988) proposed an alternate criterion based on the MDL principle for which general convergence was shown. According to this criterion, one chooses the probability measure p_k that minimizes

$$l(p_k) + d(z_1, \ldots, z_k || p_k), \tag{4.8}$$

where

$$\mathrm{d}(z_1, \ldots, z_k || p_k) = [l(p_k) - \log_2 p_k(z_1, \ldots, z_k)] - \min_q [l(q) - \log_2 q(z_1, \ldots, z_k)]\,. \tag{4.9}$$

The quantity $\mathrm{d}(z_1, \ldots, z_k || p_k)$ is essentially the number of extra bits needed to encode observations $z_1, \ldots, z_k$ using p_k instead of the probability measure q that yields the minimal encoding.

When viewed as a function of n, $\mathrm{d}(z_1, \ldots, z_n || p)$ has the interesting property that for any observation sequence $\{z_n\}_{n=1}^{\infty}$ and any computable probability measure p, either $\mathrm{d}(z_1, \ldots, z_n || p)$ has an upper bound, or it increases without bound as n tends toward infinity. Moreover, if $\mathrm{d}(z_1, \ldots, z_n || p)$ has an upper bound, then p satisfies equation 4.3. Therefore, if we find such a probability measure, it will be an appropriate model for the observations.

In equation 4.8, $l(p_k)$ is added to $d(z_1, I \ldots, z_k || p_k)$ to ensure that the number of distinct probability measures in the sequence $\{p_k\}_{k=1}^{\infty}$ is finite whenever a measure exists that satisfies equation 4.3. This fact, combined with the other properties of $\mathrm{d}(z_1, \ldots, z_n || p)$, enables one to show that there must be a point in the sequence $\{p_k\}_{k=1}^{\infty}$ beyond which all p_k's satisfy equation 4.3 whenever such probability measures exist.

Based on this convergence result, I strongly feel that a general convergence proof for the MDL principle can be found. Minimizing equation 4.8 turns out to be equivalent to minimizing

$$2\,l(p_k) - \log_2 p_k(z_1, \ldots, z_k). \tag{4.10}$$

Thus, by slightly modifying the MDL principle, we can ensure that the number of distinct probability measures in the sequence $\{p_k\}_{k=1}^{\infty}$ is finite whenever a measure exists that satisfies equation 4.3. General convergence then follows. Convergence likewise holds if we minimize

$$(1+\varepsilon)\,l(p_k) - \log_2 p_k(z_1, \ldots, z_k) \tag{4.11}$$

for any ε greater than zero. This fact has also been independently noted by Barron and Cover (1990). Because ε can be made arbitrarily small, perhaps it is that the MDL principle always yields a sequence $\{p_k\}_{k=1}^{\infty}$ containing finitely many distinct p_k's whenever a measure exists that satisfies equation 4.3. If so, the infinite case can be ruled out, and a general convergence result for the MDL principle will have been found.

4.4 Surface Reconstruction

Independent of whether convergence holds in general, both the MDL principle and its variants still have the property that they are computationally intractable in their most general forms. Finding the minimum of either equation 4.7 or equation 4.8 over all computable probability measures is impossible to do in practice because it would require a solution to the halting problem of Turing machines. Therefore, to actually apply these equations, one must limit the range of theories to a tractable subset or employ approximation techniques that attempt to find theories that are as close to the optimum as is computationally feasible. This pragmatic approach enables one to construct efficient algorithms by tailoring the optimization to specific properties of interest.

In practice, some experimentation may be required to arrive at an appropriate combination of restrictions and approximations. Thus, the following methodology is recommended for applying the MDL principle and its variants to practical problems: (1) determine the kinds of structural properties of the data that are of interest; (2) develop a language well suited for encoding data in terms of these properties; (3) develop algorithms that find short descriptions in the language; (4) run tests to find inappropriate behavior; (5) determine whether the problems lie with the language, the algorithms, or both; and (6) modify the language or algorithms accordingly and iterate.

To demonstrate this methodology, I have been applying the MDL principle to the surface reconstruction problem in computer vision (Pednault 1989). *Surface reconstruction* seeks to recover the mathematical functions that describe a surface given a set of points randomly displaced away from the surface. In this application, the surface is the theory, and the data points are the observations. The points are encoded in terms of their distances from the reconstructed surface. The optimal reconstruction is then the function S that minimizes the sum

$$l(S) + l(z_1, \ldots, z_n|S), \tag{4.12}$$

where $l(S)$ is the length in bits of a machine-readable description of S, $z_1, \ldots, z_n$ are the data points, and $l(z_1, \ldots, z_n|S)$ is the number of bits needed to encode the difference between these points and S.

In general, S will be a piecewise-continuous function that can be decomposed into a collection of regions and continuous functions, with one function per region. $l(S)$ thus incorporates the number of bits needed to specify both the region boundaries and the functions within each region. If these functions form a collection of parametric families, the function associated with a region can be described by first specifying the family it belongs to and then specifying its parameters. The number of bits needed to supply this information is included in $l(S)$. Note that $l(S)$ will increase as the number of regions and function parameters increase. Therefore, we can view $l(S)$ as measuring the complexity of the reconstructed surface.

To encode the data points, the difference between their values and S is statistically analyzed by viewing the difference as a random process. This random process, together with the function S, induces a probability distribution p on the data points. With the use of Shannon coding techniques (for example, Gallager 1968), the number of bits needed to encode the data points is given by

$$l(z_1, \ldots, z_n|S) = -\log_2 p(z_1, \ldots, z_n). \tag{4.13}$$

$l(z_1, \ldots, z_n|S)$ can thus be thought of as a degree-of-fit term. If the S exactly reproduces the data points, $p(z_1, \ldots, z_n)$ will equal one and $l(z_1, \ldots, z_n|S)$ will be zero. As the fit degrades, $p(z_1, \ldots, z_n)$ will decrease, and $l(z_1, \ldots, z_n|S)$ will increase.

Because the degree of fit can vary from region to region, we are not justified in assuming that the probability distribution p remains constant. To allow it to vary, the distribution must be specified along with the interpolating function within each region. The specification can be accomplished by treating p as a member of a parametric family of distributions and then encoding its parameters. The number of bits needed to supply this information is included in $l(S)$.

4.5 Experimental Results

For the initial round of experiments, piecewise polynomial functions were used in conjunction with a Gaussian noise model to describe surfaces and the random displacement of the data points. The algorithms developed actually allow any linear combination of basis functions. Polynomials were used in the experiments because of their familiarity to facilitate the presentation of the results. A Gaussian noise model was selected because optimal polynomial coefficients can then be determined using a computationally efficient least squares algorithm. Nonlinear families of interpolating functions can also be used within the framework, as can other noise models, but different techniques must then be employed to find optimal function parameters (the least squares algorithm presumes a Gaussian noise model and a linear combination of basis functions).

A polynomial-time algorithm was developed to find optimal reconstructions for one-dimensional surfaces (that is, curves). Finding an optimal reconstruction is computationally infeasible for a two-dimensional surface because an exponential number of regions must be examined to find the optimum. For a multidimensional surface, therefore, one has no choice but to use approximation techniques to find reconstructions that are as close to the optimum as is computationally feasible. One approach I am investigating is to use a series of optimal 1-D reconstructions to guide the reconstruction of 2-D surfaces. Early experiments with this approximation technique have proved promising.

Figures 4.1 and 4.2 illustrate the performance of the algorithm using synthetic data. In these figures, Gaussian white noise of various standard deviations is added to two different piecewise polynomial curves. The noisy curves and their resulting reconstructions are plotted side by side for comparison. The underlying curve in each figure consists of three polynomial regions of orders 0, 1, and 2, respectively. The curve in figure 4.1 is continuous, and in figure 4.2, it is discontinuous.

In figures 4.1a and 4.2a, the curves are sampled at 48 points, and the standard deviation of the noise is increased from 0 to 32 in an exponential fashion. These figures demonstrate that if the number of data points is insufficient for an exact reconstruction, then an approximation is made in which the degree of approximation decreases as the noise level increases.

In figures 4.1b and 4.2b, the standard deviation of the noise is held constant at 32, and the number of data points is increased from 48 to 768 by factors of two in figure 4.1b and from 48 to 384 in figure 4.2b. These figures demonstrate that an exact surface reconstruction is asymptotically obtained when the true surface is a member of the subset considered (in this case, polynomials), and one is minimizing the description length over this subset. The use of a high noise level illustrates that convergence occurs independent

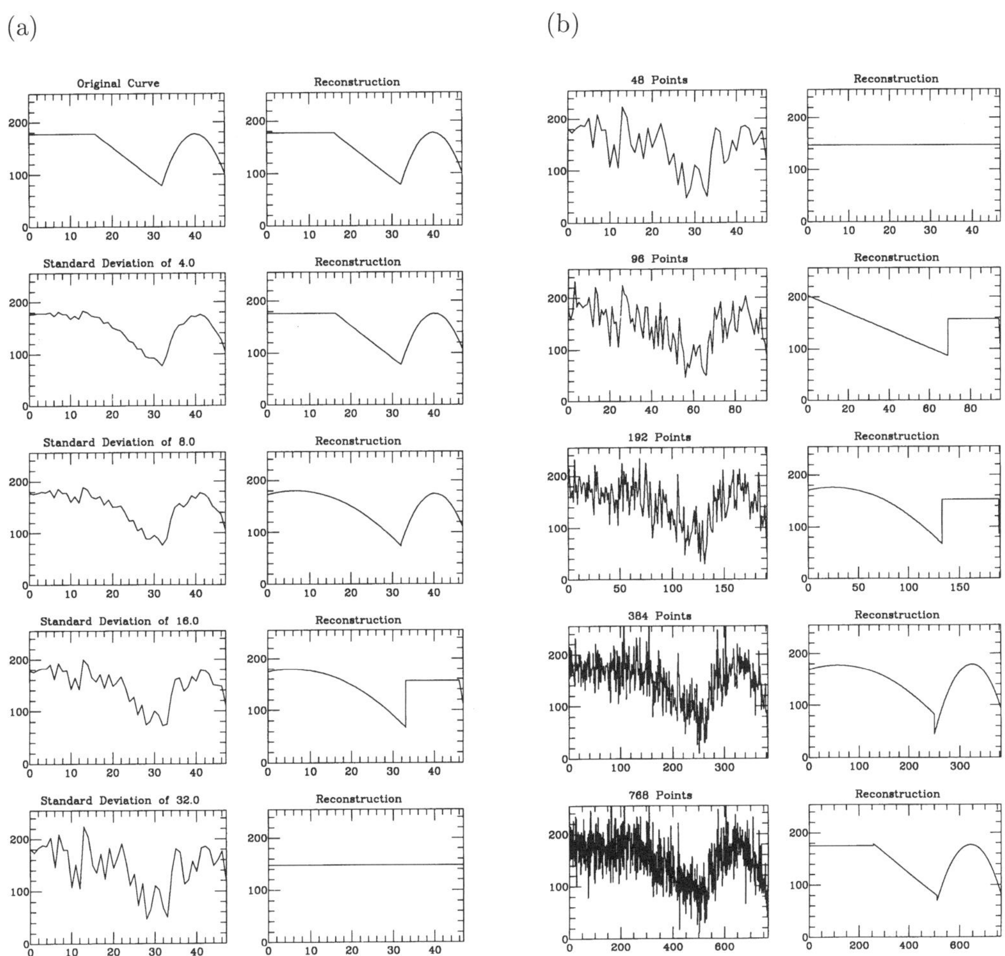

Figure 4.1
Result of Applying the Algorithm to a Continuous Piecewise-Polynomial Curve with Additive Gaussian Noise. (a) Reconstructions obtained when noise of increasing standard deviation is added to 48 sample points on the curve. (b) Reconstructions obtained when the standard deviation is held constant at 32, and the number of sample points is increased from 48 to 768.

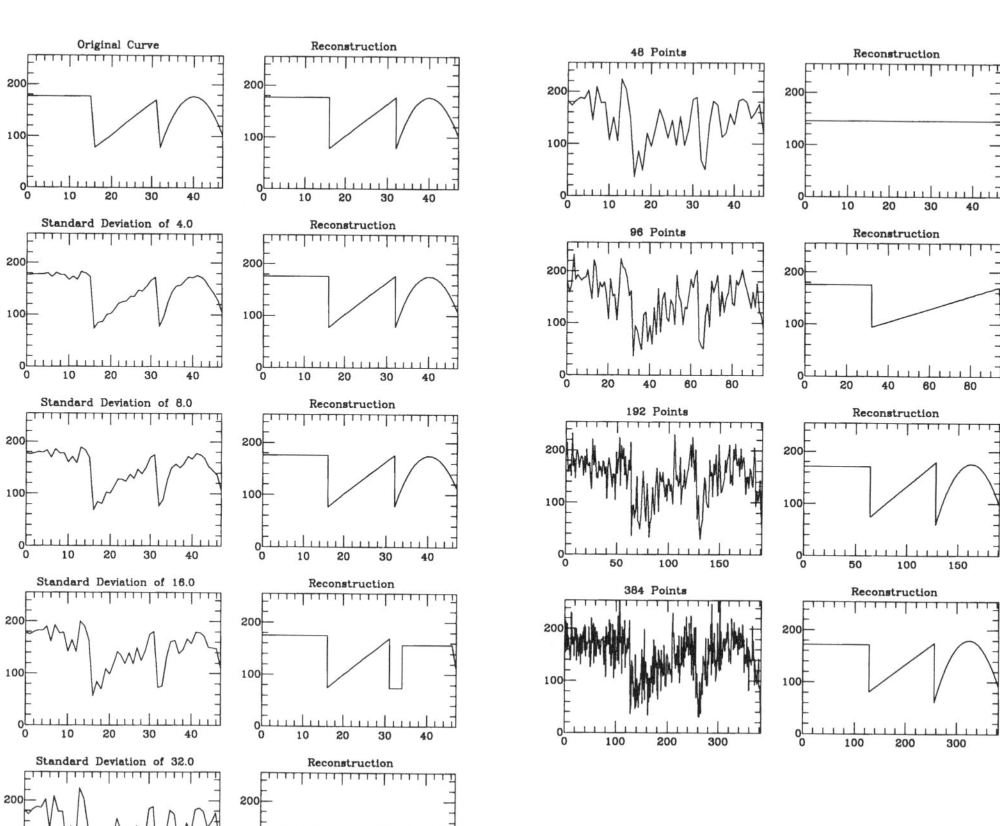

Figure 4.2
Result of Applying the Algorithm to a Discontinuous Piecewise-Polynomial Curve with Additive Gaussian Noise. (a) Reconstructions obtained when noise of increasing standard deviation is added to 48 sample points on the curve. (b) Reconstructions obtained when the standard deviation is held constant at 32, and the number of sample points is increased from 48 to 384.

of the amount of noise. The noise level does affect the rate of convergence (that is, the higher the noise, the slower the convergence) but not the eventual convergence.

Figure 4.3 shows the result of applying the algorithm to the rows of a 128-by-128 range image of a mechanical part. Figure 4.3a shows the original image, and figure 4.3b shows the row reconstruction. In figure 4.3c, a row and a column from the original image are plotted alongside their reconstructions. The positions of the row and column are indicated by horizontal and vertical marks along the borders of figures 4.3a and 4.3b.

The mechanical part does not have polynomial surfaces, yet the reconstruction produced by the algorithm is reasonably accurate. Thus, even when the true surface lies outside the subset considered, a good approximation to the surface can still be obtained. The principal requirement is for the subset to have sufficient latitude for an adequate approximation. In addition, the noise model must adequately reflect the statistical properties of the measurement errors, which happens to be the case for the mechanical part.

In all these examples, the number of intervals, their locations, and the order of the polynomials were determined entirely by minimizing the total encoding length of the data points. The initial implementation allowed as high as 15th-order polynomials. Problems with numeric instability, however, required that the polynomials be limited to at most fifth order in the examples presented. Further work is being done to resolve these stability problems.

4.6 The MDL Principle and Bayesian Inference

The MDL principle is closely related to Bayesian inference. In Bayesian inference, one seeks to find the hypothesis H_k that maximizes the posterior probability

$$p(H_k \mid z_1, \ldots, z_k), \tag{4.14}$$

where $z_1, \ldots, z_k$ are the first k observations. This choice maximizes the probability of picking the correct hypothesis given the observations made thus far. Maximizing this probability is equivalent to maximizing

$$p(H_k)p(z_1, \ldots, z_k \mid H_k) \tag{4.15}$$

because

$$p(H_k|z_1, \ldots, z_k) = \frac{p(H_k)\, p(z_1, \ldots, z_k|H_k)}{p(z_1, \ldots, z_k)} \tag{4.16}$$

and because $p(z_1, \ldots, z_k)$ does not depend on H_k. Taking the negative log of equation 4.15 yields

$$-\log_2 p(H_k) - \log_2 p(z_1, \ldots, z_k|H_k). \tag{4.17}$$

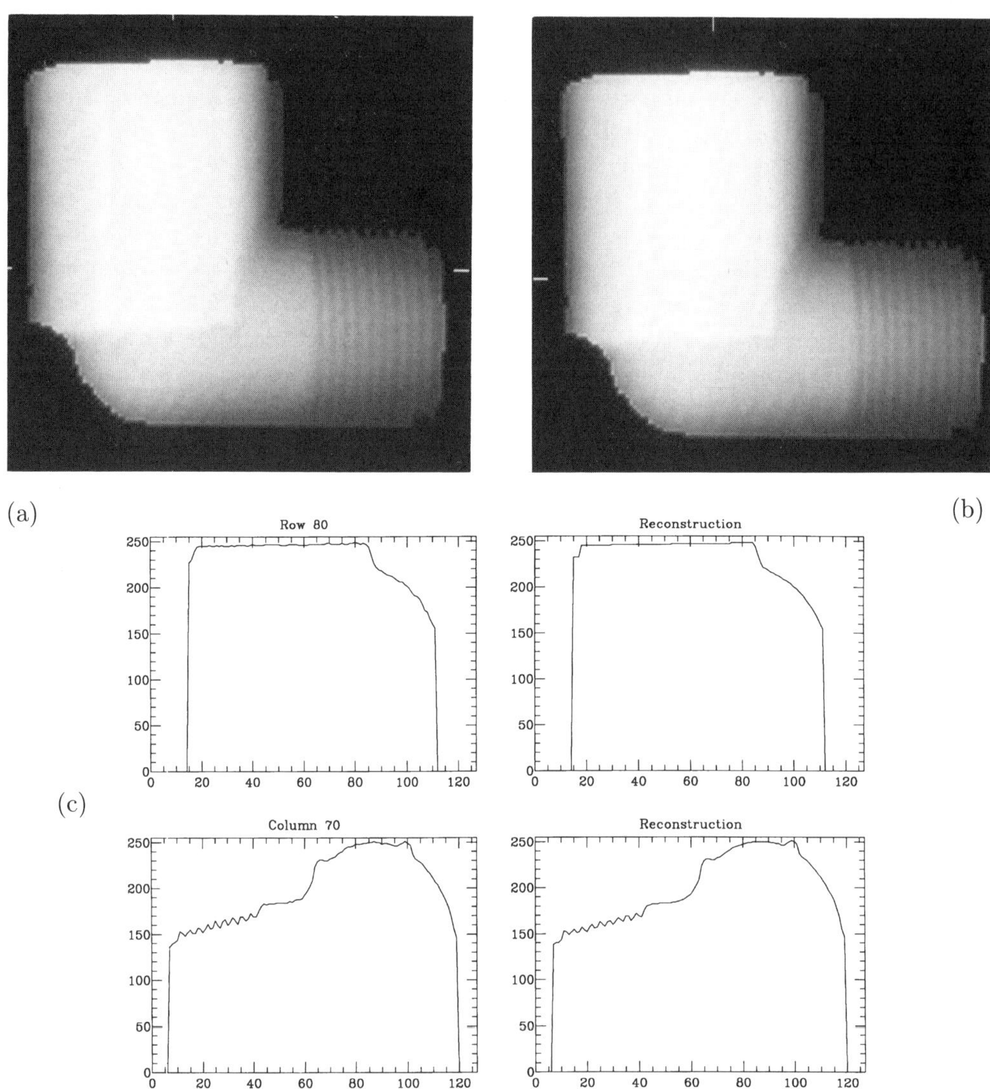

Figure 4.3
Result of Applying the Algorithm to the Rows of a 128-by-128 Range Image of a Mechanical Part. (a) The original image. (b) The row reconstruction. (c) A row and column from the original image together with their reconstructions. The positions of the row and column are indicated by marks along the borders of the images.

The connection between the MDL principle and Bayesian inference can be seen by equating H_k in equation 4.17 with p_k in equation 4.7. In so doing, we obtain

$$p(H_k) = 2^{-l(p_k)} \tag{4.18}$$

and

$$p(z_1, \ldots, z_k | H_k) = p_k(z_1, \ldots, z_k). \tag{4.19}$$

According to these equations, converting an MDL problem to a Bayesian inference problem simply requires that we view each computable probability distribution as a hypothesis. The programs for computing the distributions are viewed as Shannon codes for the hypotheses, with their lengths determining the prior probabilities of the hypotheses (equation 4.18). The distributions themselves determine the conditional probabilities of the observations given the hypotheses (equation 4.19). Equation 4.7 is then equivalent to equation 4.17, which shows that the MDL principle is essentially a form of Bayesian inference.

Converting a Bayesian inference problem to an MDL problem is more complicated, however, and the process reveals the differences between the two paradigms. In principle, one uses the prior probabilities of the hypotheses to construct a Shannon code book. This code book constitutes a language for describing the hypotheses. The coding length of hypothesis H_k is then given by

$$-\log_2 p(H_k). \tag{4.20}$$

Shannon codes are also constructed to encode the observations on the basis of their conditional probability distributions. The number of bits needed to encode observations $z_1, \ldots, z_k$ with respect to hypothesis H_k is then given by

$$-\log_2 p(z_1, \ldots, z_k | H_k). \tag{4.21}$$

However, the conversion is not always this straightforward. Because the MDL principle requires encodings to be finite sequences of ones and zeros, both the hypotheses and the possible values for each observation must be discrete (that is, countable). Many types of observations, however, are more naturally represented as continuous random variables. Likewise, hypotheses can contain real-valued parameters that must be estimated. Such real-valued parameters and random variables result in continuous, rather than discrete, observation and hypothesis spaces. To convert a Bayesian inference problem to an MDL problem, therefore, it is necessary to quantize all real-valued observations and hypothesis parameters.

Quantizing observations does not present much of a problem because physical measurements will always be quantized to reflect measurement precision (that is, there is a limit to the number of significant figures). The probability of obtaining a particular quantized value is then the probability that the actual value falls within the quantization interval. Thus, if a continuous random variable X is quantized to an accuracy of $\pm e$, the number of bits needed to encode a value of $z \pm e$ is given by

$$-\log_2 p(z|H_k) = -\log_2 \int_{z-e}^{z+e} f(x|H_k)dx, \tag{4.22}$$

where $f(x|H_k)$ is the probability density function for X with respect to hypothesis H_k. The joint probability for several quantized random variables is determined in an analogous fashion from the joint probability density function for those variables given H_k.

Quantizing hypothesis parameters is more involved. A parameterized hypothesis H_k consists of a parametric model M together with specific parameter values $a_1, \ldots, a_m$. The prior probability of such a hypothesis is, therefore,

$$p(H_k) = p(M)p(a_1, \ldots, a_m|M), \tag{4.23}$$

where $p(M)$ is the prior probability of the parametric model, and $p(a_1, \ldots, a_m|M)$ is the probability of the specific parameter values that are hypothesized. The probability of the observations is likewise conditioned on the model and its parameters:

$$p(z_1, \ldots, z_k|H_k) = p(z_1, \ldots, z_k|M(a_1, \ldots, a_m)). \tag{4.24}$$

Therefore, equation 4.17 can be rewritten as

$$-\log_2 p(M) - \log_2 p(a_1, \ldots, a_m|M) - \log_2 p(z_1, \ldots, z_k|M(a_1, \ldots, a_m)). \tag{4.25}$$

The MDL principle minimizes equation 4.25. The first term is the number of bits needed to identify the parametric model, the second term is the coding length of the arguments, and the third is the number of bits needed to encode the observations with respect to the model and its arguments.

If the arguments $a_1, \ldots, a_m$ are real valued, they must be quantized. There are two principal ways in which quantization can be accomplished. The first approach is similar to the quantization of real-valued observations and is suitable when a probability density function can be determined for the arguments, which is typically the case in Bayesian inference problems. With this approach, a set of quantization intervals is selected, and representative parameter values are chosen for each interval. If the model has more than one parameter, one selects quantization regions and representative parameter vectors. Only the representative values or vectors can be used as arguments. The probability of obtaining a particular set of representative arguments is then the probability that the nonquantized values fall within the corresponding interval or region. Thus, if a is the representative value of an argument of model M for the interval $[b, c]$, the number of bits needed to encode a is given by

$$-\log_2 p(a|M) = -\log_2 \int_b^c f(x|M)dx, \tag{4.26}$$

where $f(x|M)$ is the probability density function of the argument with respect to M. The joint probability for several arguments is determined in a similar fashion from the joint probability density function of the arguments given the model.

This quantization scheme was used in the surface reconstruction experiments described in the previous two sections. The parametric models were polynomials of various degrees plus Gaussian white noise. The parameters were the polynomial coefficients and the standard deviation of the distribution.

When using this approach, the quantization intervals and regions must be carefully chosen to keep the overall coding length as small as possible. On the one hand, a coarse quantization of the hypothesis parameters tends to increase the coding length of the observations because the quantized parameters can deviate significantly from the values that best fit the observations. On the other hand, increasing the precision of the parameters by employing finer quantizations increases the coding length of the parameters. Therefore, to minimize the total coding length, it is necessary to balance the benefit of precisely encoding hypothesis parameters against the cost of this encoding. As a rule of thumb, finer quantizations must be employed as the number of observations increases.

Rissanen (1983) proposes a general quantization methodology that minimizes the worst case coding length assuming uniform quantization steps. However, this scheme was found to produce somewhat inefficient codes in the surface reconstruction experiments previously discussed, mainly because the data points were already quantized to eight significant bits. Therefore, a nonuniform quantization scheme was developed to achieve more compact encodings.

A second approach to quantizing real-valued parameters is to insist that they be rational numbers. This restriction produces a discrete hypothesis space because the set of rationals can be placed in one-to-one correspondence with the set of natural numbers. Rationals can be represented either as the ratio of two integers or in scientific notation with integer exponents and mantissas. The former representation is more general, and the latter yields more compact representations for numbers large and small in magnitude. The integers involved can be encoded using the universal coding schemes of Elias (1975), Leung-Yan-Cheong and Cover (1978), and Rissanen (1983).

The advantage of the rational number approach is that it does not require knowledge of a probability density function for the parameters, nor does it require separate quantization schemes for each parametric model and number of observations. Instead, one determines the precision of the arguments in the process of minimizing equation 4.25. As with the quantization-interval approach, it is necessary to balance the precision of the arguments against the effect of quantization error. In this case, however, the appropriate level of quantization is determined at run time when minimizing equation 4.25, in contrast to the compile-time analysis required by the quantization-interval approach before any data can be processed.

A disadvantage of the rational-number approach is that it tends to produce longer encodings of the arguments than would be obtained using the quantization-interval approach. The precision of each rational number is implicitly encoded along with its value, which requires extra bits to convey this information. This additional overhead does not have much effect when dealing with large numbers of observations because the coding length of the observations then dominates that of the arguments. However, when the number of observations is more moderate, as is the case in the surface reconstruction experiments presented earlier, the encodings of the arguments and observations tend to be comparable in length. Consequently, the long argument coding lengths associated with the rational-number approach will bias the selection of models to those with fewer parameters. The quantization-interval approach was used for the surface reconstruction experiments to avoid this bias.

The need to quantize real-valued observations and hypothesis parameters is the key difference between the MDL principle and Bayesian inference. Remarkably, the quantization of these values can enable the MDL principle to converge to an appropriate hypothesis in cases where straightforward Bayesian inference fails to do so. The surface reconstruction problem illustrates this phenomenon.

To pose surface reconstruction as a Bayesian inference problem, a prior probability $p(m)$ must be assigned to each polynomial order m, and a conditional probability density function

$$f(a_0, \ldots, a_m, \sigma | m) \tag{4.27}$$

must be assigned to the polynomial coefficients $a_0, \ldots, a_m$ and the parameters σ of the noise model. In this case, we will assume a Gaussian noise model with the standard deviation as its parameter. If $\{< x_i, y_i >\}_{i=1}^n$ are the data points and if the polynomial is assumed to interpolate the y values given the x values, then the probability density over the y values is given by the Gaussian distribution function

$$(2\pi\sigma^2)^{-\frac{n}{2}} \cdot \mathrm{e}^{-\frac{1}{2\sigma^2}\sum_{i=1}^{n}(y_i - a_0 - \cdots - a_m x^m)^2} \tag{4.28}$$

The polynomial that interpolates the y values with the greatest posterior probability is the polynomial that maximizes the product of these three quantities:

$$p(m) \cdot f(a_0, \ldots, a_m, \sigma | m) \cdot (2\pi\sigma^2)^{-\frac{n}{2}} \cdot \mathrm{e}^{-\frac{1}{2\sigma^2}\sum_{i=1}^{n}(y_i - a_0 - \cdots - a_m x^m)^2} . \tag{4.29}$$

The difficulty with choosing the polynomial that maximizes this expression, however, is that this polynomial will always pass through all the data points in the general case. Convergence to the underlying curve does not occur except when the noise is zero. The reason for this is that the Gaussian term in equation 4.29 will be infinite for any polynomial that passes through all the points because the standard deviation σ will be zero in such cases. For all other polynomials, the Gaussian term will be finite. Because infinity is greater than any finite quantity, maximizing equation 4.29 will always produce a polynomial that passes through all the points, unless $p(m) = 0$ or $f(a_0, \ldots, a_m, \sigma | m) = 0$ for all such polynomials. Therefore, except when the noise is truly zero, convergence to the underlying curve is impossible.

By contrast, the MDL principle is not adversely affected by infinite probability densities. As discussed earlier, the observations must be quantized to use the MDL principle, requiring that the Gaussian term be integrated over the quantization intervals of the data points. This integral will have a maximum value of one when the polynomial passes through all the points and a value between zero and one in all other cases. The integration process eliminates the singularities caused by distributions with infinite probability density, thus allowing nontrivial polynomials to be selected.

The requirement that the hypothesis parameters be represented with finite precision further ensures that a nontrivial selection will be made. To encode a polynomial that passes through all the points would require that the coefficients be exactly represented. An exact representation entails a highly precise and, therefore, lengthy encoding of the arguments. If the argument coding length greatly exceeds that of the data points, chances are that a polynomial of lower degree (and, hence, a higher mean-squared error!) will achieve a shorter overall coding length by striking a better balance between the coding lengths of the arguments and the data points. This phenomenon is clearly observed in figures 4.1 and 4.2. Thus, at least for this application, quantization enables the MDL principle to asymptotically infer the correct hypothesis, whereas a straightforward Bayesian approach does not. Of course, the MDL principle can itself be viewed as a Bayesian approach, but the quantization of real-valued parameters and observations introduced in recognition of the fact that one is dealing with computable probability measures sets the MDL principle apart from standard Bayesian methods.

To be fair, a more standard Bayesian approach also works in this instance (Cheeseman 1989). Instead of choosing the order of the polynomial, the coefficients, and the standard deviation in one step, this approach calls for the choice to be made in two steps. In this case, the order of the polynomial is estimated first, followed by the coefficients and the standard deviation. The order of the polynomial is determined by finding the value of m that maximizes

$$p(m)\int_{a_0}\cdots\int_{a_m}\int_{\sigma}\left(\begin{array}{l} f(a_0,\ldots,a_m,\sigma|m)\cdot(2\pi\sigma^2)^{-\frac{n}{2}} \\ \cdot \mathrm{e}^{-\frac{1}{2\sigma^2}\sum\limits_{i=1}^{n}(y_i-a_0-\cdots-a_m x^m)^2} \end{array}\right) d\sigma\, da_m \ldots da_0, \tag{4.30}$$

which is just equation 4.29 integrated over the polynomial coefficients and the standard deviation. Once the order is selected, the coefficients and standard deviation are determined by maximizing equation 4.29 as before except that m is now held fixed.

The reason for the integration is to obtain a result proportional to the probability of the polynomial order given the data points rather than the joint probability of the order, the coefficients, and the standard deviation. Maximizing this integral expression thus yields the maximum posterior probability estimate of the polynomial order alone.

Because the order is a nonnegative integer, the hypothesis space for the first decision step is discrete. The integration over the coefficients and the standard deviation removes singularities, allowing a nontrivial polynomial order to be selected. Singularities can still appear in the second step of the decision process, leading to a polynomial that runs through all the data points but only if it has already been decided in the first step that the order of the polynomial should be sufficient to allow such a polynomial to be selected.

As this example points out, one must be careful to circumvent the singularity problems associated with real-valued variables and parameters when employing standard Bayesian methods. One-step Bayesian inference, which simply selects the hypothesis that maximizes the posterior probability, does not always work. Instead, hypotheses must sometimes be decomposed, and the posterior probabilities of the components must be sequentially maximized in the appropriate order. The MDL principle, however, avoids these problems entirely. Decisions can always be made in one step, allowing the MDL principle to be applied in a consistent manner from one problem to the next.

4.7 Summary and Conclusions

The strength of the MDL principle lies in its convergence properties. It has been shown for a large class of situations that the MDL principle enables one to eventually converge on an appropriate theory given a sufficient number of observations. Moreover, evidence was presented that convergence might hold in general.

The MDL principle is closely related to Bayesian inference. Unlike standard Bayesian approaches, however, the MDL principle requires discrete observation and hypothesis spaces. This requirement enables the MDL principle to converge to the correct hypothesis in cases where one-step Bayesian inference does not. The difficulty encountered with Bayesian inference is the result of singularities (that is, infinite probability densities) in the observation and hypothesis spaces that can arise when dealing with real-valued observations and hypothesis parameters. The MDL principle requires such values to be quantized, thus eliminating the singularities. These singularity problems can also be circumvented in standard Bayesian approaches through the use of multistep decision procedures; however, the MDL principle has the advantage that its one-step nature enables it to be applied in a consistent manner from one problem to the next.

Although the MDL principle is computationally intractable in its most general form, the benefits of its convergence properties provide strong motivation for discovering ways of overcoming these computational barriers. The results presented here and elsewhere demonstrate that these barriers can be overcome in specific applications by limiting the range of admissible theories to a tractable subset or employing approximation techniques that attempt to find theories that are as close to the optimum as is computationally feasible. Because its properties are quite attractive, the future will undoubtedly see many more applications of the MDL principle.

References

Angluin, D., and Smith, C. H. 1983. Inductive Inference: Theory and Methods. *Computing Surveys* 15(3): 237–269.

Barron, A. R. 1985. Logically Smooth Density Estimation, Technical Report 56, Dept. of Statistics, Stanford Univ.

Barron, A. R., and Cover, T. M. 1990. Minimum Complexity Density Estimation. *IEEE Transactions on Information Theory.* Forthcoming.

Barron, A. R., and Cover, T. M. 1983. Convergence of Logically Simple Estimates of Unknown Probability Densities. Presented at the International Symposium on Information Theory, St. Jovite, Quebec, Canada.

Barrow, H. G., and Tenenbaum, J. M. 1979. Reconstructing Smooth Surfaces from Partial, Noisy Information. In Proceedings of the Tenth DARPA Image Understanding Workshop, 76–86. Alexandria, Va: Defense Technical Information Center.

Cheeseman, P. 1989. Personal communication. NASA-AMES Research Center, Moffett Field, Calif.

Cover, T. M. 1985. Kolmogorov Complexity, Data Compression, and Inference. In *The Impact of Processing Techniques on Communications*, ed. J. K. Skwirzynski, 23–34. Boston: Martinus Nijhoff.

Elias, P. 1975. Universal Codeword Sets and Representations of the Integers. *IEEE Transactions on Information Theory* 21(2): 194–203

Gallager, R. G. 1968. *Information Theory and Reliable Communication.* New York: Wiley.

Grimson, W. E. L. 1983. An Implementation of a Computational Theory of Visual Surface Interpolation. *Computer Vision, Graphics, and Image Processing* 22: 39–69.

Leung-Yan-Cheong, S. K., and Cover, T. M. 1978. Some Equivalences between Shannon Entropy and Kolmogorov Complexity. *IEEE Transactions on Information Theory* 24(3):331–338.

Pednault, E. P. D. 1989. Some Experiments in Applying Inductive Inference Principles to Surface Reconstruction. In Proceedings of the Eleventh International Joint Conference on Artificial Intelligence, 1603–1609. Menlo Park, Calif: International Joint Conferences on Artificial Intelligence, Inc..

Pednault, E. P. D. 1988. Inferring Probabilistic Theories from Data. In Proceedings of the Seventh National Conference on Artificial Intelligence, 624–628. Menlo Park, Calif: American Association for Artificial Intelligence.

Rissanen, J. 1983. A Universal Prior for Integers and Estimation by Minimum Description Length. *Annals of Statistics* 11:416–431.

Rissanen, J. 1978. Modeling by Shortest Data Description. *Automatica* 14: 465–471.

Segen, J. 1979. Pattern Directed Signal Analysis, Ph.D. Dissertation, Department of Electrical Engineering, Carnegie Mellon University.

Segen, J. 1985. Learning Structural Descriptions of Shape. In Proceedings of the IEEE Computer Society Conference on Computer Vision and Pattern Recognition, 96–99. Washington, D.C.: IEEE Computer Society.

Sorkin, R. 1983. A Quantitative Occam's Razor. *International Journal of Theoretical Physics* 22: 1091–1103.

Terzopoulos, D. 1988. The Computation of Visible-Surface Representations. *IEEE Transactions on Pattern Analysis and Machine Intelligence* 10(4): 417–438.

Tukey, J. W. 1977. *Exploratory Data Analysis.* Reading, Mass: Addison-Wesley.

Wallace, C. S., and Boulton, D. M. 1968. An Information Measure for Classification. *Computing Journal* 11(2): 185–195.

Wallace, C. S., and Freeman, P. R. 1987. Estimation and Inference by Compact Encoding. *Journal of the Royal Statistical Society, Series B* 49(3): 240–265.

5 On Evaluation of Domain-Independent Scientific Function-Finding Systems

Cullen Schaffer
Rutgers University

Abstract

For more than a decade, AI researchers have designed systems to discover functional relationships in scientific data. Little has been said, however, about how to evaluate such systems once they are implemented. This chapter introduces some of the issues relevant to evaluation and suggests how attention to evaluation is likely to affect the course of AI research in function-finding discovery.

5.1 Introduction

Over the past 10 years, a number of AI researchers have proposed systems designed to discover functional relationships from data. These include the BACON programs (Langley et al. 1987), the ABACUS programs (Falkenhainer and Michalski 1986; Greene 1988), COPER (Kokar 1986), DISCOVER (Wu 1988),KEPLER (Wu and Wang, chapter 3, this volume), FAHRENHEIT (Żytkow 1987), IDS (Nordhausen 1989), E* (Schaffer 1990b), DATAX(Hamilton 1990), and others (see Schaffer (1990a) for a comprehensive survey). Given the data in table 5.1, for example, we might expect a function-finding system to note the apparent relationship $y = x^2$

The main purpose of this chapter is to ask how we might go about evaluating systems designed to handle problems of this sort. My own research experience suggests, however, that serious attention to the question of evaluation may force us to rethink much of the work of the past decade. Hence, I will also try to say something about the ramifications of developing rigorous evaluation methods.

5.2 Function-Finding Performance Is Context Dependent

Let me begin by noting two simple but critical points. First, $y = x^2$ is not the only plausible answer to the sample problem in table 5.1. An infinite number of relationships fit the given data exactly and another infinite number approximate it with varying degrees of precision. This point is critical because it shows that even for this single, simple problem, it is impossible to judge the performance of a function-finding system unless more information is given. As posed, the problem is incomplete, since criteria for evaluating answers are left unstated.

Table 5.1
A Simple Function-Finding Problem.

x	y
1	1
2	4
3	9
4	16

These criteria, in turn, depend on the goals of function finding Is the aim to guess the formula the problem poser has in mind? Or to discover the simplest formula that fits the data exactly? Or to discover a formula that balances simplicity and degree of fit satisfactorily? Or to discover a formula likely to do well in predicting future data? These goals may be related, but they are not identical, and each forms the basis of a different standard for judging proposed answers to the problem in table 5.1.

A second point is that even if goals are precisely specified, we cannot assess the performance of a function-finding system unless we know the environment in which it will be employed. A simple statistical approach might fare well in an environment producing problems like the one in table 5.1, but the same approach would be useless if variables are ordinarily related by formulas like $y = |x|$ or $y = x \bmod 3$. Function finding is induction. Induction depends on bias and an induction strategy is only as powerful as its bias is appropriate to the context in which it operates. In evaluating function-finding systems, we must not ask about performance as such but rather about *relative* performance in various environments.

In short, function-finding performance is context dependent for two reasons. First, the context in which problems are posed determines the goals of function finding and, hence, the criteria by which individual answers provided by a function-finding system may be evaluated. One answer may be more appropriate for a graph theory problem and another on an intelligence test. Second, context determines the distribution of problems a function-finding system will face and, hence, the value of its bias in prospective applications.

5.3 Scientific Function Finding

Although early work evolved in part from consideration of sequence-induction problems like those found in intelligence tests, AI research in function finding has concentrated almost exclusively on problems of *scientific* data analysis. Identifying this context is an important first step in evaluating the systems researchers have proposed, but it also introduces new difficulties.

For one thing, science may have goals, but the problem of identifying them explicitly has kept philosophers busy for centuries. Specifying objective criteria for evaluating the degree to which answers provided by a function-finding system are "scientific" would entail resolution of central issues in the philosophy of science. Of course, as naive philosophers, it is tempting for us to brush this point aside and suggest that scientists prefer simple answers that fit the given data well and yield accurate predictions. The problems here are twofold. First, as *naive* philosophers, we are likely to be wrong—even qualitatively—in this characterization of scientific goals.[1] Second, even to the extent that the characterization is correct, it leaves open a host of residual problems: how to measure the simplicity of formulas in a scientific context and compare their accuracy, how to determine the scientifically desirable balance of accuracy and simplicity, how to weigh the importance of various predictive successes, and so on. Again, we may follow our intuition in resolving these, but we run a high risk of being wrong.

The problem of determining scientific goals in function finding is complicated severely by the fact that science is far from uniform. A formula acceptable to a psychologist or an entomologist might not pass muster with a chemist or physicist. Also, even within a single field, formulas may be developed for many different and possibly conflicting purposes. Scientists may want to interpolate accurately, make predictions beyond the range of data in hand, uncover an underlying scientific law, or promote insight by a simple approximation to such a law. Clearly, no single set of criteria will suffice for all scientific fields and purposes.

Finally, it might be that the scientific value of a formula is impossible to determine purely on the basis of data. Regardless of its accuracy, simplicity, predictive value, and so on, acceptance of a formula by scientists can hinge primarily on theoretical backing or, more generally, on commensurability with accepted scientific views. The function-finding systems cited previously are domain independent, in the sense that they do not base their analyses on deep scientific knowledge of the kind that scientists acquire as a normal part of their training. Nevertheless, it can be essential to take domain knowledge into account in evaluating domain-independent systems.

The points I have discussed so far indicate the difficulty of determining general criteria for identifying good answers to scientific function-finding problems. Serious evaluation problems can arise, however, even if a desirable answer is assumed known. Suppose, for

[1] See the introductory essay in Suppe (1977) for a survey of some of the relevant philosophy of science and indications of many subtleties involved in identifying scientific goals.

example, that a function-finding system induces $y = 19.9x^2$ from a data set artificially generated on the basis of the function $y = 20x^2 + e$, where e is random noise. Is the program wrong? If so, it will always be wrong; with noisy data, it is impossible to recover coefficients precisely. Thus, we would rather say that the system is correct. But what if a system induces $19x^2$ or $15x^2$ or $10x^2$ or even $-10x^2$ from the same data? How much credit does it deserve in each case? At what point must we stop reporting that the system is essentially correct in uncovering the underlying quadratic relationship?

Again, what if a system induces $20x^{1.99}$ or $20x^{1.9}$ or $20x^{1.5}$? What if it proposes a linear relationship that is essentially a first-order approximation to the quadratic or an exponential relationship that closely follows the quadratic over the observed range? These errors seem more serious, although it is not clear that any of the answers are strictly wrong. After all, some of these are no further from the truth than Kepler was in proposing his third law: $P^2 = kD^3$. By Newton's calculations, k should be a function of the mass of the planet to which the equation is applied. By Einstein's, even the functional form is wrong. And yet, we would certainly like to give Kepler some credit for his work.

We might even imagine a function-finding system that examines the noisy quadratic data and reports that although it is confident that there is an underlying functional pattern of some sort, it is not able to identify the function. Certainly this answer, too, is not absolutely without merit.

Questions of partial credit are an unavoidable consequence of noisy data, and noise, in turn, is an essential complication of most kinds of experimental scientific work. Hence, partial credit is another tricky issue we must be prepared to tackle in evaluating function-finding systems.

Having indicated some of the subtleties involved in evaluating function-finding systems in general and scientific function-finding systems in particular, let me now move on to weigh the advantages and disadvantages of a number of evaluation schemes.

5.4 Anecdotal Evidence

With a few exceptions noted below, existing function-finding systems have been supported only by anecdotal evidence. Researchers have simply reported the results of tests on small sets of selected problems.

These tests have been marred by a number of serious methodological weaknesses, as discussed in detail in Schaffer (1990a). A majority of test problems have involved artificial data conforming exactly to a functional relationship rather than the noisy data faced in practice. In several of the few real-data tests reported, researchers have taken an active role in manipulating system parameters to ensure that acceptable answers are produced. Systems have also, sometimes, been designed with particular problems in mind and then tested on these same problems.

Leaving these difficulties aside, however, a basic one remains. When a system is tested on a finite set of problems selected by its author, we get no information about its likely performance on new problems arising in any other way. Reported successes can always be attributed to a researcher's ability to *find* problems for which a system is suited rather than to any power inherent in its approach. Moreover, anecdotal evidence does nothing to distinguish a proposed system from a straw man designed to give correct answers for—and only for—the test set.

This is not to say that existing function-finding systems are equivalent to such straw men or that the approaches they embody are without value. The point is simply that it is impossible to evaluate merit on the basis of anecdotes.

5.5 Artificial Environments

At best, anecdotes amount to isolated success stories rather than evidence regarding the general context or contexts in which a system can be expected to perform well. If we believe such a context can be specified, a much better idea is to do so and empirically evaluate performance within it.

As I have been using it, the word context suggests a real physical or social environment in which a function-finding system might be employed. From the point of view of the systems I have cited, however, little of the complexity of such environments is relevant, since only the data—and perhaps associated units of measurement—are taken as input. In testing these systems, we may abstract drastically and consider an environment as simply a generator of function-finding problems and an associated function-finding goal. Table 5.2 shows an example adapted from Schaffer (1989).

As I am interpreting the notation in the table, this specifies a generator that produces function-finding problems consisting of 20 observations for the variables x and y. Values for x are chosen at random over the interval [0,100]. Values for y are calculated from the equation $y = x^{a/b}$, with a small amount of normally distributed noise added to simulate random measurement error. The constants a and b that make up the exponent are determined, in essence, by flipping a fair coin and counting the number of tries required to flip a head: TTHTTTTH yields the exponent 3/5. Given values for x and y, the goal for the function-finding system is to recover the underlying functional relationship $y = x^{a/b}$.

Two principal advantages accrue from using environments like this one for testing.

Table 5.2
An Artificial Function-Finding Environment.

Generator G_1:

$$x \leftarrow U(20, 0, 100)$$
$$a \leftarrow G(1, .5)$$
$$b \leftarrow G(1, .5)$$
$$y \leftarrow x^{a/b} + N(20, 0, 1)$$

where $U(20, 0, 100)$ produces a vector of 20 values sampled from a uniform distribution on the interval [0,100], $G(1, .5)$ produces a single value sampled from a geometric distribution with parameter .5, and $N(20, 0, 1)$ produces a vector of 20 values sampled from a standard normal distribution.

Goal: Recover the underlying relationship $y = x^{a/b}$.

First, the environment approach allows us to obtain rigorous and purely objective assessments of function-finding power. If a system solves 85 of 100 random test problems produced by the generator, we may estimate its probability of success, under the conditions specified, at .85, and we may bound this estimate with a confidence interval to quantify its uncertainty. Although the environment I have outlined is purposely simple, an empirical demonstration of this sort would go far beyond the usual anecdotal evidence in proving that a function-finding system is of use for problems other than those selected by its authors.

Second, by specifying an environment, we facilitate comparison not only among serious function-finding systems but also between such systems and what I have called conservative alternatives. In the case of the environment of table 5.2, it seems likely that several of the function-finding systems proposed by AI researchers would perform well. On the other hand, we can also achieve excellent results with a simple statistical strategy that regresses $\log(y)$ on $\log(x)$, rounds the coefficient on $\log(x)$ to the nearest fraction with a denominator less than 10, and then uses this rounded value as its guess for a/b. To demonstrate the value of an AI approach to function finding, we must clearly show that we can specify an environment for which no such conservative alternative exists to give it serious competition.

Unfortunately, despite these advantages, tests run in artificial environments tell us nothing about the ability of function-finding systems to perform usefully in real scientific environments. A purely artificial context is likely to misrepresent both the problem distribution and the goals characteristic of any real one.

As part of the reported application of environment-based testing, for example, Nordhausen (1989) demonstrates conclusively that the function-finding component of IDS produces predictive interpolative formulas when given data generated according to the formula $y = 2x_1x_2x_3/x_4^2 + 30$, where values for the independent variables are chosen at random over the interval [10,100] and normally distributed noise with a standard deviation of as much as 150 is added to y. Nordhausen gives no evidence, however, that problems even vaguely resembling this one are likely to arise in a scientific context or that production of predictive interpolative formulas is an important or common scientific goal.

5.6 Real Data

If we want to claim that function-finding systems are of use in analyzing real scientific data, it seems clear that we will have to test them on data of precisely this kind. Simply choosing a set of real-data test problems, however, leads us back to anecdotal evidence. What we need instead is a way to specify an environment within which function-finding problems are regularly generated so that we can conduct a prospective test on a representative sample. As noted previously, we also need standards for evaluating the scientific significance of relationships hypothesized by a function-finding system. In artificial environments, we have the advantage of knowing the relationship actually employed in generating test data, although we cannot easily say how this knowledge may be used to determine the scientific significance of a functional hypothesis. With real data, we lack absolute information about the true underlying relationship. Hence, as noted earlier, the evaluation problem is doubly complicated.

My own attempt to evaluate function-finding systems on the basis of real data is reported in Schaffer (1990a). Scanning issues of the *Physical Review* journal from the first 20 years of this century, I attempted to collect *all* cases of bivariate data for which scientists had proposed a single functional relationship. After collecting a sample of 100 cases, I tested a number of prespecified function-finding systems on the data, counting each correct when it proposed a relationship matching the form of the scientist's and incorrect when it proposed any other.

This study led to a number of striking results. First, experiments with a reimplementation of the core bivariate function-finding algorithm of the BACON programs (Langley et al. 1987) showed that although the algorithm does reproduce the scientific result in roughly 30 percent of the cases studied, it gives nearly as many wrong answers as right ones. Also, although BACON is designed to detect any of an infinite number of functional relationships, its actual successes are limited to a handful of simple functional forms. Together, these points suggest that the difficulty in function finding is not so much in constructing relationships to fit the data—as previous researchers have uniformly assumed—but, rather, in judging their significance. This fact is confirmed by a second experiment demonstrating that the limited success of both the original BACON algorithm and an improved version could be duplicated by a search-free algorithm E, which simply applies BACON's elementary criterion for judging potential relationships to six common functional forms. Finally, a third experiment demonstrated the superiority of another search-free algorithm E* that extends E mainly by adopting a more sophisticated strategy in judging a handful of investigated relationships.

I call these results striking because they (1) demonstrate that an AI approach to function finding produces correct answers on real scientific problems not specially selected by program designers; (2) suggest that a widely-reported system works for very different reasons than reports have indicated; and (3) perhaps most important, lead to a radical new conception of the nature of function finding that construes the problem as one of classification rather than heuristic search.

All this is strong support for my earlier claim that shifting attention from building function-finding systems to evaluating them is likely to have a strong impact on the course of function-finding research. Nevertheless, there are serious methodological defects in the evaluation strategy I have just sketched, defects which, moreover, seem to be an unavoidable consequence of real-data testing.

One essential difficulty is the impossibility of eliminating a researcher's control over problem selection and formulation. In the case of the *Physical Review* study, I was forced to play a heavy role in identifying and interpreting examples of function finding. In doing so, I almost certainly created an important sampling bias. A second difficulty is that the test cases I drew from published reports of function finding are not likely to represent accurately the population of problems actually considered by scientists in their laboratories. This population cannot be sampled directly, however, since many problems are not recorded formally or even, perhaps, consciously recognized. In particular, scientists are relatively unlikely to record cases in which they casually examine a data set and do not detect a significant relationship. Reported or recorded function-finding cases are likely to include an unrepresentatively high proportion in which hypotheses are proposed. A third methodological weakness is in my criteria for judging hypotheses produced by function-finding systems. The fact that an individual scientist hypothesizes a relationship is certainly no guarantee of its scientific significance, and in any case, scientific significance is not necessarily preserved if a function-finding system matches the form—and not the parametric details—of this relationship.

In short, despite efforts to forge a link to scientific reality, we cannot ensure that function-finding systems are tested on representative scientific problems or ascertain the degree to which they respond with scientific answers. Moreover, in working with real data, we necessarily introduce strong elements of subjectivity in our evaluation methodology. Real-data testing is essential if we want to build systems for use in real scientific contexts, but it is not sufficient if we want hard evidence regarding function-finding performance.

5.7 Empirically Based Artificial Testing

To get hard evidence, we must return to controlled tests on artificial problems. As noted above, a serious weakness of information obtained through such tests is its possible lack of relevance to performance in a real scientific environment. If we combine artificial- and real-data testing, however, we may draw on experience with the latter to introduce strong elements of realism in artificial problems.

In my own work, as reported in Schaffer (1990a), an in-depth analysis of *Physical Review* cases for which scientists proposed linear relationships or direct proportionalities led to the problem generator G_2 shown in table 5.3. With default parameter values, G_2 generates eight data points spaced evenly over an x-interval of .65 orders of magnitude; y values are proportional to x with normally distributed noise yielding an expected correlation of .9985.[2] By varying parameters, we can alter the type and amount of noise, the number and spacing of observations, and the intercept. We can also add lack of fit or displace an endpoint to create an anomalous observation.

A first point to note about this generator is that it is hard to imagine anyone conceiving of it except on the basis of contact with real data. Defaults and options are chosen to reflect typical features of cases encountered in the *Physical Review*, and some of these are quite unexpected.

A second point is that, although generator G_1 of table 5.2 distributes problems at random over an infinite space of functional forms, G_2 uses just two functional forms and relies on external control—through the intercept parameter i—to choose between them. In fact, as the lack of a goal suggests, the new generator is not meant to be used as the basis of an artificial environment; with just two functional forms to identify, it would be easy to devise a conservative alternative to match the performance of a sophisticated function-finding system. Instead, G_2 is of use in analyzing such a system once it has been demonstrated on real data.

The E* algorithm, for example, was designed with real data in mind and tested prospec-

[2]Note that the constant of proportionality is unity. Use of this value yields no loss of generality for E*, the algorithm this environment was designed to test.

Table 5.3
An Empirically Based Generator for Function-Finding Problems.

Generator G_2:

$$x \leftarrow < 0, \tfrac{1}{n-1}, \tfrac{2}{n-1}, \tfrac{3}{n-1}, \ldots, 1 >$$
$$x \leftarrow x^u$$
$$y \leftarrow (1-q-c)x + qx^2 + c\tfrac{(2x-1)^3+1}{2}$$
$$x \leftarrow x(10^m - 1) + 1$$
$$y \leftarrow y(10^m - 1) + 1$$
$$y \leftarrow y + i\sigma$$
$$y_n \leftarrow y_n + e\sigma$$
$$\text{if } (\neg s)\ y \leftarrow y + t(n,d)\sigma/\sqrt{\tfrac{d}{d-2}}$$
$$\text{else } y \leftarrow y + (\chi^2(n,d) - d)/\sqrt{2d}$$

where $t(n,d)$ produces a vector of n values sampled from a t distribution with d degrees of freedom, $\chi^2(n,d)$ produces a vector of n values sampled from a χ^2 distribution with d degrees of freedom and default values for parameters of the generator are as follows: $n = 8, m = .65, \sigma = .054, d = 1000, i = 0, q = 0, c = 0, u = 1, e = 0, s = \text{F}$.

tively on cases drawn from the *Physical Review*, as described in the previous section. These tests show that the algorithm is able to solve some realistic problems, but they tell us nothing directly about the conditions under which E* will perform well. Also, for reasons described earlier, the tests do not yield purely objective information regarding E*'s performance. In contrast, when we report that E* solves 91 of a sample of 100 problems produced by G_2 with default settings, this finding is both precise and objective: Under specified conditions typical of those encountered in real data sets for which scientists proposed direct proportionalities, E* proposes a functional relationship of the same form with an estimated probability of .91.

Tests with nondefault parameter settings help to delimit the range of conditions under which E* does this well. One set of tests described in Schaffer (1990a) shows that the algorithm is affected very little when the size of the input data set is varied over the range observed in the *Physical Review* cases; performance is nearly as good for data sets containing just three observations as it is for those containing 25 or more. Another set of tests shows, however, that E* is highly sensitive to noise. For example, with G_2's parameter σ set at .324—yielding an expected correlation of .951—E* identifies a direct proportionality in only 21 of 100 cases. This finding is, again, relevant, because noise levels for artificial testing were chosen to span the range actually observed in the *Physical Review*. These examples show how much we can learn about the performance of a function-finding system through artificial testing. When informed by contact with real data, testing of this kind provides objective, relevant information which direct work with real data cannot.

5.8 Conclusion

I have proposed finally that we test function-finding systems on real scientific problems sampled prospectively from a reporting source and that we augment such real-data tests by measuring performance on artificial problems generated to resemble those encountered in practice. This hybrid approach still leaves a rather tenuous link between problems on which testing is based and those typically faced by laboratory scientists. It also sidesteps the tricky question of scientific goals. For real-data testing, I assume the answer provided by a scientist is the one satisfying these goals; in artificial-data testing, I leave the specification of goals to the researcher. My work has investigated the ability of E* to recover an underlying functional form, but a similar approach could be used to determine the predictive nature of its hypotheses or its tendency to converge to a correct formula or any other property deemed characteristic of scientific function finders.

Despite these flaws, however, I believe that the evaluation methods I have outlined are sufficient to shed a great deal of new light on the function-finding systems AI researchers have proposed over the past 10 years. That is, I believe that even imperfect methods may suffice for present purposes. I have attempted here to indicate the complexity and difficulty of evaluating function-finding systems. These problems must not prevent us from addressing the question, however. Without serious attention to evaluation function-finding research cannot progress.

References

Falkenhainer, B., and Michalski, R. 1986. Integrating Quantitative and Qualitative Discovery: The ABACUS System. *Machine Learning*, 1(4): 367–401.

Greene, G. H. 1988. The ABACUS.2 System for Quantitative Discovery: Using Dependencies to Discover Nonlinear Terms, Technical Report, MLI 88-17, Machine Learning and Inference Laboratory, George Mason University.

Hamilton, H. J. 1990. DATAX: A Framework for Machine Discovery of Regularity in Data. In Proceedings of the Eighth Canadian Conference on Artificial Intelligence.

Kokar, M. 1986. Discovering Functional Formulas through Changing Representation Base. In Proceedings of the Fifth National Conference on Artificial Intelligence, 455–459. Menlo Park, Calif.: American Association for Artificial Intelligence.

Langley, P.; Simon, H.; Bradshaw, G.; and Żytkow, J. 1987. *Scientific Discovery: Computational Explorations of the Creative Process.* Cambridge, Mass.:The MIT Press.

Nordhausen, B. E. 1989. A Computational Framework for Empirical Discovery. Ph.D. diss., Department of Computer Science, Univ. of California at Irvine.

Schaffer, C. 1990a. Domain-Independent Scientific Function Finding. Ph.D. diss., Dept. of Computer Science, Rutgers University.

Schaffer, C. 1990b. A Proven Domain-Independent Scientific Function-Finding Algorithm. In Proceedings of the Eighth National Conference on Artificial Intelligence, 828–832. Menlo Park, Calif.: American Association for Artificial Intelligence.

Schaffer, C. 1989. An Environment/Classification Scheme for Evaluation of Domain-Independent Function-Finding Programs. Presented at the IJCAI-89 Workshop on Knowledge Discovery in Databases. Detroit, Mich., 20 August.

Suppe, F., ed. 1977. *The Structure of Scientific Theories.* Urbana: University of Illinois Press.

Wu, Y. -H. 1988. A Practical Mechanism of Searching for Regularity in Data. In Proceedings of the Fifth International Conference on Machine Learning, 374–380. San Mateo, Calif.:Morgan Kaufmann.

Żytkow, J. 1987. Combining Many Searches in the FAHRENHEIT Discovery System. In Proceedings of the Fourth International Conference on Machine Learning, 281–287. San Mateo, Calif.:Morgan Kaufmann.

II DISCOVERY OF QUALITATIVE LAWS

6 A Statistical Technique for Extracting Classificatory Knowledge from Databases

Keith C. C. Chan
IBM Canada Laboratory

Andrew K. C. Wong
University of Waterloo

Abstract

This chapter describes a simple yet efficient method for uncovering classificatory knowledge in databases. Based on some concepts in statistics and information theory, it is capable of handling mixed-mode (mixed continuous- and discrete-valued) data that can contain inconsistent, erroneous, or missing values. The method can be divided into three phases: (1) the detection of underlying patterns in a database of preclassified records, (2) the construction of class descriptions based on the detected patterns, and (3) the use of these descriptions to determine the class membership of objects not originally in the database. The effectiveness of the proposed method was evaluated using simulated and real-life data. The results indicate that its performance is superior to many existing methods both in terms of classification accuracy and computational efficiency.

6.1 Introduction and Background

The problem-solving strategies adopted by many expert systems are intrinsically classificatory in nature in the sense that various heuristics are employed by these systems to associate data with known solutions that best explain them (Chandrasekaran 1986) For example, the tasks of MYCIN can be viewed as classifying patient data into disease categories, those of PROSPECTOR as classifying geologic descriptions into mineral formation classes, and those of SACON as classifying structural analysis problems into classes, with each class being handled by a particular family of analysis methods (Chandrasekaran 1986).

To build these expert systems, knowledge engineers are usually required to conduct interviews with domain experts to extract relevant knowledge from them. Because of communication problems between people of different backgrounds, knowledge acquisition through interviews is difficult and time consuming. It is mainly for this reason that many AI researchers advocated the use of inductive-learning techniques to automate such a process. Given a database consisting of examples of the experts' decisions, it is hoped that these techniques will be able to uncover hidden knowledge in the data for constructing expert systems.

Currently, not many of the existing learning systems can be used for such a purpose because they were primarily designed for problem domains in which it is assumed that the instances provided by the experts are perfectly described and that their desired output is always correctly specified. Recently, however, with a realization of the need to handle uncertainty in many real-world problem domains, some attempts have been made to deal with noisy data. In particular, various prepruning and postpruning techniques have been adopted by many decision-tree based learning systems to reduce the size of a tree and to prevent the problem of overfitting (Watkins 1987).

In the case of *prepruning*, branching at a node of a decision tree is terminated either when no attribute is able to increase the information gain (Breiman et al. 1984; Hart 1985; Niblett 1987; Quinlan 1986) or when branching on this node would cause more training instances to be misclassified than terminating at the node (Bratko and Kononenko 1987). Because decisions for branching or termination can only be made based on local information alone (Niblett 1987), prepruning can cause the tree-building process to terminate too early, leaving important information undiscovered (Bratko and Kononenko 1987). To overcome this problem, postpruning of decision trees was investigated.

The idea of *postpruning* is to use some optimization criteria to offset the complexity of a tree against its classification accuracy on the training data (Niblett and Bratko 1987). A branch can be pruned, for example, if there is a significant difference in the rate of misclassification over a set of test data after every nonleaf subtree of a root is replaced by the best possible leaf (Quinlan 1987). If a set of test data is not available (which is usually the case), the misclassification rate for the unseen cases at the leaves of a subtree can be estimated based on a continuity correction for the binomial distribution (Quinlan 1987) or according to a generalization of Laplace's law of succession (Bratko and Kononenko 1987; Niblett and Bratko 1987). A compromise between tree complexity and classification accuracy can also be made by using other error estimates or defining complexity in terms of the number of terminal nodes in a subtree, and so on (Breiman et al. 1984; Niblett 1987).

Instead of directly pruning decision trees, as in the systems previously described, the postpruning strategy developed for the current version of ID3 prunes a set of rules derived from following the paths in a tree (Quinlan 1987). During the pruning process, the conditions on the left-hand side of each rule are examined in turn to identify, according to Fisher's exact test, the ones that are unimportant for the classification process. These unimportant conditions are discarded from the rules to simplify them. The simplified rules are in turn omitted from the rest of the others so that the performance of the other rules on the training instances can be evaluated. The rules whose omission would not lead to an increase (or would even lead to a reduction) in the number of misclassified instances are discarded. Although this pruning method works well when compared to the others, it is rather slow and inefficient. Furthermore, because both the pruning of rules and conditions in the rules are based on hill-climbing approaches, important information can be overlooked in the event of a local optimum (Quinlan 1987). Even with postpruning, therefore, the decision-tree based systems still have to overcome some problems to effectively deal with imperfect data in classification tasks.

In the next section, a method is presented that has been demonstrated to be more effective, in terms of both classification accuracy and computational efficiency, than many existing inductive learning systems and, in particular, the decision-tree based systems. This method is based on a probabilistic inference technique evolved from the works described in Chan and Wong (1988, 1990); Chan, Wong and Chiu (1988, 1989); Chan (1989); Chiu and Wong (1986); and Wong and Chiu (1987a, 1987b). It is able to efficiently uncover hidden patterns in mixed-mode (mixed continuous- and discrete-valued) data that can contain inconsistent, missing, or erroneous values.

6.2 Acquisition of Classificatory Knowledge from Imperfect Data

Given a database consisting of the descriptions of N objects in the form of records, suppose that these N objects have been classified into P known classes, c_p, $p = 1, \ldots, P$, and that each of them is described by n distinct attributes, $A_1, \ldots, A_j, \ldots, A_n$, so that in an instantiation of object descriptions, an attribute A_j takes on the value $a_j \epsilon\, domain(A_j)$ $= \{a_{j_k} | k = 1, \ldots, K\}$. The classification task that many inductive-learning systems deal with, therefore, is to find a set of characteristic descriptions (in terms of $A_j, j = 1, \ldots, n$) for the P classes, so that based on these descriptions, an object that is not originally in the database can be correctly classified.

6.2.1 The Use of Traditional Statistical Techniques

In many real-world problem domains, the classification task previously specified is much more complicated than it might seem. The descriptions of the objects in a database can, for instance, be incomplete and erroneous. Furthermore, it might not be correctly classified. To deal with such an imperfect database, the statistical technique that is often used is the chi-square test (Bratko and Kononenko 1987; Hart 1985; Quinlan 1986). Let o_{pk} be the total number of objects in the database that belong to c_p and are characterized by a_{j_k} and $e_{pk} = o_{p+}o_{+k}/N'$ (where $o_{p+} = \sum_{k=1}^{K} o_{pk}$, $o_{+k} = \sum_{p=1}^{P} o_{pk}$ and $N' = \sum_{p,k} o_{pk} \leq N$ because of missing values) be the expected total under the assumption that being a member of c_p is independent of whether an object has the characteristic

a_{j_k}. If the statistic

$$X^2 = \sum_{p=1}^{P}\sum_{k=1}^{K}\frac{(o_{pk}-e_{pk})^2}{e_{pk}} = \sum_{p=1}^{P}\sum_{k=1}^{K}\frac{{o_{pk}}^2}{e_{pk}} - N'$$

is greater than the critical chi-square $\chi^2_{d,\alpha}$ (where $d = (P-1)(K-1)$ and α, usually taken to be 0.05 or 0.01, is the significance level), then according to the chi-square test, it can be concluded, with a confidence level of $1-\alpha$, that A_j is dependent on the class labels and, therefore, is important for constructing class descriptions as well as determining the class membership of an object.

The chi-square test is used, for example, by some decision-tree based systems during tree pruning to determine whether a node should be branched (Bratko and Kononenko 1987; Hart 1985; Quinlan 1986). It is also used in statistical pattern recognition to select a good set of features with which to perform the learning process (James 1985).

Despite its popularity, it should be noted that the chi-square test only tells us if an attribute, A_j, is, as a whole, helpful in determining the class membership of an object. It does not, however, provide us with much information about whether an object characterized by a certain value of it, say, a_{j_k}, should be assigned to a particular class, say, c_p. In view of the importance of such information—especially when A_j takes on a large number of different values or when there are many different classes to which an object could be assigned—a method is proposed here for its acquisition. Based on this method, whether an object being characterized by a certain value of an attribute is more likely to be a member of a particular class than the others can easily be determined.

6.2.2 The Proposed Method

The proposed method for acquiring classificatory knowledge from an imperfect database consists of three phases: (1) the detection of underlying patterns in the database, (2) the construction of classification rules based on the detected patterns, and (3) the use of these rules to predict the class membership of an object not originally in the database.

Detecting Hidden Patterns in an Imperfect Database. In the presence of uncertainty, an attribute value, a_{j_k}, can be considered as providing important information for determining whether an object it characterizes should be assigned to a class, c_p, if $Pr(\text{object is in } c_p | A_j = a_{j_k})$ is significantly different from $Pr(\text{object is in } c_p)$. Because $Pr(\text{object is in } c_p | A_j = a_{j_k}) = o_{pk}/o_{p+}$, and $Pr(\text{object is in } c_p) = o_{+k}/N'$, we are, in other words, interested in determining whether o_{pk} is significantly different from e_{pk}.

To make this determination, we adopt an objective criterion based on the following statistical technique described in (Chan 1989). Let

$$z_{pk} = \frac{(o_{pk} - e_{pk})}{\sqrt{e_{pk}}} \quad .$$

The maximum likelihood estimate of its asymptotic variance, ν_{pk}, therefore, is given by (Haberman 1973):

$$\nu_{pk} = (1 - \frac{o_{p+}}{M})(1 - \frac{o_{+k}}{M}) \quad .$$

In other words,

$$d_{pk} = \frac{(o_{pk} - e_{pk})/\sqrt{e_{pk}}}{\sqrt{\nu_{pk}}} = \frac{z_{pk}}{\sqrt{\nu_{pk}}} \tag{6.1}$$

has an approximate standard normal distribution.

Whether an object characterized by a specific value of an attribute, a_{j_k}, should be assigned to a class, c_p, therefore, can be determined as follows: If $d_{pk} > 1.96$, we can conclude, with a confidence level of 95 percent (or 2.576 for 99 percent), that (1) Pr(object is in $c_p|A_j = a_{j_k}$) $> Pr$(object is in c_p); (2) it is, therefore, more likely for an object characterized by a_{j_k} to belong to c_p than to other classes; and (3) c_p is characterized by the presence of a_{j_k} in most of its members. If $d_{pk} < -1.96$, we can conclude, with a confidence level of 95 percent (or 2.58 for 99 percent), that (1) Pr(object is in $c_p|A_j = a_{j_k}$) $<$ Pr(object is in c_p); (2) it is, therefore, more likely for an object characterized by a_{j_k} to belong to the other classes than to c_p; and (3) c_p is characterized by the absence of a_{j_k} from most of its members. If $-1.96 < d_{pk} < 1.96$, we can conclude, with a confidence level of 95 percent (or 2.58 for 99 percent), that (1) Pr(object is in $c_p|A_j = a_{j_k}$) is not significantly different from Pr(object is in c_p); (2) knowing that an object is characterized by a_{j_k}, therefore, does not provide us with much information about whether it should be assigned to c_p; and (3) a_{j_k} should not be in the characteristic descriptions of c_p.

Rule Generation Based on Detected Pattern. The information provided by the d_{pk}s ($p = 1, \ldots, P$ and $k = 1, \ldots, K$) whose absolute values are greater than 1.96 are utilized to construct characteristic descriptions of the various classes. These descriptions are in the form of rules such as the following:

> If A_j of an object is a_{j_k}, then it is with certainty $W(Class = c_p/Class \neq c_p|A_j = a_{j_k})$ that the object belongs to c_p ,

where W, the weight of evidence measure, is defined in terms of the mutual information, $I(c_p : a_{j_k})$, between c_p and a_{j_k} (Osteyee and Good 1974; Wang and Wong 1979) and

$$I(c_p : a_{j_k}) = \log \frac{Pr(c_p|a_{j_k})}{Pr(c_p)} \quad .$$

$I(c_p : a_{j_k})$ is positive if $Pr(c_p|a_{j_k}) > Pr(c_p)$. It is negative if $Pr(c_p|a_{j_k}) < Pr(c_p)$ and is zero if $Pr(c_p|a_{j_k}) = Pr(c_p)$. $I(c_p : a_{j_k})$ intuitively measures the decrease (if positive) or increase (if negative) in uncertainty about the assignment of an object to a certain class given that it possesses the characteristic a_{j_k}. Based on the mutual information measure, the weight of evidence provided by a_{j_k} for or against the assignment of an object characterized by a_{j_k} into class c_p can be defined as (Osteyee and Good 1974)

$$\begin{aligned} &W(Class = c_p/Class \neq c_p|a_{j_k}) \\ &\quad = I(Class = c_p : a_{j_k}) \;-\; I(Class \neq c_p : a_{j_k}) \enspace . \end{aligned}$$

In other words, W can be interpreted as a measure of the difference in the gain in information when an object characterized by a_{j_k} is assigned to c_p and when it is assigned to other classes. The weight of evidence is positive if a_{j_k} provides positive evidence supporting the assignment of an object to c_p; otherwise, it is negative. The characteristic descriptions of a class, c_p, can be considered as made up of those classification rules whose conclusion parts predict it.

Determination of Class Membership To determine the class membership of an object, *obj*, characterized by $a_1, \ldots, a_j, \ldots, a_n$, that is not originally in the database, its description can be matched against the classification rules. If an attribute value, say, a_j, of *obj* satisfies the condition part of a rule that predicts, say, $c_{obj} \epsilon \{c_p | p = 1, \ldots, P\}$, then we can conclude that the description of *obj* partially matches that of c_{obj}. Because in the presence of uncertainty, the description of *obj* might partially match that of more than one class, there is a need to decide which specific one it should be assigned to. For this purpose, the following evidence measure, the weight of evidence, W, provided by $a_1, \ldots, a_n$ in favor of *obj* being classified into c_{obj}, as opposed to other classes, is defined as (Chan 1989)

$$\begin{aligned} &W(C_{obj} = c_{obj}/C_{obj} \neq c_{obj}|a_1, \ldots, a_n) \\ &\quad = I(C_{obj} = c_{obj}|a_1, \ldots, a_n) \;-\; I(C_{obj} \neq c_{obj}|a_1, \ldots, a_n) \enspace . \end{aligned}$$

Suppose that of the n characteristics that describe *obj*, only m $(m \leq n)$ of them, $a_{[1]}, \ldots, a_{[j]}, \ldots, a_{[m]}$, $a_{[j]} \;\epsilon\; \{a_j | j = 1, \ldots, n\}$, are found to match with one or more classification rules; the previous equation can then be simplified into (Chan 1989)

$$\begin{aligned} &W(C_{obj} = c_{obj}/C_{obj} \neq c_{obj}|a_1, \ldots, a_n) \\ &\quad = W(C_{obj} = c_{obj}/C_{obj} \neq c_{obj}|a_{[1]}, \ldots, a_{[m]}) \enspace . \end{aligned}$$

If there is no a priori knowledge concerning the interrelation of the attributes, the weight of evidence provided by all the attribute values of *obj* in favor of it being assigned to

c_{obj}, as opposed to other classes, is equal to the sum of the weights of evidence provided by each individual attribute value of *obj* that matches the classification rules. In other words, W can be written as (Chan 1989)

$$W(C_{obj} = c_{obj}/C_{obj} \neq c_{obj}|a_{[1]}, \ldots, a_{[m]}) \\ = \sum_{j=1}^{m} W(C_{obj} = c_{obj}/C_{obj} \neq c_{obj}|a_{[j]}) \ .$$

Intuitively, therefore, the total amount of evidence supporting or refuting a certain class assignment is equal to the sum of the individual pieces of evidence provided by each attribute value. In fact, the value of W increases with the number and the strength of the various pieces of positive evidence supporting a specific class assignment for an object and decreases with the number and the strength of the various pieces of negative evidence refuting such an assignment.

With the weight of evidence measure, the most suitable class to which *obj* should be assigned can easily be determined. If

$$W(C_{obj} = c_p/C_{obj} \neq c_p|a_{[1]}, \ldots, a_{[m]}) \\ > W(C_{obj} = c_h/C_{obj} \neq c_h|a_{[1]}, \ldots, a_{[m]}), \ h = 1, 2, \ldots, P' \text{ and } h \neq p \ ,$$

then *obj* is assigned to c_p ($P' \leq P$ being the number of classes that are partially matched by the attribute values of *obj*).

In classifying an object, it should be noted that two or more different class assignments can have the same greatest weight of evidence. In this case, *obj* can be considered to be a member of all these classes. Also, it is possible that there is no evidence for or against *obj* being classified in any specific class. In such case, *obj* can be assigned to the most commonly occurring class in the database.

Unlike many inductive-learning systems, the proposed method has the advantage that it allows all the classes to be determined with which the description of *obj* matches (or not matches in the case $W < 0$). Furthermore, the weight of evidence for or against *obj* to be classified in each of the matched classes provides us with some idea about how typical or representative *obj* is as a member of the various classes. The ability for learning systems to uncover such knowledge is important in problem domains in which it is possible for an object to be classified in more than one class. For example, in the medical domain, a patient can be infected with more than one disease to varying degrees. Being able to determine: (1) all possible disease classes that the patient might belong to and (2) the weight of evidence associated with all such classifications, the proposed method can be employed as an aid to the physicians in medical diagnosis and prognosis.

6.2.3 Handling Mixed Continuous- and Discrete-Valued Data

It should be noted that as was described at the beginning of the section, the classification task that many AI researchers in machine learning are interested in involves symbolically represented data (Cohen and Feigenbaum 1982). In other words, the number of values that an attribute can take on (that is, $domain(A_j)$) is finite. For this reason, most of the existing classification systems are not designed to handle continuous-valued data. There are some exceptions, however. Systems such as ACLS and ASSISTANT (Bratko and Kononenko 1987; Niblett and Patterson 1982) are able to binarize a continuous-valued attribute, so that any value this attribute takes on falls either into the subinterval $A_j < k$ or $A_j > k$. Instead of taking on an infinite number of values, after binarization, the attribute takes on two discrete values, *above* k and *below* k.

Clearly, a system that can only discretize continuous-valued attributes into two subintervals might overlook many interesting patterns underlying a set of data. One way to overcome this problem is to divide the range of values that an attribute can take on into a certain number of subintervals of equal width. However, such a division can result in the loss of important information, thereby making pattern discovery difficult (Wong and Chiu 1987b). To avoid such a problem, a technique is adopted that is based on the principle of maximizing entropy in the information-theoretic sense (Wong and Chiu 1987b). This method has been mathematically shown to be able to minimize the information loss as a result of discretization. To effectively deal with mixed-mode data, we used this technique to discretize continuous-valued data in the database.

6.3 An Illustrative Example

As an illustration of how the proposed method is able to handle mixed-mode data, let us consider a database of employee records (table 6.1). Suppose that for each employee, five attributes were recorded: SEX (S), with values {M=Male, F=Female}; JOBTITLE (J), with values {A=Accountant, S=Secretary, P=Programmer, M=Manager}; OFFICE LOCATION (O), with values {T=Toronto, O=Ottawa, V=Vancouver, M=Montreal, E=Edmonton}; SALARY (SAL), with values ranging from below \$25,000 to over \$60,000; and DEPT (D), with values {M=Marketing, S=Software Development, A=Accounting, D=Data Processing}. Suppose also that because of incomplete information, there are some missing values in the data (indicated by ?). The problem is to extract classificatory knowledge from the database so that given an employee that is not originally in the database, his(her) DEPT (which is unknown) can be determined based on the extracted knowledge.

Because SALARY is a continuous-valued attribute, it is first discretized to make it

Table 6.1
An Employee Database.

#	S	J	L	SAL	D	#	S	J	L	SAL	D
1	M	A	T	$36,020	A	2	M	?	O	$42,000	D
3	?	M	?	$49,390	D	4	M	A	V	$41,120	M
5	F	A	V	$32,990	A	6	M	P	O	$30,870	S
7	M	?	M	$43,120	M	8	?	P	O	$38,700	S
9	M	M	M	$57,230	M	10	F	P	?	$29,120	D
11	?	A	V	$45,590	M	12	M	P	?	$44,400	D
13	M	M	O	$53,900	S	14	F	P	?	$39,000	A
15	F	A	V	$31,000	A	16	F	?	O	$23,000	S
17	F	P	O	$31,000	S	18	?	S	O	$26,000	S
19	M	P	?	$32,650	A	20	F	A	T	$35,000	A
21	F	A	M	$37,980	D	22	?	A	?	$34,010	A
23	M	P	O	$42,900	S	24	M	?	V	$39,990	D
25	F	?	?	$30,900	A	26	?	S	O	$22,000	D
27	F	S	?	$28,000	D	28	M	?	E	$36,900	S
29	F	M	M	$46,000	S	30	?	P	O	$34,000	D
31	M	P	O	$41,390	D	32	F	S	O	$37,000	A
33	?	S	?	$24,000	A	34	M	P	O	$33,000	D
35	F	S	E	$40,900	M	36	M	P	O	$42,000	D
37	M	P	V	$39,090	S	38	M	A	?	$44,900	M
39	F	S	T	$38,760	M	40	F	P	?	$35,000	S
41	M	P	O	$47,000	S	42	?	P	O	$42,000	D
43	F	?	T	$49,000	M	44	M	M	?	$61,000	D
45	M	?	E	$44,000	A	46	M	S	?	$39,560	M
47	?	P	O	$32,230	D	48	F	S	T	$30,000	A
49	F	P	V	$38,790	D	50	M	M	?	$36,000	A
51	M	P	O	$33,270	D	52	?	P	O	$41,000	M
53	M	M	M	$49,120	M	54	F	P	?	$38,700	D
55	F	M	O	$47,220	M	56	F	?	V	$43,410	A
57	M	M	M	$45,110	M	58	?	S	O	$24,330	S
59	M	S	?	$28,910	A						

Table 6.2
Frequency Table for DEPT and JOBTITLE.

o_{pk} e_{pk} d_{pk}	Accountant	Secretary	Programmer	Manager	TOTAL
Accounting	5 2.16 2.45	4 2.64 1.09	2 5.04 -2.04	4 2.16 -1.00	12
Software Design	0 1.98 -1.76	2 2.42 -0.35	7 4.62 1.65	2 1.98 0.02	11
Data Processing	1 2.88 -1.48	2 3.52 -1.11	11 6.72 2.63	2 2.88 -0.69	16
Marketing	3 1.98 0.91	3 2.42 0.48	1 4.62 -2.50	4 1.98 1.80	11
TOTAL	9	11	21	9	50

easier for the underlying patterns in the database to be revealed. For this example, the range of values that SALARY can take on is discretized into four subintervals based on the techniques described in Wong and Chiu (1987b): \$22,000 to \$30,870; \$30,900 to \$37,980; \$38,000 to \$41,390; and \$42,000 to \$61,000.

To determine if an attribute, say, the JOBTITLE of an employee, provides any information about the department that s/he belongs to, the chi-square test can be performed. Because $X^2 = \sum_{p=1}^{4} \sum_{k=1}^{4} \frac{(o_{pk} - e_{pk})^2}{e_{pk}} = 20.61 > \chi^2_{9,0.05} = 16.92$ from table 6.2, we can conclude, with a confidence level of 95 percent, that DEPT is dependent on JOBTITLE and that the title of an employee provides some information about the department s/he belongs to.

Unfortunately, however, based on the chi-square test, we are unable to tell which specific department an employee is in given his(her) job title. To acquire such information, the d_{pk}s given in the following table are investigated, and it is noted that d_{11}, d_{13}, d_{33}, and d_{43} are greater than the 5 percent standard normal deviate, 1.96. In fact, approximately 55 percent of the total chi-square ($X^2 = 20.61$) is concentrated at these four cells. The other 12 cells contribute little. Even though one cannot, for example, based on d_{11}, be completely certain that an employee, who is an Accountant, is likely to be in the Accounting department, there are obvious reasons for such premises.

From the signs of the deviates, one can also conclude that if an employee is an Accountant or a Programmer, it is likely that s/he is in Accounting and Data Processing respectively (d_{11} and d_{33} are positive). If, however, the employee is a Programmer, then it is quite unlikely that s/he is in Accounting or Marketing (d_{13} and d_{43} are negative). Because the absolute values of $d_{2k}, k = 1, 2, 3, 4$ are all less than 1.96, the JOBTITLE of an employee does not provide much information concerning whether s/he should be in Software Development.

Based on the significant d_{pk}s, classification rules, such as the following (based on d_{11}), can be constructed:

> If an employee is an Accountant, then it is with certainty W that s/he belongs to the Accounting department,

where

$$\begin{aligned}&W(\text{DEPT} = \text{Accounting}/\text{DEPT} \neq \text{Accounting}|\text{JOBTITLE} = \text{Accountant})\\&\quad = \log \frac{Pr(\text{JOBTITLE} = \text{Accountant}|\text{DEPT} = \text{Accounting})}{Pr(\text{JOBTITLE} = \text{Accountant}|\text{DEPT} \neq \text{Accounting})}\\&\quad = \log \frac{5/12}{4/38} = 1.98 \quad .\end{aligned}$$

The rest of the other classification rules can be similarly constructed.

To illustrate how these rules can be used during classification, let us suppose we are given an employee who is not originally in the database. Suppose that this employee is a male. He is a Programmer. He works in Ottawa and earns \$44,700 each year. From the classification rules, it is noted that knowing the sex of an employee does not provide us with any information about which department he belongs to. However, knowing that he is a Programmer, we are provided with positive evidence supporting his being in Data Processing and negative evidence against his being in Accounting or Marketing. Also, working in Ottawa suggests that he is either in Software Development or Data Processing but not in Accounting or Marketing.

To determine the specific department the employee belongs to, the weight of evidence for the employee to be in each of the four different departments can be computed; for example:

$$\begin{aligned}&W(\text{DEPT} = \text{Accounting}/\text{DEPT} \neq \text{Accounting}|\text{SEX} = \text{Male}, \text{JOBTITLE}\\&\qquad\quad = \text{Programmer}, \text{LOCATION} = \text{Ottawa}, \text{SALARY} = \$44,700)\\&\quad = W(\text{DEPT} = \text{Accounting}/\text{DEPT} \neq \text{Accounting}|\text{JOBTITLE}\\&\qquad\quad = \text{Programmer}, \text{LOCATION} = \text{Ottawa})\end{aligned}$$

$$= (-1.58) + (-2.19)$$
$$= -3.77 \ .$$

Similarly, the weights of evidence for the employee to belong to Software Development, Data Processing, and Marketing are 0.95, 2.17, and -1.73, respectively. Because the weight of evidence for the employee to be in Data Processing is the greatest given that he is male, he is a programmer, he works in Ottawa, and his salary is $44,700 (that is, in the range $42,000 to $61,000), it is likely that the department he belongs to is Data Processing. The employee could also be in Software Development, even though such a possibility is supported by less evidence ($W = 0.95$). It is, however, unlikely for him to be in Accounting or Marketing because there is negative evidence against his being in these departments.

6.4 Experimental Results

The proposed method was implemented and tested with data sets from several different domains. In the first experiment, a database consisting of the records of 120 patients was used. Each of these records was characterized by 12 components, representing 12 different symptoms (Pao and Hu 1984). Based on these symptoms, the physicians decided whether a patient should be placed in the intensive care unit (ICU) or be discharged to the main floor. Of the 120 patients, 66 of them were diagnosed as in critical condition and were placed in the ICU, and 54 of them were discharged.

In the second experiment, another patient database consisting of 99 records was available (Pao and Hu 1984). These records were characterized by the same 12 attributes, representing the 12 different symptoms in the previous experiment. Based on these symptoms, the patients were diagnosed and placed in four different disease categories by a group of physicians. Of the 99 patients, 15 were diagnosed with chest diseases, 33 with abdominal diseases, 25 with cardiac diseases, and 26 with neurological diseases.

Since the early 1930s, reports have shown that patients with Down's Syndrome have characteristic features on their palms and fingers (Cummins 1936). In the third experiment, therefore, a database consisting of 14 common fingerprint and palm patterns of 126 subjects was obtained to determine the potential of dermatoglyphics as an aid in identifying congenital diseases. These 126 subjects were classified into three groups. The first consisted of 51 myelomeningocele patients, and the second and third groups consisted of, respectively, 40 and 35 normal subjects showing different dermatoglyphic patterns (Wong, Vogel, and Wang 1975).

For performance evaluation, 10 trials for each of these three data sets were carried out. In each trial, 70 percent of the available data was randomly selected for training,

Table 6.3
Performance Comparison of Different Classification Methods (% Correct).

Data Set No.	ID3 with No Pruning	ID3 with Pre-Pruning	ID3 with Post-Pruning	Bayesian Classifier	Simple Majority	Proposed Approach
1	89.2%	82.0%	85.0%	79.2 %	51.1%	91.1%
2	79.5%	59.5%	87.0%	81.0 %	35.0%	94.0%
3	51.0%	48.2%	55.0%	44.7 %	37.5%	68.2%

leaving the rest for testing. The accuracy of the decisions made by the following methods, averaged over the 10 trials, was then determined (table 6.3): (1) the ID3 method, which builds decision trees for classification based on the top-down induction of decision tree (TDIDT) algorithm described in Quinlan (1986); (2) the ID3 method with prepruning, which terminates the branching process at a node when the attribute associated with the node is tested (by the chi-square test) to be statistically independent of the classes (Quinlan 1986); (3) the ID3 method with postpruning, which constructs a set of rules equivalent to a decision tree and then simplifies them by testing each term of each rule against the class predicted by the rule for statistical dependence (Quinlan 1987); (4) the Bayesian classifier, which classifies an object in the class with the highest conditional probability (because of small sample training data size, the attributes are assumed to be mutually independent); (5) the default or simple majority classifier, which simply assigns all objects to the most commonly occurring class in the training set, with no reference to their attributes; and (6) the proposed method without rejection (that is, an object is assigned to the most commonly occurring class when there is not enough evidence supporting it to be assigned to any specific one).

As is expected, these results indicate that the classification accuracy of the simple majority method, which served as a reference point for evaluation, was the poorest. The Bayesian classifier performed much better than the simple majority method. However, it was, in general, not as good as the decision tree-based algorithms except in the experiment with the second set of medical data.

Of the three ID3-based or decision-tree based methods, the use of a prepruning strategy during the construction of decision trees did not seem to improve the classification accuracy. In fact, it consistently made more errors than the simple ID3 algorithm in which no prepruning was performed. This result is mainly because, as a decision tree is being built, the set of training data is subdivided into smaller and smaller subsets, and at the point where the expected frequencies of each cell in the contingency table constructed for a chi-square test fall below four, the assumptions behind the use of the test cannot be justified (Quinlan 1987). Thus, without a large training set, the branching process can terminate too soon, thereby leaving important classificatory information undiscovered.

In the statistics community, it was recently suggested that the restriction of the expected frequency in each cell to at least four is too conservative. For tests conducted at a confidence level of 95 percent, the minimum expected cell frequencies can be approximately 1.0, according to Fienberg (1980). The test for the ID3 algorithm with prepruning was also performed under such an assumption. Unfortunately, it did not improve the classification accuracy of the algorithm by much. As for the ID3 methods without pruning and with postpruning, they are comparable in performance in the sense that the former is more accurate in experiments with the first set of medical data but not as accurate as in the other experiments.

Of all the six methods, the percentage of correct classification of the proposed method was the highest in all experiments. Results of a direct comparison between the proposed method and the other decision tree pruning algorithms are not yet available. However, because ID3 with postpruning has been shown to have superior performance when compared to the others (Quinlan 1987), we only compared the proposed method with ID3.

As for the time complexity of the proposed method, it should be noted that unlike the decision-tree based algorithms, its basic operation (that is, the computation of d_{pk}s) is performed only once. It is for this reason that the proposed method is substantially faster than the decision-tree based approaches whose efficiency depends on the structure of the trees. Because the d_{pk}s can be examined independently of each other, the proposed method can be employed in the implementation of an artificial neural network that not only has the advantage of being fast in its training process but also allows internal associations to be directly analyzed. Such a network has, in fact, been built and tested on simulated and real-world data. Its performance proved to be superior to a Back Propagation Network (Wong, Chan and Vieth 1991).

6.5 Conclusion

In conclusion, a simple yet efficient method was presented for the acquisition of classificatory knowledge from a database of mixed continuous- and discrete-valued attributes that can contain erroneous or null values. This method can also be used to deal with problems in relational databases, for example, where some fields are inapplicable for some tuples (for example, "pregnant" question for men) if not-applicable is considered an attribute value. The proposed method is, however, not able to discover knowledge in data sets that do not contain some sort of pattern. For example, it cannot be used to predict the behavior of a completely random process, such as the lottery.

In searching for regularities in noisy data, it should be noted that the proposed method does not assume the presence of domain knowledge to guide the search. In fact, classificatory knowledge can be accurately extracted from databases even when some of the relevant attributes that characterize the objects are not provided because of a lack of knowledge of a problem domain (Chan 1989). However, in case domain knowledge is available, the proposed method can make use of it to derive new attributes for training, guide the search for important attribute values, and classify objects.

The effectiveness of the proposed method was evaluated using both simulated and real-life data, and the results indicate that it consistently performs better than many of the existing systems in terms of classification accuracy. It is also computationally more efficient than the others. Furthermore, because it does not require all the training instances to be kept in fast memory, as is described in Quinlan (1983), large training sets can be dealt with economically, and the disadvantages (the considerable increase in processing time without significant benefits produced (Quinlan 1983)) that arise as a result of using the windowing method can be avoided. Having these advantages, the method described in this chapter provides an effective aid for uncovering hidden classificatory knowledge in databases.

References

Bratko, I., and Kononenko, I. 1987. Learning Diagnostic Rules from Incomplete and Noisy Data. In *Interactions in Artificial Intelligence and Statistical Methods,* ed. B. Phelps, 142–153. Aldershot, England: Technical.

Breiman, L.; Friedman, J. H.; Olshen, R. A.; and Stone, C. J. 1984. *Classification and Regression Trees.* Belmont, Calif.: Wadsworth.

Chan, K. C. C. 1989. Inductive Learning in the Presence of Uncertainty. Ph.D. diss., Dept. of Systems Design Engineering, Univ. of Waterloo.

Chan, K. C. C., and Wong, A. K. C. 1990. APACS: A System for Automated Pattern Analysis and Classification. *Computational Intelligence.* 6: 119–131.

Chan, K. C. C., and Wong, A. K. C. 1988. PIS: A Probabilistic Inference System. In Proceedings of the Ninth International Conference on Pattern Recognition, 360–364. Washington, D.C.: IEEE Computer Society.

Chan, K. C. C.; Wong, A. K. C.; and Chiu, D. K. Y. 1988. OBSERVER: A Probabilistic Learning System for Ordered Events. In *Pattern Recognition,* ed. J. Kittler, 507–517. London: Springer-Verlag.

Chan, K. C. C.; Wong, A. K. C.; and Chiu, D. K. Y. 1989. Discovery of Probabilistic Rules for Prediction. In Proceedings of the Fifth IEEE Conference on Artificial Intelligence Applications, 223–229. Washington, D.C.: IEEE Computer Society.

Chandrasekaran, B. 1986. From Numbers to Symbols to Knowledge Structures: Pattern Recognition and Artificial Intelligence Perspectives on the Classification Task. In *Pattern Recognition in Practice II,* eds. E. S. Gelsema and L. N. Kanal, 547–559. Amsterdam: Elsevier.

Chiu, D. K., and Wong, A. K. C. 1986. Synthesizing Knowledge: A Cluster Analysis Approach Using Event-Covering.*IEEE Systems, Man, and Cybernetics* 16: 251–256.

Cohen, P. R., and Feigenbaum, E. A. 1982. *The Handbook of Artificial Intelligence,* volume 3. Los Altos, Calif.: William Kaufmann.

Cummins, H. 1936. Dermatoglyphic Stigmata in Mongolian Idiocy. *Anatomical Record,* 64(11).

Fienberg, S. E. *The Analysis of Cross-Classified Categorical Data.* Cambridge, Mass.: The MIT Press. Haberman, S. J. 1973. The Analysis of Residuals in Cross-Classified Tables. *Biometrics* 29: 205–220.

Hart, A. E. 1985. Experience in the Use of an Inductive System in Knowledge Engineering. In *Research and Development in Expert Systems I,* ed. M. A. Bramer, 117–126. Cambridge: Cambridge University Press.

James, M. 1985. *Classification Algorithms.* London: Collins.

Niblett, T. 1987. Constructing Decision Trees in Noisy Domains. In *Progress in Machine Learning: Proceedings of EWSL 87,* eds. I. Bratko and N. Larvac, 67–78. Wilmslow: Sigma.

Niblett, T., and Bratko, I. 1987. Learning Decision Rules in Noisy Domains. In *Research and Development in Expert Systems III,* ed. M. A. Bramer, 25–34. Cambridge: Cambridge University Press. Niblett, T., and Paterson, A. 1982. *ACLS Manual.* Edinburgh:Intelligent Terminals.

Osteyee, D. B.; and Good, I. J. 1974. *Information, Weight of Evidence, the Singularity between Probability Measures and Signal Detection.* Berlin: Springer-Verlag.

Pao, Y. H., and Hu, C. H. 1984. Processing of Pattern-Based Information: Part I: Inductive Inference Methods Suitable for Use in Pattern Recognition and Artificial Intelligence. In *Advances in Information Systems Sciences,* volume 9, ed. J. T. Tou, 221–259. New York: Plenum Press.

Quinlan, J. R. 1987. Simplifying Decision Trees. *International Journal of Man-Machine Studies* 27: 221–234.

Quinlan, J. R. 1986. Induction of Decision Trees. *Machine Learning* 1(1): 81–106.

Quinlan, J. R. 1983. Learning Efficient Classification Procedures and Their Application to Chess End-Games. In *Machine Learning: An Artificial Intelligence Approach,* eds. R. S. Michalski, J. G. Carbonell, and T. M. Mitchell, 463–482. San Mateo, Calif.: Morgan Kaufmann.

Wang, D. C. C., and Wong, A. K. C., 1979. Classification of Discrete Data with Feature Space Transformation. *IEEE Transactions on Automatic Control* 24(3): 434–437.

Watkins, C. J. C. H., 1987. Combining Cross-Validation and Search. In *Progress in Machine Learning: Proceedings of EWSL 87,* eds. I. Bratko and N. Larvac, 79–87. Wilmslow: Sigma.

Wong, A. K. C., and Chiu, D. K., 1987a. An Event-Covering Method for Effective Probabilistic Inference. *Pattern Recognition* 20(2): 245–255.

Wong, A. K. C., and Chiu, D. K. Y. 1987b. Synthesizing Statistical Knowledge from Incomplete Mixed-Mode Data. *IEEE Transactions on Pattern Analysis and Machine Intelligence* 9(6): 796–805.

Wong, A. K. C.; Chan, K. C. C.; and Vieth, J. O. 1991. Training of an Artificial Neural Network for Pattern Classification: An Efficient Approach Based on Residual Analysis. In Proceedings of the SPIE Conference on Applications of Artificial Neural Network. Bellingham, Wash: Internal Society for Optical Engineering..

Wong, A. K. C.; Vogel, M. A.; and Wang, D. C. C. 1975. Computer Augmented Methodologies for Classifying Clinical Data, Internal Report, Biomedical Information Processing Program, Carnegie Mellon Univ.

7 Information Discovery through Hierarchical Maximum Entropy Discretization and Synthesis

David K. Y. Chiu
University of Guelph

Andrew K.C. Wong
University of Waterloo

Benny Cheung
GEOREF Systems Ltd.

Abstract

This chapter outlines a new approach to the synthesis of information from data. Here information is defined as a detected organization of data after a process of discretization (or partitioning) and event covering (Chiu 1986; Chiu and Wong 1986). Such organization can be reflected by how the characteristics of events defined through the discretization process deviate from prior knowledge expectation. Discretization is based on a hierarchical maximum entropy scheme that iteratively partitions the event space by minimizing the loss of information (Shannon and Weaver 1964). The event-covering process that covers or selects relevant events is based on an evaluation of the deviation of the observed event frequencies from their expectation based on prior knowledge (defined by the null hypothesis or domain knowledge). The distribution of the event occurrences in the set of detected cells through the event-covering process describes an approximate probability density function in a flexible way. The hierarchical maximum entropy discretization scheme provides a rigorous and efficient way for the probability estimation to overcome the nonuniform scaling problem in multivariate data analysis. Because our method dynamically refines the boundaries according to the detected information, it directs the synthesis and analysis process on the outcome subspace with high information content. In addition, it naturally produces a hierarchical view of information, so that data can be analyzed and synthesized with respect to an outcome context. The method was tested using simulated and real-life data with good results.

7.1 Introduction

Identifying probabilistic relationships in data can be useful in discovering a functional or a production-rule relationship in the data. For example, in the production rule of the form if-<condition>-then-<conclusion>, <condition> and <conclusion> relate certain values of two variables. The information conveyed by this rule can be reflected in a subspace of the outcome space of the variables. Identifying the subspace that contains such information will be important in the discovery process. In this chapter, we outline a new approach to the synthesis of information from data.

Here, *information* is related to the notion of data organization and is a property of the system (Stonier 1987). This view reinforces Shannon's the earlier idea of information as "a measure of one's freedom of choice," that is, entropy (Shannon and Weaver 1964, p.108). Such information (we call it relational information) can be considered as the underlying relationship of the observed outcomes. To maximize information detection is to maximize the opportunity to detect data organization by maximizing the entropy through discretization. New relational information is said to be discovered, or detected, when a significant deviation from prior knowledge (null hypothesis or domain knowledge) is found.

We describe our approach as one of data synthesis and analysis rather than merely data analysis. *Data synthesis* refers to the combining of selected observed data, as constituent elements through an analysis process, into a unified representation. It is based on the detection of probabilistic relationships in the data as a form of organization. Here, *organization* refers to a statistical characteristic of the data ensemble; it can be detected from an aggregate of samples rather than an individual sample. The methods developed in using this approach will be useful in pattern recognition or machine learning applications.

In the proposed method, a discretization scheme is first generated on the outcome space using a method called hierarchical maximum entropy discretization. Maximum entropy has been successfully used as a criterion in many engineering and scientific applications, for example, in data, signal, and image processing (Jaynes 1957; Kapur, Sahoo, and Wong 1985; Wernecke and d'Addario 1977). Our method of *hierarchical maximum entropy discretization* iteratively partitions the outcome space. The iteration produces a hierarchical scheme for analysis and synthesis with minimum information loss (Shannon and Weaver 1964). Our scheme refines the discretization boundaries dynamically based on the detected information; hence, the loss of precision is minimized. In other words, our method directs the analysis/synthesis on outcome subspace with high information content.

The analysis on the partitioned outcome subspace is performed using an approach called *event covering*, that is, the covering or selection of events with probabilistic relevancy. It is also used in identifying significant outcome subspace to which computational resources are directed. Earlier methods based on the event-covering approach are described in Chiu (1986), Chiu and Wong (1986), and Wong and Chiu (1987a, 1987b).

This chapter shows how the method can be used to detect probabilistic relations that might be piecewise continuous, multimodal, and subject to a variety of background noise. The method does not require the selection of an a priori model and the model fitting used in many regression analysis techniques (Draper and Smith 1966).

7.2 Hierarchical Maximum Entropy Discretization

Two major problems posed great concern in classical pattern recognition. One is related to the notion of scaling and distance for data represented in a Euclidean space (Marriott 1974). The other is related to the analysis of multivariate data of the mixed type, that is, a mixture of nominal, ordinal, and continuous data (Duda and Hart 1973). The first problem arises from the lack of a mathematical and logical justification for weighting and rescaling values in different dimensions in a Euclidean space. This problem affects the meaningfulness of the metric as well as nonparametric estimations such as the Parzen window (Parzen 1962) or the nearest neighbour estimation (Cover and Hart 1967), which are all metric dependent. The second problem is because of the lack of a unified framework for analyzing n-tuples whose components are of a mixed type. One approach to the analysis of multivariate data of the mixed type involves the discretization of the continuous components. Recently, we used entropy maximization as a criterion for discretizing the continuous components (Forte, Lascurain, and Wong 1987; Lascurain 1983; Wong and Chiu 1987b), thus bypassing the problem of nonuniform scaling and providing a unified treatment to mixed-mode data analysis.

Let us consider the data of interest represented by n variables or as an n-tuple $X = (X_1, X_2, \ldots, X_n)$, analogous to data in the relational model of databases. Given an ensemble of such data, in practice, the outcome space of the variables will be bounded by the limits of measurement. The *k^n-discretization process* is defined as one that finds a set of k points on each axis of the n-dimensional space. These n sets of points will partition the N-dimensional space into k^n cells, $R = \{R_i | i = 1, 2, \ldots, k^n\}$, where the projection of R_i on the jth axis will define an interval $I_{i(j)}$ on X_j, $(1 \le j \le n)$. Let P be the probability distribution on the n-dimensional space. The process produces a quantization of P into $P(R_i), i = 1, 2, \ldots, k^n$ discrete values to form a discrete probability distribution, denoted by the finite scheme

$$\Gamma = \begin{pmatrix} R_i \\ P(R_i) \end{pmatrix}, i = 1, 2, \ldots, k^n \quad . \tag{7.1}$$

The Shannon entropy H associated with Γ is defined as

$$H(R) = -\sum_{i=1}^{k^n} P(R_i) \log P(R_i) \quad . \tag{7.2}$$

The k^n*-maximum entropy discretization* (k^n*-MED) process* is to find the n sets of boundary points that partition the outcome space into cells subject to the maximization of the Shannon entropy. Given a probability distribution, let $\mathbf{R}$ be the family of all possible sets of k^n cells. We call a set of k^n cells that renders the maximum entropy the k^n-MED cells. We adopt an approximation based on the marginal maximum entropy discretization criterion. Marginal maximum entropy discretization applies the maximization criterion on each of the entropy functions defined on the marginal probability estimates rather than on the entropy function defined on the high-order probability estimate. Except in some rare situations (Ng and Wong 1987), the set of k^n-MED cells generated in most data distributions is unique.

To obtain a more restricted set of finer intervals, we can reapply the maximum entropy discretization process on each cell detected to contain a high level of data organization. The iteration of the discretization process is applied to a cell only when the deviation between the observed and expected frequency of event occurrences in the cell is found to be greater than a prescribed threshold (described in detail in section 7.5, Information Detection Using Event Covering); hence, it requires more processing resources only when necessary. We call this process the *hierarchical maximum entropy discretization.* If the availability of computational resources is not a concern, we can apply the iterative discretization process to all cells. We can then detect information at a higher level even when the cell at a lower level is not significant. This general application of the iterative process is necessary only to detect a weak relation at a higher level when the relation is not revealed at a lower level. Usually, a strong relation that is detected at a higher level will also be revealed at a lower level.

7.3 Entropy Function and Diversity between Subpopulations

In this section, we show that the entropy function has a lower bound related to the generalized Jensen difference of a diversity function (Burbea and Rao 1982). Thus, by maximizing the entropy function, the diversity between subpopulations is also maximized.

Given a set of probability measures $P_1, P_2, \ldots, P_m$ and $W = (w_1, w_2, \ldots, w_m)$, where $P_k = (p_1, p_2, \ldots, p_K)$, Rao (1984) suggests the following decomposition based on the entropy function H:

$$H(\sum_{k=1}^{m} w_k P_k) = \sum_{k=1}^{m} w_k H(P_k) + J_H(\{P_i\}, \{w_i\}) \ . \tag{7.3}$$

The second term $J_H(\{P_i\}, \{w_i\})$ in this equation is called the *generalized Jensen difference* of the function H. If $P_1, P_2, \ldots, P_m$ are probability distributions in m subpopulations with a priori probabilities (or a priori weights) $w_1, w_2, \ldots, w_m$, then the term

$H(\sum_{k=1}^{m} w_k P_k)$ is known as the *total diversity*, where the quantity $\sum_{k=1}^{m} w_k H(P_k)$ is the *average diversity* within subpopulations. Thus, $J_H(\{P_i\}, \{w_i\})$ can be interpreted as the diversity between the subpopulations.

Suppose the probability distributions $P_1, P_2, \ldots, P_m$ in the m subpopulations are unknown, but the prior probabilities $w_1, w_2, \ldots, w_m$ are known. With the Shannon entropy, the following theorem shows that the entropy of the prior probabilities is bounded by the corresponding diversity J_H.

THEOREM 1 Let $\triangle_n = \{P_i = (p_1, p_2, \ldots, p_n) \mid 0 < p_k < 1, \sum_{k=1}^{n} p_k = 1, i = 1, 2, \ldots, m\}$, and let $P_i \in \triangle_n$ for $i = 1, 2, \ldots, m$ be the m complete probability distributions. Let $W = (w_1, w_2, \ldots, w_m) \in \triangle_m$; then the inequality

$$J_H(\{P_i\}, \{w_i\}) < H(W) \tag{7.4}$$

holds, where H is the Shannon entropy.

The proof of the theorem, originally described in Sahoo and Wong (1988), is included at the end of this chapter.

Now, if we use the maximum entropy criterion on the prior probabilities for discretization, we maximize the upper bound on J_H. Because the generalized Jensen difference and the Shannon entropy are related, the diversity between the subpopulations, even though unknown, is also maximized. The theorem gives a justification for the use of the maximum entropy criterion for discretization.

7.4 Illustration of Maximum Entropy Discretization

To illustrate maximum entropy discretization, we compare it with equal-width-interval discretization. Given an ensemble of data with an unknown probability density function, the number of observations falling into each interval is a maximum likelihood estimation of the probability density function. This estimation is a maximum likelihood estimation irrespective of how the intervals are chosen. To illustrate the difference between the two methods, let us look at the following example. Consider the following 30 values observed for a given variable (X): 0.1, 0.9, 1.5, 2.0, 2.8, 3.2, 3.3, 3.5, 3.7, 3.8, 4.0, 4.5, 4.9, 5.5, 6.0, 7.3, 8.5, 8.8, 9.1, 9.2, 9.5, 9.5, 9.7, 9.7, 10.0, 10.3, 10.5, 11.1, 11.8, and 12.9. The probability density can be estimated from the histogram constructed based on these observed values. Let us arbitrarily select the number of intervals as 5. Let the range of the values to be considered be between 0.0 and 13.0. Because maximum entropy implies equal probability, maximum entropy discretization will assign 6 samples (or probability 0.2) to each of the five intervals if the observed values are distinct. If the

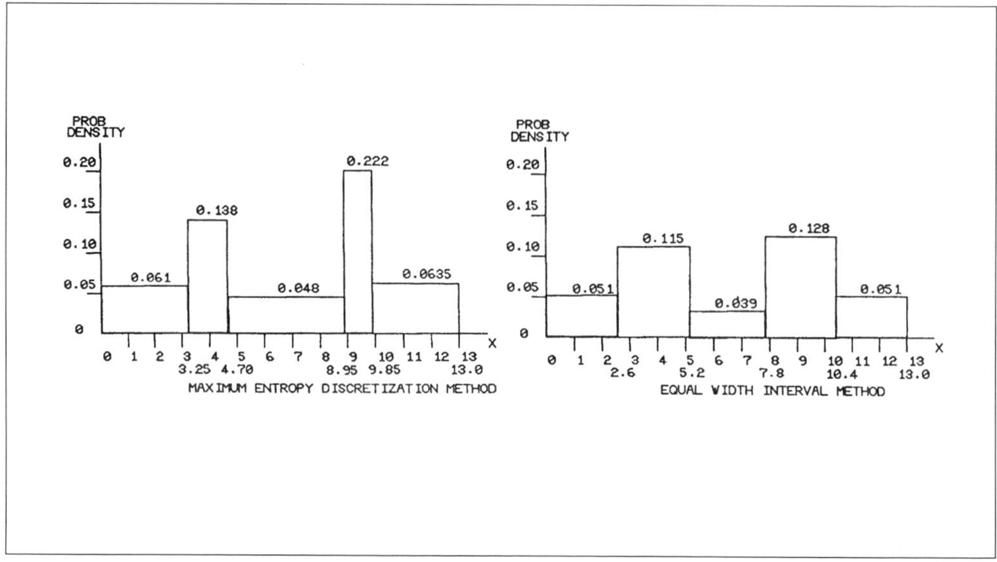

Figure 7.1
Comparison of the Histograms Generated Using the Maximum Entropy Discretization Method and the Equal-Width-Interval Method. Peaks of the probability density function are shown more clearly in the maximum entropy discretization method. The probability density is normalized to unit width.

observed values are not distinct with repeated values near the boundary point, then the maximum entropy criterion will determine the exact boundary point. The equal-width-interval method will assign the interval width to be 2.6 irrespective of the number of samples observed at the interval. The histogram, as an approximation of the probability density function using the two methods, can be plotted as in figure 7.1. Comparing the two methods, we observe that maximum entropy discretization shows the peaks of the probability density function more clearly.

7.5 Information Detection Using Event Covering

After discretization, assuming that a subset of the outcomes in the complete outcome space contains functional or relational information, we adopt event covering to detect such information.

Consider a functional relationship that relates the values of $X = (X_1, X_2, \ldots, X_p)$ and $Y = (X_{p+1}, X_{p+2}, \ldots, X_n)$. We separately apply hierarchical maximum entropy discretization on X and Y. Because the process applies to X and Y in a similar way, for simplicity, we only discuss it with respect to X.

Let $\mathbf{a} = (a_1, a_2, \ldots, a_p)$ and $\mathbf{b} = (b_1, b_2, \ldots, b_p)$ be two distinct points in the p-dimensional space, such that $a_k < b_k$, for each $k = 1, 2, \ldots, p$. The *p-dimensional open interval* $I = (\mathbf{a}, \mathbf{b})$ is defined to be the set

$$I = (\mathbf{a}, \mathbf{b}) = \{(x_1, \ldots, x_p) | a_k < x_k < b_k, k = 1, 2, \ldots, p\} \ . \tag{7.5}$$

Thus, **(a,b)** can be considered the Cartesian product

$$(\mathbf{a}, \mathbf{b}) = (a_1, b_1) \times (a_2, b_2) \times \ldots \times (a_p, b_p) \tag{7.6}$$

of the p one-dimensional intervals (a_k, b_k). The p-dimensional measure or content of I, denoted by $\mu(I)$, is defined to be the product

$$\mu(I) = (b_1 - a_2) \ldots (b_p - a_p) \ . \tag{7.7}$$

When $p = 2$, $\mu(I)$ is the area of I and when $p = 3$, $\mu(I)$ yields the volume of I. The neighborhood of **(a,b)** can be defined as the extended interval that encloses and is a proper superset of **(a,b)**.

Through the discretization process, a set of p-dimensional intervals that satisfies the maximum entropy criterion is generated for X at each iteration and similarly for Y. A set of k^n-MED cells $R = \{R_i | i = 1, 2, \ldots, k^n\}$ can then be formed as the Cartesian product of the high-dimensional intervals for X and Y. The projections of a cell R_i into the outcome subspaces of X and Y can be defined as the high-dimensional intervals I_{x_i} and I_{y_i}, respectively. Analysis and synthesis can be performed on a cell relating the projected intervals.

The event-covering process will cover a subset of the cells in R. In evaluating a cell R_i, we consider whether the observed samples that fall on R_i significantly deviate from the expectation based on either the null hypothesis or expert estimation. The relevancy of a cell can be determined by analyzing whether the observed frequency significantly deviates from the expected frequency. There are three methods in calculating the expected frequency. One is based on the uniformity assumption, another is based on the independence assumption, and the third is based on domain expert estimation.

Method 1 (uniformity assumption): If no outcome is expected to occur more than the others, the probability distribution is uniform. The expected frequency of observations in a cell R_i is estimated by

$$M \times \frac{\mu(I_{x_i})}{\mu(I_x)} \times \frac{\mu(I_{y_i})}{\mu(I_y)} \ , \tag{7.8}$$

where M is the total number of training data; I_{x_i} and I_{y_i} are the projected intervals of R_i on X and Y, respectively; and I_x and I_y are the extended intervals that enclose I_{x_i} and I_{y_i}, respectively.

The intervals I_x and I_y denote a neighborhood of the cell as a context. The context I_x and I_y can be *global* if they include all the outcome space and *local* if only an outcome subspace is considered. In hierarchical maximum entropy discretization, the intervals generated at the previous iteration naturally form the local context.

Method 2 (independence assumption): If the outcomes from I_{x_i} and I_{y_i} are independent, the expected frequency on R_i is

$$\frac{M_x(R_i) \times M_y(R_i)}{M} , \tag{7.9}$$

where $M_x(R_i)$ and $M_y(R_i)$ denote the marginal frequency of the outcomes on I_{x_i} and I_{y_i}, respectively.

Different types of information can be detected using different methods. Roughly speaking, analysis using method 1 detects a concentration of points in the outcome subspace based on the discretization scheme, irrespective of their interrelationship. However, analysis using method 2 detects the interdependence relationship; that is, the outcomes of X are related to the outcomes of Y in the sense the observation deviates from independence assumption in the respective projected intervals associated with a cell. For problems such as inference and prediction (for examples, see Wong and Chiu 1987a, 1987b), the use of method 2 is more appropriate; otherwise, method 1 is more appropriate.

Method 3 (expert estimation assumption): When expert estimation is available, the estimate can be used in calculating the expected frequencies of outcomes on certain cells. However, when this approach is used, the estimated frequencies should satisfy the constraints of the marginal frequencies. The inclusion of the expert estimation can be achieved by subtracting the expected frequency of cells with known estimates from the marginal frequencies and then calculating the expected frequencies of cells with unknown estimates based on either method 1 or method 2.

When the expected frequencies are calculated, the deviation of the observed frequency and the expected frequency can be used as a measure of discrepancy between what is observed and what is expected from the prior knowledge. Unfortunately, the absolute difference between the observed and the expected cell frequencies—$|obs(R_i) - exp(R_i)|$, where $obs(R_i)$ and $exp(R_i)$ denote the observed frequency and the expected frequency on the cell R_i, respectively—cannot be used for evaluating the relative value of the discrepancy. The reason is because the absolute difference can be affected by the marginal totals (Wrigley 1985). Hence, it is often suggested (Kalbfleisch 1985) that the difference be standardized as

$$D(R_i) = \frac{(obs(R_i) - exp(R_i))}{\sqrt{exp(R_i)}} . \tag{7.10}$$

This equation is called the *standardized residual* (Haberman 1973) and has the property that $\sum_i (D(R_i))^2$ is asymptotically distributed as chi-square if the $exp(R_i)$ terms are calculated using either method 1 or method 2. $D(R_i)$ then has an approximate normal distribution with a mean of approximately 0 and a variance of approximately 1. It must be noted, however, that the approximation of $D(R_i)$ to the standard normal distribution is useful only if the asymptotic variance for each $D(R_i)$ term is close to one (Fingleton 1984). The use of the adjusted residual provides a better approximation if the asymptotic variance substantially differs from one (Haberman 1973). The adjusted residual is defined as (Haberman 1973)

$$D'(R_i) = \frac{D(R_i)}{\sqrt{v}(R_i)} \ , \tag{7.11}$$

where

$$v(R_i) = (1 - \frac{M_x(R_i)}{M})(1 - \frac{M_y(R_i)}{M}) \ . \tag{7.12}$$

A cell R_i can be covered (selected) if the D' value is greater than a prescribed threshold T (Chan, Wong, and Chiu 1989; Chan and Wong 1990). If $obs(R_i) > exp(R_i)$, then the relation is positive on R_i; otherwise, it is negative.

7.6 Algorithm

The algorithm of hierarchical maximum entropy discretization uses a terminating criterion based on the number of samples observed for a cell. If the sample size is large enough, and the cell is covered, then the k^n-MED is reapplied to the covered cell. A rule of thumb for the smallest sample size can be chosen as $A \times k^n$, where A is 3 or 5. In our experiments, we found that if the relation is well defined, we can choose a size much smaller. In choosing the threshold of deviation in the algorithm, we can choose one for initiating the next iteration and another for detecting significant information. The following implementation of the algorithm uses a stack to store all the covered cells. The algorithm can be outlined as follows:

1. Initialize R as the complete outcome space to be analyzed;
2. Push R into stack;
3. Repeat
    - Pop R from stack;
    - If there are sufficient samples in R, then

- Apply hierarchical maximum entropy discretization on R, and generate a set of $\{R_i\}$;
- For each R_i, do
  - Identify the observed frequency on R_i;
  - Estimate the expected frequencies using different methods from prior knowledge;
  - Calculate the D' value for each of the expected frequencies;
  - If ($D' >$ threshold T)
  - Then push R_i into stack
  - Else output R_i and the results of its analysis:
    (a) D' value;
    (b) probabilistic relevancy;
    (c) probability estimate;

• Else output R and results of its analysis;

4. Until stack is empty.

The value of k is chosen a priori and can be selected by trial and error. A reasonably large k value should be used under the constraints of the sample size, so that there is enough resolution to describe the embedded relation. If k is large, the process is analogous to a breadth-first search; if k is small, the process is analogous to a depth-first search. Often, the result from the previous experiment on a given data set will provide insight into the optimal k value that will determine the exact bounds of a cell. The experiments in the next two sections use $k = 4$, and we use the chi-square test of 95 percent confidence level as a criterion of significance.

7.7 Experiment: Simulated Data

To test the behavior of the algorithm, we perform an experiment on a set of simulated data. The data are created relating two variables X and Y. The relation governing the variables is stochastic and one to many in the sense that for a certain X value, the Y values stochastically vary, as shown in the following formulas:

$$X := \pm c_1 \; cos(\theta) + \delta + c_2 \tag{7.13}$$

and

$$Y := \pm c_3 \; sin(\theta) + \delta + c_4 \quad , \tag{7.14}$$

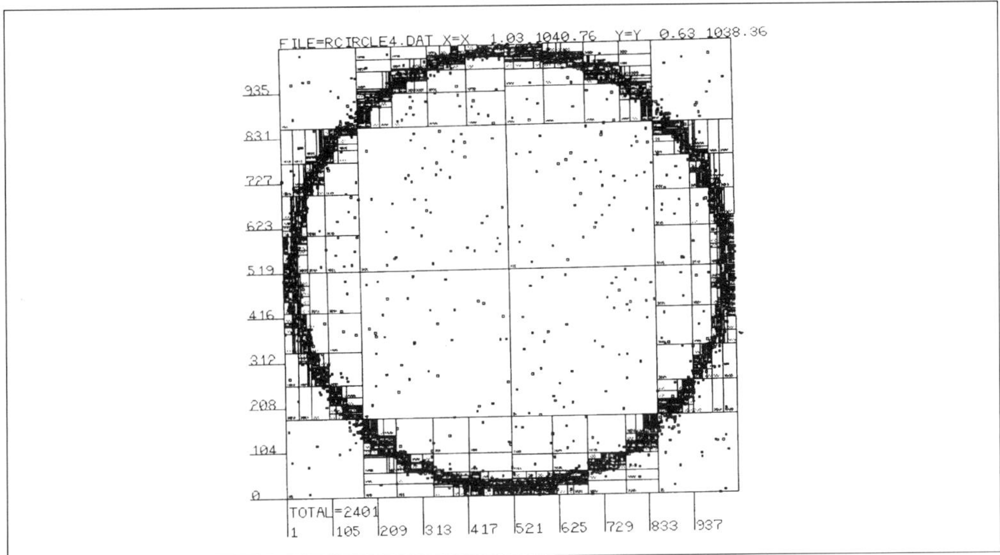

Figure 7.2
Discretized Cells in the Simulated Data Experiment. The gray cells are the detected cells.

where δ is a random variable generated from a normal distribution N(0;10.0); c_1, c_2, c_3, and c_4 are constants chosen as 500, 520, 500, and 520, respectively. The X and Y values are stochastically generated as a function of the parameter θ. Points of (X, Y) are then evenly generated based on the value of θ, with $0 \leq \theta < 2\pi$.

After 2000 points are generated, 400 points of background noise with uniform distribution are added. Hence, only a subset of the final set of 2400 sampling data conveys relevant information. Notice that the relation relating X and Y is nonlinear and bimodal and is masked by background noise.

The objective of the experiment is to see whether the algorithm can screen out the irrelevant data and produce a representation describing the original probabilistic relation. After several iterations, the algorithm stops, and the outcome space is discretized into cells, as in figure 7.2. The gray cells in the figure have a positive significant relation, indicating a deviation from the independence assumption in global context. The result is similar for evaluation based on the uniformity assumption and is consistent with the property of the simulated data in the way they are created. The set of cells identified from the algorithm also describes an approximate probabilistic density function of the detected relation. It is seen that the covered cells closely approximate the original relation even though the original relation is previously unknown.

7.8 Experiment: Genetic Sequences

The accumulation of nucleic acid and protein sequence data has grown so drastically in recent years that genetic sequence databases have been created to store these data. The molecular sequence represents the primary (one-dimensional) structure of a macromolecule. However, because of chemical bondings, the macromolecule folds into secondary (two-dimensional) and tertiary (three-dimensional) structures, and the physical and functional properties of the macromolecule are largely determined by its secondary and tertiary structure. Because it is often time consuming and difficult to obtain the secondary and tertiary structures of a macromolecule using laboratory techniques, except for a few well-studied macromolecules, the higher-order structure of many macromolecules, especially the tertiary structure, is unknown. A model of the higher-order structure of transfer RNA, which we used in this experiment, is shown in figure 7.3.

The objective of this study is to determine the statistical relationship between subsequence patterns of nucleic acid type and their positions in the sequence. When the relevant patterns and positions (in terms of their dependency) are identified, their role in the molecular structure can be inferred (Chiu and Kolodziejczak 1990a, 1990b; Wong, Liu, and Wang 1976). These detected subsequences can be used by biologists in consensus sequence analysis (for example, see Waterman 1986).

This experiment uses 79 selected sequences of eukaryotic elongator t-RNA, taken from the GenBank genetic sequence database, release 55.0 (Bilofsky and Burks 1988). These sequences are selected because they are known to be homologous and of similar length. Each sequence is a chain that varies from 76 to 79 nucleotides long, with only a few longer than 76 nucleotides. The nucleotide is one of 4 types: A (Adenine), G (Guanine), C (Cytosine), or U (Uracil).

The high-order probability distribution of a subsequence can be approximated by the product of low-order probabilities in the form of dependence tree product approximation (Chow and Liu 1968). With the length of a subsequence fixed, the dependence tree approximation can be estimated. By treating the probability of the subsequence as a variable and the subsequence position as another variable, their dependence relationship can be evaluated based on our proposed method. The advantage of using dependence tree transformation is that a subsequence, rather than a single nucleotide, can be used, and the method does not require the subsequence to be exactly matched in the data.

Because our method allows variation, exact positional alignment of the sequences is not required, thus bypassing the alignment step that can be computationally explosive in the multiple-sequence case. When nucleotide triplets (subsequence of length 3) are analyzed, the result indicates a significant relationship between certain subsequence types and their positions. Some of the significantly high-probability types, for example, GGU,

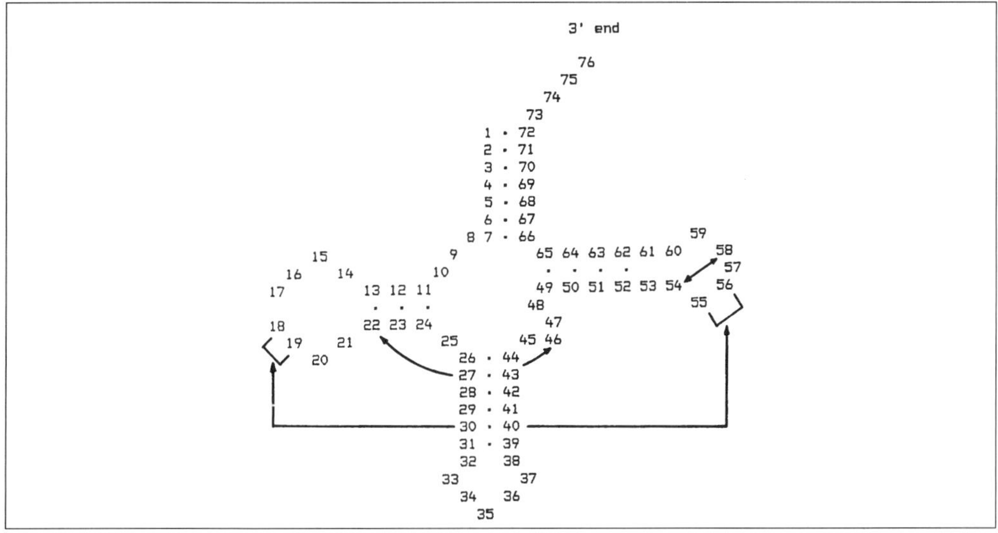

Figure 7.3
A Clover Leaf Model of Transfer RNA. The indexes show the position used in the experiment. The dots indicate the secondary bondings, and the lines indicate the tertiary bondings.

UGG, and UCG, are close to the positional sites related to tertiary bonding. Positions from 18–38 and 63–69 are found to vary, dominated by low-probability triplet types.

7.9 Theorem Proof

THEOREM 2 Let $\triangle_n = \{P_i = (p_1, p_2, \ldots, p_n) \mid 0 < p_k < 1, \sum_{k=1}^{n} p_k = 1, i = 1, 2, \ldots, m\}$, and let $P_i \in \triangle_n$ for $i = 1, 2, \ldots, m$ be the m complete probability distributions. Let $W = (w_1, w_2, \ldots, w_m) \in \triangle_m$; then the inequality

$$J_H(\{P_i\}, \{w_i\}) < H(W) \tag{7.15}$$

holds, where H is the Shannon entropy.

Proof 1 Using equation 7.3 and the Shannon entropy, we obtain

$$J_H(\{P_i\}, \{w_i\}) - H(W) = \sum_{j=1}^{m} \sum_{k=1}^{n} p_{jk} \, log_2 \frac{p_{jk}}{r_k} + \sum_{i=1}^{m} w_i \, log_2 \, w_i \ , \tag{7.16}$$

where $r_k = \sum_{i=1}^{m} w_i \, p_{ik}$ $(k = 1, 2, \ldots, n)$. Because $\sum_{k=1}^{n} p_{ik} = 1$ for all $i = 1, 2, \ldots, m$, equation 7.16 can be rewritten as

$$J_H(\{P_i\},\{w_i\}) - H(W) = \sum_{i=1}^{m}\sum_{k=1}^{n} w_i\ p_{ik}\ log_2\ \frac{w_i\ p_{ik}}{r_k} \quad . \tag{7.17}$$

The use of the inequality $log_2\ w \leq (w-1)\ log_2\ e$ in equation 7.17 results in the following:

$$J_H(\{P_i\},\{w_i\}) - H(W) < \sum_{i=1}^{m}\sum_{k=1}^{n} w_i\ p_{ik} \left(\frac{w_i\ p_{ik}}{r_k} - 1\right) log_2\ e \quad . \tag{7.18}$$

This strict inequality is because $P_i \in \triangle_n$ and $W \in \triangle_m$. Some algebraic simplifications of equation 7.18 yield

$$J_H(\{P_i\},\{w_i\}) - H(W) < log_2\ e \sum_{i=1}^{m}\sum_{k=1}^{n} \frac{w_i^2\ p_{ik}^2 - w_i\ p_{ik}\ r_k}{r_k} \quad . \tag{7.19}$$

Further simplifications of the previous inequality lead to

$$J_H(\{P_i\},\{w_i\}) - H(W) < log_2\ (e^{-1}) \sum_{k=1}^{n} \frac{1}{r_k} \sum_{s=1}^{n}\sum_{t\neq s} w_s\ w_t\ p_{sk}\ p_{tk} \quad . \tag{7.20}$$

Because w_i and p_{ik} are strictly greater than 0, we have

$$\sum_{k=1}^{n} \frac{1}{r_k} \sum_{s=1}^{n}\sum_{t\neq s} w_s\ w_t\ p_{sk}\ p_{tk} > 0 \quad . \tag{7.21}$$

Hence, from equation 7.20 and 7.21, one obtains

$$J_H(\{P_i\},\{w_i\}) < H(W) \quad . \tag{7.22}$$

which completes the proof.

7.10 Conclusion

In the proposed method, information is synthesized from detected data organization based on discretization and event covering. Relevant cells that show significant relational and functional information in the outcome subspace are covered, whereas other cells are disregarded. The covered cells represent a form of synthesized information revealed from the selected data. The set of covered cells describes the embedded relation. Compared to many AI approaches that emphasize the use of domain knowledge, our method detects information if the observed frequency of samples deviates from the expectation because of prior knowledge that can be the null hypothesis or domain knowledge. Our method also analyzes information with respect to an outcome context. By using hierarchical maximum entropy discretization, the method can iteratively refine the cells and evaluate data relationships at different resolution levels. The method was evaluated using simulated and real-life data. The experimental results show that the method can approximate the embedded relations extremely well, even when there is a large amount of noise in the data.

Acknowledgments

This work is supported by the Natural Sciences and Engineering Research Council of Canada.

References

Bilofsky, H. and Burks, C. 1988. The GenBank Genetic Sequence Data Bank. *Nucleic Acids Research* 16(5): 1861–1863.

Burbea, J., and Rao, C. R. 1982. On the Convexity of Some Divergence Measures Based on Entropy Functions. *IEEE Transaction on Information Theory* 28: 489–495.

Chan, K. C. C., and Wong, A. K. C. 1990. APACS: A System for Automated Analysis and Classification. *Computational Intelligence* 6:119–131.

Chan, K. C. C.; Wong, A. K. C.; and Chiu, D. K. Y. 1989. Discovery of Probabilistic Rules for Prediction. In Proceedings of the Fifth Conference on Artificial Intelligence Applications, 223–229.

Chiu, D. K. Y. 1986. Pattern Analysis Using Event-Covering, Ph.D. diss., Dept. of Systems Design Engineering, Univ. of Waterloo.

Chiu, D. K. Y., and Kolodziejczak, T. 1990. Inference of Consensus Structure from Nucleic Acid Sequences. Submitted to *Computer Applications in the Biosciences.*

Chiu, D. K. Y., and Wong, A. K. C. 1986. Synthesizing Knowledge: A Cluster Analysis Approach Using Event-Covering. *IEEE Transactions on Systems, Man, and Cybernetics* 16(2): 251–259.

Chow, C. K., and Liu, C. N. 1968. Approximating Discrete Probability Distributions with Dependence Trees. *IEEE Transactions on Information Theory* 14: 462–467.

Cover, T. M., and Hart, P. E. 1967. Nearest Neighbor Pattern Classification. *IEEE Transaction on Information Theory* 13(1): 21–27.

Draper, N. R., and Smith, H. 1966. *Applied Regression Analysis.* New York: Wiley.

Duda, R. O., and Hart, P. E. 1973. *Pattern Classification and Scene Analysis.* New York: Wiley.

Fingleton, B. 1984. *Models of Category Counts.* Cambridge, Mass.: Cambridge University Press.

Forte, B.; Lascurain, M.; and Wong, A. K. C. 1987. The Best Lower Bound of the Maximum Entropy for Discretized Two-Dimensional Probability Distributions, Internal Report, Dept. of Systems Design Engineering, Univ. of Waterloo.

Haberman, S. J. 1973. The Analysis of Residuals in Cross-Classified Tables. *Biometrics* 29: 205–220.

Jaynes, E. T. 1957. Information Theory and Statistical Mechanics I. *Physic Review* 108:620–630.

Kalbfleisch, J. G. 1985. *Probability and Statistical Inference.* New York: Springer-Verlag.

Kapur, J. N.; Sahoo, P. K.; and Wong, A. K. C. 1985. A New Method for Gray-Level Thresholding Using the Entropy of the Histogram. *Computer Graphics and Image Processing* 29: 273–285.

Lascurain, M. 1983. On Maximum Entropy Discretization and Its Applications in Pattern Recognition, Ph.D. diss., Dept. of Systems Design Engineering, Univ. of Waterloo.

Marriott, F. H. C. 1974. *The Interpretation of Multiple Observations.* London: Academic.

Ng, C. T., and Wong, A. K. C. 1987. On the Non-Uniqueness of Discretization of Two-Dimensional Probability Distribution Subject to the Maximization of Shannon's Entropy. *IEEE Transactions on Information Theory* 33(1): 166–169.

Parzen, E. 1962. On the Estimation of a Probability Density Function and the Mode. *Annals of Mathematical Statistics* 33: 1065–1076.

Rao, C. R. 1984. Convexity Properties of Entropy Function and Analysis of Diversity. In *Inequalities in Statistics and Probability,* volume 5, ed. Y. L. Tong, 68–77. IMS Lecture Notes.

Sahoo, P. K., and Wong, A. K. C. 1988. Upper Bound for the Generalized Jensen Difference Based on Entropy Functions. *Kybernetika* 24: 241–250.

Shannon, C. E., and Weaver, W. 1964. *The Mathematical Theory of Communication.* Urbana,Ill.: University of Illinois Press.

Stonier, T. 1987. What Is Information? In *Research and Development in Expert Systems III,* ed. M. A. Bramer, British Computer Society Workshop Series. Cambridge, Mass.: Cambridge University Press, 217–230.

Waterman, M. S. 1986. Multiple Sequence Alignment by Consensus. *Nucleic Acids Research* 14: 9095–9102.

Wernecke, S. J., and d'Addario, L. R. 1977. Two-Dimensional Maximum Entropy Reconstruction of Radio Brightness. *Radio Science* 12: 831–844.

Wong, A. K. C. and Chiu, D. K. Y. 1987a. An Event-Covering Method for Effective Probabilistic Inference. *Pattern Recognition* 20(2): 245–255.

Wong, A. K. C., and Chiu, D. K. Y. 1987b. Synthesizing Statistical Knowledge from Incomplete Mixed-Mode Data. *IEEE Transactions on Pattern Analysis and Machine Intelligence* 9(6): 796–805.

Wong, A. K. C.; Liu, T. S.; and Wang, C. C. 1976. Statistical Analysis of Residue Variability in Cytochrome c. *Journal of Molecular Biology* 102: 287–295.

Wrigley, N. 1985. *Categorical Data Analysis for Geographers and Environmental Scientists.* London: Longman.

8 Learning Useful Rules from Inconclusive Data

Ramasamy Uthurusamy
General Motors Research Laboratories

Usama M. Fayyad
The University of Michigan

Scott Spangler
General Motors Technical Center

Abstract

Learning from inconclusive data is an important problem that has not been addressed in the concept-learning literature. In this chapter, we define inconclusiveness and illustrate why ID3-like algorithms are bound to result in overspecialized classifiers when trained on inconclusive data. We address the difficult problem of deciding when to stop specialization during top-down decision tree generation and describe a decision tree–generation algorithm, called INFERULE, that addresses some of the problems involved in learning from inconclusive data. We present results showing that INFERULE outperformed ID3 (with and without pruning) in tests on a real-world diagnostic database containing automobile repair cases. We also present a set of experiments performed using synthetic data that were designed to study the behavior of INFERULE as opposed to ID3 (with pruning), under varying degrees of inconclusiveness. The results show desirable and appropriate behaviour on the part of INFERULE manifested in the discovery of dramatically more compact classifiers that have lower error rates than their ID3 counterparts.

8.1 Introduction

The application of inductive-learning techniques to real-world data is an active research area (Michalski and Chilausky 1980; Quinlan 1986a; Irani et al. 1990). Programs that induce classifiers from a set of preclassified examples constitute one approach to circumventing the difficulties associated with acquiring knowledge from domain experts. Rather than embarking on the (typically unproductive) task of collecting concise (and hopefully correct) situation-action rules from human experts, machine learning programs attempt to discover the conditions under which certain actions are appropriate by examining examples of tasks performed by experts. The situations are described in terms of a set of attributes, and the actions are represented in terms of a fixed set of classes (outcomes).

The space of all possible combinations of attribute values and classes is too large to exhaust. A practical, learning algorithm, therefore, must employ heuristics to help it discover useful rules. Furthermore, a learning program must be fast and efficient because it typically has to deal with large training sets of examples. Because of its simplicity and efficiency, Quinlan's (1986a) ID3 algorithm for inducing decision trees has met with early success and has gained widespread popularity in the machine learning research community. Much research has been devoted to improving ID3 to make it more applicable to real-world problems by finding ways to deal with noise (Quinlan 1986c); avoiding some of its inherent weaknesses (Cheng et al. 1988); and making it incremental, for example, like the ID4 and ID5 algorithms (Utgoff 1988). However, we feel that an important problem standing in the way of applying ID3 and its variants to real-world data has not been addressed in the literature. This deficiency in ID3-like programs arises from the implicit assumption that enough information is available in the data to decide exactly how each data point should be classified.

The INFERULE algorithm described in this chapter is primarily designed to address the problem of inconclusive data sets. This problem arises when the attributes used in describing a set of examples are not sufficient to specify exactly one outcome (class) for each example. In such a situation, given a training set of examples and sufficiently many (possibly irrelevant) attributes, it might be possible to uniquely classify all examples in the entire training set in their respective classes. However, such a classification will necessarily fail on future test sets of unseen examples. First, we define what we mean by inconclusive data.

Definition: Given a learning problem expressed in terms of a fixed set of attributes and classes, a training set of examples that are known to be noise free is said to be *inconclusive* if there exists no set of rules using only the given attributes that classifies all possible (observed and unobserved) examples perfectly. i.e. the available attributes do not contain the necessary information for predicting a unique outcome for each example.

Note that it is possible for the program to classify the training set perfectly even when the data are inconclusive. However, the true error rate of a rule that predicts only one class is bounded from below by a number greater than zero. The previous definition suggests that if some set of absolutely correct rules exists, then it must necessarily make use of some attribute(s) not provided to the learning program. We call such a set *the governing rule set.* Thus, the governing rule set is not discoverable by a learning program that is given an inconclusive training set. A sure sign of inconclusiveness is that given data that are known to have little or no noise, the learning program always produces a perfect classification of the training set that has a high error rate when used to classify new (test) data.

The proper way of handling inconclusive data is to resort to probabilistic rather than categorical classification rules. In this case, a rule can predict more than one outcome. Associated with each outcome is a likelihood (probability) measure (Breiman et al. 1984;

Quinlan 1986a).

In the next section, we discuss how inconclusive data differ from noisy data, as discussed in the machine learning literature. To date, induction research has not really addressed the problems arising from inconclusive data. Unfortunately, such data sets are not rare in industry. In fact, it has been our experience that most diagnostic databases commonly found in an industrial environment contain only a fraction of the information necessary to correctly classify new cases.

However, such data sets, although imperfect, are certainly far from useless. There can be many important and useful rules in the governing rule set that do not reference inaccessible attributes. In addition, it is nearly always helpful in diagnosis to narrow the possible classifications from hundreds to one of a few possibilities. Our experience with large inconclusive data sets at General Motors led us to investigate the possibility of a learning algorithm that can extract useful information from such data. Our application domain is a large database of car problems and their fixes. Using ID3 and some of its variants to induce rule sets from training subsets of this database always resulted in perfect classifiers for the particular training sets. However, the classifiers had low accuracy on predicting the outcomes of unseen cases even with large training sets.

8.2 Problems with the ID3 Algorithm

ID3 (Quinlan 1986a) induces a decision tree for classifying the examples in the training set. The decision tree is generated by setting the root node to be the set of training examples; partitioning the examples in the root node, thus creating child nodes; and recursively partitioning each of the child nodes to get the next levels in the tree. For each (nonleaf) node, ID3 selects an attribute and creates a branch for each value of the attribute appearing in the subset of examples corresponding to the node. This process of specialization is then recursively applied to each nonleaf node. A set of examples, along with the decision tree generated by ID3, is shown in figure 8.1.

The formulation of an algorithm for decision tree generation requires the specification of four steps (Breiman et al. 1984). Each step represents a decision that constitutes part of the strategy that a decision tree–generation algorithm adopts in exploring the space of possible trees.

Step 1. Select an attribute to use in partitioning the examples at a node.

Step 2. Choose a particular partition of the examples based on the attribute of step 1.

Step 3. Decide whether to stop partitioning a node.

Step 4. Assign a class to a node deemed to be a leaf in step 3.

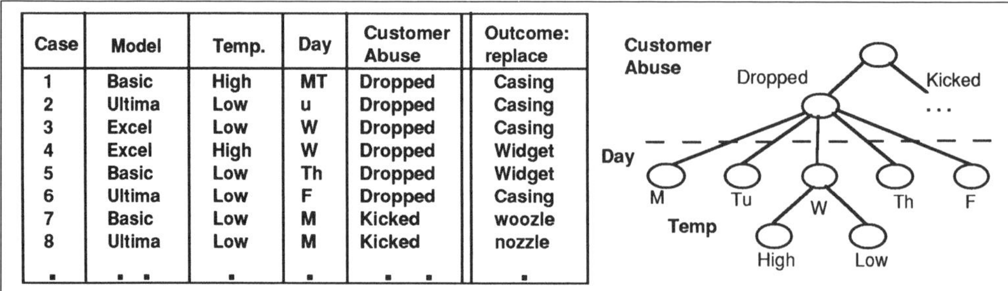

Case	Model	Temp.	Day	Customer Abuse	Outcome: replace
1	Basic	High	MT	Dropped	Casing
2	Ultima	Low	u	Dropped	Casing
3	Excel	Low	W	Dropped	Casing
4	Excel	High	W	Dropped	Widget
5	Basic	Low	Th	Dropped	Widget
6	Ultima	Low	F	Dropped	Casing
7	Basic	Low	M	Kicked	woozle
8	Ultima	Low	M	Kicked	nozzle
.	. .	.	.	. .	.

Figure 8.1
Data Set for Diagnosing Widget Failures and the Corresponding ID3 Tree.

ID3 achieves step 1 by applying an information entropy measure to select the attribute that produces the partition having the least randomness in the distribution of classes.[1] It favors partitions with an uneven distribution of classes. A set of examples in which classes are equally represented is not informative (locally). A set in which one class dominates makes for a safer class prediction. Step 2 is realized by creating a subset for each value of the attribute chosen by step 1. ID3 stops further partitioning of a node when all examples in it are of one class or when all the attributes have the same values for all the examples (step 3). In case the examples of a leaf node are not all of the same class, assignment by majority or by probability can be used for step 4 (Breiman et al. 1984; Quinlan 1986c). Steps 3 and 4 are trivially decided in the case of ID3 when the training set can be perfectly classified. Unfortunately, perfect classification of the training set is not always desirable. If the training data contain noise, a pruned tree that does not perfectly classify the training data may actually have a lower error rate than the original full tree that perfectly classifies the data. Quinlan (1986b) attempted tree pruning to deal with noise, and this approach has been somewhat successful. However, the problem is more serious when the input data are inconclusive. We discuss why we believe pruning is not appropriate in this case later in this section.

8.2.1 A Simple Example

As an example of how overspecialization occurs on inconclusive data, consider the following expert system rules for diagnosing widget failures:

IF widget was dropped	IF widget was dropped
AND fell less than 5 ft.	AND fell more than 5 ft.
THEN replace casing.	THEN replace widget.

Let these two rules be part of the governing rule set. Now assume that ID3 is given

[1] See Quinlan (1986a) and Cheng et al. (1988) for a detailed discussion of the merits of the information entropy measure.

the data set shown in figure 8.1 and that the attribute "height of widget's fall" is not provided to it. ID3 would then generate the tree shown in figure 8.1.

Obviously, the problem is that to obtain a tree that has only a single classification at each leaf node, it was necessary to specialize on irrelevant features. We would much rather see the specialization process stopped where the dotted line is drawn in the figure, thus producing the following probabilistic rule:

IF (Customer Abuse = dropped)
 THEN Fix = replace casing (67%)
 AND Fix = replace widget (33%).

This rule contributes useful knowledge about the proper classification. It is also an improvement over the ID3 output, which would ask the user for extraneous information and ultimately produce an unjustifiably narrow diagnosis. We investigate how ID3 can be modified to reduce the overspecialization problem. We primarily address the specification of step 3 of the induction algorithm. We also propose more appropriate ways for realizing steps 1, 2, and 4.

8.2.2 Tree Pruning and Inconclusive Data

Inconclusive data sets are different from noisy data sets. In a noisy domain, one can apply statistical techniques to prune away conditions (branches) that seem irrelevant to predicting a particular classification (Breiman et al. 1984; Quinlan 1986b, 1987). However, for an inconclusive data set, the assumption on which some pruning techniques are based, namely, that there is a single correct classification for a combination of attribute values, is not valid. For pruning, some algorithms assume that a single class is the proper outcome of each rule and prune with respect to this outcome, thus removing preconditions of rules based on their statistical relevance to the single (usually most probable) outcome (Quinlan 1986b, 1987). This assumption is clearly inappropriate if the attributes used can never allow a unique classification in the first place. In this case, it is not even correct for the algorithm to make the assumption that there should be only one class at each leaf node.

8.3 The INFERULE Algorithm

The INFERULE algorithm improves on ID3 to make it more applicable to inconclusive data sets. Improvement is achieved by adding a mechanism for deciding when to stop partitioning a given node in the tree (step 3). For step 4, INFERULE uses the probability method (Quinlan 1986c).

INFERULE differs from ID3 in that it generates strictly binary trees. This is a result of the fact that INFERULE specializes on the best attribute-value pair, rather than the best attribute, at any choice point. The advantage to this approach is that the data are never unnecessarily subdivided, as is the case when ID3 specializes on an attribute having many values, only a few of which are actually relevant to diagnosing the failure. Cheng, et al. (1988) provide a detailed discussion of weaknesses in ID3 resulting from this problem. Thus, to realize step 2, INFERULE chooses one of the values a_i of the selected attribute A and creates two subsets of the examples: examples with $A = a_i$ and examples with $A \neq a_i$.

8.3.1 Attribute-Value Pair Selection

We now turn our attention to the method used by INFERULE to select an attribute-value pair for partitioning the set of examples into two subsets. Let S be a set of examples. Each example consists of a specification of the values of all attributes and a class (outcome). The class is one of the m possible classes $\{c_1, \ldots, c_m\}$. Let A be an attribute that takes on one of the values $\{a_1, \ldots, a_k\}$. We now explain how INFERULE chooses one of A's values to partition S.

Let n_j be the number of examples in S that belong to class c_j. $S(a_i) \subseteq S$ is the subset of examples in S with value a_i for attribute A. $S(a_i, c_j) \subseteq S(a_i)$ is the subset of examples with $A = a_i$ and class c_j.

- $E_i(c_j) = \frac{|S(a_i)|}{|S|} n_j$, where $|S|$ denotes the number of examples in the set S. $E_i(c_j)$ is the expected number of examples in $S(a_i)$ that have class c_j; so, $E_i(c_j)$ is an estimate of the actual value: $|S(a_i, c_j)|$.
- $SE(a_i) = \sqrt{\sum_{j=1}^{m} \frac{E_i(c_j)(n_j - E_i(c_j))}{n_j}}$. $SE(a_i)$ is the standard error (Quinlan 1986b) associated with the E_is (estimates) defined previously.[2] SE adjusts for the fact that an estimate that is based on a smaller data set is less accurate than one based on a larger set.
- We define the geometric distance between the two class vectors: $\langle E_i(c_1), E_i(c_2), \ldots, E_i(c_m)\rangle$ and $\langle |S(a_i, c_1)|, |S(a_i, c_2)|, \ldots, |S(a_i, c_m)|\rangle$ to be

$$DI(a_i) = \sqrt{\sum_{j=1}^{m} [E_i(c_j) - |S(a_i, c_j)|]^2}.$$

[2] As a matter of fact, the expression for the standard error SE, as defined, can easily be simplified to an expression that is only a function of $|S(a_i)|$.

Note that the first vector is the expected class vector of the subset $S(a_i)$, and the latter is the actual class vector of $S(a_i)$.

Finally, define

$$R(a_i) = SE(a_i) \cdot \frac{1}{DI(a_i)},$$

where R is the relative goodness of the attribute-value pair $\langle A = a_i \rangle$. After evaluating all attributes and their values, the attribute-value pair with the minimum R value is the one chosen for partitioning the data. A property of R is that $R(a_i) = R(\neg a_i)$; that is, the two subsets $S(a_i)$ and $S - S(a_i)$ evaluate equally in terms of their distance from S. Roughly stated, the goal of this criterion is to choose an attribute that maximizes the difference between the outcome vectors of the resulting subsets and the expected outcome vectors. In general, the greater this difference, the more likely it is that the subset partition induced by $\langle A = a_i \rangle$ is relevant to the classification. However, a small distance indicates that the distribution of classes in the original set does not significantly change when the set is partitioned. This would indicate that $\langle A = a_i \rangle$ is probably not relevant to the classification task. The SE term allows for fair comparisons between subsets of different sizes. It adjusts for the sensitivity of the DI measure to small variations in $|S(a_i)|$ when the E_is are small.

We illustrate the notion of geometric distance with the simple example in figure 8.2. The figure shows two possible outcome vectors that can result when a set of 56 examples with four classes is to be partitioned using some attribute-value pair. It is assumed that half of the examples in the set satisfy this attribute-value pair.

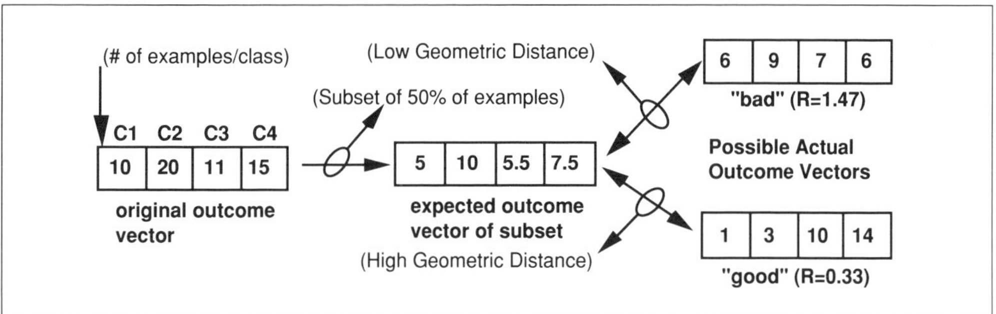

Figure 8.2
Illustration of the Geometric Distance Measure.

Note that this measure of attribute merit differs from ID3's information entropy measure. In the case of ID3, the entropy measures the discriminating power of an attribute by favoring attributes that result in outcome vectors that are unevenly distributed. Thus, an attribute value is bad if its corresponding subset of examples has equal numbers of examples from different classes. In the case of INFERULE, the merit of an attribute-value pair is indicated by the fact that the class distribution in its corresponding subset significantly differs from the class distribution in the original set.

INFERULE's attribute selection criterion appeared to give the best overall results in comparison to several others that were also tested, including Quinlan's (1986a) information entropy measure, Chi-Squared test with $m-1$ degrees of freedom (Bradley 1976), and Fisher's exact test for statistical independence using class compaction to reduce the input to a two class problem (Abramowitz and Stegun 1964).

8.3.2 To Specialize or Not to Specialize? That Is the Question

INFERULE's relative measure of improvement in classification gives a natural way of deciding when to refrain from subdividing a given data set any further. By comparing the value of the measure R against a threshold T, one can control whether INFERULE should attempt to achieve a perfect classification or stop specialization and return a probabilistic guess of possible classes. INFERULE will halt specialization at a given node whenever the value of R exceeds the threshold T for every possible attribute-value pair.

For the automobile repairs data set discussed in the next section, performance of the algorithm did not substantially vary with small changes in the value of T. Overall, it appeared that a value of $T = 0.75$ was appropriate for most data sets in this domain. A formula for how T should be varied with respect to the number of attributes and attribute values in a data set has not yet been determined. A setting of $T = 0.0$ would result in the generation of a single node tree that always predicts the most frequent class as an outcome. Setting $T = \infty$ results in the generation of a binary tree that perfectly classifies the examples in the training set. With this setting, any avoidance of overspecialization is disabled. With a setting of $T = 0.75$, INFERULE would indeed refrain from specializing the nodes below the dotted line in the tree for the example given in figure 8.1.

We investigate the sensitivity of INFERULE to the parameter T using controlled experiments conducted with synthetic data after we present results obtained on real-world automobile repair data that we believe to be inconclusive.

8.4 Results with Automobile Repair Data

The data on which the INFERULE algorithm was tested contained records of automobile repair cases and how they were fixed. The data consist of eight symptom (attribute) fields, with an average of 34 different values each. These symptom fields contain informa-

Table 8.1
Details of Automotive Data Sets.

Data Set	Number of Cases	Avg. Size of Training Set	Possible Outcomes
Check Engine	14,175	12,700	44
No Start	4,555	3,650	32
Rough Engine	11,531	10,300	47

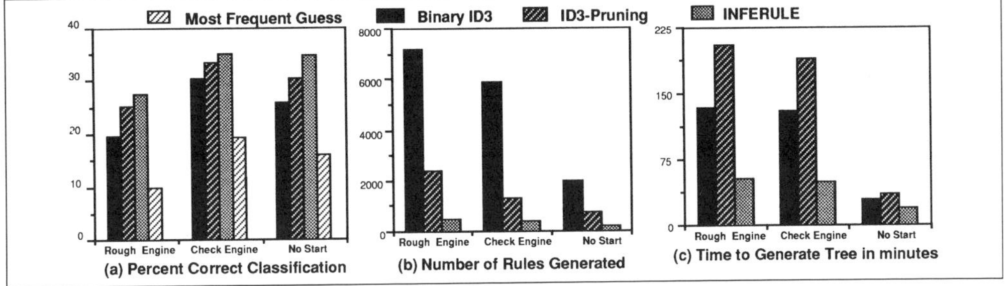

Figure 8.3
Test Results for ID3 and INFERULE on Automotive Data.

tion on the make of car and engine as well as the year and mileage of the car. They also contain codes for specific known problematic symptoms. In most cases, this information is not sufficient to uniquely diagnose the problem. Still, many useful conclusions can be drawn from these data. Our main motivation for applying machine learning techniques in this domain is to obtain rules for use in an expert system that can help Technical Assistance Staff members to quickly narrow the possible problems with a given case to a few—out of scores of—possible outcomes.

Three data sets were used, each containing different types of automobile repairs. The characteristics of each of these data sets are given in table 8.1. These three data sets were each randomly partitioned into training and test sets three different times. The results were then averaged over the different runs. The *accuracy* of a generated tree is defined to be the percentage of test cases for which the highest probability outcome suggested by the tree is the same as the actual outcome (class). Figure 8.3a shows the average accuracy for INFERULE, ID3, and ID3 with pessimistic pruning (Quinlan 1986b).

The fourth bar represents the frequency of the most common class and is given as a baseline for comparison.[3] We used a binary version of ID3 that uses only the best value of an attribute rather than branching on each attribute value. The binary ID3 performed

[3] The fourth bar corresponds to running INFERULE with $T = 0.0$, as discussed in section 8.3.2, To Specialize or Not to Specialize? That Is the Question.

better than the traditional ID3 algorithm; hence, we do not show the results of the latter. Figure 8.3b shows the average number of rules obtained for each data set, and figure 8.3c shows the average run times of the three programs.

Note two points about these results: First, one of the primary advantages of the INFERULE approach, namely, the ability to suggest several potential classifications, is ignored by the accuracy metric in figure 8.3a because it only considers whether the outcome suggested with the highest confidence agrees with the actual outcome. The percentage of test cases for which the actual outcome was among any of the ones suggested by INFERULE averaged between 80 percent and 90 percent. For ID3 with pruning, the corresponding percentage was only 40 percent to 60 percent. Including multiple guessing would enhance INFERULE's performance to significantly higher levels than those shown in the graph. Second, generating a full decision tree and then pruning it back to a smaller tree is a time-consuming process. INFERULE generates an already pruned tree without incurring the extra cost of pruning.

8.5 Studying INFERULE's Behavior

To better understand the properties of the different decision–tree generation algorithms, we conducted some experiments using artificially generated data. The prime motivation is that we do not fully understand the automotive data. We hypothesize that the data are inconclusive, but we cannot prove it. However, we have no formal method for determining whether a given set is inconclusive. Hence, we decided to generate data that we know to be inconclusive and then study the behavior of the algorithms using controlled experiments.

8.5.1 Synthetic Data Sets

First, we defined a learning problem having 15 attributes. Each attribute can have as many as 10 discrete values. We constructed a decision tree and labeled its leaves with classes. Each leaf was labeled with three to-five classes. The tree referenced only 10 of the 15 available attributes.

We used the tree to generate sets of examples. For each leaf in the tree, a random number of examples—10 on average—were generated. Of the examples generated for each leaf, 67 percent of them were of one class. The rest were randomly assigned (according to a uniform distribution) to the remaining classes. For each leaf, the values of the attributes in the conditions on the path from the root determine the conditions that the examples of the leaf must satisfy. Each example gets assigned randomly chosen values for the attributes not referenced in the preconditions of the leaf.

The examples generated in this way essentially obey the following conditions:

1. Only 10 of the attributes are relevant to the classification task. For most examples, only 4 or 5 attributes are relevant.
2. The data are definitely inconclusive because there are multiple predictions per leaf, and the irrelevant attributes for each example are assigned random values. A rule that uses only the relevant attributes for a class is expected to get no better than a 67 percent correctness rate on unseen test examples.
3. As we mask some of the relevant attributes from the learning algorithm, the data becomes increasingly inconclusive.
4. Because there are a large number of classes, an algorithm that correctly narrows the number of possible classes is expected to outperform one that guesses at random. This makes it easier to differentiate between an algorithm that is making the proper decisions during tree generation from one that is not.

8.5.2 Experiments with INFERULE

We conducted two types of experiments using the synthetic data previously described. The first type targeted studying the behavior of the algorithms as relevant attributes are masked from the data. A larger number of masked relevant attributes results in increasing degrees of inconclusiveness in the data. Results reported here were obtained by setting the parameter $T = 0.55$ in INFERULE. The second type of experiment was intended to study the effect of INFERULE's threshold parameter T on the trees generated by INFERULE.

The results reported are averaged over several randomly generated training and test sets. To obtain a reliable estimate of the error rates, test sets were chosen to be roughly twice as large as the training sets. The algorithms we compared are INFERULE, ID3, and ID3 with pessimistic postpruning.

8.5.3 Masking Relevant Attributes

We ran a series of experiments where relevant attributes were gradually masked out of the data. The number of attributes masked was varied from 0 to 10 (the number of relevant attributes). The results reported are averaged over several runs. The order in which the attributes for masking were chosen was random.

Figure 8.4a shows the average correctness on the test sets for INFERULE, ID3, and ID3 with tree pruning. A class prediction was considered correct only if the top (most common) class matched the correct class. Note that, as expected, INFERULE indeed performed better than ID3 (with or without pruning.) However, the strength of INFERULE

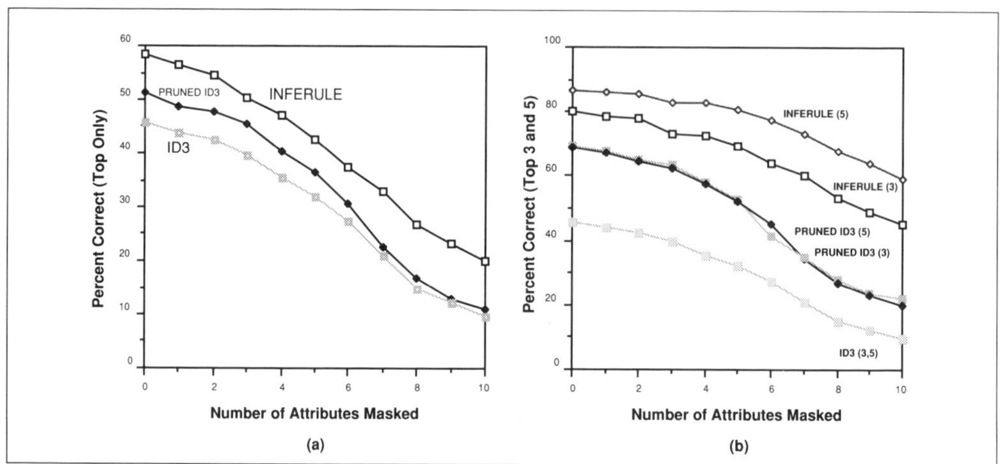

Figure 8.4
Percent Accuracy on the Test Set Classification.

really comes into play when multiple guesses are allowed. Figure 8.4b shows the percentage of correctness when one of the top three or one of the top five class predictions matches the correct class. Note that INFERULE gets a percentage that is 15 to 40 points higher than pruned ID3. ID3 without pruning typically makes one prediction. Its score, therefore, does not improve when multiple guesses are allowed.

This improvement in correctness on the part of INFERULE is coupled with dramatically smaller-sized trees. The trees generated by pruned ID3 were anywhere from 4 to 400 times larger than INFERULE's. ID3's trees were 9 to 900 times larger. The sizes are measured by the number of leaves (rules). Because all the trees are binary, the number of nodes is $2n - 1$ if the number of leaves is n. The average number of rules generated by each algorithm is shown in figure 8.5a. Note that INFERULE generates smaller trees as inconclusiveness increases, but ID3's trees grow significantly in size.

Of course, a larger tree takes a longer time to generate and an even longer time to prune. The average run times of the respective algorithms are shown in figure 8.5b. Note that INFERULE is significantly more efficient in terms of run time, which is not surprising because it generates much smaller trees.

Let us carefully examine the behavior of INFERULE as the number of masked attributes increases. Figure 8.6 shows the number of rules generated as the number of masked attributes increases. The size of the tree increases a bit after the first attribute is dropped because INFERULE gets more "confused" with the increasing degree of inconclusiveness in the data. However, as the number of masked attributes increases, INFERULE detects

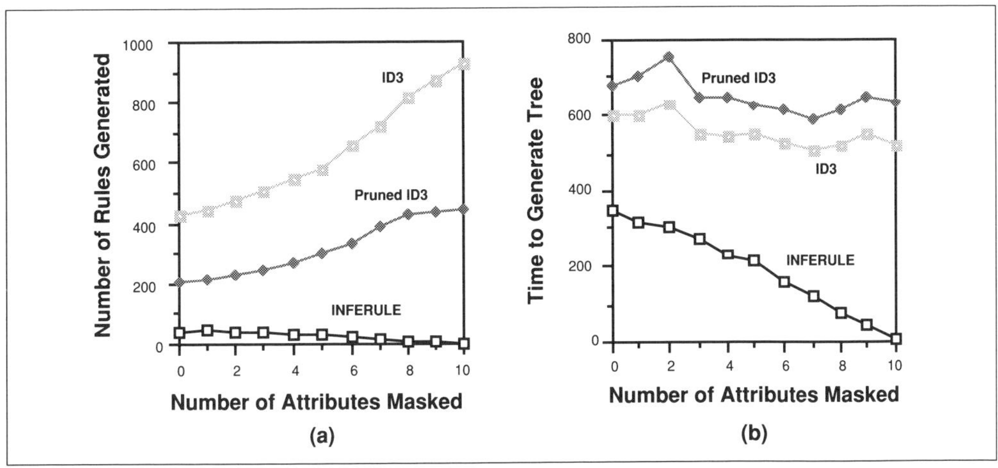

Figure 8.5
Average Number of Rules Generated with Increasing Inconclusiveness.

that learning specialized trees is no longer warranted. As a matter of fact, when all 10 relevant attributes are masked, INFERULE realizes that there is nothing to learn from the data. It exhibits proper behavior by generating a tree with a single node and simply guesses the most common classes. Figure 8.5a illustrates the behavior of the other two algorithms in this case. Note that they generate larger trees because less information is available to warrant learning. Unlike INFERULE, they do not gracefully handle decreases in available information.

8.5.4 Effect of the Parameter T on INFERULE Trees

The reader might wonder why we chose our particular setting of $T = 0.55$ for these data sets. We empirically determined a reasonable setting and used it for the experiments. Determining this threshold was easily done by examining graphs similar to the graphs of figure 8.7. Note that figure 8.7a shows that the number of rules monotonically grows with the value of T, which is expected and can actually be formally proven. However, the critical measure here is the percentage of correctness. Fortunately, as shown in the graph of figure 8.7b, the curve for the percentage of correctness versus the value of T is fairly well behaved, which made our choice of threshold setting easy. There is no guarantee that the curves will not exhibit oscillations for different data sets or different degrees of inconclusiveness. A determination of an appropriate setting for T remains for future work.

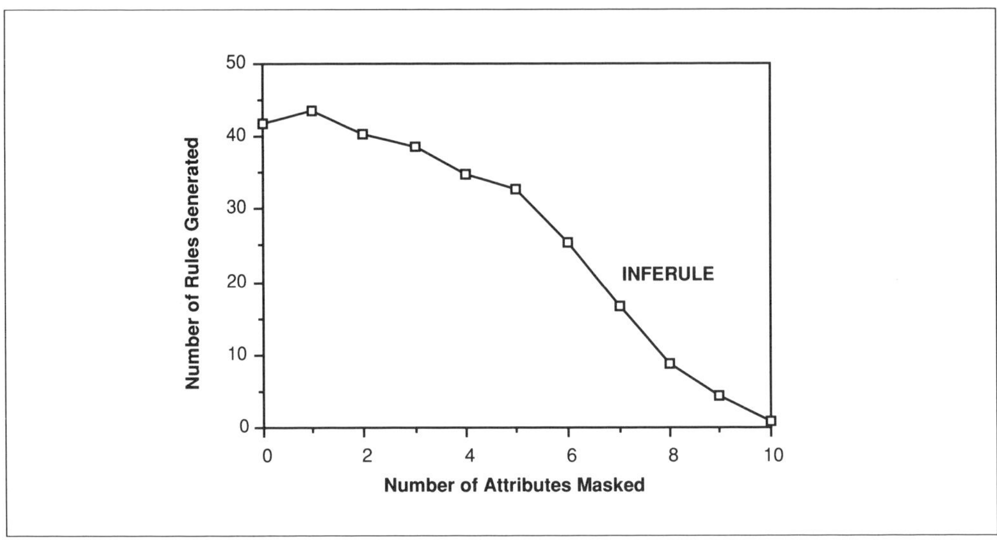

Figure 8.6
Average Number of Rules Generated by INFERULE.

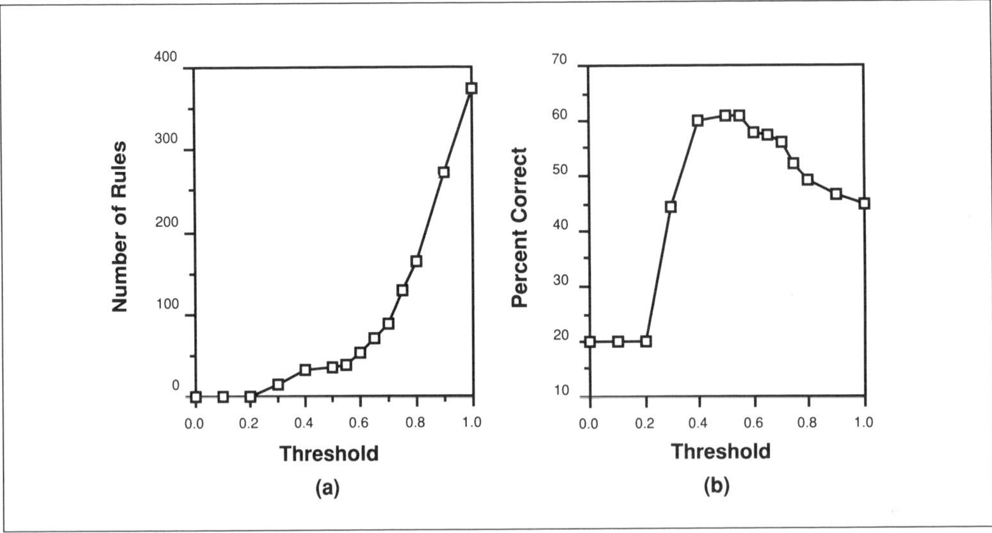

Figure 8.7
Effect of INFERULE's Threshold Parameter T.

8.6 Discussion

The results obtained from the synthetic data served to reinforce our belief that inconclusive data sets (as we defined them) exist and can be learned from. The results for this set of controlled experiments show that INFERULE generates more correct classifiers that are significantly more compact, more efficient, and easier to generate than the corresponding trees generated by ID3 with or without pruning. Higher performance was attained by INFERULE along all the performance measures.

Furthermore, finding a proper setting for the threshold parameter T turned out to be relatively easy for these data. The problem of systematically determining a proper T setting remains unsolved. We did notice, however, that as the degree of inconclusiveness in a data set increases, the effect of the small variations in the T setting on the correctness of the produced tree becomes minimal. It was reassuring to see that the setting we chose for T resulted in immediately halting tree generation when all relevant attributes were masked. Far from being coincidental, this desirable behavior is exhibited over a range of T values.

As expected, the ability to decide when to stop specializing the tree turned out to be of great importance where inconclusive data are concerned. Generating a full tree (as in ID3) and then pruning it back proved not only to be significantly more expensive but also failed to produce better trees.

There is still a question of whether inconclusiveness is different from noise. In the case of the automotive data described earlier, we happened to know that noise is not present in any significant amount. As a matter of fact, we defined inconclusiveness with the stipulation that the data are known to be noise free. For many data sets in industry, the presence or absence of noise can easily be verified from specific knowledge of the attributes, their semantics, and the method used for measuring and recording their values. However, the general question of how inconclusiveness differs from noise remains unanswered. One distinct difference is that with inconclusive data, we expect a rule to have multiple predictions. With noisy data, multiple predictions to each rule are a side effect of noise. With noisy data, it is typically desirable to determine a unique (correct) single outcome for each rule, which is not the case with inconclusive data.

8.7 Conclusions and Future Work

The primary purpose of this chapter was not to introduce yet another variant of ID3, but to hopefully influence future rule induction research to focus more on inconclusive data sets as opposed to conclusive data or data sets containing small amounts of random noise. After studying several diagnostic databases at General Motors, we are convinced that inconclusiveness is a characteristic that rule-induction algorithms must be able to deal with if they are to have any practical application in industry.

The proper way to handle inconclusive data sets is to produce probabilistic, rather than categorical, classification rules. The assumption that rules with a single outcome are desirable should be abandoned if it is not statistically supported. There is, therefore, a need for a criterion to determine when specialization is to be stopped before reaching a single classification. INFERULE addresses this issue and illustrates that the predicted improvement in performance is indeed achieved. INFERULE produced dramatically more compact trees that have significantly smaller error rates with a fraction of the computational effort required by ID3 (especially with postpruning).

For future work, we need to formulate a systematic method for determining a proper setting of the threshold parameter T. In addition, a more operational definition of inconclusiveness should be formulated along with methods for determining the existence of inconclusiveness and distinguishing it from noise.

The most important area for future research is to find a good, universal criterion for halting the specialization process. The geometric distance test used in INFERULE has some of the properties of a good criterion but can still lack generality with respect to different types of (nonautomotive) data sets, especially those with a large number of attributes. Perhaps this chapter will spark some interest and motivation for discovering this elusive criterion and thus, ultimately, producing a truly practical rule induction algorithm.

Acknowledgments

The authors would like to acknowledge the help of Andrew Chou in implementing INFERULE and formulating the distance measure used. Usama M. Fayyad is supported by a DeVlieg Industrial Fellowship and an unrestricted grant from Hughes Aircraft Company.

References

Abramowitz, M., and Stegun, M. 1964. *The Handbook of Mathematical Functions with Formulas, Graphs and Mathematical Tables.* Washington, D.C.: National Bureau of Standards.

Bradly, J.V. 1976. *Probability; Decision; Statistics.* Englewood Cliffs, N.J.: Prentice Hall.

Breiman, L.; Friedman, J. H.; Olson, R. A.; and Stone, C. J. 1984. *Classification and Regression Trees.* Monterey, California: Wadsworth and Brooks-Cole.

Cheng, J.; Fayyad, U. M.; Irani, K. B.; and Qian, Z. 1988. Improved Decision Trees: A

Generalized Version of ID3. In *Proceedings of the Fifth International Conference on Machine Learning.*, 100–107. San Mateo, Calif.: Morgan Kaufmann.

Irani, K. B.; Cheng, J.; Fayyad, U. M.; and Qian, Z. 1990. Applications of Machine Learning Techniques in Semiconductor Manufacturing. In Proceedings of The S.P.I.E. Conference on Applications of Artificial Intelligence VIII. Bellingham, Wash.: The International Society for Optical Engineering.

Michalski, R. S. and Chilausky, R. L. 1980. Learning by Being Told and Learning by Examples: An Experimental Comparison of the Two Methods of Knowledge Acquisition in the Context of Developing an Expert System for Soybean Disease Diagnosis. *International Journal of Policy Analysis and Information Systems*, 4(2): 125–161.

Quinlan, J. R. 1986a. Induction of Decision Trees. *Machine Learning* 1(1): 81–106.

Quinlan, J. R. 1986b. Simplifying Decision Trees, AI Memo, 930, Massachusetts Institute of Technology.

Quinlan, J. R. 1986c. The Effect of Noise on Concept Learning. In *Machine Learning: An Artificial Intelligence Approach*, volume 2, eds. R. S. Michalski, J. Carbonell, and T. Mitchell. San Mateo, Calif.: Morgan Kaufmann.

Quinlan, J. R. 1987. Generating Production Rules from Decision Trees. In Proceedings of the Tenth International Joint Conference on Artificial Intelligence, 304–307. Menlo Park, Calif.: International Joint Conferences on Artificial Intelligence, Inc.

Utgoff, P. E. 1988. ID5: An Incremental ID3. In *Proceedings of the Fifth International Conference on Machine Learning,* 107–120. San Mateo, Calif.: Morgan Kaufmann.

9 Rule Induction Using Information Theory

Padhraic Smyth
Jet Propulsion Laboratory

Rodney M. Goodman
California Institute of Technology

Abstract

Across a variety of scientific, engineering, and business applications, it has become commonplace to collect and store large volumes of data. For example, NASA has warehouses of data collected from interplanetary scientific missions, most of which cannot be currently processed or examined because there are simply not enough scientists and statisticians to sift through it all. However, we have at our disposal previously unimaginable amounts of computational power because of advances in VLSI technology. Hence, it seems obvious that the development of computation-intensive techniques that explore large databases is a major research challenge as both data volume and computing power continue to increase. In this chapter, we consider the problem of generalized rule induction from databases and provide an overview of our recent work on this topic. In particular, we explore the application of information-theoretic techniques to the problem of finding the best probabilistic rules relating a given set of discrete-valued domain variables. We discuss the incorporation of this approach into a practical rule-discovery algorithm called ITRULE and consider its application to a variety of problems. The chapter concludes with a general discussion concerning some of the open research issues in this field.

9.1 Introduction

The emergence of electronic and magnetic storage media as convenient and affordable methods for storing large amounts of data has led to the coining of phrases such as "the information revolution." The popular notion appears to be that the widespread availability of information will considerably accelerate human's technical progress in general, this new age being a modern-day equivalent of the industrial revolution of the last century. With the continued progress in increasing the information capacity of both storage media (for example, high-density VLSI memory chips, optical discs) and transmission media (for example, optical fibers), one can only predict that the volume of electronic data will continue to grow at a phenomenal rate.

However, despite the progress in handling this information from a hardware standpoint, progress in using the information continues to lag far behind. One of the primary reasons is the sheer quantity and volume of the data. Simply put, there is not enough manpower to analyze and examine the typical large corporate database. For example, currently in the telecommunications industry, sophisticated networks exist that automatically report a vast array of traffic information, data on module failures, system performance analyses, and so on. In turn, these reports are automatically logged on a database system as a historical record of network operations. However, although the databases contain a wealth of information in terms of system performance and fault diagnosis, they are often too complex to manually search. Another familiar example is the automatic scanners used at checkout counters in modern-day supermarkets. These "scan data" are automatically recorded and used for market research purposes. The volume of data available overwhelms what was previously a manual market-analysis task. This general trend is extremely common across a variety of disciplines.

The premise of this chapter is that the automated analysis of such large databases is obviously necessary and worthwhile. Although the lofty goals of knowledge discovery are worthy indeed, we must nonetheless begin our research at a more concrete level. We are going to look at what seems like an innocuously simple problem: Given a database described in terms of discrete or categorical attributes, what are the best rules that characterize the data? We begin by defining the problem in formal terms, defining and justifying the necessary probabilistic prerequisites underlying our approach. We then examine the idea of quantifying the quality of a probabilistic rule and demonstrate the notion of rule information content. In addition, we devote some attention to the problem of robustly estimating probabilities directly from data.

Armed with these basic tools of the trade, we can begin to address the problem of finding the most informative rules from a data set. In particular, we describe the ITRULE algorithm, which uses computationally intensive search techniques to search the data for the rules of greatest information content. The workings of the algorithm have been reported in detail elsewhere (Smyth and Goodman 1990a); hence, the focus here is more on the applications of the algorithm and the types of problems and data to which it is best suited. We conclude by discussing open problems and research issues.

9.2 The Probabilistic Rule Representation

We define a *probabilistic rule* as an if-then statement to the effect that if proposition y occurs, then there is a probability p that proposition x is true, and a probability $1 - p$ that proposition $\bar{x}$ is true. It is convenient to define the probability p as the conditional probability $p(x|y)$. Hence, our probabilistic rule corresponds to a simple statement regarding the conditional probability of one event given another. Although other methods of representing uncertainty have been proposed and are in common use, such as fuzzy logic (Zadeh1965) and certainty factors (Adams 1976), standard probability theory remains the established and preferred uncertainty model because of its theoretical foundations and proven utility.

Let **X** and **Y** be discrete random variables, x and y be letters from their respective discrete alphabets (as a notational convenience, we adopt the convention that $p(y)$ stands for $p(Y = y)$, and so on, as is customary in discussions of this nature). A common situation has **X** as the class variable, and Y as a composite variable of several discrete or categorical attribute variables. In this manner, our probabilistic rules would be classification rules of the following form:

$$\text{If } (\mathbf{Y_1} = y_1 \text{ and } \mathbf{Y_2} = y_2) \text{ then } \mathbf{X} = x \text{ with probability } p$$

Why should we look for rules at all and probabilistic ones at that? The rule-based representation plays a central role in most theories of knowledge representation, going back to the early work of Chomsky (1957), the cognitive production-rule models of Newell and Simon (1972), and the more recent work of Holland et al.(1986). Although the debate continues regarding the virtues of competing cognitive models (such as connectionism), there can be no denying the utility of the rule-based representation; that is, whether we believe that rules are truly part of human reasoning processes, they provide a practical and convenient mechanism by which to explicitly represent knowledge. For example, witness the proliferation of rule-based expert systems as a practical software engineering paradigm.

Why add probabilities to our rules? There are two ways to answer this question. The first answer is that although production-rule systems have their roots in logic, our perception of the real world tends to be couched in uncertainty. For example, most successful rule-based expert systems tend to add uncertainty measures to their rules, albeit often in an ad hoc manner. Thus, the first answer says that by necessity, we need to use probability to deal with real-world problems. The second answer to the question, that given by an information theorist, is more dogmatic. Simply put, probabilistic models are a generalization of deterministic models and, as such, provide a much more expressive and powerful mathematical language to work with. A lay person's interpretation of this statement might be that any system that correctly uses probability can always do better than a similar system that has no concept of probability.

Hence, probabilistic rules are a simple and useful technique for knowledge representation. Although far more sophisticated knowledge representation schemes exist, it seems more appropriate that we should begin work on automated knowledge discovery at a fairly simple level. As we see later, even the discovery of simple probabilistic rules in data can reveal a wealth of hidden information.

9.3 The Information Content of a Rule

Given a set of probabilistic rules, we need to be able to compare and rank the rules in a quantitative manner, using some measure of "goodness," or utility. The approach we propose is to define the information content of a rule, using ideas from information theory. *Information theory* can be considered a layer above pure probability theory. Typically, given a set of defined probabilities, we want to calculate various information-based quantities. Traditionally, information theory has a distinguished history of providing elegant solutions to communications problems, originating with Claude Shannon's (1948) pioneering work. The relation between communication theory and inductive inference is appealing. With communication systems, we are involved in the efficient transmission and reception of information from point A to point B. In inductive inference, we are effectively at point B, receiving a message (the data) through some sensory channel, from the environment (point A).

In particular, unlike communications applications, we do not know what code is being used or what the noise characteristics of the channel (measurement process) are. For example, in classification, we might be trying to infer the value of the class variable given related attribute information. In effect, the attributes form a code for the class, which is then corrupted by measurement noise. Even in the presence of perfect information (no measurement noise), the class can be ambiguously coded by the available attributes; that is, only a probabilistic (rather than deterministic) mapping might exist between the attributes and the class because of the presence of unmeasured causal variables. For the classifier design problem, we have used this analogy to improve our understanding of decision tree design techniques (Goodman and Smyth, 1988b, 1990), and in a general sense, the powerful technique of inductive inference using minimum description length encoding (Rissanen 1989; Quinlan and Rivest 1989) is also motivated by this communications problem analogy.

Hence, it seems clear that information theory should provide a theoretically sound and intuitively practical basis for our problem of finding the best rules from given data. The first task is to define the information content of a probabilistic rule; remember that a probabilistic rule is defined as

$$\text{If } \mathbf{Y} = y \text{ then } \mathbf{X} = x \text{ with probability p}$$

We recently introduced a measure called the J-measure for precisely this purpose (Goodman and Smyth 1988a, Smyth and Goodman 1991a, 1991b); it can be defined as

$$J(\mathbf{X};\mathbf{Y}=y) \;=\; p(y)\left(p(x|y)\log\left(\frac{p(x|y)}{p(x)}\right)+(1-p(x|y))\log\left(\frac{(1-p(x|y))}{(1-p(x))}\right)\right)$$

This measure possesses a variety of desirable properties as a rule information measure, not the least of which is the fact that it is unique as a nonnegative measure that satisfies the requirement that

$$\sum_y J(\mathbf{X};\mathbf{Y}=y)=I(\mathbf{X};\mathbf{Y}),$$

where $I(\mathbf{X};\mathbf{Y})$ is the average mutual information between the variables $\mathbf{X}$ and $\mathbf{Y}$, as originally defined by Shannon (1948). This equation states that the sum of the information contents (of a set of rules with mutually exclusive and exhaustive left-hand sides) must be equal to the well-known average mutual information between two variables. (The interested reader is referred to Smyth and Goodman (1990b) for a detailed treatment of the various mathematical properties of the measure.) We note in passing that other measures of rule goodness have been proposed, such as that of Piatetsky-Shapiro (see chapter 13), who proposes the use of $p(y)(p(x|y)-p(x))$. Measures such as this, based directly on probabilities, tend to assign less weight to rarer events compared to measures such as the J-measure that use a log scale (information-based). To a large extent, such information-based and correlation-based measures, in practice, often rank rules in a similar order; however, the J-measure's relation to Shannon's average mutual information makes it more desirable from a theoretical point of view.

Intuitively, we can interpret the J-measure as follows: Let us decompose the J-measure into two terms, namely, $p(y)$ and $j(\mathbf{X};\mathbf{Y}=y)$, where,

$$j(\mathbf{X};\mathbf{Y}=y)=p(x|y).\log\left(\frac{p(x|y)}{p(x)}\right)+(1-p(x|y)).\log\left(\frac{(1-p(x|y))}{(1-p(x))}\right)$$

The probability term $p(y)$ can be viewed as a preference for generality or simplicity in our rules; that is, the left-hand side must occur relatively often for a rule to be deemed useful. The other term, $j(\mathbf{X};\mathbf{Y}=y)$, is familiar to information theorists as a distance measure (namely, the cross entropy) between our a posteriori belief about $\mathbf{X}$ and our *a priori* belief. Cross entropy is a well-founded measure of the goodness of fit of two distributions (Shore and Johnson 1980). Hence, maximizing the product of the two terms, $J(\mathbf{X};\mathbf{Y}=y)$, is equivalent to simultaneously maximizing both the simplicity of the hypothesis y and the goodness of fit between y and a perfect predictor of $\mathbf{X}$. There is a natural trade-off involved here because, typically, one can easily find rare conditions (less probable y's) that are accurate predictors, but one has a preference for more general, useful conditions (more probable y's). This basic trade-off between accuracy and generality (or goodness

Table 9.1
Joint Probability Distribution for Medical Diagnosis Example.

Symptom A	Symptom B	Disease x	Joint Probability
no fever	no sore throat	absent	0.20
no fever	no sore throat	present	0.00
no fever	sore throat	absent	0.30
no fever	sore throat	present	0.10
fever	no sore throat	absent	0.02
fever	no sore throat	present	0.08
fever	sore throat	absent	0.03
fever	sore throat	present	0.27

of fit and simplicity) is a fundamental principle underlying various general theories of inductive inference (Angluin and Smith 1983; Rissanen 1989).

An example of the J-measure in action illustrates its immediate applicability. Consider the three attributes shown in table 9.1, along with their associated joint-probability distribution. The data are supposed to represent the hypothetical distribution of patients arriving at a doctor's office. In practice, we might have a large sample of patient data available, in which case, the joint distribution shown in table 9.1 might be an estimate of the true distribution. The attributes "fever" and "sore throat" represent whether a patient currently exhibits these symptoms, and "disease x" is some mysterious illness that each patient actually will or will not develop at some point.

We are, of course, interested in predictive symptom-disease rules, such as a medical practitioner might use in the course of a cursory diagnosis. Note that from table 9.1 alone or, indeed, from the original sample data, it would be difficult to manually detect the most informative rules. In table 9.2, we list the rule conditional probability $p(x|y)$, the left-hand-side probability ($p(y)$), the cross entropy $j(\mathbf{X};\mathbf{Y} = y)$, and their product $J(\mathbf{X};\mathbf{Y} = y)$ for each of six possible rules.

The three best rules, as ranked by information content, are 1, 3, and 5, in this order. Rule 5 is a perfect predictor of a patient not having the disease; however, it only occurs 20 percent of the time, limiting its use. Rules 2, 4, and 6 are of limited predictive value because for each rule, the conditional probability is relatively close to the prior probability of the right-hand side. Hence, the information content for each is low. If we use cross entropy ($j(\mathbf{X}; y)$ as the ranking criterion (and ignore the probability $p(y)$), rule 1 only ranks third. When $p(y)$ is taken into account, rule 1 provides the best generality-accuracy trade-off, with the highest J-measure of 0.229 bits of information.

In practice, because rule 3 is a specialized form of rule 1, with lower information

Table 9.2
Hypothetical Predictive Symptom-Disease Rules and Their Information Content.

Rule	Rule Description	$p(x\|y)$	$p(y)$	$j(\mathbf{X}; y)$	$J(\mathbf{X}; y)$
1	if *fever* then *disease x*	0.875	0.4	0.572	0.229
2	if *sore throat* then *disease x*	0.5285	0.7	0.018	0.012
3	if *sore throat and fever* then *disease x*	0.9	0.3	0.654	0.196
4	if *sore throat and no fever* then *not disease x*	0.75	0.4	0.124	0.049
5	if *no sore throat and no fever* then *not disease x*	1.0	0.2	0.863	0.173
6	if *sore throat or fever* then *disease x*	0.5625	0.8	0.037	0.029

content, it serves no practical purpose and would be eliminated from a simple model. Hence, a practitioner might choose to remember only rules 1 and 5 from this set and seek information regarding other symptoms if neither of these rules' conditions are met (prior to making a diagnosis). This simple hypothetical example illustrates the utility of the J-measure. The next step is to automate the rule-finding procedure, that is, to define an algorithm that automatically finds the most informative rules.

9.4 The ITRULE Rule-Induction Algorithm

Let us again formally define the generalized rule-induction problem in the context of information content: Given a set of K discrete (or categorical) random variables (called features or attributes) and a set of N sample vectors (that is, instances or samples of the attributes, perhaps a database), find the set of R most informative probabilistic rules from the data, where probabilistic rules consist of conjunctions of attribute values on the left-hand side, a single attribute-value assignment on the right-hand side, and an associated conditional probability value. Calling one of the attributes the class and simply deriving classification rules is a special case.

A cursory glance at the literature on machine learning confirms that there are many flavors and varieties of rule-induction algorithms. A significant number of these algorithms are based on symbolic, nonstatistical techniques, for example, the AQ15 algorithm of Michalski et al.(1986). Although such learning algorithms provide useful qualitative insights into the basic nature of the learning problem, we believe that a statistical framework is necessary for any robust, practical learning procedure, in particular, for real-world problems. Many rule-induction algorithms that use a statistical basis fall into the tree-based classifier category, for example, the well-known ID3 algorithm (Quinlan 1986) and its variants. These algorithms derive classification rules in the form of a tree structure. The restriction to a tree structure makes the search problem much easier than the problem of looking for general rules. Quinlan (1987) also proposed the C4 algorithm, which prunes an original ID3-like tree structure to a set of modular rules. Clark and Niblett (1988) described the CN2 algorithm, which produces a decision-list classifier structure, allowing arbitrary subsets of categorical events to be used as tests at intermediate nodes in the list. Both of these techniques, and almost all related algorithms, are strictly classifiers, and all use some form of restricted rule structure (tree, decision list) that allows the search algorithm to use a divide-and-conquer strategy in searching the data. The only vaguely similar approaches to the problem of generalized rule induction of which we are aware is a Bayesian approach presented by Cheeseman (1984) and the Entail algorithm of Gaines and Shaw (1986), which is based on fuzzy logic measures rather than probability theory. In addition, Piatetsky-Shapiro (see chapter 13) describes an approach that looks at generalized rule induction for strong rules, where strong is defined as having rule-transition probabilities near 1.

The problem of generalized rule induction is difficult. One cannot partition the data in a simple divide-and-conquer manner, making the search for rules considerably more computationally demanding than tree induction. We developed an efficient algorithm for the problem, namely, the ITRULE algorithm (Goodman and Smyth 1988a, 1988c, 1989; Smyth and Goodman 1991a).

The input to the algorithm consists of the data (a set of N discrete or categorically-valued attribute vectors), R (the number of rules required), and s, (the maximum size of the conjunctions allowed in the rules, where $1 \leq s \leq K-1$). The algorithm returns the R most informative rules as output, as high as order s, in rank order of information content. The order of a rule is defined as the number of conjunctions on the left-hand side of the rule. In addition, the user can supply a constraint matrix (size $K \times K$) of left-hand-side/right-hand-side attribute combinations, where an entry of 1 indicates that this combination is not to be considered among the candidate rules, and a 0 entry indicates the opposite. The default value for the matrix is the *identity matrix*. This constraint matrix is a simple technique to restrict the focus of attention of the algorithm to rules of interest to the user. For example, the constraint matrix allows one to enforce causal constraints or implement the special case of classification rules for a specific attribute.

The algorithm operates by keeping a list of the R best rules found as far as it searches the rule space. In turn, it considers each of the possible first-order rules for each possible right-hand side, calculates their J-measure, and includes them in the rule list if their information content is greater than that of the Rth best rule found so far. The J-measure calculations are made based on estimates from the data of the various probabilities involved. This estimation step is a critical element of the algorithm and is described in more detail in the appendix. A decision is then made about whether it is worth specializing the rule further. Specializing the rule consists of adding extra conditions to the left-hand side. The key efficiency of the algorithm lies in the fact that it uses information-theoretic bounds to determine how much information can be gained by further specialization (Smyth and Goodman 1990a, 1990b). If the upper bound on attainable information content is less than the information of the Rth rule on the list, the algorithm can safely ignore all specializations of this rule and backs up from this point. In this manner, it continues to search and apply bounds until it has covered the entire space of possible rules.

The worst-case complexity of the algorithm is exponential in the number of attributes. Precisely, for K m-ary attributes (that is, attributes that can take on m values), the number of possible rules to be examined by the algorithm is

$$R = Km\Big((2m+1)^{K-1} - 1\Big)$$

where $m = 1$ for the special case of binary attributes. However, this worst-case scenario can only occur if the attributes are all entirely independent of each other (so that none of the bounds takes effect), and the size of the training data set is significantly greater than 2^K (so that one is not limited by small-sample estimation effects). In practical situations, the combination of bounds and small sample bias ensures that the algorithm rarely searches any rules of order much greater than 3 or 4 (in Smyth and Goodman (1990a), we showed empirical results validating this effect on well-known data sets). The size of the data set N is only a linear factor in the complexity; that is, doubling the size of the data set will cause the algorithm to roughly take twice as long to run. A more significant practical limitation is the alphabet size m. In speech and computer vision problems, m can be large; for example, for the text-to-phoneme mapping problem (Sejnowski and Rosenberg 1987) , $m = 26$. A practical approach to this problem is to limit allowable order s of the rules to, say, 2 or 3, a suboptimal but necessary fix.

9.5 Applications of the ITRULE Algorithm

The ITRULE algorithm is ideally suited for problems with a large number of discrete-valued or categorical variables whose interaction is poorly understood, that is, where there is little prior domain knowledge. In particular, domains characterized by nonlinear relationships are particularly well matched by the probabilistic rule representation. Applications of the algorithm can be organized into four basic categories.

First is exploratory data analysis. Here, the algorithm is perhaps most useful for generating an initial understanding of dependencies among variables, causal relationships, and so on, in an interactive and exploratory manner. One of the early successful applications of ITRULE was for a financial database describing the characteristics and performance of a variety of mutual fund investment companies averaged over five years (Goodman and Smyth 1988c). The algorithm extracted a number of interesting (and previously unknown) general domain rules.

Second is knowledge acquisition for expert systems. The probabilistic rule output can be directly used as the knowledge base for an expert system. Hence, one can use ITRULE to automate the rule-elicitation process, circumventing the often inefficient manual knowledge-acquisition methodologies. Indeed, even when no database is available, one can, in principle, use expert-supplied case studies as a synthetic data set. We have routinely used the algorithm to produce rules from data for various commercial rule-based shells; the ability to go directly from data to a working expert system is particularly powerful, allowing for rapid prototyping of a system and iterative improvement by adding new attributes and rerunning the induction. Goodman et al. (1989) report an application of this technique for the development of expert systems for telecommunications network management and control.

Third is rule-based classifiers. By running the algorithm to find only classification rules, the resulting rule set forms a hybrid rule-based and probabilistic classifier. This classifier, which has achieved excellent classification performance in empirical tests (Smyth, Goodman, and Higgins 1990), uses appropriate conditional independence assumptions to combine rule probabilities into an estimate of the class probability. In addition, the equivalent log likelihoods, or weights of evidence (for each rule that contributes to the estimate), can be used to construct an explanation of how the classification decision was arrived at, providing the basis for a decision support system.

The fourth application category is the identification of Markov chains. By interpreting state transitions in a Markov chain as probabilistic rules, the algorithm can be used to estimate Markov chain structure from data. For example, one can directly infer general prediction and performance rules for complex engineering systems from a system simulation. In addition, the technique shows considerable potential for detecting high-order components of hidden Markov models, Markov random fields, and so on, for speech and computer vision problems.

As an example of the output of the algorithm, in table 9.3, we show the eight best rules obtained for the congressional voting records database, as described by Schlimmer (1987) (and available publicly from the University of California at Irvine machine learning database).

The algorithm was run with $s = 2$ (maximum rule order of 2) to keep the output simple. The database consists of voting records from a 1984 session of the United States Congress. Each datum corresponds to a particular politician, and the attributes correspond to the party affiliation of the voter plus 16 other attributes describing how they voted on particular budget issues, such as aid to the Nicaraguan Contras, the freezing of physician's fees, aid to El Salvador, and synthetic fuel funding. Because of the probable imposition

Table 9.3
The Eight Best Rules from the Congressional Voting Database.

Rule	Rule Description	$p(x\|y)$	$p(y)$	$J(\mathbf{X}; y)$
1	if *politics:republican* then *phys-freeze:yes*	0.980	0.387	0.428
2	if *phys-freeze:yes and syn-fuels:no* then *politics:republican*	0.967	0.318	0.363
3	if *phys-freeze:yes* then *politics:republican*	0.913	0.407	0.361
4	if *contra-aid:no and crime:yes* then *el-salv-aid:yes*	0.994	0.380	0.355
5	if *contra-aid:no* then *el-salv-aid:yes*	0.983	0.410	0.353
6	if *phys-freeze:no* then *politics:democrat*	0.988	0.568	0.352
7	if *el-salv-aid:no* then *contra-aid:yes*	0.986	0.478	0.332
8	if *phys-freeze: yes and mx-missile:no* then *el-salv-aid:yes*	0.994	0.355	0.330

of party-line voting on many of the issues, this domain is characterized by strong rules, that is, predictive accuracies in the high 90 percent region. We can see from the table that there are redundancies, that is, rules of near-equal information content that have similar left-hand sides for the same right-hand side, differing perhaps by an extra term. An obvious extension of the algorithm is to refine this original rule set by removing such redundancies; such a rule-pruning algorithm is described in Smyth, Goodman and Higgins (1990).

The ITRULE algorithm was implemented in the C programming language on both Sun and Macintosh computers. We ran the algorithm on many of the other data sets that are publicly available in the UCI database, Quinlan's (1979) chess end-game database, Sejnowski and Rosenberg's (1987) text-to-phonemes database and a variety of various character-recognition problems. Various other projects for both engineering and business applications are currently under way. In general, there is not much to be gleaned from asking how the algorithm performed in terms of rules produced on a particular data set because by definition, the rules produced are the R most informative up to order s. More important is the question of how practically large s can be. This fact is important if the structure of the dependencies is high order, for example, for certain types of Boolean functions such as parity. In practice, when running the algorithm to look for discrete-time Markov chains, the data vectors are created by successive windowing of the time-sequence system states. The size of this window effectively defines the maximum amount of memory we are able to model with the rules. If, the number of possible states at each time step is large, as in the text-to-phoneme example mentioned earlier, then practical considerations limit the amount of memory (maximum rule order) we can look at. In general, however, for most applications, there are no such constraints.

The algorithm is not directly suitable for domains characterized by continuous variables with regular functional relationships, for example, polynomial relations between real-valued variables. However, this restriction results from the choice of hypothesis space (conjunctive rules); the underlying information-theoretic ideas should, in principle, be applicable to general representations. Bridging the gap between continuous variables and symbolic representation techniques remains an open research issue, although, in practice, direct quantization of continuous variables (in an appropriate manner) rarely causes major problems. In addition, because the probability estimation procedure underlying the algorithm effectively assumes that the data are a true random sample, data sets that do not obey this assumption are not directly suitable for this technique, for example, time-series data.

9.6 Future Directions in Learning from Databases

It is worth making the general point that more cross-disciplinary research between computer scientists, information theorists, and statisticians is needed. In particular, statistics must play a basic role in any endeavor that purports to infer knowledge from data. One might say that statistical models are a necessary but nonsufficient component of knowledge discovery. Historically, statistical theory developed as a means for testing hypotheses in a controlled experiment scenario. The founding fathers of the field typically worked with pencil and paper with relatively small data sets, where each datum was painstakingly collected in a well-characterized sampling methodology. Data were expensive, and analyzing it was a purely manual operation. In contrast, many current domains are characterized by vast amounts of data that have been collected in a manner far removed from ideal random sampling techniques and that can be analyzed in any number of ways in an automated manner. In essence, the rules of the game have changed, and when applying statistical theories, it is worth remembering the original context in which they were developed.

It is interesting to note that in the 1960s, early applications of computer algorithms in the statistical field led to controversy over whether such techniques were in fact "fishing" for theories where none really existed (Selvin and Stuart 1966). This point is especially important where the number of attributes and the number of data samples are of the same order. Essentially, if one keeps applying different hypothesis tests to the same data set, it becomes more likely that one will accept a false hypothesis, that is, confuse a random correlation with a true dependency. The solution is to make one's hypothesis acceptance criteria dependent on the number of hypotheses tested so far; however, this is extremely difficult to model in all but simple problems. This type of problem can be circumvented by having large data sets; nonetheless, its relevance to any knowledge discovery algorithm is apparent.

A problem that we have not discussed is incremental or online learning, as opposed to *batch* learning, that is, the ability to incorporate new data into the model without the need for rerunning the entire induction algorithm or storing all the previous data. Various ad hoc schemes have been proposed in the machine learning or (more recently) the neural network literature. Typically, these schemes fail on two accounts: First, they confuse parameter adaptation with model adaptation; that is, they fine tune the parameters of a particular model without considering the possibility of other models. Second, they fail in any even rudimentary manner to take into account what basic statistical theory has to say about estimation over time, for example, the notion of stationarity. It is worth emphasizing that seeking universal incremental learning algorithms is probably ill advised; the engineering approach of domain-specific solutions to particular problems seems more promising (see Buntine (1990) for a similar viewpoint). The implication for database discovery algorithms might be that taking into account the nature of the data and the manner in which they were collected will prove to be the most profitable avenue for exploration rather than seeking generic, domain-independent algorithms.

Another major issue is that of prior knowledge. One of the recent paradigm shifts in machine learning has been away from the idea that a machine can acquire all knowledge starting from nothing toward a gradual realization that the machine can do much better in learning tasks with only a little (appropriate) prior knowledge. To date, most of this theory-based learning work has been largely isolated from the type of quantitative probability-based methodologies we present here. The incorporation of prior knowledge is a nontrivial problem if we consider the statistical ramifications; a priori domain theory corresponds to a priori assumptions or a statistical bias toward certain models. Despite what proponents of Bayesian inference might claim, getting accurate and consistent subjective prior estimates for complex hypothesis spaces (such as in a typical database) is difficult, and there is a dearth of practical literature and experience in this area.

As a final issue, although synthetic domains are useful for initial experimentation and comparison purposes, more work needs to be done with real databases. Typically, real databases do not consist of random samples and might contain missing and mixed-mode data. The treatment of missing data, for example, is again subject to various assumptions and can be domain dependent to a large extent. Prior work in statistical pattern recognition addressed some of these topics (Dixon 1979). Techniques such as these need to become established tools for learning and discovery algorithms.

9.7 Estimating Probabilities from Data

A necessary component of any statistical approach to rule induction is the ability to accurately estimate probabilities from data. The approach with which most people are familiar is the simple frequency ratio; that is, if we count r occurrences of an event in a total sample of size n, we then estimate the probability of this event in general as the simple frequency ratio r/n. In statistical estimation theory, this approach is known as the maximum likelihood estimate. For large values of n, this estimate is well behaved; however, for small values of n, it can cause problems.

Consider, for example, the case where a doctor arrives in a foreign country for a temporary work assignment, and of the first three patients she/he examines, all have the same particular disease. How should the doctor estimate the probability p of the disease occurring among the general population? Clearly, the maximum likelihood estimate of $p = 3/3 = 1$ is overly pessimistic and highly unlikely to be true. A proponent of Bayesian estimation methods (see Berger (1985) for a comprehensive treatment) might argue that the doctor would have an a priori belief about the value of p (perhaps the value of p that she/he has estimated from experience in his/her own country), which is then updated to a new *a posteriori* value for p on the basis of the three new observations. A conservative information theorist might argue that because this is a foreign country, the doctor has really no prior information, and hence, a maximum entropy (ME) estimate is most appropriate (the technique of ME estimation was originally proposed by Jaynes (1957) and explicitly espouses the principle of adding no extraneous information to the problem). Hence, for m mutually exclusive and exhaustive events, the ME estimate of the probability of any event is $1/m$ because no initial information is given to suggest that any one event is more likely than another.

Naturally, one can view the Bayesian and ME estimation techniques as completely compatible, differing only in the credence given to initial information. In our medical example, the Bayesian technique would likely be the most practical and appropriate given the difficulty in selecting the proper event space to construct an ME estimate. Given that selecting an initial estimate is not a problem in principle, the real issue becomes one of how to update this estimate in light of the new data. In a sense, this problem is one of choosing an interpolation formula as a function of n (the sample size), where n ranges from 0 to ∞. At $n = 0$, our formula should give the initial Bayesian-ME estimate, and it should change smoothly as a function of increasing n, approaching the maximum likelihood estimate r/n as $n \rightarrow \infty$.

Such techniques exist in the statistical literature. In our work, we chose to use the beta distribution, as described by I. J. Good (1965) in his monograph on point estimation. Without going into the technical details, one effectively parameterizes the beta distribution to encode one's beliefs about both the expectation of the probability p for $n = 0$ (the initial Bayes estimate) and the degree of confidence in our estimate for p. The latter parameter controls the effective rate at which the beta estimate changes from the prior value of p to the maximum likelihood estimate r/n as a function of n. In Good's treatment, one chooses the parameters α and β such that

$$p_0 = \frac{\alpha}{\alpha + \beta},$$

where p_0 is one's initial estimate of p having seen no data, and $\alpha > 0$ and $\beta > 0$. One's estimate for p, having seen r successes from n trials, is then

$$\hat{p}(r, n) = \frac{\alpha + r}{\alpha + \beta + n}.$$

Clearly, specifying p_0 only constrains the ratio of α and β; to solve for their actual values, Good further defines a second equation for an initial estimate of the variance of, or confidence in, p_0. We find the specification of an initial variance term somewhat nonintuitive and difficult to judge in practice. Instead, we use the following approach, which is entirely equivalent to Good's approach (in that our estimate implicitly results in a prior variance term) except that it is more intuitive for practical use.

Let us define

$$k = \alpha + \beta$$

to be the effective sample size corresponding to our prior belief p_0; that is, consider k to be the number of samples by which we wish to weight our prior belief. Hence, we can rewrite our estimator in the form

$$\hat{p}(r, n) = \frac{r + kp_0}{n + k}.$$

We have found this particular small sample estimator to be robust and easy to use in practice. In the ITRULE algorithm described earlier, one supplies the algorithm with parameter k ($k > 0$); large k makes the algorithm more conservative, and small k (such as $k = 2$) makes it more liberal in inductive inference. For our purposes, p_0 is automatically chosen by the algorithm depending on the context. Estimation of prior probabilities of simple events uses the ME technique of $1/m$, whereas estimation of conditional probabilities uses an equivalent ME technique where an initial estimate using the unconditional prior is chosen; that is,

$$p_0(x|y) = \hat{p}(x).$$

In general, we have found that the use of these relatively simple estimation techniques makes a considerable difference in the robustness of our algorithms.

9.8 Conclusion

We see the ITRULE algorithm's primary practical use as an exploratory data-analysis tool for discrete-categorical data rather than as a general-purpose "wonder algorithm." Of more fundamental significance than the algorithm itself is the basic underlying idea of intensive hypothesis search guided by information-theoretic principles as a paradigm for managing large volumes of data where we have limited prior knowledge. In this context, the work presented in this chapter—indeed, in this volume as a whole—will hopefully be viewed in retrospect as a small but important early step in the field of automated knowledge discovery.

Acknowledgments

This research was carried out in part by the Jet Propulsion Laboratory, California Institute of Technology, under a contract with the National Aeronautics and Space Administration. This work is also supported in part by Pacific Bell and by the Army Research Office under contract DAAL03-89-K-0126.

References

Adams, J. B. 1976. Probabilistic Reasoning and Certainty Factors. *Mathematical Biosciences* 32: 177–186.

Angluin, D. and Smith, C. 1983. Inductive Inference: Theory and Methods. *ACM Computing Surveys* 15(3): 237–270.

Berger, J. O. 1985. *Statistical Decision Theory and Bayesian Analysis.* New York: Springer-Verlag.

Buntine, W. 1990. Myths and Legends in Learning Classification Rules. In Proceedings of Eighth National Conference on Artificial Intelligence, 736–742. Menlo Park, Calif.: American Association for Artificial Intelligence.

Cheeseman, P. 1984. Learning of Expert Systems from Data. In Proceedings of the First IEEE Conference on Applications of Artificial Intelligence. Washington, D.C.: IEEE Computer Society.

Chomsky, A. N. 1957. *Syntactic Structures.* The Hague, Netherlands: Mouton.

Clark, P. and Niblett, T. 1989. The CN2 Induction Algorithm. *Machine Learning* 3: 261–283.

Dixon, J. K. 1979. Pattern Recognition with Partly Missing Data. *IEEE Transactions on Systems, Man and Cybernetics* 9(10): 617–621.

Gaines, B. R. and Shaw, M. L. G. 1986. Induction of Inference Rules for Expert Systems. *Fuzzy Sets and Systems* 18(3): 315–328.

Good, I. J. 1965. *The Estimation of Probabilities: An Essay on Modern Bayesian Methods*, Research monograph 30. Cambridge, Mass.: MIT Press.

Goodman, R. M.; Miller, J. W.; Smyth, P.; and Latin, H. 1989. Real-Time Autonomous Expert Systems in Network Management. In *Integrated Network Management I*, eds. B. Meandzija and J. Westcott, 588–624, Amsterdam: North Holland.

Goodman, R. M. and Smyth, P. 1990. Decision Tree Design Using Information Theory. *Knowledge Acquisition* 2(1): 1–19.

Goodman, R. M. and Smyth, P. 1989. The Induction of Probabilistic Rule Sets—the ITRULE Algorithm, *Proceedings of the Sixth International Workshop on Machine Learning*,129–132. San Mateo, Calif.: Morgan Kaufmann.

Goodman, R. M. and Smyth, P. 1988a. An Information-Theoretic Model for Rule-Based Expert Systems. Presented at the 1988 International Symposium on Information Theory, Kobe, Japan, July.

Goodman, R. M. and Smyth, P. 1988b. Decision Tree Design from a Communication Theory Standpoint. *IEEE Transactions on Information Theory* 34(5): 979–994.

Goodman, R. M. and Smyth, P. 1988c. Information-Theoretic Rule Induction. In *Proceedings of the 1988 European Conference on Artificial Intelligence.* London: Pitman, 357–362.

Holland, J. H.; Holyoak, K. J.; Nisbett, R. E.; and Thagard P. R. 1986. *Induction: Processes of Inference, Learning and Discovery.* Cambridge, Mass.: MIT Press.

Jaynes, E. T. 1957. Information Theory and Statistical Mechanics I. *Physics Review* 106: 620–630.

Michalski, R. S.; Mozetic, I; Hong, J. R.; and Lavrac, N. 1986. The Multi-Purpose Incremental Learning System AQ15 and Its Testing Application to Three Medical Domains. In Proceedings of the Sixth National Conference on Artificial Intelligence, 1041–1045. Menlo Park, Calif.: American Association for Artificial Intelligence.

Newell, A., and Simon, H. A. 1972. *Human Problem Solving.* Englewood Cliffs, N.J.: Prentice Hall.

Quinlan, J. R. 1987. Generating Production Rules from Examples. In Proceedings of the Tenth International Joint Conference on Artificial Intelligence, 304–307. Menlo Park, Calif: International Joint Conferences on Artificial Intelligence.

Quinlan, J. R. 1986. Induction of Decision Trees. *Machine Learning* 1: 81–106.

Quinlan, J. R. 1979. Discovering Rules by Induction from Large Collections of Examples. In *Expert Systems in the Micro-Electronic Age*, ed. D. Michie, 168–201. Edinburgh: Edinburgh University Press.

Quinlan, J. R., and Rivest R. L. 1989. Inferring Decision Trees Using the Minimum Description Length Principle. *Information and Computation* 80: 227–248.

Rissanen, J. 1989. *Stochastic Complexity in Statistical Inquiry.* Singapore: World Scientific.

Schlimmer, J. C. 1987. *Concept Acquisition through Representational Adjustment*, Ph.D. diss., Dept. of Computer Science, Univ. of California at Irvine.

Sejnowski, T. J., and Rosenberg C. M. 1987. Parallel Networks That Learn to Pronounce English Text. *Complex Systems* 1:145–168.

Selvin, H. C., and Stuart, A. 1966. Data-Dredging Procedures in Survey Analysis. *American Statistician* 20(3): 20–23.

Shannon, C. 1948. A Mathematical Theory of Communication. *Bell System Technical Journal* 27(3): 379–423.

Shore, J. E., and Johnson, R. W. 1980. Axiomatic Derivation of the Principle of Maximum Entropy and the Principle of Minimum Cross-Entropy. *IEEE Transactions on Information Theory* 26(1): 26–37.

Smyth, P., and Goodman, R. M. 1991a. An Information Theoretic Approach to Rule Induction from Databases. *IEEE Transactions on Knowledge and Data Engineering.* Forthcoming.

Smyth, P., and Goodman, R. M. 1991b. The Information Content of a Probabilistic Rule,*IEEE Transactions on Information Theory.*

Smyth, P; Goodman, R. M.; and Higgins, C. 1990. A Hybrid Rule-Based/Bayesian Classifier. In Proceedings of the 1990 European Conference on Artificial Intelligence. London: Pitman, 610–615.

Zadeh, L. A. 1965. Fuzzy Sets. *Information and Control* 8: 338–353.

10 Incremental Discovery of Rules and Structure by Hierarchical and Parallel Clustering

Jiarong Hong and Chengjing Mao
Harbin Institute of Technology

Abstract

In this chapter, a theoretical framework for the incremental discovery of rules and structure is presented, and a system called Thought/KD1 implementing the proposed theory is described. Similar to the process of discovering knowledge by human beings, Thought/KD1 is capable of incrementally discovering production rules by first performing classification and abstraction from given examples and then finding implications between descriptions according to containment relationships of corresponding clusters. Experimental results show that Thought/KD1 is an efficient, effective, and reasonable approach to knowledge discovery. Some applications of Thought/KD1 to the automatic construction and refinement of expert system knowledge bases are presented. Surprisingly, the knowledge base of Winston's well-known toy expert system for animal identification was entirely rediscovered by Thought/KD1.

10.1 Introduction

Knowledge-based systems, especially expert systems, are now experiencing extraordinary growth. Machine learning is commonly recognized as a fundamental way for overcoming the knowledge-acquisition bottleneck of constructing such systems, and several knowledge-acquisition approaches have begun to emerge. One can distinguish two categories of approaches: One category, in which the classification of examples and its description are given, is known as *learning from examples* and includes systems such as ID3 (Quinlan 1986), AQ15 (Hong, Michalski, and Mozetic 1986), and AE1 (Hong 1985); the other, in which classification and the corresponding description are absent, is called *machine discovery* and includes systems such as Glauber (Langley et al. 1987), ITRULE (Goodman and Smyth 1988), and Charade (Ganascia 1987).

Knowledge discovery from databases is a form of machine discovery where the discovered knowledge is represented in a high-level language. It is capable of discovering domain knowledge from given examples and, thus, has the potential for playing an important role in developing knowledge-based systems. However, the theory of knowledge discovery is still under development, and few existing methods are practical.

In this chapter, we describe a theoretical framework for knowledge discovery, which is based on the cognitive process of human discovery. The proposed methodology was implemented by an integrated learning system called Thought/KD1 incorporated in Thought (Hong and Mao 1989). Thought is a learning machine that integrates several learning strategies and is capable of cultivating existing novice-level expert systems into expert-level systems by accumulating, analyzing, and then abstracting the experiences of the existing expert systems. In this chapter, we concentrate only on Thought/KD1. The major part of Thought/KD1 comprises a conceptual clustering system called Leobs (Hong 1988) and a newly developed multipurpose system called GS that uses learning from examples (Hong and Uhrik 1988). Thought/KD1 first performs conceptual clustering using Leobs to partition the set of given examples into a certain number of subsets and then abstracts descriptions of the generated subsets. Thought/KD1 then explores some implication relations between descriptions according to the containment relationship of the corresponding subsets. Notice that similar to the process of human discovery, this approach is based on the classification and abstraction of given examples and that both Leobs and GS are efficient algorithms and have the ability to generate descriptions in disjunctive normal form (DNF). We also present an evaluation scheme for handling uncertainty and noisy data. Surprisingly, Thought/KD1 can automatically reconstruct the entire knowledge base of the toy animal identification expert system given by Winston and Horn (1984).

10.2 A Theoretical Framework

In this section, we describe a theoretical framework for incremental and constructive knowledge discovery.

10.2.1 Terminology

Suppose we are given a discrete finite attribute space of n dimensions, $E = D_1 \times ... \times D_n$, where D_j is a finite set of symbols or integers. Let $|U|$ denote the size of set U.

Definition 1: An example e is an element of E; that is, $e =< v_1 \dots v_n >$. A *selector* is a relational statement of the form $[x_j = W_j]$, where x_j is the jth attribute, $W_j \subseteq D_j$; $[x_j = W_j]$ is true if and only if x_j takes values from W_j. A *complex* cpx is either a selector or a conjunction of selectors. A *description* F is either a complex or a disjunction of complexes.

Definition 2: An example e, $e =< v_1 \dots v_n >$, satisfies a selector $[x_j = W_j]$, or alternately, the selector covers e if and only if $v_j \in W_j$; e satisfies a complex cpx if and only if e satisfies every selector of the complex cpx. An example e satisfies a description F if and only if e satisfies at least one complex of F.

Suppose that pE and nE are sets of positive and negative examples, respectively, and that pS and nS are the subsets of pE and nE, respectively.

Definition 3: A selector *Sel* covers the set pS of positive examples against the set nS

of negative examples if and only if Sel covers all positive examples in pS and excludes (that is, does not cover) any negative example in nS. A complex L covers pS against nS if and only if every selector in L covers pS against nS. A description F in terms of DNF covers pE against nE if and only if each complex in F covers a subset of pE against nE, and the union of these subsets is pE. A description in terms of selector, complex, or disjunction of complexes that covers pS against nS is also called a *cover of pS against nS* . The cover of pS against nS is denoted in this chapter by $Cover(pS, nS)$.

Definition 4: An *Extension* of description F in set S, denoted as function $Extension(F, S)$, is a subset of S in which all examples satisfy F. Note that if $F(S', S) = Cover(S', S-S')$, and $S' \in S$, then $Extension(F(S', S), S) = S'$. Thus, $F(S', S)$ is the *characteristic description* of set S'.

Definition 5: If a cover of a set S' against $S - S'$ is a complex, then it is called a *characteristic cover.* If a characteristic description consists of a sole selector, then it is called a *basic cover* of S'. Because a basic cover consists of only one selector, it is easy to find any basic cover for a set of examples by finding such an attribute value that appears in those examples in the set and not in the complement set.

Definition 6: A description F_1 implies another description F_2, denoted by $F_1 \rightarrow F_2$, if and only if the extension of F_1 is a subset of the extension of F_2. F_1 is equivalent to F_2, denoted by $F_1 <=> F_2$, if and only if they have the same extension. An implication $F_1 \rightarrow F_2$ is called a *decision rule*, and F_1 and F_2 are called the *condition part* and the *conclusion part,* respectively. Our decision rules are similar to production rules.

Lemma: Suppose $S'' \subseteq S' \subseteq S$. Suppose $F(S_1,\ S_2)$ is the description of set S_1 in set S_2; that is, $F(S_1,\ S_2) = Cover(S_1,\ S_2 - S_1)$. Then the description of S'' in S implies the description of S' in S; that is, $F(S'',\ S) \rightarrow F(S',\ S)$. The description of S'' in S is equivalent to the conjunction of the descriptions of S'' in S' and S' in S; that is, $F(S'',\ S) <=> F(S'',\ S')\ \&\ F(S',\ S)$.

Proof: (1) According to the assumption of the lemma, $F(S'', S)$ covers S'' and excludes $S - S''$. Therefore, $Extension(F(S'', S), S) = S''$.

In a similar fashion, $Extension(F(S', S), S) = S'$. Thus, $F(S'', S) \rightarrow F(S', S)$ because $S'' \subseteq S'$.

(2) Because $F(S'', S')$ covers S'' and excludes $S' - S''$, $F(S', S)$ covers S' and excludes $S - S'$, and $S'' \subseteq S' \subseteq S$, we have $F(S'', S')\ \&\ F(S', S)$ covers S'' and excludes $S - S''$, which is equivalent to $F(S'', S)$.

10.2.2 Theory and Methodology of Knowledge Discovery

It is often observed that human beings define concepts by first finding their extensions by a way of classification and then abstracting the connotations from corresponding extensions. In this way, they discover a production rule by finding containment relationships of concept extensions. In this section, we describe a methodology of knowledge discovery that is based on the previous observations.

10.2.3 A Methodology of Knowledge Discovery

Suppose we are given a set S of examples. For classification, group the given examples into clusters in the following two ways: First, in *hierarchical clustering* (HC), recursively group S into a hierarchy of clusterings $\{S_1, ..., S_k\}$, $\{S_{11}, ..., S_{1k}\}$, ..., $\{S_{k1}, ..., S_{kk}\}$, ..., where S_{ij} is a subset of S_i, and k is usually 2.

Second, in *parallel clustering* (PC), for $k = 2, 3, \ldots, r$, group in turn the same set S into different clusterings, $\{S_1^{(2)}, S_2^{(2)}\}$, ..., $\{S_1^{(r)}, ..., S_r^{(r)}\}$.

For abstraction; first generate descriptions of clusters structured by HC: $\{F_1, ..., F_k\}$, $\{F_{11}, ..., F_{1k}\}$, ..., $\{F_{k1}, ..., F_{kk}\}$, ... where $F_i = Cover(S_i, S - S_i)$, and $F_{ij} = Cover(S_{ij}, S - S_{ij})$;

Second, generate descriptions of clusters structured by PC: $\{F_1^{(2)}, F_2^{(2)}\}$, ..., $\{F_1^{(r)}, ..., F_r^{(r)}\}$, where $F_i^{(2)} = \text{Cover}(S_i^{(2)}, S - S_i^{(2)})$, $i = 1, 2$, and $F_i^{(l)} = \text{Cover}(S_i^{(l)}, S - S_i^{(l)})$, $i = 1, \ldots, l$ and $l = 3, \ldots, r$;

Third, generate a certain number of characteristic covers, if any, and all possible basic covers of each cluster structured in the classification step.

For rule formation, there are four algorithms of knowledge discovery in Thought/KD1: hierarchical knowledge discovery (HKD), parallel knowledge discovery (PKD), characteristic knowledge discovery (CKD), and inheritance knowledge discovery (IKD) (to be described later). HKD is based on hierarchical clustering and its corresponding abstraction. PKD is based on parallel clustering and its corresponding abstraction. CKD is based on classification and characteristic cover and basic cover abstraction. The validity of the methodology of rule formation is shown as follows:

Theorem 1: First, suppose S_{ij} and S_i and corresponding F_{ij} and F_i are obtained by HKD; then $F_{ij} \rightarrow F_i$. Second, suppose $S_i^{(l)}$ and $S_j^{(t)}$ and corresponding $F_i^{(l)}$ and $F_j^{(t)}$ are obtained by PKD; then if $S_i^{(l)} \subseteq S_j^{(t)}$, $F_i^{(l)} \rightarrow F_j^{(t)}$. Third, in each subset S' of S, the covers of S' against the complement $S - S'$ of the subset S' in the whole set S are logically equivalent. Particularly, the characteristic covers and basic covers are all equivalent to each other.

Proof: According to the lemma, it suffices to note that in HKD, $S_{ij} \subseteq S_i \subseteq S$. The second and third points of theorem 1 also follow from the lemma.

In Thought/KD1, the HKD and CKD subsystems are used to discover domain knowledge, but the PKD subsystem is used to discover not only the domain knowledge but also knowledge with uncertainty, noise, or exceptions.

From the proposed methodology, the following can be observed: First, rule discovery is based on classification, which follows the human cognitive law that a concept is only a description of a class of those facts that share the property in common. Second, this methodology allows the discovery of rules in the form of DNF. Third, in general, the validity of the discovered decision rules based on the methodology depends on the whole set S of given examples. The larger the size of S is, the greater the degree of confidence in the rules. Fourth, it was already shown that in learning from examples, the problems of finding a maximal complex with the minimum number of selectors and finding an optimal cover with the minimum number of complexes are *NP-hard* (Hong 1985; Haussler 1988). Thus, the optimal knowledge discovery problem, that is, finding those decision rules whose condition parts and conclusion parts are both optimal, is NP-hard, and any practical knowledge discovery algorithm has to be heuristic and approximate.

10.2.4 Implementation of Thought/KD1

As described in Theory and Methodology of Knowledge Discovery, the process of rule discovery in Thought/KD1 is composed of two major steps. The first step conceptually clusters sets of given examples using Leobs and then generates the corresponding descriptions (including characteristic and basic covers) using GS. For HKD, the result is a hierarchy of clusterings and corresponding descriptions, each of which comprises a family of clusters of its father clustering. For PKD, k clusterings are independently obtained. The second step is rule formation, as described in the previous section. That is, for hierarchical discovery, new knowledge is discovered by finding all possible implications between the descriptions of clusters (including characteristic and basic covers) in a clustering and those in its father clustering and then making all characteristic and basic covers in each cluster logically equivalent for CKD. The same holds for parallel discovery except implications are found between cluster descriptions and clusterings corresponding to larger k's.

Leobs, implemented on a SUN3 workstation, is an extension of the well-known conceptual clustering system Cluster/2 (Stepp and Michalski 1986) and is capable of conceptually partitioning a set of examples into k disjoint subsets, as described in A Methodology of Knowledge Discovery, where k is either given by the user or determined by a conceptually interrelated degree (Hong 1988). GS is a new multipurpose system of learning from examples, which generates a description in DNF of a class of (positive) examples compared with the union of the rest of the classes of (negative) examples, as described in A Methodology of Knowledge Discovery. The complexes are constructed, in turn, by first using generalization to select a selector that covers the maximum number of positive examples and then using specialization to exclude those negative examples that are incorrectly covered by the chosen selector.

10.2.5 Complexity of Thought/KD1

The complexity of Thought/KD1 is mainly dependent on GS and Leobs. Suppose that in a clustering, the numbers of positive and negative examples are p and q, respectively; there are n attributes; and each attribute takes d values on average. In each GS cycle, two evaluation matrices are built. An element in the evaluation matrix of a set of examples is the frequency of occurrences of an attribute value (Hong and Uhrik 1988). Hence, the complexity of building the evaluation matrix for the set of positive (negative) examples is about dpn (dqn). The complexity of searching for the element with the maximum number of occurrences in the matrix is about dn comparisons; that is, the cost of building a selector is about dn. Thus, the worst-case cost of building a complex is about dn^2. Finally, the worst-case cost of building a cover of the set of positive (negative) examples is dn^2p (dn^2q). Now, suppose Leobs constructs a binary tree with $s = \mid S \mid$ leaves. Without much difficulty, we can see that the worst-case cost of building the binary tree is about $dn^2 s \log_2 s$. That is, the worst-case run time of Thought/KD1 is on the order of $dn^2 s \log_2 s$.

10.3 Sample Results

In this section, we show sample results of Thought/KD1 using the HKD, PKD, and CKD methods and running on the set of animal examples illustrated in table 10.1.

10.3.1 Hierarchical Knowledge Discovery

By running the HKD subsystem of Thought/KD1 on the data in table 10.1, we obtain a hierarchy of clusterings with corresponding descriptions, as shown in figure 10.1. The discovered knowledge is shown in table 10.2.

Table 10.2 shows nontautological rules discovered by HKD. For example, rule 2 states that if an animal has hooves, then it must give milk. Surprisingly, this conclusion, drawn from only a few animal examples, is always true in zoology. Moreover, rule 3 says that if an animal has claws and is able to swim, then it must give milk, which also holds in the real animal kingdom. It is interesting that rule 1—stating that if an animal has webs, then it isn't a mammal because it gives no milk—is true except for the platypus.

10.3.2 Parallel Knowledge Discovery

Table 10.3 shows the results, including clusters and descriptions, of running the PKD subsystem on the data in table 10.1 for k = 2, 3, 4. The discovered rules are listed in table 10.4. In table 10.4, rules 1 and 2 are the same as rules 2 and 1 in table 10.2, which are discovered by HKD. Rule 3, a specialization of rule 2, is almost true.

Table 10.1
Data for Animal Identification.

#	Animal	Feet	Ears	Eats	Gives_milk	Flies	Swims
1	tiger	claw	external	meat	yes	unable	able
2	dog	claw	external	grain	yes	unable	able
3	horse	hoof	external	grass	yes	unable	able
4	sheep	hoof	external	grass	yes	unable	unable
5	frog	web	middle	meat	no	unable	well
6	penguin	web	middle	meat	no	unable	able
7	bat	claw	external	meat	yes	well	unable
8	chicken	claw	middle	grain	no	able	unable
9	rat	claw	external	grain	yes	unable	able
10	crane	claw	middle	meat	no	well	unable
11	rabbit	claw	external	grass	yes	unable	unable
12	camel	hoof	external	grass	yes	unable	unable
13	pig	hoof	external	grain	yes	unable	able
14	duck	web	middle	grain	no	able	well
15	ox	hoof	external	grass	yes	unable	able
16	swallow	claw	middle	meat	no	well	unable
17	bear	claw	external	meat	yes	unable	able
18	ostrich	claw	middle	grain	no	unable	unable
19	horse	hoof	external	grass	yes	unable	well
20	eagle	claw	middle	meat	no	well	unable

10.3.3 Characteristic Knowledge Discovery

The CKD subsystem gives the results in terms of logical equivalence. For example, for cluster S_2 in hierarchical clustering or cluster $S_2^{(2)}$ for parallel clustering, CKD discovers the equivalence [Gives_milk=yes] <=> [Ears=external].

Moreover, by substituting one description in the equivalences for another in the discovered rules, we can obtain other results, for example, [Feet=hoof] → [Ears=external] from rule 4 in table 10.4 and [Feet=web] → [Ears=middle] from rule 5 in table 10.4.

10.4 Incremental Knowledge Discovery

Thought/KD1 can do two kinds of incremental knowledge discovery, characterized by incrementally adding new attribute values and adding new examples to the database, respectively. The former is called *hierarchical refinement of the knowledge base,* and the

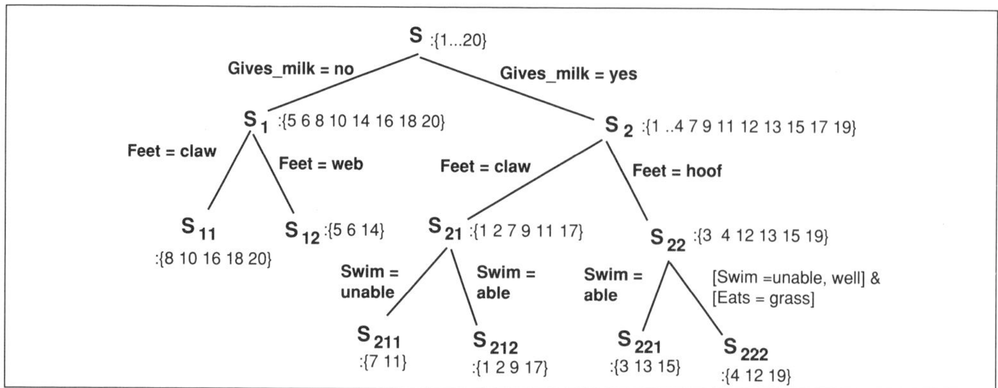

Figure 10.1
A Hierarchy of Clusters and Corresponding Descriptions Generated by HKD.

Table 10.2
Nontrivial Rules Discovered by Hierarchical Knowledge Discovery (HKD).

#	Decision Rules Discovered by HKD
1	[Feet=web] → [Gives_milk=no]
2	[Feet=hoof] → [Gives_milk=yes]
3	[Feet=claw][Swims=able] → [Feet=claw][Gives_milk=yes]

latter is called *incremental refinement of the knowledge base.* Hierarchical refinement of the knowledge base is used in HKD and is capable of making the discovered knowledge more accurate and meaningful because the newly added attribute values give the data in a cluster more information (details) for the next clustering. For example, in simply running HKD on cluster S_1, as shown in figure 10.1, HKD inappropriately separates the birds into two sets S_{11} and S_{12} and in S_{12} mixes the frog and two birds (penguin and duck). By adding the new attribute Feathers into these examples in S_1 and rerunning HKD, a new clustering is constructed that comprises a set of all birds, $S'_{11} = \{6, 8, 10, 14, 16, 18, 20\}$, and a set containing frog, $S'_{12} = \{5\}$. In the rest of this section, we focus on the incremental refinement of the knowledge base.

10.4.1 Inconsistency and Incompleteness of Discovered Knowledge Bases

In incremental refinement of the knowledge base, the previously discovered knowledge needs to be modified to preserve consistency and completeness.

Definition 7: A rule is inconsistent with the database if an example exists in the database that satisfies the condition part of the rule but not the conclusion part. A knowledge base is inconsistent with the database if there is an inconsistent rule in the

Table 10.3
Clusters and Corresponding Descriptions Generated by Parallel Knowledge Discovery.

Name	Cluster	Description	Content
$S_1^{(2)}$	{5, 6, 8, 10, 14, 16, 18, 20}	$F_1^{(2)}$ $F_1^{'(2)}$	[Gives_milk=no] [Ears=middle]
$S_2^{(2)}$	{1..4, 7, 9, 11..13, 15, 17, 19}	$F_2^{(2)}$ $F_2^{'(2)}$	[Gives_milk=yes] [Ears=external]
$S_1^{(3)}$	{7, 10, 16, 20}	$F_1^{(3)}$	[Flies=well]
$S_2^{(3)}$	{5, 6, 8, 14, 18}	$F_2^{(3)}$	[Gives_milk=no][Flies=able, unable]
$S_3^{(3)}$	{1..4, 9, 11..13, 15, 17, 19}	$F_3^{(3)}$	[Gives_milk=yes][Flies=able, unable]
$S_1^{(4)}$	{1, 2, 7, 9, 11, 17}	$F_1^{(4)}$	[Feet=claw][Gives_milk=yes]
$S_2^{(4)}$	{8, 10, 16, 18, 20}	$F_2^{(4)}$	[Feet=claw][Gives_milk=no]
$S_3^{(4)}$	{3, 4, 12, 13, 15, 19}	$F_3^{(4)}$	[Feet=hoof]
$S_4^{(4)}$	{5, 6, 14}	$F_4^{(4)}$	[Feet=web]

Table 10.4
Non-Trivial Decision Rules Discovered by Parallel Knowledge Discovery (PKD).

#	Decision Rules Discovered by PKD	Containment
1	[Feet=hoof] → [Gives_milk=yes]	$S_3^{(4)} \subseteq S_2^{(2)}$
2	[Feet=web] → [Gives_milk=no]	$S_4^{(4)} \subseteq S_1^{(2)}$
3	[Feet=web] → [Gives_milk=no][Flies=able, unable]	$S_4^{(4)} \subseteq S_2^{(3)}$

knowledge base. A knowledge base is incomplete with respect to the database if an example exists in the database that does not satisfy the condition part of any consistent rule.

Theorem 1 guarantees that the knowledge base discovered by Thought/KD1 is both consistent and complete with respect to the database. Hence, in incremental refinement of the knowledge base, any inconsistency or incompleteness of the knowledge base must be caused by new data. If new examples cause the inconsistency of a rule, the rule should be modified to exclude these new examples. Also, if some newly added examples cause incompleteness of the knowledge base, some new knowledge should be discovered to cover these newly added examples that are not yet covered by the rules in the previous knowledge base. The following example causes knowledge base inconsistency and incompleteness:

Suppose in a previous discovery, we obtained relevant rules as follows:

R_1: [Feet=web] → [Gives_milk=no],

R_2: [Feet=claw] $\rightarrow$ [Gives_milk=yes],

R_3: [Feet=hoof] $\rightarrow$ [Gives_milk=yes].

Now, suppose that a new example for a platypus is added to the database:

[Feet=web] [Ears=external] [Eats=meat] [Gives_milk=yes] [Flies=unable] [Swims=well].

We can see that rule R_1 is inconsistent with platypus because a platypus has webbed feet but gives milk and that the knowledge base is incomplete because neither R_2 nor R_3 covers platypus.

10.4.2 An Incremental Learning Procedure

In Thought/KD1, a procedure called Refine is a modification of the incremental learning algorithm implemented in AQ15 (Hong, Michalski, and Mozetic 1986; Michalski et al. 1986) and is used to refine the knowledge base to preserve its consistency and completeness. Suppose KB is the knowledge base discovered in the past and DB is the database comprising a set OLDD of old data that were used in the past knowledge discovery and a set NEWD of new data to be handled by Thought/KD1. To make KB consistent, do the following:

1. Find a rule R_i in KB such that it is inconsistent with NEWD, where $R_i = F_1 \rightarrow F_2$. If there is no such rule to be found, then exit.
2. Find the set DP of those examples in DB that satisfy both F_1 and F_2 and a set DN of those examples in DB that satisfy F_1 but not F_2.
3. Generate $pc := Cover$(DP, DN).
4. Make intersection: $F_1' := F_1$ & pc.
5. Replace rule R_i with the modified rule $R_i' = F_1' \rightarrow F_2$.
6. goto 1.

To make KB complete, do the following:

1. Find those new examples that are not covered by either the conclusion part or the condition part of any discovered rule in KB; then run Thought/KD1 on these new data to discover new knowledge, and add it to KB. Label all rules in KB as unmarked.
2. Find an unmarked rule $R_i = F_1 \rightarrow F_2$ from KB such that F_2 covers the new examples and F_1 does not, and mark R_i and all other rules that have the same conclusion part F_2 as R_i. If no unmarked rule can be found, then exit.

3. Find a set NEWP of those examples in NEWD that are covered by F_2 and a set OLDN of those in OLDD that are not covered by F_2.
4. Generate $cv = Cover$(NEWP, OLDN).
5. Make $F_1' = F_1 \vee cv$.
6. goto 2.

For the inconsistency case of the platypus example, the condition part [Feet=web] of R_1 covers three old examples, that is, frog, penguin, and duck, and a new one, that is, platypus. $pc := Cover(\{$frog, penguin, duck$\}, \{$platypus$\})$ = [Ears=middle]. Thus, the modified knowledge is R_1' = [Feet=web][Ears=middle] $\rightarrow$ [Gives_milk=no], which is consistent with platypus.

For the completeness case of the platypus example, because the conclusion parts [Gives_milk=yes] of both R_2 and R_3 cover platypus, Refine chooses one, say, R_3, and builds NEWP = {platypus} and OLDN = S_1, as shown in figure 10.1. Then cv = $Cover$(NEWP, OLDN) = [Ears=external]. Thus, R_3 is changed into the form [Feet=hoof] $\vee$ [Ears=external] $\rightarrow$ [Gives_milk=yes].

Theorem 2 shows the correctness of the incremental learning algorithm Refine.

Theorem 2: After being processed by the incremental learning procedure Refine, the knowledge base is consistent and complete.

Proof: It suffices to show that any example e in DB that satisfies the condition part F_1 and the conclusion part F_2 of the original rule R_i must also satisfy the new condition part of the modified rule R_i' and that any new example that caused the original inconsistency (that is, it satisfied F_1 but F_2) cannot satisfy the new condition part of F_1'. Suppose example e satisfies F_1 and F_2. According to the procedure Refine, $F_1' = F_1 \& pc$, and pc = $Cover$(DP, DN), where DP is a set of those examples in DB that satisfy both F_1 and F_2, and DN is a set of those examples that satisfy F_1 but do not satisfy F_2. Thus, $e \in$ DP, and e satisfies pc and the new condition part F_1' as well. That is, e satisfies the modified rule R_i'. Now, suppose e satisfies F_1 but not F_2. Then it must be the case that $e \in$ DN, and thus, e does not satisfy pc or the new condition part F_1'. The completeness part is similarly proved.

10.5 Using Domain Knowledge

Domain knowledge can be used to constrain the search space of Thought/KD1 and generate new meaningful high-level concepts that will make the discovered knowledge more comprehensible and more useful. This use of domain knowledge is called *constructive learning* and was implemented earlier in AQ15 (Hong, Michalski, and Mozetic 1986).

In Thought/KD1, the domain knowledge is represented in terms of decision rules, facts (complexes), and arithmetic expressions; for example, [Class=mammal] is a fact, and volume = length * width * height is an example of an arithmetic expression. In this section, we outline how domain knowledge is used and illustrate how powerful the constructive learning is.

10.5.1 Labeling Clusters

In general, the clusters structured by the conceptual clustering system Leobs are meaningful. For instance, in figure 10.1, cluster S_{12} is a group of mammals, cluster S_{22} is a group of ungulates, and the newly generated cluster S'_{12} is a group of birds. Therefore, such clusters can be labeled by domain knowledge such as [Class=mammal], [Class=ungulate], and [Class=birds].

Definition 8: A *label* of a cluster U is either explicitly defined by the user in terms of domain knowledge (usually basic cover) or is implicitly implied by the name of the cluster, denoted by function $Label(U)$.

According to point 3 of theorem 1, the label for a cluster is logically equivalent to the characteristic descriptions of the cluster, including characteristic covers and basic covers. Like the importance of category labeling by human beings, cluster labeling plays an important role in knowledge discovery. In fact, from the labeled clusters, we can discover significant knowledge, as follows: (1) the implications between the label and characteristic descriptions of the cluster, for example, [Gives_milk=yes] $\rightarrow$ [Class=mammal] and [Feet=hoof] $\rightarrow$ [Class=ungulate]; (2) those implications in which a *partial cover* of the cluster (that is, a cover of a subset of the cluster) is the condition part, and the label serves as the conclusion part, for example, [Flies=well][Lays_eggs=yes] $\rightarrow$ [Class=bird]; (3) those implications in which the conjunction of descriptions of its ancestor clusters is the condition part, and the label serves as the conclusion part, for example, [Gives_milk=yes][Eats=meat] $\rightarrow$ [Class=carnivorous_mammal]; and (4) those implications in which the label serves as a conjunct of the condition part, for example, [Class=bird][Flies=able] $\rightarrow$ [Class=flying_bird].

10.5.2 Inheritance Knowledge Discovery

The given labels of clusters enable Thought/KD1 to conduct inheritance knowledge discovery (IKD), which is a modification of HKD. In IKD, the classification is the same as in HC, but the abstraction is different: A description generated by IKD is a cover of the set against all brothers of the set except the complement of the whole set S; that is, $F_i = Cover(S_i, S - S_i), \ldots, F_{ij} = Cover(S_{ij}, S_i - S_{ij}), \ldots$
The corresponding rule formation is changed into the form

$F_i \; \& \; F_{ij} \; \& \; ... \; \& \; F_{ij..kl} \rightarrow Label(S_{ij..kl})$,
where the condition part of the rule consists of the conjunction of all descriptions of clusters in the path from the root S to the current cluster $S_{ij..kl}$, or

$Label(S_{ij..k}) \; \& \; F_{ij..kl} \rightarrow Label(S_{ij..kl})$,
where the condition part of the rule consists of the conjunction of the description of the current cluster and the label of its father cluster.

Without much difficulty, we can show that the IKD method is correct. For example, according to part 2 of the lemma, the condition part of each rule, as previously defined, is equivalent to $F_{ij..kl}(S_{ij..kl}, S - S_{ij..kl})$, which is the same as the description of $S_{ij..kl}$ in the whole set S.

10.5.3 Constructive Knowledge Discovery

Suppose we pick the data for birds from table 10.1, as shown in table 10.5. In table 10.5, there are seven examples of birds, each of which has eight attribute values (not including Class). Notice that some values are missing and marked by an * and that the attribute Class is absent in the original input file (see table 10.1); Class will be constructed by GS later. In this case, GS generates a description [Feet=web ∨ claw] ∨ [Eats=grain], which is meaningless.

However, if we add the following domain knowledge as decision rules to the input file and rerun GS, then a new attribute Class is constructed (see the last column in table 10.5), and a more comprehensive and simpler description, that is, [Class=bird], is generated:

[Flies=able][Lays_eggs=yes] → [Class=bird]

[Flies=well] → [Flies=able]

[Feathers=yes] → [Class=bird],

with the result that [Class=bird] covers all seven examples.

As shown in the bird example, an advantage of using correct domain knowledge is the ability to construct high-level concepts that are usually more abstract, simple, and representative than the original concepts. Hence, when a new concept (attribute) is constructed, its value should make a strong pattern and be shared by most examples. Thus, this value is more likely to be selected by GS, often serving as a characteristic or basic cover, because GS is based on the frequency of occurrences of an attribute value. If the domain knowledge is incorrect, the new concept will be less representative, and its value will be somewhat sparse in the newly constructed columns (for example, Class). In this case, like AQ15, GS has a filter that ignores those new attributes that give a weak pattern.

Table 10.5
Data for Birds Extracted from the Data in Table 10.1.

#	Flies	Feet	Swims	Feathers	Eats	Gives_milk	Ears	Lays_eggs	Class
1	unable	web	able	yes	meat	no	middle	*	bird
2	*	*	unable	yes	grain	no	*	yes	bird
3	well	claw	*	*	meat	*	middle	yes	bird
4	able	web	well	*	*	no	middle	yes	bird
5	well	claw	unable	*	meat	no	middle	yes	bird
6	well	claw	unable	*	meat	no	middle	yes	bird
7	unable	claw	unable	yes	meat	no	middle	yes	bird

* = missing attributes.

10.6 Handling Uncertainty, Noise, and Exception

As shown in Hierarchical Knowledge Discovery, the validities of the discovered rules are different: Some of them are tautological; some are always true (for example, rules 2 and 3); and some hold only within the training set S of given examples, for example, rule 1. Thus, there is a need for handling uncertainty of the discovered rules. Similarly, there is also a demand on handling noises and exceptions of given data. Chapter 13 by Piatetsky-Shapiro presents a good and reasonable scheme for handling uncertainty and noisy data. In this section, we present a scheme for judging the validity of the discovered rules.

10.6.1 Evaluation of Uncertainty

Suppose we are given a rule $F \rightarrow H$. Let $|E| = |D_1| \times \ \ldots \ \times |D_n|$ be the number of all possible different tuples, where $|D_i|$ is the number of different values for field i. The *confidence degree* (CD) of the rule is defined as follows:

$$CD(F,H) = 1 - e^{\frac{-|E|}{|E|-|S|}} \times (1 - \frac{|Extension(F,S)|}{|S|} \times \frac{|Extension(F,S)|}{|Extension(H,S)|}) \qquad (10.1)$$

Function $CD(F,H)$ has the following properties:

1. $1 - 1/e \ \leq \ CD(F,H) \ \leq \ 1$.
2. $CD(F,H)$ increases as the size $|S|$ of S increases, and it will be close to 1, the maximum degree of confidence, when $|S|$ is close to $|E|$; that is, $\lim_{|S|\rightarrow|E|} CD(F,H) = 1$.
3. With increasing $Extension(F,S)$, $CD(F,H)$ increases.

4. $CD(F, H)$ increases as the ratio of $|Extension(F, S)|/|Extension(H, S)|$ increases, which can be considered a measurement of closeness between descriptions F and H.

10.6.2 Evaluation of Noise and Exception

In table 10.4, set $S_1^{(3)}$ is a subset of set $S_1^{(2)}$ except for example 7, that is, the bat. In other words, $S_1^{(3)} - \{7\} \subseteq S_1^{(2)}$. If we consider example 7 as noise or an exception, then we can discover a meaningful rule with certainty α:

[Flies=well] $\rightarrow$ [Gives_milk=no] (α).

In general, given a rule $F_1 \rightarrow F_2$, the certainty α of this rule can be defined as

$$\alpha(F_1, F_2) = CD(F_1, F_2) \times (1 - \frac{|Exc(F_1, F_2)|}{|Extension(F_1, S)|}) \tag{10.2}$$

where Exc is an exception set defined as $Extension(F_1, S) - Extension(F_2, S)$

10.7 Applications to Construction and Refinement of Knowledge Bases

In this section, we discuss the construction and refinement of knowledge bases.

10.7.1 Automatic Construction of Knowledge Bases for Expert Systems

Thought/KD1 is capable of automatically constructing knowledge bases for expert systems by discovering meaningful decision rules from input data. Suppose we are given data for the animal world, as shown in table 10.6.

Table 10.6
Data for Animal World. **BOLD** values are taken by basic covers.

#	Animal	Hair	Teeth	Eyes	Feathers	Feet	Eats	Milk	Flies	Eggs	Swims
1	tiger	**YES**	pointed	forward	no	claw	meat	**YES**	unable	no	able
2	cheetah	**YES**	pointed	forward	no	claw	meat	**YES**	unable	no	able
3	giraffe	**YES**	blunt	side	no	hoof	grass	**YES**	unable	no	able
4	zebra	**YES**	blunt	side	no	hoof	grass	**YES**	unable	no	unable
5	ostrich	no	no	side	**YES**	claw	grain	no	unable	yes	unable
6	penguin	no	no	side	**YES**	web	fish	no	unable	yes	able
7	albatross	no	no	side	**YES**	claw	grain	no	yes	yes	unable
8	eagle	no	no	forward	**YES**	claw	meat	no	yes	yes	unable
9	viper	no	pointed	forward	no	no	meat	no	unable	yes	unable
10	bee	no	no	side	no	*	nectar	no	able	*	unable

* = missing attribute.

By running Thought/KD1 on the data, a hierarchy of clusters structured by HC and the corresponding descriptions generated by IKD are illustrated in figure 10.2, with the discovered knowledge shown in table 10.7. Surprisingly, by using a few examples,

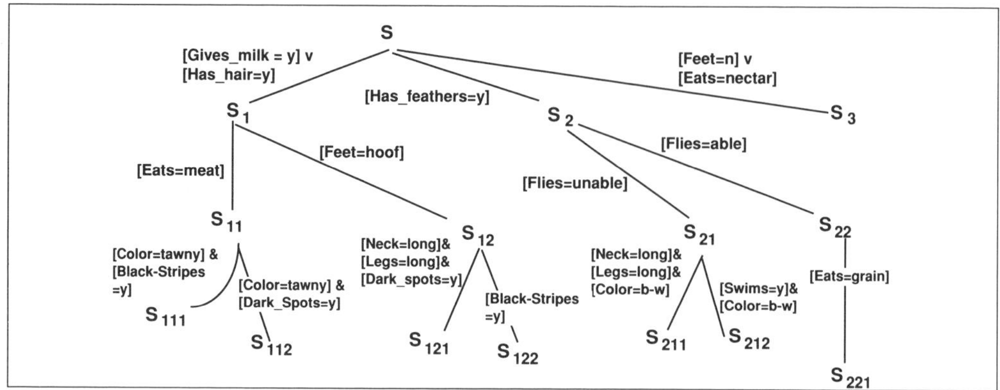

Figure 10.2
Clusters and Corresponding Descriptions Generated by Inheritance Knowledge Discovery.

the knowledge base of Winston's animal identification toy expert system was entirely discovered by Thought/KD1.

Notice that in figure 10.2, some new attribute values for individual animals are added to the database, such as [Color=tawny] and [Has_dark_stripes=yes] for tiger and that the new additional examples, such as eagle, viper, and bee, are needed to discover more accurate knowledge. For example, without the bee example, an inaccurate decision rule [Flies=able] → [Class=bird] would be discovered.

Other decision rules discovered by Thought/KD1 include:

[Class=Carnivorous_mammal] → [Class=mammal] because $S_{11} \in S_1^{(3)}$
and [Class=Carnivorous_mammal] → [Class=carnivore] because $S_{11} \in S_1^{(2)}$.
We can see that the rules discovered by Thought/KD1 are more accurate and reasonable than those given by Winston.

10.7.2 Refinement of Knowledge Bases

Similar to IKD, Thought/KD1 can be applied to refine the knowledge bases of expert systems. For example, consider again Winston's knowledge base, two rules of which are [Class=mammal][Feet=hoof] → [Class=ungulate] and [Gives_milk=yes] → [Class=mammal].

As shown in table 10.7, Thought/KD1 discovered a new rule for ungulate:

[Feet=hoof] → [Class=ungulate]. We see that by replacing the two original rules with the new rule, the knowledge base is refined.

Table 10.7
Rediscovering Knowledge Base of Animal World in Winston and Horn, *LISP,* (Addison Wesley,1984).

Name	Clusters	Knowledge Discovered
	Parallel Clustering	Combination of Parallel and Characteristic Discovery and Labeling
$S_1^{(3)}$	{1, 2, 3, 4}	[Has_hair=yes] ∨ [Gives_milk=yes] → [Class=mammal]
$S_2^{(3)}$	{5, 6, 7, 8}	[Has_feathers=yes] → [Class=bird]
$S_3^{(3)}$	{9, 10}	[Feet = no] ∨ [Eats=nectar] → $Label(S_3^{(3)})$
$S_1^{(2)}$	{1, 2, 8, 9}	[Eats=meat] → [Class=carnivore]
	Hierarchical Clustering	Combination of Hierarchical and Characteristic Discovery and Labeling
S_1	{1, 2, 3, 4}	[Has_hair=yes] ∨ [Gives_milk=yes] → [Class=mammal]
S_2	{5, 6, 7, 8}	[Has_feathers=yes] → [Class=bird]
S_3	{9, 10}	[Feet=no] ∨ [Eats=nectar] → $Label(S_3)$
S_{11}	{1, 2}	[Teeth=pointed][Feet=claw][Eyes=forward] → [Class=carnivorous_mammal]
S_{12}	{3, 4}	[Feet=hoof] → [Class=ungulate]
S_{21}	{5, 6}	[Has_feathers=yes][Flies=unable] → [Class=unflying_bird]
S_{22}	{7, 8}	[Flies=yes][Lays_eggs=yes] → [Class=flying_bird]
	Hierarchical Clustering	Combination of Labeling and Inheritance Discovery
S_1		[Has_hair=yes] ∨ [Gives_milk=yes] → [Class=mammal]
S_2		[Has_feathers=yes] → [Class=bird]
S_3		[Feet=no] ∨ [Eats=nectar] → $Label(S_3)$
S_1 S_{11}		[Class=mammal][Eats=meat] → [Class=carnivorous_mammal]
S_1 S_{12}		[Class=mammal][Feet=hoof] → [Class=ungulate]
S_2 S_{21}		[Class=bird][Flies=unable] → [Class=unflying_bird]
S_2 S_{22}		[Class = bird][Flies=able] → [Class=flying_bird]
S_{11} S_{111}		[Class=carnivorous_mammal][Color=tawny][Black_stripes=yes] → [Animal=tiger]
S_{11} S_{112}		[Class=carnivorous_mammal][Color=tawny][Dark_spots=yes] → [Animal=cheetah]
S_{12} S_{121}		[Class=ungulate][Neck=long][Legs=long]& [Dark_spots=yes] → [Animal=giraffe]
S_{12} S_{122}		[Class=ungulate][Black_stripes=yes] → [Animal=zebra]
S_{21} S_{211}		[Class=unflying_bird][Neck=long] & [Legs=long][Color=b-w] → [Animal=ostrich]
S_{21} S_{212}		[Class=unflying_bird][Swims=able][Color=b-w] → [Animal=penguin]
S_{22} S_{221}		[Class=flying_bird][Eats=grain] → [Animal=albatross]

10.8 Conclusion

The major contributions of this chapter are the presentation of a theoretical framework and the description of reasonable methods of incremental and constructive knowledge discovery. This theory is based on the observation of the cognitive process of human discovery. That is, knowledge discovery depends on the classification and abstraction of given examples, facts, and observations. The methodology is implemented by an integrated learning system, Thought/KD1, which mainly comprises a conceptual clustering system Leobs and a general-purpose, concept-learning system GS. Some interesting sample results show that Thought/KD1 is efficient and effective and can be applied to discover more complicated knowledge and refine knowledge bases in expert systems. In the future, we plan to test Thought/KD1 with large, real-world databases.

Acknowledgments

The authors would like to thank Gregory Piatetsky-Shapiro for his many valuable suggestions and discussions and his help in preparing this chapter. We would also like to thank Chris Matheus for revising this chapter. The research was supported in part by grants from the National Natural Science Foundation of China, 6875016 and 68973044.

References

Ganascia, J. G. 1987. Charade: A Rule System Learning System. In Proceedings of the Tenth International Joint Conference on Artificial Intelligence, 345–347. Menlo Park, Calif.: International Joint Conferences on Artificial Intelligence, Inc.

Goodman, R. M., and Smyth, P. 1988. Information-Theoretic Rule Induction. In Proceedings of the 1988 European Conference on Artificial Intelligence, 357–362. London: Pitman.

Haussler, D. 1988. Quantifying Inductive Bias: AI Learning Algorithms and Valiant's Learning Framework. *Artificial Intelligence* 36(2): 177–221.

Hong, J. R. 1988. Leobs: A System Learning by Observation (in Chinese), HIT-88-236, Dept. of Computer Science, Harbin Institute of Technology, China.

Hong, J. R. 1985. AE1: An Extension Matrix Approximate Method for the General Covering Problem. *International Journal of Computer and Information Sciences* 14(6): 421–437.

Hong, J. R., and Mao, C. J. 1989. Thought: A General Intelligence Architecture for Making Existing Expert Systems Rival the Performance of True Experts. Presented at the Second Workshop on Machine Learning, Guilin, China, August.

Hong, J. R., and Uhrik, C. 1988. A New Similarity Based Learning Algorithm GS and a Comparison with ID3. Presented at the International Computer Science Conference, Hong Kong, December.

Hong, J. R.; Michalski, R. S.; and Mozetic, I. 1986. AQ15: Incremental Learning of Attribute-Based Descriptions from Examples, The Method and User's Guide, ISG 86-5, UIUCDCS-F-86-949, Dept. of Computer Science, Univ. of Illinois at Urbana-Champaign.

Langley, P.; Simon, H. A.; Bradshaw, G.; and Żytkow, J. M. 1987. *Scientific Discovery: Computational Explorations of the Creative Processes.* Cambridge, Mass.: MIT Press.

Michalski, R. S.; Mozetic, I.; Hong, J. R.; and Lavrac, N. 1986. The Multi-Purpose Incremental Learning System AQ15 and Its Testing Application to Three Medical Domains. In Proceedings of the Fifth National Conference on Artificial Intelligence, 1041–1045. Menlo Park, Calif.: American Association for Artificial Intelligence.

Quinlan, J. R. 1986. Induction of Decision Trees. *Machine Learning* 1(1): 81–106.

Stepp, R. E., and Michalski, R. S. 1986. Conceptual Clustering: Inventing Goal-Oriented Classifications of Structured Objects. In *Machine Learning: An Artificial Intelligence Approach,* volume 2, eds. R. S. Michalski, J. Carbonell, and T. Mitchell, 471–498. San Mateo, Calif.: Morgan Kaufmann.

Winston, P., and Horn, B. K. 1984. *LISP.* Reading, Mass.: Addison-Wesley.

11 The Discovery, Analysis, and Representation of Data Dependencies in Databases

Wojciech Ziarko
University of Regina, Canada

Abstract

A technique for the identification and the analysis of data dependencies or cause-effect relationships in databases is presented. The technique is based on the mathematical theory of rough sets, which provides the necessary formalism to conduct the analysis. I demonstrate how to evaluate the degree of the relationship and identify the most critical factors contributing to the relationship. Identification of the most critical factors allows for the elimination of irrelevant attributes prior to the generation of rules describing the dependency.

11.1 Introduction

The perception and empirical discovery of cause-effect relationships is one of the most fundamental features of intelligent behavior. The discovery is based on experience accumulated through taking measurements, that is, by memorizing observations concerning states, processes, individuals, and so on. For example, in the medical domain, the statistical analysis of past patient records is one of the primary means of scientific research. The past records provide an invaluable repository of information that if used properly would improve our understanding of the nature of different diseases and, in effect, lead to more accurate diagnostic decisions. The databases of information of this kind have been built in different domains for years. The real-life cause-effect relationships assume the form of data dependencies in such databases. Consequently, discovering and analyzing data dependencies is of primary importance among the goals for reasoning from data.

Until recently, the only methodology available for reasoning from data was based on statistical methods. In many data analysis problems, however, statistical methods are not suitable either because of the strong statistical assumptions, such as the adherence to a particular probability distribution model, or the fundamental limitations of the statistical approach. The primary limitation is the inability to recognize and generalize relationships such as set inclusion from the structural data set after being entirely confined to arithmetic manipulations of probability measures. Although this approach frequently yields useful results, it also involves an information loss that in many problems is not acceptable. Problems of this kind arise in machine learning, particularly in empirical learning where the discovery and description of structural set relationships is of primary importance. A number of rule-extraction algorithms have been developed to achieve this task more efficiently (Michalski 1983; Quinlan 1986), and clearly, none of them could be substituted with existing statistical methods. The rule-generation algorithms, however, are narrow in their objective of finding a generalized description of a relationship because they are not designed to perform multiaspect data analysis. Many useful properties of data, such as functional data dependencies, are not explicitly analyzed by rule-extraction methods. A technique is needed to allow for comprehensive analysis of structural properties of data, that is, on the same detail level on which the rule generation is performed. The use of such a technique would allow for better understanding of data dependencies and some conclusions regarding the quality of the extracted rules prior to initializing the rule-generation process. The rule generation would be the final step in the data analysis and reduction procedure during which a body of knowledge would be established about what the degree of data dependencies is, what is relevant and what is possibly irrelevant with respect to an outcome, which factors are the most important, and so on.

Several years ago, a mathematical technique suitable for performing this kind of analysis, called *rough set theory*, was introduced by Pawlak (1982, 1984a, 1984b, 1986a, 1986b). This technique, which is complementary to statistical methods of inference, provides a new insight into properties of data. The main focus of this technique is on the investigation of structural relationships in data rather than probability distributions, as is the case in statistical theory. The rough set-based methods are particularly useful for reasoning from qualitative or imprecise data. Better-known experimental applications of this methodology include a control algorithm acquisition for process control (Mrozek 1987), the building of knowledge-acquisition interfaces for expert systems by using rough set-based machine learning techniques (Wong and Ziarko 1986a), decision table analysis and reduction (Pawlak 1986b; Ziarko 1987), conceptual engineering design (Arciszewski and Ziarko 1986), medical diagnosis (Pawlak, Slowinski, and Slowinski 1986), machine learning (Pawlak 1986a; Wong and Ziarko 1986b; Ras and Zemankowa 1987; Grzymala-Busse 1988), information retrieval (Gupta 1988), and approximate reasoning (Rasiowa and Epstein 1987; Wasilewska 1989).

In this chapter, I want to demonstrate a rough set-based technique for identifying and analyzing dependencies in data. By using a number of examples, I attempt to convey the basic ideas of the data analysis, data reduction and rule-extraction process based on rough sets. I try to compromise between minimizing the mathematical formalism and maximizing the clarity of the presentation. The computational results presented in this chapter were obtained with a personal computer–based system called Rough.

11.2 Principal Notions of Rough Sets

In this section, the principal notions of the rough set model will be introduced and illustrated with examples.

11.2.1 The Problem

The primary problem addressed by the technique of rough sets is the discovery, representation, and analysis of data regularities. The methodological approach that underlies the whole technique is based on the intuitive observation that lowering the degree of precision in the representation of objects, for example, by replacing the numeric temperature measurements by qualitative ranges of HIGH, NORMAL, or LOW, makes the data regularities more visible and easier to characterize in terms of rules. Lowering the representation accuracy, however, might lead to the undesired loss of information expressed in the reduced ability to discern among different concepts. To analyze and evaluate the effect of different representation accuracies on concept discernibility levels, a number of analytic tools, which are described in the following sections, were developed. By using these tools, one can attempt to find a representation method that would compromise between sufficient concept discernibility and the ability to reveal essential data regularities.

11.2.2 Limits of Discernibility

The bottom line of the presented approach is the analysis of limits of discernibility of a subset of objects X belonging to the domain, or universe, U. In other words, the central issue is the determination of how well subset X can be characterized in terms of the information available to represent objects of the universe U.

For example, if U is the collection of cars represented in terms of weight and engine size, and X is the subset of those cars that achieve high gas mileage, we could ask whether knowing the car weight and engine size is enough to tell the mileage.

In the model of rough sets, we always assume that an object-representation method, for example, in terms of attributes and their values, is available that would allow us to classify objects into indiscernibility classes. The representation technique (or the knowledge representation system) reflects adapted means of perception or observation whose natural resolution leads to the classification of objects. The limits of discernibility of objects are formally expressed by an equivalence relation IND over the set of objects U. In this context, the pair $APP = (U, IND)$ is called an *approximation space.* The equivalence classes of IND are also called *elementary sets* because they represent the smallest discernible groups of objects.

Let IND' be a collection of all elementary sets of the relation *IND*. Any subset X of U can be approximately characterized by the following two sets:

$$\underline{IND(X)} = \bigcup \{Y \in IND' : X \supseteq Y\}$$

and

$$\overline{IND(X)} = \bigcup \{Y \in IND' : Y \cap X \neq \emptyset\} \ ,$$

which are called the lower and the upper approximation of the set X, respectively. That is, the *lower approximation* of X is a union of those elementary sets Y that are completely included in X, whereas the *upper approximation* of Y is the union of those elementary sets that have non-empty intersection with Y. Whenever the lower approximation of the set X is different from its upper approximation, the set X cannot be precisely characterized by means of elementary classes of *IND*, and we say that the set X is *rough*. The degree of the imprecision is expressed by the accuracy measure

$$m(X) = card(\underline{IND}(X))/card(\overline{IND(X)}),$$

where *card* is a cardinality of a set.

The boundary area of the set X

$$BND(X) = \overline{IND(X)} - \underline{IND(X)}$$

consists of those objects whose membership status with respect to set X cannot be determined in a given knowledge representation system.

For any object in the lower approximation, it can be determined without ambiguity that it belongs to X, whereas we can only say about objects in the upper approximation that they possibly belong to X.

The negative region of the set X

$$NEG(X) = U - \overline{IND(X)}$$

consists of those objects of U about which we know with certainty that they do not belong to set X.

These three basic areas—lower approximation, boundary region, and negative region—are shown in figure 11.1. In this figure, the small rectangular blocks correspond to indiscernibility classes of an approximation space defined on U.

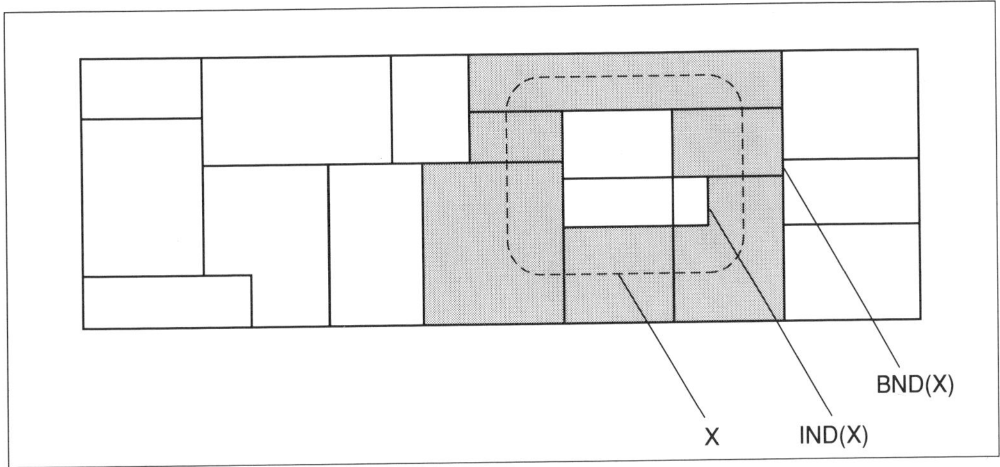

Figure 11.1
The Set X, its Lower Approximation, and the Boundary Region. The small rectangular blocks correspond to indiscernibility classes of an approximation space defined on U.

11.2.3 Analysis of Attribute-Value Systems

The notions of lower and upper approximations determine the discernibility limits of a knowledge representation system. Most commonly, objects are represented by sets of features, that is, by attributes and their values. By employing the definitions of lower and upper approximations, one can evaluate the usefulness of the given set of features with respect to the discrimination of the concept X from its complement U-X.

Formally, an attribute-value system (also known as an information system or knowledge representation system) is a quadruple (Marek and Pawlak 1973)

$$S = (U, A, V, f),$$

where U is a non-empty, finite set called universe, A is a finite set of attributes, $V = \cup V_a$ is a union of domains V_a of attributes a belonging to A, and $f : U \times A \rightarrow V$ is an information function such that $f(x, a) \in V_a$ for every $a \in A$ and $x \in U$.

The information function assigns attribute values to objects belonging to U.

The attribute-value system allows for convenient tabular representation of data describing objects, as is illustrated in example 1.

Example 1: In table 11.1, a collection of cars is described in terms of such attributes as overall length (**size**), number of cylinders (**cyl**), presence of a turbocharger (**turbo**), type

Table 11.1
An Example Attribute-Value System

U	size	cyl	turbo	fuelsys	displace	comp	power	trans	weight	mileage
1	compact	6	yes	EFI	medium	high	high	auto	medium	medium
2	compact	6	no	EFI	medium	medium	high	manual	medium	medium
3	compact	6	no	EFI	medium	high	high	manual	medium	medium
4	compact	4	yes	EFI	medium	high	high	manual	light	high
5	compact	6	no	EFI	medium	medium	medium	manual	medium	medium
6	compact	6	no	2-BBL	medium	medium	medium	auto	heavy	low
7	compact	6	no	EFI	medium	medium	high	manual	heavy	low
8	subcompact	4	no	2-BBL	small	high	low	manual	light	high
9	compact	4	no	2-BBL	small	high	low	manual	medium	medium
10	compact	4	no	2-BBL	small	high	medium	auto	medium	medium
11	subcompact	4	no	EFI	small	high	low	manual	light	high
12	subcompact	4	no	EFI	medium	medium	medium	manual	medium	high
13	compact	4	no	2-BBL	medium	medium	medium	manual	medium	medium
14	subcompact	4	yes	EFI	small	high	high	manual	medium	high
15	subcompact	4	no	2-BBL	small	medium	low	manual	medium	high
16	compact	4	yes	EFI	medium	medium	high	manual	medium	medium
17	compact	6	no	EFI	medium	medium	high	auto	medium	medium
18	compact	4	no	EFI	medium	medium	high	auto	medium	medium
19	subcompact	4	no	EFI	small	high	medium	manual	medium	high
20	compact	4	no	EFI	small	high	medium	manual	medium	high
21	compact	4	no	2-BBL	small	high	medium	manual	medium	medium

of fuel system (**fuelsys**), engine displacement (**displace**), compression ratio (**comp**), type of transmission (**trans**), and mileage (**mileage**). The information was collected from car test results published by *Popular Science*. To analyze such an information system with respect to the relationship between car mileage and other parameters, the mileage attribute was declared as a decision attribute Q, and all remaining attributes form a set of conditions P.

With every subset of attributes P of A, we can associate the structure of approximation space in S by defining the equivalence relation $IND(P)$ over U as follows:

$$(x, y) \in IND(P) \text{ iff } f(x, a) = f(y, a) \text{ for all } x, y \in U \text{ and } a \in P \ .$$

Relation $IND(P)$ induces a classification of objects into classes, each of which consists of objects with the same values of attributes belonging to P.

11.2.4 Dependency of Attributes

One of the main problems in the analysis of attribute-value systems with respect to discovering cause-effect relationships in data is the identification of dependencies among different groups of attributes.

Let P, Q be two groups of attributes called condition and decision attributes, respectively. Also, let Q' be the family of elementary sets of the relation $IND(Q)$.

In the approximation space $APP = (U, IND(P))$ we introduce the notion of a positive region of Q', $POS(P,Q)$ as a union of lower approximations of all elementary classes of the relation $IND(Q)$:

$$POS(P, Q) = \bigcup \{\underline{IND}(P, Y) \ : \ Y \in Q'\} \ ,$$

where $\underline{IND}(P, Y)$ is a lower approximation of the set Y in terms of elementary classes of the relation $IND(P)$.

According to this definition, to find the positive region of the partition Q', we have to compute the lower approximation of each class of Q' in the approximation space corresponding to the relation $IND(P)$. The set union of such lower approximations will form the positive region of the partition Q'. The positive region of Q' is a discernible part of U; that is, any object in $POS(P, Q)$ can be uniquely classified into one of the classes of Q' based solely on values of attributes in P.

We say that the set of attributes Q depends in degree $k(0 \leq k \leq 1)$ on the set of attributes P in S if

$$k(P, Q) = card(POS(P, Q))/card(U).$$

The value $k(P, Q)$ provides a measure of dependency between P and Q. If $k = 1$, then the dependency is full or functional; if $0 < k < 1$, then there is partial dependency; if $k = 0$, then the attributes P and Q are independent.

A dependency close to 1 gives reason to hypothesize that generally, there is a strong cause-effect relationship between attributes P and Q, and a dependency close to 0 suggests weak, if any, cause-effect relationship between P and Q.

Example 2: Suppose that we are interested in factors affecting car mileage. From table 11.1, we can compute the degree of dependency between condition attributes $P =$ {**size, cyl, turbo, fuelsys, displace, comp, power, trans, weight** } and the decision attribute $Q =$ **mileage** as

$$k(P, Q) = 1.$$

The full functional dependency means that the mileage of a car is affected by interactions of all or some possible causes represented by attributes contained in the set P. There is still an open question, however, about which combinations or interactions really affect the mileage and which are irrelevant. For instance, by assuming $P =$ { **size, power** }, we obtain

$$k(P, Q) = 0.269,$$

which implies that **size** and **power** are definitely not good enough to determine the **mileage**. This problem leads to the notion of a minimal set of attributes, or a *reduct*, as described in the next subsection.

11.2.5 Minimal Sets of Attributes

Another important issue in the analysis of dependencies among attributes is the identification and information-preserving reduction of redundant conditions. The objective is to find a minimal subset of interacting attributes that would have the same discriminating power as the original attributes. Finding such a subset would allow for the elimination of irrelevant, or noisy, attributes without any loss of essential information.

We say that the set of attributes P is independent with respect to the set of attributes Q if for every proper subset R of P

$$POS(P,Q) \neq POS(R,Q);$$

otherwise, P is said to be dependent with respect to Q.

The set of attributes R is a *minimal subset* of, or a *reduct*, of P if R is an independent subset of P with respect to Q such that

$$POS(R,Q) = POS(P,Q).$$

Intuitively, the minimal subset R satisfies the following conditions: (1) it preserves the degree of dependency between P and Q and (2) none of the attributes can be eliminated from the minimal subset R without affecting point 1. Although a single reduct can be computed relatively easily, the general problem of finding all reducts is NP-hard. An algorithm for solving that problem was implemented in Rough.

Example 3: The idea of a minimal subset can be used to find a nonredundant group in the set of condition attributes, as defined in example 2. Based on this minimal subset, we will be able to discern cars with respect to their acceleration with the same accuracy as when we use the full set of condition attributes.

Seven different minimal sets of attributes can be computed from the information system presented in table 11.1: (1) **cyl**, **fuelsys**, **comp**, **power**, **weight**; (2) **size**, **fuelsys**, **comp**, **power**, **weight**; (3) **size**, **fuelsys**, **displace**, **weight**; (4) **size**, **cyl**, **fuelsys**, **power**, **weight**; (5) **cyl**, **turbo**, **fuelsys**, **displace**, **comp**, **trans**, **weight**; (6) **size**, **cyl**, **fuelsys**, **comp**, **weight**; and (7) **size**, **cyl**, **turbo**, **fuelsys**, **trans**, **weight**.

Each of these minimal sets of attributes can be used to represent information about cars instead of all condition attributes.

One of the possible minimal subsets computed from table 11.1 is

$$R = \{\textbf{size}, \textbf{fuelsys}, \textbf{displace}, \textbf{weight}\}.$$

This subset means that with respect to the prediction of car mileage, based on the information in table 11.1, it is enough to consider only the car size, type of fuel, engine displacement, and car weight. Other factors can be disregarded, which is of practical value in real applications (for instance, costly but irrelevant tests can be eliminated from a diagnostic procedure).

11.2.6 Selection of the Best Minimal Set

Every minimal set of attributes can be perceived as an alternative group of attributes that could be used instead of all available attributes in the decision making based on cases. The main difficulty here is how to select an optimal reduct. This selection depends on the optimality criterion associated with attributes. If it is possible to assign a cost function to attributes, then the selection can be naturally based on the combined minimum cost criterion. For example, in the medical domain, some diagnostic procedures are much more expensive than others. By selecting the least expensive series of tests represented by the minimum cost reduct, considerable savings can be achieved without compromising the quality of the diagnosis. In the absence of an attribute cost function, the only source of information to select the reduct is the contents of the table. Two approaches are possible. First, the reduct with the minimal number of attributes is selected. Second, the reduct with the least number of combinations of values of its attributes is selected. The second approach favors a reduct that represents the strongest pattern or data regularity.

For instance, in the collection of reducts presented in example 3, the best reduct is the third, **size**, **fuelsys**, **displace**, **weight**, which only has 12 combinations of attribute values.

11.2.7 Significance of Attributes

The relative contribution or significance of an individual attribute a belonging to the minimal set R with respect to the dependency between R and Q is represented by significance factor SGF, given by

$$SGF(a, R, Q) = [k(R, Q) - k(R - \{a\}, Q)]/k(R, Q)$$

if $k(R, Q) > 0$.

Formally, the *significance factor* reflects the relative degree of decrease of dependency level between R and Q as a result of the removal of the attribute a from R. In practice, the stronger the influence of the attribute a is on the relationship between R and Q, the higher the value of the significance factor is.

Example 4: By computing the significance of attributes in the minimal set R as derived in example 3 with respect to $Q =$ **mileage**, we obtain the distribution shown in table 11.2.

The significance of each attribute given in table 11.2 is measured by the relative decrease of the dependency degree between reduct attributes and mileage caused by eliminating the attribute from the reduct. As we see, the size of the car is the most important factor, followed closely by weight and engine displacement.

Table 11.2
Significance of Reduct Attributes

Attribute	Significance
size	0.654
fuelsys	0.154
displace	0.500
weight	0.615

11.2.8 Core Set of Attributes

In some practical problems, it is often necessary to find the subset of attributes contained in all reducts, if one exists. The attributes contained in all reducts are also contained in the reduct that represents the real cause of a cause-effect relationship. Therefore, finding such attributes is equivalent to identifying some, if not all, features responsible for the causal relationship. As is demonstrated later, the computational procedure to find this set of attributes is relatively simple and, in some cases, can replace the more complex computation of all minimal subsets, which is, in fact, NP-hard (Wong and Ziarko 1985).

We say that an attribute $a \in P$ is superfluous if

$$POS(P,Q) = POS(P - \{a\}, Q);$$

otherwise, a is said to be *indispensable* in P.

The core is defined as a set of all indispensable attributes in P ; that is,

$$CORE(P,Q) = \{a \in P : POS(P,Q) \neq POS(P - \{a\}, Q)\} \ .$$

From this definition follows a simple rule that can be used in the computation of the core attributes. According to this rule, to determine whether an attribute a belongs to the core set, it suffices to compute the dependencies $k(P,Q)$ and $k(P, Q - \{a\})$, that is, before and after removing the attribute a from the set Q. If the dependencies are different, then a is one of the core attributes.

An important property of the core is given by proposition 1.

Proposition 1: Core equals the intersection of all minimal sets of P; that is,

$$CORE(P,Q) = \bigcap MIN(P,Q) \ ,$$

where $MIN(P,Q)$ is the family of all minimal sets of P with respect to Q.

In other words, core attributes are the ones that are included in every minimal subset. They can never be eliminated in the process of computation of reducts unless we are ready to disturb the dependency between condition and decision attributes.

Table 11.3
Data from Table 11.1 after Attribute Reduction

size	fuelsys	displace	weight	mileage
compact	EFI	medium	medium	medium
compact	EFI	medium	light	high
compact	2-BBL	medium	heavy	low
compact	EFI	medium	heavy	low
subcompact	2-BBL	small	light	high
compact	2-BBL	small	medium	medium
subcompact	EFI	small	light	high
subcompact	EFI	medium	medium	high
compact	2-BBL	medium	medium	medium
subcompact	EFI	small	medium	high
subcompact	2-BBL	small	medium	high
compact	EFI	small	medium	high

11.3 Generation of Decision Rules

One of the most fundamental features of the knowledge discovery system based on rough sets is a module for the generation of decision rules characterizing the dependency between condition and decision attributes. In what follows an example set of rules produced from table 11.1 is presented and explained.

11.3.1 Rules in the Decision Table Format: An Example

The decision rules are generated according to a new algorithm derived from the theory of rough sets. The system generates a set of production rules in the decision table format based on the reduced set of condition and decision attributes. In table 11.3, the current set of condition attributes is the best selected reduct computed from table 11.1 with respect to the decision attribute **mileage**.

Table 11.4 illustrates the set of rules produced from the reduced table. Rules are represented in the tabular form with the blank meaning "do not care." For example, row 5 in table 11.4 corresponds to the rule

if (**displace** = small) *and*
(**fuelsys** = EFI) *then* **mileage** = high.

All rules for a single decision are connected by an implied *or* Boolean operator. For instance, for medium mileage, the rule is as follows:

if [(**size** = compact) *and*
(**displace** = medium) *and*

Table 11.4
The Set of Rules Produced from the Reduced Table

CNo	DNo	size	fuelsys	displace	weight	mileage
13	16	compact		medium	medium	medium
4	16	compact	2-BBL		medium	medium
3	8			light		high
6	8	subcompact				high
4	8		EFI	small		high
2	2				heavy	low

(**weight** = medium)] *or*
[(**size** = compact) *and* (**fuelsys** = 2-BBL) *and*
(**weight** = medium)] *then* **mileage** = medium.

Two numeric columns (CNo and DNo in the rule display table) are used to evaluate the quality, or the strength, of the generated rules. CNo is the number of cases in the original table that support each given rule. For example, for rule 1 (CNo = 13), 13 cases in the table match rule conditions and have the decision value "medium". DNo is the number of cases with a particular decision value. For example, DNo = 16 means that 16 cases in the knowledge table have the decision value "medium". CNo provides a measure of strength or confidence associated with the rule. The higher CNo is, the more the rule is confirmed. Clearly, we would not rely on a rule based on one or a few cases unless it is known that the contents of the knowledge table exhaust all feasible combinations of attribute values.

11.3.2 Decision Tables Versus Decision Trees

Unlike other systems (Quinlan 1986), the generated rules do not form a decision tree that leads to a smaller number of conditions that would otherwise be required to maintain the tree structure. The primary format for the representation of original data and computed rules here is the decision table rather than the decision tree. Decision tables have already proven their usefulness in other areas, such as software engineering, planning, or, hardware logic design, and this system is essentially expanding their applicability into the knowledge discovery domain. Clearly, it is possible to express each decision tree in the decision table format, but the advantages of using decision tables containing decision trees are questionable. The main advantages of decision trees, such as the naturalness of hierarchical presentation of conditions and the efficiency of sequential processing, are lost when the decision tree is presented as a decision table. However, if for a particular application the hierarchical arrangement of conditions is not important, and the compactness and generality of rules are the critical factors, then the decision tables have a definite advantage.

11.4 Final Remarks

The technique described in this chapter is primarily appropriate for analyzing or generating rules from data in the decision table format. The decision table format means that the domain of each attribute should consist of a finite, preferably not large, set of values such as true or false or predefined qualitative categories such as Low, Medium, or High. To deal with continuous data, a conversion procedure must be provided to transform real numbers into several discrete categories. The definition of the conversion procedure, for instance, the specification of the qualitative ranges, is considered a part of the problem domain knowledge. It is hoped, however, that automatic conversion routines will be developed that make the approach domain expert independent.

Handling uncertainty and dealing with incomplete data are other issues to be addressed here. The pure rough set technique does not attempt to use the information in the boundary area of a concept, which, in some situations, leads to information loss and the inability to take advantage of statistical information. Some extensions to the original model have been proposed to rectify this limitation (Pawlak, Wong, and Ziarko 1988), but the general issue is still open.

The method of rough sets can help in filtering noisy data, in particular, the procedure for reduct computation, to discover groups of interacting attributes whose values form strong patterns in the data collection. In this way, the highly unstable noise attributes can be eliminated without information loss.

The techniques reported in this chapter were implemented in Turbo Pascal on an IBM AT. A general system for knowledge discovery called Rough was developed. The system consists of a spreadsheet-like table editor; a comprehensive data analysis module incorporating the ideas of rough sets; a rule-generation module; and an advisory subsystem to respond to user queries. In the most recent version, Rough can handle nondeterministic rules and incomplete data. The system has been used to experiment with data analysis and rule generation in different domains, including the analysis of speech. In this application, the method of reduct computation was used to eliminate unnecessary spectral frequencies to find the best representation for a group of spoken words. In the medical domain the method of rough sets was used with encouraging results for analysis of records of patients who suffered from duodenal ulcer (Pawlak, Slowinski, K., and Slowinski, R. 1986) A group of researchers at Wayne State University, Detroit, Michigan, have been using the approach of rough sets for structural design optimization (Arciszewski et al. 1987; Arciszewski and Ziarko 1986). The objective of the data analysis in this case is to find, based on the database of existing designs and verified performance data, a set of characteristic design rules that would relate design parameters with the degree of satisfaction of a particular optimality criterion.

Acknowledgments

Thanks are owed to Dr. Gregory Piatetsky-Shapiro and Dr. Larry Saxton whose remarks contributed to an improved version of this chapter. The research reported here was supported in part by a grant from the Natural Sciences and Engineering Research Council of Canada.

References

Arciszewski, T., and Ziarko, W. 1986. Adaptive Expert System for Preliminary Engineering Design. In Proceedings of the Sixth International Workshop on Expert Systems and Their Applications, 695–712. Paris: Agence de L'Informatique.

Arciszewski, T.; Ziarko, W.; and Mustafa, M. 1987. A Methodology of Design Knowledge Acquisition for Use in Learning Expert Systems. *International Journal of Man-Machine Studies* 27: 23–32.

Grzymala-Busse, J. 1988. Knowledge Acquisition under Uncertainty—A Rough Set Approach. *Journal of Intelligent and Robotic Systems* 1: 3–16.

Gupta, D. 1988. Rough Sets and Information Retrieval. In Proceedings of Eleventh International Conference on Research and Development in Information Retrieval. New York: Association for Computing Machinery.

Marek, W., and Pawlak, Z. 1973. Information Storage and Retrieval Systems—Mathematical Foundations, 149, Institute of Computer Science, Polish Academy of Sciences.

Michalski, R. S. 1983. A Theory and Methodology of Inductive Learning. *Artificial Intelligence* 20: 111–161.

Mrozek, A. 1987. Rough Sets and Some Aspects of Expert System Realization. In Proceedings of the Seventh International Workshop on Expert Systems and Their Applications, 597–611. Paris: Agence de L'Informatique.

Pawlak, Z. 1986a. On Learning–Rough Set Approach. *Lecture Notes* 208: 197–227. New York: Springer-Verlag.

Pawlak, Z. 1986b. Rough Sets and Decision Tables. *Lecture Notes* 208: 186–196. New York: Springer-Verlag.

Pawlak, Z. 1984a. On Rough Sets. *Bulletin of the European Association for Theoretical Computer Sciences* 24: 94–109.

Pawlak, Z. 1984b. Rough Classification. *International Journal of Man-Machine Studies* 20: 469–483.

Pawlak, Z. 1982. Rough Sets. *International Journal of Computer and Information Sciences* 11(5): 341–356.

Pawlak, Z.; Slowinski, R.; and Slowinski, K. 1986. Rough Classification of Patients after Highly Selective Vagotomy for Duodenal Ulcer. *International Journal of Man-Machine Studies* 24: 413–433.

Pawlak, Z.; Wong, S. K. M.; and Ziarko, W. 1988. Rough Sets: Probabilistic versus Deterministic Approach. *International Journal of Man-Machine Studies* 29: 81–95.

Quinlan, J. R. 1986. Learning Efficient Classification Procedures and Their Application to Chess and Games. In *Machine Learning: An Artificial Intelligence Approach,* eds. R. Michalski, J. Carbonell, and T. Mitchell, 463–482. San Mateo, Calif.: Morgan Kaufmann.

Ras, Z., and Zemankowa, M. 1987. On Learning with Imperfect Teachers. In Proceedings of the Second International Symposium on Methodologies for Intelligent Systems, 256–263. New York: North-Holland.

Rasiowa, H., and Epstein, G. 1987. Approximation Reasoning and Scott's Information Systems. In Proceedings of the Second International Symposium on Methodologies for Intelligent Systems, 33–42. New York: North Holland.

Wasilewska, A. 1989. Syntactic Decision Procedures in Information Systems. *International Journal of Man-Machine Studies*, 30: 273–285.

Wong, S. K. M., and Ziarko, W. 1986a. INFER–An Adaptive Decision Support System Based on Probabilistic Approximate Classification. In Proceedings of the Sixth International Workshop on Expert Systems and Their Applications, 713–726. Paris: Agence de L'Informatique.

Wong, S. K. M., and Ziarko, W. 1986b. On Learning of the Evaluation of Decision Rules in the Context of Rough Sets. In Proceedings of the International Symposium on Methodologies for Intelligent Systems, 308–324. New York: Association of Computing Machinery.

Wong, S. K. M., and Ziarko, W. 1985. On Optimal Decision Rules in Decision Tables. *Bulletin of Polish Academy of Sciences*, 33 (11–12): 693-696.

Ziarko, W. 1987. On Reduction of Knowledge Representation. In Proceedings of the Second International Symposium on Methodologies for Intelligent Systems (Colloquia Program), 99–113. Charlotte N.C.: Oak Ridge National Laboratory.

III USING KNOWLEDGE IN DISCOVERY

12 Attribute-Oriented Induction in Relational Databases

Yandong Cai, Nick Cercone, and Jiawei Han
Simon Fraser University

Abstract

An attribute-oriented induction method is developed to extract characteristic rules and classification rules from relational databases. The method adopts the AI learning from examples paradigm and applies in the learning process an attribute-oriented, tree-ascending technique that integrates database operations with the learning process and provides a simple and efficient way of learning from large databases. The method learns conjunctive rules as well as restricted forms of disjunctive rules. Moreover, incremental learning and learning in databases containing noise and exceptions can be performed by collecting quantitative information in the generalization process. Our analysis of the algorithms shows that attribute-oriented induction substantially reduces the complexity of the database learning processes.

12.1 Introduction

Learning is one of the most important characteristics of human and machine intelligence. Because relational database systems are pervasive and widely used in many applications, it is advantageous to learn knowledge in the form of rules from data in relational databases.

Relational database systems provide many attractive features for machine learning. They store a large amount of information in a structured and organized manner. Each tuple in the database can be viewed as a typed logical formula in the conjunctive normal form. Such uniformity facilitates the development of efficient learning algorithms. Moreover, well-developed database implementation techniques promote efficient learning algorithms in large databases.

Two types of rules, characteristic rules and classification rules, can easily be learned from relational databases. A *characteristic rule* is an assertion that characterizes the concept satisfied by all the data stored in the database. For example, the symptoms of a specific disease can be summarized as a characteristic rule. Alternatively, a *classification rule* is an assertion that discriminates the concepts of one class from that of others. For example, to distinguish one disease from another, a classification rule should summarize the symptoms that discriminate this disease from the other.

In this chapter, we develop an attribute-oriented induction method that extracts characteristic rules and classification rules from relational databases. Our method is demonstrated by two algorithms, learning characteristic rules (LCHR) and learning classification

Table 12.1
A Student Relation in a Sample University Database.

Name	Category	Major	Birth_Place	GPA
Anderson	M.A.	history	Vancouver	3.5
Bach	junior	math	Calgary	3.7
Carey	junior	literature	Edmonton	2.6
Fraser	M.S.	physics	Ottawa	3.9
Gupta	Ph.D.	math	Bombay	3.3
Hart	sophomore	chemistry	Richmond	2.7
Jackson	senior	computing	Victoria	3.5
Liu	Ph.D.	biology	Shanghai	3.4
Meyer	sophomore	music	Burnaby	2.9
Monk	Ph.D.	computing	Victoria	3.8
Wang	M.S.	statistics	Nanjing	3.2
Wise	freshman	literature	Toronto	3.9

GPA = grade point average.

rules (LCLR). Following the learning from examples paradigm, both algorithms apply an attribute-oriented, tree-ascending technique that integrates database operations with the learning process and provides a simple and efficient way of learning from large databases.

The chapter is organized as follows: The concepts of learning from relational databases are introduced in the next section. The learning of characteristic rules is then studied, followed by the learning of classification rules. Finally, a comparison with other learning algorithms is made.

12.2 Concepts of Learning from Databases

The large amount of facts stored in databases can be viewed as rich examples for various kinds of learning processes. Clearly then, learning from examples (Genesereth and Nilsson 1987) should be an important strategy for learning from databases.

The problem of learning from databases can be characterized by a triple (D, C, Λ), where D represents a set of data stored in the database, C represents a set of conceptual biases (generalization hierarchy, and so on) useful for defining particular concepts, and Λ is a language used to phrase definitions.

Example 1: We examine a small sample university database that consists of one relation, Student, as shown in table 12.1.

First, D is the set of data in the database relevant to a specific learning task. We call the class undergoing learning the *target class* to distinguish it from other classes. For example, to characterize the features of the target class Graduate Students, only the data relevant to graduates (table 12.2) are useful in the learning process. If the relevant data are spread over several relations, join operations should be performed on these relations to collect the relevant data before the algorithm is applied.

Most studies on learning from examples partition the set of examples into positive and negative sets. However, because a relational database usually does not explicitly store negative data, no specified negative examples can be used to perform specialization in learning. All the data stored in the database that characterize the features of a property are positive examples. For instance, the tuples relevant to graduates are positive examples because they represent the characteristics of graduates.

However, by adopting *the closed-world assumption* (Reiter 1984), which assumes that all the information about a property is stored in the database, negative data are implicitly given in databases. The task-relevant data that are not in the target class can be grouped into one class, called the *contrasting class.* Then the properties of the contrasting class should be taken as negative data. For instance, to distinguish a graduate from a nongraduate, the properties that belong to nongraduates define negative examples. It is necessary to incorporate such negative examples in learning classification rules.

We then examine C, the conceptual bias. It is often necessary to incorporate higher-level concepts in the learning process (Genesereth and Nilsson 1987). By organizing different levels of concepts into a taxonomy of concepts, a rule space can be partially ordered according to a general-to-specific ordering. The most general point in the rule space is the null description, and the most specific points correspond to the specific values of attributes in the database. Moreover, we restrict our candidate rules to formulas with a particular vocabulary, that is, a basis set that we call the *conceptual bias*, permitting the learned rules to be represented in a simple and explicit form.

The specification of conceptual bias is a necessary and natural process for learning. Usually, the conceptual bias is provided by knowledge engineers or domain-specific experts. Some conceptual hierarchies can also be discovered automatically using some

Table 12.2
The Set of Data Relevant to Graduate Students.

Name	Category	Major	Birth_Place	GPA
Anderson	M.A.	history	Vancouver	3.5
Fraser	M.S.	physics	Ottawa	3.9
Gupta	Ph.D.	math	Bombay	3.3
Liu	Ph.D.	biology	Shanghai	3.4
Monk	Ph.D.	computing	Victoria	3.8
Wang	M.S.	statistics	Nanjing	3.2

{ computing, math, biology, statistics, physics } $\subset$ science
{ music, history, literature } $\subset$ art
{ freshman, sophomore, junior, senior } $\subset$ undergraduate
{ M.S., M.A., Ph.D. } $\subset$ graduate
{ Burnaby, Vancouver, Victoria, Richmond } $\subset$ British Columbia
{ Calgary, Edmonton } $\subset$ Alberta
{ Ottawa, Toronto } $\subset$ Ontario
{ Bombay } $\subset$ India
{ Shanghai, Nanjing } $\subset$ China
{ China, India } $\subset$ foreign
{ British Columbia, Alberta, Ontario } $\subset$ Canada
{ 2.0 - 2.9 } $\subset$ average
{ 3.0 - 3.4 } $\subset$ good
{ 3.5 - 4.0 } $\subset$ excellent

Figure 12.1
A Concept Hierarchy Table of the University Database.

interesting techniques (Michalski 1983). We assume that conceptual clustering produces a small taxonomy for each attribute (that is, a hierarchy of classes in which the subclasses of each class are mutually exclusive and jointly exhaustive), which is represented as a concept tree. Such a concept tree is specified using an IS_A hierarchy and stored in a relation table, the *concept hierarchy table.*

For example, the concept hierarchy table of figure 12.1 can be specified for a university database, where $\{ A_1, \ldots, A_k \} \subset$ B indicates that B is a generalization of A_i, for $1 \leq i \leq k$, that is, A_i *IS_A B.*

Finally, we examine the language Λ. We use the first-order predicate calculus as the primitive language for learning from databases. From the logical point of view, each relation tuple is a formula in a conjunctive normal form. For example, the tuple

Name	Category	Major	GPA
Jackson	senior	computing	3.5

represents a logic formula,

$\exists\, t$ ((*Name(t)* = Jackson) $\bigwedge$ (*Category(t)* = senior) $\bigwedge$ (*Major(t)* = computing) $\bigwedge$ (*GPA(t)* = 3.5)) .

The intermediate and final learning results can also be represented using relational tables. Such a relation is called a *generalized relation.* The final generalized relation can contain several tuples that represent a disjunction of several conjunctions (tuples). Therefore, our logic bias (Genesereth and Nilsson 1987) on the learned rules (hypotheses) is not limited to conjunctive definitions but to a small number of disjuncts. Such relaxation makes learning more effective because it is often necessary to represent the learning results in disjunctive forms. A maximum number of disjuncts of the resulting formula, that is, the maximum number of tuples in a final generalized relation, can be specified by users as a *threshold* value of the learning process. For example, if a threshold value is three, the learning process will derive a rule consisting of at most three disjuncts, with each being a sequence of conjuncts. There is a trade-off between a reasonably large threshold and a small one. A smaller threshold leads to a simple rule with fewer disjuncts, but it can result in overgeneralization and the loss of some valuable information. However, a large threshold can preserve some useful information, but it can result in a relatively complex rule with many disjuncts and some inadequately generalized results. Therefore, fine tuning of thresholds is often necessary in the learning process.

12.3 Learning Characteristic Rules

For learning characteristic rules, the LCHR algorithm is developed as follows: An attribute-oriented, tree-ascending technique is applied that substitutes the lower-level concept (attribute value) in a tuple with its corresponding higher-level concept and, thus, generalizes the relation. As a result, different tuples may be generalized to the same concept. By eliminating identical tuples and using a threshold to control the generalization process, the final generalized relation consists of only a small number of tuples, which can be transformed into a simple logic formula. The process is illustrated in the following example. The detailed algorithm is presented in Cai, Cercone, and Han (1990b).

Example 2. This example concentrates on learning a characteristic rule for graduate students from the database in example 1. The algorithm consists of four steps.

Step 1 is the selection of the task-relevant data. The task-relevant data can be extracted by performing selection, projection, and join on the relevant relations. Clearly, in our example, the task-relevant data for learning characteristic rules for graduates can be so obtained, as shown in table 12.2. Then the attribute on which the data selection is based should be removed from the working relation because it is not relevant to the learning task afterwards. In this example, the task is to learn characteristics of graduates rather than to distinguish M.S. and Ph.D. students. Thus, the attribute Category should be removed after finding the set of relevant data.

Step 2 is the attribute-oriented induction process. If there are many distinct values in an attribute, and there are higher-level concepts provided for them in the concept

Table 12.3
A Generalized Relation.

Major	Birth_Place	GPA
art	B.C.	excellent
science	Ontario	excellent
science	B.C.	excellent
science	India	good
science	China	good

hierarchy table, generalization should be performed on this attribute by substituting each attribute value with its higher-level concept. For example, in table 12.2, "physics" can be replaced by "science," and "Vancouver" by "B.C.," and so on. This process corresponds to the generalization rule, *climbing generalization trees* (Michalski 1983). Such substitutions can result in having identical tuples in the relation which should be merged into one.

If there is a large set of distinct values of an attribute, but there are no higher-level concepts in their concept hierarchy tree, the ascending of the concept tree cannot be performed, and the attribute should be eliminated in generalization. A tuple is viewed as a set of conjuncts in a logical form. The removal of an attribute eliminates a conjunct and, thus, generalizes the rule. Such a removal of attributes corresponds to the generalization rule, *dropping conditions*, in learning from examples (Michalski 1983). For instance, the first attribute, Name, is the key of the relation in table 12.2. Because it contains a large set of distinct values that should be generalized, but there is no higher-level concept provided for this attribute in the concept hierarchy tree, the attribute should be eliminated.

By removing two attributes, Category and Name, and generalizing the three remaining ones, the relation depicted in table 12.2 is generalized to a small relation, shown in table 12.3.

As discussed in Concepts of Learning from Databases, the generalization process can be controlled by a threshold, a specified upper bound on the number of tuples in the final generalized relation. The generalization should be performed repeatedly until the number of tuples of the resulting relation is no more than the threshold.

In our example, suppose that the threshold value is set to three. Because the attribute Birth_Place in table 12.3 contains four distinct values, generalization should be performed on this attribute by ascending one level in the concept tree of the attribute, which results in the relation shown in table 12.4.

Notice that generalization can be performed on one attribute by ascending several levels up a concept tree without generating intermediate relations if such intermediate

Table 12.4
Further Generalization of the Relation.

Major	Birth_Place	GPA
art	Canada	excellent
science	Canada	excellent
science	Foreign	good

Table 12.5
Simplification of the Generalized Relation.

Major	Birth_Place	GPA
ANY	Canada	excellent
science	Foreign	good

relations still contain too many distinct values in an attribute. By such a multilevel tuple substitution, the processing cost can be reduced, which can be seen in our example. Because a generalization on Birth_Place generates more distinct values than the threshold, further generalization can be performed immediately to produce table 12.4 without generating the intermediate result, table 12.3.

Generalizing the relation ensures that the number of distinct values in each attribute of the resulting relation is no larger than the specified threshold. However, the total number of tuples in the resulting relation can still be above the threshold. In this case, further generalization on some attribute(s) should be performed. The choice of the attribute(s) to be generalized can depend on the tuple reduction ratio, simplicity of the final learned rule, and so on.

Step 3 is the simplification of the generalized relation. Simplification should be performed on the generalized relation when possible. For example, if several tuples share the same values in all their attributes except one, they can be reduced to one by taking the distinct values of this attribute as a set.

In table 12.4, the first two tuples can be reduced to one by taking "art" and "science" as one set. Because art and science cover all the Major's areas, {art, science} can further be generalized to ANY, as shown in table 12.5.

Step 4 is the transformation of the final relation into a logic formula. Based on the correspondence between relational tuples and logical formulas (Gallaire, Minker, and Nicolas 1984), the final relation can be transformed into a logic formula. That is, each tuple is transformed to a conjunctive normal form, and multiple tuples are transformed to a disjunctive normal form.

The relation of table 12.5 is equivalent to rule 1, a graduate is either a Canadian with an excellent GPA or a foreign student majoring in science with a good GPA:

$$\forall(x)\ \text{graduate}(x) \Longrightarrow (\text{Birth\_Place}(x) \in \text{Canada} \bigwedge \text{GPA}(x) \in \text{excellent}) \bigvee (\text{Major}(x) \in \text{science} \bigwedge \text{Birth\_Place}(x) \in \text{foreign} \bigwedge \text{GPA}(x) \in \text{good}).$$

Similarly, the characteristic rule for undergraduates is rule 2: An undergraduate is a Canadian.

$$\forall(x)\ \text{undergraduate}(x) \Longrightarrow (\text{Birth\_Place}(x) \in \text{Canada}).$$

THEOREM 1 Algorithm LCHR correctly learns characteristic rules from relational databases.

Proof: (Sketch) Step 1 collects the relevant data in the database for the target class. Step 2 generalizes the concepts in each attribute either by ascending the concept tree or by removing attributes, which simulates the generalization process of learning from examples. Moreover, the specified threshold ensures that the process of ascending the tree terminates when it reaches the threshold-controlled number of disjuncts. Steps 3 and 4 perform simplification and transformation based on the logic transformation rules. Thus, the obtained rule should be the desired result that characterizes the property of the data.

12.4 Learning Classification Rules

Here, we consider a second database learning algorithm, LCLR (Cai, Cercone, and Han 1990). The attribute-oriented induction process can also be applied to learning classification rules. The facts that support the target class serve as positive examples, and those that support the contrasting class serve as negative examples. To distinguish the target class from the contrasting class, the portion of the target class that overlaps with that of the contrasting class should be removed from the description of classification rules. We illustrate the algorithm using example 3.

Example 3. This example concentrates on learning a classification rule that distinguishes graduate students from undergraduate students in the relation of table 12.1. The algorithm has the following four steps:

Step 1 is the extraction of the data relevant to the learning task. This step is similar to step 1 of LCHR. Because all the classes relevant to the learning task are used in the learning process (as both positive and negative examples), it is necessary to extract them and cluster them according to the target class and the contrasting class.

Step 2 is the attribute-oriented induction process. Similar to LCHR, this algorithm repeatedly performs generalization by ascending the concept tree or removing attributes. Because different classes can share tuples, care must be taken in the generalization process. The tuples shared by both the target and constrasting classes (called *overlapping*

Table 12.6
A Generalized Relation.

Learning Concept	Major	Birth_Place	GPA	Mark
graduate	art	Canada	excellent	*
	science	Canada	excellent	*
	science	Foreign	good	
undergraduate	science	Canada	excellent	*
	art	Canada	average	
	science	Canada	average	
	art	Canada	excellent	*

tuples) should be marked, and such marks should be inherited in their generalized tuples. Because generalization can produce new overlapping tuples, a check for overlap should be performed at each level of ascent of the concept tree. The judgment of further generalization or attribute removal should rely on the number of unmarked tuples in the target class. The process iterates until the number of distinct values of each attribute of the unmarked tuples in the generalized relation is not beyond the threshold specified for the target class. After this point, if the portion of the resulting relation in the target class still contains more unmarked tuples than the threshold value, further generalization is still needed, which is similar to the LCHR process.

In our example, the attributes Name and Category are removed, and the remaining three attributes are generalized by ascending the concept tree. The resulting relation is shown in table 12.6. The first three tuples belong to the class of graduates, and the last four tuples belong to the class of undergraduates.

Step 3 is the simplification of the final generalized relation. In this step, the marked tuples are eliminated, and the simplification process is performed similar to that of LCHR.

Step 4 is the transformation of the final relation into logic formulas. This step is similar to step 4 in LCHR. However, the resulting formula in LCLR is a sufficient condition of the target class, but that in LCHR is a necessary condition of the target class. This is explained in more detail in the next section.

In our example, the classification rule for graduates is rule 3: If a student is from a foreign country, majoring in sciences with a good GPA, s/he is a graduate student:

$$\forall(x)\ \text{graduate}(x) \Longleftarrow \text{Major}(x) \in \text{science} \bigwedge \text{Birth\_Place}(x) \in \text{foreign} \bigwedge \text{GPA}(x) \in \text{good}.$$

Similarly, the classification rule for undergraduates is rule 4: If a student is a Canadian with an average GPA, s/he is an undergraduate student.

$$\forall(x)\ \text{undergraduate}(x) \Longleftarrow \text{Birth\_Place}(x) \in \text{Canada} \bigwedge \text{GPA}(x) \in \text{average}.$$

THEOREM 2 Algorithm LCLR correctly learns classification rules from relational databases.

Proof: (Sketch) Step 1 collects relevant data in the database for the learning task. Step 2 generalizes the concepts in each attribute either by removing attributes to get rid of the attribute that cannot be effectively generalized or by ascending the concept tree to generalize the values under the conceptual bias. The marked tuples, which are overlapped between classes, are eliminated in the rule formation, which guarantees that the learned rule has the discriminating property. The specified threshold limits the generalized rules to a small number of disjuncts. The simplification and transformation in steps 3 and 4 are based on the logic transformation rules and the correspondence between relational tuples and logic formulas. Thus, the algorithm correctly learns classification rules from databases.

12.5 Discussion

We first analyze our learning algorithms; compare them with traditional learning methods; and then discuss some important issues, such as the incorporation of statistical information to handle noise and exceptions and incremental learning from database updates.

12.5.1 Algorithm Analysis

We developed two interesting algorithms, LCHR and LCLR, for learning from databases. Both algorithms are attribute oriented and data driven. They start with a large number of data and perform generalization, attribute by attribute and step by step, without referring to a fixed model.

The first algorithm, LCHR, takes tuples relevant to the target class as positive examples and adopts the *least commitment principle* (that is, commitment to minimally generalized concepts) by ascending the concept tree only when necessary. Because the generalized rule covers all the positive examples in the database, it forms the necessary condition of the target class; that is, the rule is in the form

$$\text{target\_class(x)} \Longrightarrow \text{condition}(x),$$

where condition(x) is a formula containing x. The condition holds for all the examples in the target class. However, because data in the contrasting class are not taken as negative examples in the learning process, there could be data in the contrasting class that also meet the specified condition. Therefore, the learned rule might not be a sufficient condition of the target class.

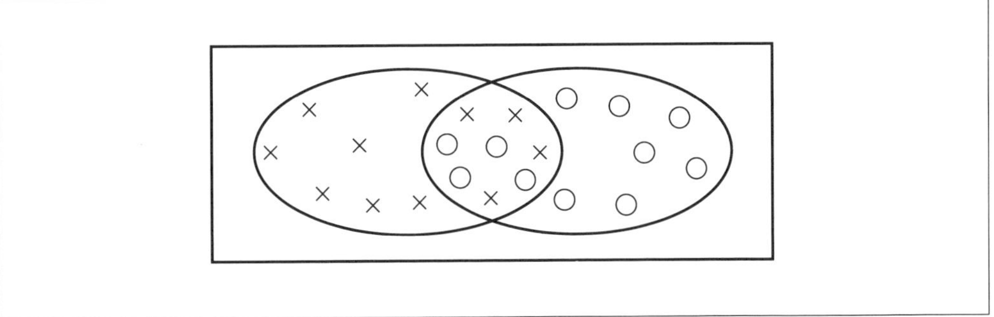

Figure 12.2
Problem Space in Learning Classification Rules.

The second algorithm, LCLR, treats the tuples of the target class as positive examples and tuples of the contrasting class as negative examples. Nevertheless, LCLR adopts the least commitment principle by ascending the concept tree only when necessary. Figure 12.2 shows schematically the problem space in learning classification rules, where $\bigcirc$ represents a tuple in the target class, and $\times$ represents a tuple in the contrasting class. Because the generalized rule excludes the concepts that cover the tuples in the contrasting class, it distinguishes the target class from the contrasting class. However, the generalization usually does not cover all the positive examples in the database. Therefore, the learned rule forms the sufficient condition of the target class but not the necessary condition, that is, the rule should be in the form

$$\text{target\_class}(x) \Longleftarrow \text{condition}(x).$$

That is, if an instance x meets the specified condition, it must be in the target class.

As a special case in which there are no overlapping data discovered (marked) in the learning process by the LCLR algorithm, the learned rule represents both necessary and sufficient conditions of the target class because it covers all the positive examples but no negative examples. The rule is of the form

$$\text{target\_class}(x) \Longleftrightarrow \text{condition}(x).$$

12.5.2 Comparison to Other Learning Algorithms

Our algorithms can be considered as implementations of a typical method of learning from examples, the *version space method* (Cohen and Feigenbaum 1983; Russell and Grosof 1987), in relational database systems. However, our approach has some distinct features.

First, the version space method learns classification rules from both positive and negative examples. The positive instances are for generalization, and the negative instances are for specialization. However, our approach mainly relies on the generalization process, that is, the least commitment generalization and the threshold control. Negative data are never used in the LCHR algorithm. They are used in the LCLR algorithm to extract the features not shared by the contrasting class. The specialization in the LCLR algorithm is based on overlapping instances, which is different from the specialization based on negative instances in learning from examples.

Second, the version space method adopts tuple-oriented generalization. In contrast, we adopt the attribute-oriented generalization, which treats a concept hierarchy of each attribute as a factored version space and performs generalization on individual attributes. Factoring the version space can significantly improve the computational efficiency. Suppose there are p nodes in each concept tree and k concept trees (attributes) in the relation; then the total size of k factorized version spaces is $p \times k$, and the size of the unfactorized version space for the same concept tree is p^k (Subramanian and Feigenbaum 1986). The search space for attribute-oriented generalization is much smaller than the space for tuple-oriented generalization.

The efficiency of the attribute-oriented generalization can also be demonstrated by analyzing its worst-case time complexity. Suppose there are N tuples in the database that are relevant to the learning task, A attributes for each tuple, and H levels for each concept tree; the run-time complexity in the worst case is then analyzed as follows: For each attribute, the time for substituting the lower-level concepts by the higher-level concepts is N, and the time for checking redundant tuples is $NlogN$. Because the height of the concept tree is H, the time spent on each attribute is at most $H \times (N + NlogN)$. Obviously, the upper bound of the total time for processing A attributes is $A \times H \times (N + NlogN)$. In general, A and H are much smaller than N in a large database. Therefore, the time complexity of our approach is $O(NlogN)$ in the worst case, which is more efficient than tuple-oriented generalization (Russell 1988).

Third, our approach integrates the learning process with database operations. Most of the operations in the algorithms are traditional relational database operations, such as selection, join, and projection (for extracting relevant data and removing attributes), tuple substitution (for ascending concept trees), and intersection (for discovering overlapping tuples). Such operations are set oriented and have been efficiently implemented in relational systems. Although most other learning algorithms suffer from inefficiency problems in a large database environment because of their tuple-oriented exhaustive search, our approach provides an efficient solution to learning in databases (Dietterich and Michalski 1983).

Furthermore, our algorithms can learn disjunctive rules, which provides additional flexibility over the version space method. By incorporating statistical information in the learning process, our approach can handle noise or exceptional data and perform incremental learning elegantly, as discussed in the following subsection.

12.5.3 Using Statistics to Handle Noise and Exceptions

In many applications, a generalization might not cover all the instances in a database. For example, 95 percent of the patients suffering from a disease might have similar symptoms, but 5 percent of them might have some unusual symptoms. If the unusual cases are not excluded, no universally generalized rule can be found under such circumstances.

Many researchers consider a small number of unusual cases as noisy or exceptional data, and techniques have been developed to cope with noise and exceptions (Manago and Kodratoff 1987; Wong and Chan 1988). The LCHR and LCLR algorithms can be extended to handle noise and exceptions. Our technique is to incorporate quantitative information in the learning process. A special attribute, *votes*, is attached to each tuple in the generalized relation, which registers the number of tuples in the initial relation that are generalized to the tuple in the current generalized relation. The vote of each tuple in the initial data relation is assumed to be one. In the generalization process, the vote of each tuple is propagated to its generalized tuples and accumulated in the preserved tuple when other identical (thus redundant) tuples are removed from the generalized relation.

Based on the votes information, two weights, t-weight and d-weight, can be calculated and associated with the learned rule. The *t-weight* represents the typicality of each disjunct in the rule, and the *d-weight* indicates the discriminating ability of each disjunct in the rule.

Suppose there are n tuples $\{q_1, q_2, ..., q_n\}$ in the generalized relation. The t-weight for the tuple q_j is the ratio of the votes in the original tuples covered by q_j to the total number covered by all the tuples; that is,

$$t\_weight = \frac{votes(q_j)}{\sum_{i=1}^{n} votes(q_i)} .$$

However, suppose there are k classes $\{C_1, C_2, ..., C_k\}$ in the generalized relation in which C_j is the target class. (In our discussion, we assume $k = 2$, that is, there are only two classes: the target class and the contrasting class.) The d-weight for the tuple q_j (referring to the target class) is the ratio of the number of original tuples in the target class covered by q_j to the total number of tuples in both the target class and the remaining classes covered by q_j; that is,

$$d\_weight = \frac{votes(q_j \; in \; C_j)}{\sum_{i=1}^{k} votes(q_j \; in \; C_i)} .$$

Because t-weight and d-weight carry database statistics, they can be used to prune noisy and exceptional data in the generalization process (Han, Cai, and Cercone 1990). A high t-weight implies that the concept is induced from the majority of data, and a low t-weight implies that the concept is induced from some rare, exceptional cases. By pruning low t-weighted tuples, the final generalized relation characterizes the majority number of facts in the database. Similarly, the d-weight of a nonoverlapping tuple is always one. A tuple with a high d-weight (close to one) indicates that the tuple is mainly generalized from the original tuples in the target class with only some exceptional cases from the contrasting class; a tuple with a low d-weight (close to zero) indicates that it is mainly from the contrasting class with only some exceptional cases from the target class. Because only the tuples with high discriminating behavior are able to discriminate one class from others, only the high d-weighted tuples should be included in the classification rule.

In practice, we can specify *pruning thresholds* for t-weights and d-weights to prune exceptional cases and noisy data in generalization. Moreover, similar pruning can also be performed during the generalization process. For example, the selection of a candidate attribute for further generalization can be based mainly on the examination of those tuples that carry a majority number of votes.

12.5.4 Incremental Learning on Database Updates

Because updates are frequently encountered in many databases, a flexible database learning technique should allow learning to be performed incrementally on database updates (Kulkarni and Simon 1988). Incremental learning avoids restarting the costly learning process from scratch on database updates.

Interestingly, using the votes information obtained in the previous learning process, incremental learning can be performed efficiently and effectively on database insertions. We assume that the generalized relation of a learning task is stored and associated with the special attribute votes. When a tuple is added to the database, each attribute of the new tuple is first generalized to the same concept level as those in the original generalized relation. The newly generalized tuple is then merged into the generalized relation. If there is an identical tuple in this relation, the effect is simply an increment of the votes of the identical tuple. Otherwise, it is inserted as a new tuple in the final generalized relation. If the size of the newly formed generalized relation is larger than the threshold value, further generalization should be performed on it to derive a new final generalized relation. Similarly, this incremental learning method can be applied to database deletions and updates as well.

12.6 Conclusion

It is attractive and challenging to automatically extract knowledge rules from large databases. We studied the process of learning characteristic rules and classification rules from relational databases and developed two efficient database learning algorithms, LCHR and LCLR. Both algorithms adopt an attribute-oriented induction approach, which integrates database operations with the learning process and provides an efficient way of learning knowledge from relational databases.

The algorithms were implemented in a prototyped database learning system, DBLearn, which is written in C, using the Oracle relational database system and the Unix facilities LEX and YACC. The system is running on a Sparc workstation, and preliminary experiments have demonstrated that attribute-oriented induction is an efficient and promising approach for the discovery of knowledge rules in relational databases.

There are many interesting research issues related to learning from data and knowledge bases. The automatic discovery of concept hierarchies in databases, the discovery of knowledge from deductive databases, and the integration of deduction and induction processes in databases are the important topics for future research.

Acknowledgments

The work was supported in part by the Natural Sciences and Engineering Research Council of Canada under grant A-4309 and in part by a research grant from the Centre for System Science at Simon Fraser University.

12.7 References

Cai, Y.; Cercone, N.; and Han, J. 1990a. An Attribute-Oriented Approach for Learning Classification Rules from Relational Databases. In Proceedings of the Sixth International Conference on Data Engineering, 281–288. Los Angeles, Calif.

Cai, Y.; Cercone, N.; and Han, J. 1990b. Learning Characteristic Rules from Relational Databases. In *Computational Intelligence II*, eds. Gardin and G. Mauri, 187-196. New York: Elsevier.

Cohen, P., and Feigenbaum, E. A. 1983. *The Handbook of Artificial Intelligence,* volume 3. Los Altos, Calif.: William Kaufmann.

Dietterich, T. G., and Michalski, R. S. 1983. A Comparative Review of Selected Methods for Learning from Examples. In *Machine Learning: An Artificial Intelligence Approach*, volume 1, eds. R. S. Michalski, J. G. Carbonell, and T. M. Mitchell, 41–82. San Mateo, Calif.: Morgan Kaufmann.

Gallaire, H.; Minker, J.; and Nicolas, J. 1984. Logic and Databases: A Deductive Approach. *ACM Computing Surveys*, 16(2): 153–185.

Genesereth, M., and Nilsson, N. 1987. *Logical Foundations of Artificial Intelligence*. San Mateo, Calif.: Morgan Kaufmann.

Han, J.; Cai, Y.; and Cercone, N. 1990. Discovery of Quantitative Rules from Large Databases. In *Methodologies for Intelligent Systems*, 5, eds. Z. W. Ras, M. Zemankova, and M. L. Emrich, 157–165. New York: Elsevier.

Kulkarni, D., and Simon, H. A. 1988. The Process of Scientific Discovery: The Strategy of Experimentation. *Cognitive Science* 12: 139–175.

Manago, M. V., and Kodratoff, Y. 1987. Noise and Knowledge Acquisition. In Proceedings of the Tenth International Joint Conference on Artificial Intelligence, 348–354. Menlo Park, Calif.: International Joint Conferences on Artificial Intelligence, Inc.

Michalski, R. S. 1983. A Theory and Methodology of Inductive Learning. In *Machine Learning: An Artificial Intelligence Approach*, volume 1, eds. R. S. Michalski, J. G. Carbonell, and T. M. Mitchell, 83–134. San Mateo, Calif.: Morgan Kaufmann.

Reiter, R. 1984. Towards a Logical Reconstruction of Relational Database Theory. In *On Conceptual Modeling*, eds. M. Brodie, J. Mylopoulos, and J. Schmidt, 191–233. New York: Springer-Verlag.

Russell, S. J. 1988. Tree-Structured Bias. In Proceedings of the 7th National Conference on Artificial Intelligence, 641–645. Los Altos, Calif.: Morgan Kaufman.

Russell, S. J., and Grosof, B. N. 1987. A Declarative Approach to Bias in Concept Learning. In Proceedings of the Sixth National Conference on Artificial Intelligence, 505-510. Menlo Park, Calif.: American Association For Artificial Intelligence.

Subramanian, D., and Feigenbaum, J. 1986. Factorization in Experiment Generation. In Proceedings of the Fifth National Conference on Artificial Intelligence, 518-522. Menlo Park, Calif.: American Association For Artificial Intelligence.

Wong, A. K. C., and Chan, K. C. C. 1988. Learning from Examples in the Presence of Uncertainty. In Proceedings of the International Computer Science Conference '88, 369–376. Hong Kong.

13 Discovery, Analysis, and Presentation of Strong Rules

Gregory Piatetsky-Shapiro
GTE Laboratories Incorporated

Abstract

I address the problem of the discovery of exact or almost exact rules in databases. First, I discuss rule-interest measures and present several desirable properties of such measures. I then describe KID3, a near-optimal algorithm for discovery of all simple strong rules, and outline methods for structuring and presenting the discovered rules. Finally, I derive general formulas for estimating the accuracy of sample-derived rules on the full data set. Tests using real data showed good agreement between the predicted and actual rule accuracy. Tests also revealed several ways to improve on statistical estimation by using domain knowledge.

13.1 Introduction

The increasing computerization of all parts of life, especially in the industrial world, creates an ever-increasing stream of data. Transactions such as making a telephone call, using a credit card, and even shopping in a supermarket are being routinely recorded, with all the corresponding details, and stored in some database. Many companies are now looking at ways to use this data resource.

The type of rule or pattern that exists in data depends on the domain. Discovery systems have been applied to real databases in medicine (Blum 1982), computer-aided design (see chapter 22), astronomy (Cheeseman et al. 1988), the stock market (Beard 1989), and many other areas (see also chapter 1).

Scientific data are likely to have quantitative patterns such as Boyle's law, $PV = c$. If the experiment is properly controlled to deal with only one cause, then usually a single pattern exists in data. Systems such as BACON (Langley et al. 1987) or those in part I of this volume address the discovery of quantitative patterns.

Business databases are different. The collected data typically reflect the uncontrolled real world, where many different causes overlap, and many patterns are likely to exist simultaneously. The patterns are likely to have some uncertainty: if A, then B with certainty C. Many methods for deriving such rules have been proposed, including Gaines and Shaw (1986), Quinlan (1987), Cendrowska (1987), Clark and Niblett (1989), and parts II and III of this collection.

The eventual use of the pattern determines the approach to finding it. The most studied problem has been *classification*: Given examples that belong to one of the pre-specified classes determine a method for classifying them (Quinlan 1986; Breiman et al.

1984). The problem I address here is the discovery of interesting rules in data when no prespecified classes exist. It can also be described as discovery of characteristic rules or data summarization.

At GTE Laboratories, I am involved in building a knowledge discovery workbench, an interactive system for intelligent data analysis, that is designed to integrate several different discovery tasks (including classification and summarization); access existing large databases and data dictionaries; use domain knowledge in many aspects of discovery; and present the discovered patterns in a visual, human-oriented way. The work on finding strong rules reported in this chapter is part of this effort.

An *exact* rule is one that is always correct. Most exact rules in a database represent some domain dependency and are usually (but not always) known to database users. Exact rules are part of the domain knowledge and, thus, are useful for any application. In addition, they can be used directly for providing high-level answers to user requests (Imielinski 1987) or semantic query optimization (Malley and Zdonik 1986).

A *strong* rule is one that is almost always correct. Such approximate rules are useful for decision support and the giving of approximate answers to statistical queries. Expert system rules are usually strong ones.

In this chapter, I propose several intuitively correct principles that all rule-interest functions should satisfy. I show how to precompute field statistics and describe KID3 (knowledge in databases 3), a fast algorithm for parallel discovery of all simple exact rules in data. The algorithm is asymptotically optimal because it accesses each data tuple just once. The discovered rules can be structured and presented in visually appealing ways.

I also derive formulas for estimating the accuracy of sample-derived rules on the full data set. The formulas are general and are independent of the rule-generation method. Testing the prediction formulas on real data produced good results. Testing also indicated where domain knowledge can be used to improve on purely statistical prediction.

13.2 Database Rules

A database rule is $(C_1 \rightarrow C_2)$, where C_1 and C_2 are conditions on a database universal relation. This universal relation is a logical file combining all fields of interest and, possibly, using joins and arbitrary user-specified computed fields. Here, I do not consider the details of obtaining a universal relation (see Ullman 1982) and assume that it can be materialized as a single file. I also limit myself to simple one-field comparisons in both a rule's left-hand side (LHS) and right-hand side (RHS). I do, however, show how to extend my approach to more complex conditions.

Different comparisons are meaningful for different field-value domains. There are two basic kinds of domains: An *ordered* or *interval* domain has a linear order among all its values. For example, field Charge has values between 0 and 10,000. The meaningful comparisons for an interval field A are $A \leq a$, $A \geq a$, $a_1 \leq A \leq a_2$, and similar comparisons with strict inequalities. An *unordered* or *nominal* domain is a simple unordered list of values. For example, possible values for Customer-Type are BUS (business customers), FED (federal government), GTE (GTE internal account), IXC (interexchange carrier), and so on. The meaningful comparisons for a nominal field A are $A = a$ or $A = a_1 \vee ... \vee a_k$.

Frequently, values in an unordered domain have an externally defined structure (see Figure 13.1). For example, customers of the type Federal government, GTE internal account, or Inter-exchange carrier have many properties common to large organizations. Defining the node Large-organization = FED or GTE or IXC in the hierarchy of Customer-Type values makes it easier to find rules about large organizations and allows for a natural expression of rules where Customer-Type = FED or GTE or IXC. Domains with such hierarchies of values are called *structured* and have an additional comparison operator, A is-a *concept*.

Many business databases have extensive data definition manuals that contain such hierarchical structures. In other cases, we can find the structure from exact rules, such as discovered by the KID3 algorithm.

13.3 Rule-Interest Measures

Different functions for rule-utility measures have been introduced by Quinlan (1987), Gaines (chapter 29), Goodman and Smyth (chapter 9), Hong and Mao (chapter 11) and others. Some of these functions require substantial computation. Usually, the interest of rule $A \rightarrow B$ is computed as a function of $p(A)$—the probability of A; $p(B)$; $p(A\&B)$; rule complexity, and, possibly, other parameters, such as the mutual distribution of A and B or the domain sizes of A and B. User-specified interest weights for different fields can also be considered.

The typical rule-discovery task is to find K rules with the highest rule-interest function RI. Later, I propose several intuitive principles that all rule-interest functions should satisfy. I conjecture that all RI functions satisfying these principles will assign high values to strong rules and low values to weak rules. The specific ordering among rules can be different, but the separation of strong and weak rules would approximately be the same. This conjecture is supported by two recent studies by Mingers (1989a, 1989b) that show that the decision tree accuracy is almost independent of the measure used to select the splitting node. If so, the simplest function that satisfies these principles can

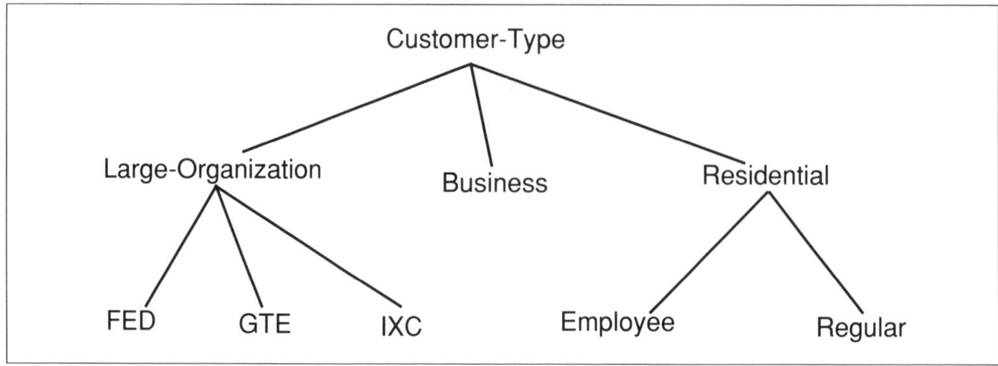

Figure 13.1
The Structure of a Customer-Type Domain.

be used for faster computations.

Let N be the file size or the total number of tuples. Let $|A|$ denote the number of tuples that satisfy a condition A. Then $|B|$ tuples satisfy B, and $|A\&B|$ tuples satisfy $A \rightarrow B$. I examine the behavior of a rule-interest function RI with respect to these parameters. The proposed principles are as follows:

1. $RI = 0$ if $|A\&B| = \frac{|A||B|}{N}$. If A and B are statistically independent, the rule is not interesting.
2. $RI \nearrow$ (monotonically increases with) $|A\&B|$ when other parameters remain the same.
3. $RI \searrow$ (monotonically decreases with) $|A|$ (or $|B|$) when other parameters remain the same.

These principles have some interesting implications. First, $RI > 0$ if $|A\&B| > |A||B|/N$ (that is, A is positively correlated to B), and $RI < 0$ if $|A\&B| < |A||B|/N$ (that is, A is negatively correlated to B). In this respect, RI is similar to the correlation coefficient between A and B. Second, because we always have $|A\&B| \leq |A| \leq |B|$, principles 2 and 3 imply that RI has local maxima when $|A\&B| = |A|$ or $|A| = |B|$ and a global maximum when $|A\&B| = |A| = |B|$.

The simplest function that satisfies these principles is $|A\&B| - \frac{|A||B|}{N}$. This function can intuitively be understood as the difference between the actual number of data tuples with $A\&B$ and the number expected if B were independent of A.

Measuring the significance of the correlation between A and B is a standard statistical problem for 2 x 2 contingency tables. The usual measurement is

$$\phi = \frac{|A\&B| - |A||B|/N}{\sqrt{|A||B|(1 - |A|/N)(1 - |B|/N)}}, \tag{13.1}$$

which is approximately normally distributed (Iman and Conover 1983). It also satisfies the proposed principles.

These principles can be extended to other rule parameters, for example, $RI \searrow$ rule complexity or $RI \nearrow$ sample size (see also chapter 11). These principles are also symmetric with respect to A and B, which appears to be counterintuitive. However, work on discovery of causal theories (Verma and Pearl 1990) has shown that different models can be equivalent with respect to the same data. Further analysis of these principles is an interesting research problem.

13.4 Precomputing Field-Value Statistics

Never use statistics
when you know what you are talking about.

To speed interactive discovery on large databases, we can precompute answers to frequent run-time computations, such as "How many tuples satisfy a particular condition?" For simple conditions such as $A = a$ or $a_1 \leq A \leq a_2$, the answer can easily be obtained from field statistics as described in the following paragraphs.

For fields with unordered domains (for example, Customer-Type), I store all value frequencies that exceed a user-specified threshold. For the remaining values, I store their total count and the number of distinct values. With these statistics, the cardinality of conditions such as $A = a_1 \vee \ldots \vee a_k$ can be estimated efficiently and accurately.

For fields with ordered domains (for example, Charge), I have developed the *adjustable buckets method*, which is a refinement of the field distribution steps method described by Piatetsky-Shapiro and Connell (1984). The distribution steps method sorts all field values and then keeps the first value; the last value; and values in positions $S+1$, $2S+1$, and so on, where S is the step size (example 1).

Example 1. Steps for the Sorted List of Charges (step-size S = 3).

Charge	0.0	0.0	0.0	0.0	0.0	1.5	2.7	19.7	19.7	19.7	19.7	94.5
Position	1	2	3	4	5	6	7	8	9	10	11	12
	|			|			|			|		|
Steps	0.0			0.0			2.7			19.7		94.5

Although this method minimizes the worst-case estimation error for any range comparison (the error is no more than S), it is not adequate when a precise count is needed (for example, when testing equivalence or subsumption of conditions). It is also insensitive when values (such as 19.7 in example 1) fall across step boundaries. Such situations are typical for fields such as Charge, where a charge for a popular service can occur many more times than the average. Steps also do not measure gaps in the domain. From the steps in example 1, it is not possible to infer that there are no values between 19.7 and 94.5.

The adjustable buckets method divides the sorted values into approximately equal buckets, according to a user-specified default bucket width W. Each bucket has low and high bounds and a count of values between the bounds. Initially, bucket-low = $value(start)$, bucket-high = $value(end)$, where $end = start + W - 1$, and bucket-count = W. Here, $start = 1$ for the first bucket or 1 + the end of the previous bucket. However, if $value(end) = value(end + 1)$, the end pointer is incremented until $value(end) < value(end + 1)$, or the end of the value list is reached. At this point, if $value(start) < value(end)$, and frequency of $value(end)$, f_{end}, is W or more, the bucket is split in two:

1. [low= $value(start)$, high= $value(end - f_{end})$, count= $end - f_{end} - start + 1$].
   This bucket describes values from $value(start)$ up to, but not including $value(end)$.
2. [low=high=$value(end)$, count= f_{end}].
   This bucket describes the frequency of $value(end)$.

The purpose of this approach is to keep a precise count of any value with a frequency of at least W and combine less frequent values into approximately equal buckets.

For the values in example 1, we would have the following buckets:

Example 2. Buckets for Charges (W = 3)

Charge	0.0	0.0	0.0	0.0	0.0	1.5	2.7	19.7	19.7	19.7	19.7	94.5
Buckets	[0.0				0.0]	[1.5	2.7]	[19.7			19.7]	[94.5 94.5]
Counts			5				2			4		1

Computation of these statistics is on the order of sorting and, thus, very fast.

13.5 KID3 Algorithm for Discovery of Exact Rules

To find rules of the form $cond(A) \rightarrow cond(B)$, one needs to check whether all tuples satisfying *cond(A)* also satisfy *cond(B)*. For example, if among all tuples with Customer-Type = FED, it is true that Credit = Excellent (this hypothetical example is clearly based on old data), then we can infer the rule:

$$(\text{Customer-Type} = \text{FED}) \rightarrow (\text{Credit} = \text{Excellent})$$

I present here the KID3 algorithm that finds, in parallel, all simple exact rules of the form $(A = a) \rightarrow cond(B_i)$. The algorithm requires only one access to each database tuple. Thus, it is optimal to within a constant factor because at least one access is needed to each tuple to check whether this tuple refutes any of the previously inferred rules. A similar method was also proposed by Cai, Cercone, and Han (chapter 12).

The KID3 algorithm is extensible to finding rules with more complex conditions on a left-hand side. For example, rules such as $(a_1 \leq A \leq a_2) \rightarrow cond(B)$ can be found by first discretizing the values of A into disjoint intervals using the adjustable buckets method.

To find rules implied by different fields, the algorithm is run once on each field. An approach to structuring the set of rules is discussed in the next section.

The idea of the algorithm is to hash each file tuple by A. (A slower but simpler to implement version sorts all tuples by A and then compares adjacent tuples). Each hash cell keeps a running summary of all tuples with the same A value. When a tuple is hashed to an empty cell, the summary is initialized with the tuple value. When a tuple is hashed to an occupied cell, the cell summary is updated by comparing it with the tuple. The algorithm is suitable for a parallel implementation because in its inner loop the Summary-Update test can be done independently and in parallel on all fields of file tuple and cell summary.

```
Procedure Kid3(A, File)
for Tuple in File
    get Cell corresponding to Tuple.A
    if empty Cell then
      Cell.Summary = Tuple , Cell.Count = 1 ;; initialize cell
    else
      Cell.Count = Cell.Count + 1 ;; update cell
      for field C in Cell.Summary
          when Cell.Summary.C ≠ NIL
          do <field-type>-Summary-Update(Cell.Summary.C, Tuple.C)
      end for
    end if
end for
```

At the end, a cell for $A = a$ contains the summary of all the file tuples satisfying $A = a$. The summary can be presented to the user or used for deriving rules implied by $A = a$.

13.5.1 Updating Cell Summary for Different Field Types

The procedure Summary-Update(Cell-value, Tuple-value) updates the current cell summary for a field C by comparing it with the C value in the tuple. Depending on the field type, different procedures are used. When the field summary is too general (as defined by user criteria), the summary value is set to NIL, a special value indicating that the field is to be excluded from further computation. What intermediate information has to be kept is determined by the type of the summary description we want to have at the end.

For nominal fields, the cell summary is a list of as many as K (a user-specified limit) values. Currently, I only keep the first K different values. If there are more than K values, the summary is set to NIL. It is also possible to keep more complex summaries, such as the K most frequent values and their frequencies.

For interval fields, the cell summary tracks the smallest and largest field values. Complex summaries can include the average value, the standard deviation, and so on.

At first glance, the appropriate summary for fields with structured domains is a minimal generalization of all the tuple values using the field-value hierarchy (such as in figure 13.1). However, the minimal generalization is expensive to compute incrementally, especially if the domain hierarchy is not a tree; so, we collect all the field values and compute the generalization at the end. A method for finding minimal generalizations, given a list of values and a generalization hierarchy, is described by Shum and Muntz (1988).

The running time of KID3 is $O(NM)$, where N is the number of tuples, and M is the number of fields. For databases with a large number of fields, a significant speedup can be achieved by using the precomputed field statistics to estimate the cardinality of the summary condition after each update (or each Jth update). If the cardinality is greater than the allowed maximum (which can be either user defined or obtained from the required minimum rule significance for ϕ [equation 13.1]), then the summary for this field is set to NIL.

13.5.2 Inferring Rules from Field Summaries

When all tuples have been hashed by A, a cell for $A = a$ contains the cell count and summaries of all tuples with $A = a$. Each non-NIL summary for field C corresponds to a condition *scond*(C) satisfied by all tuples with $A = a$:

- *scond*(C) is $C = c_1 \vee ... \vee c_k$ for nominal fields
- *scond*(C) is $c_1 \leq C \leq c_2$ for interval fields.

The number of tuples that satisfies *scond*(C) can be either computed by direct file access or, when speed is desired, estimated using the predefined field statistics.

Each summary corresponds to a potential rule $(A = a) \rightarrow scond(C)$. The significance of this rule is measured by $\phi(Cell.Count, |scond(C)|)$, where ϕ is defined in equation 13.1. Rules whose significance is less than the user-specified threshold are rejected. There is also an option to reject rules whose cell count is less than a user-specified minimum.

The entire algorithm was implemented in ALLEGRO COMMON LISP on a Sun Sparcstation 1. Working on a 1000-tuple file with 77 fields, it takes about 2 seconds to summarize a file and find all rules for a particular field.

13.5.3 Extending KID3 to Complex Conditions

The algorithm can also be extended to handle complex right-hand side conditions, such as a list of the K most frequent field values and their frequencies or multifield value combinations. However, the more complex the rule RHS is, the more computationally expensive it is to find such rules. Although finding rules with an unrestricted RHS is NP-hard, there are many important special classes where efficient algorithms exist (Haussler 1988).

In general, if the correctness of a condition $cond(B)$ can be computed incrementally by tracking only a limited number of values, then an efficient Summary-Update procedure can be written for testing rules of the form $(A = a) \rightarrow cond(B)$.

It is also possible to infer rules with a more complex left-hand side. We can allow fields with structured domains and infer rules (A is-a *concept*) $\rightarrow cond(B)$ by hashing each value of A into all concepts that are more general than the hash key. For example, given the Customer-Type domain in figure 13.1, a tuple with Customer-Type = FED will be hashed into a cell for FED and also into a cell for Large-Organization—a superconcept of FED. The rules on higher-level concepts need to be inferred before the rules on lower-level concepts.

Multifield LHS conditions, for example, $A_1 = a_1$ & $A_2 = a_2$, can be handled by hashing on a combined key $A_1\&A_2$. Knowledge of one-field rules is useful in guiding a search for multifield rules.

13.6 Capturing and Presenting Interrule Structure

A large database with complex records can have many exact dependencies. In a 1000-tuple, 77-field medical records database I found several thousand exact rules. To help users make sense of these rules, it is necessary to structure them. For example, if we found $(A = a) \rightarrow (B = b)$, $(B = b) \rightarrow (C = c)$, and $(A = a) \rightarrow (C = c)$, then the third rule is a consequence of the first two and can (even should) be omitted from presentation. Business databases are especially likely to have many interrelated strong rules, because the data codes are, typically, a product of corporate rules and policies.

Here, I outline an algorithm that computes a structured tree of all conditions that explain a given condition C_1. The general idea of the algorithm is to perform a topological sort of the relevant rules selected from a precomputed list of all rules. However, care has to be taken when dealing with rules that define equivalent conditions, for example, $(C_1 \rightarrow C_2)$ and $(C_2 \rightarrow C_1)$.

```
Procedure Explanation-Tree(A)
    let A-rules = all rules of the form (B → A)
    let A-tree = (node A count |A|)
    sort A-rules by decreasing |B|
    while A-rules not-empty do
          remove first rule (B1 → A) from A-rules
          if |B1| = |A| then add B1 to node(A-explanation)
          else
              let B1-explanation = Explanation-Tree(B1)
              make B1-explanation a child of A-explanation
              remove all concepts in B1-explanation from A-rules
          end if
    end while
    return A-explanation
```

For example, analyzing the condition **Toll Billed Minutes = 0** produced the following computer-generated output. The actual database field names and values are changed by the program into their english translations, on user request.

```
Toll Billed Minutes is equal to 0 [count 80]
    Service Type is Public Coin [count 20]
    == equivalent–to == Billing Code is Public Paystation

    Customer Class is Inter–Exchange Carrier [count 32]
        Area-Code is 183 [count 26]
            Service Type is AT&T InterState Private Line [count 18]
            Service Type is AT&T InterSvc Private Line [count 8]
        Service Type is Other Common Carrier [count 6]
```

When such structures become complex, they can be better presented visually, to take

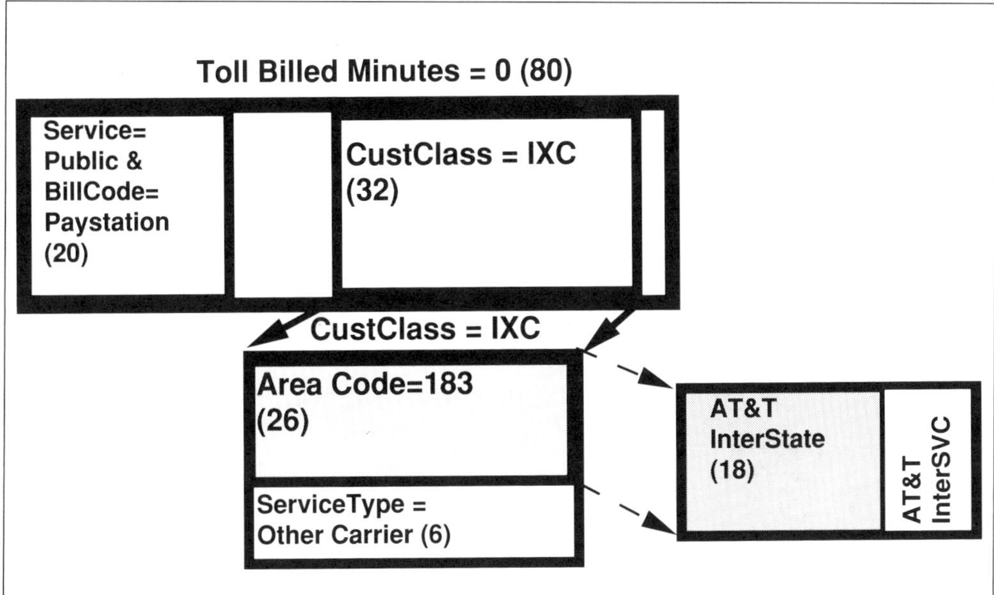

Figure 13.2
Containment Diagram

advantage of our innate pattern-recognition abilities (Bergeron and Grinstein 1990, Tufte 1990). If a rule has about 10 words, then a picture is worth 100 rules!

An interesting alternative to the obvious tree structure is a containment diagram (figure 13.2). This diagram has several advantages, such as the immediate visual comprehension of relative concept sizes, completeness of coverage, and containment. It is also possible to show the degree of overlap between concepts on the same level. I feel that a visual representation of the discovered knowledge would significantly enhance its comprehension.

13.7 Accuracy of Sample-Derived Rules

For large databases, even the fastest algorithms for rule discovery can be too expensive to apply to all data. In such cases, we can apply the discovery algorithms to a random sample of data. However, the rules discovered in a sample can be invalid on the full data set.

In this section, I present a formal statistical analysis of the accuracy of sample-derived rules when applied to a full data set. I analyze two types of rules: equality rules, $cond(A) \rightarrow (B = b)$, and range rules, $cond(A) \rightarrow (b_1 \leq B \leq b_2)$, with $b_1 < b_2$ This analysis is independent of the LHS condition *cond*(A). It is also independent of the rule-discovery algorithm; it applies to rules derived by any algorithm.

I tested the formulas for estimating the accuracy of sample-derived rules on real data and found a good agreement. Testing also revealed several ways to use domain knowledge to improve on purely statistical prediction.

I assume that the sampling is random and without replacement. Formulas for sampling with replacement are similar except that binomial distribution is used in place of hypergeometric distribution in the derivation.

Notation: In the following, let N be the size of the full file **F**, S be the size of the sample **S**, s be the number of tuples satisfying *cond*(A) in the sample, and n be the number of tuples satisfying *cond*(A) in **F**. Because n is unknown, I estimate it as $s * N/S$.

Let $C(I, J) = \frac{I!}{(I-J)!J!}$ be the number of combinations of J things taken from a group of I things. The following analysis relies on these combinatorial equalities:

$$\sum_{k=s}^{n} C(k,s) = C(n+1, s+1) \quad \text{(well known)} \tag{13.2}$$

$$\sum_{k=s}^{n} (k+1)\, C(k,s) = (s+1)\, C(n+2, s+2), \tag{13.3}$$

which was derived from equation 13.2 by using $(k+1)\, C(k,s) = (s+1)\, C(k+1, s+1)$, and

$$\sum_{k=s}^{n} k\, C(k,s) = \frac{sn+n+s}{s+2}\, C(n+1, s+1), \tag{13.4}$$

which was derived by subtracting equation 13.2 from equation 13.3.

The following analysis is different for equality rules and range rules. Rules where B is compared to a list of values and range rules where $b_1 = b_2$ are treated the same way as equality rules.

13.7.1 Equality Rules

Given that *cond*(A) $\rightarrow$ ($B = b$) in the sample **S**, what can we say about the accuracy of *cond*(A) $\rightarrow$ ($B = b$) in **F**?

The expected rule accuracy in **F** is the conditional probability $p(B = b|cond(A))$, which is the number of **F** tuples satisfying $cond(A) \& (B = b)$ divided by n. Without a priori information about $p(B = b|cond(A))$, we can give an a posteriori estimate using the urn model (Feller 1968). In this model, there are n different urns, each with n balls. All urns have red balls, corresponding to tuples with $(B = b)$, and black balls, corresponding to tuples with $(B \neq b)$, but in different proportions. Urn number k has exactly k red balls, corresponding to rule accuracy k/n.

The experiment corresponds to choosing an urn at random and then randomly and without replacement drawing s balls from this urn. After finding that all selected balls are red (corresponding to the rule being true in the sample), we want to estimate the proportion of red balls in the chosen urn (corresponding to rule accuracy). Clearly, the chosen urn has at least s red balls, because this number is the number of red balls in the sample. Hence, we need to consider only urns numbered from s to n.

Let r be the number of red balls in the urn, and let $p(r|\mathbf{S})$ denote the a posteriori probability for r, given that sample $\mathbf{S}$ contains only red balls. In the absence of any domain knowledge to the contrary, we can assume the apriori probabilities of $p(r = k)$ to be equal. Then, the Bayesian formula gives us the probability for r:

$$p(r = k \mid \mathbf{S}) = \frac{p(\mathbf{S} \mid r = k)}{\sum_{i=s}^{n} p(\mathbf{S} \mid r = i)} \tag{13.5}$$

There are $C(n, s)$ different samples of size s. For an urn with i red balls, there are $C(i, s)$ samples with only red balls. Therefore, $p(\mathbf{S} \mid r = i) = C(i, s) \ / \ C(n, s)$, and, using equation 13.2, we get

$$p(r = k \mid \mathbf{S}) = C(k, s) / \sum_{i=s}^{n} C(i, s) = \frac{C(k, s)}{C(n + 1, s + 1)} \tag{13.6}$$

Let $ra = r/n$ denote rule accuracy. Its expected value, given $\mathbf{S}$, is

$$\begin{aligned} E(ra \mid \mathbf{S}) &= \sum_{k=s}^{n} \frac{k}{n} p(r = k \mid \mathbf{S}) = \sum_{k=s}^{n} k \frac{C(k, s)}{C(n + 1, s + 1)} = \text{(by eq.13.4)} \\ &= \frac{\frac{sn+n+s}{s+2} C(n + 1, s + 1)}{C(n + 1, s + 1)} = 1 - \frac{1 - s/n}{s + 2} \simeq 1 - \frac{1 - S/N}{s + 2} \end{aligned} \tag{13.7}$$

S/N is a good approximation for s/n when $s/n < 0.5$, which is almost always the case. Thus, we can use this formula even though n is unknown.

In the remainder of this section I omit $\mathbf{S}$ from probability formulas, but it should be clear when a probability is computed a posteriori.

13.7.2 Finding Confidence Intervals for Rule Accuracy

Besides the expected value, it is useful to know a confidence interval for rule accuracy, for example, given $\epsilon > 0$, we want to find ra_ϵ such that $p(ra \geq ra_\epsilon) \geq 1 - \epsilon$. The desired formula is

$$\begin{aligned} p(ra \geq k/n) &= \sum_{i=k}^{n} p(ra = i/n) = \sum_{i=k}^{n} \frac{C(i,s)}{C(n+1,s+1)} \\ &= \frac{1}{C(n+1,s+1)}(\sum_{i=s}^{n} C(i,s) - \sum_{i=s}^{k-1} C(i,s)) = \frac{C(n+1,s+1) - C(k,s+1)}{C(n+1,s+1)} \\ &= 1 - \frac{k!/(k-s-1)!}{(n+1)!/(n-s)!} = 1 - \frac{(n-s)!/(k-s-1)!}{(n+1)!/k!} \\ &= 1 - \frac{n-s}{n+1} \cdots \frac{k-s}{k+1} = 1 - (1 - \frac{s+1}{n+1}) \ldots (1 - \frac{s+1}{k+1}) \end{aligned} \tag{13.8}$$

For $s \ll n$ this formula can be approximated as

$$1 - (1 - \frac{s+1}{(n+k+2)/2})^{n-k+1} \simeq 1 - e^{-Y} \tag{13.9}$$

where

$$Y = 2(s+1)(n-k+1)/(n+k+2) \tag{13.10}$$

The desired confidence interval for $p(ra \geq ra_\epsilon) \geq 1 - \epsilon$ is therefore given by $Y = \ln 1/\epsilon$. By solving equation 13.10 for k we get

$$ra_\epsilon = k/n = 1 - \frac{\ln 1/\epsilon - (s + 1 - \ln 1/\epsilon)/n}{s + 1 + 0.5 \ln 1/\epsilon} \simeq 1 - \frac{\ln 1/\epsilon}{s} \quad . \tag{13.11}$$

The approximation is good when $\ln 1/\epsilon \ll s, s \ll n$.

13.7.3 Range Rules

Here we have $cond(A) \rightarrow (b_1 \leq B \leq b_2)$ in the sample. The expected accuracy of this rule in the entire file can be estimated using the following approach.

Let us redefine the sampling in the following way: Instead of the original file population, we consider only the AB population consisting of all the B values in file tuples satisfying $cond(A)$. The AB sample from this population is all the B values in the original sample tuples satisfying $cond(A)$. The AB population size is estimated as $n = s * N/S$. I solve the problem of estimating the accuracy of rules derived on AB sample, when applied to the AB population. From this solution, it is trivial to estimate the accuracy of the rule $cond(A) \rightarrow (b_1 \leq B \leq b_2)$ on the full population. In the rest of this section, I refer to AB sample as sample and to AB population as population.

Let sample *Span* be the proportion of population items that fall between the maximum and minimum sample values. By definition, the expected rule accuracy is equal to the expected sample *Span*. Let *Rank(v)* be the rank of value v among all population values. Let $MaxR(sample)$ denote the rank of the maximum value in a sample—equal to the number of values $\leq max(sample)$. $MinR(sample)$ is the rank of the minimum sample value; then

$$Span(sample) = \frac{MaxR(sample) - MinR(sample) + 1}{n} \tag{13.12}$$

We assume that neither maximum nor minimum values are tied in rank. The effect of ties is negligible unless the number of ties is comparable to $MaxR(sample)$.

In the rest of this chapter, I abbreviate $MaxR(sample)$ as $MaxR$ and $MinR(sample)$ as $MinR$. The probability of $MaxR \leq i$ is $C(i,s)/C(n,s)$; therefore,

$$p(MaxR = i) = p(MaxR \leq i) - p(MaxR \leq i-1) = \frac{C(i,s) - C(i-1,s)}{C(n,s)} \tag{13.13}$$

The expected value of this equation is

$$\begin{aligned} E(MaxR) &= \sum_{i=s}^{n} i\,(C(i,s) - C(i-1,s)) \;/\; C(n,s) \\ &= \frac{1}{C(n,s)}\,(n\,C(n,s) + \sum_{i=s}^{n-1} i\,C(i,s) - \sum_{i=s}^{n} i\,C(i-1,s)\;) \end{aligned} \tag{13.14}$$

Because $C(s-1,s) = 0$, we can omit the first term from the second sum and reindex it with $i = i-1$, obtaining $\sum_{i=s}^{n-1}(i+1)C(i,s)$. Therefore

$$\begin{aligned} E(MaxR) &= \frac{1}{C(n,s)}\,(n\,C(n,s) + \sum_{i=s}^{n-1} i\,C(i,s) - \sum_{i=s}^{n-1}(i+1)C(i,s)\,) \\ &= \frac{1}{C(n,s)}\,(n\,C(n,s) - \sum_{i=s}^{n-1} C(i,s)) \\ &= \frac{n\,C(n,s) - C(n,s+1)}{C(n,s)} \;=\; n - \frac{n-s}{s+1} \end{aligned} \tag{13.15}$$

By an argument of symmetry, $E(MinR) - 1 = n - E(MaxR)$. Therefore, $E(MinR) = 1 + (n-s)/(s+1)$, and the expected rule accuracy is

$$E(ra) = E(MaxR - MinR + 1)/n = 1 - 2\frac{1 - s/n}{s+1} \simeq 1 - 2\frac{1 - S/N}{s+1} \quad (13.16)$$

13.7.4 Range Rules including Extreme Values

An important special case occurs when one of the rule range values is equal to a known minimum or maximum value. For example, the rule is $cond(A) \rightarrow (0 \leq B \leq b_2)$, and it is known that $0 \leq B$ is always true. This type of domain knowledge approximately doubles the estimation accuracy, as I show in the following paragraphs.

Let us assume that the sample includes the minimum value (the maximum value case is analogous). Its population rank is 1. We can assume that the first sample element is fixed to be the minimum value, and we need to take the remaining $s - 1$ sample values from the remaining $n - 1$ population. From equation 13.15, we get

$$E(MaxR \mid \text{sample } s-1 \text{ from } n-1) = n - 1 - \frac{n-s}{s} \quad (13.17)$$

Hence,

$$\begin{aligned} E(MaxR \quad | \quad & \text{sample has } minVal) = \\ & 1 + E(MaxR \mid \text{sample } s-1 \text{ from } n-1) = n - (n-s)/s \end{aligned} \quad (13.18)$$

In this case, the expected sample span is equal to *MaxR*, and the expected rule accuracy is

$$E(ra) = E(MaxR)/n = 1 - \frac{1 - s/n}{s} \simeq 1 - \frac{1 - S/N}{s} \quad (13.19)$$

The standard deviation and confidence intervals for rule accuracy can be computed using a similar approach.

13.7.5 Testing the Estimation Formulas

I conducted an experiment using a file of 2000 randomly selected records of telephone customer data. Only 12 fields from each record were used. From this file, a random sample of 500 records was extracted, and exact rules on this sample were computed using the KID3 algorithm. I found 150 rules—52 range rules (including 17 with extreme range value) and 98 equality rules. These rules were then tested on all 2000 records, and the actual accuracy was compared with that predicted by the derived formulas.

From 52 range rules only 14 remained exact on the entire file. However, the *predicted* rule accuracy, averaged over all range rules, was 89.75 percent, which is close to the average *actual* rule accuracy of 90.47 percent. The difference is only about 0.7 percent.

The difference between the actual and predicted rule accuracy further decreases when the predicted rule accuracy increases. For example, for 15 rules with predicted accuracy above 95 percent, the difference was only approximately 0.3 percent on the average. These results indicate that within a range specified by the rule, the value distribution is essentially random and statistical techniques can be used effectively.

From 98 equality rules, the vast majority (92) remained exact on the entire file. The actual rule accuracy was, on the average, 99.57 percent, and the predicted accuracy was, on the average, 95.25 percent. Thus, rules on nominal fields seem to be stronger than statistically indicated. The following subsection shows how domain knowledge can be used to explain this anomaly.

13.7.6 Using Domain Knowledge to Improve Estimation

Database fields can be divided into two classes: static and dynamic. *Static fields* carry information that encodes the domain model. For example, Customer-Type is a static field because customer type cannot be changed for a given customer entry. The information in static fields is essentially permanent. Thus, if A and B are static and $A \rightarrow B$ on a small sample, then it is likely that $A \rightarrow B$ on the entire database. If there are exceptions, then they can probably be explained and stored.

Dynamic fields represent the current state of events. Almost all numeric measurements, such as charges, are dynamic fields. They have a random component, which is why the accuracy of range rules can be so well predicted by statistical techniques. Some nominal fields are also dynamic, for example, credit class or subscriber interexchange carrier: these fields can change at any time.

Domain knowledge of which fields are static can significantly improve the estimation accuracy. In our example, all the sample rules that did not remain 100 percent correct on the full file had dynamic fields (credit class or inter-exchange carrier) in either rule LHS or RHS.

Functional dependencies are another source of domain knowledge. Dependencies among database fields are usually an indication that one or both fields in the dependency are static.

An additional way of using domain knowledge is to use domain concepts in rules. Because a concept is a union of several field values, a rule using a concept is stronger, has a higher predicted accuracy, and is also more understandable to a human. The total number of rules is also reduced.

13.8 Summary and Future Directions

I focused on the problem of finding strong (exact or almost exact) rules in databases. Such rules reflect the existing domain theory and can be useful for intelligent data analysis.

First, I examined rule-interest measures and presented a set of intuitively correct principles that a rule-interest measure should satisfy. I conjecture that all measures satisfying these principles produce approximately the same rule ordering.

I then described the KID3 algorithm for fast discovery of all simple exact rules. The algorithm uses precomputed field statistics and domain knowledge about data types and the hierarchy of field-domain values. I outlined a method for finding structure in discovered rules and visually presenting it to the user.

I also analyzed the problem of estimating the accuracy on a full database of rules found on a random sample. I derived formulas for predicting rule accuracy and tested them on real data. These tests indicate several areas where using domain knowledge can improve on statistical estimation.

Many interesting research directions remain unexplored. The rules found in the current state of a database can be violated by updates. However, the incremental nature of the algorithm allows the incremental change in rules by considering only the new data.

I would like to measure how much the use of field-domain hierarchies improves accuracy and reduces rule-set size. I am also interested in automatically generating domain hierarchies that minimize the number of strong rules. Another possible direction is extending the rule-discovery algorithm to more complex, multifield rule conditions.

The KID3 algorithm has already been adapted to perform data summarization of user-specified concepts and is a part of the knowledge discovery workbench that is being developed at GTE Laboratories. Because we are working with real business databases, the ultimate test is discovering some information of practical value.

Acknowledgments

I am most grateful to Shri Goyal for his strong support of this work; to Bud Frawley, Sunny Ludvik, Marvah Moore, Usama Fayyad, and M. Rajinikanth for their comments on the draft of this work, and to Jaime Carbonell, Gabriel Jakobson, Larry Kerschberg, Mary McLeish, Kamran Parsaye, Michael Siegel, and Samy Uthurusamy for their encouragement and stimulating discussions.

References

Beard, P. 1989. Automated Arbitrage Expert System Developed: It Outperformed S&P's 500 in First Quarter. *AIWeek* 6(13): 1–3.

Bergeron, R. D., and Grinstein, G. 1990. A Conceptual Model for Interactive Multidimensional Visualization. *Transactions on Graphics* (Special Issue on Scientific Visualization).

Blum, R. 1982. Discovery and Representation of Causal Relationships from a Large Time-Oriented Clinical Database: The RX Project. *Lecture Notes in Medical Informatics* 19. New York: Springer-Verlag.

Breiman, L.; Friedman, J. H.; Olson, R. A.; and Stone, C. J. 1984. *Classification and Regression Trees.* Monterey, Calif.: Wadsworth and Brooks.

Cendrowska, J. 1987. PRISM: An Algorithm for Inducing Modular Rules. *International Journal of Man-Machine Studies* 27: 349–370.

Cheeseman, P.; Kelly, J.; Self, M.; Stutz, J.; Taylor, W.; and Freeman, D. 1988. AutoClass: A Bayesian Classification System. In *Proceedings of the Fifth International Conference on Machine Learning,* 54–64. San Mateo, Calif.: Morgan Kaufmann.

Clark, P. and Niblett, T. 1989. The CN2 Induction Algorithm. *Machine Learning* 3(4): 261–283.

Feller, W. 1968. *An Introduction to Probability Theory and Its Applications,* Volume 1, 3d ed. New York: Wiley.

Gaines, B. R., and Shaw, M. L. G. 1986. Induction of Inference Rules for Expert Systems. *Fuzzy Sets and Systems* 18: 315–328.

Haussler, D. 1988. Quantifying Inductive Bias: AI Learning Algorithms and Valiant's Learning Framework. *Artificial Intelligence* 36(2): 177–221.

Iman, R. L., and Conover, W. J. 1983. *A Modern Approach to Statistics.* New York: Wiley.

Imielinski, T. 1987. Intelligent Query Answering in Rule-Based Systems. *Journal of Logic Programming* 4: 229–257.

Langley, P.; Simon, H.; Bradshaw, G.; and Żytkow, J. 1987. *Scientific Discovery: Computational Explorations of the Creative Process.* Cambridge, Mass.: MIT Press.

Malley, C., and Zdonik, S. 1986. A Knowledge-Based Approach to Query Optimization. In Proceedings of the First Expert Database System Conference, 243–257. Columbia, S. C.: Univ. of South Carolina.

Mingers, J. 1989a. An Empirical Comparison of Pruning Methods for Decision-Tree Induction. *Machine Learning* 4(2): 227–243.

Mingers, J. 1989b. An Empirical Comparison of Selection Measures for Decision-Tree Induction. *Machine Learning* 3(4): 319–342.

Piatetsky-Shapiro, G., and Connell, C. 1984. Accurate Estimation of the Number of Tuples Satisfying a Condition. In Proceedings of the ACM-SIGMOD Conference, 256–276. New York: Association of Computing Machinery.

Quinlan, J.R. 1987. Generating Production Rules from Decision Trees. In Proceedings of the Tenth International Joint Conference on Artificial Intelligence, 304–307. Menlo Park, Calif.: International Joint Conferences on Artificial Intelligence, Inc.

Quinlan, J.R. 1986. Induction of Decision Trees. *Machine Learning* 1(1): 81–106.

Shum, C., and Muntz, R., 1988. Implicit Representation of Extensional Answers. In Proceedings of the Second Expert Database System Conference, 257–273. Fairfax, Va.: George Mason University.

Tufte, E. R. 1990. *Envisioning Information.* Cheshire Conn.: Graphics Press.

Ullman, J. D. 1982. *Principles of Database Systems,* 2d ed. Rockville, Md: Computer Science Press.

Verma, T. S., and Pearl, J. 1990. Equivalence and Synthesis of Causal Models. Presented at the Sixth Conference on Uncertainty in AI, Cambridge, Mass., July.

14 Integration of Heuristic and Bayesian Approaches in a Pattern-Classification System

Q. Wu, P. Suetens, A. Oosterlinck
Catholic University of Leuven, Belgium

Abstract

To overcome the practical limitations of traditional statistical methods, efforts were made to develop pattern-classification systems that integrate knowledge-based and statistical techniques. This chapter presents a method to solve a class of pattern-classification problems characterized by the hierarchical structures of the hypothesis space and domain-context dependency. For such problems, the hypothesis hierarchy can be utilized to construct a classification tree. Domain knowledge can be incorporated to guide heuristic search in the tree and determine the scope of subsequent Bayesian classification. The proposed method was applied to a well-known problem of biomedical pattern classification: human chromosome analysis. Test results using this method confirm the expected improvement of classification performance over the use of the traditional Bayesian method.

14.1 Introduction

Human societies are confronted with ever-growing amounts of information. Pattern-recognition systems are increasingly in need today, especially in dealing with all sorts of sensor data (ranging from one dimensional to multidimensional). Among the major components of a pattern-recognition system, the classification strategy that provides the ultimate decision-making mechanisms is of vital importance.

Most pattern-classification systems use traditional statistical methods (Davies 1971; Chen 1973; Batchlor 1974; Habbema 1979; Landeweerd, Bins, and Gelsema 1980). Because of the real-world constraints on time and computational complexity, various simplifying assumptions need to be made about the statistical characteristics of the input data. Typically, these assumptions include statistical independence or models of normal distributions of data. Although these domain-independent assumptions remain popular in use, the fact that unacceptably high error rates are associated with many systems under such schemes indicates limitations to the approaches.

To overcome such limitations, efforts have been recently made to develop pattern-classification systems that integrate knowledge-based and statistical techniques (Oosterlinck et al. 1987; Wu , Suetens, and Oosterlinck 1987, 1989). In the following discussion, a method is described that aims at solving a class of pattern-classification problems characterized by the hierarchical structures of the hypothesis space and domain-context dependency. Such problems are often encountered in biomedical fields. To exemplify the use of the method, a case study is described that uses a well-known application field of biomedical pattern classification—human chromosome analysis; in this study, considerable early investigations were made using traditional statistical techniques, but only limited success was achieved. Such a case study compares the classification performance of a traditional Bayesian classification system with the method described here.

14.2 Limitations of Traditional Statistical Methods

A statistical pattern-classification system can be briefly described as follows: Given the problem of classifying a set of patterns or objects $a_j, j = 1, ..., n$, each pattern is perceived in terms of a measurement vector $\mathbf{F}_j$ acquired by a sensing device capable of capturing its features. According to the domain of discourse, for each pattern a_j, we associate a classification set C_j that contains all the possible classes that can be assigned to pattern a_j. In general, the classification sets can be distinct, but for the sake of simplicity, we consider all classification sets identical; that is,

$$C_j = C = \{c_1, ..., c_m\}, \forall j.$$

Thus, each pattern admits one of m possible classes $c_i, i = 1, ..., m$. Also, we discuss only the case in which the same feature measurements are made from each pattern, so that

$$\mathbf{F}_j = \mathbf{F} = \{f_1, ..., f_l\}, \forall j.$$

To classify a pattern into one of m classes, a feature hyperspace is constructed based on the measurement vector $\mathbf{F}$, which can be regarded as measurements of true feature values corrupted by random noises. The uncertainty in discovered knowledge is represented by the multiclass conditional probability density functions estimated from a learning data set:

$$p[\mathbf{F}|c_i], i = 1, ..., m.$$

The calculation of the a posteriori probability or likelihood using the Bayes formula results in

$$P[c_i|\mathbf{F}] = L_i = \frac{p[\mathbf{F}|c_i]P[c_i]}{p[\mathbf{F}]}, i = 1, ..., m,$$

where $p[\mathbf{F}]$ is actually a normalizing factor that can be dropped, and $P[c_i]$ is easy to estimate and usually can also be dropped under equal a priori conditions. Subsequently, statistical decision criteria are applied for classification. In most cases, the Bayesian minimum error decision rule is applied (also known as maximum likelihood classification) to obtain the theoretically optimal solution. This is achieved by minimizing wrong classification (error); that is, a pattern is assigned into class i with the highest likelihood or a posteriori probability:

$$L_i = \max_j \{L_j\}, j = 1, ..., m.$$

Such a procedure can be summarized as in figure 14.1.

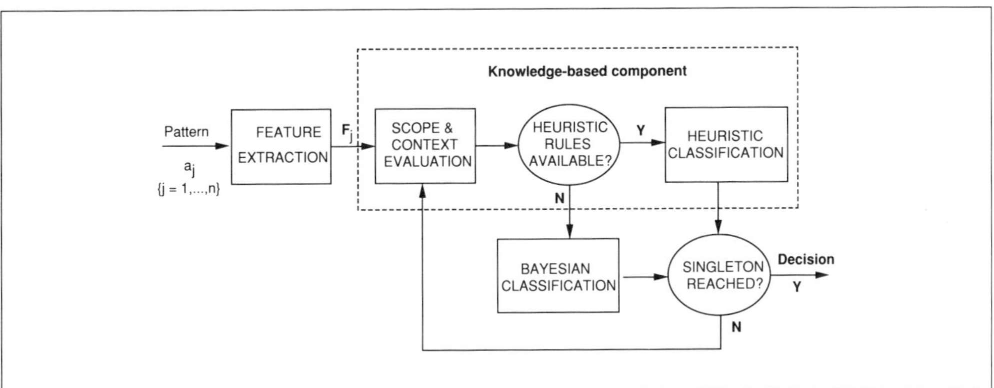

Figure 14.1
The Bayesian Classification System.

However, in practice, to solve real-world problems, the effectiveness of the previous traditional statistical methods is affected by the difficulties in obtaining a reliable estimation of multiclass and multivariate conditional probability density functions and incorporating domain expert knowledge. The first difficulty is the result of two elements. First is dimensionality and sample size, which are known to play an important role in statistical pattern classification (Kanal and Chandrasekaran 1977). For most biomedical pattern classification problems, the number of features and measurement spaces is usually quite large. To obtain a good estimation of $p[\mathbf{F}|c_i], i = 1, ..., m$, the complexity can be NP-hard, and the size requirement of the learning set turns out to be impractical. Second is the existence of serious natural variation or diversity in data. Typically, for biomedical data, accurate interspecimen normalization of feature measurements for classification is difficult to obtain.

Because of these problems, in reality the following simplifications are often made: First, an educated guess is made about the form of statistical models of multivariate probability density functions, which are actually domain independent. In this way, one only has to estimate parameters describing these functions; the approach is often referred to as the *parametric method.* For example, a popularly used assumption is normal distribution; that is,

$$p[\mathbf{F}|c_i] = \frac{1}{(2\pi)^{n/2}|\mathbf{C}_i|^{1/2}} \exp[-\frac{1}{2}(\mathbf{F}-\mathbf{M}_i)'\mathbf{C}_i^{-1}(\mathbf{F}-\mathbf{M}_i)], i = 1, ..., m$$

by which the learning problem is reduced to one of estimating the covariance matrixes $\mathbf{C}_i$ and mean vectors $\mathbf{M}_i$, and the complexity of the likelihood computation is reduced to $O(ml^2)$, where l stands for the number of features measured from each pattern. Second, an assumption about the statistical independence of each feature is made; that is,

$$p[\mathbf{F}|c_i] = \prod_{k=1}^{l} p[f_k|c_i], i = 1, ..., m.$$

In this way, the estimation of $p[\mathbf{F}|c_i]$ can be facilitated by estimating $p[f_k|c_i]$, that is, learning each feature respectively, resulting in an easy solution for the problem of learning set size requirement and a further reduction in time and space complexity to $O(ml)$. This approach is often referred to as the *nonparametric method.*

The second difficulty is incorporating domain expert knowledge. Typically, experts apply heuristic search and constraint satisfaction in their manual classification procedures, but such mechanisms are not incorporated in the framework of traditional statistical classification methods.

14.3 Integration of Heuristic and Bayesian Approaches

In this section, a method that enables the integration of heuristic and Bayesian approaches in pattern classification is described. It aims at solving a class of pattern classification problems characterized by the hierarchical structures of the hypothesis space and domain-context dependency. Such problems are often encountered in biomedical fields where classification is highly hierarchically structured and domain-context dependent.

14.3.1 Classification Tree and Search

The proposed scheme is essentially an adaptation of the traditional Bayesian classification system, integrated with a domain knowledge-based component (figure 14.2).

To classify a pattern into one of the predefined classes concerned, instead of globally applying the Bayesian classification procedure to each pattern with respect to the whole list of singleton classes in the classification set (a strategy of exhaustive search that we consider inefficient), we make use of the hierarchical structures of hypothesis space to construct a classification tree. Depending on the different problems at hand, the structure of the classification tree can be different. For instance, in figure 14.3a is a *strict tree* in the sense that each subset has a unique parent set that contains it. Figure 14.3b is a

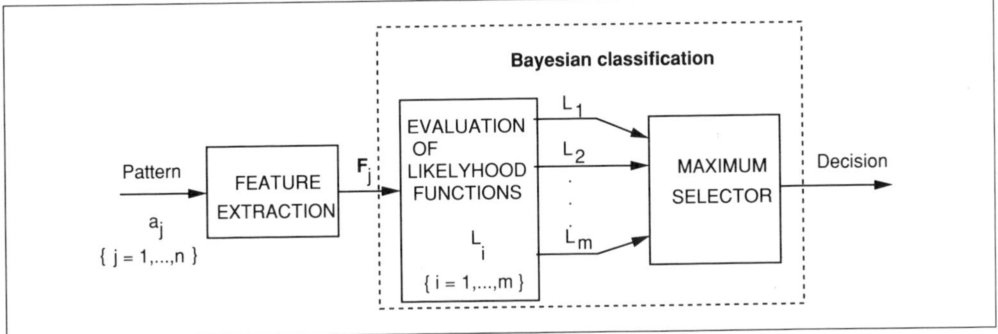

Figure 14.2
A Classification Scheme that Integrates Heuristic and Bayesian Approaches.

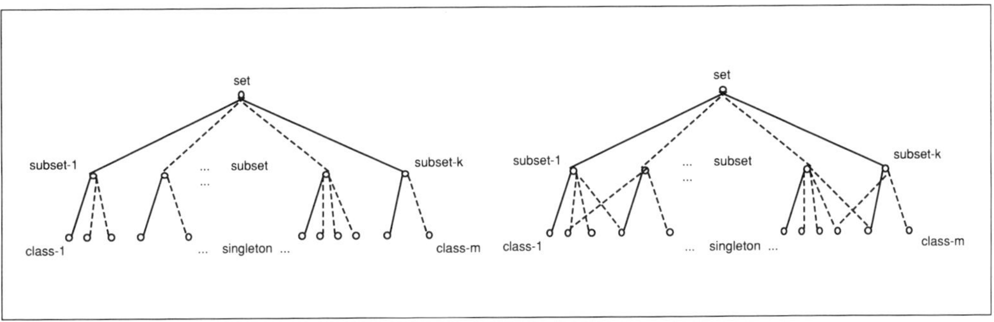

Figure 14.3
Classification Trees: (A) Strict. (B) Nonstrict.

nonstrict tree. Also different can be the depth (that is, number of levels) of the tree based on different categorizations of classification sets and subsets.

For many pattern-classification problems, expert knowledge exists in the forms of domain heuristics and contextual constraints. Such knowledge should be incorporated to guide search in the classification tree, pruning inconsistent branches and avoiding exhaustive search. At the level where uncertainties or ambiguities overwhelm so that no heuristic rule is available, conventional Bayesian procedure can be called for evaluation. In this way, a search can be performed by alternately applying heuristic and Bayesian classification rules until an end node (singleton classification) is reached. The result of combining both decision rules in the classification procedure is that the global optimization using traditional Bayesian classification (which can be inconsistent with the domain constraints) is replaced by domain consistency and local optimization.

14.3.2 The Classification Algorithm

The algorithm of the proposed classification scheme is summarized in figure 14.2 and described as follows: Domain knowledge is used to guide the search in the tree which involves the application of domain-contextual constraints and heuristic rules. However, an evaluation of the classification context and the search scope is carried out first. After the search scope is determined, depending on whether heuristic rules are available, a pattern is classified by either a heuristic rule or the Bayesian procedure based on its measured features. After a classification search has been conducted, the pattern under classification is checked to see whether it has reached a leaf of the tree, that is, whether its singleton classification has been obtained. If it has, the decision is made, and the system proceeds to the next unclassified pattern. If not, its classification context and scope are evaluated again in step 1, and steps 2 and 3 are repeated. The whole procedure terminates when the search for the classification of each pattern has been completed. In the next section, a case study is presented in which a well-known biomedical pattern-classification problem is attempted to exemplify the use of the proposed scheme.

14.4 A Case Study: Human Chromosome Analysis

Chromosome analysis as an important constituent of automated cytogenetics, as well as as an outstanding pattern-classification problem, has attracted extensive study during the past decades (Castleman and Melnyk 1976; Oosterlinck et al. 1977; Piper et al. 1980; Granum 1980; Ledley, Ing, and Lubs 1980; Zimmerman et al. 1986; Piper and Lundsteen 1987; Wu, Suetens, and Oosterlinck 1987). Its significant applications include clinical diagnosis, biological research, and mutagen dosimetry. In brief, the task is to recognize the chromosomes in metaphase images (figure 14.4a) digitized from a microscope view of metaphase cells and to classify them into 24 predefined classes (figure 14.4b).[1] Until now, work on automation has mainly focused on human chromosome analysis because of its obvious clinical value. Methods using traditional statistical classification techniques were studied by many early investigators but met with only limited success, in the sense that error rates of the classification were still too high to make the method of practical use.

The application of the proposed scheme to human chromosome classification can be

[1] Cell division undergoes several stages. The stage at which the chromosomes are most suitable for analysis is the metaphase.

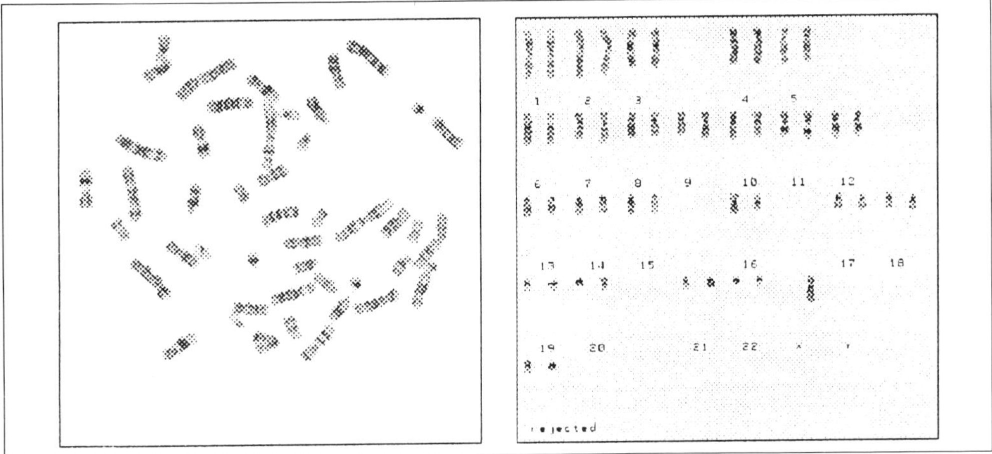

Figure 14.4
Chromosome Analysis: (A) A Giemsa-Banded Human Metaphase Cell Image. (B) Classification of the Chromosomes in (a).

carried out as follows: To classify a set of chromosomes in a metaphase cell, we make use of the readily available hierarchical classification structure, as specified by the domain notation of "Denver group," to construct a two-stage classification tree:[2] classification first into the group and then into the class. We have chosen to use a nonstrict tree here to allow an adequate search scope and avoid or reduce dead-end search.

The domain knowledge we acquired in our early studies (Wu, Suetens, and Oosterlinck 1987) and used here can be formulated as (1) a set of rules to guide search for chromosome group classification based on the feature measurements of chromosomes and the context in relation to other chromosomes within the same cell and (2) contextual constraints. In a normal cell, each class except class 24 (Y chromosome) should contain two chromosomes at most; there can only be either two class 23 (X) chromosomes (female cases) or one X chromosome and one Y chromosome (male cases).

14.4.1 The Chromosome Classification Algorithm

The algorithm for chromosome classification is summarized as follows: First, an evaluation of the classification context and search scope is carried out to check how many chromosomes have already been classified into different groups and classes and to determine the search scope for the chromosome currently under classification. Second, if

[2]Denver groups: A (containing numbers or classes 1-3), B (4-5), C (6-12, X), D (13-15), E (16-18), F (19-20), G (21-22), and Y.

available, the rules are applied to guide the search in the tree for the classification of the chromosome. If not, Bayesian classification is applied. Third, the chromosome is checked to determine whether it has reached a leaf of the tree, that is, whether its singleton classification has been obtained. If it has, the decision is made. If not, its classification context and scope are evaluated again in step 1, and steps 2 and 3 are repeated. Fourth, the system proceeds to the next unclassified chromosome, and the previous loop is repeated. The whole procedure terminates when the search for the classification of all chromosomes has been completed; that is, all chromosomes in the metaphase are classified.

A null face branch or reject class is set up to handle the case of unclassifiable chromosomes for which neither a heuristic rule nor the Bayesian procedure can be applied because it is highly uncertain, or its maximum likelihood is below a certain threshold.

At the first stage of the classification tree, rules are available for group-level classification, but at the second stage, only rules to apply the contextual constraints are currently available; that is, each class except class 24 (Y chromosome) should contain two chromosomes at most and either two X chromosomes or one X chromosome and one Y chromosome are allowed at a time for one cell. If a violation of these constraints occurs after applying the Bayes decision rule, the maximum likelihoods of these chromosomes being assigned to the same class are compared, and the allowed number of chromosomes with the highest maximum likelihoods remains. The others are then attached to the classes with the next maximum likelihoods. For those Bayes-classified chromosomes that are consistent with the constraints, no constraint rule is applicable.

To demonstrate the algorithm at work, given an unclassified chromosome, the evaluation in step 1 first determines its classification context based on how many chromosomes have already been classified into different groups and classes and then determines the scope of the search. It is decided then that the search should involve all different groups. At this point, the procedure goes on to step 2, where heuristic rules are available for group classification. A typical rule for a full-set (all 46 chromosomes present) cell at this stage reads: "If the chromosome is among the longest four and is metacentric ($0.35 <$ centromeric index < 0.5), it is assigned to group A." As a result of the application of this rule, the chromosome is grouped into group A. Because group A is not a singleton classification, the chromosome is reevaluated in step 1. By this point, the context is updated so that the number of chromosomes already in group A is incremented, and the scope for the next search is determined to be from classes 1-5 if these classes do not already contain two chromosomes. Now, in step 3, because no rule is applicable for further classification of this chromosome, the Bayesian classification procedure is called for resolution. In case two chromosomes are indeed already classified into the class for which the unclassified chromosome has the maximum likelihood, the contextual constraint rule becomes applicable. The maximum likelihood of the chromosome under classification is

Table 14.1
Results of the Classification Experiment.

Number of cells	40
Number of chromosomes	1792
Error rate by the Bayes classifier	38.57%
Rejection rate by the Bayes classifier	0%
Error rate by the proposed classifier	34.13%
Rejection rate by the proposed classifier	0.01%

then compared to the maximum likelihoods of the two chromosomes belonging to the same class; only the two chromosomes with the highest likelihoods are assigned to this class. The other one is then attached to the class with the next maximum likelihood. A decision is made after confirming that the singleton classification has been reached in step 4, and the system proceeds to classify the next chromosome in the cell, if any.

14.4.2 Experimental Results

The proposed classification scheme was implemented in C on a VAX Workstation 3100. An experiment was carried out on a data set of 1792 ASG-stained metaphase chromosomes of 40 cells from a large database originally collected in Edinburgh (Piper 1986, 1987). The true classification information was also provided in the database. The input to the algorithm are the chromosome feature measurements computed by an existing chromosome analysis software system. These features were described and used in several early studies (ten Kate 1985; Groen et al. 1989) and were found suitable for chromosome classification. A traditional nonparametric Bayes classifier was used for both pure Bayes classification as reference and its use in the proposed scheme. Only a set of 11 rules was used for the experiment; they are discussed in Wu, Suetens, and Oosterlinck (1990). During the experiment, the database was divided into two subsets, A and B, of similar size. The average error rate was then taken by using A as the training set and B as the test set, and vice versa. By using a separate testing set and training set in this way, we intended to avoid a biased estimate of the classification performance. Table 14.1 summarizes the results of the classification experiment.

From table 14.1, a 4.44 percent decrease in the average error rate using the proposed classification scheme was observed compared to using the traditional Bayes classifier. The slight increase in the rejection rate (the percentage of the chromosomes that cannot be classified and are assigned to the reject class) can be accounted for by the scope evaluation during the search, which in few cases could still lead to dead-end classification. However, this drawback is trivial compared with the achieved improvement because the cost of rejection is regarded as minor as opposed to misclassification when one considers the effort needed during interactive correction by the operator.

14.5 Conclusions

We proposed and described a method that enables the integration of heuristic and Bayesian approaches in a pattern-classification system. The method is designed to solve a class of pattern-classification problems characterized by the hierarchical structures of the hypothesis space and domain-context dependency. It takes into account a priori domain knowledge about hierarchical classification structures, heuristic search, and contextual constraints, which are believed to play an important part in the expert manual solution of many pattern-classification problems, and uses such knowledge to guide the application of somewhat domain-independent traditional statistical decision rules. In this way, the misclassifications that are inconsistent with the domain constraints can be avoided by pruning the classification tree using heuristic search rules. Another major advantage is that as exhaustive search is integrated with heuristic search and might no longer be needed. An efficiency gain can thus be achieved without a loss of performance. Test results of the case study confirmed the expected improvement of classification performance over using the traditional Bayesian method.

Acknowledgments

The authors want to thank Dr. Jim Piper for providing the chromosome database. This work was supported in part by the Belgium National Incentive Program for Fundamental Research in Artificial Intelligence, initiated by the Belgium State—Prime Minister's Office—Science Policy Programming, and the Commission of the European Communities within the frame of its Medical and Health Research Program, project II.1.1/13.

References

Batchlor, B. G. 1974. *Practical Approach to Pattern Classification.* New York: Plenum.

Castleman, K. R., and Melnyk, J. H. 1976. Automatic System for Chromosome Analysis—Final Report, JPL 5040-30, Jet Propulsion Laboratory, Pasadena, Calif.

Chen, C. H. 1973. *Statistical Pattern Recognition.* Rochelle Park, N.J.: Spartan.

Davies, R. G. 1971. *Computer Programming in Quantative Biology.* New York: Academic Press.

Granum, E. 1980. Pattern Recognition Aspects of Chromosome Analysis, Ph.D. thesis, Electronics Lab. Technical Univ. of Denmark.

Groen, F.; ten Kate, T. K.; Smeulders, A.; and Young, I. T. 1989. Human Chromosome Classification Based on Local Band Descriptors. *Pattern Recognition Letters* 9: 211–222.

Habbema, J. D. F. 1979. Statistical Methods for Classification of Human Chromosomes. *Biometrics* 35:103–118.

Kanal, L. N., and Chandrasekaran, B. 1977. On Dimensionality and Sample Size in Statistical Pattern Classification. In *Machine Recognition of Patterns*, ed. A. K. Agrawala, 192-197. Washington, D.C.:IEEE Press.

Landeweerd, G. H.; Bins, M.; and Gelsema, E.S. 1980. Interactive Pattern Recognition of White Blood Cells Using ISPAHAN. In *Pattern Recognition in Practice*, E. S. Gelsema and L. N. Kanal (eds.). North-Holland. Amsterdam.

Ledley, R. S.; Ing, P. S.; and Lubs, H. A. 1980. Human Chromosome Classification Using Discriminant Analysis and Bayesian Probability. *Comput. Biol. Med.* 10: 209–219.

Oosterlinck, A.; Suetens, P.; Wu, Q.; and Baird, M. 1987. Pattern Recognition and Expert Image Analysis System in Biomedical Image Processing. In: International Symposium on Pattern Recognition and Acoustical Imaging, Proceedings of the International Society for Opitcal Engineering, 44–52. Bellingham, Wash.: International Society for Optical Engineering.

Oosterlinck, A.; van Daele, J.; de Boer, J.; Dom, F.; Reynaerts, A.; and van den Berghe, H. 1977. Computer-Assisted Karyotyping with Human Interaction. *J. Histochem. Cytochem.* 25: 754.

Piper, J., and Lundsteen, C. 1987. Human Chromosome Analysis by Machine. *Trends in Genetics*, 3(11): 309–313.

Piper, J. 1987. The Effect of Zero Feature Correlation Assumption on Maximum Likelihood Based Classification of Chromosomes. *Signal Processing* 12: 49–57.

Piper, J. 1986. Classification of Chromosomes Constrained by Expected Class Size. *Pattern Recognition Letters* 4: 391–395.

Piper, J.; Granum, E.; Rutovitz, D.; and Ruttledge, H. 1980. Automation of Chromosome Analysis. *Signal Processing* 2(3): 203–221.

ten Kate, T. K. 1985. Design and Implementation of an Interactive Karyotyping Program in C on a VICOM Image Processor. Master's thesis, Delft Univ. of Technology.

Wu, Q.; Suetens, P.; and Oosterlinck, A. 1990. Knowledge-Base Supported Chromosome Classification. Forthcoming.

Wu, Q.; Suetens P.; and Oosterlinck, A. 1989. On Knowledge-Based Improvement of Biomedical Pattern Recognition: A Case Study. Proceedings of the Fifth IEEE Conference on Artificial Intelligence Applications, 239–244. Washington, D.C.:IEEE Computer Society.

Wu, Q.; Suetens, P.; Oosterlinck, A. 1987. Toward an Expert System for Chromosome Analysis. *Knowledge-Based Systems* 1(1): 43–52.

Zimmerman, S. O.; Johnston, D. A.; Arrighi, F. E.; and Rupp, M. E. 1986. Automated Homologue Matching of Human G-Banded Chromosomes. *Comput. Biol. Med.* 16(3): 223–233.

15 Using Functions to Encode Domain and Contextual Knowledge In Statistical Induction

William J. Frawley
GTE Laboratories Incorporated

Abstract

This chapter discusses the notion and use of attribute-value decision trees in representing classification functions that are known only through their behavior on databases. In function-based decision trees, nodes represent arbitrary functions over the database, combining database fields with functions and data external to the database. Mathematically, tree-structured functions implemented by decision trees are seen to be approximators (approximating or estimating functions) over the space of functions having finite range. In particular, this use of functions allows the introduction of domain knowledge and contextual information into the process of deriving approximate rule sets from examples. Further, the function-based paradigm supports the reuse of concepts discovered as the disjunctions of separate paths leading to maximal replicated subtrees. These ideas are embodied in the program FBI (function-based induction), whose use is described. The chapter concludes by describing how the function-based technique fits into a user-centered knowledge discovery system.

15.1 Introduction

Statistical techniques of knowledge discovery in databases often employ top-down induction to produce a decision tree whose nodes are database field names (attributes), whose branches are attribute values or sets of values, and whose leaf nodes identify values of a classifier function being synthesized (Quinlan 1986). Among the limitations of attribute-based induction as a tool for automated knowledge acquisition from large sets of examples is its inability to incorporate logical primitives and domain knowledge. Some things are known about virtually any domain, such as which attributes are likely to be correlated, which are likely to be combined, and how they are likely to be combined. For example, in a personnel database the concept of "pensionable" might involve the sum of the employee's age and his (her) seniority, which cannot be represented naturally in an attribute decision tree. However, if $P(x) := age(x) + seniority(x)$ were treated as a primitive building block, a decision tree would conveniently represent concepts involving *pensionable*. In function-based decision trees, nodes represent arbitrary functions over the database of examples rather than attributes of examples, so that the tree-structured functions implemented by decision trees are viewed in a more general sense as approximators (approximating or estimating functions) over the space of functions having finite range. In particular, this approach allows the introduction of domain knowledge and contextual information into the process of deriving approximate rule sets from databases and supports the reuse of disjunctive concepts discovered in already computed trees.

The typical induction problem is to approximate a finite-range classifier function over a database. That is, given a database of examples and their class values, such as diagnoses, assigned to them by a function known only in terms of these values, construct a set of rules that compress the data, accurately portray the unknown function over the data, and generalize the classification process so that cases encountered in the future will be classified reasonably. When a carefully crafted expert system already exists for the classification problem, its performance can be compared to that of the example-derived rules to assess the effectiveness of the induction. The next section provides a simple illustration of the power of domain and contextual knowledge in inducing useful rules and the value of formulating the induction problem in terms of functions over the database of examples.

Approximating functions of finite range is different from the usual numeric approximation in which the functions of interest share both their domain spaces and their range spaces. In traditional numeric approximation, comparisons of fit are made in the range space, which carries a metric. Here, the domain is common, namely, the database itself, but the ranges can be different sets of values. Measures of fit are expressed in terms of conditional predictions, such as "When $g(x) = a$, it is such-and-so believable that $f(x) = b$." To prepare for the formal analysis, the section Databases and Views introduces terminology and notation. Next, Approximating Finite-Range Functions details how comparisons can be made between functions using only domain space considerations and presents an approximation theorem for finite-range functions. Then, the section Tree-Structured Functions formally defines tree functions and presents an existence theorem for exact decision tree approximators.

Function-Based Induction describes FBI (function-based induction), a program to compute tree-structured functions, which is designed for iterative knowledge discovery, and how domain and contextual knowledge guide the calculation. Next, Function Discovery and Reuse discusses FBI's discovery of two forms of function: simple classifiers and certain disjunctive concepts. In particular, a discovered function can be used in building further decision trees, including reconstructing the tree from which it was discovered. Recognizing the current-day separation between discovery methods and database technique, the concluding section discusses steps toward a user-centered approach in knowledge discovery by function-based induction.

15.2 Attributes Are Not Sufficient: An Example

PROPHET (Prerau, Gunderson, and Levine 1988) is a rule- and frame-based diagnostic system developed at GTE Laboratories that successfully accomplishes a telephony customer access facility task that formerly required human expertise. It embodies knowledge acquired from specialists in the manner typical of AI expert systems. As part of an ongoing experiment, the PROPHET developers provide example sets and, piecemeal over time, elements of domain knowledge for analysis by FBI, described later, to examine the process of building expert systems from examples and limited domain knowledge rather than from highly specific human expertise.

A severely compressed description of the domain is as follows: Customers' telephone lines routinely are automatically tested during late-night hours. A maintenance database records facts regarding the line for each telephone line, for example, telephone number, central office, and service type, along with the date and test results for the last 15 days. Other databases record the network topology so that partial paths shared by various lines can be inferred. Because measured electrical faults can be the result of various causes and are not of individual importance, specialists examine the maintenance records looking for patterns suggestive of imminent failure because of bad transmission sections in the network. The purpose of this activity is to identify and repair such bad sections before any customer complaints are noted; the purpose of PROPHET is to automate this activity.

Each record consists of 24 fields, 15 of them being the automatically recorded day-to-day line status, which has four possible values: OK, SP (suspect), MD (moderate electrical fault), and SV (severe fault encountered). In attempting to build a rule set (decision tree) to approximate the category field, the first helpful aspect of domain knowledge was to use only line-status attributes, DAY-1, ... , DAY-15. This attribute set worked in all cases of data sets recorded on a given day, but some rules generated would involve as many as all 15 attributes. For data sets of only some few hundred records, the computed rules would not be so deep, but they would be too numerous (for example, 29 rules of a maximum depth of 6 to categorize 409 cases). Even when they are accurate, rules too deep or too numerous are not intelligible to humans who must rely on them (Quinlan 1987) and usually indicate poor statistics at the nodes. Another simple domain concept is reliance on the number of hits, that is, the count of all SPs, MDs, and SVs in the 15-day history, in interpreting patterns. In one experiment, this domain function alone accounted for a 62 percent accurate approximation over 1238 examples (figure 15.1). Over time, other functions of the history data were disclosed, for example, the maximum number of consecutive days with hits, leading to rule sets that are compact and accurate.

Experience in computing rules from examples to mimic the performance of an expert diagnostic system has shown the importance of certain simple types of domain knowledge, namely, knowledge of just which database attributes are useful or meaningful and knowledge of effective ways (functional forms) of combining these attributes. As important as this information can be, it need not be difficult to acquire. It can be included in the first-order knowledge of the field under study.

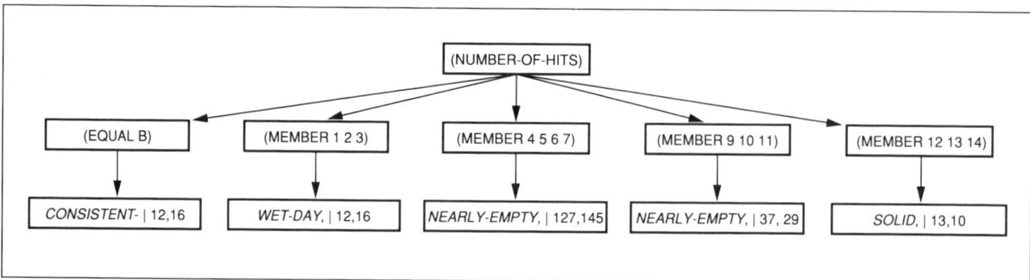

Figure 15.1
Decision Tree Representing Five Simple Rules Computed from 1238 PROPHET Examples Using FBI. Leaf nodes show the category and the numbers of associated correct and incorrect examples. The single domain function number of hits correctly categorizes 62 percent of the cases.

This domain provides a similar argument regarding the importance of the knowledge of functional forms combining context knowledge and database attributes to the construction of rule sets from examples. For example, weather plays a role in the PROPHET domain: Hits (faults) during dry weather are more important than those after rains. Obtaining weather information involves either applying some query function to another database or determining context by separate analysis of the given database (for example, a day on which hits are recorded on an exceptional number of phone lines might be rainy). Thus, a mixed concept accessing more than one database, such as $f(x) := (status(x) = \text{SV}) \wedge not(weather(x) = \text{RAIN})$, might be required in diagnostic rules.

15.3 Databases and Views

Within the scope of this research, a *database* is a finite collection of objects, $D = \{d\}$, organized for efficient storage and rapid access and update, that represents aspects of various real-world entities. Its *attributes*, sometimes called fields, slots, or properties, are a set of given primitive functions, $\mathcal{A} = \{A\}$, defined over D, having arbitrary domains, possibly including objects of D itself such as when the value of the supervisor field of an employee is another employee. The state of an object is defined at any time by the values of its attributes. More complex functions over D can be constructed by combining attributes among themselves, for example, $f(d) := age(d) + seniority(d)$, or with other functions that might access information external to D, for example, $g(d) := weather(birthdate(d))$. This use of terms follows the practice of object-oriented databases (Bertino 1989), where objects whose attribute values are other objects are called *nested objects* and functions defined in terms of attributes are called *derived property methods.*

The contents of a typical database change over time: New entries are added, some existing entries are deleted, and some are modified. (Note that modification can be modeled as a deletion-addition sequence: Throw away the entry to be updated, then create a new one just like the old one except for the slots that are to be changed.) In the work reported here, calculations are based on a particular state of the contents, but calculated structures that are stored in the database, such as decision trees, are *active* database entries; that is, to the extent that they make reference to database entries, when an item is deleted from the database, references to it are deleted, and when an item is added to the database, appropriate references are created.

Not every object in D need provide a value for every attribute of D, for example, when an employee's age is not recorded in the database. For uniformity, attributes and any functions defined on some elements of D are extended to apply to all of D. This extension is achieved by adding a special symbol such as $\perp$ to any domain and taking this symbol to be the value of functions at points where they would otherwise be undefined. Thus, all functions considered here are regarded as defined on all of D. (Note that this approach requires that operators on all associated domains be extended to handle the special symbol. For example, $18 + \perp$ should equal $\perp$.)

A particular application can involve only some attributes or special ways of combining them. Rather than making use of all the attributes of a database, one might choose to use only a subset; rather than using attributes alone, one might choose to use a set of functions built from attributes and other available sources of information. Starting with a finite family of functions $\mathcal{F}$ defined on D, one defines a virtual database $D_{\mathcal{F}}$, the *view of D through $\mathcal{F}$*, which has the elements of $\mathcal{F}$ as its attributes and whose objects, $d \in D$, have as their attribute values the values $f(d)$ for $f \in \mathcal{F}$. (Note that the database D can be identified with the view $D_{\mathcal{A}}$.)

Within a view $D_{\mathcal{F}}$, certain objects can be indistinguishable and are termed *equivalent* according to the following definition:

$$d \equiv d' \bmod \mathcal{F} \quad \text{iff} \quad \forall f \in \mathcal{F},\ f(d) = f(d')\ .$$

Thus, in a personnel database, two employees whose ages in years are the same integer and who have the same number of years of service are equivalent with respect to the view defined by the family $\{age, seniority\}$. For any set $\mathcal{F}$ of functions defined on D, the associated relation $\equiv$ is an equivalence relation; that is, it is reflexive, symmetric, and transitive and, hence, defines a partition of D.

As is seen, a goal of this work is to partition the entries of a database into subsets small enough that all members of each subset belong to the same class. The database is partitioned according to the equivalence classes defined by a view, whose defining family of functions (called approximator functions) is chosen so that the elements of the partition are small with respect to the regions of constancy of the class function to be approximated.

Before going on to the formal mathematical development, a comment is in order regarding the attention paid in the discussion to one approximating function rather than to a set of functions defining a database view. The correspondence between the two is made by the *cross-product mapping*: Given $\mathcal{F}$, $\times\mathcal{F}$ is that function on D that maps $d \in D$ to the tuple $< f_1(d), \ldots, f_m(d) >$. In this way, $D_{\mathcal{F}}$ can be thought of as a database of vectors.

15.4 Approximating Finite-Range Functions

Using a well-established definition of measure of information, this section provides an answer to the following question: Given two functions defined on the same database, how helpful is knowledge of the value of one function in guessing the value of the other? Because the range spaces of such functions are not specified, the conceptual tool available is the partition of a database induced by a function defined on it, so the development concentrates on partitions of a probability space. Based on the answer to the previous question, it is possible to define conditions and an algorithm for effective tree-function approximation of functions having finite ranges.

A *partition* P of a set D is a collection of nonoverlapping subsets of D whose union is D. This is denoted by $P \in \Pi(D)$. The individual subsets of a partition are called its *blocks* or *elements*. For partitions P and Q of the same set, Q is a *refinement* of P, denoted by $Q \leq P$, if every element of Q is a subset of some element of P; P is said to be *coarser* than Q. A partition then carves up a set; a refinement of a given partition slices the pieces into smaller ones. The refinement relation $\leq$ partially orders $\Pi(D)$ so that given arbitrary partitions P and Q, it is possible to compute the coarsest refinement of both; namely, $P \wedge Q = \{ A \cap B \mid A \in P \, and \, B \in Q\}$.

A function, f, maps its domain, $D(f)$, onto its range, $R(f)$. Associated with f is its *inverse*, f^{-1}, which maps any subset B of f's range into the set of x's such that $f(x) \in B$. The following simple relationship between functions and partitions is crucial to achieving the previous goal and is what motivates the subsequent mathematical development. Every function f induces a partition of its domain, $P(f) = \{f^{-1}(\{r\})|r \in R(f)\}$. For A, a subset of the domain of f, the restriction of f to A, $f|_A$, maps A onto $f(A)$, being equal to f on A and not defined elsewhere. Then $P(f|_A) = \{A \cap S|S \in P(f)\}$.

Let $(D, \mathcal{M}, \mu)$ be a probability measure space, with D being a set, $\mathcal{M}$ a σ-algebra of measurable subsets of D, and μ a measure on $\mathcal{M}$ with $\mu(D) = 1$. Note that any non-null member, A, of $\mathcal{M}$ defines a relativized probability space $(A, \mathcal{M}_A, \mu_A)$ whose measurable sets are intersections of members of $\mathcal{M}$ with A and whose measure is defined by $\mu_A(B) = \mu(B)/\mu(A)$ (Bartle 1966). Associated with each partition of D into disjoint measurable subsets, $\mathcal{A} = \{A\}$, is a nonnegative real number, $i(\mathcal{A},\ \mu)$, called the "information content of the partition $\mathcal{A}$ with respect to μ", which is meant to assess the difficulty of guessing to which element A of $\mathcal{A}$ a point d randomly selected from D belongs. One form of the function i, used in information theory and related to the physicist's entropy, is

$$i(\mathcal{A},\ \mu) \ = \ -\sum_{A \in \mathcal{A}} \mu(A) \ \cdot \ \log\ \mu(A)\ ,$$

where the base-two logarithm is used. (To treat sets of measure zero, the form $0 \cdot \log 0$ is assigned the value zero.) This venerable formula has its roots in nineteenth-century statistical mechanics. Wiener (1948) uses the base-two logarithm to compare knowledge of something before an event to knowledge of it after the event, calling the difference the *information* associated with the event. Shannon and Weaver (1949) prove that the form given here uniquely possesses certain desired properties and name it *entropy.* Brillouin (1956), noting the sign difference between it and traditional entropy, calls information *negentropy.*

This information-theoretic form of i has three desirable properties. First, $i(\{D\}, \mu) = 0$, corresponding to the notion that no information is associated with a choice that is a priori certain. Second, given two partitions of D, $\mathcal{A}$ and $\mathcal{B}$, the information content of the partition formed by all possible intersections of A's from $\mathcal{A}$ and B's from $\mathcal{B}$ is given by

$$i(\mathcal{A} \cap \mathcal{B},\ \mu) \ = \ i(\mathcal{A},\ \mu) \ + \ \sum_{A \in \mathcal{A}} \mu(A) \ \cdot \ i(\mathcal{B}_A,\ \mu_A)\ ,$$

where $\mathcal{B}_A$ is the partition of A induced by $\mathcal{B}$ consisting of intersections of A with members of $\mathcal{B}$. (Note that an equivalent form of this equation can be obtained by reversing the roles of $\mathcal{A}$ and $\mathcal{B}$ on its right-hand side.) In particular, this same result holds for $i(\mathcal{B},\ \mu)$ for all refinements, $\mathcal{B}$, of $\mathcal{A}$. Thus, refining a partition increases its information content by the μ-average of the information contents of the induced partitions of its elements.

Consider two arbitrary partitions, $\mathcal{A}$ and $\mathcal{B}$, of D. Prior knowledge of which B in $\mathcal{B}$ contains a selected point d can lessen the difficulty of guessing which A in $\mathcal{A}$ contains d. An intuitive but reasonable definition of the "conditional information content of $\mathcal{A}$ given $\mathcal{B}$ with respect to the measure μ" is

$$i(\mathcal{A} \mid \mathcal{B},\ \mu) \ = \ \sum_{B \in \mathcal{B}} \mu(B) \ \cdot \ i(\mathcal{A}_B,\ \mu_B)\ .$$

The third useful characteristic of the specific form of i previously defined is that the expression for conditional information is seen to occur in the expansion of $i(\mathcal{A} \cap \mathcal{B},\ \mu)$, so that $i(\mathcal{A} \cap \mathcal{B},\ \mu) = i(\mathcal{A} \mid \mathcal{B},\ \mu) + i(\mathcal{B},\ \mu)$. It can be shown that $i(\mathcal{A} \mid \mathcal{B},\ \mu) = 0$ if and only if $\mathcal{B}$ is μ-almost a refinement of $\mathcal{A}$, which means that any element B of the partition $\mathcal{B}$ either has measure zero, or there is one element A of $\mathcal{A}$ for which $\mu(A \cap B) = \mu(B)$ that for all other members A' of $\mathcal{A}$, $\mu(A' \cap B) = 0$. (Note that if $\mathcal{B}$ is a refinement of $\mathcal{A}$, then $\mathcal{B}$ is μ-almost a refinement of $\mathcal{A}$.)

These notions apply directly to functions. First, note that for finite-range functions the ideal situation in approximating f by g occurs when $P(g) \leq P(f)$. In this case, $|R(f)| \leq |R(g)|$ and a finite number of rules of the form "if $g(x) = a_i$ then $f(x) = r_i$" exactly describe f. More generally, for a finite-range function f defined on D, the difficulty in guessing the value of f on a randomly chosen $d \in D$, called the *uncertainty in f* and denoted by $i(f)$, is defined as $i(P(f),\ \mu)$. In addition, for finite-range f and g defined on D, "the uncertainty in the value of f supposing that the value g is known," denoted by $i(f; g)$, is defined as $i(P(f) \mid P(g),\ \mu)$. Taking the average over all values of g yields

$$i(f; g) = \sum_{A \in P(g)} \mu(A) \cdot i(f|_A) .$$

Note that $0 = i(f; f) \leq i(f; g) \leq i(f)$. Carried to more detail than space here permits, this analysis leads to the following theorem.

THEOREM 1 **(approximation theorem for finite-range functions):** For finite-range μ-measurable functions f and g on $(D,\ \mathcal{M},\ \mu)$, there exists a function G defined by a finite set of rules of the form $g(x) = a_i \Rightarrow f(x) = r_i$ which equals f μ-almost everywhere if and only if $i(f; g) = 0$.

15.5 Tree-Structured Functions

A *linear combination of functions* is a new function built from a set of given functions. Its structure is simple; its coefficients, however, range over all real or complex numbers. This section introduces the formalism of a *tree-structured function*, tree function for short, which has a hierarchical structure built from a set of given functions and which generalizes the notion of decision tree mentioned earlier. What is intended is to capture the notion of a tree whose root node is a function and whose branches represent the different possible values or sets of values of this function. Each branch points to a subtree, which can be a constant. Evaluating the tree for an argument consists of evaluating the root node function for this argument and selecting the branch corresponding to its value. The selected branch either leads to a constant, which is the value of the tree for this argument, or another tree for further evaluation. It is convenient to require that no function occur more than once along a path from the root to a terminal node of the tree.

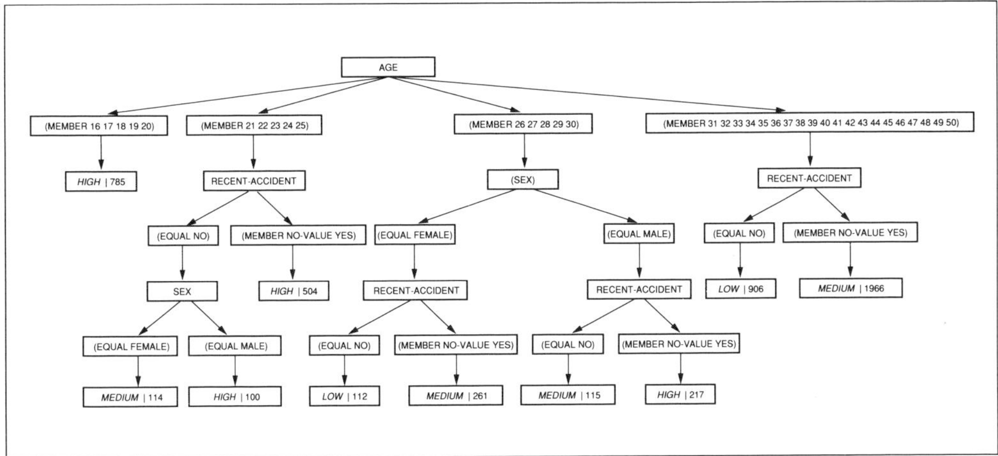

Figure 15.2
Decision Tree Computed by FBI Approximating Risk over an Artificial Database of 5000 Examples. Each example has as many as 7 fields. Tree height is 3; it has 10 leaves.

As an example, figure 15.2 shows a tree function of height 3 computed by FBI over an artificial database consisting of 5000 records with 7 fields: age, sex, race, seniority, recent-accident, retirable, and risk. This tree portrays risk, that is, automobile insurance risk, in terms of the other six attributes. Note that only age, sex, and recent-accident occur in the tree, which has 10 leaves. Each leaf displays a count of the number of successful cases it represents. (In this contrived database, there are no errors.) The formal definition is now given.

Definition 1 Let D be a nontrivial set and $\mathcal{F} = \{f: D \rightarrow R(f)\}$ a family of functions on D, each having a finite range. The function F is a tree-structured function on D based on the family of functions $\mathcal{F}$, denoted by $F \in T(D, \mathcal{F})$, if and only if F is either a constant function or F has the form $(f, \{(V_i, F_i)\})$ for some f in $\mathcal{F}$, where $\{V_i\}$ is a partition of the range of f on D, each F_i is a member of $T(D, \mathcal{F}/\{f\})$, and the form $(f, \{(V_i, F_i)\})$ maps any d from D to the value $F_i(d)$ for that i satisfying $f(d) \in V_i$.

Constant tree functions are termed *trivial.* (For any particular x, $\underline{x}$ represents the constant function that maps any $d \in D$ to x. That is, $\underline{x}(d) = x$.) A *height*, h, is defined for tree functions as follows: Trivial tree functions have zero height; $F = (f, \{(V_i, F_i)\})$ has height given by $1 + max_i \ \{h(F_i)\}$. Once a particular function occurs in the tree function F, it cannot appear in any of F's subtrees; thus, the height of F is no greater than the size of its base family $\mathcal{F}$.

Tree-structured functions are different in nature from the numeric functions used in linear approximation. Computationally, they are nested multiway branches or *case* statements. There are no numeric weights. Rather, the *weight*, or importance, of a function f to F is determined by its position in F's hierarchical arrangement. In $F = (f, \{(V_i, F_i)\})$, for example, f is the most important constituent, dominating other members of $\mathcal{F}$ used in constructing the various F_i. Looked at in another way, a typical tree-structured function represents a set of rules, one for each path from the top node to a constant node, with each rule conjoining conditions of the form $f(d) \in V$.

A top-down method of approximating one function, g, by a tree function based on the view $D_{\mathcal{F}}$ of the database D, where $\mathcal{F} = \{f_1, \ldots, f_m\}$, involves choosing the single best approximating function to head the tree structure and then, for each value in the range of the best approximator, recursively applying the same method of approximation to the original problem with all the functions under consideration restricted to the subdomain defining that value. The conditions under which an exact approximation is possible are stated in terms of the cross-product of the approximators.

THEOREM 2 **(existence theorem for exact decision tree approximators):** Under the conditions of definition 1 and with g and members of $\mathcal{F}$ being μ-measurable, there exists a $F \in T(D, \mathcal{F})$ that is μ-almost everywhere equal to g if and only if $i(g; \times\mathcal{F}) = 0$.

The goal of computing an exact approximation is not always achievable: If D contains points d and d' such that $(d \equiv d' \bmod \mathcal{F}) \wedge g(d) \neq g(d')$, then no tree function based on $\mathcal{F}$ can equal g on all of D. Points of this type are called *g-$\mathcal{F}$-inconsistent* on D.

15.6 Function-Based Induction

FBI is an object-oriented research prototype program that computes tree-structured functions according to the top-down approach previously described. It is designed for use as an element in an iterative user-centered knowledge discovery system in which domain and contextual knowledge is incrementally supplied. It is written in Common Lisp and New Flavors and presently runs on Symbolics computers.

The arguments to FBI include (1) an object-oriented database, D; (2) a measure (importance function), μ, defined on (some) subsets of D; (3) a set, $\mathcal{F}$, of μ-measurable functions, called approximators, defining a database view, $D_{\mathcal{F}}$; (4) a μ-measurable function, g, to be approximated over $D_{\mathcal{F}}$; and (5) a functional, I, used to select the best approximator to g. The default value of μ is the counting measure, $\mu(S) = |S|$. (It is not required that μ be a probability measure. Normalization and relativization are automatically handled.) The best-approximator selector I takes four arguments: $I(g, \mathcal{F}', D', \mu)$, where $D' \subseteq D$ and $\mathcal{F}' \subseteq \mathcal{F}$, computes that f in $\mathcal{F}'$, which minimizes some notion of conditional uncertainty in g over D'. The default behavior is to minimize the conditional entropy, described in Approximating Finite-Range Functions.

By means of the arguments $\mathcal{F}$, μ, and I, the user can guide the inductive process with domain and contextual knowledge. First and most obvious is to include in $\mathcal{F}$ functions that combine D's attributes with external data sources in ways typical of the domain at hand. Also, already computed decision trees and functions discovered from decision trees (see the next section) can be used as approximators. Second, μ provides a degree of importance to data subsets, such as giving greater weight to more recently acquired data. An example of using μ to provide domain information is seen in the integrated learning system of Silver et al. (1990). There, FBI monitors a history of telephone network traffic control episodes. When decision trees are being computed, FBI queries another (knowledge-based) program for a weight for each example; these weights represent the other program's assessment of the degree to which experimental assumptions pertain to the examples. Finally, I can encode domain knowledge and user preference. For example, in the telephone network traffic domain, it is known that the actions taken in a situation should be considered in the context of which network controls are then in effect. For this domain, the approximator selector encodes this knowledge as a rule that can override a numerically based selection: If actions taken is about to be selected and if network controls does not occur above this node in the tree as calculated thus far, then take network controls as the best approximator. Clearly, customization of I is a powerful mechanism.

Trees computed by FBI are integrated into the database. Each leaf of a tree encodes the associated value of g and retains pointers to all the database entries used in its construction. Each nonleaf node retains pointers to its inconsistent database entries, computed as follows: First, during tree construction, classes of g-$\mathcal{F}$ inconsistencies are identified, and for each class, those having the most likely g value on the class are used to construct the tree. Then, the inconsistent data that were not used are passed through the nodes and branches down to those nonleaf nodes having no suitable branch, where they are recorded as inconsistent. (These two steps constitute FBI's default way of dealing with noisy data; it is computationally expensive. Other modes can be selected using an input parameter.) In addition, FBI adds a metalevel field to the database itself to record all trees computed over it, making it possible to update the trees as the database changes. Each new database entry is passed through the structure of each tree. If it is consistent with a tree's approximation to g, it is indexed by some leaf node of the tree; otherwise, it is noted as inconsistent at some nonleaf node.

15.7 Function Discovery and Reuse

FBI supports the discovery of two forms of function: simple classifiers and certain disjunctive concepts. Taken together, these are called *functions defined implicitly by computed decision trees.* The presumption underlying both forms of discovery is that the repeated occurrence of a subtree within a decision tree indicates a potentially valuable domain concept. In fact, replicated subtrees can occur and not represent useful or novel knowledge; they might be the result of a statistical anomaly or due to the particular database sample used to construct the tree. They also might depend on the specific function being approximated and have narrow utility. (For related methods, see Pagallo [1989], Pagallo and Haussler [1989], and Matheus [1990].)

To be precise, it is the occurrence of two or more *equivalent subtrees* that is noted. The constant functions (leaf nodes) $\underline{x}$ and $\underline{y}$ are equivalent if and only if $x = y$; the tree-structured functions $(f, \{(V_i, F_i)\})$ and $(g, \{(W_j, G_j)\})$ are equivalent if and only if the functions f and g are identical and there is a permutation of $\{(W_j, G_j)\}$ under which, for all i, $V_i = W_i$ and F_i is equivalent to G_i. Equivalence classes are formed by inspecting the tree function from the bottom up. Maximal equivalence classes are used for discovery. A class is *maximal* if it contains more than one tree function, and no two of its members are subtrees of distinct but equivalent trees.

To exemplify function discovery from tree-structured functions, consider the branches below age in figure 15.2. During tree construction age defines 35 distinct, direct subtrees that, on inspection, are found to belong to only 4 equivalence classes; the values leading to them are coalesced. The discovered classifier function (not shown) is age-class-function-1 which maps the ages of database entries (persons) into one of four classes, age-class-1, ..., age-class-4, each of which represents a set of values of age, shown in boxes in the figure. (The boxes are numbered from left to right.) Again turning to figure 15.2, note that the subtrees labeled A and B are equivalent. The paths from the top of the tree to A and B are conjoined into a concept that maps a typical database entry d to either true or false:

$$(age(d) \in \text{age-class-3} \ \wedge \ sex(d) \ = \ \text{female}) \ \vee \ age(d) \in \text{age-class-4}\ .$$

The discovered age classifier and the discovered conjunctive concept can be used in the construction of decision trees, including the reconstruction of the original tree, as shown in figure 15.3. Note that the tree in this figure is of greater height than the one in figure 15.2, but that 89 percent of the cases are resolved in only two steps.

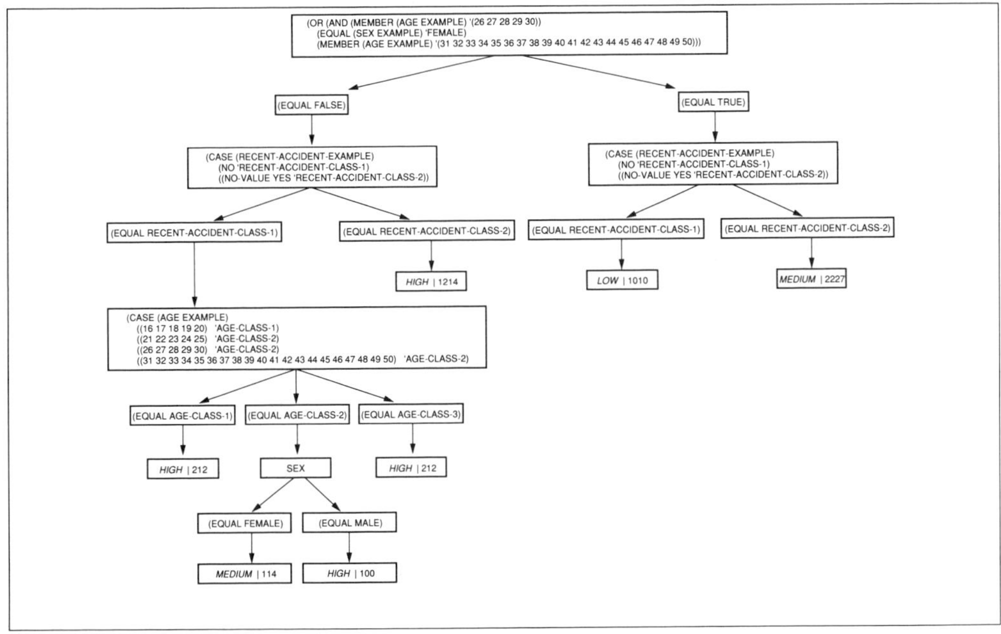

Figure 15.3
The Decision Tree of figure 15.2 Recomputed Using the Two Functions Discovered from Figure 2: An Age Classification and a Conjunction.

15.8 Steps Toward a User-Centered Approach

Function-based induction is a generalization of attribute-value statistical induction over a database that provides the means for the incorporation of domain and contextual knowledge, encoded in functional form, into the process of compressing and generalizing classifier functions known only in terms of their values over database entries. The program FBI implements function-based induction and includes the ability to discover certain classifiers and disjunctions. It is designed for iterative use by a person who examines results and provides additional knowledge of domain and context over time. Computed and discovered functions can be used in subsequent approximation and discovery. This chapter concludes with the following advice for making function-based induction a part of a user-centered knowledge discovery system of the type described in figure 15.1: Function-based induction should be incorporated into databases so that they maintain a number of decision trees as active, persistent database entities.

In contrast to the typical focus on one particular decision tree approximating some function over a database, the approach here presumes a multiplicity of decision trees constructed over a database. Expressed in the terminology previously introduced, this multiplicity corresponds to various choices for g, $\mathcal{F}$, the best approximator selector algorithm, and μ.

First, because a single database can serve many purposes, such as when medical records contain information about diagnosis and therapy along with financial data concerning the cost of treatment in different locales, or because one database service can provide access to a number of distinct databases, for example, tying together pharmacological and disease databases, different users will want to predict different functions. Next, in treating even one target function, users will experiment with different approximators: attributes, functions of attributes, knowledge of domain and context, recently computed decision tree functions, and recently discovered concepts. Third, users will experiment with different ways to choose the best approximator for the data at each level of tree construction. For example, maximizing the information gained yields bushy trees; maximizing the information gained for each approximator branch keeps tree branching factors small. (*Branching factors* relate to how understandable a tree is to the user.) Finally, users will compute versions of one particular tree over different subsets or samplings of the total database, for example, distinct trees for sex = female and sex = male or a tree based on the earliest 30 percent of the database entries.

Not only must many trees be considered simultaneously, they must also be made permanent database objects. Discovery in a large database will not be a one-run or even a one-month enterprise. Discovered knowledge will emerge as the result of repeated and increasingly refined computations devised not by one user but at the direction of many users, some possessing expert domain knowledge, referring back to, and building on, earlier results. Moreover, not only should computed trees and discovered functions be persistent database entities, they should also be active participants in database modifications. For example, a decision tree maintains counts of, or pointers to, bad or good examples, that is, those entities for which the approximation fails and doesn't fail, and can be queried about its error rate. Over time, as the database contents change, these counters or pointers should automatically be updated so that a tree's error rate can be monitored. It will be the continued successful performance over time that validates a decision tree or a discovered function, not the statistics that describe it when it is newly created.

At this time, discovery methods and databases are separate and distinct. To make discovery methods valuable to users, they must be incorporated into the databases themselves.

Acknowledgments

I acknowledge the influence of J. Ross Quinlan, who has led the way for so many in this field; the assistance of Sam Levine, Alan Gunderson, and Dave Prerau, who supplied data and information on the Prophet domain; the Learning in Expert Domains team, Bernard Silver, Glenn Iba, Tom Fawcett, Kelly Bradford, John Doleac, and John Vittal, for maintaining a stimulating intellectual environment; and my knowledge discovery colleagues, Gregory Piatetsky-Shapiro and Chris Matheus.

References

Bartle, R. G. 1966. *The Elements of Integration.* New York: Wiley.

Bertino, E. 1989. Indexing Techniques for Queries and Nested Objects. *IEEE Transactions on Knowledge and Data Engineering* 1(2): 196-214.

Brillouin, L. 1956. *Science and Information Theory.* New York: Academic.

Matheus, C. J. 1990. Adding Domain Knowledge to SBL through Feature Construction. Proceedings of the Eighth National Conference on Artificial Intelligence, 803–808. Menlo Park, Calif.: American Association for Artificial Intelligence.

Pagallo, G. 1989. Learning DNF by Decision Trees. Proceedings of the Eleventh International Conference on Artificial Intelligence, 639–644. Menlo Park, Calif.: International Joint Conferences on Artificial Intelligence.

Pagallo, G., and Haussler, D. 1989. Two Algorithms That Learn DNF by Discovering Relevant Features. *Proceedings of the Sixth International Machine Learning Workshop,* 119–123. San Mateo, Calif.: Morgan Kaufman.

Prerau, D.; Gunderson, A.; and Levine, S. 1988. The PROPHET Expert System: Pro-Active Maintenance of Company Outside Plant. *Proceedings of the Fourth Annual Artificial Intelligence and Advanced Computer Technology Conference,* 384–389. Long Beach, Calif.

Quinlan, J. R. 1987. Generating Production Rules from Decision Trees. Proceedings of the Tenth International Conference on Artificial Intelligence, 304–307. Menlo Park, Calif.: International Joint Conferences on Artificial Intelligence.

Quinlan, J. R. 1986. Induction of Decision Trees. *Machine Learning,* 1(1): 81–106.

Shannon, C. E., and Weaver, W. 1949. *The Mathematical Theory of Communication.* Urbana, Ill.: Univ. of Illinois Press.

Silver, B.; Frawley, W.; Iba, G.; Vittal, J.; and Bradford, K. 1990. ILS: A Framework for Multi-Paradigmatic Learning. *Proceedings of the Seventh Annual Conference on Machine Learning,* 348–356. San Mateo, Calif.: Morgan Kaufman.

Wiener, N. 1948. *Cybernetics.* New York: Wiley.

16 Integrated Learning in a Real Domain

F. Bergadano, A. Giordana, and L. Saitta
Universita' di Torino

F. Brancadori and D. De Marchi
SOGESTA s.p.a.

Abstract

This chapter describes the results obtained in applying the learning system Enigma to a fault diagnosis problem of electromechanical devices at Enichem-Anic (Ravenna, Italy). Enigma is capable of learning structured knowledge from examples and a domain theory, using an integrated inductive-deductive paradigm. The results are compared with those obtained by an expert system, designed for the same task, in which the knowledge base was acquired using the traditional method of expert interview. The comparison indicates that performance obtained by the learning system is systematically better than that of the manually developed expert system. The conclusion, based on demonstrated performance and the ability to limit development time and costs, is that, even with room for improvement, automated learning is a viable approach to the construction of expert systems.

16.1 Introduction

It is widely recognized that the feasibility of expert systems exhibiting human-like levels of performance strongly depends on the possibility of developing mechanisms for automating the processes of knowledge acquisition and maintenance. During the last decade, a number of research projects have been devoted to combining machine learning and knowledge acquisition. Although advances have been made, especially with learning concept descriptions from examples, the problem remains extremely difficult. This fact is confirmed by the scarcity of applications of learning systems to real applications in which machine learning techniques generate knowledge bases with the same or better utility as those constructed by human experts. Successes do exist. Note the results obtained in developing automatic classification systems for agricultural and medical applications (Michalski and Chilausky 1980; Michalski et al. 1986) and those obtained using decision trees in domains where the learning events can be represented by vectors of attribute-value pairs (Quinlan 1986; Cestnik, Kononenko, and Bratko 1987).

Many of the previously mentioned results in classification systems were based primarily on inductive methods. However, an important requirement, which characterizes many applications, is that the learned rules be understandable in light of preexisting knowledge of the domain. This requirement holds true particularly for diagnostic systems.

This chapter describes a pilot project aimed at assessing the possibilities offered by the state of the art in machine learning to automate the process of knowledge base construction for an electromechanical troubleshooting expert system. To achieve these goals, the prototype system ENIGMA, based on an integrated inductive-deductive paradigm (Bergadano and Giardano 1988) was developed, and extensive experimentation was performed. The performance of the ENIGMA knowledge base is compared with that of MEPS, a rule-based expert system, whose knowledge was manually acquired by interviewing a domain expert (Brancadori and Radicchi 1989). However, performance is not the only useful parameter for the comparison: Knowledge understandability and meaningfulness and development time were also considered. The results were encouraging enough for a research sponsor to justify funding a project to develop an industrial version of this learning system.

16.2 The Learning Problem

The case study was supplied by the Enichem-Anic chemical plant in Ravenna, Italy. In this plant, a technique of predictive maintenance is applied to a large set of apparatuses, including motor pumps, turboalternators, and ventilators. All these devices have rotating shafts to which various rotors are connected. When a machine has rotating elements, several unavoidable vibratory motions are induced in its parts; these vibrations occur during normal machine operation and are not dangerous as long as the amplitudes are limited. When some fault occurs in the machine, new, anomalous vibrations, as well as other manifestations, appear. The aim of predictive maintenance is to locate failures (still in initial stages) and diagnose their severity through an analysis of these vibrations, a process called *mechanalysis*. Mechanalysis basically involves a Fourier analysis of the vibratory motions taken at prespecified and labelled points, typically at the supports of the machine components. By means of a special analyzer, the technician obtains the amplitude and velocity of the global vibration for each support in the vertical, horizontal and axial directions. In addition, the same data can be taken for each of the harmonic components of the vibrations, and qualitative evaluation of the vibrations' phases can be carried out.

Mechanalysis has a strong mathematical foundation in vibration theory, and, hence, the relationships between anomalous frequencies and faults can, in principle, be predicted. In practice, however, the situation is not so simple: Usually, many more vibrations occur than are predicted because of mechanical imperfections in the parts, mutual influence among motions, resonance phenomena, fault co-occurrence, and so on. Moreover, a vibration does not begin abruptly; its intensity increases until a level that is considered severe is reached.

The proposed task was to automatically learn from mechanalysis examples and, with the help of background knowledge, to develop a knowledge base suitable to derive diagnoses of the type produced by human experts. Although this task can be thought of as a classic case of learning concept descriptions (Michalski 1983), it shows many difficulties in the kind of available data and in the conceptualization of the problem that are not present in other learning tasks described in the literature.

First, the examples are complex; those for motor pumps consist of from 20 to 60 measurements taken at different points and conditions of the machine. Each has two or three attributes (value, direction, and frequency if appropriate). Beyond that, the examples are noisy; in fact, all the measurements are affected by large uncertainty margins, that depend both on the intrinsic limits of the measurement apparatus and on the human subjectivity in recording the observed values.

Conceptually, the principal difficulty is that the expert's conclusion arises mainly from a global evaluation of the mechanalysis measures: A particular frequency pattern (or value) might have great relevance in one context and little in another. Moreover, only a few of the many measures are important for any one diagnosis, and the human expertise is knowing how to identify them. This global characteristic makes it difficult to define an adequate description language. In fact, as features, the individual mechanalysis measures are too low level and cannot be directly used to build a description space. However, features of a higher level, defined in terms of groups of items, are introduced to describe hypotheses. This form of constructive learning was strongly guided in the current implementation by the domain theory (Muggleton 1988).

16.3 The Learning System

ENIGMA is basically an evolution of an earlier system, ML-SMART (Bergadano, Gemello, et al. 1989; Bergadano, Giordana, and Saitta 1988), which was enhanced to include deductive capabilities (Bergadano and Giardano 1988). Several attempts to apply the original, purely inductive ML-SMART to the described case study produced knowledge that was difficult to understand in light of the existing domain theory. We do not describe ENIGMA here, but we mention some points that are necessary to understand how the system was applied. (For a detailed description, see Bergadano, Brancadari, et al. [1989a]; Bergadano, Giordana, and Saitta [1988]; and Brancadori and Radicchi [1989].)

ENIGMA receives a set of learning events and a body of background knowledge described as a Horn theory as input and produces a structured knowledge base of classification rules as output. What makes this system suitable to deal with structured domains is that the learning events are described as vectors of items. Each item is, in turn, a vector of attribute-value pairs and corresponds to a part (subpattern) of a concept instance. In the current case, the learning events correspond to the mechanalysis data that are collected in a table of the type shown in figure 16.1.

Figure 16.1
Organization of the Data Collected during Mechanalysis. i = Unstable phase.

Support	Direction	TOTAL VIBRATION Amplitude [μm]	Speed [mm/s]
A	Hor	7/11	2.4/2.6
A	Vert	4/8	1.2/1.4
A	Ax	20	12

FOURIER ANALYSIS ω [CPM]	v [mm/s]		ω [CPM]	v [mm/s]
3000^i	0.7/0.9	...	18K	0.7
3000	0.2/0.7	...	18K	0.4
3000	3/3.2	...	18K	0.8/1

Inside the table, the data are arranged in groups of three rows; each group corresponds to a given support and each row to one spatial direction (horizontal, vertical, or axial). The first group of two columns (total vibration) contains the measures of amplitude and velocity of the total vibration, and the second group (Fourier analysis) contains the measures of frequency, velocity, and (possibly) phase of the harmonic components of the vibration. Notice that for the harmonics, the measured value of velocity v (for which reliable analyzers exist) provides an estimate of the amplitude, which is proportional to v through the (known) ω. In some cases, the measurement consists of a single value (when the index of the analyzer is stable), but in others, it consists of a range of values (when the analog index of the analyzer oscillates between two extremes). This distinction is important for the differential diagnosis. The qualitative behavior (stable, unstable, oscillating, rotating, fixed) of the vibration phase, when observed, is denoted by a letter attached to the corresponding frequency value. For instance, the i occurring in figure 16.1 denotes an unstable phase.

A mechanalysis table is described to ENIGMA by supplying an item for each non-empty entry. Each item is described by a vector of attributes characterizing the support, the direction, the amplitude, the type (total vibration or Fourier analysis), the value of the measure, the normal value, and the rotation speed of the shaft. These attributes correspond to what are called *operational predicates* (elementary features) in explanation-based learning. Other predicates (higher-level features) can be defined using a Horn theory. In particular, it is possible to let ENIGMA work by applying pure explanation-based generalization, if a complete theory that defines a nonoperational description of the concept is given (Mitchell, Keller, and Kedar-Cabelli 1986). However, a complete theory is difficult to formulate, and ENIGMA was given a theory that defines only high-level features capturing contextual information.

The rules learned by ENIGMA take the following general form:

$$r :\ H_j;\ \phi \stackrel{w}{\rightarrow} H_k \,|\, H_l \,.$$

Rule r can be interpreted as follows: Suppose that H_0 is the set of all classes, and $h \in H_0$ is the concept to be identified in a given event f. Suppose also that because of some reasoning based on other rules of this type, h can belong only to the subset $H_j \subset H_0$. Then, if the assertion ϕ is verified on f, rule r concludes that h belongs to H_k with probability w or H_l with probability $1 - w$. The relations $H_k \cap H_l = \emptyset$ and $H_j \supset H_k, H_l$ always hold. H_j is called the *context* of the rule, H_k the *primary implication*, and H_l the *secondary implication.* If the probability w is one, the secondary implication is not present. As a special case, the set H_k can consist of a single concept h.

The assertion ϕ is a first-order logic formula expressed only with operational predicates. Numeric quantifiers such as Atleast n, Atmost n, Exactly n, and negation are also allowed. Usually, the primary implication of a rule coincides with the context of another formula. Formulas having the same primary implication are implicitly considered as being disjunctively joined. As a consequence, the knowledge base learned by ENIGMA can be described as a graph of rules. ENIGMA produces such a graph by searching in the rule space using a general-to-specific strategy, starting from the most general formula, *true* $\rightarrow H_0$, and generating more specific formulas until classification rules are discovered. This process is guided by statistical heuristics that trade consistency for completeness and by the background knowledge supplied at the start. The strategies and the heuristics are described in Bergadano et al. (1989b); Bergadano, Giordana, and Saitta (1988); Bergadano and Giordana (1988); and Brancadori and Radicchi (1989).

16.4 The Learning Set

All the experiments were performed using a set F of $N = 209$ mechanalysis tables (examples) that were filled by an experienced domain expert and refer to diagnoses of motor pumps. The considered faults can be grouped into six classes:

- C_1 = Problems in the joint
- C_2 = Faulty bearings

- C_3 = Mechanical loosening
- C_4 = Basement distortion
- C_5 = Unbalance
- C_6 = Normal operating conditions.

However, as mentioned in The Learning Problem, these faults rarely occur in isolation, and even then, it is not always possible to precisely individuate them. Thus, not all the N examples were uniquely classified by the human expert, but the diagnoses generated by him followed the taxonomy shown in figure 16.2. These are the intermediate classes that were used by the expert:

- C_7 = Shaft misalignment ($C_7 = C_1 \cup C_4$)
- C_8 = Problems in the pump ($C_8 = C_2 \cup C_3 \cup C_5$)
- C_9 = Problems in the motor ($C_9 = C_2 \cup C_3 \cup C_5$)
- C_{10} = Problems in the machine ($C_{10} = C_8 \cup C_9$).

The *ambiguity* $a(f)$ of a classified example f is the minimum number of classes that f is hypothesized to belong to; for instance, an example f classified in class C_8 has an ambiguity of 3. Moreover, a diagnosis H_i is said to be *more specific* than a diagnosis H_j if and only if H_j is an ancestor of H_i in the diagnostic taxonomy. Obviously, we want the automated system to be at least as specific as the expert. The ambiguity parameter a roughly corresponds to the amount of effort required to exactly individuate the cause of a single fault. In fact, the higher the ambiguity, the greater the number of components that need to be examined. For example, if faulty bearings in the pump are assessed, then only the bearings have to be disassembled; however, if nothing more specific than problems in the pump can be hypothesized, then the whole pump must be dismounted.

In table 16.1, the expert's classification of the N examples is reported; the average ambiguity of the examples is 2.08. Note that an internal node of the diagnostic taxonomy denotes uncertainty about the right choice among the descendant nodes; the intersection $C_i \cap C_j$ denotes a co-occurrence of C_i and C_j. Thus, the ambiguity of the diagnosis $C_i \cap C_j$ is taken to be the minimum of those assigned to C_i and C_j. In regard to the expert's classification, in many cases the expert was able to generate a less ambiguous hypothesis than the one reported in table 16.1. However, the error rate for these more specific expert diagnoses was 5 percent; the diagnoses reported in table 16.1 are the most precise ones that are error free. Here, we say that a diagnosis is in *error* when the true class is not included in the set of those proposed.

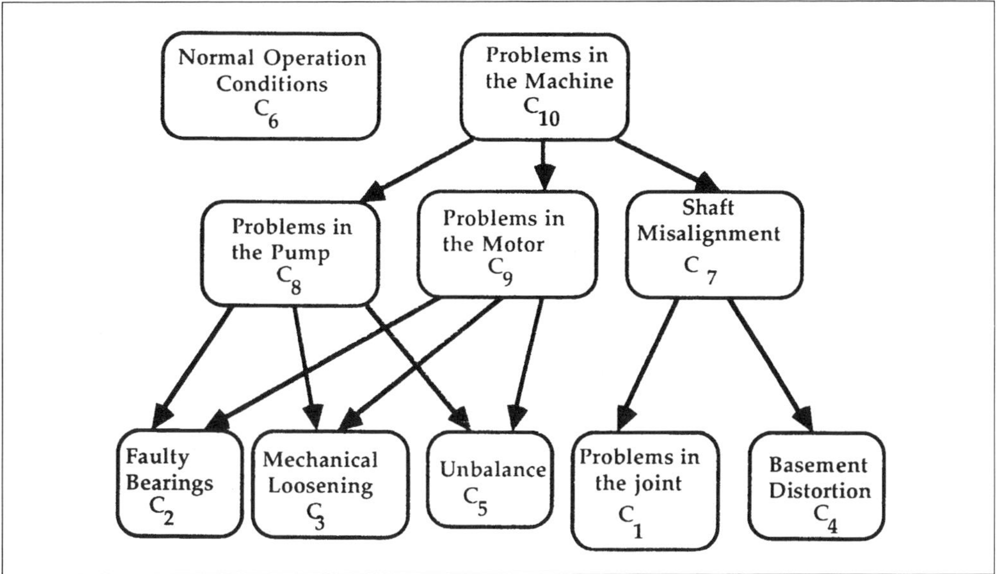

Figure 16.2
Diagnostic Taxonomy of Motor Pump Faults.

16.5 Results with the Expert System MEPS

MEPS is a prototype expert system that was manually developed by means of interviews with the same domain expert who supplied the classified examples (Michalski 1983). The knowledge is represented by means of rules and frames and contains both diagnostic and structural information. The chosen implementation environment is the Gold-Works shell on an IBM personal computer. The system contains about 290 diagnostic rules and 70 structural frames. Its representation language is a first-order logic-based language with an associated continuous-valued semantics. The process of designing and implementing the MEPS prototype took about 18 months, 12 of which were devoted to the acquisition, encoding, and maintenance of the knowledge base.

In table 16.2, the results obtained from MEPS are reported. On a given case, MEPS performs evidential reasoning and generates a list of possible faults in decreasing value of evidence. The recognition rate was evaluated in two ways: pessimistically and optimistically.

In the pessimistic case, only the best scored hypothesis, h_{best}, was considered; if h_{best} was a descendant in the diagnostic taxonomy of the node corresponding to the diagnosis

Table 16.1
Diagnoses Generated by the Expert. The classes correspond to the taxonomy in figure 16.2

	No. of Examples	Ambiguity	Class	No. of Examples	Ambiguity
C_{10}	29	5	$C_7 \cap C_5$	2	1
C_7	42	2	$C_7 \cap C_2$	2	1
C_8	26	3	$C_1 \cap C_3$	2	1
C_9	8	3	$C_1 \cap C_8$	1	1
C_1	13	1	$C_7 \cap C_3$	1	1
C_2	23	1	$C_1 \cap C_2$	4	1
C_3	6	1	$C_1 \cap C_9$	1	1
C_4	5	1	$C_4 \cap C_9$	1	1
C_5	13	1	$C_4 \cap C_8$	1	1
C_6	27	1	$C_3 \cap C_4$	1	1
			$C_1 \cap C_5$	1	1

Table 16.2
Results of MEPS on the Examples of the Set F_0.

Ambiguity	No. of Cases	The Best Hypothesis Was the Correct One	The Correct Hypothesis Was Included in the Proposed Set
1	131	122	122
2	60	49	59
3	18	15	18

given by the expert and was an ancestor of the correct diagnosis, then h_{best} was considered to be correct (the system gave an answer of equal or higher specificity than the expert and it contained the correct class). In the optimistic case, all generated hypotheses were considered; the MEPS diagnosis was considered correct if at least one of the generated hypotheses satisfied the two preceding characteristics. The obtained average ambiguity was 1.46, the pessimistic error rate was 0.86, and the optimistic error rate was 0.95.

16.6 Results Obtained Using ENIGMA

Learning experiments with ENIGMA were performed by exploiting the incremental abilities of the system and consisted of a sequence of six runs (phases). In the first phase, 60 randomly chosen cases were used as a learning set (LS) and the remaining 149 examples as a test set (TS). Then, 20 examples were randomly selected from the 149 to update the current knowledge base; the remaining 129 now became the test set. The error rate on the

Table 16.3
Results of the Automatic System ENIGMA with Incremental Learning. LS = Learning Set; VTS = Variable Test Set; FTS = Fixed Test Set.

	Phase 1	Phase 2	Phase 3	Phase 4	Phase 5	Phase 6
Cardinality of the LS	60	80	104	125	145	167
Cardinality of the VTS	107	87	63	42	22	0
Cardinality of the FTS	42	42	42	42	42	42
LS Recognition Rate	0.97	0.99	0.96	0.98	0.97	0.96
VTS Recognition Rate	0.93	0.94	0.94	0.90	0.91	//
FTS Recognition Rate	0.90	0.90	0.86	0.90	0.86	0.86
Recognition Rate Complete Set	0.94	0.95	0.93	0.95	0.94	0.94
Average Ambiguity	1.15	1.24	1.18	1.18	1.23	1.19
No. of Subproblems	13	13	13	17	18	18
No. of Generated Formulas	2788	3817	4067	1801	1643	1635
No. of Rules in the Knowledge Base	39	70	128	131	142	147
No. of Deleted Rules	//	20	28	40	46	47
No. of Added Rules	//	51	86	43	57	52
CPU Time (sec)	47826	43617	44252	36464	19992	19876

80 (60 plus 20) training examples was computed. Notice that the first 60 examples were test examples for the knowledge acquired with the next 20 examples. The whole process was repeated five times by randomly choosing the examples to be added in each phase (but keeping their number fixed). The average results are reported in table 16.3. As an example, here is one of the rules learned by ENIGMA: "If the shaft rotating frequency is ω_0, and the harmonic at ω_0 is reported to have high intensity, and the harmonic at $2\,\omega_0$ is reported to have high intensity in at least two measurements, then the example is an instance of one of the classes C_1, C_4, or C_5."

16.7 Discussion

In regard to the results of the automatic learning, the performance is stable as we increase the number of examples, but eventually it degrades slightly. Because of the ambiguity inherent in the examples, adding new ones to the training set does not necessarily contribute any new information; instead, it mixes information from different faults. In fact, denoting the average ambiguity of the learning examples added in the jth phase by $a_j(LS)$, we notice (table 16.4) an increment in the confusion of this set, which is responsible for this phenomenon. More precisely, the confusion arises with the five fault classes;

Table 16.4
Ambiguity of the Learning Set in Each Learning Phase. The last column refers to examples of classes C_1-C_5.

	Ambiguity in the Added Learning Set	Ambiguity in the Global Learning Set	Ambiguity of the Examples of Classes C_1–C_5
Phase 1	1.98	1.98	2.18
Phase 2	2.23	2.04	2.24
Phase 3	2.36	2.11	2.31
Phase 4	2.23	2.13	2.33
Phase 5	2.85	2.23	2.43
Phase 6	2.36	2.25	2.44

Table 16.5
Comparison between ENIGMA and MEPS.

	Ambiguity	Recognition Rate on Complete Set	Recognition Rate on Test Set	Development Time
ENIGMA	1.21	0.95	0.94	4 Months
MEPS	1.46	0.95	—	18 Months

the examples in class C_6 (nonfaulty machine) are always good examples.

Next, we compare the knowledge base acquired by ENIGMA to that of MEPS. For ENIGMA, the knowledge base used for this comparison was the one acquired during the second phase. As seen in table 16.5, the performance of the two systems is comparable, but the knowledge base acquired automatically was developed far more quickly than that of MEPS. One point of interest is that one-third of the rules acquired by ENIGMA corresponded directly to rules in MEPS.

In regard to the development time, an initial phase of problem mastering was common to both projects (about 2 months) and another month was spent preparing and recording the data. For MEPS, the manual knowledge acquisition and updating lasted 12 months, whereas ENIGMA acquired the knowledge base in a few hours. To make the acquired knowledge more understandable to the expert, the system was given a domain theory, defining higher-level features. An example of rules in this domain theory is: "If the shaft rotating frequency is ω_0, and a vibration has frequency ω, and ω is a multiple of ω_0, then ω is a *harmonic* of ω_0." The process of defining and implementing this theory took one additional month.

It should be noted that the 209 cases, whose acquisition spanned a time period of 25 years, are the source of the knowledge of the human expert who supplied the MEPS rules. He did not have a teacher, nor was there expertise available in advance; he formed his knowledge by dealing with this set of cases. In a sense, then, the MEPS knowledge base is tested on its own learning set.

16.8 Conclusions

In this chapter, we described an application of the learning system ENIGMA to a real problem of mechanical troubleshooting. The problem was a difficult one because of the complexity and high degree of noise in the data as well as the effort required to choose a suitable description language and a problem conceptualization. The results indicate that it is realistic to apply machine learning techniques to significant problems, largely reducing the development time of expert systems while maintaining a performance level comparable to that of expert systems developed with classic methodologies.

Acknowledgments

This chapter is a revised and extended version of a paper presented at the Seventh International Machine Learning Conference (1990) in Austin, Texas.

References

Bergadano, F., and Giordana, A. 1988. A Knowledge Intensive Approach to Concept Induction. In *Proceedings of the Fifth International Conference on Machine learning,* 305–317. San Mateo, Calif.: Morgan Kaufmann.

Bergadano, F.; Giordana, A.; and Saitta, L. 1988. Automated Concept Acquisition in Noisy Environments. *IEEE Transactions on Pattern Analysis and Machine Intelligence* 10(4): 555–577.

Bergadano, F.; Brancadori, F.; Giordana, A.; and Saitta, L. 1989. A System that Learns Diagnostic Knowledge in a Database Framework. Presented at the IJCAI-89 Workshop on Knowledge Discovery in Databases, Detroit, Mich. 20 August..

Bergadano, F.; Gemello, R.; Giordana, A.; and Saitta, L. 1989. Smart: A Problem Solver for Learning from Examples. In *Fundamenta Informaticae*, volume 12, 29–50. Amsterdam: Elsevier.

Brancadori, F., and Radicchi, S. 1989. Acquisizione Automatica della Conoscenza. *Informatica Oggi* 9(53): 81–93.

Cestnik, B.; Kononenko, I.; and Bratko, I. 1987. Assistant 86: A Knowledge Elicitation Tool for Sophisticated Users. In Proceedings of the Second European Working Session on Learning.

Michalski, R. S. 1983. A Theory and Methodology of Inductive Learning. *Artificial Intelligence* 20: 111–161.

Michalski, R., and Chilausky, R. 1980. Learning from being Told and Learning from Examples. *International Journal of Policy Analysis and Information Systems* 4: 125–161.

Michalski, R.; Hong, J.; Lavrac, N.; and Mozetic, I. 1986. The AQ15 Inductive Learning System: An Overview and Experiments. In Proceedings of the First International Meeting on Advances in Learning.

Mitchell, T.; Keller, R. M.; and Kedar-Cabelli, S. 1986. Explanation Based Generalization: A Unifying View. *Machine Learning* 1:47–80.

Muggleton, S. 1988. Machine Invention of First Order Predicates by Inverting Resolution. In *Proceedings of the Fifth International Conference on Machine Learning,* 339–352. San Mateo, Calif.: Morgan Kaufmann.

Quinlan, R. 1986. Induction of Decision Trees. *Machine Learning* 1: 81–106.

17 Induction of Decision Trees from Complex Structured Data

Michel Manago
CNRS & IntelliSoft

Yves Kodratoff
CNRS & George Mason University

Abstract

The ID_3 induction algorithm has been shown to be remarkably effective for automatically generating expert systems from databases. Nevertheless, as it is shown in this chapter, ID_3 cannot handle complex databases, such as relational databases or object-oriented databases. The KATE system uses the same induction techniques as ID_3 (same search technique, same preference criterion), but it drastically improves its knowledge representation capabilities. Examples are represented by frames (structured objects), which allows constraining the search space during induction. KATE's frame-based language is also used to represent classes of objects with slots and facets, hierarchies of classes (taxonomies), constraints, and procedural calls that deduce descriptors from other descriptors (goal-driven or data-driven reasoning). In this chapter, we show the extensions that had to be made to the ID_3 architecture to handle complex examples with objects and relations and to use background knowledge.

17.1 Turning Data into Knowledge

Since the early 1980s, the ID_3 induction algorithm (Quinlan 1983) has been successfully used for automatically generating expert systems from databases. From a set of training cases, ID_3 produces a knowledge base in the form of a decision tree. For instance, from a database of patients whose diseases are known, this induction engine learns how to efficiently predict the diseases of new incoming patients. Each case, or record in the database, is called a *training example.*

Numerous descendants of ID_3 offer improvements to the vanilla flavor algorithm (for example, being able to handle numeric attributes and unknown values, prune the decision tree based on statistical measures, generate production rules or run-time systems, and optimize user-defined costs as well as the depth of the tree). These descendants have been used for building numerous real-life, large-scale, industrial applications (Michie 1989), such as diagnostic systems (more than five medical expert systems generated from case libraries and patient records, a fault diagnostic system for printed circuit boards at ITT), decision support systems (shuttle landing control at the National Aeronautics and Space

Administration, military decision support systems), financial risk evaluation systems (credit card assessment, life and vehicle insurance), design support (design of a gas-oil separator at British Petroleum), and quality control in the manufacturing industry (Westinghouse Electric Corporation).

17.2 Learning from Complex Data

Not all potential knowledge-based-system applications can be tackled by ID_3. We show in this chapter that the knowledge representation capabilities of ID_3 (that is, vector of attributes) are too limited to cope with the training data when they are made up of complex entities: ID_3 lacks the ability to handle objects and relations. With the increasing sophistication of database management systems (relational and object-oriented DBMSs), there is a clear gap between what can be done using ID_3 and its descendants and the needs that are to be fulfilled. This gap was our motivation for developing a tool that is able to use induction for problems that call for a more powerful data model. In this section, we discuss why attribute-value vectors cannot be used for learning from complex data. Examples are drawn from a real-life application that was solved using KATE. In this application, there was no database to start with, and a lot of work was invested in accurately modeling the data (that is, choice of a representation language and the actual terms used to describe the data).

17.2.1 Using Commonsense Knowledge about the Domain

We begin by contrasting the notion of a complex data object with that of an attribute-value vector. In particular, we argue that the use of attribute-based representations increases the number of both the needed data features and legal values for objects' features.

Consider the domain of tomato plant diagnosis. A diseased tomato plant can be affected by several different symptoms. Each symptom is a complex entity whose description depends on both the type of symptom and its location. For instance, the symptom tache-ou-plage-sur-folioles (spot-on-leaves) is described by the following 17 features:

REPARTITION-SUR-PLANTE, REPARTITION-SUR-FEUILLE, NOMBRE,
COULEUR, ZONATIONS, MESURE, LIMITES, LOCALISATION-SUR-FOLIOLE,
PROPORTION-SUR-FOLIOLE, REPARTITION-SUR-FOLIOLE,
JAUNISSEMENT-POURTOUR, MYCELIUM-FRUCTIFICATIONS,
ASPECT-DU-MYCELIUM, TOUCHER, FORME, RELIEF.[1]

[1] distribution-on-plant, distribution-on-leaf, number, color, spherical-zones, measure, limits, localization-on-folioles, proportion-on-folioles, distribution-on-folioles, yellowing-of-edges, fructification-

Another symptom, called chancre-extérieur-collet (canker-on-the-outside-of-the-stem) is described by the following 14 features:

ZONATIONS, TOUCHER, MESURE, FORME,
LIMITES, RELIEF, LIEN-SYMPTOME-INTERNE, DEGRE-D-ATTAQUE,
MYCELIUM-FRUCTIFICATIONS, REPARTITION-SUR-PLANTE,
LOCALISATION-SUR-EXTERIEUR-TIGE,
REPARTITION-SUR-EXTERIEUR-TIGE, NOMBRE, COULEUR.[2]

These two kinds of symptoms are described by a different number of features; share some common features: COULEUR (color) and FORME (shape); and have some unique features: JAUNISSEMENT-POURTOUR (yellowing-around-the-edges) for the spot on the leaves, LOCALISATION-SUR-EXTERIEUR-TIGE (location-on-the-outside-of-the-stem) for the canker on stem, and so on.

How can a symptom be represented with a flat attribute-value vector knowledge representation language such as the one used in ID_3? One solution is to introduce an attribute for each type of symptom (for example, exists-spot-on-leaves) and one for each of its features (for example, color-of-spot-on-leaves). However, because there are 147 different symptoms with an average of nine features per symptom, there is a total of 147 * 9 = 1323 attributes. Such a large number of attributes will prevent ID_3 from finding a solution because at the root node, ID_3 will make 1323 information-gain computations, 1322 for each child node, and so on. (Although ID_3 can handle databases with a large number of examples, the examples are usually described by fewer than 100 attributes.) Moreover, with this representation, it is impossible to have two or more symptoms of the same type in the same example.

A second solution for modeling the data with attribute-value vectors appears to be a little more economical in terms of the total number of attributes. A special attribute, called type-of-symptom, which has one of 147 values (the 147 kinds of symptoms), is introduced. An attribute is associated with each feature of the 147 symptoms even when this feature is not relevant for all the symptoms. For example, color is not a relevant feature for describing a hole, but it must still appear in its description because color is useful to describe some other symptom, such as a spot. When an attribute is not useful for describing a specific symptom, it has the special value irrelevant in the examples. This value is then processed by the induction engine in a special way so that it will not disrupt the information-gain computation. (During induction, the training examples with value irrelevant are propagated in each branch of the decision node.)

of-myceliums, aspect-of-mycelium, feel, form, scraps

[2]spherical-zones, feel, measure, limits, scraps, link-to-internal-symptom, state-of-damages, fructification-of-myceliums, distribution-on-plant, localization-on-the-outside-of-the-stem, distribution-on-the-outside-of-the-stem, number, color

There are other applications where this special value might be needed. For instance, in the cancer database (Quinlan 1986) with 30 attributes to each example, a patient is described by the sex and state of pregnancy. When the sex of a patient is male, the feature pregnant is not relevant, and we could write "pregnant = irrelevant" in all examples where "sex = male." We now show why in the tomato diseases application, this simple approach will produce such a large number of computations that the induction system will fail to complete its task. Consider a symptom represented by a vector of attributes:

	TYPE-SYMPTOME	COULEUR	...	JAUNISSEMENT-POURTOUR	REPARTITION SUR-EXTERIEUR-TIGE
EX109	TACHE-OU-PLAGE-SUR-FOLIOLES	BRUN	...	OUI	IRRELEVANT
EX206	CHANCRE-EXTÉRIEUR-COLLET	GRIS-BEIGE	...	IRRELEVANT	GÉNÉRALISÉE

The attributes that describe a symptom are the union of the features that describe each kind of symptom. In the tomato plant domain, 147 different types of symptoms are described by an average number of nine features. If the data are represented with attribute-value vectors, each symptom is described by a total of 80 attributes (some features are shared by several symptoms). On the average, there are 71 attributes with value irrelevant. Therefore, during induction, as soon as the type of the symptom is known, ID_3 makes 71 useless computations of information gain at each subsequent node of the decision tree. Because the same tomato plant (that is, an example) can have as many as six different symptoms, these figures are multiplied by six (we have type-of-symptoml, colorl, . . . , type-of-symptom-2, color2, and so on), which yields a total of 480 attributes for describing all the features of the symptoms in an example, 429 of which have the value irrelevant.

Furthermore, the number of features needed to describe a symptom is not the only number that is drastically increased because ID_3 does not use commonsense descriptive knowledge about the objects it classifies. The set of possible values for features is also increased. For instance, the set of possible colors for a symptom of type TACHE-OU-PLAGE-SUR-FOLIOLES is different from the one of a symptom of type CHANCRE-EXTÉRIEUR-COLLET. With ID_3's attribute-value representation, the set of legal values for each feature is the union of the set of values possible for the feature when it is attached to any symptom. In this case, the allowed values for the attribute color include the ones for a symptom of type TACHE-OU-PLAGE-SUR-FOLIOLES and a symptom of type CHANCRE-EXTÉRIEUR-COLLET (the set of legal colors for these two symptoms is different). In the tomato domain application, this yields an average number of 30 different possible values for each feature. Because in its computation of information gain, ID_3 evaluates the entropy of each branch (that is, each possible value for the attribute), ID_3 makes 429 * 30 = 12870 useless computations of entropy for irrelevant features plus a large number of entropy computations of irrelevant feature values for the remaining relevant features at each node of the decision tree.

As we saw, because ID_3 lacks the ability to use commonsense knowledge about the domain, it can do a massive amount of completely useless computation. Although these computations turn out to be marginal for some applications, they simply cannot be afforded when the training data become complex (combinatorial explosion during induction). In this case, commonsense background knowledge about the domain can be used to constrain the search space during induction and prune irrelevant features; one does not need to test for the information gain of being pregnant for male patients!

17.2.2 Learning from Examples Made from Several Objects

The fact that there is more than one object of the same type in the training examples might cause ID_3 to learn incorrect rules. To represent that there can be six symptoms to each example with a feature-value vector, one would introduce six features called exists-symptom1,..., exists-symptom6 and several other features to describe each symptom (such as type-of-symptom1, color-symptom1,..., type-of-symptom6, color-symptom6). The choice of labels symptom1,..., symptom6 for a given symptom is purely random. There are no valid reasons to decide that a particular spot-on-leaves should be called symptom1 instead of symptom2. One cannot devise an ordering of the symptoms that would force a kind of symptom to always have the same label because any 6 out of 147 symptoms can appear in an example. Unfortunately, the choice of label might drive the induction system into learning incorrect rules. Consider what would happen if in every example of a disease A, there is a spot-on-folioles with label symptom1.

Exmpl. 1 (A): <exist-symptom1 = yes> <type-of-symptom1 = spot-on-folioles>
<color-symptom1 = yellow> ... <type-of-symptom1 = canker-on-stem>
<exist-symptom2 = yes> <color-symptom2 = white>...
Exmpl. 2 (A): <exist-symptom1 = yes><type-of-symptom1 = spot-on-folioles>
<color-symptom1 = brown> ... <exist-symptom2 = yes>
<type-of-symptom2 = hole-in-folioles> <color-symptom2 = irrelevant>...
Exmpl. 3 (B): <exist-symptom1 = yes> <type-of-symptom1 = mold-on-fruit>
<color-symptom1 = white> ... <exist-symptom2 = yes>
<type-of-symptom2 = spot-on-folioles> <color-symptom2 = brown>

ID_3 might possibly learn the rule [IF <type-of-symptom1 = spot-on-folioles> THEN disease A]. However, if there is a spot-on-folioles that is called symptom2 in an example of disease B this rule is syntactically consistent with the data, but it is semantically incorrect. What is needed here is a way to express a test of the form "Is there any symptom of type spots-in-folioles?" instead of the tests "Is symptom1 of type spots-in- folioles?" "Is symptom2 of type spots-in-folioles?" and so on. The induction engine then computes information gain of this more generic test. In other words, this application requires a more powerful knowledge representation language and a more powerful pattern-matching algorithm. The pattern matcher must handle variables, and it must be based on some form of first-order logic instead of propositional calculus.

There are other reasons why ID_3 cannot be used for the tomato data. For example, it cannot handle relations between objects that might be discriminant (for example, the fact that the mold is on the spot is important). Our point is that ID_3 cannot be used in the tomato application because its knowledge representation capabilities are insufficient, not because its induction mechanism is faulty (the hill-climbing search strategy, the heuristic-preference criterion based on entropy). Thus, the obvious idea is to build an induction tool with the same learning mechanism as ID_3 but a more powerful knowledge representation language. The idea sounds simple, but the technical difficulties to be overcome in achieving this goal are considerable. In the next section, we show how the notion of objects is represented in KATE and describe the fundamental changes that had to be made to the induction algorithm so that it could process complex databases of this kind.

17.3 Constraining Search during Induction

This section discusses the ways that KATE constrains search. First, the underlying mechanism of the frame is examined, then how the frame-based approach makes it possible to restrict inductive search to relevant attributes and relevant values of attributes. Finally, we discuss how examples that are made up of a variable number of objects are handled.

17.3.1 The Frame-Based Language in KATE

About 20 years ago, researchers in knowledge representation for AI systems came up with the notion of frames (Minsky 1975). Frame-based languages rapidly invaded most of the AI tools: expert system shells, blackboard systems, image-recognition systems, natural language parsers, planning systems, and so on. The practical interest of these languages has been well demonstrated; they are powerful and efficient, the knowledge is made of modular reusable entities, the formalism is natural, and they enable object-oriented programming. Starting with figure 17.1, we briefly present KATE's frame-based language and show how it is used to represent background knowledge about the domain so that the induction engine can overcome the problems described in the previous section.

A frame can be viewed as a data structure. It represents a set of objects (a *class*) or the

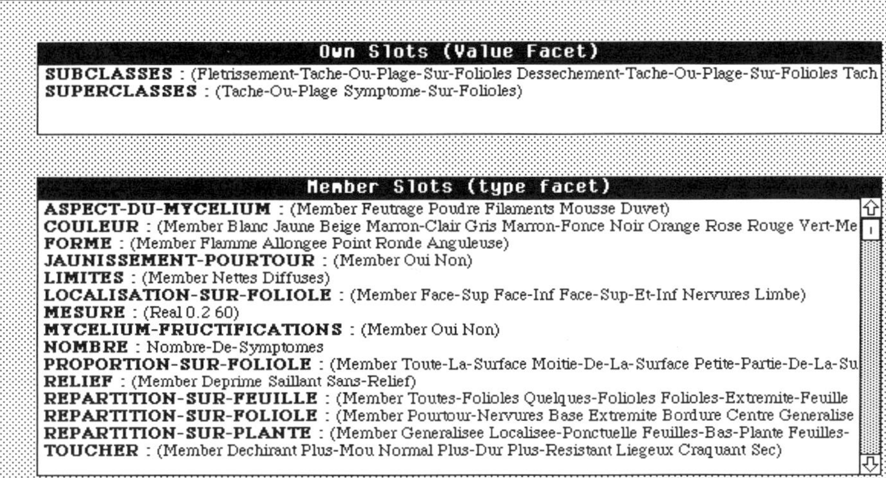

Figure 17.1
With KATE's Frame Editor, the User Manually Enters the Class Definitions Used during Induction.

objects themselves (the *instances* of the class). Properties and relations are attached to the frame and are called *slots*. Facets are attached to the slots. Facets enable representing different kinds of information about the slots. For example, there are facets that represent the actual value of the slot (*value facet*), the type or legal range of values for the slot (*type facet*), procedures to deduce features from other features in backward or forward chaining (*demons*), and the number of values allowed for a slot (*cardinal facet*). Consider the following class frame:

[TACHE-OU-PLAGE-SUR-FOLIOLES
own slots:
<SUPERCLASSES (**VALUE** TACHE-OU-PLAGE SYMPTOME-SUR-FOLIOLES)>, etc. ..

member slots:
<LOCALISATION-SUR-FOLIOLE
(**TYPE** (FACE-SUP FACE-INF FACE-SUP-ET-INF NERVURES LIMBE)
(**CARDINAL** (1 2))>
<MESURE
(**TYPE** (**REAL** 0.2 60))> , etc. ..]

The type facet of member slot LOCALISATION-SUR-FOLIOLE indicates the range of possible values for this nominal attribute. The value of this slot is one of the values in the set {FACE-SUP FACE-INF FACE-SUP-ET-INF NERVURES LIMBE}. The cardinal facet attached to this slot indicates that it can simultaneously have one or two values. Thus, in some of the examples, this feature will have one value, and in others, it will have two values in the above set of legal values. The type facet attached to the MESURE slot indicates that the slot expects a real value between 0.2 and 60. In KATE, predefined data types include nominal (the value is in a set of discrete values), ordered nominal (the value is in a list of ordered values), integer (or subranges), real (or subranges), Boolean, or the name of a class. In the last case, the slot is a relation that links an instance of a class to another instance of a class. For example, [MEN <SPOUSE (TYPE WOMEN)>] indicates that an instance of class MEN will be linked to an instance of class WOMEN by the SPOUSE relation.

17.3.2 Constraining the Set of Test Nodes during Induction

The notion of a slot is similar to the notion of an attribute in ID_3. The difference lies in the fact that a slot is always attached to an object (that is, a frame). For instance, the slot LOCALISATION-SUR-FOLIOLE of TACHE-OU-PLAGE-SUR-FOLIOLES is a different attribute (that is, it has a different range of allowed values and a different cardinal) from the slot LOCALISATION-SUR-FOLIOLE of FLETRISSEMENT-SUR-FOLIOLE. The induction engine will behave differently when it computes information gain for this slot depending on whether it is attached to one object or the other. For example, it will build different branches at this test node because the range of allowed values is different.

The notion of an attribute in ID_3 has thus been replaced in KATE with the notion of a slot attached to an object. Because a frame contains a description of all the features that are relevant to describe a certain concept (that is, the slots), KATE never considers an irrelevant feature in a given context for the information-gain computation. For example, we might have a class called MEN with Boolean slot BEARDED and a class called WOMEN with Boolean slot PREGNANT. Because KATE always tests for the information gain of a slot attached to an object, it never tests for the state of pregnancy of a person whose class is MEN. In other words, KATE computes the information gain of PREGNANT(WOMEN) and BEARDED(MEN) instead of the information gain of PREGNANT or BEARDED in general. We see in Handling Examples with Different Objects what happens when an example does not have an object of this type in its description.

By using knowledge represented by frames, KATE knows which features are relevant for describing a particular object. The induction engine uses this knowledge when building the decision tree. This is achieved by always introducing a slot with the type of the object to which it is attached. On subsequent nodes in the decision tree, the features that are possible are constrained because of the type of the object. For example, if at the first node of the decision tree, the most informative feature has been the SIZE slot of a symptom of type HOLE-IN-A-LEAF, for subsequent nodes in the tree, only the slots attached to the frame HOLE-IN-A-LEAF are used in the information-gain computation. Descriptors such as COLOR and TEXTURE that are not relevant for this concept are simply discarded, and information gain is no longer computed for these. Thus, at different nodes of the decision tree, different features are considered. The search strategy (hill climbing) and preference criterion (maximize information gain) used in KATE are the same as in ID_3. The difference lies in what is considered during the search. ID_3 considers all remaining features that do not appear in the tree for the computation of information gain, and KATE does more work to dynamically constrain the set of features considered.

17.3.3 Constraining the Number of Branches for a Test Node

Information gain is thus computed for a slot that is attached to an object of a certain type. For example, KATE tests information gain of COLOR(SYMPTOM-ON-LEAVES) and not information gain of COLOR by itself, as ID_3 would. As we saw previously, the information about the type of the slot (expected values of the slot) is represented by a facet, called *type*, that is attached to the slot. Two different frames can have different type facets, and KATE is able to represent and use the fact that the range of values for the same slot is different for two different frames. Because the range of values for a slot of a frame is known, and information gain is computed for a slot attached to a frame, KATE is able to constrain the set of legal values for this slot; each branch for the candidate node in the tree is meaningful in the given context.

To summarize, the frame-based language is used to represent commonsense knowledge about the entities that describe the training examples. This knowledge is used during induction to constrain the set of features that are relevant in a given context (that is, reduce the number of test nodes considered for the information-gain computation) and constrain the set of values for these features (that is, reduce the number of branches for the test nodes). Using this background knowledge prevents a combinatorial explosion during induction when the training data are complex. (The set of irrelevant features can rapidly become overwhelming, as we saw in Learning from Complex Data.) Note that any data set that can be represented by ID_3's attribute-value vectors can also be trivially represented by frames. One simply introduces a single frame whose slots correspond to the ID_3 attributes, and KATE's induction engine behaves like ID_3's.

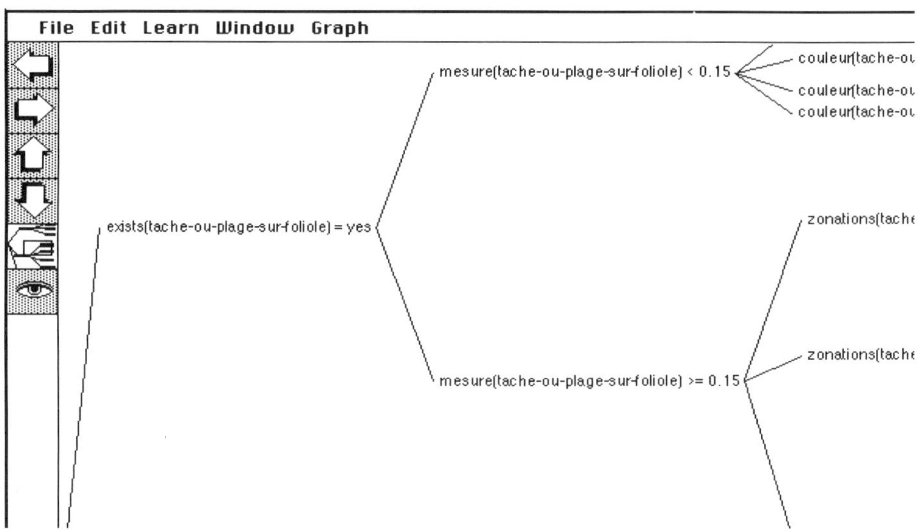

Figure 17.2
When the Training Examples Contain a Variable Number of Objects, Information Gain of the Special Test "exists(object-type)" Is Considered When Building the Tree.

17.3.4 Handling Examples with Different Objects

As we showed, the tests considered for the information-gain computation at different nodes in the decision tree are different. The procedure that dynamically generates candidate nodes for the information-gain computation in KATE is as follows:

When all the examples at the current branch of the decision tree contain an object of the same type, information gain of the nonrelational slots of this object is computed (that is, nominals, ordered nominals, integers, and reals). This can either introduce a new object or specialize an object that already appears in the current path of the decision tree. Numeric tests are binarized to maximize information gain. When a certain type of object does not appear in the description of all the examples at the current decision node, information gain of the special test "exists(type-of-object)" is computed (figure 17.2). Information gain of relational slots is computed when the relation links two existing objects or when the relation introduces one new object. Information gain of a relation that introduces two new objects is not computed. This design choice is motivated by the need to constrain the search space.

In KATE, the first test "exists(object-type)" that appears in the decision tree means "is there any object of this type in the example?" The second test means "is there a second object of this type in the example?" and so on. Each object that appears in the tree is given a name that can be indexed further down in the tree. This identifier is actually a typed variable that is bound to the actual objects in the training examples, so that we can index the features of a particular object when computing information gain afterward.

This method enables dealing with examples described by a different number of objects. For instance, when all the examples contain a symptom of type SYMPTOM-ON-LEAVES, KATE computes information gain only for the slots that describe an instance of the class SYMPTOM-ON-LEAVES. Once the first symptom appears in the tree, the information gain of the remaining relevant features of the symptom is computed. The information gain of introducing a second symptom is also computed. The system does not consider features attached to a second symptom until there is already a symptom that appears in the tree, features attached to a third symptom until two symptoms already appear in the tree, and so on. This, of course, introduces a certain bias in the behavior of the system because some tests that might be discriminant are hidden at certain nodes until the symptom becomes visible. Again, this design choice is motivated by the need to constrain the search space.

When information gain has been computed at a decision node for all these tests, the test with the highest information gain is retained as the current decision node. The search strategy and preference criterion are, thus, similar in KATE and ID_3. As we saw, the difference lies in the generation of the tests that are considered for the information-gain computation at each decision node of the tree.

To conclude this section, let us note that although we chose to use frames in KATE, we are well aware that alternative knowledge representation languages could have been used (for example, predicate calculus). The extensions that were introduced in ID_3's induction engine are general, and they do not depend on the fact that the data are represented using a frame language. Nevertheless, the frame structure provides all that is needed for the induction algorithm; the slots and legal slot values for a particular object can be efficiently retrieved to build the decision tree (that is, dynamically generate test nodes and test branches to compute information gain), and deductive knowledge can be represented and used by the induction engine.

17.4 Object-Oriented Programming in KATE

Object orientation is a unifying factor for all the tools in KATE (graphic browsers, object editors, spreadsheet, interface to programming languages, interface to databases, induction engine, and decision tree editor). It not only enables modeling the domain entities and the training examples using an object-oriented approach, but also object-oriented programming. Object-oriented programming can be useful for deducing knowledge (goal-driven or data-driven reasoning) or interfacing the different tools with themselves or the external world. Here, we highlight the use of deductive knowledge.

Procedural calls (demons) are used to deduce features from other features. For example, the values of slots "type-of-culture" and "heating-mode" of frame "cultures" can be deduced from the slot "kind-of-culture." When "kind-of-culture" is "in-the-fields," "type-of-culture" is "in-ground" (in a glass house, it could be sand), and "heating-mode" is "cold" (in a plastic tunnel or a glass house, it could be heated). The backward-chaining rule [IF <kind-of-culture=in-the-field> THEN <heating-mode=cold>] can be efficiently implemented by a method attached to the slots "type-of-culture" and "heating-mode." The following method is attached to the "heating-mode" slot of frame "culture." Message is a primitive of the KATE language, and *self* is a system variable bound to the original recipient of the message, as it is classically done in object-oriented programming. The $ prefix denotes an entity in the current knowledge base.

```
IF (EQUAL (message *self* $kind-of-culture) $in-the-field) THEN $cold.
```

In addition to using KATE's object language to program the method, the user has access to the full power of external programming languages such as Lisp, Pascal, and C.

KATE uses deductive knowledge in several tools. In the spreadsheet used to collect the database of training examples when none is available to start with, deductive knowledge saves the work of filling information that can easily be deduced, as shown in figure 17.3. The deduction of the values of "type-of-culture" and "heating-mode" is automatically performed by the methods attached to slots "type-de-culture" and "mode-de-chauffage" of frame "culture" (goal-driven reasoning). The methods are activated when accessing the unknown value of these slots. The methods dynamically compute the values of these slots and deduce that when the slot "kind-of-culture" has value "in-the-fields," its value is "cold." Note that if the value of "kind-of-culture" was itself dynamically computed by another method, we would have a backward-chaining deduction.

Deduction can also be achieved in forward chaining (event driven) by attaching an active value demon to the slot. For example, one could attach an active value to slot "kind-of- culture" that would update the values of "heating mode" and "type-of-culture."

Demons are naturally indexed by the frame structures, and the induction engine can also use deductive domain knowledge encoded this way, as shown in Manago (1989). Note that the issue of whether to use deductive knowledge during induction is still highly controversial; should a learning system empirically discover everything from scratch, or can it use deductive domain knowledge when it is available? One of the advantages of the knowledge-intensive approach is that noisy data can be filtered by using deductive knowledge, as shown in Manago and Kodratoff (1987). One of its disavantages is that it

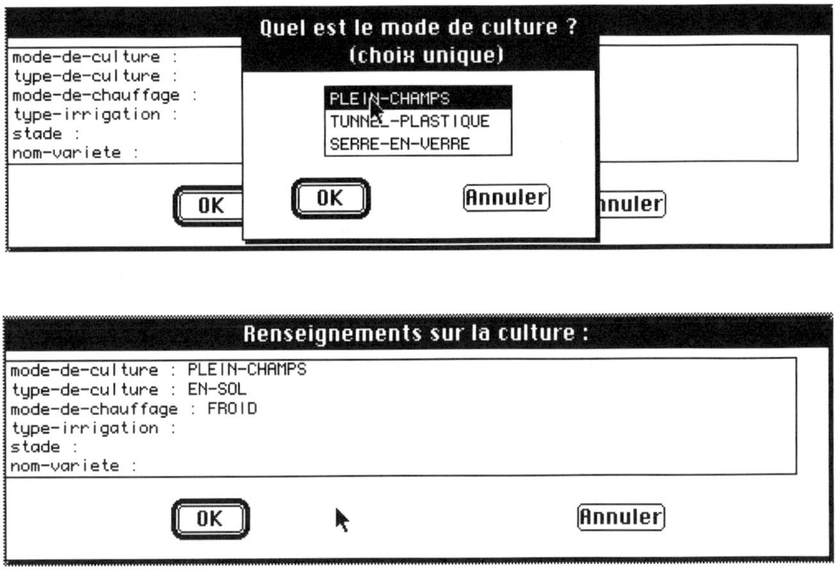

Figure 17.3
The Spreadsheet Directly Uses Deductive Knowledge to Collect the Database of Examples.

introduces a bias on the behavior of the learning system. We feel at this point that this is application dependent; for some applications, it is better to use deductive knowledge during induction, and for some, it is better to use knowledge-poor induction. The user, therefore, has the option to enter deductive knowledge but is not forced to do so to use KATE.

17.5 Interface to Databases

KATE offers an interface to DBMSs and external spreadsheets through ASCII files. A description of the file's content is provided in the class definitions by attaching a position-in-datafile facet to the slots. KATE is then able to directly read the training examples from the data file. Each record is separated by carriage returns in the data file, and each component of a record is separated by tabulations or blank spaces. In figure 17.4, we show the class description of a data file (figure 17.5) for lending money to companies. This ASCII file was generated by MicroSoft Multiplan on a compatible PC. It contains 700 records that were processed by KATE's induction engine.

Clearly, a classical ID$_3$ could have been used for this bank loan application. In KATE,

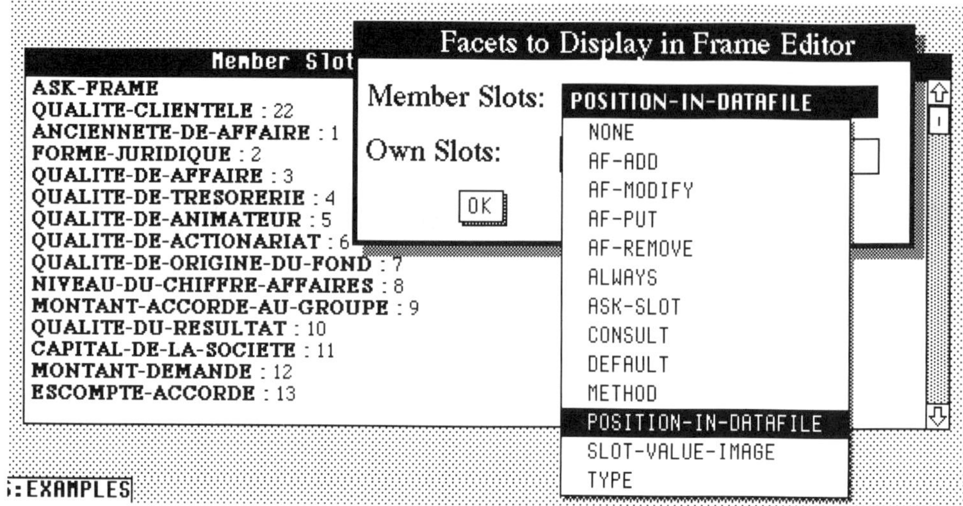

Figure 17.4
KATE Can Be Linked to External Databases and Spreadsheets Using Classes and Facets. The value of the facet is the position of the slot value within the record in the data file.

1	95	SARL	S	S	?	?	B	P	?	J
100	?	?	S	?	S	?	?	?	95	?
?	?	?	?	?	?	S	J	?		

Figure 17.5
A Data Record for a Company Asking for a Bank Loan. Question marks denote unknown values.

a single object was introduced with the slots shown in figure 17.5. KATE's induction engine behaved exactly like a sophisticated ID_3 (the attributes correspond to the slots of the object). KATE is thus able to handle any application that ID_3 can handle. However, for applications that require a more powerful data model, such as the tomato disease application or a military decision support application, KATE can still be used, but ID_3 cannot. In figure 17.6, we present the ASCII file definition of a training example for the tomato application. This example well demonstrates that these data are much too complex to be handled by a classical ID_3 (note the differences in the description of the four symptoms):

17.6 Applications

KATE is a commercial product. It is specifically aimed at applications such as the maintenance of industrial machines; the design and validation of decision systems; the computer-aided generation of diagnostic expert systems; expert system maintenance; the analysis, interpretation, and classification of complex data; and quality control in manufacturing.

KATE has been used to generate and maintain an expert system on tomato plant diseases at the Institut National de Recherche en Agronomie. Some promising preliminary results in the area of tomato plant diseases have been achieved throughout the course of the INSTIL ESPRIT project (Blythe et al. 1988; Manago 1988). The french Compagnie Bancaire has used KATE to evaluate risks when lending money to companies (700 training cases with 80 percent unknown values, 7 classes to identify). The results of the inductive system were tested using KATE's auto consultation mode on an additional data set of 400 examples that were not presented during induction. The results were satisfactory; 73 percent of KATE's predictions were perfect (same response as the expert), and an additional 10 percent were correct (the right answer was suggested with the highest probability). Note that for the same test data, a single expert made correct predictions at less than 70 percent, and a panel of 10 experts was at slightly below 80 percent. KATE outperformed an in-house expert system by over 20 percent (generation of its knowledge base took six person-months). The rules found by KATE were more efficient but were different from the ones manually generated by the experts. In fact, before generating the tree, we were told by the expert that the test "montant-demandé" was weakly discriminant. This test was identified by KATE as one of the most discriminant and appeared near the root of the decision tree! An analysis of the cases that were wrongly classified by KATE during auto consultation also revealed that the errors of the system generated by induction were not as damaging as the errors made by the expert system generated through expert interviews.

```
[EX5
        (CLASSES  EXAMPLES)
        (DISEASE  CORYNEBACTERIUM)
        (EST-DECRIS-PAR (CULTURE6 PROBLEME7))]
[CULTURE6
        (CLASSES  CULTURE)
        (DECRIS  EXEMPLE5)
        (MODE-DE-CULTURE  SERRE-EN-VERRE)
        (TYPE-DE-CULTURE  HORS-SOL)
        (MODE-DE-CHAUFFAGE  CHAUFFE)
        (TYPE-IRRIGATION  LOCALISEE)
        (STADE  ADULTE-FRUITS-MURS)
        (NOM-VARIETE  PRISCA)]
[PROBLEME7
        (CLASSES PROBLEME)
        (DECRIS  EXEMPLE5)
        (REPARTITION-SUR-CULTURE
            EN-LIGNES-PLUS-OU-MOINS-LONGUES-SUR-LES-RANGEES)
        (ETAT-VEGETATION-MALADE  VEGETATION-MAUVAISE)
        (ASPECT-ANORMAL-DES-PLANTES  PLANTES-JAUNIES)
        (DATE-D-APPARITION-DU-PROBLEME  18)
        (HUMIDITE-AUTOUR-DE-L-APPARITION-DU-PROBLEME  OUI)
        (EVOLUTION-DU-PROBLEME  RAPIDE)
        (ONE-PART-IS  (SYMPTOME8 SYMPTOME9 SYMPTOME10 SYMPTOME11)]
[SYMPTOME8
        (CLASSES  FLETRISSEMENT-DES-FOLIOLES)
        (PART-OF  PROBLEME7)
        (REPARTITION-SUR-PLANTE  GENERALISEE)
        (REPARTITION-SUR-FEUILLE  TOUTES-FOLIOLES)
        (LOCALISATION-SUR-FOLIOLE  LIMBE)
        (PROPORTION-SUR-FOLIOLE  TOUTE-LA-SURFACE)
        (REPARTITION-SUR-FOLIOLE  GENERALISEE)
        (REVERSIBILITE  NON)
        (VITESSE-EVOLUTION  RAPIDE)]
[SYMPTOME9
        (CLASSES  JAUNISSEMENT-DES-FOLIOLES)
        (PART-OF  PROBLEME7)
        (REPARTITION-SUR-PLANTE  GENERALISEE)
        (REPARTITION-SUR-FEUILLE  TOUTES-FOLIOLES)
        (LOCALISATION-SUR-FOLIOLE  FACE-SUP-ET-INF)
        (PROPORTION-SUR-FOLIOLE  TOUTE-LA-SURFACE)
        (REPARTITION-SUR-FOLIOLE  GENERALISEE)
        (INTENSITE  PALE)
        (HOMOGENE  OUI)
        (LIMITES  NETTES)
        (ASPECT  NECROSE)
        (TOUCHER  NORMAL)]
[SYMPTOME10
        (CLASSES  TACHE-OU-PLAGE-SUR-FOLIOLES)
        (PART-OF  PROBLEME7)
        (REPARTITION-SUR-PLANTE  GENERALISEE)
        (REPARTITION-SUR-FEUILLE  TOUTES-FOLIOLES)
        (NOMBRE  NOMBREUX)
        (CONFLUENCE  OUI)
        (VARIABILITE  FAIBLE)
        (COULEUR  MARRON-FONCE)
        (ZONATIONS  2-ZONES)
        (MESURE  20)
        (LIMITES  DIFFUSES)
        (MYCELIUM-FRUCTIFICATIONS  NON)
        (LOCALISATION-SUR-FOLIOLE  FACE-SUP-ET-INF)
        (PROPORTION-SUR-FOLIOLE  TOUTE-LA-SURFACE)
        (REPARTITION-SUR-FOLIOLE  GENERALISEE)
        (TOUCHER  SEC)
        (FORME  ALLONGEE)
        (RELIEF  SANS-RELIEF)
        (JAUNISSEMENT-POURTOUR  OUI)]

[SYMPTOME11
        (CLASSES  AUTRES-ANOMALIES-DE-COLORATION-INTERIEUR-TIGE)
        (PART-OF  PROBLEME7)
        (REPARTITION-SUR-PLANTE  TIGE-BAS-PLANTE)
        (LOCALISATION-INTERIEUR-TIGE  VAISSEAUX)
        (COULEUR  GRIS)]
```

Figure 17.6
ASCII File Definition of a Training Example for the Tomato Disease Application.

KATE has also been used for generating and validating a fault diagnosis expert system (errors of transmission in a circuit) and a military decision support system (interpretation of two-dimensional pictures) at the Centre d'Electronique de l'Armement (CELAR). A second military system for identifying targets is currently being built at CELAR.

17.7 Conclusion

In this chapter, we presented a tool that extends the scope of applications that can be addressed through induction. KATE can represent complex training cases that could not be handled by earlier tools such as ID3. It can handle the notion of objects, relations between objects, several objects in an example, a different number of objects from one example to the other, hierarchies of objects, and deductive knowledge. Any application for which ID3 can be used can also be tackled by KATE; the data are represented by a single object whose slots correspond to the ID3 attributes. KATE is, therefore, an extension of ID3 as opposed to a new induction system. The induction mechanism is similar to the one used by ID3; KATE uses the same search strategy (hill climbing) and the same preference criterion (information gain based on Shannon's entropy measure). However, KATE does more work than ID3 when generating candidate nodes in the decision tree. In KATE, a test is a slot attached to an object as opposed to being a stand-alone attribute, as in ID3. The set of tests for which information gain is computed is dynamically generated, and it is constrained by the class description of the objects; at different decision nodes, different tests are considered for the information-gain computation. The frame-based representation of KATE is used to generate these tests. The slots of the class frames are used to build the candidate test nodes, and their ranges of legal values (represented by facets) are used to build the branches. By using commonsense knowledge about the domain entities represented by frames, KATE's induction engine is able to test the information gain of features that are relevant given a certain context.

Acknowledgments

We would like to thank *IntelliSoft* for allowing us to publish this work and Noël Conruyt, Jacques Lerenard, and Dominique Blancard (Institut National de Recherche en Agronomiet) who developed the tomato application. *IntelliSoft* would also like to thank all the organizations that support machine learning research at *IntelliSoft*, the European economic community (ESPRIT project 2154, Machine Learning Toolbox), l'Agence Nationale pour la Valorisation de la Recherche, le Ministre de la Recherche et de la Technologie, and Apple Computers. KATE is a trademark of *IntelliSoft* Inc. and is available on the microExplorer from Texas Instruments and the Macintosh from Apple. KATE-runtime (KATIOUCHA) is available on the Macintosh (with an interface to Apple's Hypercard).

References

Blythe, J.; Needham, D.; McDowell, R.; Manago, M., Rouveirol, C.; Kodratoff, Y.; Lesaffre, F. M.; Conruyt, N.; and Corsi, P. 1988. Knowledge Acquisition by Machine Learning: The INSTIL Project. In *ESPRIT 88: Putting the Technology to Use*, volume 1, 769–779. Amsterdam: North Holland.

Manago, M. 1989. Knowledge Intensive Induction. In *Proceedings of the Sixth International Workshop on Machine Learning*, ed. A. M. Segre, 151–155. San Mateo, Calif.: Morgan-Kaufmann.

Manago, M. 1988. Intégration de Techniques Numériques et Symboliques en Apprentissage Automatique. Ph.D. diss., Univ. of Orsay.

Manago, M., and Kodratoff, Y. 1987. Noise and Knowledge Acquisition. In Proceedings of the Tenth International Joint Conference on Artificial Intelligence, 348–354. Menlo Park, Calif.: International Joint Conference on Artificial Intelligence.

Michie, D. 1989. New Commercial Opportunities Using Information Technology. In *Proceedings of the Third International Gi-Kongress*, eds. W. Brauer and C. Freska, 64–71. New York: Springer Verlag.

Minsky, M. 1975. A Framework for Representing Knowledge. In *The Psychology of Computer Vision*, ed. P. H. Winston. New York: McGraw-Hill.

Quinlan, J. R. 1986. Simplifying Decision Trees. In Proceedings of the First AAAI Workshop on Knowledge Acquisition for Knowledge Based Systems, 36.0–36.15. Menlo Park, Calif.: American Association for Artificial Intelligence.

Quinlan, J. R. 1983. Learning Efficient Classification Procedures and Their Application to Chess End Games. In *Machine Learning: An Artificial Intelligence Approach*, volume 1, eds. R. S. Michalski, J. G. Carbonell, and T. M. Mitchell, 463–482. San Mateo, Calif.: Morgan Kaufmann.

IV DATA SUMMARIZATION

18 Summary Data Estimation Using Decision Trees

Meng Chang Chen[1] and Lawrence McNamee
University of California, Los Angeles

Abstract

Unlike other applications of decision trees that extract knowledge from databases for classification, in this chapter, summary data estimation uses decision trees to estimate the summarized attributes of a category of individuals in a database. Another difference is the adoption of the closed-world assumption in summary data estimation. From scanning a database, two kinds of decision trees are generated for summary data estimation. The first tree is utilized to estimate the cardinality of the queried category, the second to estimate the value of the summarized attribute(s). Together, the summary data of the queried category can be estimated. Many systems using a decision support mechanism, such as query optimization of database management, are possible applications of summary data estimation.

18.1 Introduction

A *summary datum*, represented as a trinary tuple <statistical function, category, summary>, is metaknowledge summarized by a statistical function on a category of individual information typically stored in a database. For instance, <average-income, female engineer with 10 years experience and master's degree, $45,000> is a summary datum, read as "the average income of the female engineers with 10 years experience and a master's degree is $45,000." For a *statistical query*, a query about a category of a number of individuals or objects, a conventional database management system (DBMS) needs to exhaustively scan a large portion of the database, which is inefficient. A good approach for solving this problem is the use of a summary data management system that stores and manages properly selected precomputed results, called *summary data*. The stored summary data can then be utilized to derive new summary data (Chen, McNamee, and Melkanoff 1988; Chen and McNamee 1989). However, by itself, this approach is not capable of accurately estimating summary data. With the knowledge discovery approach introduced in this chapter, the accuracy of summary data estimation can be increased. Together, they can achieve a remarkable improvement in performance for many applications. For instance, in applications such as decision support and statistical query processing, summary data can directly answer questions; in other cases, summary

[1]Currently with AT&T Bell Laboratories, New Jersey.

data can be applied in choosing an effective way to solve problems, for example, as in conventional and semantic query optimization.

A *decision* tree is a data structure that facilitates a decision-making process. In a decision tree, each intermediate node represents a condition or a test, and each leaf is assigned a tag. The decision-making process flows along the branches from the root to the lower-level nodes and finally to the leaves. From an evaluation of all the tags collected from a traversal of the tree, a decision is made. One of the most popular decision trees is the classification tree (Breiman et al. 1984; Quinlan 1986).

Unlike the classification tree that is utilized for estimating the class of an individual datum, summary data estimation estimates summary data of a category of individuals in a database. In this chapter, two types of decision trees are employed: the cardinality tree and regression tree. The *cardinality tree* is used to estimate the cardinality of data in a category, and the *regression tree* estimates the value of a numeric attribute or the product of several attributes of a category.

The cardinality tree is similar to the ordinary classification tree in that it is used to discriminate the two artificial classes, "exist" and "non-exist." Given a data space and a database, the class "exist" is assigned to a data point in the data space if it appears in the database. Otherwise, the class "non-exist" is assigned. However, although the ordinary classification tree partitions the data space such that each leaf (that is, a subset in the partition) has a pronounced majority for one of the classes in a cardinality tree, the data of the two classes, "exist" and "non-exist," should be homogeneously distributed in each leaf. The estimation of the subset cardinality of a leaf in a cardinality tree is calculated by assuming a uniform distribution in the leaf. The regression tree for numeric attributes is generated using a procedure similar to that in Breiman et al. (1984), so that the data in each leaf of a regression tree is subject to a bound of the regression error. Once the cardinality tree and regression tree are generated, an estimation of summary data of a category can be answered by traversing the trees. First, the regression tree is traversed to partition the queried category into a collection of subcategories and collect their associated tags. Next, the cardinality tree is used to estimate the cardinality of each category. Finally, a sum of products of the tags and cardinalities gives an estimate of the statistical queries.

In the next section, definitions and notations used in this chapter are defined. Estimation Using the Cardinality Tree presents the algorithms and theorems for generating a cardinality tree and using the cardinality tree for estimation. Regression Tree Generation deals with the regression tree, and in Summary Data Estimation, summary data estimation using the results from the previous two sections is discussed. Future research and conclusions are presented in the last section.

18.2 Notations and Definitions

An attribute can be categorical or ordered according to its domain. For an *ordered attribute*, there is an ordering relation $\leq$, such that for every element e_1 and e_2, either $e_1 \leq e_2$ or $e_2 \leq e_1$; there is no ordering relationship among the elements in the categorical attribute domain. A *simple condition* (called condition hereafter) for an ordered attribute is composed of an ordering operator and a value in the attribute domain, $\leq c$, or a set membership operator and a subset of the attribute domain, $\in S$, for a categorical attribute. A *split* on a set partitions the set into two subsets so that all the elements of one subset satisfy the associated condition, and the others do not.

A *data space*, denoted R^*, is the cross-product of the domains of all the attributes in a data model. A *category* is defined as all the data in a data space satisfying a predicate. Apparently, a database or a category is a subset of R^*. A category is called *orthogonal* if it can be presented as a cross-product of subsets of each attribute domain. Given a database, a *category instance* is the set of data in the database also belonging to the category.

A *statistical function* is defined as a set function that inputs a set of data and generates a *summary*, which can be a real number result or a null value. A statistical function, S, is called a *semiadditive function* if

$$\forall R_i,\ R_i \subseteq R^*,\ and\ R_i \cap R_j\ =\ \emptyset\ \ s.t.\ \ S(R_i \cup R_j)\ =\ S(R_i)\ +_S\ S(R_j)\ ,$$

where $[Real \cup \{\lambda\}, +_S]$ forms a commutative monoid. Note that λ is a null value. Although some functions are not semiadditive, they can still be directly computed by using the summaries of other semiadditive statistical functions or computed results of other nice statistical functions. For example, the average function can be directly computed by dividing the result of the sum function by the result of the cardinality function. We call these nice functions *computed* statistical functions. A statistical function S is called computed from the results of other semiadditive or computed statistical functions $S_1, \ldots, S_n$ that are called the *component functions* of S if S can be represented as

$$\exists f,\ \forall R_i \subseteq R^*,\ S(R_i)\ =\ f(S_1(R_i), \ldots, S_n(R_i))\ ,$$

where $f : (Real \cup \{\lambda\}^n \rightarrow (Real \cup \{\lambda\})$, and there is no cycle (that is, quasi order) in the definition of computed functions. The definition of a computed statistical function also indicates its computing procedure. Hereafter in this chapter, the term summary data, meaning "summary data with a semiadditive statistical function," is used for brevity.

18.3 Estimation Using the Cardinality Tree

In Mannino, Chu, and Sager (1988), a recent survey on the estimation of a statistical profile of database queries is given. Some important work was done by Christodoulakis (1981), who proposes a parametric method to describe the distribution of records using a family of distributions, including normal distribution, and Pearson type 2 and type 7 distributions. In addition, a variable-width histogram is presented for one-dimensional data. There are also some ad hoc approaches for selectivity estimation. For instance, Kamel and King (1975) propose textual analysis, which has been applied in image processing, to cluster blocks with similar values of some ad hoc functions. In Piatetsky-Shapiro and Connell (1984), the equidepth histogram approach is used for one-dimensional selectivity estimation. A multidimensional extension of the equidepth method (Muralikrishna and DeWitt 1988) partitions the data domain into blocks having the same amount of data. The equidepth histogram approach outperforms the equiwidth approach because the former tends to produce more homogeneous blocks. However, the equidepth concept is not sufficient to describe the data distribution.

Under the assumption of uniform distribution, to estimate the cardinality of data satisfying a query, it is apparent that the more homogeneous the data distribution is, the better the estimation can be. However, the distribution of data in a database is not homogeneous, nor is it independent among its attributes in general. This distribution of data in the database makes most of the current cardinality estimation models inaccurate. In addition, to the best of our knowledge, the literature only discusses the selectivity problem.

This section presents a new approach for organizing a large collection of multidimensional data with unknown distribution by partitioning the data space so that the data are relatively homogeneously distributed in each block. A multidimensional decision tree, the cardinality tree, is generated according to this partition. After the tree is generated, a cardinality estimation can be done using a tree traversal. This approach is applicable to data spaces with both ordered and categorical attributes.

18.3.1 Homogeneity Measurement on a Data Block

Envision an orthogonal category (or *data block*) as an urn and each data point in the data block as a ball. If a data point exists in the database, assign class 1 to the data point; otherwise, assign 0. Define $p_1(B)$ and $p_0(B)$, respectively, as the probabilities of drawing 1 and 0 randomly from data block B. The probabilities $p_1(B)$ and $p_0(B)$ are abbreviated as p_1 and p_0 if they present no confusion.

Example 1: Let a data space $R^* = \{1, 2, 3, 4\} \times \{a, b, c, d\}$ and a database, as shown in table 18.1.

Table 18.1
A Simple Database.

X	Y
1	a
1	d
3	b
3	c
3	d
4	d

Then $p_1(R^*) = 6/16$, and $p_0(R^*) = 10/16$.

Given a data block B and its associated p_1, for a fraction s of B, if no other information is available, $|s| * p_1$ is the best estimate of the number of 1's in s in terms of the mean square error, where $|s|$ is the size of s. Heuristically, the more homogeneous a data block B is, the lower the mean estimation error is because estimation of cardinality will, on encountering a partial block, prorate its estimate according to the proportion of the block's volume that overlaps the query. Define the function f as the probability function of the orthogonal subsets of B being queried. A measure of homogeneity for the data block B with f, called the *homogeneity index*, is defined as

$$\sum_{s \subseteq B} f(s) * [p_1(s) - p_1(B)]^2 \quad .$$

The homogeneity index is the *mean square error* between $p_1(s)$ and $p_1(B)$ under f. It is clear that the lower the homogeneity index value of B is, the more accurate the estimation will be.

The homogeneity index of a data block B is the measurement of how uniformly distributed its associated relation instance is, assuming the value of f is the same everywhere. Intuitively, the data block with either an absolute majority of 1's or 0's or evenly mixed 0's and 1's has a low homogeneity index value. The number of all possible orthogonal subsets of B is $\prod \alpha_i u(\alpha_i)$, where $u(\alpha_i)$ is equal to $C(|Dom(\alpha_i)|, 2)$, where C is the combinatorial function for ordered attributes, and $2^{|Dom(\alpha_i)|}$ is the number of categorical attributes. Because of the large number of orthogonal subsets, the homogeneity index would be expensive to calculate and suffers from the problem that f might be unknown.

Because of the difficulty in obtaining the homogeneity index value of a data block B, a simplified measure function, the *Gini index*, is adopted as a proxy for the homogeneity index. For a data block B, the Gini index G(B) (Breiman et al. 1984) is defined as $2 * p_1 * (1 - p_1)$ as well as $2 * p_0 * (1 - p_0)$. The Gini index can be interpreted as the expected error rate of randomly drawing a data point from the data block and guessing its class to be 1 with probability p_1 and 0 with probability p_0. Another interpretation of the Gini index is in terms of variances because $2 * p_1 * (1 - p_1)$ is equal to the variance of the data block.

18.3.2 Partitioning Data Space

Most likely a database is not deliberately constructed to be homogeneous. However, it can be viewed as a collection of relatively homogeneous disjoint small blocks of data, from which the estimation of the cardinality of a query is more accurate than can be obtained from the original relation instance.

Classification and regression trees (CARTS) (Breiman et al. 1984) have been proposed for use in biology and social science for data analysis. The goal of CART is to predict the classification or value of an attribute by using certain predictor variables. CART employs a nonparametric approach to generate a decision tree according to the contents of the data and the measure functions. Although CART seems unrelated in our context because there is no classification to be done, we show that by defining artificial classes according to the existence of the data point in the database, an appropriate method of cardinality estimation can be obtained. When CART identifies the data blocks that have a pronounced majority of 1's or 0's, those areas that are not qualified for further splits might have a homogeneous distribution of both 1's and 0's as a side effect. An important property of the Gini index that is useful in this regard follows.

Theorem 1: Apply a split on a data block B, and obtain two data blocks B_1 and B_2. Then

$$G(B) \geq r_1 * G(B_1) + r_2 * G(B_2), \text{ where } r_i \text{ is defined as } |B_i| \, / \, |B| \ .$$

Proof: Because the Gini index, $2 * p_1 * (1 - p_1)$, is a concave function and by the definition of a concave function, if v is a concave function (Papadimitriou and Steiglitz 1982), then

$$v(\lambda x + (1 - \lambda)y) \geq \lambda v(x) + (1 - \lambda)v(y), \text{ where } 0 \leq \lambda \leq 1 \ .$$

The previous inequality is satisfied.

From theorem 1, every split reduces the average error rate; that is,

$$G(B) - r_1 * G(B_1) - r_2 * G(B_2) \geq 0 \ .$$

There is no reduction for the case when the probabilities p_1 (or p_0) of B, B_1, and B_2 are the same. Denote the difference, that is, the reduction of the split using condition c, as $\Delta c(B)$. If the number of possible splits is finite, a maximal split exists that, among other things, maximizes the reduction of the split. In other words, the maximal split minimizes $r_1 * G(B_1) + r_2 * G(B_2)$. Because the Gini index is a concave function and symmetric in p_0 and p_1, the maximal split tends to separate clusters of 1's from clusters of 0's, so that one of the B_is has a higher p_1, and the other has a higher p_0. Moreover, the reduction of the maximal split is small when the maximal split fails to separate 0's and 1's in B. The small reduction happens when both subblocks resulting from every possible split have similar p_0s and p_1s with the original block, that is, when the block might be fairly homogeneous.

In this chapter, ordered attributes are assumed bounded; that is, there are an upper bound and a lower bound for each ordered attribute, and by definition, categorical attributes have finite domains. When the domain of an ordered attribute is continuous, some discretization process is needed to map the continuous data space to a discrete data space to guarantee a finite number of possible splits. A discretization algorithm is called *legitimate* if every data point in the database is mapped into a discrete data space with the same density everywhere. The density of a discrete space is defined as the number of data points in a unit interval of the discretized attribute. However, more processing time is needed when the density increases. Hence, the density of a discretized space is a major factor in performance. The following theorem shows that a maximum split is invariant to various densities of discretized spaces resulting from different legitimate discretization processes.

Theorem 2: For a continuous attribute α, the data blocks of a database discretized using different legitimate discretization algorithms have the same maximum split.

Proof: Let D_1 and D_2 be two legitimate discretization algorithms with density d_1 and d_2, respectively, that generate data blocks B and Q, respectively. Let S_i be a split that divides the data block B (or Q) into $B_{i,1}$ and $B_{i,2}$ ($Q_{i,1}$ and $Q_{i,2}$). Let $p_{k,i}$ and $q_{k,i}$ be the probability of drawing 1 randomly from data blocks $B_{k,i}$ and $Q_{k,i}$, respectively. Assume S_k is a maximum split of the data block B. Then, with $\forall S_i$ when a split is made on B_1, where $i \neq k$, the following inequality is satisfied:

$$r_k * G(B_{k,1}) + (1 - r_k) * G(B_{k,2}) - r_i * G(B_{i,1}) - (1 - r_i) * G(B_{i,2}) \leq 0 \ ,$$

where $r_j = \frac{|B_{j,1}|}{|B_1|}$, and $G(B_{j,l}) = 2 * p_{j,l} * (1 - p_{j,l}), l = 1, 2$.

The previous inequality can be rewritten as

$$(\frac{d_2}{d_1})^2 * [r_k * (\frac{d_1}{d_2})^2 * G(B_{k,1}) + (1 - r_k) * (\frac{d_1}{d_2})^2 * G(B_{k,2})$$

$$- r_i * (\frac{d_1}{d_2})^2 * G(B_{i,1}) - (1 - r_i) * (\frac{d_1}{d_2})^2 * G(B_{i,2})] \leq 0 \ .$$

Because $p_{j,l} * \frac{d_1}{d_2} = q_{j,l}$, and $(1 - p_{j,l}) * \frac{d_1}{d_2} = (1 - q_{j,l})$, this inequality reduces to

$$(\frac{d_2}{d_1})^2 * [r_k * G(Q_{k,1}) + (1 - r_k) * G(Q_{k,2}) - r_i * G(Q_{i,1}) - (1 - r_i) * G(Q_{i,2})] \leq 0 \ .$$

The previous inequality shows the split S_k is also a maximum split of the data block Q generated from the discretization algorithm D_2.

Theorem 2 cannot only be used for discretizing a continuous domain but also for condensing a sparse discrete-ordered domain to reduce the computation time. For an ordered attribute, there are exactly $m - 1$ different splits, where m is the number of distinct values of this attribute in the relation instance. However, for a categorical attribute, there are as many as $2^{(m-1)}$ different splits, which makes finding a maximum split intractable for large m. The following theorem provides a method that limits the number of potential maximal splits of a categorical attribute to $m - 1$.

Theorem 3: Let $d_1, \ldots, d_m$ be the distinct values of a categorical attribute α. Define a rearrangement of these values, with the ith denoted d_i', such that

$$p\,(1 \mid \alpha = d_1') \geq p\,(1 \mid \alpha = d_2') \geq \ \ldots \ \geq p\,(1 \mid \alpha = d_m') \ ,$$

where $p(1 \mid \alpha = d_i')$ is the conditional probability of drawing 1 when the value of α is d_i'. Then the subset S of $Dom(\alpha)$ that yields the maximum split is one of the sets $\{d_1', d_2', \ldots, d_j'\}, j = 1, 2, \ldots, (m - 1)$.

Proof: See Breiman et al. (1984).

18.3.3 Generation of the Cardinality Tree

The purpose of partitioning the data space R^* is to have a collection of subsets, so that in each subset-block, the data in a relation instance are relatively homogeneously distributed. During the partition, a tree data structure is created. When splitting a data block B, take B as the father node and the two resulting blocks from the split as sons, and label the branches by the condition and the logical values. After applying several splits on a data block B, a tree rooted by B with disjoint fractions of B as leaves is generated. Denote the tree as T(B). If every split is a maximal split, call the tree a *maximal tree.* Define the Gini index of T(B), G(T(B)), as $\sum_{B_i} (\mid B_i \ / \ \mid B \mid) G(B_i)$, where B_i is a leaf of T(B).

If a tree is grown from a data block until all the bits of every leaf are 1's (or 0's), the Gini index value of the tree will become zero. When G(T(B)) is zero, T(B) is called *complete.* Otherwise, T(B) is called *incomplete.* Although a complete tree benefits from the zero error of estimation, the potentially large number of small blocks that result from a large number of splits to separate 0's and 1's makes the complete tree infeasible. To prevent an undesirably large number of splits and guarantee the performance of the resulting tree, some control of the tree growth is required. One method is to introduce a threshold value, t, so that if the reduction of the maximal split is less than t, further splits of the block can be stopped. However, this method does not take the sizes or the number of 1's of the blocks into account and tends to favor the splits on small blocks; the tree growth will terminate with many small blocks and some large blocks. In our approach, the number of 1's, n_1, is adopted as the weighting factor, so that the stop-split test becomes "$\Delta B(c) * n_1 \geq \mathit{threshold} - \mathit{value}$," where c is a maximal split. Under this new constraint, blocks with many 1's are favored to continue further splits, thereby reducing the absolute estimation error.

Example 2: The split s_1 with condition $y \in \{d\}$ is the maximum split of the data block in example 1. $\Delta B(y \in \{d\})$ is

$$G(B) - r_1 * G(B_1) - r_2 * G(B_2)$$
$$= 2 * \frac{6}{16} * \frac{10}{16} - \frac{1}{4} * 2 * \frac{3}{4} * \frac{1}{4} - \frac{3}{4} * 2 * \frac{3}{12} * \frac{9}{12} = \frac{3}{32}\ .$$

If the threshold value is set as $\frac{20}{32}$, then there will be no split on the block because the stop-split test $\Delta B(\ y \in \{d\}\ ) * n_1 \geq \frac{20}{32}$, where $n_1 = 6$, is not satisfied.

Note that splitting the data block using the maximal split is a one-step optimization that cannot always guarantee global optimization. Thus, the incomplete maximal tree might suffer from poor performance for some ill-defined situations. The following is the algorithm for cardinality tree generation.

Algorithm for Cardinality Tree Generation:
Input: Threshold value t and a data block B.
Output: A cardinality tree, root $\rightarrow$ T(B).

1. Set root = B.
   Put B in the queue *Avail.*

2. While *Avail* is not empty, do 3–6:

   3. Get the first of *Avail.* Call it *Head.*

   4. Find the maximal split, c of *Head.*
      If $\Delta c * n_1 \geq t$,
      split *Head,* else skip to the end of this while loop.

5. Store *Head* with its p_1, its size, the associated condition, and pointers to its sons.

6. Store the two sons of *Head* in *Avail.*

7. End.

18.3.4 Cardinality Estimation

Because the distribution of the 1's and 0's of a leaf of a cardinality tree is more homogeneous than all its ancestor nodes, using $p_1(l) * fac_i$ would be more accurate to estimate the contribution of a leaf l to the query, where fac_i is the area of the intersection of the leaf and the query. Thus, given a cardinality tree, the estimation of the number of tuples satisfying a query can be done using a tree search on the cardinality tree. The following is the algorithm of cardinality estimation using traversal of a cardinality tree. An example is also included.

Algorithm for Estimation Using Cardinality Tree:
Input: A cardinality tree root → T(B) and a query box Q.
Output: An estimation *Est.*

1. Put the root in the queue *Avail.*
   Set $Est = 0$.

2. While *Avail* is not empty, do 3:

   3. Get the first of *Avail.* Call it *Head.*
      Case 1. If $Head \subseteq Q$, add $p_1 * \mid Head \mid$ to *Est.*
      Case 2. If $Head \cap Q \neq \phi$, and *Head* is a leaf, add $p_1 * \mid Head \cap Q \mid$ to *Est.*
      Case 3. If $Head \cap Q \neq \phi$, and *Hcad* is a not leaf, move two sons of *Head* to *Avail.*
      Case 4. If $Head \cap Q = \phi$, discard *Head.*

4. The value of *Est* is the estimation of Q.

5. End.

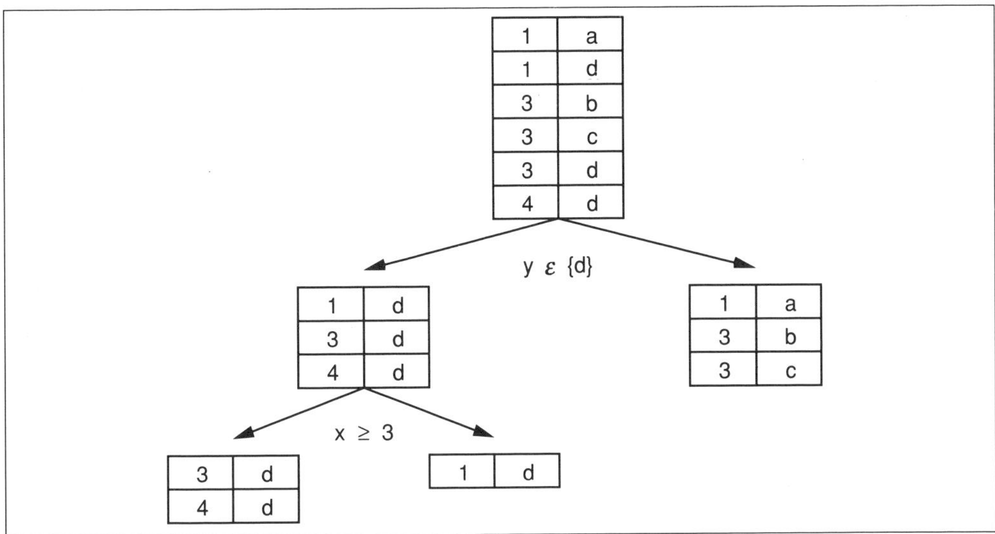

Figure 18.1
Cardinality Tree for the Database in Example 1

Example 3: Set the threshold value = 1/4. The cardinality tree generated from the database in example 1 is shown in figure 18.1.

18.4 Regression Tree Generation

In the previous section, we introduced a data-space partitioning method for cardinality estimation that can be modified for the summary estimation. A cardinality tree partitions the data space, so that in each block, data points distribute homogeneously; however, a regression tree partitions the data space so that for all the data in each block, values of a particular attribute or products of some attributes are close to each other. In our approach, the closeness is measured by the least squares method. Measurement by the Gini index for cardinality tree generation is replaced by the least squares measurement in the regression tree generation. Let $X = \{x_1, \ldots, x_n\}$ be the set of data points. Suppose the attribute α is selected for estimation. Then it is well known that

$$L_\alpha(X) = \frac{1}{n} \sum_i (\alpha(x_i) - \bar{\alpha}(X))^2$$

is the least squares measurement, where $\bar{\alpha}(X)$ is the mean value of α of the data in X. That is, for every data point x_i in X, the predictor function that achieves the least squares error is equal to $\bar{\alpha}(X)$. The methodology using this measurement is called *least squares regression.*

In addition, it is easy to show that $L_\alpha(X)$ is a concave function. Thus, for a split c that divides the data space X into X_1 and X_2, the reduction $\Delta L(X, c) = L_\alpha(X) - L_\alpha(X_1) - L_\alpha(X_2)$ is positive. After the split, either $\bar{\alpha}(X_1)$ or $\bar{\alpha}(X_2)$ will be larger than $\bar{\alpha}(X)$, and the other will be less. Similar to cardinality tree generation, after several splits, the square error of the whole data space should be lower. To efficiently split the data space, the concept of a maximal split is adopted. In regression tree generation, the maximal split c is defined as the split that produces the largest reduction $\Delta L(X, c)$. By slightly modifying the cardinality tree generation algorithm, replacing the measurement function Gini index with a least squares measurement, an algorithm to generate a regression tree by partitioning the data space can be obtained.

Algorithm of Regression Tree Generation:
Input: Threshold value t and a data block B.
Output: A regression tree, root $\rightarrow$ T(B).

1. Set root = B.
   Put B in the queue *Avail.*

2. While *Avail* is not empty, do 3–6:

   3. Get the first of *Avail.* Call it *Head.*

   4. Find the maximal split, c, of *Head.*
      If $\Delta L(Head, c) * n(Head) \geq t$, split *Head*, else skip to the end of this while loop.

   5. Store *Head* with $\bar{\alpha}$ (Head), the associated condition, and pointers to its sons.

   6. Store the two sons of *Head* in *Avail.*

7. End.

The complexity order of the generating regression tree algorithm should be the same as the cardinality tree generation algorithm because theorems 2 and 3 both apply to regression tree generation (Breiman et al. 1984). In this algorithm, the blocks with more data are favored to reduce the average absolute error.

18.5 Summary Data Estimation

The summation estimation of an attribute α for a query box Q can be obtained using the following algorithm, where Est(B) denotes the cardinality estimation of B.

Algorithm of Summary Data Estimation:
Input: A cardinality tree $root_1 \rightarrow T_1(B)$, a regression tree $root_2 \rightarrow T_2(B)$, and a query box Q.
Output: An estimation *EstSum*.

1. Put the $root_2$ in the queue *Avail*. Set *EstSum* = 0.

2. While *Avail* is not empty, do 3:

    3. Get the first of *Avail*. Call it *Crnt*.
    Case 1. If $Crnt \subseteq$ Q, add $\bar{\alpha}$ $(Crnt) *$ Est$(Crnt)$ to *EstSum*.
    Case 2. If $Crnt \cap$ Q $\neq \phi$, and *Crnt* is a leaf, add $\bar{\alpha}$ $(Crnt) *$ Est$(Crnt \cap$ Q) to *EstSum*.
    Case 3. If $Crnt \cap$ Q $\neq \phi$, and *Crnt* is a not leaf, move two sons of *Crnt* to *Avail*.
    Case 4. If $Crnt \cap$ Q $= \phi$, discard *Crnt*.

4. The value of *EstSum* is the estimation of Q.

5. End.

18.6 Conclusion

In this chapter, a new approach was presented to estimate the summary data of an arbitrary orthogonal category. This approach is an extension of the Cart mechanism and was modified to develop a summary data estimator. The Gini index was adopted to approximate the homogeneity index and proved to be appropriate from simulation studies, as indicated by Chen (1989). With a properly tuned threshold value, the cardinality tree performs well in estimating the error rate and requiring moderate storage. In addition, the cardinality tree can handle multidimensional and arbitrarily distributed data with both ordered and categorical attributes.

A number of enhancements could be added to improve the performance of the proposed summary estimation method. The first one involves the introduction of a complex condition instead of the simple condition described herein. For instance, a complex condition can have more operators, such as logical operators and arithmetic operators, and more than one attribute. Another approach might be the application of the complex condition " $X < c \& Y \in S$ " on two attributes at the same time, which might achieve a global optimization that could never be reached by a stepwise local optimization method. Also, some study is warranted to investigate alternative indexes other than the Gini index or the least squares error to approximate the homogeneity index.

There are other methods, such as the maximum-reduction-first approach that always selects the node with the highest reduction among all the nodes in the tree to be split. It stops any further split when the number of leaves reaches a predefined number. This method is useful in a storage-critical environment. A combination of the maximum-reduction-first method and the threshold test method is also feasible. The trade-off between a large decision tree and good estimation performance is controlled by the threshold values. However, no other methods are known to us for deciding these values except by a trial-and-error approach. As a final remark, it is believed that the sampling mechanism can be applied to generate the cardinality tree and the regression tree when the amount of data is large.

References

Breiman, L.; Friedman, J.; Olshen, R.; and Stone, C. 1984. *Classification and Regression Trees.* Belmont, Calif.: Wadsworth.

Chen, M. C. 1989. Estimation and Derivation of Summary Data, Ph.D. diss., Computer Science Dept., Univ. of California at Los Angeles.

Chen M. C., and McNamee, L. 1989. On the Data Model and Access Method of Summary Data Management. *IEEE Transactions on Knowledge and Data Engineering* 1(4): 519–529.

Chen, M. C.; McNamee, L.; and Melkanoff, M. 1988. A Model of Summary Data and Its Applications in Statistical Databases. In Proceedings of the Fourth International Working Conference on Statistical and Scientific Database Management, 246–273. Rome: Artigiana.

Christodoulakis, S. 1981. Estimating Selectivities in Data Bases, Ph.D. diss., Computer Science Dept., Univ. of Toronto.

Kamel, N. and King, R. 1985. A Model of Data Distribution Based on Texture Analysis. In Proceedings of ACM SIGMOD, 319–325. New York: Association of Computing Machinery.

Mannino, M.; Chu, P.; and Sager, T. 1988. Statistical Profile Estimation in Database Systems. *ACM Computing Surveys* 20(3): 191–221.

Muralikrishna, M., and DeWitt, D. 1988. Equi-Depth Histograms for Estimating Selectivity Factors for Multi-Dimensional Queries. In Proceedings of ACM SIGMOD, 28–36. New York: Association of Computing Machinery.

Papadimitriou, C., and Steiglitz, K. 1982. *Combinatorial Optimization: Algorithms and Complexity.* New York: Prentice-Hall.

Piatetsky-Shapiro, G., and Connell, C. 1984. Accurate Estimation of the Number of Tuples Satisfying a Condition. In Proceedings of ACM SIGMOD, 256–276. New York: Association of Computing Machinery.

Quinlan, J. 1986. Induction of Decision Trees. *Machine Learning* 1(1): 81–106.

19 A Support System For Interpreting Statistical Data

Peter Hoschka and Willi Klösgen
German National Research Center for Computer Science (GMD)

Abstract

EXPLORA is an integrated system for conceptually analyzing data and searching for interesting relationships within the data. The knowledge base of EXPLORA includes the objects and semantic relations of the real system that produces the data. The interpretation process of the system can be summarized as follows: Various statement types can be embedded into a general search algorithm to find the true statements in the data. The statement types represent patterns of possibly interesting statements and are associated with computable predicates, mostly incorporating statistical criteria of significance. Redundancy filters prune the search graph, so that the search algorithm generates only true and nonredundant statements. Generalization and selection criteria are used to further reduce the set of statements to the true, nonredundant, and interesting statements. Interactive navigation in the space of statements supports the composition of a summary report about the findings, optionally arranged under the control of a text model.

19.1 Introduction and Background

Exploring databases to find the contextual meaning or implication of stored data, with other words to extract information or knowledge from databases, is an increasing challenge. New solutions such as intelligent databases (Parsaye et al. 1989) have to be developed that complement traditional tools such as query languages or statistical packages. To infer the meaning of data requires an interpretation process based on domain knowledge. Therefore, the central questions of such new approaches are: what kind of domain knowledge is needed, how can this knowledge be represented, and how can it be manipulated to support the interpretation of data?

Various approaches already treat the problem of knowledge discovery. Many of them focus on rule discovery. In this case, the inferred statements about the data are formulated as if-then rules. Frequently, the rule formalism is chosen to subsequently process the acquired knowledge, for instance, in expert systems.

Rules set one example of a formalism to represent knowledge in an understandable form. A statement expressed as a rule is, in general, more readable than the usual output of purely statistical discovery techniques. In a rule-discovery system, a rule mostly relates two sets in a logical form. The right-hand side of a rule usually captures a target group, namely, that set of objects that is of special interest. One searches for sufficient conditions for a target group; this left-hand side of a rule represents a set of objects specified by some descriptor variables.

According to the strength of the relation between the left- and the right-hand side of a rule, one can distinguish exact, strong, or weak rules. For an *exact rule*, it is necessary that all elements of the set on the left-hand side also belong to the set on the right-hand side. However, in the case of statistical data, one has to deal with noise. Therefore, one can demand that nearly all elements (*strong rules*) or only as many as necessary, such as "much more than on average" (*weak rules*) must also belong to the set on the right-hand side. With this differentiation between exact, strong, and weak rules, three subtypes of the statement type "rule" are given, each associated with separate criteria to establish and verify a rule in a set of data.

Statements expressed as rules mostly represent static correlations between situations or events that remain constant over some period of time. However, frequently, the real system that produces the data is dynamic, so one has to deal with change and also infer statements about the change between two time points or about the long-term trend. Statements such as "For the first time stagnation of sales for product A in customer group B" can be important for management decisions.

Therefore, one has to deal with the stability of rules over time. This can be regarded as a special comparison problem for rules. The underlying database can consist of several similarly structured sections such as data about succeeding time points. Rules can be derived for each section. Then, the question arises of whether there are any significant differences between similar rules (for example, with equal right-hand sides) over the sections.

However, rules need not necessarily be the only formalism in which the derived information about a data set can be appropriately represented in an understandable, not purely statistical form. An interpretation and discovery system, therefore, needs statements of different types to be searched for in the data. Three of these statement types are treated in this chapter in detail: a rule searcher, a change detector, and a trend detector.

19.1.1 Fundamentals of the EXPLORA Approach

Common to most approaches that deal with knowledge discovery is a search in spaces of hypotheses, where the search can be pruned by domain knowledge, frequently represented in the form of taxonomical structures defined for the values of the variables. Our approach for content interpretation provides the user with an integrated system (EXPLORA) for conceptually analyzing data and searching for interesting relationships within the data. The central point of this approach is a general graph search under semantic control.

Various statement types such as rules and change and trend analyses can be integrated into EXPLORA to detect interesting and nonredundant statements controlled by its general search algorithm.

Therefore, EXPLORA, in contrast to rule-discovery systems, is not only based on a single statement type. Each statement type that is appropriate to capture—that is to reliably discover and clearly formulate—pieces of knowledge of a special kind can be included in the system. Instances of each statement type are searched and presented in an understandable form. To verify such an instance in the given data, a computable predicate (*verification method*) is associated with each statement type.

We specifically address the discovery of knowledge from data sets that are collected regularly and often. Our target environment can be described as follows. Analyzing and interpreting data is a day-to-day task for many knowledge workers: Investment consultants at a bank interpret stock quotations, marketing specialists study sales statistics, and politicians analyze their election results. The interpretation of data is a task of human experts who are versed in the domain and who know how one has to analyze the data to discover their meaning. The result of their work is a report constituting a content interpretation of the data. The aim of our EXPLORA system is to support a part of this interpretation process by a knowledge-based system for data exploration.

EXPLORA is a system that has a set of data as input and produces a content interpretation (figure 19.1), mostly as the result of an interactive process. The system needs both application-specific context knowledge and statistical knowledge for such an interpretation process. The representation of this knowledge in the system requires some effort; therefore, we concentrate on a system supporting regular and routine interpretation tasks, because for these tasks, a lot of specific experience is available, making it easier to formalize the needed knowledge.

The interpretation process in EXPLORA is based on domain knowledge and can be summarized by the following approach: Various *statement types* (patterns of possibly interesting statements) with associated computable predicates, mostly incorporating statistical criteria of significance, are embedded in a general search algorithm to generate true statements (*facts*) about some vectors of objects in a (large) product space. Redundancy filters prune the search graph, so that the search algorithm generates only true and nonredundant statements. Generalization and selection criteria are used to identify true, nonredundant, and interesting statements (*messages*). Interactive navigations in the space of messages (and facts) support the composition of a summary report, optionally scheduled by a text model that contains ordering criteria.

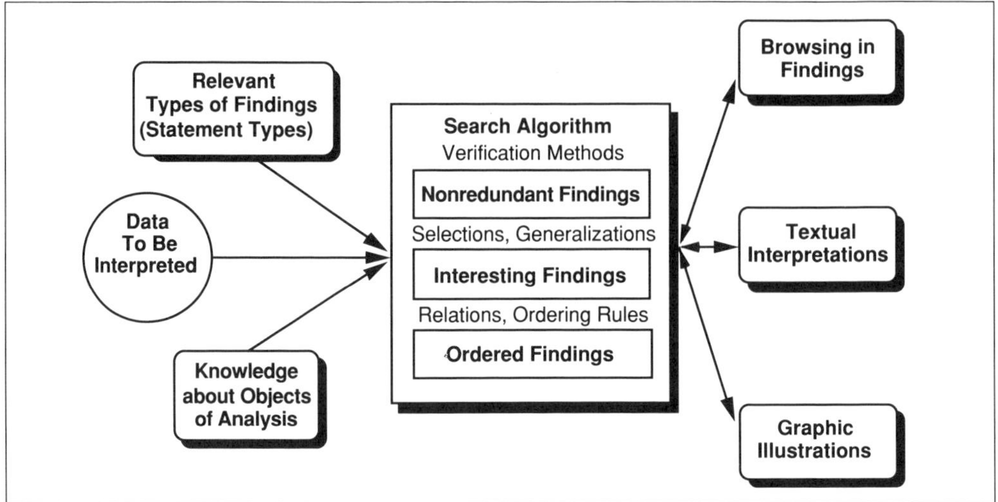

Figure 19.1
Summary View of EXPLORA.

19.1.2 Application Environment of EXPLORA

We evaluated the usefulness of our approaches by having EXPLORA work for selected pilot users in the area of survey analysis. The applications belong to the application class "market research." Homogeneous applications of the same structure are gathered in EXPLORA in an application class to facilitate the incorporation of an application into the system. The market research class is characterized by the following structures:

Data consist of records about units of analysis, such as persons, companies, or regional districts. A lot of variables are collected for the total or a sample of these units. There are dependent variables, such as about the buying behavior of persons and independent variables that characterize the units, such as socioeconomic variables. Other types and structures of variables are important for selecting relevant statement types, appropriate statistical tests, and certain parameters. Of primary interest in these applications are statements about remarkable patterns of the aggregated dependent variables for socioeconomic classes of units or about patterns of comparison between target classes and socio- economic classes. Target classes are built by taxonomies defined on the dependent variables, and socioeconomic classes are constructed by the independent variables and their taxonomies. The files, structured by records (units) and variables, are collected regularly so that an additional time dimension is available. Moreover, several files (for companies and equipment, persons and contracts, and so on) can be connected.

Examples of this application class are given in market research, where interviews of companies concerning their investment behavior or persons concerning their financial behavior constitute the units of analysis. Another example of this type is the analysis of political elections, where the units are given as a total of regional districts; the dependent variables are not values of interviews but the actual votings for political parties. This example was used as an alpha test for our first prototype.

Results are typically presented in the form of tabulation and graphics. Two or three independent variables are selected to structure the rows and columns. The aggregated values of a dependent variable appear within the tabulation. This is how the notorious bulk of information arises: The users are drowned by tabulations (corresponding to the large number of possible combinations of variables) in which they have to identify unusual values, for example, by comparing the values with the margins.

EXPLORA overcomes this situation so that its user obtains the most interesting messages concerning the data. Interactively, the user can focus the themes of the exploration and browse through the presented messages. These messages are constructed on the basis of statement types referring to longitudinal or cross-section analyses.

19.1.3 Research Environment of EXPLORA

Besides the fields of knowledge discovery in databases or intelligent databases, other related fields apply knowledge-based techniques for data analysis. First are *statistical consultation systems*, which advise their users on the selection and operation of statistical methods. These systems not only advise the user but also execute the proposed procedures. Some early examples of this type of statistical expert system are a prototype consultation system for regression analysis (Gale 1986) and a system for the construction of generalized linear models (Nelder and Wolstenholme 1986). These attempts to model data analysts in statistical expert systems do not aspire to deal with context; they provide a set of statistically supported conclusions and let the user choose the particular conclusions that are consistent with his (her) knowledge of the context. Because these systems hold no semantic knowledge about the application, the domain-specific content interpretation has to be performed by the user.

Another approach can be found in the area of *natural language generation systems* (McDonald and Bolc 1988). A long-term view of these efforts is the paradigm of a system that can function as an author. Only a few examples in this area, such as the stock report generation system Ana (Kukich 1988), operate in the area of data analysis. However, the focus of these systems is directed toward producing a natural language report, and the discovery of interesting statements within the data is only rudimentarily treated.

Given:
- A descriptional model of a domain using objects, relations, and operations
- Data D about the domain organized by the objects
- A formal language L; statements expressed in L verified in D by using (statistical) methods
- Constraints C (for example redundancy, selection, ordering rules)

Wanted:
All true statements about the domain (and the data D) expressed in L satisfying C

Figure 19.2
Formal Description of the Problem.

Other fields to be mentioned are *data fusion*, with the special aim of combining data from separate sources (frequently for supervision and primarily in military applications), and *data navigation*, with the distinct emphasis on the interactive support with special branches for retrieval of information and for authoring (Halasz 1988). A large number of discovery methods can be found in the field of machine learning (Michalski 1986).

19.1.4 A Formal Description

The approach of EXPLORA can be characterized as a semantic method for the exploration of statement spaces. Formally, the problem can be stated as described in figure 19.2.

A similar, more specific formulation was developed by Hajek and Havranek (1977) for the Guha approach. The basics of the formal language used in EXPLORA are summarized in figure 19.3. In this chapter, we do not refer to this formal description; for a formal discussion, see the short BNF description at the end of the chapter or Latocha (1989).

19.1.5 EXPLORA and the Assisting Computer

The EXPLORA project is part of a key project, the Assisting Computer (AC), at the German National Research Center for Computer Science. The vision of this project is the paradigm of the computer as a personal-assisting machine. The goal of this long-term activity is to create intelligent, active support systems that have the abilities to complete inexact user commands, render them more precise, and correct them if necessary. In addition, these systems will learn and adapt themselves to their users, consult and criticize

- L has a categorical grammar.
- There are primary and derived syntactical categories.
- Objects and statements are primary syntactical categories.
- Predicates and operations belong to the derived syntactical categories.
- The vocabulary of L is given by a set of primary objects.
- Primary objects can only have the syntactical categories object, predicate, operation.
- The set of all objects represents the set of all expressions generated by the grammar.
- At least one syntactical category is associated with an object.
- All categories are subcategories of object.
- Objects of the subcategory predicate are applied to objects and deliver objects of the subcategory statement.
- Objects to which a predicate is applied are not necessarily primary objects.
- Quantors are represented by predicates.

Figure 19.3
Basis of the Formal Language Used in EXPLORA.

them, and explain themselves. The final result of AC will be an ensemble of machine assistants adaptable to specific requirements and consisting of universal office assistants, domain assistants (such as EXPLORA), and communication assistants.

19.2 Statement Types

Fundamental to generating knowledge in EXPLORA is a pool of statement types. For each application class, all statement types are collected that can be investigated by the system for verification in the set of data. A first statement type can be conceived as a rule searcher of the kind developed for learning by example. Here, we have examples and counterexamples of a concept and a space of hypotheses built by descriptors. Those hypotheses that are consistent with the given examples and counterexamples have to be found by the learning algorithm. In our case, the examples are given by those units, such as persons, contracts, companies, equipment, or districts, stored in the database that take a special value of a dependent variable. We call these units the *target group*. Target groups, for instance, are persons having initiated a life insurance policy or are mortgages being contracted. The descriptors are given by taxonomies defined for the values of the independent variables. Statistical databases usually constitute a noisy domain, so that no exact rules or strong rules are primarily searched. A typical weak rule is given by the following:

> If the income of a person is higher than 2000, and his (her) educational status is at least high school, then his (her) probability of holding bonds is much higher than it is in the total population.

The amount of noise in our applications requires a statistical model handling the degree of interest of a rule and, further, a search approach that is model driven and not data driven (compare Mitchell 1982). The search approach is treated in the next section, but first we want to show how this type of rule-like statement is represented in EXPLORA and how the statistical model is chosen. The following template characterizes this statement type:

> **Target group** shows **outstanding behavior** within **population** for **subpopulation** in **year**.

An instance of this type is given by

> **Persons having initiated an insurance policy at company A** are **highly overrepresented** within the **clients of A** for **high-income people in the South** in **1987**.

This statement type has five arguments: target group, outstanding behavior, population, subpopulation, and year. An object structure is associated with each argument of a statement type. Such an *object structure* consists of a set of objects and a partial ordering on this set. The object structure "outstanding behavior" has several patterns of behavior as elements, such as "overrepresented" and "highly overrepresented." A "stronger" relation supplies a partial ordering on this set of behavior patterns. The object structures "target group," "population," and "subpopulation" each have a lot of classes of database units as elements, such as classes of persons or contracts. Each class of units is constructed by the combination of several attributes or relations. Sociodemographic and financial variables of the data set, for instance, form the basis for these attributes and relations. Hierarchical taxonomies are defined for the values of the variables. The taxonomies induce a partial ordering on the set of classes of units. The argument "target group" represents the right-hand side of a rule, and the left-hand side is given by "subpopulation." "Population" and "year" can be considered as a preselection on the database: Only the selected units of the database are classified in rules. The argument "outstanding behavior" is used to hold the degree of strength of a rule.

Further, a *verification method* is associated with each type of statement. This method includes statistical criteria used to exclude fortuitous results and indicate the degree of interest of a concrete instance of a statement type (Gebhardt 1988). It is characteristic for exploratory analyses that the statistical criteria of a verification method are not rigid tests with strict assertions of significance. An instance of a statement type is given by an application of the statement type; for each of its associated object structures, an element of its object set is taken as argument. The verification method checks whether this instance of a statement type is true (in the given data). A *statement type*, therefore, defines a search space with dimensions corresponding to the object structures existing in the statement type. A fact is now defined as a true instance of a statement type in this search space.

The verification method for the previous statement type is given by a simple statistical model. A target group holds a percentage p_0 in the population, and in a subpopulation, a percentage p. The standard deviation s for p is estimated. Patterns of outstanding behavior are defined in terms of $q = (p - p_0)/s$ ("highly overrepresented" as $q > 5$ and "overrepresented" as $q > 3$). These bounds of significance are parameters of the statement type and can be adapted by the user to his (her) special requirements. The statements that are statistically significant might be too weak to a user, especially when a large sample size (20,000 persons) is given. Then he (she) can specify higher bounds, so that the difference in percentages $(p - p_0)$ for a subgroup to be declared as outstanding becomes larger. Other statistical models associated with such a rule searcher or modifications of this parametric model can be chosen; for instance, several kinds of estimating of the standard deviation s are possible considering the problem of weighted samples. The verification method constitutes a clear interface to introduce such modifications or even other rule types.

If the database is divided into several sections, and the rules are generated section specifically, the problem arises of comparing similar rules over the sections. An important subcase is given when these sections correspond to different time points. Then one has to detect changes in the rules over time: Is a subpopulation still characteristic for a target group, or are other subpopulations becoming more characteristic for this target group? Besides elementary comparisons of the left-hand sides of rules generated for different time points, for instance, for the data of two succeeding years, one can again introduce statistical models. These statistical models treat accidental fluctuations or noisy data. One possible analysis of change can also be represented by the previous template of a statement type. However, in this case, other definitions for "outstanding behavior" have to be defined, such as (strong) decreases or increases: The percentage of **target objects** in a **subpopulation** has **strongly increased** within the **population** in **time range**. A two-sample problem is one way to use a statistical foundation for the verification method of this statement type, which in its general form compares two sections of the database, such as two time points. One has to compare two shares of different samples and test if the underlying probabilities can be equal. Here, we use a test that is equivalent to a chi-square test (leading to a hypergeometric distribution that is approximated by a normal distribution). The derived statements of this type can be considered as information in its own right, which can be interesting for a user, especially if he (she) wants an answer to the question, what has changed? However, it can also be used to validate the stability of a rule characterizing a target group by a subpopulation. Then, one has to decide whether the changes lead only to a gradual difference in the degree of strength of this rule or these changes are so considerable that this rule can't be maintained any longer.

Another fundamental statement type for this application has to deal with long-term trends. Dependent on the periodicity and the overall time range of the data, a broad spectrum of methods for analyzing time series is available and could be incorporated into various statement types. We use some simple methods to detect patterns, for example, in short yearly series. These patterns can be represented by such formulations as "fact holds for the first time since . . . ," "fact holds for the . . . time in sequence," "the best result since . . . ." In these overall statement types, one has to include another predicate formalizing the kind of possible facts and results. Such a predicate can represent facts such as gains or losses and exceeding bounds.

The verification methods of these statement types related to series are simple. Much flexibility is gained by the indicated possibility of fitting one predicate into another (the argument of a statement cannot only be an elementary object structure but also a derived structure, such as the result of the application of another predicate). The overall flexibility of EXPLORA, however, is given by the possibility of including various statement types in the system and its search approach. Some examples of other statement types, such as "ranking list." "cumulations," "functional dependencies," and "necessary conditions for target groups" are compiled in figure 19.4, and some statement types are listed in the appendix.

19.3 Graph Search in EXPLORA

We already indicated that each statement type determines a search space. For each of the arguments of a statement type, the concrete object structures have to be fixed. The search space is given by the product of the sets of elements belonging to the object structures that are chosen as arguments. Each element of this product space corresponds to an instance of the underlying statement type. In principal, each element in the product space has to be checked by the verification method of the statement type to verify that it

Chrysler holds second largest sales for high-income people.
Chrysler holds largest sales for old-aged, high-income people.

More than 50% of stock of PCs is in companies with less than 20 employees.
Less than 10% of stock of PCs is in companies with more than 200 employees.
More than 50% of stock of PCs is not older than 3 years.

Stock of older text systems decreases with size of company.
Contracting rate of insurances decreases after age 35.

The top 50 districts are in southern areas.
The top 20 districts are in southern metropolitan areas.

Figure 19.4
Examples of Statements Belonging to Other Statement Types.

is a fact. To reduce this search for facts and delimit the number of facts for presentation, we now introduce a partial ordering on this product space.

This partial ordering is induced by the partial orderings already in existence in the associated object structures. It is defined as the product of the adapted partial orderings over the associated object structures. To adapt a given partial ordering of an object structure, one has to define whether this ordering is essential for the ordering of statements as well and, if so, in what direction (that is, stronger, weaker) it is essential. This definition is done by redundancy filters.

With the *redundancy elimination* in EXPLORA, facts are either selected or rejected as uninteresting. It is at this point that the partial ordering over the statement space comes in. This partial ordering is used to compare instances of a statement. The comparison determines whether one instance is stronger than another, and only the strongest statements are selected. As an example of such a redundancy rule, let us consider the previous statement type for rule searching. We have basic partial orderings over the object structures of "behavior patterns" (one pattern might be stronger than another pattern), as well as "target group," "population," and "subpopulation." The last three structures are given by the intensional structure of class descriptions by attributes: the class "high-income people in southern Germany" is more general than the class "very-high-income people in Bavaria" (that is, a subregion of southern Germany). Then, one instance of this statement is stronger than (or equal to) another if the pattern of the first instance is

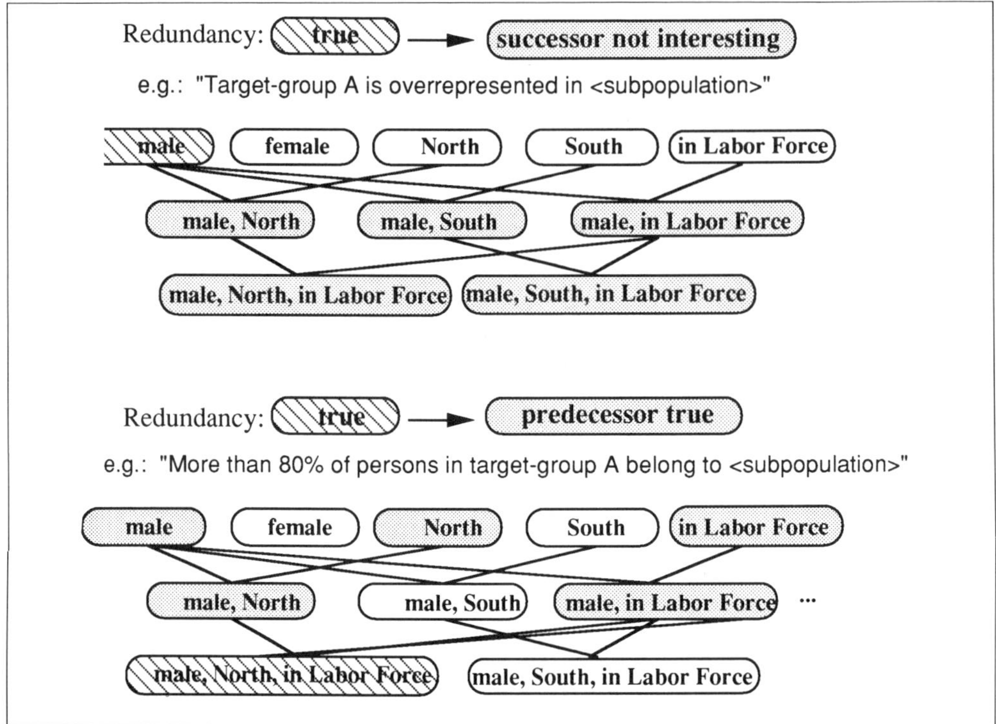

Figure 19.5
Small Sections of Search Graphs of Subpopulations with Two Redundancy Filters.

stronger than (or equal to) the pattern of the second instance and if the class appearing in the first instance is more general than (or equal to) the second. For partially ordered sets, we can apply one of several possible redundancy filters. In our example, this filter is a heuristic of the form

> If a statement is true for an element in the partial-ordered set, then for all successor elements this statement is not interesting.

Further redundancy filters are given by other combinations of the specifiers true, false, not interesting; and successor, predecessor. These are local rules for the single dimensions of the search space of statements. They are combined by the search algorithm (Latocha 1989) when looking for true statements in the statement space.

In case of the filter "Statement about object true -> Statement about successor true," this algorithm starts searching at the leaves, and if it finds a true statement, it looks for the strongest true statements compared to this one. Then it can eliminate all stronger statements because they are false and all weaker ones because they are redundant. In case of the filter "Statement about object true -> Statement about successor not interesting," it starts at the root, and if a true statement is found, then all successors are eliminated. When the specifier "predecessor" is involved, the inversed ordering of the graph is taken. In figure 19.5, the search is demonstrated by regarding only one argument of a statement type and a small class structure with no hierarchies of taxonomic values.

The search algorithm uses this partial ordering, which can be represented as a graph, to reduce the search for true statements and present only the nonredundant statements to the user. The control strategy of this algorithm is determined by the semantics, for example, of the taxonomies belonging to the structures of the search dimensions and the semantics behind the redundancy filters.

Fundamental to the EXPLORA approach is this central search into which any statement type associated with a verification method can be embedded. Therefore, the complexity of the search depends on the associated search space of a statement type. Different statement types can be incorporated so that a general assessment of the complexity seems impossible. For special statement types such as rule searchers, some theorems about the complexity of learning algorithms can be applied (Haussler 1988). Computationally efficient learning algorithms are available, assuming that the hypothesis space has a polynomially bounded growth function.

We have accomplished some empirical investigations for single examples. Two factors are of interest in the context of EXPLORA. The first measures the *efficiency* of the search algorithm, that is, the number of elements in the search space that are explicitly checked by the verification method compared to the total number of elements in the search space (the inverse of this ratio). The second measures the redundancy elimination (*effectiveness*), that is, the number of statements that are presented to the user as nonredundant compared to the number of true statements in the search space. These factors largely depend on the topology of the search space and the kind and number of redundancy filters. For instance, a redundancy rule such as "If a statement about an object is true, then statements about its successors are not interesting" only reduces the number of true statements. In the investigated examples, the efficiency varies between 4 and 2000 and the effectiveness between 40 and 1000.

19.4 Generalization

The system discovers true statements by working through the statement pool (according to the directions and the focus of the user) and applying the verification methods to the data that are associated with the objects of the statement. The search is controlled by the graph structure and the redundancy filters. This is basically how facts are derived from data, and only nonredundant facts are presented to the user. Through this systematic proceeding, EXPLORA turns out to be a discovery aid for its user, even identifying facts that might be hidden in the data.

However, not everything that is true and nonredundant is also of interest. This ability to separate the essentials from the obvious is an important condition for a good interpretation of data. Therefore, the next task is the further condensation of facts to obtain the most important and interesting messages. Two approaches can be taken: Facts can be selected, or several facts can be compiled into a new, more general statement.

As a further technique to reduce the number of presented facts and combine facts, we use *inductive generalization* (or *learning*) approaches (Michalski 1986). We apply methods of attributive and relational generalization: The objects of a structure can hold attributes, so that each object takes, for each attribute, a value out of a structured set of possible values. The goal of the generalization methods is to find classes of objects defined by means of the attribute values with a high density of true statements or some other measure evaluating the class. These classes are constructed by attributive and relational descriptions (Klösgen 1989). This approach is similar to that described previously in Statements Types, where an example of a statement type for rule searching is discussed.

In this example, the class structures, such as "target group," are already represented in the statement type; they appear as explicitly introduced object structures for some arguments of the statement type. A target group is defined relative to a set of basic units of analysis, such as persons or companies in a survey. In the case of a sample, we are not interested in statements about the individual units of analysis but in statements about some classes of units. These classes are constructed by using the attributes available for the units of analysis. A partial ordering is defined on the set of all possible attributive generalizations. A class is more general than another if the values of the attributes in its description are more general (referring to the structure defined on the values) or if its description holds only a subset of the attributes used for the other class.

The other possibility is given when statements about individual objects (such as products or companies) are interesting as well as statements about classes of these objects. In this case, the statement type (and the associated verification method) has to refer to the individual objects. The class structures are then investigated in a second subordinated search process in which common values of attributes of the identified facts are discovered, and corresponding classifications of facts are presented. As a simple example, let us assume that a record sale was achieved in the sales district Munich. Then, it is checked to see if there was a record sale in every southern German sales district in the analyzed time range. If so, then the fact about Munich is surely not interesting, but the message about southern Germany is. As another example, if in successive periods a certain fact has been discovered, then these facts can be summarized into a single message about this space of time. Such generalizations are also possible if only a few exceptions exist: record sales in nearly all reorganized districts.

Special approaches are introduced in EXPLORA to deal with overlapping generalizations (Gebhardt 1989). This problem appears because of attributes that are highly correlated, such as income, education, and age. A special problem of overlapping is to determine more flexible conditions for a subclass to suppress a class. The measure of evidence for a class (for example, a statistical significance or simply an arithmetic value such as a proportion of positive examples) is combined with a similarity measure for classes that also considers extensional structures of the classes (the objects belonging to the class and the degree of overlapping and not merely the ordering derived on the basis of the descriptions).

We use *selection rules* as another way to condense the number of facts and find interesting messages. These are semantic (context- or application-specific) rules that represent further criteria to select, as a filter, those facts that will be presented to the user. In comparison to the verification method that primarily holds statistical criteria, these criteria are application oriented.

To demonstrate the necessity for condensing the derived nonredundant facts (sometimes in a postprocessing step), we now discuss some of these aspects in more detail for the rule-type statement. If only the previously mentioned redundancy filters limit the elimination of facts, then some problems emerge with taxonomies, especially of the interval type and, to a lesser degree, the hierarchical type. Consider, for instance, the variables age or income, where intervals must be generated. The elementary redundancy formalism compares, for example, statements for age groups 20–59 and 30–49. Both statements can be statistically significant (as determined by the verification method) and the significance for the age group 30–49 might be higher than that for the age group 20–59. Then, a redundancy formalism has to decide whether both statements are important or only one of them will be presented: the one with the stronger significance or the one that refers to a more general subpopulation (left-hand side of the rule). More flexible solutions to this problem than using fixed categories of significance are described in Gebhardt (1989). One can also introduce additional domain knowledge: The group 20–59 is perhaps more natural than the group 30–49 because it relates to people in the labor force.

Nonapplicable values can constitute a similar problem, for example, for combinations of taxonomies, such as the class of pregnant men or the metropolitan area with a low population density. If only the intensional structure of the hypothesis space is regarded, one has to use some additional domain knowledge to exclude statements such as: "The 20 top districts lie in metropolitan areas with a high population density." This class is more specific than the classes "metropolitan area" and "high population density." If, as in the case of this statement type, the system searches for the most specific class (because of redundancy filter "true -> predecessor true"), additional knowledge about meaningful combinations can be used to eliminate some nonmeaningful combinations from the search space. Again, the methods developed to choose between overlapping generalizations can be used to treat this problem. Because this method also analyzes the *extensional structure* of the classes (the individual objects belonging to the classes), it detects that the classes "metropolitan area" and "metropolitan area with a high population density" (nearly) contain the same objects.

Another problem connected with these intervals can be the heterogeneous distribution of significance within a group. Although the group 20–59 is positively significant, it might be that the range 50–59 is negatively significant and, therefore, is dominated by the rest. By iteratively cutting countercurrent bordering intervals, we can prevent the group 20–59 instead of the group 20–49 from being presented as positive. Therefore, the countercurrent part 50–59 must be cut off, which is also done in the multidimensional case, when, for example, age and income groups are combined.

A typical overlapping problem because of correlation relates to descriptions with different attributes covering nearly the same objects. The algorithm (Gebhardt 1989) selects between such descriptions as "high-income, married" and "high-school-education, living with spouse or partner."

19.5 Browsing

As a result of the search, optionally supplemented by selections and generalizations, we arrive at a set of messages that represent nonredundant and condensed facts. Several relations exist for this set of messages: A message can, for instance, be an example orcounterexample of another message, or it can be a message about a subordinate object or an object that stands in contrast to another object (appearing in another message).

These relations can be used in two ways: We apply methods of text organization (Mann 1988) to order the set of messages in a coherent report. Ordering and discourse rules refer to these relations on messages. The process of surface generation (or text generation), however, is represented in EXPLORA only by some elementary techniques because natural language generation is not of primary interest in our approach. In particular, we use text templates to transform the internal representation of the message into a natural language representation that is presented to the user.

However, in an interactive mode, the user has the ability to browse or navigate in the spaces of messages. Using these relations, he (she) can, for instance, call (counter-)

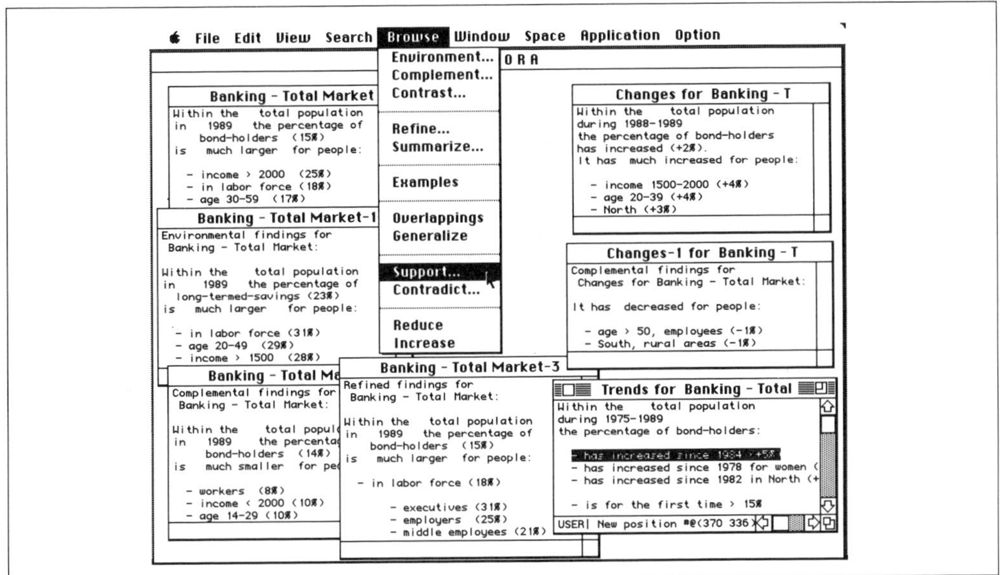

Figure 19.6
Browsing in the Analysis Space: A Supporting Finding for a Selected Statement is Called.

examples for an active message, he (she) can fade in (out) all subordinate messages of selected hierarchies, or he (she) can request all the messages about contrasting objects. Some sets of messages that are connected by the comparison or intensification relation are shown in the windows in figure 19.6.

Three activity spaces (Streitz, Hannemann, and Thüring 1989) are available to support the user in interactively composing a report of analysis: an analysis space, an outlining space, and an argumentation space. The *analysis space* contains several windows, each containing statements of one of those statement types that were tentatively selected by the user for a current analysis. Special menus for browsing are offered in this space. In the *outlining space*, the final report is composed in a window. Single statements of the analysis space that were selected by the user as the most interesting concerning the subject of his (her) report can be dragged to the outlining space. There they can be organized and commented on with tools similar to those available in an outlining system. Options for outlining are offered in special menus in this space. The *argumentation space* allows the organization of the findings into a series of argumentation structures. Menu options allow the user to specify predefined as well as offhand, annotated argumentation structures. These structures can also be transferred to the outlining space.

The browsing menu available in the analysis space offers commands to navigate in the environing, refining, exemplifying, overlapping, and supporting findings of a single statement or group of statements. Further, the amount of presented statements can be regulated by reduce or increase sliders. Some examples of these browsing commands follow: To the *environment* of findings about bond holders belong findings about owners of savings; to the *complemental* part of the environment belong rules characterizing people that hold no bonds. The *contrasting* part of the environment of a group of statements about X-Cola is given by group of statements about Y-Cola. The *refinement* of a statement concerning the southern districts refers to a similar statement about the districts of a southern subregion or industrialized southern districts. An *example* associated with a statement about southern districts is given by a statement about a single southern district. *Overlapping findings* refer to groups of objects that contain nearly the same objects but are described by different attributes because of correlated variables. A *supporting finding* for a statement is given by a statement of another statement type but one that is related in substance: "Target districts are overrepresented in high-income regions" is supported by the statement: "the top 20 target districts lie in high-income regions." Most of these browsing commands have a counterpart, given by the inverse relation: contradict versus support, generalize versus overlap, summarize versus refine, and so on.

The direction of search can be specified for most of these browsing commands in the view menu by choosing among the options stronger, weaker, and countercurrent. These options relate to the numeric value of significance: Secondary statements must respectively have a larger, smaller value or a value with inversed sign compared to the primary statement. The view menu additionally offers selections among textual, graphic, or tabular presentations of a statement or group of statements.

The reduce and increase sliders can influence several parameters of a verification method or of the approach for dealing with overlapping generalizations (compare section on generalization). For instance, the bounds of significance applied in the verification method of the statement type in figure 19.6 can be increased, so that some statements about subgroups with only small differences in percentages will be eliminated.

19.6 Statement Types And Formal Language

This section summarizes the statement types implemented in the applications as well as the formal language used in EXPLORA.

19.6.1 Statement Types

The following templates summarize various statement types we implemented in our applications. The statistical approach included in a verification method belonging to a statement type can depend on the application and the statistical nature of its associated data (for example, a weighted sample of 20,000 persons versus a totality of all 248 election districts).

Cross-Sectional Analyses

At <point of time> for <population>:
<target-value> shows <outstanding behavior> in <subpopulation>.

<point of time>::= usually the current point of time (new data)
<population>::= selection on the database: subset of units of analysis determined by a logical selection-formula (e.g., conjunction of selector terms defined by taxonomies on attributes of the database)
<target-value>::= aggregated value of a <dependent variable> over <subpopulation>
<dependent variable>::= attribute of the database, domain can be restricted to a <target population>
<target-population>::= selection on the database
<subpopulation>::= selection on the database
<outstanding behavior>:: = one of various (partially ordered) sets of patterns, e.g.:

percentage of <target-population> is overrepresented in <subpopulation>
percentage of <target-population> in <subpopulation> is larger than threshold value
mean of <dependent variable> is significantly above the average in <subpopulation>
share of <dependent variable> is significantly above the average in <subpopulation>

<target-value> in <subpopulation> shows <pattern of functional dependency>
e.g.: . . . is decreasing from <value of ordinal variable>

<target-value> in <subpopulation> shows <ranking-pattern>
e.g.: . . . is <the nth largest> for <object>

Analyses of Changes between Two Time Points

From <prior point of time> to <point of time> for <population>:
<target-value> shows <change-pattern> in <subpopulation>.

e.g.: percentage of <target-population> in <subpopulation> has significantly increased

<change of target-value> shows <outstanding behavior> in <subpopulation>
<outstanding behavior>::= see Cross-Sectional Analyses

Analyses of Trends over a Series of Time Points

Between <first point of time> and <last point of time> for <population>:
<target-value> shows <trend-pattern> in <subpopulation>.

<trend-pattern>::= various (simple) patterns of time series (nth largest since . . .)

19.6.2 Formal Language

A summary of the formal language L used in EXPLORA is described in BNF:

<object>::= <primary object> | <secondary object>
<primary object>::= <elementary object> | <predicate> | <operation>
<secondary object>::= (<operation> <object>+) | <statement>
<statement>::= (<predicate> <object>+)
<elementary object>::= $O_1|O_2|\ldots O_k$
<predicate>::= $P_1|P_2|\ldots P_m$
<operation>::= $OP_1|OP_2|\ldots OP_n$

19.7 Conclusion

EXPLORA addresses applications with regularly produced data that have to be analyzed in a routine way. The system systematically searches for statistical results (facts) to detect relations that could possibly be overlooked by a human analyst. However, EXPLORA will contribute to overcome the large bulk of information that today is usually still produced when presenting the data. Therefore, a second knowledge process in EXPLORA works to discover messages about the data by condensing the facts. Approaches for inductive generalization that have been developed for machine learning are utilized to identify common attribute values of the objects to which the facts relate. In addition, the system searches for interesting facts by applying redundancy filters and domain-dependent selection criteria. EXPLORA formulates the messages in terms of the domain, groups and orders them, and provides flexible tools for navigating through the data. A prototype is implemented for Apple Macintosh and Symbolics using Common Lisp and Common Lisp Object System.

Acknowledgments

This research was done at the German National Research Center for Computer Science in the EXPLORA project. The conception, design, and implementation of the EXPLORA system is the result of cooperative work within the project. The other members of the project are F. Gebhardt, F. Kellermann, and P. Latocha.

References

Gale, W. A. 1986. REX Review. In *Artificial Intelligence and Statistics*, ed. W. A. Gale, 173–227. Reading, Mass.: Addison Wesley.

Gebhardt, F. 1989. *Choosing among Competing Generalizations.* Sankt Augustin: GMD (Arbeitspapiere der GMD, 421).

Gebhardt, F. 1988. Prospects for Expert Systems to Analyze Election Data. In *Classification and Related Methods of Data Analysis*, ed. H. Bock, 691–696. Amsterdam: North Holland.

Hajek, P. and Havranek, T. 1977. On Generation of Inductive Hypotheses. *International Journal of Man-Machine Studies* 9(4): 415–438.

Halasz, F. G. 1988. Reflections on Notecards: Seven Issues for the Next Generation of Hypermedia Systems. *Communications of the ACM* 31(7): 836–852.

Haussler, D. 1988. Quantifying Inductive Bias. *Artificial Intelligence* 36(1): 177–221.

Klösgen, W. 1988. The Generalization Step in a Statistics Interpreter. In *Data Analysis, Learning Symbolic and Numeric Knowledge*, ed. E. Diday, 473–480. New York: Nova Science.

Kukich, K. 1988. Fluency in Natural Language Reports. In *Natural Language Generation Systems*, eds. D. McDonald and L. Bolc, 280–311. New York: Springer-Verlag.

Latocha, P. 1989. Exploration von Aussagenräumen. Sankt Augustin: GMD (GMD-Studien 164).

McDonald, D., and Bolc, L. 1988. *Natural Language Generation Systems.* New York: Springer-Verlag.

Mann, W. C. 1988. Text Generation: The Problem of Text Structure. In *Natural Language Generation Systems*, eds. D. McDonald and L. Bolc, 47–68. New York: Springer-Verlag.

Michalski, R. S.; Carbonell, J. G.; and Mitchell, T. M. 1986. *Machine Learning, An Artificial Intelligence Approach*, Volume II. San Mateo, Calif.: Morgan Kaufmann.

Mitchell, T. M. 1982. Generalization as Search. *Artificial Intelligence* 18(2): 203–226.

Nelder, J. A., and Wolstenholme, D. E. 1986. A Front-End for GLIM. In *Expert Systems in Statistics*, ed. R. Haux, 155–177. Stuttgart: Fischer.

Parsaye, K.; Chignell, M.; Khoshafian, S.; and Wong, H. 1989. *Intelligent Databases.* New York: Wiley.

Streitz, N. A.; Hannemann, J. M.; and Thüring, M. 1989. *From Ideas and Arguments to Hyperdocuments: Travelling through Activity Spaces.* Sankt Augustin: GMD (Arbeitspapiere der GMD, 421).

20 On Linguistic Summaries of Data

Ronald R. Yager
Iona College

Abstract

I introduce a new approach to the summarization of data based on the theory of fuzzy subsets. This new summarization allows for a linguistic summary of the data and is useful for both numeric and nonnumeric data items. It summarizes the data in terms of three values: a summarizer, a quantity in agreement, and a truth value. I also discuss a procedure for investigating the informativeness of a summary.

20.1 Introduction

The ability to summarize data provides an important method for getting a grasp of the meaning of a large collection of data. It enables humans to help understand the environment in a manner amenable to future useful manipulation.

At one extreme lies the large mass of undigested data, and at the other extreme lies the usual summarization in terms of the mean or average value of the data. The mean does help in understanding the content of data, but in some respects, it might provide too terse a summarization. The variance provides a means of judging the validity of the mean as the summary. In many instances, especially in situations involving presentations to nonquantitatively oriented people, an alternative form of summarization can be useful. This form of summarization can be especially useful if it can provide us with a summary that is not as terse as the mean and if it can be used for the summarization of nonnumeric data. In this chapter, I present a new approach to the summarization of data based on the theory of fuzzy sets (Bellman and Zadeh 1977; Zadeh 1965, 1978a, 1978b; Yager 1981b). This new approach will provide us with a linguistic summary of data. These linguistic summaries will be less terse than the mean and will allow us a myriad of possible ways to summarize data.

The facility to summarize data or observations has much to do with communicating observations about the world in a useful and understandable manner. It also provides a starting point for the ability to make useful inferences from large collections of data. The statement that "many Chinese like rice," which is a summarization of some observations, allows us to make inferences about the viability of opening a rice shop in China.

20.2 Summarizing Data

Assume V is some observable quality that can take values in the set $X = \{x_1, x_2, \ldots\}$. We allow V to take on numeric values or nonnumeric values. For example, V could be age, salary, hair color, years of education, or any other conceivable quality. Let $Y = \{y_1, \ldots, y_n\}$ be a set of objects that manifests the quality V. I use $V(y_i)$ to indicate the value of the quality V for object y_i; thus, $V : Y \rightarrow X$.

The data to be summarized consists of the collection $D = V(y_i),\ V(y_2), \ldots,\ V(y_n)$, the observations of the property V for the elements in the set Y. If Y is a group of n people, and V is the quality age, then the data would be the ages of the n people.

Definition: A summary of the data set D consists of three items, a summarizer, S; a quantity in agreement, Q (the term quantifier can also be used); and measure of validity or truth of the summary, T.

Given a data set D, I can hypothesize any appropriate summarizer S and any quantity in agreement Q; the measure T will then indicate the truth of the statement that "Q objects satisfy the statement S." We see the summarizer plays a role similar to the mean. The quantity in agreement has a role similar to the variance, and T is analogous to the confidence.

Example: If D is a set of data representing the ages of people, we can hypothesize the summary:

$S =$ *about 25*
$Q =$ *most* .

Then T, obtained by a procedure that I describe, will indicate the truth of the statement, "Most people in D are about 25." It is important to note that we are not restricted in our selection of S to the mean but can select any value of S useful for the purpose for which we are summarizing the data. A similar statement holds for the value Q. It is with the evaluation of T that we determine the validity of the summary.

Example: If $D =$ 25, 13, 12, 19, 37, 25, 56, 45, 73 is a set of ages of a group of people, we can discuss summaries in the form:

1. $S =$ *about 15*
   $Q =$ *some*

Hence, *some people are about 15.*

2. $S =$ *middle age*
   $Q =$ *most*

Hence, most people in the sample are at middle age. Again, the evaluation of T will determine the validity of the summary. T will be a number in the unit interval such that the closer T is to 1, the more truthful the proposed summary.

20.3 On the Form of Summarizer S

As I indicated, I summarize the data by means of a summarizer S. These summarizers will be allowed to take the form of a linguistic value (Zadeh 1978b). For example, in summarizing ages, some useful linguistic summaries could be *old*, *young*, *about 30*, *middle age*, *over 40*, and *exactly 15*.

The ability to use linguistic values for summarizers is based on the faculty of being able to quantitatively represent these linguistic values as fuzzy subsets of the base set X, a set containing all the possible observed values of our data.

Assume X is a set of elements. A fuzzy subset H of X is a generalization of the idea of a subset of X. The fuzzy subset H associates with each element $x \in X$ a value $H(x) \in [0,1]$, called the *membership grade* of x in H. $H(x)$ indicates the degree to which x satisfies the concept indicated by H. If H were an ordinary subset, then $H(x)$ would be restricted to the set $\{0,1\}$.

Consider the set

$$X = \{1,\ 2,\ 3,\ 4,\ 5,\ 6,\ 7,\ 8,\ 9,\ 10\}.$$

We could represent the value *near 5* as

$$\mathit{near}\ 5 = \left\{\frac{0}{1}, \frac{0.5}{2}, \frac{0.7}{3}, \frac{1}{4}, \frac{1}{5}, \frac{1}{6}, \frac{0.7}{7}, \frac{0.3}{8}, \frac{0}{9}, \frac{0}{10}\right\}.$$

We could represent the value *large* as

$$\mathit{large} = \left\{\frac{0}{1}, \frac{0}{2}, \frac{0}{3}, \frac{0}{4}, \frac{0}{5}, \frac{0}{6}, \frac{0.3}{7}, \frac{0.5}{8}, \frac{0.8}{9}, \frac{1}{10}\right\}.$$

We could represent the value *exactly 3* as

$$\mathit{exactly}\ 3 = \left\{\frac{0}{1}, \frac{0}{2}, \frac{1}{3}, \frac{0}{4}, \frac{0}{5}, \frac{0}{6}, \frac{0}{7}, \frac{0}{8}, \frac{0}{9}, \frac{0}{10}\right\}.$$

Thus, we see that we can take linguistic values, that is, words, and associate with them a fuzzy subset expressing the meaning of the word in terms of membership grades.

In the context of our methodology for summarizing data, a summarizer S is associated with a fuzzy subset over X. The meaning of the summarizer is equivalent to the membership function of the fuzzy subset. In applications, a user would suggest a summarizer

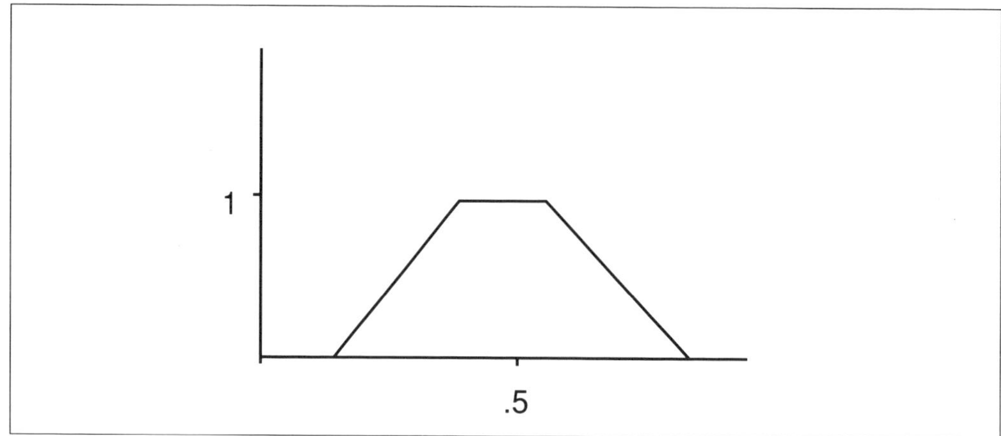

Figure 20.1
The Quantity *about 50%*

and would be asked the meaning of the term S. The user would then be prompted to provide a fuzzy subset representing S. One promising approach to developing the meaning of linguistic terms is to have the user directly plot the meaning of the word into the machine and then store it as a matrix.

20.4 On the Form of the Quantity in Agreement

The second component of the data summary is the quantity in agreement, Q. Q is a proposed indication of the number of pieces of data that satisfy the summary S. Q can be one of two types. The first is an absolute type of quantity, and the second, is a proportional or relative type of quantity. Examples of the first type are: *about five*, *at least 30*, *exactly 3*, *less than 50*, *several*, and so on. With the absolute type of quantity, we are specifying how many pieces of data satisfy S. The second type, relative quantities, is exemplified by such terms as *more than half*, *most*, and *at least 25%*. The relative quantities are characterized by indicating what proportion of the data satisfies S.

In either of these two cases, we are stipulating Q in terms of a linguistic value, just as we did to stipulate S. Thus, Q can also be represented as a fuzzy subset. However, when we use a relative quantity, Q is specified as a fuzzy subset of the unit interval [0,1]. For example, the quantity "about 50%" can be represented by the fuzzy subset shown in figure 20.1.

When we use an absolute quantity, then Q is specified as a fuzzy subset of the set R^+ of real numbers. For example, the quantity *few* can be represented as shown in figure

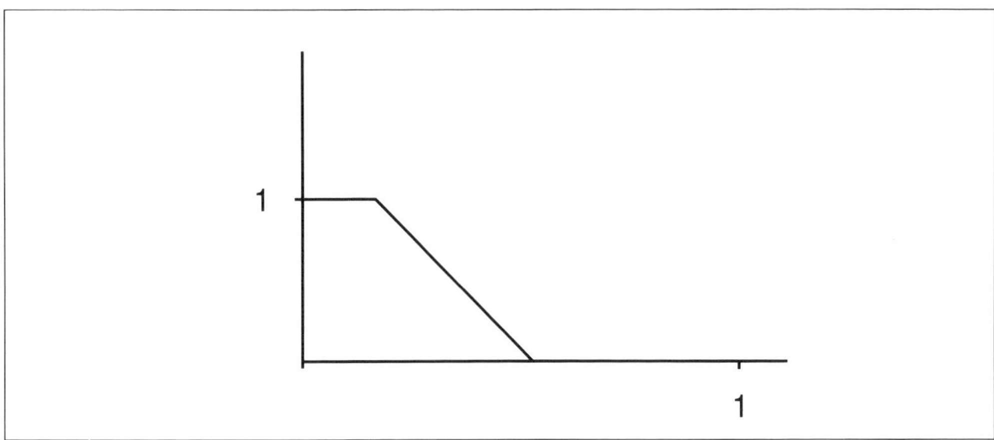

Figure 20.2
The Quantity *few*

20.2.

It is important to note that the meaning of the quantity Q is its fuzzy subset representation. Because a user is providing the quantity Q, she (he) must also provide the meaning of the Q, just as she (he) must provide the meaning of the summarizer S. Furthermore, with respect to the definition of both summarizers and quantities in agreement, the user is free to provide any fuzzy subset she (he) wants to specify the meaning.

20.5 Calculation of the Truth of a Summary

Assume we have a set of data

$$D = \{d_1,\ d_2, \ldots, d_n\}$$

corresponding to the readings for some variable V for all the elements in a population of n people, where each d_i is drawn from some set X. For example, if V is a subject's weight, then X could be a set of real numbers. If V is hair color, then X would be a set of hair colors. Let S be a proposed summarizer of the elements in D, expressed as a user-defined fuzzy subset of X. Finally, let Q be a quantity in agreement expressed as a fuzzy subset of either $[0,\ 1]$ or R^+. I show a method for determining the validity T of this proposed summary S, Q in light of the data D.

I first consider the case where Q is a relative quantifier:

$$Q:\ [0,\ 1] \rightarrow [0,\ 1]\ \ .$$

The procedure for obtaining T in this case is as follows:

1. For each $d_i \in D$, calculate $S(d_i)$, the degree to which d_i satisfies the summarizer S.
2. Let $r = \frac{1}{n} \cdot \sum_{i=1}^{n} S(d_i)$

   the proposition of D that satisfies S.
3. Then $T = Q(r)$, the grade of membership of r in the proposed quantity in agreement.

Example: Assume we have a population of six people, and we have measured the ages of these people:

$$D = 25,\ 37,\ 22,\ 36,\ 31,\ 30.$$

Assume a proposed summary of these data is:

Summarizer = *about 30*

Quantity in agreement = *most*

The value *about 30* is defined by the user as the fuzzy subset S, where the membership function is

$$S(x) = \exp\left(-\left(\frac{x-30}{6.6}\right)^2\right).$$

Thus, we get

$$\begin{array}{ll} d_1 = 25 & S(d_1) = .56 \\ d_2 = 37 & S(d_2) = .32 \\ d_3 = 22 & S(d_3) = .23 \\ d_4 = 36 & S(d_4) = .44 \\ d_5 = 31 & S(d_5) = .98 \\ d_6 = 30 & S(d_6) = 1 \end{array}$$

and therefore,

$$r = 3.53/6 = .588 \ .$$

If the user's definition for *most* is defined by the fuzzy set where $Q(r) = r^2$, then

$$T = Q(.58) = (.58)^2 = .3364 \ .$$

Thus, the validity of the summary *about 30 for most elements in D*, given the definition of *most* and *about 30*, is .3364.

If we choose a different summarizer for our data, then we would get a different truth. For example, if our summarizer S is *at least 25 years old*, and our quantity in agreement is still *most*, then the following results are obtained:

Because S is such that

$$S(d) = 1 \; for \; d \geq 25$$
$$S(d) = 0 \; for \; d < 25,$$

then

$$S(d_1) = S(d_2) = S(d_4) = S(d_5) = S(d_6) = 1$$
$$S(d_3) = 0,$$

then

$$r = 5/6 = .833$$

and then

$$Q(.833) = .69$$

Thus, given our data and our definition for *most*, the validity of the summary *most people in this sample are over 25* is .833.

In the case where our amount in agreement Q is an absolute quantity, then our procedure remains the same, except that in step 2,

$$r = \sum_{i=1}^{n} S(d_i),$$

the total amount of satisfaction to S.

20.6 Some Concepts from Fuzzy Set Theory

Because we are using fuzzy subsets to represent the linguistic terms used to specify a summarization S and a quantity in agreement Q in our model, we must first present some concepts from fuzzy set theory.

Definition: If F is a fuzzy set of X, then F is said to be *normal* if there exists some x such that F(x) = 1.

Definition: Assume F and G are two fuzzy subsets of X. Then F is said to be *contained* in G, denoted $F \subset G$, if $F(x) \leq G(x)$ for all $x \in X$.

Definition: If F is a fuzzy subset of X, *the* α *level set* of X, denoted F_α, is the crisp subset of X defined by

$$F_\alpha = \{x \mid F\,(x) \geq \alpha,\ x \in X\}.$$

Definition: If F is a fuzzy subset of X, then the *negation* of F, denoted $\overline{F}$, is also a fuzzy subset of X in which $\overline{F}(x) = 1 - F(x)$.

For example, if the fuzzy set T represents *tall*, then $\overline{T}$ represents *not tall.*

Definition: If F is a fuzzy subset of X, then (1) there exists some $n > 1$, such that F^n, where $F^n\,(x) = (F(x))^n$, is representative of *very* F and (2) There exists some $0 < n < 1$, such that F^n, where $F^n\,(x) = (F(x))^n$ is representative of *sort of* F.

Note that if $n_1 > n_2$, then $F^{n_1} \subset F^{n_2}$.

Definition: Assume X is a set on which there exists a negation operation, N, such that $N\,(x) = \overline{x}$. If F is a fuzzy subset of X, then the *antonym* of F, denoted $\hat{F}$, is the fuzzy subset of X, such that $\hat{F}\,(x) = F\,(\overline{x})$. In particular, if X is the unit interval, then $\hat{F}(x) = F(1 - x)$.

Examples of antonym pairs would be true-false, tall-short, big-small.

Definition: Assume F is a normal fuzzy subset of the set of real numbers. Then a representative value for F, denoted $R(F)$, is defined as

$$R\,(F) = \int_0^1 M(F_\alpha)\ d_\alpha,$$

where $M(F_\alpha)$ is the mean value of α level sets F_α (Yager 1981a).

Definition: Assume F is a fuzzy subset of the finite set X. Then the *specificity* of F is defined as

$$S(F, X) = \int_0^1 \frac{1}{card(F_\alpha)} d_\alpha,$$

where $card(F_\alpha)$ is the number of elements in the α level set F_α.

The specificity measures the degree to which F suggests one and only one element of X as its manifestation.

We note the following properties of specificity

1. $0 \leq S(F, X) \leq 1$.
2. $S(F, X) = 1$ if $F(x) = 1$ for one element in X, and $F(x) = 0$ for all the rest.
3. If A and B are two normal fuzzy subsets of X, such that $A \subset B$, then $S(A) \geq S(B)$.
4. If F and $\hat{F}$ are antonyms, then $S(\hat{F}, X) = S(F, X)$ (Yager 1982).

20.7 Properties of the Summarization

Most naturally used quantities in agreement fall into one of three classes. Assume Q is a fuzzy subset of X (X is either R^+ or the unit interval I): (1) Q is said to be a monotonically nondecreasing quantifier if $r_1 > r_2 \Rightarrow Q(r_1) \geq Q(r_2)$. Examples of this type of Q are *at least 30%*, *almost all*, and *most*. (2) Q is said to be a monotonically nonincreasing quantifier if $r_1 > r_2 \Rightarrow Q(r_1) \leq Q(r_2)$. Examples of this type of Q are *at most 30%*, *few* and *almost none*. (3) Q is said to be a unimodal-type quantifier if there exist two values $a \leq b \in I$, such that for all $r < a$, Q is monotonically nondecreasing, for all $r > b$, Q is monotonically nonincreasing, and for all $r \in [a, b]$, $Q(r) = 1$. Examples of this type of Q are *close to 30%*, *exactly 5* and *some*.

THEOREM 1 Assume we have a set of data D. Let S and Q be a proposed summary and quantity in agreement having an associated truth value T. Consider another proposed summary $\overline{S}$ and $\hat{Q}$, where $\overline{S}$ is the negation of S, and $\hat{Q}$ is the antonym of Q. If T' is the associated truth value of this proposed summary, then

$$T = T' \quad .$$

Proof:

$$T = Q\left(\frac{1}{n}\sum_{i=1}^{n} S(d_i)\right) \quad .$$

$$T' = \hat{Q}\left(\frac{1}{n}\sum_{i=1}^{n} \overline{S}(d_i)\right) = \hat{Q}\left(\frac{1}{n}\sum_{i=1}^{n} (1 - S(d_i))\right)$$

$$T' = \hat{Q}\left(1 - \frac{1}{n}\sum_{i=1}^{n} S(d_i)\right) = Q\left(\frac{1}{n}\sum_{i=1}^{n} S(d_i)\right)$$

This result implies, for example, that if "many" and "few" are antonyms, then given a data set D about heights, the summarization "tall" for "many" will have the same truth value as the summarization "not tall" for "few."

THEOREM 2 Assume we have a data set D. Let S and Q be a proposed summarization having the truth value T. The summarization S and $\overline{Q}$, where $\overline{Q}$ is the negation of Q, has the truth value T' where

$$T' = 1 - T \quad .$$

Proof:

$$T' = \overline{Q}(r) = 1 - Q(r) = 1 - T \ .$$

These two theorems provide an equivalence rule for summaries, where two summaries are said to be equivalent (or more precisely semantically equivalent) when they supply the same information about the data set D.

Equivalence Rule: The summary (S, Q, T) is equivalent to the summary $(\overline{S}, \hat{Q}, T)$, and both are equivalent to the summary $(S, \overline{Q}, 1 - T)$; thus,

$$(S, Q, T) \Leftrightarrow (\overline{S}, \hat{Q}, T) \Leftrightarrow (S, \overline{Q}, 1 - T) \ .$$

THEOREM 3 Assume D is a collection of data drawn from a set X. Let S be a proposed summary described as a fuzzy subset of X. Let Q_1 and Q_2 be two quantities in agreement, such that $Q_1 \subset Q_2$. Then if T_1 is the truth of the summary S with quantity of agreement Q_2 and if T_2 is the truth associated with S and Q_2, then $T_2 \geq T_1$.

Proof: In both cases, because the S value is the same for each d_i, then both cases have the same value for r. However, because $Q_1 \subset Q_2$, then $Q_1(r) \leq Q_2(r)$, and hence, $T_1 \leq T_1$.

This theorem implies that a tradeoff exists between the specificity with which we state our value Q and the degree of truth we get for our summarization. Thus, we run the risk of finding our summarization to be false, if we attempt to be too specific in the formulation of Q.

THEOREM 4 Assume D is a collection of data drawn from a set X:

(1) Let Q be a monotonically nondecreasing quantity in agreement, and let S_1 and S_2 be two summaries, fuzzy subsets of X, such that $S_2 \subset S_1$. Then if T_1 is the truth of summary S_1, Q and if T_2 is the truth of summary S_2, Q, then $T_1 \geq T_2$.

(2) If Q is monotonically nonincreasing, and $S_2 \subset S_1$, then $T_2 \geq T_1$.

Proof: Because $S_2 \subset S_1$, for any observation d_i, $S_1(d_i) \geq S_2(d_i)$, and hence,

$$\sum_{i=1}^{n} S_1(d_i) \geq \sum_{i=1}^{n} S_2(d_i).$$

Therefore, $r_1 \geq r_2$. If Q is monotonically nondecreasing, $r_1 \geq r_2 \Rightarrow Q(r_1) \geq Q(r_2)$; hence, $T_1 \geq T_2$. If Q is monotonically nonincreasing, $r_1 \geq r_2 \Rightarrow Q(r_1) \leq Q(r_2)$; hence, $T_1 \leq T_2$.

Thus, this theorem states that if Q is a monotonically increasing-type quantity, such as *at least 30%* or *almost all* and if we are too specific in the statement of our summarizer S, we run the risk of obtaining a low validation of our summary.

20.8 Informativeness about the Data Set from a Summary

Assume a data set D, drawn from a measurement space X. In providing a summary of the data, we are attempting to present the information contained in the data set in a more concise manner, one that is easier for the human mind to comprehend. However, in making this summary, we lose some information about the data set because the most informative way of presenting the data is the data set itself. A question that naturally arises is whether a summarization about the data set D is informative. A first inclination might be to assume that the truth associated with a summarization is the indication of the informativeness of a summary. The following example is intended to illustrate the inappropriateness of this conjecture.

Example: Assume $X = \{1, 2, 3, 4, 5\}$. Consider the summary:

$S =$ greater than or equal to 2

$Q =$ few

$T =$ false.

Even though we obtained a false result, we learned a lot about the data.

In the following discussion, I present an outline of an approach to indicating the informativeness of a summarization with respect to capturing the original data set D. Assume we have a summary (S, Q, T) of some unknown data set D having elements drawn from some measurement space X. Let the elements of this summary be S, a fuzzy subset of X; Q, a fuzzy subset of I; and T, a truth value from the set I.

We now ask what the possible sets are that could have been our original data set? Let Ω be a set whose members are all collections of elements drawn from X^*. The elements of Ω are multisets consisting of n elements. The first observation we can make is that $D \in \Omega$. That is, D is an element of this set; it is a collection of n values drawn from X. Our summary (S, Q, T) gives us more information about our unknown data set D. If $d_1, \ldots, d_n$ are the elements of our unknown collection, then

$$T = Q\left[\frac{1}{n}\sum_{i=1}^{n} S(d_i)\right].$$

This observation implies the following criteria: Let $Q^{-1}(T)$ be the set of elements in the unit interval such that $r \in Q^{-1}(T)$ implies $Q(r) = T$; then only those elements in Ω satisfying

$$\frac{1}{n}\sum_{i=1}^{n} S(d_i) \in Q^{-1}(r)$$

are possible manifestations of our unknown data set. Let us denote this subset of Ω by Ω_s, $\Omega_s \subset \Omega$. We call Ω_s the set of possible data sets.

We note that if Ω_s has just one element, that is, one possible data set, then our summarization can be used to exactly obtain the unknown data set. As the number of elements in Ω_S increases, we are less certain about which is the unknown data set D. Note that if Ω_S is empty, then our summary is incompatible with Ω.

In situations when X is finite, then Ω is finite, and we can use our measure of specificity to indicate the informativeness of the data summary with regard to the set D. Let us denote $I(S, Q, T)$ as the measure of information from the summary about D. Because $(S, Q, T) \to \Omega_S$, we can say that

$$I\,(S,\,Q,\,T) = 0 \quad if\; card\,\Omega_S = 0$$

and

$$I\,(S,\,Q,\,T) = 1/K \quad if\; card\,\Omega_S = K.$$

We note the close connection to Shannon's entropy, which would be measured for this situation as $-\ln K$.

Assume we have two summaries associated with this unknown data set, $(S_1,\,Q_1,\,T_1)$ and $(S_2,\,Q_2,\,T_2)$. Each summary suggests a subset of Ω of possible values of D; these subsets can be denoted as Ω_{S_1} and Ω_{S_2}. The possible values for the data set D suggested by this pair of summaries is

$$\Omega_S = \Omega_{S_1} \cap \Omega_{S_2} \quad .$$

Because $\Omega_S \subset \Omega_{S_1}$ and $\Omega_S \subset \Omega_{S_2}$, if *card* $\Omega_{S_1} = K_1$, *card* $\Omega_{S_2} = K_2$, and *card* $\Omega_S = K_3$, then

$$K_3 \le K_1$$

$$K_3 \le K_2 \quad ,$$

and hence, Ω_S is telling us more about the potential value for D. Thus, in general, as we add more and more summaries, we gain more information about the possible value for the original data set D.

20.9 Properties of Informative Summaries

Let us recapitulate. We have a data set D. In providing a summary of this set, we are reducing the amount of information we know about this set for the convenience of being able to see what the data are saying in a more compact form. However, each particular summary reduces the information we know about the data set in a different way. In some instances, our goal is to provide informative summaries, that is, summaries that give as much information about the data set as possible and still provide a summary. Let us continue our investigation into the possibility of measuring the informativeness of summary triplets (S, Q, T).

First, let us consider the case where Q is *all* and has membership 1 for $r = 1$ and 0 elsewhere. Assume that S has a membership of 1 for $x^* \in X$ and 0 for all others. In this case, Q and S are highly specific, and Q is increasing. If $T = 1$, we can use this summary to easily deduce that all elements in D are s^*. Thus, this summarization is highly informative about the data set D.

Let us consider Q again as previously defined but let us now assume S to be less specific. In particular, some subset A of X exists for which S has membership 1. If the truth of this summary is 1, we can only say that D is made up of elements from the set A. In particular, the larger A is, that is, the less specific S is, the larger the possible set of potential values is for D. Thus, the more specific S is in this case, the more informative the summarization is.

Consider again the case where S is highly specific; that is, only one value exists having nonzero membership, x^*. Let Q be a monotonically increasing quantifier. Consider two possible associated truth values $T_1 > T_2$. Because Q is increasing, then r_1, associated with T_1, must be such that $r_1 \geq r_2$, where r_2 is associated with T_2. Because $r_1 \geq r_2$ fixes more of the elements in the unknown D as having membership grade 1 and less having membership grade 0 for the first case than for the second. Because we know with certainty that the observed value was x^* for the situation when membership grade is 1 and that while when membership grade is 0 a multitude of possible values exist for our observation, we can conclude that the situation with T_1 is more informative about D.

Consider now a situation where we have two increasing quantities Q_1 and Q_2, such that $Q_1 \subset Q_2$; that is, Q_1 is more specific than Q_2. Let S again be the highly specific summary, and let our truth be T. Because $Q_1 \subset Q_2 \Rightarrow Q_1(r) \leq Q_2(r)$, if $Q_1\ (r_1) = Q_2(r_2) = T$, then $r_1 > r_2$. This fact implies that for Q_1, more of the elements of D are fixed at x^*.

From this discussion, we can conclude that one way to achieve highly informative summaries is to obtain summarizations in which Q is monotonically nondecreasing; S and Q are highly specific; and T is high, close to 1. However, our quest for these types of summarizations is affected by the theorems, in which we have shown that as S and Q become more specific, T becomes smaller. Thus, some optimal summary, not easily apparent, appears that provides the most information. Further, we note that the elements in the data set D impose some limit on the degree to which any summary can be informative.

Let us again consider Q to be increasing but this time unspecific; that is, only one value of r exists with membership grade 0. Because of the monotonicity, this must occur at $r =$

0. Let S be unspecific: For example, $S(\hat{x}) = 0$, and for all other $x \in X$, $S(x) = 1$. If for this situation, T is low (for example, $T = 0$), then we can see that because $Q(r) = T = 0$, $r = 0$. Now $r = 0$ implies that $S(d_i) = 0$ for all i. Hence, from our characterizations of S, under this condition, all the d_is must be equal to $\hat{x}$; thus, D is completely known. By continuing in this manner, we can conclude that if Q is monotonically nondecreasing and if S and Q are highly nonspecific, then if T is false, we obtain a highly informative summarization.

However, we note that these two situations are closely related. We note the following observations: (1) If Q is monotonically nondecreasing, then the antonym of Q, $\hat{Q}$, where $\hat{Q}(r) = Q(1-r)$, is such that $\hat{Q}$ is monotonically nonincreasing, and the specificity of $\hat{Q}$ is the same as Q. (2) If Q is monotonically nonincreasing, then $\overline{Q}$, not Q, is monotonically nondecreasing. Furthermore, if Q is nonspecific but with at least one element having 0 membership grade, then $\overline{Q}$ becomes specific. (3) Similarly, if S is nonspecific but with at least one element having 0 membership, then $\overline{S}$ becomes highly specific.

Consider a summary S, Q, and T in which S is nonspecific, Q is monotonically nonincreasing and nonspecific, and T is low. As I showed in theorem 1, the summary $\overline{S}$, $\hat{Q}$ will have the same truth T as S, Q. However, $\overline{S}$ becomes specific, and $\hat{Q}$ remains nonspecific as it becomes monotonically nonincreasing.

Finally, consider the summary $\overline{S}$, $(\overline{\hat{Q}})$ from theorem 2, with truth $T' = 1 - \mathrm{T}$. Thus, in this final case, we have $\overline{S}$, $(\overline{\hat{Q}})$, and T', where $\overline{S}$ is highly specific, $\overline{\hat{Q}}$ is monotonically increasing and highly specific, and T' is high.

Thus, we see for summaries of monotonically increasing quantities Q, that if T is high, then we have a highly informative summary when both S and Q are highly specific. However, where T is low, we have highly informative summaries if $\overline{S}$ and $\overline{\hat{Q}}$ are highly specific.

As an attempt to get a measure of the informativeness of a summary (S, Q, T), we can suggest the following:

$$I = \max\left[T \cdot Sp(Q) \cdot Sp(S)\,,\ (1-T) \cdot Sp(\overline{\hat{Q}}) \cdot Sp(\overline{S})\right] \ ,$$

where T is the truth, and Sp indicates the specificity of the associated fuzzy set. The larger I is, the more informative it is.

Let us now turn our attention to monotonically nonincreasing quantifiers such as *few* or *less than 20%*. Assume Q is monotonically nonincreasing and specific. For example, $Q(r) = 1$ if $r = 0$, and elsewhere $Q(r) = 0$; S is nonspecific (for example, $S(x^*) = 0$, but for all other, $x \in X$, $S(x) = 1$). If our truth value is $T = 1$, we can see that $Q(r) = 1$, which implies that $r = 0$, in turn implying that x^* is the only possible value for elements in D. Analogous to the case where Q is monotonically nondecreasing, we can see that the following holds: A summary T, Q, S, in which Q is highly specific and monotonically nonincreasing, S is highly specific, and T is true, gives a lot of information about the members of D. For example, if we have $X = \{0, 1, 2, 4, 5\}$, $Q =$ *very few*, $S =$ *at least one*, and $T = 1$, then we know that the elements in D are 0.

This observation could have been obtained from our equivalency rule for summarizers. Assume we have a summary S_1, Q_1, T_1, where Q_1 is monotonically nondecreasing and highly specific, S_1 is highly specific, and T_1 is true. I previously showed that this summary is an informative type.

Consider the summary $(\overline{S}, \hat{Q}_1, T_1)$. This summary is equivalent to the summary (S_1, Q_1, T_1) and, therefore, must be equally informative about the elements in D. However, this summary is a new one in which the quantity in agreement $\hat{Q}_1$ is still highly specific but monotonically nonincreasing, and the truth T_1 is high, but the summarizer S_1 is nonspecific.

We have also shown that if (S_2, Q_2, T_2) is a summary in which S_2 is nonspecific, Q_2 is monotonically nondecreasing and nonspecific, and T_2 is false, then this summary is highly informative about the elements in D. If we apply our equivalency rule, we get $(\overline{S}_2, \hat{Q}_2, T_2)$, in which $\hat{Q}_2$ is now monotonically nonincreasing and nonspecific, $\overline{S}_2$ is specific, and T_2 is false. This new summary must also be highly informative about the elements in D.

Thus, if (S, Q, T) is a summary of some data set D, and Q is a monotonically nonincreasing quantity, then a possible indicator of the informativeness of this summary is

$$I\,(S,\,Q,\,T) = \max[T \cdot Sp(Q) \cdot Sp(\overline{S})\,,\,(1 - T) \cdot Sp(S) \cdot Sp(\overline{Q})]\quad .$$

Let us now consider the information content in a unimodal type summary, such as *about 40%* or *near 5*. Consider the case where S is highly specific (for example, $S(x^*) = 1$, and all other x-s have membership grades 0). Q is unimodal and highly specific (for example, $Q(a/n) = 1$, $Q(r)$ for all other $r \in [0, 1]$), and $T = 1$. Analyzing this case, we see that because $T = 1$, then $Q(r) = 1$; thus, $r = a/n$. Because S only equals something other than zero for $x*$, then a of the readings in D must be x^*, and the remaining $n - a$ readings can be anything but x^*.

From the previous discussion, we can conclude that for summaries with unimodal quantities Q that are highly specific, summarizers S that are highly specific, and truth that is high, the information content about D is high. Furthermore, the closer the location of the peak of Q is to 1 along the r axis, the more information there is. For example, very close to 60% of the sample is almost 30 years old is highly true tells us more about the elements in D than the statement close to 40% of the sample is almost 30 years is true.

We have shown then that a summary (S_1, Q_1, T_1) will be informative about the data set D if S_1 is highly specific; Q_1 is unimodal, highly specific, and centered about a; and T_1 is high. We also note that the higher a is, the more informative it is; thus, the limit, when $a = 1$, is the most informative. Applying our equivalence rule to this situation, we get a new summary ($\overline{S}_1$, $\hat{Q}_1$, T_1), which is equivalent to (S_1, Q_1, T_1). However, we note that $\overline{S}_1$ is broad, and Q_1 is still unimodal and specific, but its center is about $1 - a = b$. We can conclude that for unimodal summaries, good information is obtained when the summarizer is broad (unspecific), Q is specific but centered about a low value, and T is high.

We can now hypothesize a measure of informativeness for unimodal summaries. Assume (S, Q, T) is a unimodal summary. Let a be the center of the range where $Q(r) = 1$. Then a measure of the informativeness can be expressed as

$$I = \max\left[a \cdot T \cdot Sp(Q) \cdot Sp(S), (1 - a) \cdot T \cdot Sp(Q) \cdot Sp(\overline{S})\right]$$

20.10 Conclusion

The ability to summarize is an important mechanism in the analysis of information. It provides a means of answering particular questions about the data and a way of formatting the information to enable an analyst to comprehend the content of the data in a holistic manner. The procedure presented in this chapter has a number of advantages over the classic, that is, mean, way of summarizing data. Among these advantages are the abilities to summarize nonnumber, as well as numeric, data; provide numerous different summaries for special purposes; and provide linguistic summaries.

References

Bellman, R. E. and Zadeh, L. A. 1977. Local and Fuzzy Logics. In *Modern Uses of Multivalued Logics*, eds. J. M. Dunn, and G. Epstein, 103–165. Dordect, Holland: Reidel.

Yager, R. R. 1982. Measuring Tranquility and Anxiety in Decision Making. *International Journal of General Systems* 8: 139–146.

Yager, R. R. 1981a. A Procedure for Ordering Fuzzy Subsets of the Unit Interval. *Information Science* 24: 143–161.

Yager, R. R. 1981b. Quantified Propositions in a Linguistic Logic. In *Proceedings of the Second International Seminar on Fuzzy Set Theory*, 69–124. Linz, Austria: University of Linz.

Zadeh, L. A. 1978a. Fuzzy Sets as a Basis for a Theory of Possibility. *Fuzzy Sets and Systems* 1: 3–28.

Zadeh, L. A. 1978b. PRUF–A Meaning Representation Language for Natural Languages. *International Journal of Man-Machine Studies* 10: 395–460.

Zadeh, L. A. 1965. Fuzzy Sets. *Information and Control* 8: 328–353.

V DOMAIN-SPECIFIC DISCOVERY METHODS

21 Extracting Reaction Information from Chemical Databases

C.-S. Ai, P. E. Blower, Jr., and R. H. Ledwith
Chemical Abstracts Service

Abstract

This chapter describes a system that extracts chemical reaction information from a database created by the American Chemical Society and used to publish the *Journal of Organic Chemistry.* The extraction process is divided into four phases: (1) preprocess documents to extract the experimental sections from journal articles; translate data to a representation that captures font information; isolate words, numbers, and punctuation; and build Lisp data structures for the documents; (2) classify words mainly by dictionary lookup and word morphology; (3) transform the text of an experimental section into frames representing the meaning of the text in a simplified and canonical form; and (4) build a synthesis frame for each experiment using heuristic rules. Following an analysis of the data, each of the phases is discussed.

21.1 Introduction

As the volume of scientific literature continues to grow, scientists increasingly rely on online databases to support their work. Entering original information into the online databases and verifying it makes online database building expensive. However, using advanced natural language processing (NLP) techniques and accessing large files of computerized natural language text, it is feasible to develop automatic database-building techniques.

Presentations given at a recent workshop on knowledge discovery in databases indicate that extracting knowledge from databases has become an active AI research area (Piatetsky-Shapiro and Frawley 1989). The reports covered areas such as rules for medical diagnosis, drug side effects, chemical reaction information, and rules for semantic query optimization. AI literature contains other reports of systems using NLP techniques for text understanding, including systems that process patent abstracts that describe the physical structures of objects (Lebowitz 1988) and that describe newspaper articles about corporate takeovers (Jacobs and Rau 1988) and international terrorism (Lebowitz 1980). However, extracting information from chemical text has received little attention.

The goal of our research is to develop techniques for extracting information about chemical reactions from the text of the *Journal of Organic Chemistry* (JOC). These techniques could provide the basis for a system that generates a summary of all preparative reactions from the experimental section of a journal article. The system could be integrated into the Chemical Abstracts Service (CAS) editorial production stream to generate reaction records from JOC manuscripts and, thus, support production of the database for our online reaction search service called CASREACT.

The next section gives background information on the current database-building procedure at CAS and reasons for doing NLP research in reaction information extraction. Some interesting characteristics of chemical text are described followed by a description of the methods we developed to extract reaction information from primary journals. Finally, our current research status is reported, and future research directions are outlined.

21.2 Background

CAS databases are generated by an editorial staff consisting of highly trained scientists who perform an intellectual analysis of journal articles and patents in chemistry and related sciences. CASREACT allows users access to chemical reactions reported in the chemical literature. To build the CASREACT database, editorial staff members in the Organic Chemistry Department of CAS manually extract chemical reaction information from approximately 100 journals. It is labor intensive and time consuming to locate and record the reaction information because it requires a detailed analysis.

Using NLP techniques to analyze chemical text offers an attractive alternative. With increasing amounts of the primary literature available in computer-readable form, it is reasonable to assume that if practical NLP-based techniques could be developed, they could be applied to a significant proportion of the literature processed by CAS. However, NLP applications reported to date have concentrated on areas such as query interpretation or the understanding of financial news and medical text; little attention has been paid to chemical text. CAS, therefore, initiated research toward understanding chemical text.

CAS studied the feasibility of extracting information on chemical reactions from primary journal articles (Zamora and Blower 1984; Ai, Blower, and Ledwith 1990). We developed an NLP system that generates a summary of the preparative reactions reported in the experimental sections of JOC. The summary identifies each participating substance, its reaction role, and its quantity. It also records information, such as the order of mixing the chemical substances and the duration and temperature of individual steps. For multistep experiments, the system identifies generic class names of intermediate products. The summary does not record workup procedures (for example, methods for isolating and purifying the product) or analytic data.

The area of reactions was selected for our initial study for two reasons: First, the analysis of synthetic descriptions in experimental sections seems to have the right level of difficulty for experiments using NLP techniques for information extraction. Although the application domain is restricted, and the text format is stylized and predictable, the text uses natural language, which exhibits considerable variation. Second, there is a potential for using the results to build the CASREACT database.

21.3 Characteristics of Chemical Text

We studied numerous experimental sections from JOC and found that the format of these sections is stylized; that is, the authors use a few basic templates to describe experiments in organic chemistry. The following subsections discuss some important characteristics of this format.

21.3.1 Presentation Style

A simple synthetic procedure has a discourse structure consisting of a heading, synthesis description, workup, and characterization of the product (figure 21.1). The *heading*, typically not a complete sentence, contains the reaction product. The *synthesis descriptions* consist of sentences that mention the reactants; their quantities; and reaction conditions, such as time, temperature, and solvents. The *workup* describes how the reaction was terminated and the procedures for isolating and purifying the product. The yield information is given before the end of the workup. Finally, the *characterization* provides analytic data to confirm the product.

21.3.2 Numeric Data

The high proportion of numeric data present in the synthetic description in figure 21.1 is typical of text taken from an experimental section. The numeric data help simplify our processing in several ways: (1) Part of these data provides precise quantities of the substances involved; the percentage yield of the product; and details of the reaction conditions: time, temperature, and pressure. (2) The numeric data are often associated with units of measure (for example, 2.0 g, 4.4 mmol, 16 h), which allows us to interpret their meaning and how they are related to other data in the paragraph. (3) The spectral and analytic data given in the last two sentences of figure 21.1 are superfluous for our purpose, but these data are recognized because of their form and the high density of numeric data.

21.3.3 Chemical Substances

The large number of references to chemical substances is also typical of the text we are processing. Authors name chemical substances in a variety of ways. The most commonly used substances are referred to by trivial names, acronyms, empirical formulas, and

Heading
2,6-Bis [3-(bromomethyl)-2-methoxy-5-methyl-phenyl]-4-phenylpyridine(**14e**).

Synthesis
To a solution of **14d** (2.0g, 4.4 mmol) in 20 mL of benzene was slowly added phosphorous tribromide (0.45 mL, 4.8 mmol) at 5 degrees C, whereupon the reaction mixture was stirred for 16 h at room temperature.

Workup
After the addition of 50 mL of water, the mixture was neutralized with 10 percent $NaCO_3$. After the layers were separated, the aqueous phase was extracted with chloroform (2 X 50mL). The combined organic phases were dried ($MgS0_4$), and the solvent was evaporated in vacuo to give **14e** as a white foam: yield 82 percent;

Characterization
mass spectrum, $m|e$ 579.035 (M^+, calcd 579.041); ^{1}H NMR 8.06 (s, 2 H, pyridine H), 7.73-7.26 (m, 9 H, Ar H), 4.64 (s, 4 H, CH_2), 3.63 (s, 6 H, OCH_3), 2.69 (s, 6 H, CH_3).

Anal. Calcd for $C_{29}H_{27}Br_2N0_2$: C, 59.91; H, 4.68; N, 2.41. Found: C, 59.88; H, 4.74; N, 2.20.

Figure 21.1
Components of a Synthetic Procedure.

pseudo-formulas, for example, acetone, ether, THF, NBS, $MgSO_4$ and EtOAc. Authors usually name the most important substances, in particular, the reaction product, using systematic chemical nomenclature, as illustrated by the substance in the heading in figure 21.1. Embedded digits and a variety of punctuation marks are present in the systematic nomenclature. Because this name is so long and unwieldy, an author usually substitutes a temporary label or substance identifier, as s/he does with **14e** in the heading of figure 21.1. These identifiers are always rendered in boldface type, so they are readily recognized.

Substance and quantity information are closely associated and almost always presented using one of two patterns:

<substance> (<quantity>) (for example, **14d** (20g, 4.4 mmol))

<quantity> of <substance> (for example, 20mL of benzene)

Both patterns are illustrated in figure 21.1.

21.3.4 Limited Numbers of Verbs

Although many verbs can be used to describe the same action, typically, a small group of verbs is for one action in this domain. Figure 21.2 contains a set of commonly used verbs. The verbs are classified into categories. For example, the verbs add, dissolve, and

COMBINE	add, dissolve, treat, etc.
REACT	heat, reflux, stir, etc.
PREPARE	make, onvert, prepare, etc.
RESULT	give, provide, yield, etc.
WORKUP	collect, extract, filter, etc.
MISC	agree, appear, calculate, etc.

Figure 21.2
Commonly Used Verbs.

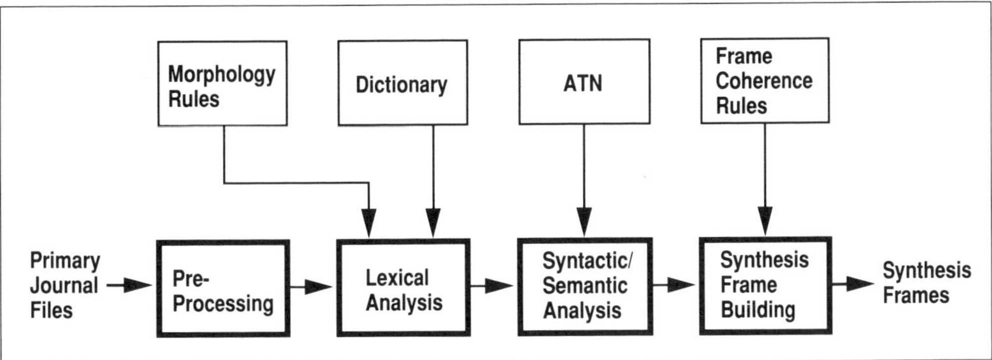

Figure 21.3
Overall System Architecture.

treat all describe the combining process in a synthesis.

21.4 Reaction Information Extraction Process

This section summarizes the reaction information extraction process, which is divided into four phases. The overall system architecture is shown in figure 21.3. The system takes the primary journal file as input and extracts the experimental section from each article. An example of text describing a synthetic procedure is shown in figure 21.4, and the conceptual representation (called a *synthesis frame*) of the output generated from the text is shown in figure 21.5.

21.4.1 Preprocessing

The *preprocessing phase* extracts experimental sections from articles on the primary journal tapes; transforms each section to an ASCII representation that captures font information; marks boundaries of words, sentences, and paragraphs; and builds Lisp structures for each section.

21.4.2 Lexical Analysis

The *lexical analysis* treats a document as a stream of independent words and tags syntactic and semantic information to each word using the following information: (1) a dictionary with about 1300 entries, (2) a grammar for valid chemical formulas, (3) suffix stems, (4) chemical name morphemes and N-grams, and (5) hyphenated word patterns. The tagging algorithm used for the lexical analysis is as follows:

```
If the word is in the dictionary
Then tag information in the dictionary to the word
Elseif a suffix stem is found and the root form is in the dictionary
  Then the word is recoded into its root form, and tag the information
    in the dictionary and suffix stem to the word
  Elseif the word can be parsed using the chemical formulae grammar
    Then tag the word as a chemical formula
    Elseif an N-gram is found
      Then If a specific suffix, e.g., "tion" is found
        Then tag the word as a chemical process
        Else tag the word as a chemical name
      Elseif a hyphenated word pattern is found
        Then tag the word with the information associated with the pattern.
```

Using this algorithm to classify words, we can assign definitely correct information to known words, highly likely information to unknown words that follow known patterns, and default information to ill-formed words. This approach permits a gradual degradation from perfect knowledge to unknown information. Examples of the output of this analysis for the first two sentences in figure 21.4 are shown in figure 21.6. Each sentence is represented by a list starting with *SEN TEXT and followed by a list of words. Each word is represented by a list consisting of the word and pairs of a property name and a property value. Property names are in upper case, and values are in lower case.

```
  2,6-Bis[3-(bromomethyl)-2-methoxy-5-methyl-phenyl]-4-phenylpyridine(14e).
To a solution of 14d (2.0 g, 4.4 mmol) in 20 mL of benzene was slowly added
phosphorous tribromide (0.45 mL, 4.8 mmol) at 5 ! C, whereupon the reaction
mixture was stirred for 16 h at room temperature. After the addition of 50 mL
of water, the mixture was neutralized with 10% NaC03. After the layers were
separated, the aqueous phase was extracted with chloroform (2 X 50 mL). The
combined organic phases were dried (MgS04), and the solvent was evaporated in
vacuo to give 14e as a white foam: yield 82%; mass spectrum, m/e 579.035 (M+,
calcd 579.041); 1H NMR 8.06 (s, 2 H, pyridine H), 7.73-7.26 (m, 9 H, Ar H),
4.64 (s, 4 H, CH2), 3.63 (s, 6 H, OCH3), 2.69 (s, 6 H, CH3).

  Anal. Calcd for C29H27Br2N02: C, 59.91; H, 4.68; N, 2.41. Found: C, 59.88; H,
4.74; N, 2.20.
```

Figure 21.4
A Sample Synthetic Paragraph.

Product:	2,6-Bis[3-(bromomethyl)-2-methoxy-5-methyl-phenyl]-4-phenylpyridine (14e)	Yield: 82%
Step: 1.1	Event: COMBINE	Temp: 5 deg C
Role Reactant Solvent Solvent	Substance 14d phosphorous tribromide benzene	Amount 2.0 g, 4.4 mmol 0.45 mL, 4.8 mmol 20 mL
Step: 1.2 -	Event: REACT Time: 16 hr	Temp: room

Figure 21.5
A Sample Conceptual Synthetic Frame.

21.4.3 Syntactic-Semantic Analysis

The *syntactic-semantic analysis* involves a partial parse of the sentence using augmented transition network (ATN) parsing. The traditional ATN syntax, for example, the one given in Amsterdam (1986), is cumbersome to write and difficult to understand. We developed a new ATN syntax modeled on the one given in Charniak and McDermott (1986). The syntax uses flow-of-control constructs borrowed from programming languages. Three flow-of-control constructs follow:

First, SEQ describes a sequence of patterns that is to be matched against the input word list. Each <pattern> must match the word list in the stated order unless it is an OR or an OPTIONAL pattern:

```
(*SEN TEXT ((
 12.6-Bis[3-(bromomethyl)-2-methoxy-5-methyl-phenyl]-4-phenylprydine
 CUCS
 l.BOLD.2.6-Bis[3-(bromomethyl)-2-methoxy-5-methyl-phenyl]-4-phenylpyridine
 CHEM name SYN noun )(( PUNC () (14e CUCS .BOLD.14e SYN unknown)
 PUNC ))(. PUNC .) ))

(*SEN TEXT
    ((To SYN prep) (a SYN art) (solution SYN noun CHEM generic)
    (of SYN prep )(14d CUCS .BOLD.14d SYN unknown) (( PUNC ))
    (2.0 SYN num) (g SYN noun UNIT wt )(, PUNC ,) (4.4 SYN num)
    (mmol SYN noun UNIT mass) (( PUNC ) )(in SYN prep) (20 SYN num)
    (ml SYN noun UNIT vol) (of SYN prep) (benzene CHEM name SYN noun)
    (was SYN aux ROOT (be SYN verb)) (slowly ROOT (slow SYN adj)SYN adv)
    (added ROOT (add SYN verb) SYN verbpast)
    (phosphorous CHEM name SYN noun FORM plural)
    (tribromide CHEM name SYN noun) (( PUNC ))(0.45 SYN num)
    (ml SYN noun UNIT vol) (, PUNC ,) (4.8 SYN num )
    (mmol SYN noun UNIT mass )(( PUNC )) (at SYN prep) (5 SYN num)
    (.degree. SYN noun UNIT temp )(, PUNC ,) (whereupon SYN conj)
    (the SYN art) ( reaction ROOT (react SYN verb) SYN noun SEM state )
    (mixture SYN noun CHEM generic )(was SYN aux ROOT (be SYN verb))
    (stirred ROOT (stir SY verb) SYN verbpast )(for SYN prep) (16 SYN num)
    (h SYN noun UNIT time) (at SYN prep) ( room SYN noun )
    (temperature SYN noun) (, PUNC .) ))
```

Figure 21.6
Examples of Lexical Analysis Output.

Syntax: (SEQ <pattern>+).

Second, OR allows alternative patterns. Only one <pattern> is used in the match, and the patterns are tried in the order given:

Syntax: (OR <pattern>+).

Third, OPTIONAL allows a single pattern to be used zero or more times in matching against the input list. The required number of matches is specified by <range>:

Syntax: (OPTIONAL [<range>] <pattern>).

An ATN using this alternative syntax for the graphical representation of figure 21.7 is shown in figure 21.8. This ATN recognizes two substance descriptions, for example, **14d** (2.0 g, 4.4 mmol) and 20 mL of benzene. The subordinate ATNs, NQ (quantity expression) and SID (substance ID), are not shown. These constructs permit more compact and readable ATNs and also eliminate the need for many explicitly named nodes.

The analysis has two phases: Phase 1 searches each sentence for phrases such as substance information and reaction conditions and splits compound sentences into clauses. Phase 2 then converts each clause into an event frame.

Phase 1: The search in phase 1 is a simple loop, proceeding left to right through the sentence, one word at a time. At each word, the remainder of the sentence is parsed using ATN grammars. The grammars define phrases describing (1) substance information, (2) reference to external procedures, (3) time-temperature data, (4) verb phrases, and (5) characterization data.

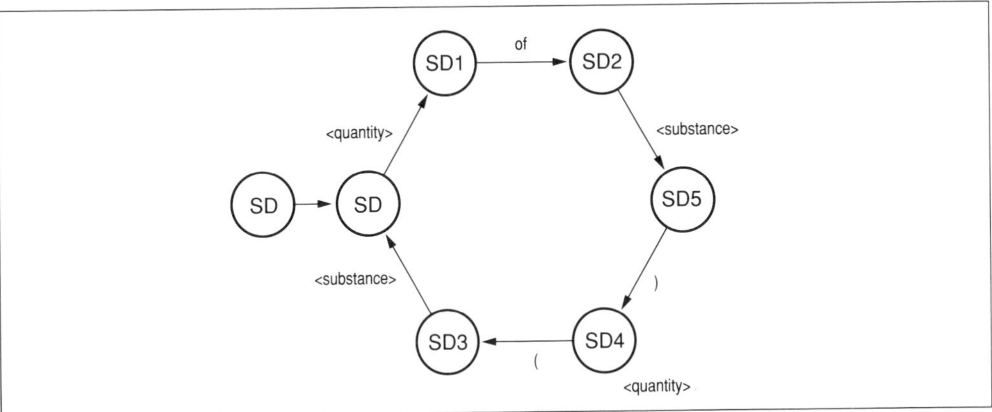

Figure 21.7
A Sample Augmented Transition Network.

If the ATN parsing is successful, then a frame representation of the parsed phrase and the unprocessed portion of the sentence are returned. The text of the parsed phrase is replaced by the frame representation, and parsing continues with the unprocessed portion of the sentence.

Each compound sentence is split into clauses using the following algorithm, where

CW = current word

VERB = last verb encountered

CONJ = last conjunction encountered.

```
If CW is a verb,
Then if VERB is not nil,
     Then if CONJ is not nil,
     Then split sentence before CONJ
  Set CONJ = nil and VERB = CW
     Elseif VERB is not marked as active,
        Then set VERB = CW
     Else If the sentence starts with "After",
  Then split sentence before the noun group preceding CW
  Else Split sentence before CW
        Set VERB = CW
ElseIf (VERB is not nil) and
        (CW is a conjugation) and
        (or (CONJ is nil) (or (CONJ is ",") (CONJ is "and"))),
        Then Set CONJ = CW.
```

```
[defnet SD
 (OR (SEQ (PARSE NQ (SETR QUANT *value*))
          (PARSE SID (SETR SUB *value*)))
      (SEQ (PARSE SID (SETR SUB *value*))
          (WORD ()
          (PARSE NQ (SETR QUANT *value*))
          (WORD ))))
(BUILDQ (SUBSTANCE NAME (+) QUANTITY (+)) SUB QUANT)]

Where:

 BUILDQ = builds a structure which is returned as the value if the parse
          is sucessful.
 *value* = holds the return value of a sucessful parse.
```

Figure 21.8
A Sample Augmented Transition Network Using the New Syntax.

Phase 2: Phase 2 converts each clause in the output of phase 1 into an event frame. Assigning a frame to a clause is based on the verb phrase in the clause using chemical heuristics, such as "If the verb phrase contains the word 'obtained,' then use the PREPARE frame, fill the PRDS slot with the last substance encountered, and fill the RCTS slot with the substances following the preposition 'from'." Another example is "If the verb is UNKNOWN and has a CHEM property, then use the REACT frame." (The PRDS slot holds the products of an experiment; RCTS contains the reactants of a chemical reaction; CHEM stores chemical properties.) The output of phase 1 and phase 2 for the first two sentences in figure 21.4 are shown in figure 21.9 and figure 21.10, respectively. In these figures, *C represents the start of a clause, and *P represents the start of a phrase.

21.4.4 Synthesis Frame Building

The *synthesis frame building process* first extracts reaction-related event frames and then organizes them into a tree structure, as shown in figure 21.11. Of eight event frames, five frames, namely, TITLE, COMBINE, PREPARE, RESULT, and REACT, contain reaction information and are included in the final output. The rest of the frames, that is, WORKUP, UNKNOWN, and MISC, are discarded because they contain irrelevant information. The tree represents the experimental section of a document. Each experiment description starts with a title and is followed by one or more synthetic steps. The title

```
(*S PARA TITLE t PRDS ((SUBSTANCE NAME
 (2.6-Bis[3-(bromomethyl)-2-methoxy-5-methyl-phenyl]-4-phenylpyridine)
 CHEM name ID 14e )))


(*SEN TEXT
 ((*C TEXT ((To SYN prep) (a SYN art) (solution SYN noun CHE generic) (of SYN prep)
 (*P TYPE sub ID 14d QUANTITY (VALUES WEIGHT (2.0 g) NORMALIZED
     (4.4 mmol)))(in SYN prep)
 (*P TYPE sub NAME (benzene) CHEM name QUANTITY (VALUES VOLUME (20 mL)))
 (*P TYPE verb TEXT (was added) ROOT (add SYN verb) FORM active)
 (*P TYPE sub NAME (phosphorous tribromide) CHEM name QUANTITY
     (VALUES VOLUME (0.45 mL) NORMALIZED (4.8 mmol)))(at SYN prep)
 (*P TYPE temp TEMP (5 .degree.C))(, PUNC ,)))(*C TEXT ((whereupon SYN conj)
     (the SYN art)(reaction ROOT (react SYN verb) SYN noun SEM state)
     (mixture SYN noun CHEM generic)(*P TYPE verb TEXT (was stirred) ROOT
     (stir SYN verb) FORM active)(for SYN prep) (*P TYPE time TIME (16 h))
     (at SYN prep) (*P TYPE temp TEMP (room))(, PUNC .)))))
```

Figure 21.9
Examples of Phase 1 Output.

```
(TITLE PRDS
  ((SUBSTANCE NAME
         (2.6-Bis[3-(bromomethyl)-2-methoxy-5-methyl-phenyl]-4-phenlpyridine)
          CHEM name
          ID 14e)))


(COMBINE COMPONENTS
  ((SUBSTANCE ID 14d
          QUANTITY
            (VALUES WEIGHT (2.0 g) NORMALIZED (4.4 mmol)))
   (SUBSTANCE NAME (benzene) CHEM name
          QUANTITY (VALUES VOLUME (20 mL)))
   (SUBSTANCE NAME (phosphorous tribromide)
          CHEM name
          QUANTITY
           (VALUES VOLUME (0.45 mL) NORMALIZED (4.8 mmol))))
          TEMP(5 .degree.C)
          VERB add)
(REACT TIME (16 h) TEMP (room) VERB stir)
```

Figure 21.10
Examples of Phase 2 Output.

contains information about the products of the synthesis. The synthesis step contains a list of actions that are represented in event frames. Each substance mentioned in the event frames is then assigned a role using chemical heuristics. An algorithm (Ai, Blower, and Ledwith 1990) was developed to handle complex paragraphs, which usually involve some sort of interparagraph reference. Figure 21.12 shows the final output for the text in figure 21.4.

21.5 Current Status of the Research Work

In our reaction information extraction research, we found interesting and important features of chemical text, built a dictionary of 1300 entries, developed a grammar for valid chemical formulas and morphology rules for classes of words and chemical names, defined heuristic rules for assigning roles to substances and converting a stream of an event frame to a synthesis frame, resolved interparagraph references, and implemented a prototype reaction information extraction system.

Our system was written in Franz Lisp on Vax 11/785 and tested with 89 paragraphs of text from two experimental sections. The system handles simple paragraphs well but does not handle complex paragraphs (for example, paragraphs containing interparagraph references) as well as desired. Although these preliminary results are encouraging, the system is not yet robust or reliable enough to deal with a large volume of text. More research needs to be done to improve the system performance.

21.6 Future Research Directions

Our future research involves performing empirical analysis of a large amount of documents to discover new syntactic or semantic patterns, replacing the lexical and syntactic-semantic processing with an integrated parsing technique based on conceptual analysis (CA), implementing a rule-based system for creating the synthesis frames, and exploring methods for detecting errors in the reactions generated by the system.

21.6.1 Empirical Chemical Text Analysis

A *sublanguage* is the language a particular group of people use to communicate ideas with each other (Sager 1986). Sublanguages often have limited vocabularies, syntactic patterns, and semantic subclasses (Johnson 1987), which can simplify and facilitate the knowledge discovery process. In our previous research projects, we studied numerous synthesis papers from JOC using an informal approach. As expected, we found that the text in experimental sections is stylized, as mentioned in Characteristics of Chemical

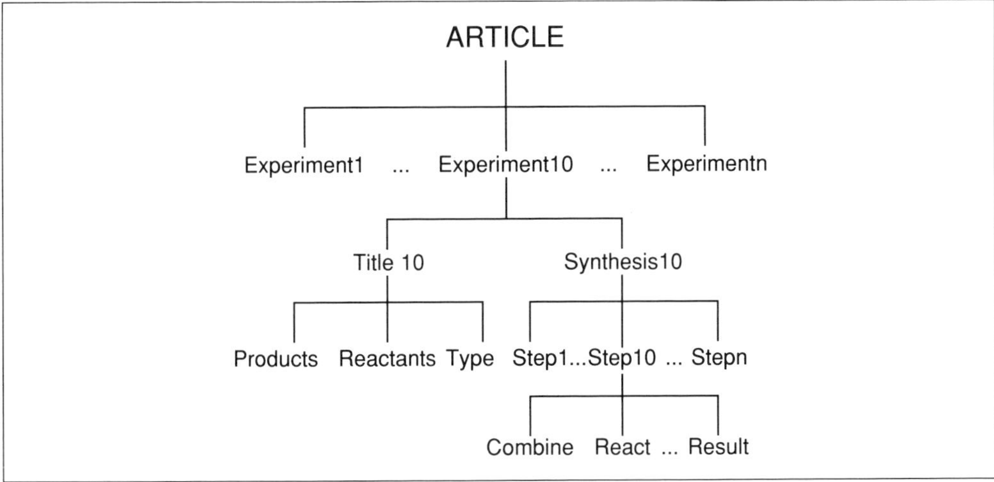

Figure 21.11
Tree Representation of an Experimental Section.

Text. We plan to analyze more synthesis papers from JOC using systematic methods such as those described in Grishman and Kittredge (1986) and Kittredge and Lehrberger (1982). We will also use statistical techniques, such as word frequencies and co-occurrence patterns.

21.6.2 Conceptual Analysis

The syntactic-semantic processing currently done by the system focuses on important noun and verb phrases, ignoring any words or phrases it considers unimportant. It does not attempt a complete syntactic analysis of the text because this analysis seems unnecessary for our application. This part of our processing is similar to some of the integrated parsing techniques developed as an outgrowth of conceptual analysis. CA was developed at Yale (Riesbeck 1975) and was used in a number of experimental systems, for example, Riesbeck and Schank (1978). The goal of CA is to map natural language sentences into conceptual structures that capture their meanings. CA focuses on semantic analysis and uses syntactic information when useful. It allows a partial parsing and concentrates on information that is of interest to a particular application.We intend to replace the lexical and syntactic-semantic processing in the current program with an integrated parsing technique based on CA.

```
(frame experiment34
[TITLE = title34]
[SYNTHESIS = synthesis34 ])

(frame title34
[PRDS =
   (SUBSTANCE NAME
     (2.6-Bis[3-(bromomethyl)-2-methoxy-5methyl-phenyl]-4-phenylpyridine)
   ID 14e)) ])

(frame synthesis34
[STEPS =
  (STEPl
    ((COMBINE COMPONENTS
        ((SUBSTANCE ID 14d
                 QUANTITY
                   (VALUES WEIGHT (2.0 g) NORMALIZED (4.4 mmol))
                 ROLE Reactant)
        (SUBSTANCE NAME (benzene)
                 QUANTITY (VALUES VOLUME (20 mL))
                 ROLE Solvent)
        (SUBSTANCE NAME (phosphorous tribromide)
               QUANTITY
                 (VALUES VOLUME 90.45 mL) NORMALIZED (4.8 mmol))
               ROLE Solvent)
               TEMP (5 .degree.C))
               (REACT TIME (16 h) TEMP (room))
               (RESULT PRDS ((SUBSTANCE ID 14e)) YIELD (VALUES PERCENT (82)))))
])
```

Figure 21.12
Final Output.

21.6.3 Rule-Based Expert System Development

We developed three sets of rules: (1) rules for assigning substance roles, (2) rules for converting event frames to a synthesis frame, and (3) rules for resolving interparagraph references. Currently, these rules are embedded in Lisp code. We plan to implement a rule-based expert system with rules in an English-like if-then format.

21.6.4 Error Analysis

We want to develop the capability to detect errors in the reactions generated by the program. This area has not received much attention in the NLP literature. Because the goal of our system is to generate reaction records for CASREACT, errors cannot be tolerated to the extent that they might be used later in an experimental system. We intend to devote substantial effort to exploring methods for detecting errors (Cater 1983) in the reactions generated by the program.

21.7 References

Ai, C. S.; Blower, P. E., Jr.; and Ledwith, R. H. 1990. Extraction of Chemical Reaction Information from Primary Journal Text. *Journal of Chemical Information and Computer Science.*

Forthcoming.

Amsterdam, J. 1986. Augmented Transition Networks for Natural Language Parsing. *AI Expert* 1: 15–21.

Cater, A. 1983. Request-Based Parsing with Low-Level Syntactic Recognition. In *Automatic Natural Language Parsing*, eds. K. Sparck Jones and Y. Wilks. Chichester, England: Ellis Horwood.

Charniak, E., and McDermott, D. 1986. *Artificial Intelligence.* Reading, Mass.: Addison Wesley.

Grishman, R., and Kittredge, R., eds. 1986. *Analyzing Language in Restricted Domains: Sublanguage Description and Processing.* Hillsdale, N.J.: Lawrence Erlbaum.

Johnson, S. 1987. Mathematical Building Blocks. *AI Expert.*

Kittredge, R., and Lehrberger, J., eds. 1982. *Sublanguage: Studies of Language in Restricted Semantic Domains.* Walter De Gruyter.

Lebowitz, M. 1988. The Use of Memory in Text Processing, *Communications of the ACM.* 31(12).

Lebowitz, M. 1980. Generalization and Memory in an Integrated Understanding System. Technical Report, 186, Dept. of Computer Science, Yale Univ.

Piatetsky-Shapiro, G., and Frawley, W., eds. 1989. IJCAI-89 Knowledge Discovery in Databases Workshop, Detroit, Mich., 20 August.

Riesbeck, C. 1975. Conceptual Analysis. In *Conceptual Information Processing,* ed. R. C. Schank. Amsterdam: North Holland.

Riesbeck, C., and Schank, R. C. 1978. Comprehension by Computer: Expectation-Based Analysis of Sentences in Context. In *Studies in the Perception of Language*, eds. W. Leviet and G. Flores d'Arcais. New York: John Wiley.

Sager, N. 1986. Sublanguage: Linguistic Phenomenon, Computational Tool. In *Analyzing Language in Restricted Domains: Sublanguage Description and Processing,* eds. R. Grishman and R. Kittredge. Hillsdale, N.J.: Lawrence Erlbaum.

Zamora, E. M., and Blower, P. E., Jr. 1984. Extraction of Chemical Reaction Information from Primary Journal Text Using Computational Linguistic Techniques. *Journal of Chemical Information and Computer Science* 24(3): 176–188.

22 Automated Extraction of Knowledge from Computer-Aided Design Databases

Avelino J. Gonzalez, Harley R. Myler, Massood Towhidnejad
Frederic D. McKenzie, Robin R. Kladke, and Raymond Laureano
University of Central Florida

Abstract

The development of expert systems and other knowledge-based systems is frequently slowed by the arduous task of knowledge acquisition. For a particular domain, the required knowledge can be extensive, and its extraction from the appropriate source can be astonishingly time consuming. For model-based diagnostic systems, one proposed partial solution to this knowledge acquisition bottleneck is automated knowledge extraction from computer-aided design (CAD) databases.

To build a knowledge base (model) for a model-based diagnostic system, both system structure and component function need to be described. The automated knowledge generation (AKG) system extracts descriptive information about the components of a system as well as their interconnectivity data from CAD databases. Instead of simply performing a direct translation of the CAD data, the modules that compose the AKG system cooperatively correct any inconsistencies in the CAD representations and supply the function information. This information is not found in CAD but is vital for the effective modeling of the systems to be diagnosed and their individual components. The AKG goal is to automatically build a functional knowledge base for a model-based diagnostic system with minimal human intervention.

22.1 Introduction

The process of extracting knowledge from a database is different from that of discovering knowledge. *Discovering knowledge* implies that facts or implicit relationships have been found that were previously unknown to humans. For instance, seemingly unrelated measurements of voltage and current might have led Ohm to discover his famous law when he noted that the behavior of one was dependent on the other and that the dependence was linear. This phenomenon always existed as a law of physics, but its discovery led to new knowledge. *Extracting knowledge*, however, deals with taking knowledge that was explicitly put in by humans (directly or indirectly) and retrieving it in a manner that satisfies the stated purpose. Diagnostic knowledge for man-made devices has always existed because its designers have known enough about it to be able to diagnose most of its problems. Inclusion of such knowledge in a database is, therefore, explicit in nature. The exception to this occurs when the correlation of measurements indicates a previously unknown relationship between parameters in the device or system being diagnosed; in this case, the knowledge is also implicit.

Explicit knowledge, along with its extraction from a database, is the topic of this chapter. We focus on the automated extraction of diagnostic knowledge. In particular, this knowledge is in the form of a model to be used in model-based reasoning systems. *Model-based reasoning* attempts to represent the internal structure of the system or device for which diagnosis is to be performed. In contrast, *rule-based systems* tend to concentrate on the input/output behavior of the device being diagnosed. Model-based techniques are useful in the control and diagnosis of process, electrical, and mechanical systems. The knowledge required by model-based techniques is different from that for rule-based systems. It consists of a model that simulates the operation of all the devices composing the system in question. It can be thought of as design knowledge, as opposed to operating knowledge, which is the type associated with rule-based systems. Design knowledge lends itself very well to being automatically acquired because a good amount of it is available in the databases found in computer-aided design (CAD) systems.

The database used is part of a CAD tool in which the knowledge about the design of the system whose model is to be extracted is represented. This chapter describes a technique that is used to perform these functions and that can deliver a ready-made knowledge base for a model-based diagnostic and control system with minimal or no human interaction.

22.2 Requirements for Model-Based Diagnostics

The inference engine in a diagnostic model-based system has several functions. It simulates the behavior of the real system by means of the model, compares the values calculated in the model with those measured in the real system, and then searches for the cause of any disagreement between these values. Such discrepancies are a sign of the malfunctioning of one or several components (Scarl, Jamieson, and Delaune 1987).

However, to carry out these activities, the inference engine requires a knowledge base (model) that supplies information about both the physical connections and the function of the components of the system being modeled. Thus, the system needs to be described in terms of both its structure and its functions. Knowledge of system structure includes the type and number of input and output for each component and the direction of flow in connections. System function information involves transfer functions, delays, and tolerances associated with the different output of the components.

Frames are the usual means of representing the knowledge base in model-based systems. Each frame represents a specific component or concept, which is related in some way to other components and objects in the same system. Slots in a frame represent attributes of

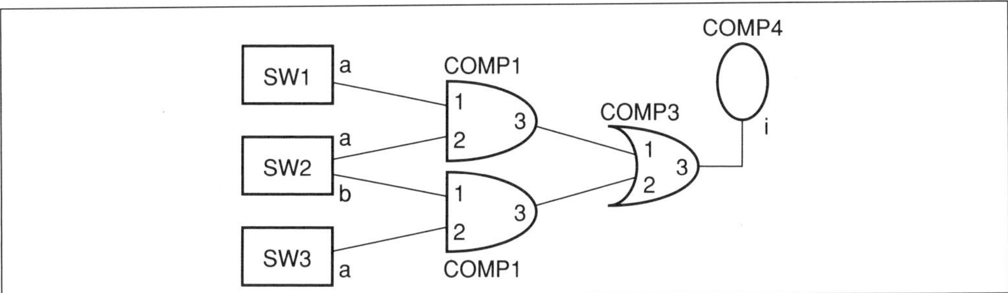

Figure 22.1
Simple Logic Diagram.

the object that include the description of the component itself and information about its physical connections to other components and its behavior when interacting with others in the system. In figure 22.1, the diagram of a simple logic system is shown. Figure 22.2 displays the corresponding frame-based model representation for the component COMP3 in the logic diagram. The format of the frames might vary in relation to the model-based system being used.

The first frame in figure 22.2 is called an *upper-level frame.* This type of frame groups common attributes for a set of components and, by the inheritance property, passes down the information to the lower-level or instance-level frames, such as the second frame shown in figure 22.2 that includes attributes more specific to the component. In a large frame-based model, the advantage of this feature can be better appreciated because it helps reduce the size of frames and, consequently, the knowledge base size.

The most important observation that can be made from the example in figures 22.1 and 22.2 is the fulfillment of the requirement that both structure and function be represented. In this specific model, the INPUT, OUTPUT, and NOMENCLATURE slots are associated with structure, and the OUTPUT-FUNCTIONS, TOLERANCE, UNITS, and OUTPUT-RANGES slots are associated with functions. The combination of both structure and function in the representation of each component allows for the effective modeling of the entire system to be diagnosed.

22.3 Knowledge Extraction from Computer-Aided Design Data

When a designer makes use of a CAD system to draw the schematics of an engineering system or device, all the information entered to perform such activity is generally kept in a database system. This design information is precisely what is needed to satisfy the structural description requirements of model-based systems, and because it is already electronically stored, automated knowledge extraction seems attractive.

```
(deframe OR-GATE
  (nomenclature "an OR gate")
  (ako LOGIC-GATE)
  (instances COMP3)
  (input  ELEC-INPUT1 ELEC-INPUT2)
  (output ELEC-OUTPUT)
   (output-functions (ELEC-OUTPUT
                     (IF (OR (> ELECT-INPUT1 3.7)
                            (< ELECT-INPUT2 3.7)
                      5.0
                      0)))
  (units (ELECT-OUTPUT "VOLTS"))
  (tolerances (ELECT-OUTPUT 0.2))
  (output-ranges
      (ELECT-OUTPUT (*RANGES* -5 5 T T))))

(deframe COMP3
  (nomenclature "the OR gate")
  (aio OR-GATE)
  (input   (ELEC-INPUT1 (COMP1 ELEC-OUTPUT))
           (ELEC-INPUT2 (COMP2 ELEC-OUTPUT)))
   (output  (ELEC-OUTPUT (COMP4 ELEC-INPUT))))
```

Figure 22.2
Frame-Based Representation Model of the OR Gate.

Component Name	Component Description
COMP1	AND GATE
COMP2	AND GATE
COMP3	OR GATE
COMP4	LIGHT BULB
SW1	TWO-POSITION SWITCH
SW2	TWO-POSITION SWITCH
SW3	TWO-POSITION SWITCH

Figure 22.3
Sample COMPOC.DAT File That Contains Descriptions of Components.

22.3.1 Problems with Computer-Aided Design Data

It might seem simple to access the CAD database to extract the knowledge to build the model for the diagnostic system. One might think that by rearranging and making some minor changes in format of the information in CAD, the knowledge base for the model-based system could easily be generated. For this situation, a direct translator from one format to another would presumably suffice.

However, the task of knowledge extraction from such a source is not at all straightforward. CAD data present problems that a simple translator cannot handle. These include the absence of function information problems as well as misinterpretations because of the designer's drawing style. Structure information for a system is taken from CAD files with data similar to that shown in figures 22.3 and 22.4, which refer to the simple logic diagram previously discussed. Even though fairly complete structure information for a system is found in a CAD database, CAD drawings have traditionally not included function information because it is assumed that whoever reads the schematics knows what each component does just by looking at it. Nevertheless, function is as important as structure information for the generation of a model.

Misinterpretation of the drawings by the CAD system itself is another cause of problems. Drawings of the same system done by two different designers can lead the CAD system to store two different sets of information in the databases because of the interpretation made of the graphic data. This means that some information in the database might not truly reflect what is in the CAD drawing. For example, figure 22.5 shows a diagram of a component with a single output that feeds the input of three different components. Instead of representing this information in its database, in some cases, CAD has misinterpreted the to-from connections, as shown in figure 22.6. When in reality component A is the only input to B, C, and D, the CAD database incorrectly interpreted

From	@	To	@
SW1	a	COMP1	1
SW2	a	COMP1	2
SW2	b	COMP2	1
SW3	a	COMP2	2
COMP1	3	COMP3	1
COMP2	3	COMP3	2
COMP3	3	COMP4	i

Figure 22.4
Sample TOFROMC.DAT File That Contains the Connections of the Components.

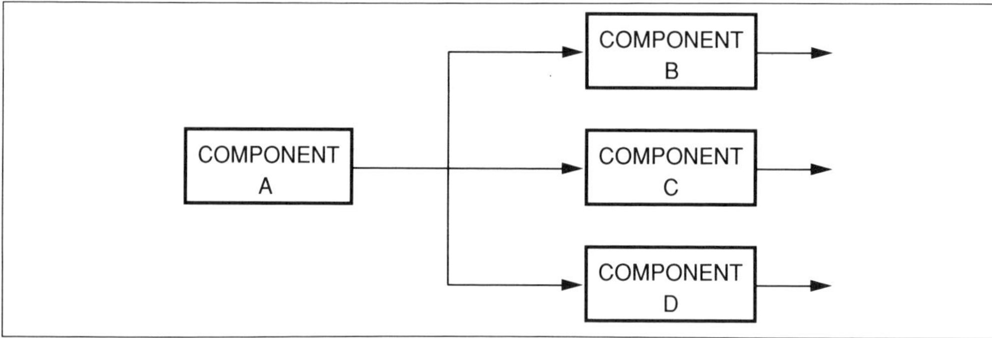

Figure 22.5
Correct Interpretation of a Single Output Feeding Multiple Input.

that components C and D have no input and multiple output. At the same time, this error leads to the interpretation of C and D as starting points of flow when only A is. This problem is related to the order in which the connections were made by the draftsperson. When drawing a line of connection, CAD generally considers the starting point to be an output of a component and the ending point of the connection line to be an input of a component.

In figure 22.7, a measurement tapping into a connection between components is added. Its representation in CAD can also cause a problem. Because CAD cannot distinguish measurements from normal components, the database might contain the interpretation of figure 22.8. Instead of being interpreted as an output node or end point, it is considered a starting point of flow. Component B is interpreted as having two input: component A and the measurement. Here, the problem could become more serious if the designer

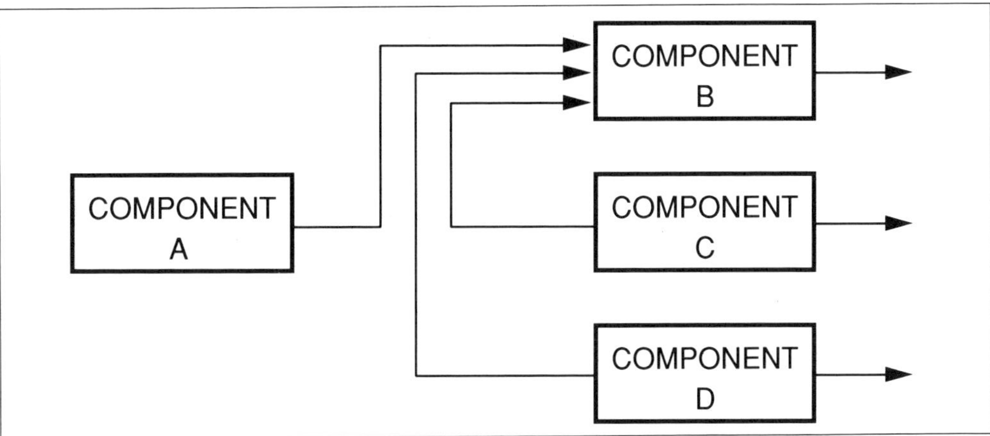

Figure 22.6
Incorrect (Actual) Interpretation of a Single Output feeding Multiple Input.

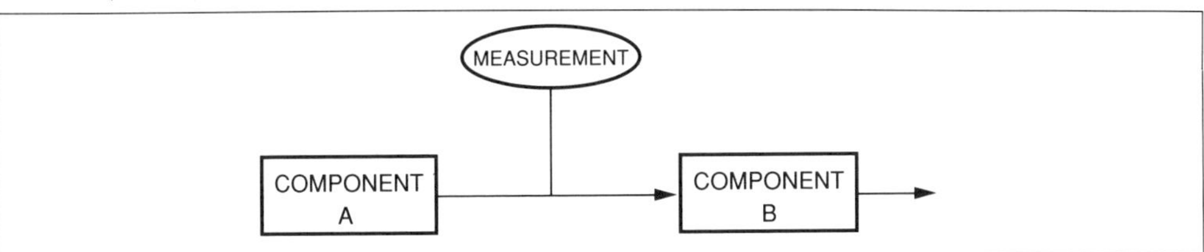

Figure 22.7
Correct Interpretation of a Measurement Tapping into a Connection.

makes the connection between A and B by selecting B as the starting point and A as the ending point. In such a situation, A would be seen as downstream of B regardless of other connections already made.

22.3.2 The Intelligent Interpreter Approach

Because a simple translator cannot handle CAD data problems, a more intelligent program is needed to automate knowledge extraction. The ability to correct and expand input information by supplying missing values and resolving inconsistencies and other conflicts is needed to effectively extract knowledge from CAD databases. This service may only be provided by an intelligent interpreter. The difference may seem to be in the terminology at this point, but a simple example can demonstrate the difference.

Consider the following Persian sentence:

۵۰۰ سال پیش اربابان حقوق بردگان خودشان را می خوردند.

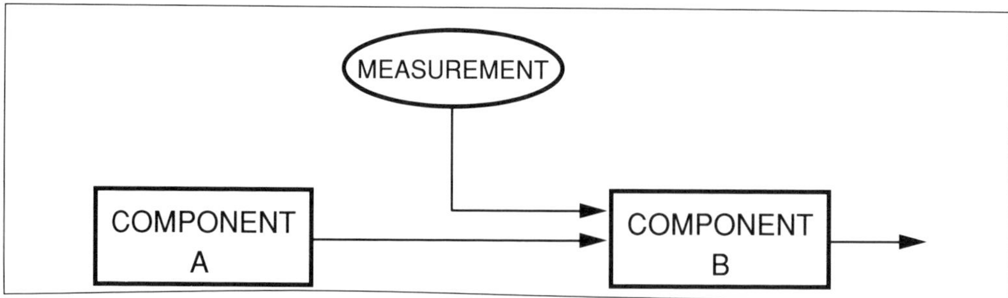

Figure 22.8
Incorrect Interpretation of a Measurement Tapping into a Connection.

If a literal translation into the English language were made, the following would result:

Five hundred years ago, the masters were eating the right of their slaves.

This literal translation is not really communicating the intended message. The statement is confusing unless the person has some previous knowledge about the relationship of masters and slaves in ancient Persia. The actual meaning of the Persian sentence is

Five hundred years ago, the masters were discriminating against their slaves.

This time, in addition to the translation technique, some knowledge related to the intended message (Persian history of 500 years ago) was utilized to make an interpretation of the Persian statement. As seen, a word-by-word translation is not enough in language-to-language conversion. A similar concept applies to knowledge extraction from CAD, in which an interpreter, rather than a direct translator, is needed.

To perform the challenging task of creating a knowledge base for a diagnostic system with information from CAD, the intelligent interpreter needs to abide by the following guidelines: After extracting the structural information from the CAD databases, it must check for consistency to avoid the CAD data problems already discussed. It must also supply the functional information missing in CAD. To effectively carry out the two previous activities, the intelligent interpreter can have its own database with the functional description of virtually all the components that typically appear in the type of systems that are being modeled. With the help of this knowledge of function, nonsensical connections from CAD can be recognized by the system and flagged with low confidence. The correct identification of components in the system to be modeled is required for the proper assignment of functional characteristics. This leads to the additional requirement that the interpreter be able to resolve any conflicts arising during the process of component identification. All these activities must be done by the interpreter with minimal human intervention and with a generic approach in terms of the CAD system being accessed and the diagnostic system knowledge base being produced.

22.4 The Automated Knowlege Generation System

With an understanding of the problems that CAD data present to automated knowledge extraction, ongoing research at the University of Central Florida concentrates on the development of an intelligent interpreter called the automated knowledge generator (AKG). The AKG system, which currently consists of approximately 6000 lines of code, is being implemented in Symbolics 36XX Series machines using Symbolics Lisp Windows and Flavors. The Flavors object-oriented programming (OOP) facilities allow each component from the CAD database to be represented as an object. The development and later modifications of the system are simplified because OOP lends itself to design modularity.

As shown in figure 22.9, the system is divided into several modules: Access, Spawn, Constraint Generator, Resolver, Parser, Component Knowledge Base (CKB), and Builder.

The first three modules are involved in knowledge extraction from the CAD files (connectivity). The second set of three work together in the resolution process of components, and the last module, the Builder, takes care of the actual generation of the knowledge base in the proper format for the target model-based system.

22.4.1 Computer-Aided Design Information Extraction in the Automated Knowledge Generator

The input to the AKG system are the CAD database files COMPOC.DAT and TOFROM-C.DAT, which contain the description and connectivity of components in the system to be modeled. The Access module is responsible for obtaining these files from remote computers where the CAD resides. This module uses a file, which can be customized, that contains the communication configurations needed by the host to make the data transfer possible. Once the files are available, the Spawn module creates an object (flavor) for each component in the target system by using the information from COMPOC.DAT. Then, the Constraint Generator adds interconnectivity data from the TOFROM.DAT file to the newly created objects. These connectivity data are used to correct any inconsistencies noted in the flow of the system. At this point, all the information available in CAD has been extracted, and an initial model has been created in which the connectivity data impose the first set of constraints on the system.

22.4.2 Resolution Process

The second stage in the AKG process is the *resolution process.* Its driving force is the Resolver module, which is responsible for the identification of the components so that the function information can be properly assigned. In this task, the Resolver is assisted by

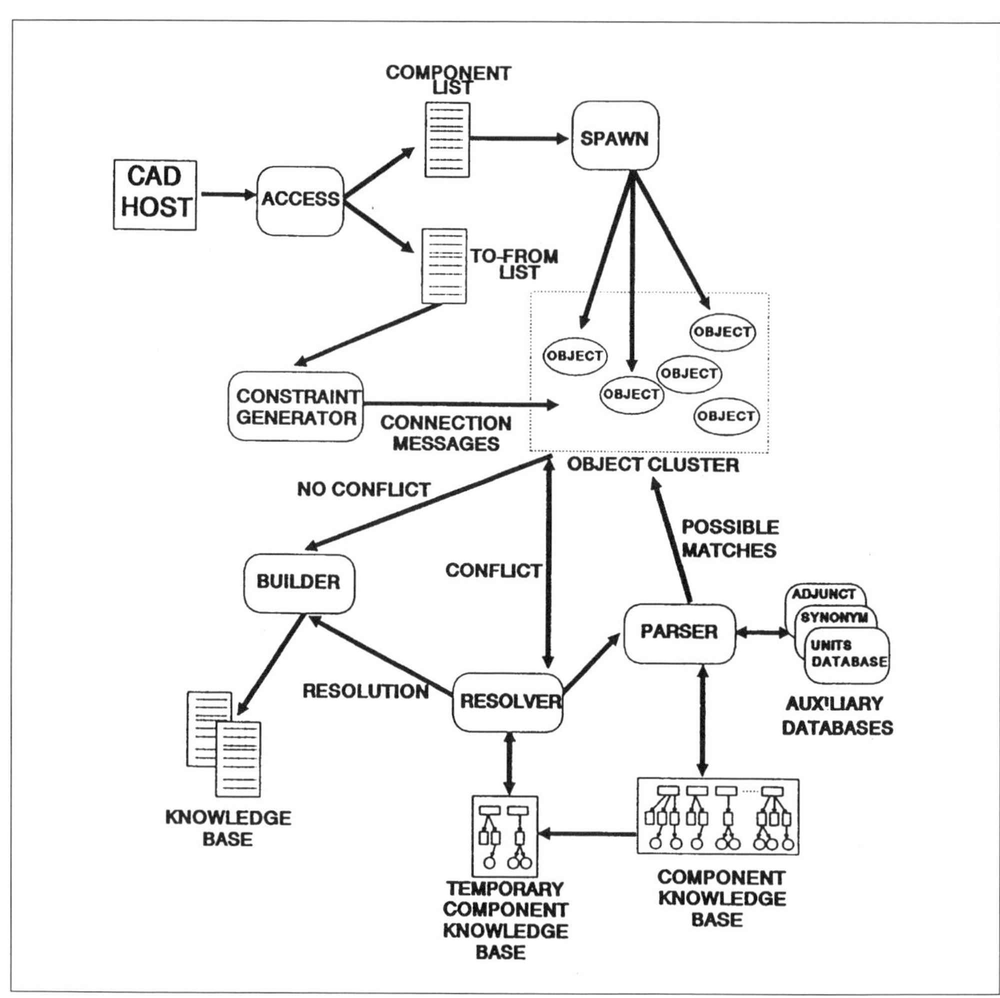

Figure 22.9
A Graphical Representation of the Automated Knowledge Generator Process.

CKB and the Parser. In this discussion, components from CKB are referred to as *generic components* or CKB components; components obtained from CAD for identification are called *component objects.*

Domain knowledge is an integral part of the identification or resolution of CAD components. It consists of a data store of potentially all the generic components in the world. This knowledge is collected in the CKB. Its role is to supply the information necessary to complete the functional description of a component object. This information includes the transfer function of the device and other related parameters, such as delays and tolerances. CKB is represented in a tree structure of object frames representing generic components. The root nodes or upper-level frames of this structure are generalized devices. They represent types of devices and contain information that govern the accepted behavior of these device types. This information is carried through to the children of these upper-level devices as a result of inheritance. Upper-level devices are the parents of more specific devices, which, in turn, might have even more specific children. Any of these components in the structure can have instances of themselves in the CAD components.

In AKG, the Resolver manages uncertainty with the use of confidence factors (CFs) in describing the correctness of the connectivity between component objects and the correctness and completeness of the component objects themselves. Based on the amount of data extracted from CAD about a component, an initial CF is assigned to it by the Resolver. Because each component is a flavor object composed of a group of slots of information, this CF is equal to the weighted sum of the slots filled, where the weight of each slot corresponds to its importance in the identification process of the component itself.

A *global threshold* CF is established by the user at run time; it represents the minimum CF required to label a component as identified. If, as expected, the CAD input knowledge is incomplete and inconsistent, most of the components fail the global confidence threshold and are sent to the Parser for identification. By means of a set of string-matching heuristics (Kladke 1989), the Parser examines the NOMENCLATURE (description) and UNITS slots of each component object received from the Resolver. Thus, the Parser determines a group of possible matches to components in CKB. These possible matches from CKB, each one with a CF reflecting the certainty of the match, are added to a list in the POSSIBLE-MATCHES slot of their corresponding component flavor.

During the interaction of the Parser and CKB, a temporary CKB is created. All the components in CKB accessed by the Parser are placed within this space. This highly constrained knowledge base, a subset of CKB, is the Resolver's key to accessing CKB when trying to identify a component object. If the desired target component does not lie within the temporary CKB but is only a sibling or child of a component within the space to be searched, the Resolver can request to dynamically increase the search space by accessing related components that reside in the rest of CKB.

Beginning from the *islands of certainty*, that is, the component objects containing the most information and, therefore, the highest confidence factor for identification, the Resolver uses the technique of *relaxation labeling* (Rosenfeld, Hammel, and Zucker 1976; Thathachar and Sastry 1986) to propagate confidence through the system. Relaxation labeling, borrowed from image understanding, is a subset of constraint labeling. To produce as many islands of certainty as possible, there is local constraint propagation. That is, the Resolver attempts to identify which CKB generic component in the list of possible matches is the best match for the object under consideration by comparing their respective property or constraint values. If a match is verified, the Resolver assigns the information in the component from the CKB to the system component object, thus increasing its CF. To further fill in the rest of the information in the component objects that have no best match, islands of certainty and their neighbors are taken as starting points to begin the process of combining constraints between component objects and their possible matches by applying techniques for global constraint propagation and elimination. Final component information is obtained through prediction and search. This entire process is performed iteratively until no component within the object cluster experiences a CF increase greater than a preset convergence factor. If any component object is not successfully resolved through this process, the human user is asked to identify it. Once identified, this new information is learned by AKG, and the Resolver resumes the iteration.

The Resolver deals with change following an incremental approach. If an object's label, that is, the object's assigned identity, changes during the resolution process, this change affects the consistency of the connections between the object itself and the surrounding components. If this change makes the connectivity inconsistent, then all the labels of the surrounding components are affected. This process continues until either no other label is changed, or the components that serve as starting or ending points of flow in the system are reached. This process is similar to the region-growing technique in image processing. Another aspect of the resolution process is the reuse of learned information to reduce processing time when similar components are all considered identified when at least one of them is completely resolved.

22.4.3 Target Knowledge Base Construction

Following resolution, the final phase of AKG is carried out by the Builder module. The output for AKG consists of a frame-based model of the schematic drawing in CAD. The Builder module formats the internal model into a file conforming to the requirements of the target diagnostic system. The diagnostic system for which AKG has been producing models is known as the knowledge-based autonomous test engineer or KATE (Cornell 1987; Gonzalez et al. 1988; Gonzalez, Myler, and Towhidnejad 1989), and is located at the Kennedy Space Center of the National Aeronautics and Space Administration (NASA). For the KATE target, a two-level structure is created composed of mid-level (generic or categorical) and instance-level (specific) knowledge base frames.

22.4.4 Automated Knowledge Generator Performance and Applications

The second stage of the AKG process, the resolution of components, is the most time consuming. The optimal time complexity predicted for this algorithm assuming backtrack-free solutions is $O(nk^2)$, where n is the number of components and k is the number of possible matches from CKB during the process of component identification. However, backtrack-free solutions are possible only with a 100 percent correct and complete CKB. Therefore, the actual time complexity could vary to $O(nk^3)$. The run-time complexity is a function of the number of components, the quality of the information, and the completeness of CKB with regard to the target system environment.

AKG can be applied to all domains subject to the availability of a CAD schematic with interconnected components and the viability of having transfer functions between the system components. The following domains can be handled by AKG and are ordered according to how well AKG works on them: electrical systems, process systems, and mechanical systems.

The largest data set to which AKG has been applied is the environmental control system section of the Orbiter Maintenance and Refurbishment Facility at the NASA Kennedy Space Center. The information used in this application, which consists of 138 components, was obtained from Intergraph CAD schematics. At this point, resolution of 70 percent of the components is being obtained. Work is continuing to increase the percentage of resolved components to at least 95 percent.

22.5 Summary

A method to extract knowledge from CAD databases to construct knowledge bases for model-based diagnostic systems was discussed. Because model-based systems require that both structure and function be described and because the representation of systems in CAD usually needs compensation because of their inconsistencies and lack of function information, it was shown that a simple translator would not suffice to generate a useful knowledge base for a diagnostic system.

An intelligent interpreter such as AKG is needed to accomplish the task of automated knowledge extraction from CAD. By means of its knowledge of the internal structure of the system to be diagnosed and the behavior of the individual components, AKG is able to predict missing functional information and detect conflicts in the identification process of components. It is by local and global propagation of constraints, starting from islands of certainty, that discrepancies in the resolution process of components are gradually eliminated.

Acknowledgments

The AKG project is supported by the NASA Kennedy Space Center under contract NAG-10-0043.

References

Cornell, M. 1987. The KATE Shell—An Implementation of Model-Based Control, Monitor, and Diagnosis. In Proceedings of the First Workshop on Space Operations Automation and Robotics.

Gonzalez, A. J.; Myler, H. R.; and Towhidnejad, M. 1989. Automated Knowledge Generation in Support of Shuttle Ground Operations. In Proceedings from the Artificial Intelligence in Government Conference, 268–74.

Gonzalez, A. J.; Myler, H. R.; Owen, B. C.; and Towhidnejad, M. 1988. Automated Generation of Knowledge from CAD Design Data Bases. In Proceedings of the First Florida Artificial Intelligence Research Symposium, 75–80.

Kladke, R. R. 1989. A Mega-Heuristic Approach to the Problem of Component Identification in Automated Knowledge Generation. Master's thesis, Univ. of Central Florida.

Rosenfeld, A.; Hammel, R. A.; and Zucker, S. W. 1976. Scene Labeling by Relaxation Operations. *IEEE Transactions on Systems, Man, and Cybernetics* SMC-6: 420–433.

Scarl, E. A.; Jamieson, J. R.; and Delaune, C. I. 1987. Diagnosis and Sensor Validation through Knowledge of Structure and Function. *IEEE Transactions on Systems, Man, and Cybernetics* SMC-17(3): 360–368.

Thathachar, A. L., and Sastry, P.S. 1986. Relaxation Labeling with Learning Automata. *IEEE Transactions on Pattern Analysis and Machine Intelligence* PAMI-8(2):256–267.

23 Justification-Based Refinement of Expert Knowledge

Jeffrey C. Schlimmer, Tom M. Mitchell, and John McDermott
Carnegie Mellon University

Abstract

This chapter considers the problem of refining task-specific formulations of problem-solving knowledge by relating it to task-independent domain facts and knowledge about domain terms, goals, and problem-solving methodology. We describe an approach and a prototype computer program that accepts rules from a knowledge base developer, attempts to justify the behavior of each rule, and then utilizes these justifications to suggest refinements to the rules. The approach is illustrated using rules from an existing expert system for computer configuration (XCON). From the perspective of previous work in knowledge acquisition, this work proposes a novel method for assimilating and maintaining manually provided expertise. From the perspective of previous work in explanation-based learning (EBL), it raises new issues such as (1) how to extend EBL to allow explaining general rules rather than specific training instances and (2) how to justify rules that are pragmatically useful but not logically entailed by task-independent background knowledge.

23.1 Introduction

The task of building an expert system often involves creating and refining a large knowledge base over the course of many months or years. For example, the knowledge base of the XCON (R1) expert configuration system (Bachant and Soloway 1989) has grown over the past 10 years from 300 component descriptions and 750 configuration rules to 31,000 component descriptions and 10,000 rules (Barker and O'Connor 1989). Despite modular knowledge representations, extending an agent's knowledge of how to perform a task often necessitates modifying other, prior knowledge. For instance, in XCON, creating a new component's description might require creating new configuration rules and updating old ones. These latter modifications require expert attention, and in the case of rule-based knowledge representations, the expert must (re)define the actions the rule will perform (its right-hand side) and the conditions under which these actions are appropriate (its left-hand side). The problem of defining the rule's conditions can be viewed as specifying the rule's correct level of generality. If its conditions are too specific, its actions will be omitted when needed, and if too general, they will be performed when inappropriate.

This chapter describes Cobble, a system that can assist developers as they create and refine a knowledge base. Principally, it can point out reasons why rule conditions appear

Figure 23.1
Sample Rule to be Justified and Refined.

If The current problem-solving step is to propose an operator, and
An operator O proposes placing device D in container C, and
Device D is a box-mountable TK50 tape drive, and
Container C is the CPU box of a micro-expansion system;
Then Reject operator O because D should be placed in a different container.

to be overly specific or overly general. Cobble uses two classes of knowledge: (1) the target knowledge base being created or refined and (2) supplementary knowledge describing task-independent facts, domain terms, goals, and problem-solving methodology. As applied to the XCON system, the former includes configuration rules, and the latter includes component descriptions and definitions of configuration properties, acceptable configurations, and XCON's propose-apply method. In general, much of this latter knowledge is implicitly represented in the former; rules in the target knowledge base are task-specific formulations that alleviate the need for search. Given these two classes of knowledge, Cobble basically elucidates mismatches between them, identifying whether a rule's conditions are appropriately general, overly general, or overly specific. If a mismatch is found, Cobble points out the problem to the developer and suggests remedies.

In a typical scenario, an XCON developer would request analysis for a rule, such as the one listed in figure 23.1 because it was newly written, recently revised in light of some configuration problems, or flagged by a truth maintenance system (TMS) as out of date. To analyze a rule, Cobble follows a two-step process. First, it *justifies* the rule in terms of the supplementary knowledge. This process involves explaining why the rule's action (rejecting an operator) is appropriate when the rule's conditions are satisfied. In this case, the rule is justified because it correctly prevents configuring a low bus priority device (a tape drive) in a high bus priority container (the central processing unit [CPU] box). Second, Cobble *generalizes* the justification and proposes refinements to the rule. Tracing through the inferred justification for this rule reveals that the rule's action is appropriate in a more general class of situations than its conditions indicate—it is overly specific. In particular, the rule's action is appropriate if the TK50 tape drive is either box or rack mountable; this observation identifies a candidate refinement of the original rule.

In the remaining sections of this chapter, we describe our research in the context of related work. Then in Justifying and Refining Rules, we enumerate each of the types of knowledge Cobble uses and describe how it identifies problems and suggests remedies.

In the next section, we provide a detailed example of Cobble at work on a sample rule from XCON's knowledge base. Finally, in the last section, Issues, we identify three issues uncovered by our preliminary explorations.

23.2 Background

The general task of maintaining knowledge has been a topic of great interest (compare Davis 1977). One approach to this task is based on the automatic programming paradigm. If one were able to identify all the knowledge relevant to a task and the conditions under which it would be relevant, it should be possible to efficiently encode it for use in a performance system. Then, whenever the underlying knowledge is modified, the efficient knowledge could be reencoded. Swartout (1983) describes this type of approach; given a high-level problem-solving goal hierarchy and task-specific knowledge, the XPLAIN system derives rules for use in expert consulting systems. Compared to hand coding the target knowledge, this approach has the advantage that the derivation trace can be used in explaining the performance program's behavior.

In contrast, a second approach is based on the truth maintenance paradigm. If one were able to identify the underlying support for a target knowledge rule, then it should be possible to apply TMS to identify when and, perhaps, even how the rule should be revised. Smith et al. (1985) describe this type of approach; given a set of expert rules and a background theory of task-specific knowledge, their methodology builds a justification identifying how basic domain knowledge is incorporated in rules. In use, their method would be demand driven. When a problem arises from the use of target knowledge, the method recursively identifies the source of the error and reasons about the error types and propagation through the rule base. In the context of the dipmeter advisor system, they demonstrate that analysis of a rich, hand-derived justification can lead to an interesting revision of a sophisticated rule.

Our approach is a combination of these two paradigms. Like Swartout (1983), our method derives target knowledge bottom up from supplementary knowledge, and like Smith et al. (1985), it uses a preexisting target rule top down to guide the revision process. Using a target rule top down improves the expected comprehensibility of the resulting rule and the expected computational complexity.

Methodologically, our approach is similar to explanation-based, or analytic, learning (EBL) methods (compare DeJong and Mooney 1986; Mitchell, Keller, and Kedar-Cabelli 1986). In EBL, the task is to construct an efficient recognizer of a general class given a class instance and a domain theory characterizing the relationships between instance features and class properties. At its simplest, EBL uses the domain theory to prove that the instance is a member of the class and then derives from this proof the weakest preconditions necessary for instances to class members. In our task, a target rule is justified and generalized rather than an instance. The proof must show that the rule's actions achieve problem-solving goals given that its conditions are satisfied. Weak preconditions extracted from this proof are used to suggest revisions to the rule's conditions. Following this basic outline, a prototype implementation, Cobble, justified a handful of rules drawn from XCON, indicating the feasibility of automated rule maintenance.

23.3 Justifying and Refining Rules

Given that task-specific knowledge can be encoded in the form of rules and that a need to maintain these rules exists, a straightforward approach to the problem would be to compare individual rules with underlying, supplementary knowledge about the domain of study. The latter should be somewhat simpler to update, consisting largely of simple assertions. If a contradiction is found between the two, the rule could be appropriately modified to reflect changes. This type of comparison between a rule and domain knowledge involves showing that the former is a useful formulation of the latter or that when the rule's tests are satisfied, its actions make progress toward the overall problem-solving goal.

23.3.1 Knowledge Types

Our specific methodology relies on the availability of two classes of knowledge: the target knowledge to be created and revised and supplementary, background knowledge. The former includes relations between situations and appropriate actions; XCON's configuration rules (compare figure 23.1) are an example of this type of knowledge. Rules map from two types of facts to two types of actions: those that are task independent and those that are dependent on the particular problem-solving method. The sample rule in figure 23.1 tests both fact types, including task-independent tests such as whether the tape drive is box mountable and problem-solving method-specific tests such as whether the current problem-solving step is to propose an operator. This rule's actions are limited to method-specific actions. This mixture of information encodes problem-solving control knowledge and undoubtedly leads to more efficient problem solving, but it also complicates justification. In the upcoming example, the justification must consider not only how computer components should be arranged into an acceptable partial configuration but also that any arranging should be done at a certain point in problem solving, using a particular problem-solving notation.

The latter, background or supplementary knowledge, can be broken down into several subtypes: (1) task-independent facts, (2) task-specific definitions, (3) relationships between goals and facts, (4) relationships between actions and the goals they help achieve, and (5) intergoal relationships. (Goal-oriented types of knowledge are not explicitly represented by XCON.) Examples of these include (1) XCON's component descriptions (for example, the TK50-AA tape drive draws 2.4 amperes of 12 VDC, uses the TQK-50 controller, ...), (2) conceptual distinctions (for example, low bus priority devices are those that have high transfer rates and low interrupt priorities), (3) goal achievement conditions (for example, achieving efficient bus operation is violated by low bus priority devices in high bus priority containers), (4) actions' effects (for example, rejecting an operator can eliminate an error of commission), and (5) goal hierarchies (for example, to appropriately configure a system, configure each device in an appropriate container). Each of the above types can include both knowledge about the domain of interest and knowledge about the problem-solving method that uses the target knowledge.

A key component of this knowledge about XCON includes some cursory knowledge about its propose-apply method. This method relies on an application of successively more specialized knowledge. Initially, plausible partial solutions are proposed using weak knowledge to ensure including all acceptable solutions. Then, potentially unacceptable solutions are rejected or eliminated to exclude unacceptable solutions. One of the remaining solutions is randomly chosen and applied. If there are none, new knowledge is brought to bear in another propose-reject eliminate-apply cycle.

23.3.2 Justification

The justification process uses these knowledge types as input and follows the basic EBL outline: prove and generalize. First, assume that the rule's conditions are satisfied. Second, based on the rule's actions, determine which goal the rule intends to address. Then in this context, attempt to prove that the rule's action(s) help achieve the goal, using the task-independent facts and supplementary knowledge as required.

In the first step, rather than assuming that any condition was potentially satisfied, the context of justification is restricted by assuming that only the rule's conditions are satisfied. This is a major constraint on the number of alternative justifications; in some cases, it is possible that a rule's action might have many justifications. Finding a justification supporting the rule's conditions can help ensure that subsequent suggested revisions make sense. This restriction also has computational advantages; constructing the proof can involve using variablized knowledge, and matching this knowledge is exponential. Using only the rule's conditions effectively lowers the exponent's base.

Restricting the justification context has its drawbacks. If the rule to be justified is overly general, and only the rule's conditions are given, it cannot be proved that the rule's actions achieve the goal. The current implementation of Cobble uses a fixed justification context and can only revise overly specific rules. Justification failure then can indicate the need to relax an overly restrictive context, perhaps by also including a successful problem-solving application of the rule. (Justification failure can also indicate that there is insufficient supplementary knowledge.) If this is done, justification can succeed, and the rule can be specialized. Although this approach is limited to those rules that have been successfully applied (that is, it could not be used on new rules), the additional information is easily retained. In addition, although expanding the justification context increases the number of alternate justifications, it might be possible to constrain them by imposing a priority on components of a large justification context.

23.3.3 Revision

Cobble also follows the second half of the basic EBL outline: generalize by analyzing the proof to derive weak preconditions. This results in sufficient conditions for the rule's action to help achieve the goal. The differences between these generalized conditions and the rule's original conditions identify potential refinements.

The generalizer used is based on a trace of the justification process and is similar in spirit to Rosenbloom and Laird (1986). Unreferenced portions of the justification context are simply omitted. Constants that have been tested in some way are replaced by constrained variables (for example, interrupt priority = 2, which is greater than 5). The resulting generalized conditions are then partitioned into two groups: those that will be recommended as conditions for the revised rule and those that will be added as TMS assumptions. This partitioning is simply done. Conditions referring to assumed rule conditions are included in the first group, and conditions referring to task-independent facts are included in the latter. Then the new conditions are partially evaluated to reduce their complexity. Finally, Cobble reduces the number of tests in the revised rule's left-hand side by iteratively removing each test and trying to derive its value using only the other tests. If successful, the test is deleted, and the process repeats. Figure 23.2 lists Cobble's sequence of operations. (Our specific implementation of Cobble uses the Theo problem solver (Mitchell et al. 1990) to justify and revise XCON rules.)

23.4 Detailed example.

As a concrete example, reconsider the sample inference rule listed in figure 23.1. This rule was drawn from the XCON system and is listed in detail in figure 23.3. As part of XCON's propose-apply problem-solving method, this rule can be applied after potential partial solutions have been proposed. It is designed to reject the option of configuring a specific type of tape drive in the CPU box, even though it might appear appropriate for

Figure 23.2
Cobble's Pseudo Code.

Given: A rule, task-independent facts, and supplementary knowledge;
Produce: A set of revised rule conditions, and
A set of TMS assumptions.

Cobble(Rule,Facts,K):
1. Assert each condition of Rule in a new context C.
2. Using K, determine which goal G Rule helps achieve.
3. Proof ← Prove that each action of Rule helps achieve G given C + Facts + K.
4. Conditions and Assumptions ← Generalize (Proof):
   a. Omit unreferenced parts of C,
   b. Replace constrained constants by variables,
   c. Separate new conditions from TMS assumptions,
   d. Partially evaluate single conditions, and
   e. Remove provably redundant conditions.
5. Return Conditions and Assumptions.

other reasons. (The basic reason is that the tape drive has a low bus priority, and the space in the CPU box should be reserved for high bus priority devices.) This rule also includes a test for the absence of a second, yet-to-be-configured tape drive; although it is undesirable to put a tape drive in the CPU box, if there are two tapes, one must be configured there.

Following the pseudo code listed in figure 23.2, Cobble first asserts each of the conditions in a new context; namely, that there is a goal (that is, gc) whose status (activity-phase) is current, whose method step is propose-operator, whose problem-space is select-device, and so forth, for the other conditions listed in figure 23.3, lines 0–9.

To justify the rule's action, Cobble draws on supplementary knowledge describing how actions can achieve goals and what these goals are. Figure 23.4 lists three levels of justification goals, from the most accurate to two simpler versions. In contrast to goal 3, goal 1 involves many aspects of the XCON problem-solving method. In fact, the goals in figure 23.4 are ordered by increasing independence from specifics of the problem-solving method. At the top level, the derivation must show that the rule's actions achieve goal 1 given the rule's conditions.

Given that our interest is primarily in maintaining the task-specific information contained in a competent problem-solving system, we adopted an approach that allows

```
(p select-device:reject:100a:prefer-another-container
; Justification: On some systems, there are reasons to prefer
;                particular containers.
; Specificities: Specific for the tk50 on a micro-expansion system.
;                The tk50 should be configured in the second box if
;                there is only one.
; Loop Inhibitor: Defined-value - operator ^status
; Subgroups: 1. prefer-another-container
;
0  (gc ^activity-phase current ^step propose-operator
1      ^problem-space select-device)
2 {(operator ^activity-phase pending ^status proposed ^token <token>
3           ^problem-space select-device ^subtask primary-task)
4   <operator>}
5  (system-data ^configuration-type micro-expansion)
6  (device ^status not-configured ^token <token> ^subtype tk50
          ^floor-category box-mountable)
7 -(device ^status not-configured ^token { <> <token> }
          ^subtype tk50 ^floor-category box-mountable)
9  (container ^capacity-phase current ^class box ^type cpu)
  -->
   (modify <operator> ^status rejected
                      ^rejected-reason prefer-another-container)
)
```

Figure 23.3
Sample XCON Rule.

Cobble to sidestep much of the complicated justification that would otherwise be involved in moving from goal 1 to goal 3. Rather than extensive supplementary knowledge describing the programming-like, problem-solver-specific notation in goal 1, a simple rule template identifies a number of XCON-specific conditions for a class of rule actions. Figure 23.5 lists the rule template that allows the justification to proceed from goal 1 to goal 2. It specifies a number of attribute-value tests that must be present in any rule that rejects an operator, with ?X denoting unique values and *X denoting zero or more items. Similar subtemplates allow the derivation to proceed from goal 2 to the problem-solver-independent goal 3. Conveniently, the XCON project includes an effort to develop just this type of rule template as part of a syntactic knowledge checker (McDermott 1988). Given this type of goal knowledge, together with task-specific knowledge about the capacities, requirements, and compatibilities of different components, Cobble is able

Figure 23.4
Justification Goals.

1. Reject an operator that proposes configuring an unconfigured TK50 tape drive if
   - This is the propose-operator step,
   - The operator's activity-phase is pending,
   - The problem-space is select-device, and
   - The current container is the cpu box of a micro-expansion system.
2. Reject an operator that proposes configuring an unconfigured TK50 tape drive if
   - The problem-space is select-device and
   - The current container is the cpu box of a micro-expansion system.
3. Reject the configuration of a TK50 tape drive configured in the cpu box of a micro-expansion system.

Figure 23.5
Template for Propose-Apply-Reject XCON Rules.

```
(p reject
   (gc ^activity-phase current ^step propose-operator ^problem-space ?P)
  {(operator ^activity-phase pending ^status proposed ^problem-space ?P)
   <operator>}
   *(<> gc)
  -->
   (modify <operator> ^status rejected ^rejected-reason ?R)
)
```

to derive the actions of the rule in figure 23.3 by assuming that its conditions are true.

Figure 23.7 lists Cobble's justification trace for the first action of the rule in figure 23.3. In the first part of the trace, lines 2-21, the justification assesses the part of the rule that is specific to XCON's problem-solving method. (Indented lines are the justification support for the lines above them.) This is a justification for the control structure of the rule. In the second part of the trace, lines 22 and following, the justification measures the part of the rule that is domain specific. This is a justification for the configuration knowledge in the rule.

Generalizing the justification (compare figure 23.2) yields a new rule incorporating recommended revisions shown in figure 23.6. First, note that the revised rule is identical

Figure 23.6
Revised XCON Rime Rule.

```
(p r:select-device:reject:100a:prefer-another-container
0  (gc ^activity-phase current ^step propose-operator
1      ^problem-space select-device)
2 {(operator ^activity-phase pending ^status proposed ^token <token>
3             ^problem-space select-device ^subtask primary-task)
4   <operator>}
5  (system-data ^configuration-type micro-expansion)
6  (device ^token <token> ^subtype tk50)
7 -(device ^status not-configured ^token { <> <token> }
8          ^subtype tk50 ^floor-category box-mountable)
9  (container ^capacity-phase current ^class box ^type cpu)
 -->
  (modify <operator> ^status rejected
                     ^rejected-reason prefer-another-container)
)
```

to the original where the justification template in figure 23.5 was applied, including most of lines 0-4 in both rule figures. Second, note that the fourth test on line 6 is greatly simplified. Knowing that the operator in lines 2 and 3 has been proposed is enough to ensure that (1) the status of the first device is not-configured and (2) it is of the appropriate floor-category for mounting in the current container. Omitting unnecessary conditions is the simplest type of generalization. None of these simplifications applies to the negated test for another, competing device on line 7 because as far as this rule knows, no operator has been proposed for this device.

Experiments with other XCON rules demonstrate the utility of partial evaluation. For instance, a constant is variablized to the expression {cpu <> nil <> extension} and is subsequently reduced to cpu through partial evaluation.

After generalizing the conditions, Cobble removes redundant tests. Although this is effective in reducing the syntactic size of the rule, it does not improve simplicity and has no effect whatsoever on the revised rule's generality. In fact, recent consultation with XCON developers indicates that an approach that augments the revised rule's left-hand side would be more useful. Instead of removing provably redundant conditions, adding them could increase novice developers' understanding of configuration situations and potentially improve the performance of the rule matcher.

Figure 23.7
Justification Trace for Rule in Figure 23.3.

```
 The MODIFY of the STATUS of TEST-2 is REJECTED because
 2 TEST-2 matches the REJECT-TEMPLATE because
     TEST-1 is a GC, and
     The ACTIVITY-PHASE of TEST-1 is CURRENT, and
     The STEP of TEST-1 is PROPOSE-OPERATOR, and
     The PROBLEM-SPACE of TEST-1 is SELECT-DEVICE, and
     SELECT-DEVICE <> NIL, and
     TEST-2 is an OPERATOR, and
     The ACTIVITY-PHASE of TEST-2 is PENDING, and
     The STATUS of TEST-2 is PROPOSED, and
     The PROBLEM-SPACE of TEST-2 is SELECT-DEVICE, and
     TEST-2 matches the PROBLEM-SPACE-REJECT-SUBTEMPLATE because
       TEST-4 is a DEVICE, and
       The PROBLEM-SPACE of TEST-2 is SELECT-DEVICE, and
       The SUBTASK of TEST-2 is PRIMARY-TASK, and
       The TOKEN of TEST-2 is <TOKEN>, and
       <TOKEN> <> NIL, and
       The TOKEN of TEST-4 is <TOKEN>, and
       TEST-2 matches the SELECT-DEVICE-PRIMARY-REJECT SUBTEMPLATE because
         TEST-6 is a CONTAINER, and
21       The CAPACITY-PHASE of TEST-6 is CURRENT.
22 The POSSIBLE-ERROR-TYPE of TEST-2 is COMMISSION because
     TEST-4 is a DEVICE, and
     The POSSIBLE-VIOLATION of TEST-2 is BUS-ORDER because
       TEST-4 is a DEVICE, and
       TEST-6 is a CONTAINER, and
       The TOKEN of TEST-2 is <TOKEN>, and
       The TOKEN of TEST-4 is <TOKEN>, and
       The CAPACITY-PHASE of TEST-6 is CURRENT, and
       The BUS-PRIORITY of TEST-6 is HIGH because
         The BUS-PRIORITY of CPU-BOX is HIGH, and
         The CLASS of TEST-6 is BOX, and
         TEST-6 is a CONTAINER, and
         The TYPE of TEST-6 is CPU, and
         The TYPE of CPU-BOX is CPU, and
         HIGH <> NIL.
       ...                                           (continued)
```

23.5 Issues

Applying this methodology to actual rules led us to three observations. First, justifying a rule requires more than showing that the rule's actions logically follow from its pre-

Figure 23.7
Justification Trace for Rule in Figure 23.3 *(cont.)*.

```
      ...
    The BUS-PRIORITY of TEST-4 is LOW because
      TEST-4 is a DEVICE, and
      The SUBTYPE of TEST-4 is TK50, and
      The CONTROLLER of TK50 is TQK50, and
      The BUS-PRIORITY of TQK50 is LOW because
        The TRANSFER-RATE of TQK50 is 99, and
        99 > 50, and
        The INTERRUPT-PRIORITY of TQK50 is 2, and
        2 < 5.
    LOW <> HIGH.
  There is AN-ALTERNATE-LOC? for TEST-2 because
    TEST-4 is a DEVICE, and
    TEST-6 is a CONTAINER, and
    The TOKEN of TEST-2 is <TOKEN>, and
    The TOKEN of TEST-4 is <TOKEN>, and
    The SUBTYPE of TEST-4 is TK50, and
    The CAPACITY-PHASE of TEST-6 is CURRENT, and
    TEST-6 is not THE-LAST-CONTAINER? because
      TEST-3 is a SYSTEM-DATA, and
      The TYPE of TEST-6 is CPU, and
      The CONFIGURATION-TYPE of TEST-3 is MICRO-EXPANSION.
  The TOKEN of TEST-2 is <TOKEN>, and
  The TOKEN of TEST-4 is <TOKEN>, and
  There is NO-COMPETING-DEVICE? to TEST-4 because
    TEST-4 is a DEVICE, and
    TEST-5 is a DEVICE, and
    The CLASS of TEST-5 is DEVICE, and
    The TEST-STATUS of TEST-5 is NEGATED, and
    The STATUS of TEST-5 is NOT-CONFIGURED, and
    The TOKEN of TEST-4 is <TOKEN>, and
    The TOKEN of TEST-5 is TOKEN-1, and
    TOKEN-1 <> <TOKEN>.
```

conditions and task-independent facts. In fact, the actions of rules we examined do not logically follow from these. To justify these rules, one must consider relations between goals and problem-solving facts and relations between actions and the goals they help achieve. Further, one must prove that its actions are sensible given these various criteria rather than prove that its actions are entailed by its preconditions. We are still in the process of precisely articulating the property that must be proved of the rule for it to be justified.

Second, a complete but shallow encoding of the relationships between problem-solving actions and goals reduces justification complexity to proving that task-specific actions help achieve a task-specific goal. Cobble uses rule templates for this purpose—an idea shared with XCON's syntactic knowledge-checker project. Adopting this strategy limits Cobble's ability to refine problem-solving method-specific information in rules. If this information is likely to require maintenance, then in-depth supplementary knowledge of problem solver-specific facts, definitions, actions, and goals might also be required.

Third, overly specific rules can be refined by assuming the rule's conditions, determining its goal, proving that the rule's actions help achieve the goal, and then generalizing the justification. Our prototype implementation of Cobble demonstrates the feasibility of this approach. However, Cobble is currently incapable of refining overly general rules. We intend to add this capability by allowing Cobble to expand the justification context to include positive applications of the rule, but this will increase the likelihood that inappropriate justifications will be found. Balancing the scope of the justification context and retaining an appropriate justification structure is another open issue.

Acknowledgments

We would like to thank Judy Bachant and Keith Jensen for helping us understand the current XCON system and its configuration task, Tom Cooper for assisting in formulating the rule templates, and the Carnegie Mellon University gripe group for providing a quality computing environment. This research is supported by a grant from Digital Equipment Corporation.

23.6 References

Bachant, J., and Soloway, E. 1989. The Engineering of XCON. *Communications of the ACM* 32: 311–317.

Barker, V. E., and O'Connor, D. E. 1989. Expert Systems for Configuration at Digital: XCON and Beyond. *Communications of the ACM* 32: 298–310.

Davis, R. 1977. Interactive Transfer of Expertise: Acquisition of New Inference Rules. In Proceedings of the Fifth International Joint Conference on Artificial Intelligence, 321–328. Menlo Park, Calif.: International Joint Conferences on Artificial Intelligence, Inc..

DeJong, G., and Mooney, R. 1986. Explanation-Based Learning: An Alternative View. *Machine Learning* 1: 145–176.

McDermott, J. 1988. Preliminary Steps toward a Taxonomy of Problem-Solving Methods. In *Automating Knowledge Acquisition for Expert Systems*, ed. S. Marcus, 225–256. Boston: Kluwer.

Mitchell, T. M.; Keller, R. M.; and Kedar-Cabelli, S. T. 1986. Explanation-Based Generalization: A Unifying View. *Machine Learning* 1: 47–80.

Mitchell, T. M.; Allen, J.; Chalasani, P.; Cheng, J.; Etzioni, O.; Ringuette, M.; and Schlimmer, J. C. Theo: A Framework for Self-Improving Systems. In *Architectures for Intelligence*, ed. K. VanLehn. Hillsdale, N.J.: Lawrence Erlbaum. Forthcoming

Rosenbloom, P. S., and Laird, J. E. 1986. Mapping Explanation-Based Generalization onto Soar. In Proceedings of the Fifth National Conference on Artificial Intelligence, 561–567. Menlo Park, Calif.: American Association for Artificial Intelligence.

Smith, R. G.; Winston, H. A.; Mitchell, T. M.; and Buchanan, B. G. 1985. Representation and Use of Explicit Justifications for Knowledge Base Refinement. In Proceedings of the Ninth International Joint Conference on Artificial Intelligence, 673–680. Menlo Park, Calif.: International Joint Conferences on Artificial Intelligence, Inc.

Swartout, W. R. 1983. XPLAIN: A System for Creating and Explaining Expert Consulting Programs. *Artificial Intelligence* 21: 285–325.

24 Rule Discovery for Query Optimization

Michael Siegel
Sloan School of Management, MIT

Edward Sciore
Boston College

Sharon Salveter
Boston University

Abstract

Semantic query optimization has been shown to be a useful method for reducing query processing costs. Savings result from the use of rules, or integrity constraints, supplied by experts. However, a methodology for experts to establish a set of useful rules has not been developed. In this chapter, we define an automatic method for deriving and maintaining a useful rule set in which intermediate results from the optimization process direct the search for learning new rules. Rules derived from the current state of the database are later used for semantic query optimization to reduce query processing costs.

24.1 Introduction

Semantic query optimization has been shown to be a useful method for reducing query processing costs (Hammer and Zdonik 1980; King 1981a, 1981b; Xu 1983; Jarke 1984; Chakravarthy, Fishman, and Minker 1984; Chakravarthy 1985; Shenoy and Ozsoyoglu 1987; Siegel 1988a, 1988b). Savings result from the use of rules, or integrity constraints, supplied by experts. However, a methodology for experts to establish a set of useful rules has not been developed. Thus, semantic query optimization has not been used in numerous applications where it could contribute to more efficient database operation. In this chapter, we describe automatic methods for deriving rules for use in query optimization.

The success of semantic query optimization depends on the existence of a set of useful rules. However, these rules are not necessarily those that would or could be specified by an expert. We developed an automatic method for deriving a useful rule set in which intermediate results from the optimization process direct the search for learning new rules. Unlike user-specified rules, a system with an automatic capability can derive rules that might be true only in the current state of the database. An example of such a derived rule is, "No employee makes more than $65,000." Although such rules might not always be true, it is useful for the system to take advantage of them as long as they are true. In addition, as the database is modified, some derived rules can become invalid, and others become true. Some derived rules can lose their usefulness. A system that maintains a set of derived rules is flexible in a time-varying world.

The process of automatic rule derivation is known in the field of AI as inductive or heuristic learning (Blum 1982; Davis and Lenat 1982; Lenat 1983a, 1983b; Lindsay et al. 1980; Michalski, Carbonell, and Mitchell 1983; Waterman 1970). Given a domain such as medical diagnosis (Blum 1982), a learning system derives appropriate rules and constraints by examining data or sequences of operations on the data. Usually, heuristics are used to limit the search for effective rules. They also determine the effectiveness of the system. In a similar manner, we can use heuristics to identify the characteristics of the rules to be derived and to search the database for these rules. It seems promising and natural to apply the techniques of inductive learning to rule derivation for database systems.

Automatic rule derivation for semantic query optimization uses the database usage pattern to identify the characteristics of desirable rules. It also considers past database performance when making decisions about deriving rules. The information from the database use pattern and database performance statistics can be used to limit the search required to find new rules. These methods can be used to derive rules for query optimization in conjunction with, or in lieu of, a human expert. The savings that result from this method will accrue when rules that are derived can be repeatedly used in the optimization process.

Compared to other learning problems, automatic rule derivation for semantic query optimization is a well-defined and restricted problem with the following advantages: the existence of an automated process for defining specifications for what needs to be learned, a restricted set of rule characteristics used to limit the search through the data, a database environment providing the procedures needed for search through the data, and a built-in mechanism for determining the value of what has been learned.

In the next section, we present an introduction to semantic query optimization. A detailed discussion can be found in Siegel (1988b). In Automatic Rule Deviation, we describe automatic rule derivation as a method for supplying the optimizer with a set of useful rules. Finally, we present our conclusions and suggestions for future research.

24.2 Semantic Query Optimization

Semantic query optimization (Hammer and Zdonik 1980; King 1981a, 1981b; Xu 1983; Jarke 1984; Chakravarthy, Fishman, and Minker 1984; Chakravarthy 1985; Shenoy and Ozsoyoglu 1987; Siegel 1988b) is a two-phase process: The optimizer must first identify possible query transformations and then select those transformations that, when applied, result in the least cost query. *Semantic query transformation* is the addition or removal of constraints to a query in accordance with a given rule set. The transformed query is semantically equivalent to the original query in the sense that if the database state satisfies the rules, then the transformed query will return the same answer from the database. The choice of which transformations to use is crucial; leaving out a transformation can miss an important optimization, and including an irrelevant transformation can add (remove) a useless (useful) constraint and increase execution time. Deciding on the optimal subset of transformations takes time; therefore, limiting the size of the rule set can help in reducing the cost of query optimization.

24.2.1 Rules and Semantic Transformations

As an example of semantic query optimization, we begin by introducing the following sample database scheme:

SHIPS(Shipname, **Shiptype**, Deadweight, Draft, Length, Registry)

CARGOES(Shipname, **Cargotype**, Dollarvalue, Weight, Destination)

The SHIPS relation has a cluster index on Shiptype, and the CARGOES relation has a cluster index on Cargotype.

Queries are specified by a select-project-join query language that is equivalent to a subset of QUEL. As an example, query Q_1 asks for the name of all ships with deadweight greater than 250:

retrieve SHIPS.Shipname (Q_1)
where SHIPS.Deadweight > 250.

We consider only integrity constraints that can be represented as simple rules, where a *simple rule* is an implication that involves two attributes at most. Additionally, we require that simple rules contain an antecedent constraint that involves a single restriction at most, and the consequent constraint can contain a disjunction of restrictions on a single attribute. For example, figure 24.1 shows two simple rules. Rule R_1 says that all ships with deadweight greater than 200 are tankers. Rule R_2 says that all tankers with a cargo carry oil. Simple rules of these types are known to be useful for semantic query optimization (Chakravarthy, Fishman, and Minker 1984; Hammer and Zdonik 1980; Jarke 1984; King 1981a, 1981b; Shenoy and Ozsoyoglu 1987; Siegel, 1988b).

As an example of the transformation process, consider query Q_1. Because rule R_1 holds, we know that every tuple satisfying the query must have *tanker* as its Shiptype; thus, the constraint $SHIPS.Shiptype = tanker$ belongs to the transformation set of the

R_1	attribute	constraint
antecedent	SHIPS.Deadweight	(> 200)
consequent	SHIPS.Shiptype	(= tanker)
R_2	**attribute**	**constraint**
antecedent	SHIPS.Shiptype	(= tanker)
consequent	CARGOES.Cargotype	(= oil)

Figure 24.1
Simple Rule Types.

query. By selecting this transformation, we can derive the semantically equivalent query Q_2:

retrieve SHIPS.Shipname (Q_2)
where SHIPS.Deadweight > 250
and SHIPS.Shiptype = tanker.

24.2.2 Heuristic-Based Transformation

Because the transformation set for a query might be large, it is impractical to consider all possible transformations. Moreover, only a small percentage of the possible transformations might actually be useful. For example, in query Q_1, adding the restriction on Shiptype is potentially useful because it allows us to take advantage of an index. However, a transformation that adds a restriction on the Length attribute will most likely result in a higher-cost query. A common approach to identifying the most promising transformations is to use transformation heuristics to limit the size of the transformation set (Hammer and Zdonik 1980; King 1981a, 1981b; Xu 1983; Chakravarthy 1985; Shenoy and Ozsoyoglu 1987; Siegel 1988b).

We consider an implementation of heuristic-based semantic query optimization with the architecture shown in figure 24.2. A complete description of this system can be found in Siegel (1988b).

The semantic transformation module takes the query tree as input and tries to find a transformation heuristic that applies to some subtree. Figure 24.3 contains an example of a transformation heuristic known as Index Introduction (King 1981b). If it finds such a subquery, it returns a proposed rule. A *proposed rule* is a template: It indicates the sort of rule that would be useful to transform the query. For example, when H_1 is applied to query Q_1, it discovers that *Shiptype* is an unrestricted cluster attribute and returns proposed rule PR_1.

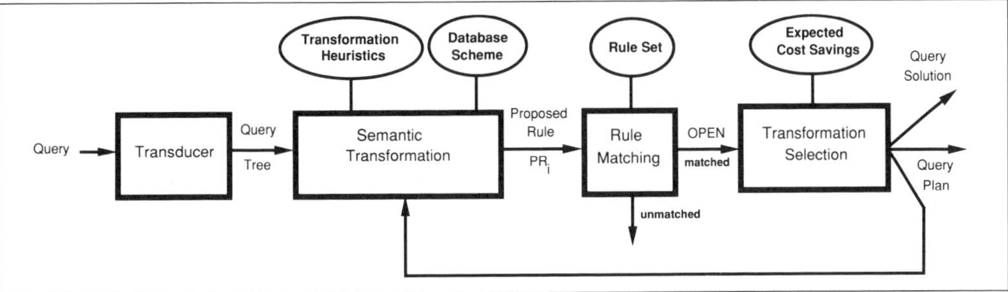

Figure 24.2
Query Optimizer.

If a relation R in the query has a restricted attribute A and an unrestricted cluster index attribute B, then look for a rule where the restriction on A implies a restriction on B.

Figure 24.3
Heuristic H_1 - Index Introduction.

PR_1	**attribute**	**constraint**
antecedent	SHIPS.Deadweight	(> 250)
consequent	SHIPS.Shiptype	

Proposed rules represent wish lists. The heuristic that generates the proposed rule has no idea of what rules actually exist; it simply asserts that if such a rule did exist, then it would be useful. The rule-matching module is responsible for examining each proposed rule to see if there is a relevant existing rule. A rule *matches* the proposed rule if the antecedent of the rule is implied by the antecedent of the proposed rule. For example, rule R_1 matches proposed rule PR_1. When a match occurs, the consequent of the existing rule can be added to the transformation set.

In the following section, we show how intermediate results from the optimization process can be used to direct the search for new rules that can be used by the optimizer to reduce query processing costs.

24.3 Automatic Rule Derivation

Automatic rule derivation is a two-part process: The characteristics of worthwhile rules are first identified, then a query is issued to the database in an attempt to derive rules having these characteristics. The performance of the automatic rule-derivation process is determined by its ability to derive rules that are useful in the optimization process. The identification of desirable rule characteristics uses information obtained from the semantic query optimizer. The ability to derive useful rules from the database requires

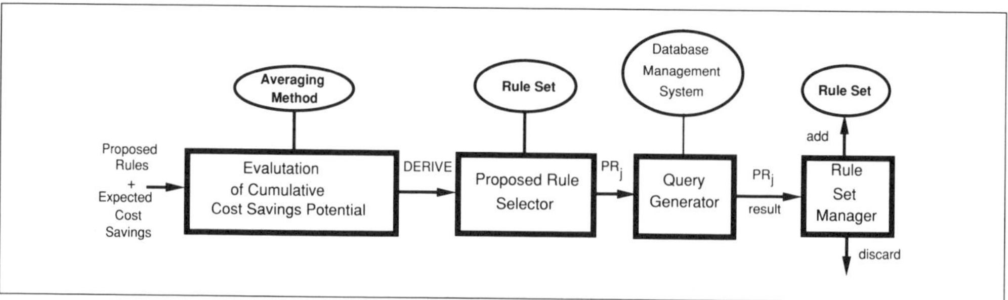

Figure 24.4
The Rule-Derivation Process.

intelligent management and selection of these characteristics as well as the existence of correlations in the database that fit the selected characteristics.

Unfortunately, no one approach to rule derivation works for all database systems. Algorithms for selecting rule characteristics will differ depending on the availability of various types of statistics and semantic information. This additional information can either be explicitly supplied by a domain expert or automatically generated by the database system as an assessment of past performance. Because there are many variables that affect the implementation of the derivation process, we begin by describing a basic approach to automatic rule derivation that does not assume the existence of such additional information. In Enhancements to Automatic Rule Derivation, we describe how additional information can be used to enhance the performance of the derivation process. Ultimately, improvements in the derivation process will lead to improvements in the performance of the semantic query optimizer. Finally, we describe the maintenance requirements in the presence of updates for a set of derived rules.

24.3.1 A Basic Approach to Automatic Rule Derivation

A flow diagram of the rule-derivation process is shown in figure 24.4. The first module takes a stream of proposed rules and their expected cost savings as input and uses them to manage a list called Derive. The Derive list consists of those proposed rules whose cumulative potential cost savings is considered sufficiently high. The second module examines the value of proposed rules on Derive and compares these values with those of rules in the existing rule set. If appropriate, a proposed rule is selected and sent to the third module for derivation. This module automatically generates a query from the proposed rule and executes it on the database. The result of the query is then sent to the final module, which decides whether a new rule should be added to the rule set. In the following subsections, we discuss each of these modules in detail.

Defining Rule Characteristics An important principle behind our approach is that it is not sufficient to simply derive rules from the database; we must derive worthwhile rules. Consequently, the rule-derivation process must be directed by the query optimizer, so that only rules that would have been useful to the optimizer during previous queries are derived.

The process of defining characteristics of desirable rules begins by examining a continuous stream of proposed rules. These proposed rules are a by-product of the optimization process. Only unmatched proposed rules that are the result of failed transformations are used as input to the derivation process; they define the characteristics of desirable rules. Because these proposed rules failed to match rules in the existing rule set, it seems promising to attempt to derive rules that would match similar proposed rules in the future. As an example, suppose that proposed rule PR_1 was generated by some transformation but that rule R_1 is not yet in the existing rule set. The transformation will fail, and the proposed rule will be sent to the derivation process. Intuitively, the proposed rule, PR_1, symbolizes the following:

> "It is desirable to have a rule in the rule class $RC(Deadweight, Shiptype)$. This rule should have an antecedent that matches the constraint $Deadweight > 250$. If such a rule existed, we could add the consequent to the query and have a restriction on the previously unrestricted cluster index attribute."

During its operation, the semantic query optimizer sends every unmatched proposed rule, along with its expected cost savings, to the rule deriver. The expected cost savings of a proposed rule is an estimate of how much the failed transformation would have saved had there been a matching rule in the rule set. The cost-estimation formulas used by the optimizer are a function of the rule class and the transformation heuristic used and do not depend on the existence of a matching rule. Thus, the expected cost savings for a failed transformation can be calculated by the optimizer just as easily as that for a successful transformation.

This value of expected cost savings acts as an estimate of the potential cost savings for the yet-to-be-derived rule. This estimate of potential cost savings will enable the system to select the most promising proposed rules for derivation. Other factors described in Enhancements to Automatic Rule Derivation can be used to more accurately estimate the potential cost savings.

All proposed rules examined by the derivation process are entered onto the list Derive along with the estimate of their potential cost savings. If an entry for this proposed rule already exists, then a cumulative potential cost savings must be calculated for this proposed rule. The cumulative value of potential cost savings is a weighted average of the potential cost savings attributed to the proposed rule. As in the calculation of expected cost savings, a sliding average method is used to determine this cumulative statistic. To account for the passage of time, at set intervals, the value of each proposed rule on Derive is reduced by a fixed percentage. Proposed rules with a cumulative potential cost savings below a threshold are removed from Derive. Thus, a proposed rule that is less likely to lead to the derivation of a useful rule is eventually deleted.

Selecting Proposed Rules A selection process is needed to identify the most promising proposed rules. Because there is no way to determine in advance which proposed rules will derive useful rules, we suggest that the selection process be based on past experience. That is, the cumulative expected cost savings computed during optimization is the basis for the estimate of potential cost savings—the value used to select proposed rules for derivation.

The selection of proposed rules for derivation must be carefully controlled because the size and quality of the rule set has a significant impact on optimization. Thus, a proposed rule is selected for derivation only if its potential cost savings is considerably larger than the worth of the least valuable rule in the rule set. The method used to determine the worth of each member of the rule set is described in Maintaining Derived Rules.

Proposed rules can be selected for derivation as long as a rule on Derive exists whose potential value is sufficiently high. At the same time, existing rules that no longer contribute to the optimization process should be removed from the rule set. Ideally, a function based on the performance of the semantic query optimizer with respect to size and quality of the rule set would be used to justify the selection of a proposed rule. As a simplification of this process, we impose a limit on the maximum size of the rule set and on the minimum value of a rule in the rule set. Rules with a value below this minimum value are removed from the rule set.

Query Generation After a proposed rule is selected for derivation, it is sent to the query generation module. This module automatically generates a query from the proposed rule and executes the query against the database in an attempt to instantiate it. For example, figure 24.5 shows proposed rule PR_1 and the query corresponding to it. The consequent of the proposed rule determines the *retrieve* part of the query, and the antecedent determines the *where* part.

If the proposed rule involves attributes from different relations, then the generated query must include a condition in the *where* clause connecting these two relations. An example of such a proposed rule is PR_2:

PR_2	**attribute**	**constraint**
antecedent	SHIPS.Shiptype	(= tanker)
consequent	CARGOES.Cargotype	

PR_1	**attribute**	**constraint**
antecedent	SHIPS.Deadweight	($>$ 250)
consequent	SHIPS.Shiptype	

retrieve SHIPS.Shiptype (Q_3)
where SHIPS.Deadweight $>$ 250.

Figure 24.5
Query Inferred by Proposed Rule PR_1.

The query generated by this proposed rule is as follows:

retrieve CARGOES.Cargotype (Q_4)
where SHIPS.Shiptype = tanker
and SHIPS.Shipname = CARGOES.Shipname.

The join conditions appearing in the generated query can be derived either from explicit specifications in the database scheme or by use of universal instance techniques (Sciore 1991).

Rule Management After the generated query for a proposed rule is executed on the database, its result and the proposed rule are sent to the rule manager module. This module first tries to construct a derived rule from its input. If the result of the query is null, then no rule is possible for the proposed rule, and it is discarded. If the proposed rule is from a constraint-removal heuristic, then the consequent of the proposed rule must be verified. That is, if the result of the query does not imply the consequent of the proposed rule, then the proposed rule is discarded; otherwise, it is considered a derived rule.

Even if a derived rule is found, it might not be useful. A rule derived from a constraint-introduction heuristic is promising if the selectivity of the derived consequent is below a threshold selectivity. If a derived rule is promising, then it is added to the rule set.

24.3.2 Enhancements to Automatic Rule Derivation

In this subsection, we describe a number of enhancements to automatic rule derivation. These enhancements can be applied when additional information is available from a domain expert, the database implementer, or the statistics maintained by the database system. For example, the database implementer might specify that any proposed rule whose antecedent has a selectivity greater than 0.1 will probably not derive a useful rule. If such information is specified, then the derivation process can filter any proposed rule whose antecedent selectivity is greater than 0.1. If this heuristic is good, then its application will improve the performance of the derivation process.

Most of the examples of rule derivation in this chapter have involved a single heuristic being applied to a simple query and producing a single proposed rule. In general, a query will have many transformations, leading to the generation of many proposed rules. Because only a few of these proposed rules are likely to lead to the derivation of useful rules, it is important to limit the quantity and increase the quality of the proposed rules being placed on Derive. In the following subsections, we describe a number of enhancements to the basic approach. Based on available information, these methods can be used to identify the most promising proposed rules.

User-Specified Domain Knowledge Our basic approach to automatic rule derivation defines a method for deriving rules in the absence of a rule set specified by a domain expert. However, varying levels of domain-specific knowledge might be available and should be used to improve the derivation process. It is important to note that automatic rule derivation is not required to be independent of a domain expert. If domain-specific knowledge is available, the derivation process can improve its effectiveness by using this information.

One category of useful domain-specific knowledge is the indication of which rule classes have meaningful correlations and which do not. This knowledge about correlations is used to increase the value of proposed rules in promising rule classes and decrease the worth of proposed rules in less likely classes.

For example, assume that the following rule classes are known to be unlikely to contain meaningful correlations:

$RC(SHIPS.Shiptype, CARGOES.Destination)$

$RC(SHIPS.Shiptype, CARGOES.Shipame.)$

As query Q_5 enters the optimizer, heuristic H_2 is used to generate the set of proposed rules shown in figure 24.6:

retrieve SHIPS.Shipname (Q_5)

    where SHIPS.Shiptype = tanker

    and SHIPS.Shipname = CARGOES.Shipname.

If this transformation fails (that is, no matching rules are found for any of the proposed rules), then all these proposed rules are sent to the derivation process. The potential cost savings for the first and the last proposed rule is reduced because both of these proposed rules are in a rule class that is not likely to produce a useful rule.

Statistical Enhancements Statistics obtained from past database and rule-derivation performance can also be used to improve the performance of rule derivation. One example of such statistics is the *derivability factor*, which tracks past attempts to derive a rule for a given rule class. The assumption is that if previous attempts to derive rules have been unsuccessful, then future attempts will be equally unsuccessful. In other words, the derivability factor denotes the degree to which the attributes in a rule class are correlated. Thus, it extends the notion of correlation, which corresponds to a derivability factor of either 1 or 0. A second useful statistic is called the maintenance factor. The *maintenance factor* tracks the cost of rule maintenance required by the presence of updates. Maintenance costs include the cost of checking for violations during updates and the cost associated with maintaining rules in the presence of violations. Given a proposed rule, the derivation process can use these statistics to estimate the maintenance cost of the corresponding derived rule. The estimated potential cost savings of a proposed rule is then appropriately adjusted.

SHIPS.Shiptype = tanker → CARGOES.Shipname
SHIPS.Shiptype = tanker → CARGOES.Cargotype
SHIPS.Shiptype = tanker → CARGOES.Dollarvalue
SHIPS.Shiptype = tanker → CARGOES.Weight
SHIPS.Shiptype = tanker → CARGOES.Destination

Figure 24.6
Proposed Rule Generation-Scan Reduction.

A third useful statistic is the *antecedent selectivity factor*. It considers to what extent the selectivity of the antecedent condition in a proposed rule determines the value of a derived rule. If the antecedent of a proposed rule is too general, then it is likely that the corresponding derived rule will not be worthwhile. For example, consider the query Q_6:

retrieve SHIPS.Shipname (Q_6)
where SHIPS.Length (< 1000).

The application of Index Introduction (see figure 24.3) generates proposed rule PR_3:

PR_3	**attribute**	**constraint**
antecedent	SHIPS.Length	(< 1000)
consequent	SHIPS.Shiptype	

Based on the assumption that the transformation failed, this proposed rule would be sent to the derivation process, added to Derive, and perhaps later chosen for derivation.

However, such a derived rule would be practically useless because the restriction on the Length attribute is much too general.

All three of these factors are examples of statistics that are difficult for a human expert to specify well. The assessment of these factors requires a detailed understanding of the application data, the database use pattern, and semantic query optimization. Because it is unlikely that a human expert can assess all these parts of the system and come up with the required factors, it seems more appropriate for the system to determine the factors from past database experience. Although maintaining these statistics increases system overhead, this added expense can be justified by the improvement in both the performance of automatic rule derivation and, as described in Enhancements to Automatic Rule Derivation, semantic query optimization.

Heuristic Knowledge Another type of useful knowledge is an indication of what kinds of rules are more likely to be derived. This knowledge can be represented in various heuristic specifications. For example, a proposed rule with an antecedent constraint on extreme values of a range attribute is a good candidate for derivation. Proposed rules that satisfy this heuristic can have their value enhanced when they are added to Derive.

Other heuristics indicate whether certain kinds of attributes are more or less likely to appear in a rule. For example, the key attributes of a relation usually do not belong to worthwhile rules. Conversely, category attributes (Elmasri 1985), such as Shiptype or Cargotype, often do. If a proposed rule containing one of these attributes is sent to the derivation process, then its value is modified appropriately.

Although such heuristics are often true, they might not be true for a particular database or relation. Thus, we can also consider keeping statistics that track the past performance of these heuristics. In this way, the system can learn the types of proposed rules that are likely to lead to a successful derivation and those that are not.

Managing Derive We now turn to the problem of how to manage the proposed rules on Derive. Thus far, we have assumed that all proposed rules placed on Derive are treated equally. However, this assumption is not necessarily reasonable if several proposed rules belong to the same rule class. For example, assume that the following proposed rules are entries on Derive:

PR_4	**attribute**	**constraint**
antecedent	SHIPS.Deadweight	($>$ 160)
consequent	SHIPS.Shiptype	

PR_5	**attribute**	**constraint**
antecedent	SHIPS.Deadweight	($>$ 180)
consequent	SHIPS.Shiptype	

Based on their respective potential cost savings, either proposed rule can be selected for derivation. Assume that proposed rule PR_4 is selected, and the following rule R_3 is derived:

R_3	**attribute**	**constraint**
antecedent	SHIPS.Deadweight	(> 160)
consequent	SHIPS.Shiptype	(= tanker ∨ passenger)

Because the antecedent of proposed rule PR_5 implies the antecedent of proposed rule PR_4, rule R_3 matches both proposed rules, which can be removed from Derive.

In general, if a useful rule has been derived from some proposed rule, and there are other proposed rules on Derive that match the derived rule, the value of their potential cost savings will automatically be reduced. For example, if rule R_3 is derived, then later transformations involving either of these proposed rules will succeed. Thus, proposed rule PR_5 will no longer be sent to the derivation process, and its cumulative potential cost savings will be depreciated over time. Consequently, if space on Derive is at a premium, then it is reasonable for the derivation process to immediately remove all proposed rules that are implied by a newly derived rule.

Another issue involves the benefits of combining proposed rules. For example, it might be the case that the cumulative cost savings of PR_5 and PR_4 are individually too small. However, we could combine them by assigning the cost savings for PR_4 to PR_5. Such a combination might then produce a high enough value to warrant selection. Combining proposed rules in this way can be effective. The liability is that the derived rule will not be sufficiently selective. One solution to this dilemma is to compute all possible rules for a given rule class, which can be done by simply deriving a view over the rule class (Siegel 1988b).

Semantic Query Optimization Revisited The techniques for enhancing the performance of the rule-derivation process can also be used to improve the optimization process. In particular, the use of domain-specific knowledge, statistics, and heuristics limits the types of rules that can be derived; thus, it can also be used to limit the set of proposed rules considered during the matching phase of optimization. The optimization process can be improved if the proposed rule-generation function has access to the same knowledge used to enhance the derivation process.

This added phase of the transformation process reduces the search required to locate applicable transformations. In addition, the derivation process no longer needs to filter through the set of proposed rules after a failed optimization. Unlikely candidates are eliminated by the proposed rule generator before entering the matching phase of optimization.

24.3.3 Maintaining Derived Rules

It is important to monitor the performance of the derived rule set. Performance statistics are needed to determine when rules should be removed from the rule set and when new rules should be derived. In addition to performance concerns, the set of derived rules must remain valid in the presence of updates to the database. A system that uses derived rules must detect violations and modify the rule set to account for the new database state. In this section, we examine methods for monitoring rule-set performance and maintaining derived rules in the presence of updates.

Monitoring Rule Performance The performance of each rule can be monitored by considering the successful applications of this rule. A rule is *successful* if it is used to establish a transformation that appears in the final version of a query. The value of a rule in a transformation can be determined by the semantic query optimizer. Cost formulas included in the specification of transformations are used to estimate the cost savings. *Cumulative cost savings*, the sum of the savings resulting from all successful applications of this rule, are maintained by the system. The averaging method evaluates the time-weighted value of each rule, and at set intervals, the value of each rule is depreciated by a fixed percentage. Simple maintenance procedures can control the size of the rule set by deleting rules whose values are below a threshold. The cost savings statistics in the rule set are directly comparable to the potential cost savings of proposed rules on Derive. Thus, the derivation process can attempt to derive rules to replace less valuable ones found in the rule set.

Ideally, the system should maintain a rule set that is optimal both in size and in worth. A simple approach to managing the contents of the rule set uses an upper limit on the size of the rule set and a lower limit on the value of a rule in set. Using these limits, the rule set manager can supply the optimizer with a useful rule set.

Maintaining Derived Rules in the Presence of Updates Unlike updates that violate integrity constraints (user-specified rules), updates that violate derived rules are accepted; the derived rule must be modified. The impact of updates on derived rules is similar to the impact of updates on indexes or derived views. Careful index selection in relational databases can help to reduce query processing costs (Finkelstein, Schkolnick, and Tibero 1988). However, careful analysis is required because the savings resulting from the use of these indexes can easily be eliminated by the high cost of maintaining them in the presence of updates. Similarly, methods are required to determine the cost of updates on the use of derived rules.

Rule derivation for semantic query optimization is similar to this index-selection problem (Chan 1976). Like the index-selection problem, the selection process for rule derivation must consider the cost of maintaining derived rules. Desirable rule characteristics are determined from the past performance of the optimizer. Maintenance costs depend on the implementation and, as in index selection, can be estimated by considering a sample database workload. Siegel (1988b) proposes methods for maintaining a valid rule set in the presence of updates.

24.4 Summary

In this chapter, we defined a method for automatic rule derivation, where rules are derived for use in the optimization process. The process of rule derivation reduces the dependency on human experts and provides a means for the optimization process to follow changes in the database use pattern, making semantic query optimization possible and effective in applications that have limited access to expert knowledge.

By considering automatic rule derivation for use in semantic query optimization, this research goes beyond prior connections to AI research (King 1981a, 1981b). As we described it, automatic rule derivation combines methods of machine learning and heuristic search. The automatic rule-derivation process is made tractable by a number of well-defined procedures. First, the set of semantic transformation heuristics used by the semantic query optimizer and the database use pattern help to define the characteristics of what must be learned. Using selected characteristics, the database management system provides the search methods needed for deriving rules. Finally, the performance of the optimizer provides a measure of the success or failure of the learning process.

Automatic rule derivation can be used to derive rules for query optimization without the assistance of a human expert. Thus, it makes semantic query optimization possible in systems where no rules are supplied by the database implementer. In a system where additional expert knowledge is available, automatic rule derivation can use this knowledge to improve the derivation process. This, in turn, will improve the performance of the optimization process. Finally, in addition to providing rules for use in semantic query optimization, automatic rule derivation can provide a human expert with new knowledge in the form of derived rules.

Numerous questions remain about the derivation process. First, we need to determine the savings that can be realized from semantic query optimization using automatic rule derivation. In particular, when is it likely that we will generate meaningful rules? What types of rules are most likely to be derivable? What types of data models (Siegel 1988b) are appropriate for semantic query optimization using automatic rule derivation? What types of applications are appropriate for these methods? We hope to address these questions and others using the current implementation.

Once rules have been derived from the database, they must be maintained in the presence of updates. Several methods for maintaining a valid set of derived rules are described in Siegel (1988b). These methods include explicit reference to exceptional instances and the rewriting of rules to account for violations. It is a matter of future research to implement these and other methods to discover which are cost effective in a given application. Managing derived rules in the presence of updates poses many challenges for both AI and database research—to name two, giving a system the ability to learn from exceptions and making explicit use of exceptions in rule maintenance and database operations.

This research focuses on the importance of learning to support database optimization. However, these same learning techniques can be useful in finding rules that are of interest to a domain expert. It is important to consider such learning procedures for use in areas other than semantic query optimization.

A prototype system was developed for deriving simple rules from the database. We used a semantic query optimizer generator (Siegel 1988b) to produce an executable semantic query optimizer. Rules were derived from shipping data provided by Lloyd's of London.

In summary, this chapter described a method for deriving knowledge from data, where the knowledge can be used to supply an optimizer with a set of useful rules. The success of semantic query optimization in reducing query processing costs will depend on learning methods, such as this one, to provide the database with a useful set of rules in a changing database environment.

Acknowledgments

The authors would like to thank David Corbin of Lloyd's of London for providing them with test data. This work was funded by National Science Foundation grants DCR8407688, IST8408551, and IST8710137.

References

Blum, R. 1982. Discovery, Confirmation, and Incorporation of Causal Relationships from a Large Time-Oriented Clinical Data Base: The RX Project. *Computers and Biomedical Research* 15: 164–187.

Chakravarthy, U. 1985. Semantic Query Optimization in Deductive Databases. Ph.D. diss., Univ. of Maryland.

Chakravarthy, U.; Fishman, D.; and Minker, J. 1984. Semantic Query Optimization in Expert

Systems and Database Systems. In *Proceedings of the First International Conference on Expert Database Systems*, 326–340. Univ. of South Carolina.

Chan, A. 1976. Index Selection in a Self-Adaptive Relational Database Management System. Master's thesis, Massachusetts Institute of Technology.

Davis, R. and Lenat, D. 1982. *Knowledge-Based Systems in Artificial Intelligence*. New York: McGraw-Hill.

Elmasri, R. 1985. The Category Concept: An Extension to the Entity-Relationship Model. *Data and Knowledge Engineering* 1(1): 75–116.

Finkelstein S.; Schkolnick, M.; and Tibero, P. 1988. Physical Database Design for Relational Databases. *ACM Transactions on Database Systems* 13(1): 91–128.

Hammer, M., and Zdonik, S. B. 1980. Knowledge-Based Query Processing. In Proceedings of the Sixth VLDB Conference, 137–146. Washington, D.C.: IEEE Computer Society.

Jarke, M. 1984. Semantic Query Optimization in Expert Systems and Database Systems. In Proceedings of the First International Conference on Expert Database Systems, 467–482. Univ. of South Carolina.

King, J. J. 1981a. Query Optimization through Semantic Reasoning. Ph.D. diss., Stanford Univ.

King, J. J. 1981b. QUIST: A System for Semantic Query Optimization in Relational Databases. In Proceedings of the Seventh VLDB Conference, 510–517. IEEE N.Y., N.Y.

Lenat, D. 1983a. EURISKO: A Program That Learns New Heuristics and Domain Concepts. The Nature of Heuristics III: Program Design and Results. *Artificial Intelligence* 21(1): 61–98.

Lenat, D. 1983b. Theory Formulation by Heuristic Search. The Nature of Heuristics II: Background and Examples. *Artificial Intelligence*, 21(1-2): 31–60.

Lindsay, R.; Buchanan, B.; Feigenbaum, E.; and Lederberg, J. 1980. *Applications of Artificial Intelligence for Organic Chemistry: The* DENDRAL *Project*. New York: McGraw-Hill.

Michalski, R.; Carbonell J.; and Mitchell, T. 1983. *Machine Learning: An Artificial Intelligence Approach*. San Mateo, Calif.: Morgan Kaufmann.

Sciore, E. 1991. An Extended Universal Instance Model, *Information Systems* 16(1).

Shenoy, S., and Ozsoyoglu, M. 1987. A System for Semantic Query Optimization. In Proceedings of the 1987 ACM-SIGMOD International Conference on the Management of Data, 181–195. New York: Association for Computing Machinery.

Siegel, M. B. 1988a. Automatic Rule Derivation for Semantic Query Optimization. In Proceedings of the Second International Conference on Expert Database Systems, 371–385. Washington, D.C.: George Mason Foundation.

Siegel, M. B. 1988b. Automatic Rule Derivation for Semantic Query Optimization. Ph.D. diss., Boston Univ.

Waterman, D. 1970. Generalization Learning Techniques for Automating the Learning of Heuristics. *Artificial Intelligence*, 1: 27–120.

Xu, D. 1983. Search Control in Semantic Query Optimization, Technical Report, TR83-09, Dept. of Computer Science, Univ. of Massachusetts.

VI INTEGRATED AND MULTI-PARADIGM SYSTEMS

25 Unsupervised Discovery in an Operational Control Setting

Barry G. Silverman, Michael R. Hieb, and Toufic M. Mezher
George Washington University

Abstract

An approach is proposed to the problem of discovering knowledge bases, in the absence of experts or human trainers, for operational control domains where large-scale simulators exist. That is, rather than having access to human trainers or a real device, the discovery system has access to a software simulator of a real device or situation. This approach attempts to integrate and extend several known learning algorithms (the bucket brigade and Eurisko) to exploit their proven capabilities. Two initial investigations and preliminary findings are presented and discussed along with the rudiments of a theory of parameters.

25.1 Introduction

The purpose of this chapter is to describe a computational model of discovery that is applicable to symbolic, rather than neural or genetic, learning, including instructionless learning of knowledge base rules, rule discovery by perturbing a real-time process, and conceptual clustering and generalizing at the symbolic level

The general approach to rule discovery from unsupervised observation is not new; for example, see Buchanan and Feigenbaum (1978); Langley, Bradshaw, and Simon (1981); or Lenat (1983). This approach is not often repeated, however (Buchanan et al. 1988), and much is still unknown about the strengths, weaknesses, limiting conditions, and techniques of symbolic learning in the absence of human trainers. For these reasons alone, it is worth further researching computational models in the discovery field.

Our discovery process applies to operational control processes. There are a large number of process domains for which an environment simulator exists that is accurate, detailed, and of large scale. Examples include system testing and human training simulators used in life- or cost-critical situations found, for example, in the military, the aerospace industry, the airline industry, and power plant control. Such simulators are painstakingly crafted by experts and hold an often unparalleled wealth of expertise on the subject matter, particularly so if the original experts have dispersed or are otherwise too busy to act as interview subjects for knowledge engineering activities. The documentation of these simulators rarely captures the depth or the dynamics of the expert know-how built into the simulator itself. Human study of more than a million lines of partially documented simulator code is far from fruitful if faster techniques for extracting its knowledge exist. This avenue is the more focused and pragmatic, although longer-term, purpose of the research documented here.

A general model of discovery applicable to the problems described is introduced and elaborated in Discovery System Overview. Details are explored in Investigations using a set of examples and empirical investigations. Convergence strategies and properties are discussed in the next section. A discovery system architecture is discussed in Architecture of a Discovery System, and Discussion, Origins, and Contributions is a discussion of the research that has been conducted in this field.

25.2 Discovery System Overview

The goal of the system described here is the unsupervised learning of a rule base by having a Learner observe how well a Performer controls the Environment (simulator) and by exploring and experimenting with the Environment. In exploration, the Learner perturbs the Environment by having the Performer enact a control action (that is, alter a control variable setting) and then observes the results to obtain environmental feedback. In experimentation, the Learner makes a formal prediction about the proper setting that a set of control variables should assume. In exploration the Learner might be interested in discovering what happens to a simulated battery and related parameters of performance when its heating pad is set to 100°C, but in experimentation, the Learner would be more interested in testing a hypothesized rule base about how best to set the heating pad's thermostat. In either exploration or experimentation, a critic exists that notices the result of making a control action and that assigns blame and rewards accordingly.

In particular, this system is a model of theory formation by inductive elimination that proceeds according to the following steps (we focus here primarily on how the Learner works): (1) given starting knowledge, conduct explorations (collect parameter data); (2) notice patterns (screen the data for abnormalities and select parameters of interest); (3) if possible, generate and experiment with theories (create rule sets and test them); (4) criticize and evaluate results (assign credit); (5) repeat from 1 exhaustively; and (6) refine and improve the process.

Each of these six steps is discussed in detail in the sections that follow. The input to this algorithm is a problem or abnormal situation. The output is a set of symbolic rules. In the following, added attention is paid to exploring, hypothesizing, experimenting, criticizing, and refining.

Conduct explorations: As already mentioned, this step involves collecting parameter data in the Environment by altering one of the Performer's control parameters and waiting until it fires the appropriate rules, and the Environment reacts to this control parameter setting. For these purposes, the Learner must have some starting knowledge, including (1) a list of control parameters available to be perturbed, (2) parameter-type information (for example, continuous, discrete, or nonnumeric valued), (3) starting metarules for incrementing or randomly varying control parameters (in step 6, these metarules are evaluated and, if necessary, adapted) and (4) the control actions available. Although these assumptions are restricting in terms of the power of the algorithm, few discovery systems have ever worked with less starting knowledge (Lenat 1983). Other starting conditions include the Performer being able to detect what has happened in the Environment and then to affect the Environment. The Learner must also have a well-structured set of rules about the domain and threshold values for critical control parameters, which are needed to initialize, start, and operate the simulator under steady-state conditions. This information is usually readily available from the simulator design specifications, process control diagrams, and similar documents and is comparable to what other symbolic discovery systems invariably begin with. The output of step 1 is a set of data that have been screened for abnormalities (for example, high or low parameter readings) plus the past history of these parameters.

Notice patterns: Humans can recognize and understand the new only in terms of what they already know. In step 2, pattern recognizing is left to agents that fire demons and metarules that assess which values of the control parameter subset are relevant for hypothesizing given the current parameters' values and their history. Either induction- or model-based knowledge can be used to narrow the search space. Where several hundred control parameter candidates exist, the accuracy of this step becomes critical. The output of step 2 is a list of parameters to explore.

Generate and experiment: Control action rule creation is derived from the existing parameter data and the list of parameters from step 2. The second phase of this step involves experimentation, giving generated rules to the Performer and observing how well they control the Environment.

Criticize: In broad terms, the purpose of this step is to analyze the Simulator results beyond what the initial screening indicates and attempt to ascribe fault or success to individual rules and rule terms. As such, this step is an important adjunct to the planning in steps 2 and 3. In specific terms, the criticize step is intended to mitigate several convergence and suboptimal obstacles encountered in the algorithm.

Repetition: Simulators often represent large search spaces, particularly if several hundred control parameters exist that, in turn, can range over thousands of value levels. Further, the effects of setting a control variable aren't often noticeable until significant amounts of time have passed, so that variables can fully interact, and process dynamics can complete themselves. The repetition cycle lag time must be tuned to a duration that accounts for such effects.

Refine the process: Often, the functionality of the preceding steps will carry the discovery process to a given point (for example, suboptimum) and then fail to move past this point. Much of the research has been and continues to be interrupting the first five steps, finding where the process fails, fixing the errant functionality or adding new functionality, and then letting the first five steps resume again. Much of the ensuing sections captures the fixes that have been made to date.

25.3 Investigations

To force the investigations to a higher degree of realism, an actual domain is used. This domain concerns real-time battery operation, diagnosis, and repair for an electrical power subsystem (EPS) of the space telescope orbital satellite. Specifically, the goal of the Performer component of the discovery system is to act as a ground station that monitors telemetry from sensors in the solar-powered EPS for anomalous behavior, isolates the causes of the anomalies, and attempts fixes by forming and linking commands in spacecraft language. The full EPS would take about 2000 rules to command and control. Little would be gained by having the discovery system work with the entire EPS except to cause the investigations to take much longer to run. Hence, a subset of EPS components is simulated, including three networks; several switches; two solar panels; one bus; a number of sensors, fuses, and users; and a battery. The reduced Simulator requires only about 200 rules be discovered for the Performer agent to command and control it. However, to properly test the discovery system, a few EPS performance and anomaly situations have been added to the Simulator that are not overly faithful to the actual EPS components but that help illustrate convergence difficulties that research must overcome.

25.3.1 Investigation 1—Asymptotic Convergence

As a starting knowledge base, the Performer is given about 100 rules in 11 knowledge bases (organized as agents in four blackboard panels–one each for detection, isolation, repair, and command packet formation). These 100 rules are primarily able to notice whether EPS (hereafter called the Environment) is staying within acceptable performance thresholds for battery voltage, battery condition, and cabin and battery temperature. These rules can also perform low-level repairs, involving opening and shutting switches to shift networks if they have managed to isolate in which network or component the anomaly might be. The Performer cannot repair some anomalous conditions and is unaware of control parameter settings that would have avoided the anomalies to begin with. A Screener agent, however, will screen the data to determine abnormal parameter values.

A Selector agent, in turn, collects parameter data packets and the Screener's results and in conjunction with the Performer's prior actions recommends which parameters should be utilized to form new rules from the global control parameter list. (For example, amperage-related problems might be blamed on the component fault, user drawdown, or, possibly, temperature-related control parameters but would not be attributed to gate control parameters and their current settings.) In the current investigation, either model-based knowledge is used in simple lookup tables that give the relationships between parameters, or an inductive-classification system such as ID3 is used. Although this step could be ignored in the current investigations, such a feature is particularly vital for the full-scale space telescope problem, which involves over 400 control parameters.

A Proposer agent fires metarules that hypothesize new control actions (parameter value settings) for the Performer to experiment with. As a software detail, the Learner components (the Selector and Proposer agents) use separate blackboards and are on a separate machine from either the Simulator or the Performer (which also occupy one machine each) to enhance both parallel processing and knowledge insulation. Discovery transpires while the spacecraft is still orbiting, and the Performer must still perform its duties to the best of its ability.

To illustrate, imagine that the average battery voltage is not being maintained at the goal of 34 volts (V). Instead, voltage fluctuates in harmony with cabin temperature, gradually dropping below 34 V whenever the spacecraft orbits behind earth's shadow and gradually increasing to 34 V after it reenters the sunlight. A trend line would show average voltage maintained at near 34 V. Try as it might, the Performer cannot mitigate this oscillating behavior (it has no thermostat control rules), and it detects conditions when the battery voltage drops below 34 V as abnormal. The Selector attributes blame to temperature-related control parameters (through induction over the past sets of parameter values), and then the Proposer agent recommends that the Performer use the thermostat control parameter starting at the zero setting. After each cycle that fails, it increments the thermostat value until successive cycles lead to the voltage achieving and maintaining its goal level.

Each complete discovery system cycle consists of an abnormal situation detected, parameter(s) recommended, new rules formed and sent to the Performer, commands sent to spacecraft, the spacecraft completing one full orbit with new commands, telemetry sent back to the ground station, and evaluation of the telemetry (to determine the result of the control action). As seen from figure 25.1, the discovery system eventually invents the correct rule set that causes the Environment to remain within the desired limits. This invention occurs monotonically and slowly converges on the asymptote (thermostat setting = 11°C). Unfortunately, not all inventions can be so neatly converged on.

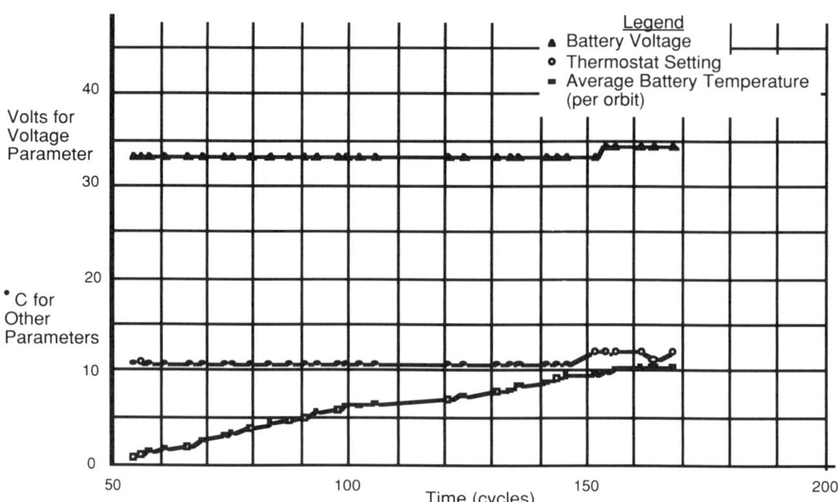

Figure 25.1
Actual Results from Running the Discovery System (convergence on a 34-V parameter goal by incrementing the thermostat from 0° to 11°C).

25.3.2 Investigation 2—Theory of Parameters, Ranges, and Thresholds

The rate and strategy of convergence is highly dependent on the metarules the Learner chooses to fire as well as on the quality of these rules. The metarule for investigation 1 simply increased the recommended parameter by a small delta on each cycle, as follows:

IF: (1) Recommended Parameter Threshold = Not Acceptable, AND
(2) Recommended Parameter = Numeric (Continuous Positive), AND
(3) Convergence Strategy = Increment, AND
(4) Lower Bound = Origin, AND
(5) Increase Rate = Slowly

THEN: Recommended.Parameter Threshold (t) = A + Recommended.Parameter Threshold (t - 1).

If A is set to .25 percent of range, and the range of the ordinate is 0° to 100°C, the threshold is eventually reached.

This metarule presumes a naive theory of parameters, ranges, and thresholds. First, it converges too slowly (several hours of clock time) given the large number of parameters potentially requiring discovery system services. One is tempted to alter the increase rate. For example, if A = 5°C on each time step, the asymptote (11 deg) is almost reached in two time steps but is then exceeded in the third. Two interesting problems arise at this juncture. First, the goal has been overshot, but the Screener will only continue to detect the outcome as abnormal. There is no directional information, and because the cases were abnormal beneath the goal (threshold) and because they are still abnormal, there is no way to assign blame to the increase rate. A possible solution is to give the Screener a more detailed knowledge of what is abnormal that would indicate elements such as NEGATIVE-TOO-LOW or NEGATIVE-TOO-HIGH. This additional knowledge would allow the Learner to realize it needs to alter the increase rate and direction (new term to be added to metarules) in a fashion to dampen oscillations until convergence is achieved.

There are a number of drawbacks to this approach, the most obvious of which is that if the Performer knew what was too high versus too low, the problem would already be solved. However, the Performer will not generally know this information and cannot properly utilize complicated procedures to detect abnormalities.

25.3.3 Apparatus for Storing and Retrieving Theories

Several other issues immediately arise as well (such as the nature of the parameter, its range and direction, types of control action, and selection of threshold settings) indicating that the discovery system needs a more robust understanding of general parameter theory. With a better understanding, the discovery system, hopefully, can make more intelligent guesses about what subsets of parameter space to search and at what speed. The easiest way to introduce the reader to a more robust theory is to show a more robust form of a metarule and to discuss the rationale for each of its terms. An improved metarule is

IF: (1) Recommended Parameter Threshold = Not Acceptable, AND
(2) Recommended Parameter = Type (T), AND
(3) Lower Bound = Type (U), AND
(4) Upper Bound = Type (V), AND
(5) Parameter Type = Type (W), AND
(6) Threshold Type = Type (X), AND
(7) Convergence Strategy = Type (Y), AND
(8) Convergence Rate = Type (Z)

THEN: Recommended Parameter Threshold (t)
A + Recommended Parameter Threshold (t - 1).

The terms of the metarule have been variablized and can be bound to the lists of values discussed in figure 25.2. For a given parameter on the recommended parameter list, much of the information the metarule needs can be obtained from the parameter object, which has slots with the information in figure 25.2 (legal values are in parentheses):

```
[Parameter Name:
Parameter Type:  (Numeric Nonnumeric)
Number Type:  (Real Real-Positive
                    Real-Negative   Integer
                 Integer-Positive   Integer-Negative)
Symbol Type:  (Atom    List    One-of-List
                   Range-of-List    Some-of-List)
Upper Bound:  ( (Number  #)  (Number  #)  ...)
Lower Bound:  ( (Number  #)  (Number  #)  ...)
Related Parameters:  (Candidate Parameter Names)
Related History:  ( (Name Tried   Values Tried  #)
                   (Name Tried   Values Tried  #)  ...)
Threshold Type:  (Single Value   Step Function)
Threshold:  ( (Number Predicate  #)
              (Number Predicate  #)  ...)].
```

Figure 25.2
Lists of Values.

Many of these slots are self-explanatory. As mentioned earlier, the parameter name is a given, so, too, is the parameter type and the number or symbol type. Although one could add code to discover these slots for new parameters, this ability was felt to be beyond the realm of interest because of the early stages of this research. Even with this starting knowledge, there are still a half dozen (or more) slots of unknowns, a significant search space.

Recall the discovery steps delineated in the discussion of investigation: In step 1, the abnormalities are detected, and in step 2 the history trends in the slots of the recommended parameter objects are studied, and the parameters for the Proposer to use with each problem detected are recommended. In step 3, the metarules are created, the metarules are applied to isolate threshold value estimates, and the parameter object slots are updated by adding the relevant aspects of the previous items. For example, the Proposer would provide the Performer with the current guess on upper and lower bounds, parameters being tried, and threshold assumptions. The # symbol is a placeholder that is later substituted by a symbol indicating whether it is the final (that is, presumed correct) or interim value, as determined by the Screener's evaluation and the Critic's blame (credit) assignment (see the next section).

The description of the apparatus for the discovery system to form theories of environmental parameters is almost complete. Initially, it was hoped that in step 3 the estimates of unknown values could be selected, as was done in earlier discovery systems (for example, Eurisko, genetic algorithms, or self-organizing neural nets), that is, with the aid of a random number generator. The results reveal that even for a small search space of 100 integers, the convergence time is slow. If the parameters' upper and lower bounds, plus the space of all the additional related parameters, also had to be explored, the convergence time would become prohibitive. This does not begin to approximate the convergence obstacles of the full 400+ parameter set. One way to reduce search time would be to redouble efforts to acquire knowledge from human experts. Another way, which is focused on here, is to explore alternative convergence strategies—the remaining metarule terms yet to be discussed.

25.4 Convergence Strategies and Properties

The convergence problem is not just a question of speedup but a way to elevate the discovery system past local optima so that it will also delete irrelevant rule terms (generalizing further than it already does), regroup the parameters and their values (another aspect of generalizing), notice and manage situational shifts (a form of specializing for appropriate situations), work incrementally, and reason about situations it has seen before (analogical reasoning). In addition to speedup, generalization, specialization, incrementalism, and analogical properties, the discovery system should offer hope of avoiding suboptimalities and converging to near-optimal conditions in relatively short order. The research to isolate a convergence strategy with these properties is still in its beginning stages, and this section presents preliminary ideas and designs currently being pursued.

25.4.1 Extensions to a Classical Credit-Assignment Algorithm

One way to achieve the desired properties is to adopt one (or more) known algorithm(s) and extend it (them) to fit the stated purposes. This approach should permit the performance advantages of the previously demonstrated algorithm without, hopefully, overly degenerating its behavior because of the modifications and extensions. The first algorithm to be so used is the bucket brigade algorithm (BBA). The implementation pursued closely follows Holland (1985).

BBA is a technique normally used for assigning credit to a Performer's rules that win a competition or that set the stage for a winner as well as for assigning punishment or reward to the winning rule based on the rule's impact on the Environment. What is called for by the discovery system, however, differs in several respects, as is summarized in the next paragraph and is elaborated on in the following sections:

First, two separate competitions are called for, one in the conventional sense within the Performer's rule base and a separate one between the metarules of the Proposer. Second, the strength payments normally transmitted from the winning rule to its stage setter must also be passed to its metarule (that is, its creator), as must any feedback payments or losses from the Environment. In this fashion, the metarules can detect when their offspring have been successful. Third, BBA is normally applied in smaller applications than those suggested here; in which case, domain knowledge of goal states is considered unnecessary to affect the convergence (in fact, such knowledge is normally eschewed as compromising the generality of BBA). In domains with several hundred parameters, each posing dozens of unknown items requiring discovery services, a compromise to BBA's elegance seemed warranted, and thus, goal proximity knowledge is permitted (and exploited) where readily available. This knowledge is necessary to prune the search space as well as to send evidence to guide the selection of metarule operations.

25.4.2 Bookkeeping during Rule-Strength Competitions

The easiest way to clarify these departures, alterations, and extensions is to discuss their impact on the metarules. To begin with, it should be noted that there are three types of environmental outcomes in abnormal situations:

First, a failure outcome (failure) originates when the Environment has to simulate a shutdown. Although this criterion is the sole one normally used in smaller domains by BBAs, it leads to costly results and can be avoided through judicious study of the other two outcomes. If a simulated failure state is reached in the domain, it can have serious repercussions. In most simulator domains, one must avoid simulator failures and crashes (for example, having an airplane crash or a spacecraft go into its safe mode) by a careful study of potential problems.

Second, a problem outcome (problem) is used when the Performer decides its rule base is insufficient to permit it to solve a condition likely to lead to a failure. Conversely, the Problem outcome is a sign that the Performer was missing rules that would allow it to chain to a repair goal. When the Problem result is issued, it leads to the creation of a Problem parameter object, a slot that includes the parameter name, the goal that cannot be reached (for example, 34 V in the earlier example), and the situation that includes the values of parameters thought relevant to the goal (as identified by Selector).

Third, the trend outcome (better, worse, same) is issued by an adjunct to the Performer called the Trend Analyst. The Trend Analyst is a relatively simple agent that plots history traces of all parameters; uses regression to extrapolate their future progress; and notices when cautionary thresholds of known goals are about to be exceeded, so it can alert the Performer to initiate repairs before thresholds are seriously exceeded. This generic type of strip-chart recording agent (as generic as the parameter concepts discussed here) knows nothing about the domain beyond what is conveyed in parameter object slot values.

The bookkeeping of the two competitions is kept as simple as possible, and as with the classical BBA algorithm, the accounting can be achieved in a single update step on each cycle. During this step, classical BBA would simply pass environmental feedback (credit quantity with plus or minus sign corresponding to credit or punishment) to the most recently fired rule, which, in turn, would pay off its stage-setter rule. The only changes required during this one bookkeeping step for the approach described here are as follows: First, because in most cases, it is undesirable to wait for the Environment to encounter a (harshly) negative situation, the feedback quantity and sign are computed by the Trend Analyst agent instead. Thus, the credit assignment step waits for the Trend Analyst to determine whether the goal has been achieved. This must not, of course, preclude the Environment from signaling a failure condition. It simply adds more information to the signals that emanate from the Environment. Second, the goal proximity information is also easily added to the credit-assignment computations. Recall that goals only exist for parameters that are fully defined (that is, all slots defined a priori or all slots already filled out and confirmed by earlier discovery services) and that discovery experiments are conducted on control parameters that by definition are yet to be fully defined. Goal proximity information is computed as

$$\text{Trend} = \text{B} * \frac{[\text{P}_\text{k}\,(\text{goal}) - \text{P}_\text{k}\,(\text{actual})]}{\text{UB}_\text{k} - \text{LB}_\text{k}}$$

where

P_k(Goal)	=	Goal Parameter value.
P_k(Actual)	=	Actual Parameter value.
UB_k	=	Upper-bound slot value of known parameter.
LB_k	=	Lower-bound slot value of known parameter.
B	=	A constant that scales the bracketed ratio to a numeric level consistent with the other credit equation terms (such as the size of environmental feedback).

This trend equation captures directional and quantitative effects of the experimental parameter on the known parameter's value. IF: P_k (actual) $>$ P_k (goal), Then Trend $<$ 0, but IF: P_k (actual) $<$ P_k (goal), Then Trend $>$ 0. This term thus provides directional indications. Because Trend is not a straight delta but is instead normalized over the P_k ordinate range (upper and lower bounds), it provides fractional or percentile indications of how far off the experimental parameters are. By comparing Trend(t) versus Trend(t –

1) with the changes made in the experimental parameters, the discovery system can better infer what changes to the metarule might be warranted. The metarule thus receives both the Trend(t) value, as well as a credit number, as the feedback from the fired Performer rule.

In short, the metarule's strength is modulated by both (1) a classical BBA style feedback (and stage-setter payoff) often computed by the Trend Analyst rather than from Environment's failure outcome and (2) a new trend term that gets added to the metarule's strength through the same bookkeeping step. As a result, a metarule that has been converging on a goal gains strength, and once it causes (the experimental parameter to cause) the Environment to pass the goal (from either direction), the metarule begins to lose strength.

As a metarule loses strength, Proposer consults the metarule's Trend(t) values for sign changes and first attempts to alter the increase rate and increase direction values. If these alterations fail, it tries other slots of the experimental parameter. With each successive trial that fails, this metarule loses more strength from its bid, its stage-setter payoffs, and its potentially decreasing or negative environmental (that is, the Trend Analyst) payoff.

25.4.3 Focus of Attention in Strategy Planning

Besides BBA, the Proposer has two other convergence strategies that are vying for attention with respect to a given situation. If the current metarule and its variants are labeled the "current line of investigation," the two alternative strategies available are the "similar lines of investigations" and "new lines of investigation." The similar lines of investigation strategy attempts to analogize, specialize, or generalize off the current line of investigation, and the new lines strategy is drawn by the randomizer, suggesting other parameters and slot values to begin experimenting on.

These three convergence strategies correspond to a focus-of-attention problem. That is, the Learner needs to decide whether it is exploring or experimenting with the correct set of recommended parameters and within this set whether it is pursuing the best guesses at the given parameter object slot values (bounds, related parameters, thresholds, and so on). Rather than using exhaustive search or purely random guesses, the credit strengths passed back from the Performer build the strength of hypotheses under each of the three strategies up or down. When the competition is held, the metarules or metastrategies that make the highest bids will be chosen, which, in turn, gives the Proposer its focus of attention, the metarule instantiations and bindings to use, and the parameter list and values for it to use after the instantiations and bindings are fixed.

25.4.4 Specialization, Generalization, and Analogy

It was previously mentioned that a number of properties of the convergence strategy could elevate the discovery system above the problems of irrelevant, overly general, or inappropriate rule tree elements. These properties were called generalization, specialization, and analogy and were referred to under the strategy for pursuing similar lines of investigation. That is, rather than randomizing and starting over, an alternative focus might be to explore regions in proximity to the current metarule bindings. As an example, consider the following:

Specialization: Specialization begins with the current line of investigation and tries to add more specific terms, conditions, or values to include in a metarule. For example, rather than just pursuing a different increase rate and direction with respect to a single abscissa, specialization might add a second and third parameter type to be simultaneously searched within the construct of the current metarule. A new metarule is formed that is a child of the current line of investigation. A tree of such children—and of their children's children, and so on—is likely to be created. Each node of the tree obtains some of the original parent's rule strength and, thereby, is able to enter the bidding competition and, possibly (eventually), win a chance to fire. Specialization is an important strategy that is pursued whenever search of a given parameter range has proved fruitless.

Generalization: Several forms of generalization have already been mentioned: (1) generalizing a given rule tree (or a rule) by deleting terms from it; (2) regrouping parameters or their values into a combined, more general parameter; and (3) generalizing (as opposed to specializing) the recommended parameter list by moving higher up the classification hierarchy. Here, only the second and third definitions are of interest, and their occurrence is largely the reverse of specialization, that is, parents are added to a given metarule's lineage tree that can enter the competition. Generalization normally occurs when trying to back off a parameter's values that discovery services previously indicated were stable. For example, after the proper thermostat setting was discovered, suppose the heating pad began to steadily deteriorate, in the sense that it would respond to a given thermostat setting by a gradually decreasing amount. Discovery without generalization would eventually begin to slowly increase the thermostat threshold to an offset corresponding to the errant heating pad behavior. Generalization, however, could lead the discovery system to generalize the thermostat parameter threshold by allowing it to abstract from its current type of single value back to a list of legal types, and then specialization could pick a new type, such as "slowly decreasing," which, in turn, would keep the metarule active and speed future (re)discoveries.

Analogy: Specialization and generalization are relatively clever heuristics for guiding search when the current line of investigation is stuck as opposed to resorting to the

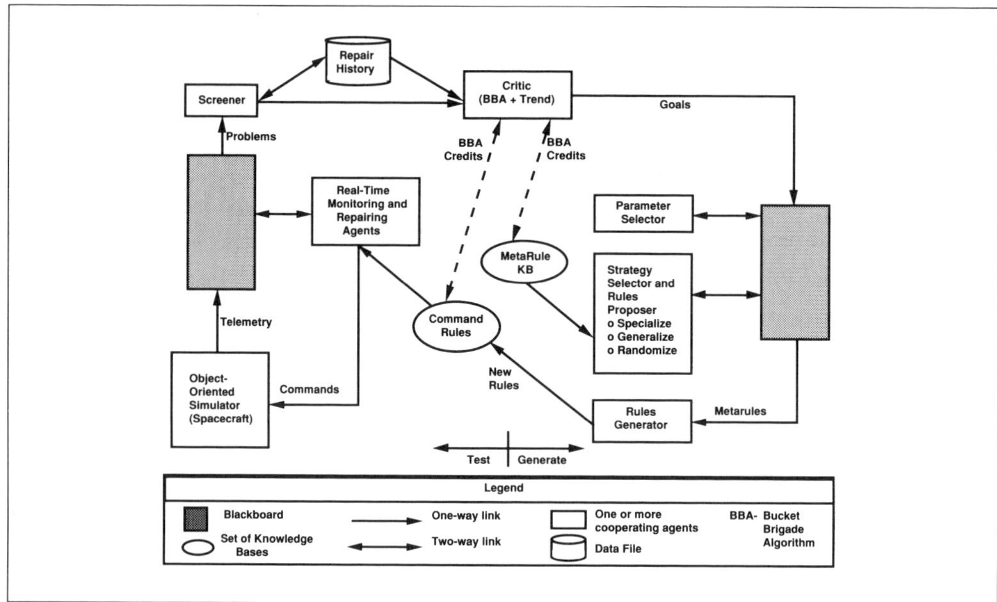

Figure 25.3
Diagram of Discovery System.

random search-and-selection strategy. Analogy, however, is an attempt to avoid search either altogether if the analogy is perfect or as much as possible when it is imperfect (although the analogies are applicable in part). For the sake of simplicity, it is assumed that only exact match analogs (that is, identities) can be reused to avoid search effort. Analogy will be useful for any periodic, harmonically oscillating, or Markovian chaining types of situations.

25.5 Architecture of a Discovery System

Figure 25.3 is a depiction of the proposed architecture for the discovery system, which is being built according to the following steps. This operational system description draws from the elements and strategies of the preceding sections.

First, given starting knowledge, attempt to operate the simulator and control anomalous situations through a series of cooperation agents that specialize in monitoring, repairing anomalies, analyzing trends, and assembling spacecraft simulator commands. These agents know the ultimate goals to achieve to keep the simulator in a stable condition but are missing rules to reach these goals when anomalies arise in the simulator's behavior. If and when such anomalies arise, a flag is set, and a goal is sent to the Critic. As a result, this side of the system serves as a test capability of any rules generated by the right-hand side. The test side produces histories of all anomalies to be used by the generate side for future reference when generating new rules. It also produces a parameter problem statement (goal that can't be reached equals parameter theory inadequacy).

Second, the Critic criticizes and evaluates the results. The Critic evaluates the parameter data, updates the strengths of the most recently fired parameter problem-solving rules and their stage setters through BBA, looks up the metarules that generated the recently fired rules and adjusts their strengths, and places a problem (goal) on the blackboard.

Third, the Parameter Selector notices patterns (selecting parameters and values of interest). The Parameter Selector sets subgoals to reduce the search space from the several hundred parameter sets of most simulators to a few parameters known to be relevant to the current problem parameter. The Parameter Selector stores relevancy trees as a priori knowledge but does not know precise relationships. Finding these relationships is the purpose of the system, constituting *theory formation* (forming a theory of the parameters of the simulator), which is the job of the Strategy Selector and Rules Proposer.

Fourth, a competition among differing metastrategies that are vying to form new theories is conducted by the Strategy Selector and Rules Proposer, which pursues three parallel lines of investigation: same line as already pursued (for example, just increase the current parameter's threshold); similar lines of investigation, including analogizing, generalizing, or specializing the rule-generation template; and new lines of investigation, such as random jumps through the subgoal search space. The output of this blackboard is a list of metarules from which rules will be formed.

Fifth, new rules are generated that instantiate the current theory about the simulator's parameters.

Sixth, continue from step 1 until the simulator anomaly is resolved, and normal (stable) operation is resumed.

25.6 Discussion, Origins, and Contributions

This chapter described two investigations into an existing discovery system that highlighted several weaknesses that need correcting. A third investigation has been initiated, offering further design features for credit assignment, specialization, generalization, analogy, incrementalism, and speedup. These features are currently being coded in an effort to overcome the rule base optimization and convergence obstacles of the instructionless learning system. In addition, the rudiments of a theory of parameters and their ranges and thresholds have been proposed to permit the discovery system to form, test, and confirm (or disconfirm) more robust parameter theories under its own experimentation powers.

The long-term goal of this research is to automate the acquisition of knowledge bases suitable for real-world application from simulators or, at least, to shorten the acquisition time and effort of such systems. This goal is clearly a long way off and, as we indicate, methodological issues are still the basic research concern. In this regard, an interesting question is, How do the methods presented here compare to others found in the literature?

In terms of supervised learning methods, several classical ones fit symbolic rules to training cases (for example, Michalski's [1977] AQ, Mitchell's [1983] Lex, or Langley's [1981] Amber). Żytkow's (1987) Fahrenheit system designs its own experiments to collect data in static, rather than dynamic, environments. As a class of unsupervised learning methods, the discovery system presented here bears both similarities to, and differences from, Eurisko's theory of accretion (Lenat 1983).

The similarities to Eurisko are as follows: (1) the steps of the inductive-elimination algorithm closely parallel those of Lenat's theory of accretion, (2) both systems attempt to be general-purpose (cross-domain) discovery systems, and (3) both work in an unsupervised mode. Eurisko has several major strengths not evident in this work, including the following: (1) Eurisko does not need the parameter list a priori, as does our discovery system, because it has large chunks of code that infer, discover, and attempt to name new parameters, attributes, and so on (humans are asked by Eurisko to approve or modify the machine-generated names) and (2) the refinement step (step 6 in Discovery System Overview) is automated to a large extent in Eurisko, and the discovery process itself is adaptive (although requiring close human supervision) as opposed to manually refined, as pursued to date in this work. These and other aspects of Eurisko establish it as the highest degree of machine discovery system yet achieved. However, the approach pursued here includes several off-the-shelf techniques (BBA, ID3 for induction, and case-based reasoning) that have more fully known and studied behavior and convergence properties than Eurisko and that are intended to avoid some of the nonreproducibility issues that seem to surround less formal methods (for example, Ritchie and Hanna [1984] and Walker [1987]).

In addition, Eurisko's generate rule step is fully random, but its search space pruning and critic steps are entirely based on specific heuristics that might be somewhat generic but tend to be domain oriented. BBA and inductive classification, however, are equivalent to generic entropy minimization and energy maximization schemes, respectively, which guarantee near optimality in many situations. BBA has weaknesses, many of which have already been alluded to; however, among its strengths are its clarity, reproducibility, and validity for certain known problem sets. As a final note, the proposed system offers a rudimentary theory of parameters that is generic to simulator-oriented domains, whereas

Eurisko's starting Knowledge base was largely altered from domain to domain (although its metarules weren't).

A number of other systems fall into this category of theory formation and plan adaptation by noticing and reacting to minimize failures in predicted or hypothesized theories. A few examples include but are not limited to case-based reasoning by Kolodner, Simpson, and Sycara-Cyranski (1985); analogical reasoning by Carbonell (1983); and view application by Shrager (1987). Each of these systems relies on abstraction of the model or problematic behavior of the system, searching a classification hierarchy (or associative memory) for similar problems and transferring in the solutions to these problems as potential solution hypotheses suitably altered to the current context. This type of knowledge-rich problem solving is not included in the discovery system presented here (which relies more on brute force search of the problem space). In addition, with the abilities of abstraction, categorization, association, and analogy across nonidentical situations, we are moving in an important future research direction for discovery systems such as the one presented here.

Acknowledgments

The support of the National Aeronautics and Space Administration, GSFC code 522.3, of the work presented here is gratefully acknowledged, although the positions taken are those of the authors alone.

References

Buchanan, B. G., and Feigenbaum, E. A. 1978. Dendral and Meta-Dendral: Their Application Dimension. *Artificial Intelligence* 11: 5–24.

Buchanan, B. G.; Sullivan, J.; Cheng, T.-Z.; Clearwater, S. H. 1988. Simulated-Assisted Inductive Learning. In *Proceedings of the Seventh National Conference on Artificial Intelligence*, 552–557. Menlo Park, Calif.: American Association for Artificial Intelligence.

Carbonell, J. 1983. Derivational Analogy in Problem Solving and Knowledge Acquisition. In *Proceedings of the International Machine Learning Workshop*, 12–18. San Mateo, Calif.: Morgan Kaufmann Publishers.

Holland, J. 1985. Properties of the Bucket Brigade. In *Proceedings of the First International Conference on Genetic Algorithms and Their Applications*, 1–7. Hillsdale, N.J.: Lawrence Erlbaum.

Kolodner, J. L.; Simpson, R. L.; and Sycara-Cyranski, K. 1985. A Process Model of Case-Based Reasoning in Problem Solving. In *Proceedings of the Ninth International Joint Conference on Artificial Intelligence*, 284–290. Menlo Park, Calif.: International Joint Conferences on Artificial Intelligence.

Langley, P. 1981. Language Acquisition through Error Recovery, IP Working Paper, 432, Carnegie-Mellon Univ.

Langley, P.; Bradshaw, G. L.; and Simon, H. A. 1981. Bacon5: The Discovery of Conservation Laws. In *Proceedings of the Seventh International Joint Conference on Artificial Intelligence*, 121–126. Menlo Park, Calif.: International Joint Conferences on Artificial Intelligence.

Lenat, D. B. 1983. Theory Formation by Heuristic Search. *Artificial Intelligence* 21:31–59.

Michalski, R. S. 1977. A System of Programs for Computer-Aided Induction: A Summary. In *Proceedings of the Fifth International Joint Conference on Artificial Intelligence*, 319–320. Menlo Park, Calif.: International Joint Conferences on Artificial Intelligence.

Mitchell, T. M. 1983. Learning and Problem Solving. In *Proceedings of the Eighth International Joint Conference on Artificial Intelligence*, 1139–1151. Menlo Park, Calif.: International Joint Conferences on Artificial Intelligence.

Ritchie, G. D. and Hanna, F. K. 1984. AM: A Case Study in AI Methodology. *Artificial Intelligence*, 23: 249–268.

Shrager, J. 1987. Theory Change via View Application in Instructionless Learning. *Machine Learning* 2:246–276.

Walker, T. 1987. How Feasible Is Automated Discovery? *IEEE Expert* 69–82.

Żytkow, J. M. 1987. FAHRENHEIT Discovery System. In *Proceedings of the Fourth Workshop on Machine Learning*, 281–287. San Mateo, Calif.: Morgan Kaufman.

26 Mining for Knowledge in Databases: Goals and General Description of the INLEN System

Kenneth A. Kaufman, Ryszard S. Michalski, and Larry Kerschberg
George Mason University

Abstract

The INLEN system combines database, knowledge base, and machine learning techniques to provide a user with an integrated system of tools for conceptually analyzing data and searching for interesting relationships and regularities in them. Machine learning techniques are used for tasks such as developing general rules from facts, determining differences between groups of facts, creating conceptual classifications of data, selecting the most relevant attributes, determining the most representative examples, and discovering equations governing numeric variables. The equations discovered are accompanied by conditions under which they apply. These techniques are implemented as inference operators that a user can apply to a database or knowledge base to perform a given knowledge extraction function. Examples of three major inference operators are provided, one for learning general rules differentiating between groups of facts, one for creating conceptual classifications of facts, and one for discovering equations characterizing numeric and symbolic data.

26.1 Introduction

This chapter briefly describes the goals and general design of the INLEN system for conceptually analyzing databases and discovering regularities and patterns in them. The name INLEN derives from the terms inference and learning, which represent two major capabilities of the system. INLEN integrates a relational database, a knowledge base, and a number of machine learning and inference capabilities. The latter two enable the system to perform tasks such as creating conceptual descriptions of facts in the database, inventing classifications of data, discovering rules and unknown regularities, and formulating equations together with the conditions of their applicability. We present here a general system design and explain all the basic functions. Major operators, specifically those for determining rules from examples, creating classifications, and discovering equations, are illustrated with examples.

The motivating goal of the INLEN system is to integrate three basic technologies—databases, expert systems, and machine learning and inference—to provide a user with a powerful tool for manipulating both data and knowledge and extracting new or better knowledge from these data and knowledge. INLEN evolved from the QUIN system (query and inference), a combined database management and data analysis environment (Michalski, Baskin, and Spackman 1982; Michalski and Baskin 1983; Spackman 1983). QUIN was designed both as a stand-alone system and as a subsystem of Advise, a large-scale inference system for designing expert systems (Michalski and Baskin 1983; Michalski, Mozetic, et al. 1987; Baskin and Michalski 1989). In the last few years, new tools have been developed, in particular, more advanced inductive-learning systems, for example, AQ15 (Michalski et al. 1986) and ABACUS-2 (Greene 1988), and expert database systems (Kerschberg 1986, 1987, 1988). These systems have influenced the development of INLEN. INLEN also draws on the experiences with Agassistant, a shell for developing agricultural expert systems (Katz, Fermanian, and Michalski 1986), and Aurora, a general-purpose PC-based expert system shell with learning and discovery capabilities designed by Michalski and Katz (International Intelligent Systems 1988).

However, INLEN is more than just a tool. Its modular architecture enables it to incorporate many discovery tools. INLEN can be viewed as a toolbox, a methodology, or an environment for making all sorts of discoveries in databases. It is especially appropriate to apply INLEN to data systems that are constantly changing or growing; among the systems capabilities are the ability to detect changes over time and explore the ramifications of these changes.

26.2 INLEN System Design

As previously mentioned, INLEN combines database, expert system, and machine learning capabilities to create an environment for analyzing and extracting useful knowledge from a data or knowledge base. It includes ideas from the recently developed expert database technology to combine the storage and access abilities of a database system with the ability to derive well-founded conclusions from a knowledge-based system (Kerschberg 1986, 1987, 1988). INLEN integrates several advanced machine learning capabilities that until now have only existed as separate experimental programs. Many learning systems are capable of but a small subset of what can be learned from factual data. By integrating a variety of these tools, a user will have access to a powerful and versatile system.

The general design of INLEN is shown in figure 26.1. The INLEN system consists of a relational database for storing known facts about a domain and a knowledge base for storing rules, constraints, hierarchies, decision trees, equations accompanied with preconditions, and enabling conditions for performing various actions on the database or knowledge base. The knowledge base not only can contain knowledge about the contents of the database but also metaknowledge for the dynamic upkeep of the knowledge base itself.

The purpose of integrating these capabilities is to provide a user with a set of advanced tools for searching for, and extracting useful knowledge from, a database; organizing this knowledge from different viewpoints; testing this knowledge on a set of facts; and facilitating its integration within the original knowledge base.

Information in the database consists of relational tables (RTs), and information in the knowledge base consists of units called knowledge segments (KS). A KS can be simple or compound. Simple KSs include rule sets, equations, networks, and hierarchies. Compound KSs consist of combinations of any of these elements or combinations of simple KSs and RTs. The latter form can be used, for example, to represent a clustering that consists of groups of objects (represented as an RT) and the associated descriptions of the groups (represented as rules). Another example of such a representation is a relational table with a set of constraints on, and relationships among, its attributes. These constraints and relationships are represented as rules. Compound KSs also consist of directory tables that specify the locations of their component parts in the knowledge base or, in the case of RT components, in the database.

A justification for such knowledge types is that they correspond to natural forms of representing human knowledge, especially technical knowledge. Also, by distinguishing between these different forms of knowledge and selecting appropriate data structures to represent them, we can achieve greater efficiency in storing and manipulating such structures. Meanwhile, the KS architecture allows for an object-oriented structure in which the user need not be overly concerned about the form taken by a piece of knowledge.

INLEN employs three sets of operators: *data management operators* (DMOs), *knowledge management operators* (KMOs), and *knowledge generation operators* (KGOs). DMOs are standard operators for accessing, retrieving, and manually altering the information in the database. Thus, they operate on RTs. KMOs perform analogous tasks on the knowledge base in situations in which manual input, access, or adjustments are required. The knowledge generation operators interact with both the database and the knowledge base. These operators evoke various situations in which manual input, access, and adjustments are required. KGOs take input from both the database and the knowledge base. These operators invoke various machine learning programs to perform tasks such as developing general rules from facts, determining differences between groups of facts, creating conceptual classifications of data, selecting the most relevant attributes, determining the most representative examples, and discovering equations governing numeric variables. The results of KGOs are stored as KSs. Examples of the performance of a few basic knowledge generation operators are given in An Illustration of Selected Knowledge Generation Operators: Cluster, Diff, and Diseq. A brief description of DMOs, KMOs, and KGOs follows.

26.2.1 Data Management Operators

DMOs form a standard set of relational database operations for the purpose of manipulating the system's collection of facts:

Create generates a new relational table. It takes an attribute list as an argument.

Append adds a new tuple (row) to a relational table.

Change alters some or all of the values in some or all of the tuples of a table.

Delete removes rows or columns from a table, as specified, respectively, by Select or Project operations. Alternatively, entire tables can be removed from the system.

Select retrieves a relational table from a database and returns the complete table or part of it. The part represents the subset of its rows that satisfy criteria specified in the arguments of the operator. Project reduces a table by removing columns. Columns that are kept correspond to attributes specified in the arguments of the operator.

Join creates a relational table combining the columns of two tables. The rows are the subset of the rows of the Cartesian product of the two tables whose attributes satisfy criteria provided by the user.

Union, performed on two tables with the same set of attributes, returns the set of tuples (rows) that appear in either of the two tables.

Intersect, performed on two tables with the same set of attributes, returns the set of tuples that appear in both of the input tables.

26.2.2 Knowledge Management Operators

KMOs are used to create, manipulate, and modify INLEN's knowledge base, thereby allowing the knowledge base to be handled in a manner analogous to handling a database. Knowledge can take the form of simple or compound KSs. Consequently, most of KMOs shown in figure 26.1 are generalized for any of these forms. Unless otherwise specified, they should be thought of as operating on any KS; that is, they can operate on rules, equations, hierarchies, and so on.

Diverse representations of knowledge can be culled from the same database and, therefore, will represent distinct viewpoints obtained using the knowledge generation operators. For example, a dynamic system whose behavior is governed by a set of differential equations could have its time series input-output behavior represented as a relation consisting of all measurable input-output variables. Each tuple would consist of the input-output variable value at some time. KGOs could be used to create knowledge viewpoints such as functional and multivalued dependencies from relational database theory, a set of decision rules, a causal and temporal semantic network, and so on. Each of these viewpoints is valid and should be managed by KMOs.

Expert database tools and techniques can be used to manage the evolution of the combined knowledge database by incorporating knowledge discovered in the database. The arrow in figure 26.1 linking the database and the knowledge base components represents such an interaction.

KMOs listed in the following are depicted as analogues of INLEN's data management operators. Without intensive testing of the system in different domains, one cannot tell how useful these operators are, but they represent our first approximation based on the analogy with DMOs. Further research might lead to the development of other operators and also other knowledge representations, including the likely use of a more object-oriented approach in which one data representation is replaced by an active link with the concept of a formula, a rule set, or some other representation.

Under the current design, these are KMOs and their functions:

Create is used to generate a new KS with a structure and set of attributes specified by the user. KS will be empty until knowledge is added using either an Append operator or one of the knowledge generation operators.

Append is used for the manual addition of new knowledge to KS.

Change is used for the manual alteration of part of one or more items in KS.

Delete is used to remove selected portions of KS from the knowledge base. Alternatively, an entire KS can be erased by giving no qualifying conditions to the operator.

Select is used to retrieve KS from the knowledge base (and from the database in the case of component RTs). Criteria can be provided to return only selected items (such as rules, subtrees, rows in tables, and so on) in this KS.

Project is used to return a subset of a compound KS that ignores entire components (for example, rule sets, decision trees, columns of tables) of KS. The items specified in the operator's arguments will be included.

Join is used to combine a pair of simple KSs or components of compound KSs. For example, a set of rules and a data table can be united into a compound KS, or two rule sets can be combined by finding conditions in the first rule set that are satisfied by decisions in the second rule set. Rules can then be expanded by replacing the matching conditions in the first rule set with the conditions leading to the corresponding decisions in the second rule set.

Union is applied to two or more KSs of the same type. It generates a list of the elements present at least once in any of the segments.

Intersect is applied to two or more KSs of the same type. It generates a list of the elements present at least once in each of the segments.

26.2.3 Knowledge Generation Operators

KGOs perform complex inferences (often approximating NP-complete tasks) on KSs to create new knowledge. It should be noted that KGOs also consist of primitives (such as

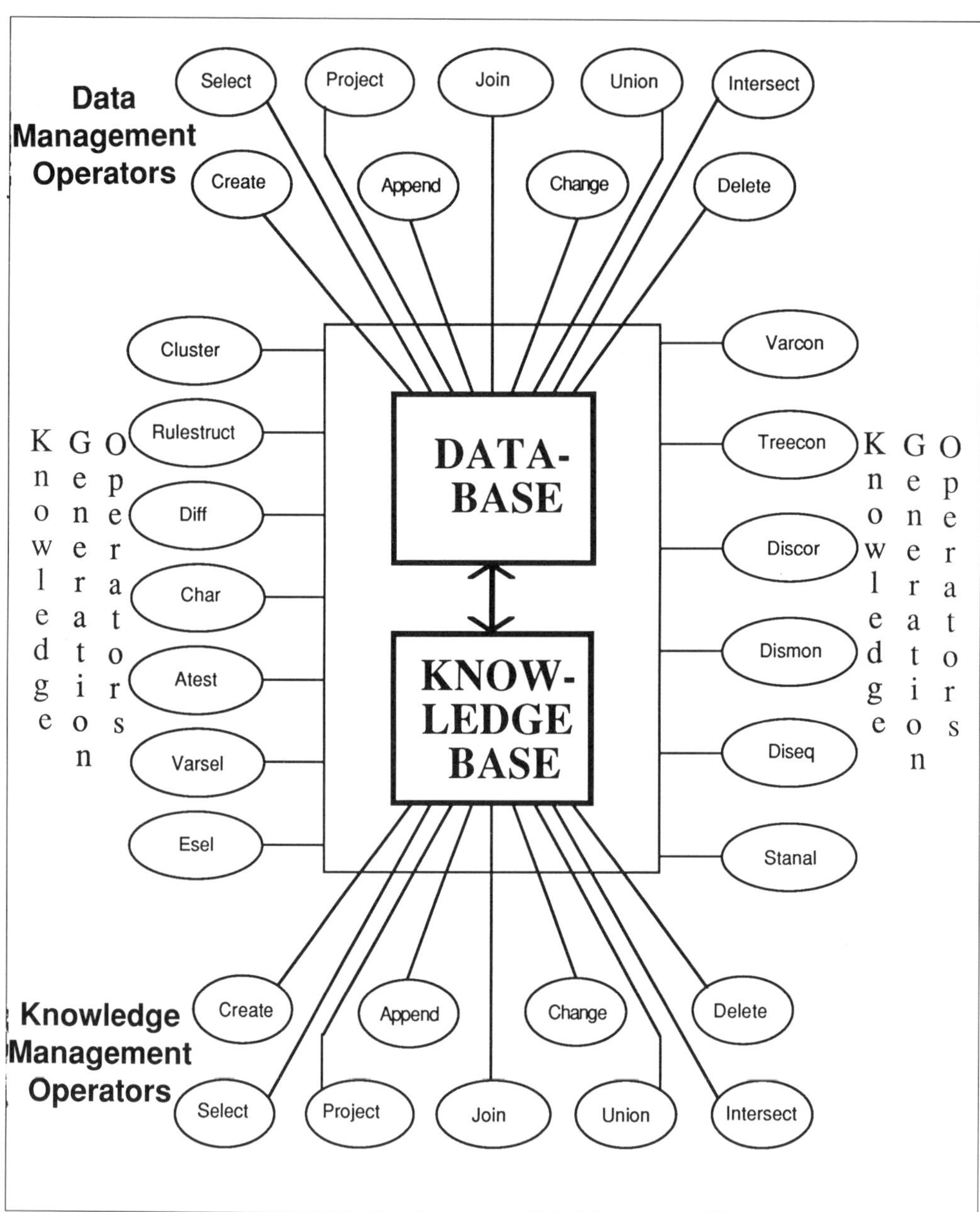

Figure 26.1
A Functional Diagram of INLEN.

save and retrieve) to facilitate access to the structures they generate. These structures will generally be compound KSs that include tables in the knowledge base that locate their other components.

Many of these operators work with or generate rules. Rules in INLEN consist of a decision part implied by a condition part. The decision part consists of a conjunction of one or more statements or actions, and the condition part consists of a disjunction of conjunctions, each consisting of one or more elementary conditions (for examples, see tables 26.1 and 26.2).

Under the current design, these are the basic KGOs employed by INLEN:

Cluster performs conceptual clustering of tuples in a relational table to create logical groupings of objects or events represented by the tuples. It also determines a set of rules characterizing the created groups. Specifically, the operator divides rows of a relational table into two or more groups and returns KS consisting of a relational table similar to the input table and containing additional information indicating the groups and a rule set characterizing the individual groups. An example of this operator is given in the next section. User-defined parameters can influence the creation of the groups. Detailed descriptions of the conceptual clustering algorithm that performs this operator are in Michalski, Stepp, and Diday (1981) and Stepp (1983, 1984).

Rulestruct also performs conceptual clustering but applies it to a rule set rather than a relational table. A compound KS is returned consisting of the original rule set with grouping information plus a new rule set to explain the grouping.

Diff (differentiate) takes two or more classes of objects (each object represented as a tuple in a relational table) and induces general rules characterizing the differences between the classes. The output KS consists of the rule set created by the operator and the object classes represented by RTs. The AQ program that executes this operator is described in Michalski and Larson (1983). The rules produced are called *discriminant descriptions*; that is, they specify sufficient conditions for distinguishing one class of objects from the other class(es).

Char (characterize) determines descriptions characterizing a class of objects. This operator also falls into the domain covered by the AQ program. Here, the emphasis is on finding characteristic rules describing all examples of a class of objects, without concern about the differences between this class and other classes. Output includes the initial class plus the generated descriptions.

Atest tests a set of decision rules for consistency and completeness on a set of examples (specified in a relational table). Consistency implies that no event in the example space is covered by two different rules. Completeness refers to the condition that every possible example will be covered by the conditions applying to at least one rule. The output KS consists of the input rules, example sets, and a relational table containing Atest's analysis. Atest is described in detail in Reinke (1984).

Varsel determines attributes in a relational table that are most relevant for differentiating between various classes of objects. Output consists of a rule describing the selection of the variables given the input classes and the subtable generated by projecting on the chosen variables. By keeping only the most relevant attributes in the object (example) descriptions, one can significantly reduce the computation time required by the Cluster or Diff operators (Baim 1982).

Esel determines the examples (objects) that are most representative for given classes. Promising examples are returned as output with a rule specifying the input classes and the chosen examples, and other examples are rejected (Michalski and Larson 1978; Cramm 1983).

Varcon applies mathematical operators specified in its argument to combine variables into useful composites. The output KS will consist of the new composite variables and a rule specifying the original table, the mathematical operators, and the created variables. For example, Varcon can be used if the sum or product of two variables might be more useful than either individual value (Davis 1981).

Treecon takes a set of rules or decision examples and organizes them into a decision tree, which can be a more efficient way for storing or using this knowledge (Michalski 1978; Layman 1979).

Discor discovers correlations between the values of attributes in a set of examples. It is implemented as a standard statistical operation of correlation and returns a table of its results.

Dismon seeks out monotonic relations between attributes in a set of examples and in doing so can discover an interesting relationship within the data. It is an operator that is used in the Diseq operator.

Diseq discovers equations that describe numeric data in a set of examples and formulates conditions for applying these equations. Diseq returns a set of equations and the rules that determine when they apply. It is based on the ABACUS-2 system for integrated qualitative and quantitative discovery (Falkenhainer and Michalski 1986; Greene 1988). ABACUS-2 is related to programs such as BACON (Langley, Bradshaw, and Simon 1983), FAHRENHEIT (Żytkow 1987), and COPER (Kokar 1986).

Stanal performs a statistical analysis of the data to determine its various statistical properties.

Table 26.1
An Example of the Cluster Operator.

	Input					Output	
Microcomputer	Display	RAM	ROM	Processor	No_Keys	2-Group	3-Group
Apple II	Color_TV	48K	10K	6502	52	1	1
Atari 800	Color_TV	48K	10K	6502	57-63	1	1
Comm. VIC20	Color_TV	32K	11-16K	6502A	64-73	1	2
Exidi Sorceror	B/W_TV	48K	4K	Z80	57-63	1	2
Zenith 118	Built_in	64K	1K	8080A	64-73	2	3
Zenith 1189	Built_in	64K	8K	Z80	64-73	2	3
HP 85	Built_in	32K	80K	HP	92	1	2
Horizon	Terminal	64K	8K	Z80	57-63	1	2
Challenger	B/W_TV	32K	10K	6502	53-56	1	1
O-S 11 Series	B/W_TV	48K	10K	6502C	53-56	1	2
TRS-80 I	B/W_TV	48K	12K	Z80	53-56	1	1
TRS-80 III	Built_in	48K	14K	Z80	64-73	1	1

Two-Group Clustering:
[Group 1] $\Leftarrow$ [RAM = 16K..48K] or [No_Keys $\leq$ 63]
[Group 2] $\Leftarrow$ [RAM = 64K] & [No_Keys $>$ 63]

The Cluster operator takes as the input the relational table, marked Input, and a parameter requiring it to partition the rows in the table into two- and then three-group clusterings. The two rightmost columns show the partitions generated. Cluster also generates rules describing the groups stored in the knowledge base

Three-Group Clustering:
[Group 1] $\Leftarrow$ [Processor = 6502 v 8080A v Z80] & [ROM = 10K..14K]
[Group 2] $\Leftarrow$ [Processor = 6502A v 6502C v HP] or [ROm = 1K..8K] & [Display $\neq$ Built_in]
[Group 3] $\Leftarrow$ [Processor = 6502 v 8080A v Z80] & [ROM = 1K..8K] & [Display = Built_in]

26.3 An Illustration of Selected Knowledge Generation Operators: Cluster, Diff, Diseq

This section gives examples of how some basic KGOs work, specifically, the Cluster, Diff, and Diseq operators.

26.3.1 Cluster

Cluster is capable of creating groupings of objects or events and, when used recursively, can generate an entire taxonomy. Unlike traditional clustering methods, Cluster also returns the rules that describe its grouping. The presented example is based on the results described in Michalski and Stepp (1983), which involves creating a classification of microcomputers. Variables considered include the type of processor, the amount of random-access memory (RAM), the read-only memory (ROM) size, the type of display, and the number of keys on the keyboard. Dividing the examples into two groups, the system grouped them according to RAM size and keyboard; clustering into three groups was based on the processor type, ROM size, and the display type. Table 26.1 presents the original data and the classifications generated by the Cluster operator. The input to Cluster was a table of the characteristics of the microcomputers, and the output consisted of a table with new columns indicating the groups of the objects along with rules characterizing the groups.

Table 26.2
An Example of the Diff Operator.

Microcomputer	Display	RAM	ROM	Processor	No_Keys	2-Group	3-Group
Apple II	Color_TV	48K	10K	6502	52	1	1
Atari 800	Color_TV	48K	10K	6502	57-63	1	1
Comm. VIC20	Color_TV	32K	11-16K	6502A	64-73	1	2
Exidi Sorceror	B/W_TV	48K	4K	Z80	57-63	1	2
Zenith 118	Built_in	64K	1K	8080A	64-73	2	3
Zenith 1189	Built_in	64K	8K	Z80	64-73	2	3
HP 85	Built_in	32K	80K	HP	92	1	2
Horizon	Terminal	64K	8K	Z80	57-63	1	2
Challenger	B/W_TV	32K	10K	6502	53-56	1	1
O-S 11 Series	B/W_TV	48K	10K	6502C	53-56	1	2
TRS-80 I	B/W_TV	48K	12K	Z80	53-56	1	1
TRS-80 III	Built_in	48K	14K	Z80	64-73	1	1

Diff takes as input a relational table in which the last column indicates group (class) membership. In this example, the Diff operator tries to rediscover the rules, invented by Cluster, from the examples of groups.

Rediscovered rules for Two-Group Differentiation:

[Group 1] $\Leftarrow$ [Display $\neq$ Built_in] or [ROM $\geq$ 14K]
[Group 2] $\Leftarrow$ [RAM = 64K] & [No_Keys = 64-73]

Rediscovered Rules for Three-Group Differentiation:

[Group 1] $\Leftarrow$ [Processor = Z80 v 6502] & [ROM = 10K..14K]
[Group 2] $\Leftarrow$ [Processor = 6502C v 6502A v HP] or [ROM = 4K..8K] & [Display = B/W_TV v Term.]
[Group 3] $\Leftarrow$ [ROM = 1K..8K] & [Display = Built_in]

These rules were generated by Diff directly from examples. They are similar but not identical to the rules originally created by Cluster. They provide an alternative, logically consistent, characterization of individual groups.

26.3.2 Diff

The Diff operator is based on the AQ inductive-learning method that has been effectively used for many rule-learning tasks in areas such as medicine, agriculture, physics, computer vision, and chess. One recent application for diagnosing potential breast cancers, given a few training examples, is described in Michalski, Iwanska, et al. (1986). The rules generated performed well on new cases of the disease. An application of the Diff system to concisely describe the groups created by the Cluster operator (table 26.1) is shown in table 26.2. The groups of examples are given as input, and Diff creates rules that describe the differences between these groups. Note that the found rules are a little simpler than the descriptions produced by Cluster (a redundant condition specifying the processor type in the third group of the three-grouping cluster was removed). Diff often produces a significantly simpler description.

Although this example shows an application of Diff to create the discriminant rules for groups of examples, the AQ algorithm that it employs can also be used to determine characteristic rules that describe classes of events (Michalski 1983). In the INLEN system, this function is represented by the Char operator. In case of large example sets, there can be large differences between characteristic and discriminant rules.

Table 26.3
The Diseq Operator Formulates Stoke's Law.

Substance	Radius (m)	Mass (kg)	Height (m)	Time (s)	Velocity (m/s)
Vacuum	0.05	1	6	0.1	0.98453
Vacuum	0.05	2	2	0.4	3.93812
Vacuum	0.10	1	3	0.5	2.95359
Vacuum	0.10	2	7	0.1	0.98453
Glycerol	0.05	1	5	0.1	19.11200
Glycerol	0.05	2	8	0.3	38.22400
Glycerol	0.10	1	6	0.5	9.55600
Glycerol	0.10	2	7	0.2	19.11200
CastorOil	0.05	1	9	0.4	14.67200
CastorOil	0.05	2	3	0.1	29.34400
CastorOil	0.10	1	5	0.3	7.33600
CastorOil	0.10	2	8	0.5	14.67200

Diseq searches for relationships among the data objects. It discovers that equations for the ball's velocity exist, but they depend on the medium through which the ball is falling.
Here are the rules Diseq discovered:
If [Substance = Vacuum] **then** v = 9.8175 * t
If [Substance = Glycerol] **then** v * r = 0.9556 * m
If [Substance = CastorOil] **then** v * r = 0.7336 * m,

where v = velocity, r = radius, t = time, and m = mass.

26.3.3 Diseq

The Diseq operator is based on the Abacus-2 discovery system that is described in Greene (1988). The operator is capable of learning equations that fit a set of tabular data. It is also capable of subdividing a set of examples into subsets in which different rules apply and coping with noisy data. It specifies conditions under which different rules apply. Abacus-2 expands the capabilities of the earlier system Abacus (Falkenhainer and Michalski 1986) and can discover more complex regularities.

The Abacus programs have formulated equations characterizing a number of different empirical data, for example, data specifying planetary motion, the distances between atoms in a molecule, and Stoke's law of falling bodies. Stoke's law specifies the velocity of an object falling through different media and is presented in table 26.3. As shown in the table, the velocity of an object falling through a fluid is governed by an equation involving different variables from those found in the equation describing the velocity of an object falling through a vacuum. Diseq was able to find the equations for both cases.

26.4 Conclusion

INLEN is a large-scale integrated system capable of performing a wide variety of complex inferential operations on data to discover interesting regularities in them. These regularities can be detected in qualitative data and quantitative data as well as in the knowledge base itself. In addition, INLEN provides functions that facilitate manipulation of both the data and the knowledge base.

A major novelty of INLEN is that it integrates a variety of knowledge generation operators that permit a user to search for various kinds of relationships and regularities in the data. To achieve such an integration, the concept of KS was introduced. The KS stands for a variety of knowledge representations, such as rules, networks, and equations, each possibly associated with a relational table in the database (as in the case of a set of constraints), or for any combination of such basic KSs.

Because INLEN serves to collect learning and discovery systems as operators, it is more of a methodology than a simple tool. Because it incorporates many diverse knowledge generation operators, INLEN carries the possibility of extending the limits of discovery systems' capabilities.

Many of INLEN's modules have already been implemented as stand-alone systems or parts of larger units. Other tools and the general integrated interface are under development. Future work involves bringing these systems together and completing the control system to facilitate access to the systems in the form of simple, uniform commands.

Acknowledgments

The authors thank Pawel Stefanski, Jianping Zhang, and Jan Zytkow for their comments and criticism. They are also grateful to Peter Aiken, Kathleen Byrd, and Joyce Ralston for their assistance in preparing earlier versions of the manuscript.

This research was done in the Artificial Intelligence Center at George Mason University. The activities of the center are supported in part by the Defense Advanced Research Projects Agency under a grant administered by the Office of Naval Research N00014-87-K-0874 and in part by the Office of Naval Research, grants N00014-88-K-0226 and N00014-88-K-0397.

References

Baim, P. W. 1982. The PROMISE Method for Selecting Most Relevant Attributes for Inductive Learning Systems, UIUCDCS-F-82-898, Dept. of Computer Science, Univ. of Illinois.

Baskin A. B., and Michalski, R. S. 1989. An Integrated Approach to the Construction of Knowledge-Based Systems: Experiences with ADVISE and Related Programs. In *Topics in Expert System Design*, eds. G. Guida and C. Tasso, 111–143. Amsterdam: Elsevier.

Cramm, S. A. 1983. ESEL/2: A Program for Selecting the Most Representative Training Events for Inductive Learning, UIUCDCS-F-83-901, Dept. of Computer Science, Univ. of Illinois.

Davis, J. H. 1981. CONVART: A Program for Constructive Induction on Time Dependent Data, Master's thesis, Dept. of Computer Science, Univ. of Illinois.

Falkenhainer, B., and Michalski, R. S. 1986. Integrating Quantitative and Qualitative Discovery: The ABACUS System, UIUCDCS-F-86-967, Dept. of Computer Science, Univ. of Illinois.

Greene, G. 1988. Quantitative Discovery: Using Dependencies to Discover Non-Linear Terms, Master's thesis, Dept. of Computer Science, Univ. of Illinois.

International Intelligent Systems, Inc. 1988. User's Guide to AURORA 2.0: A Discovery System, International Intelligent Systems, Inc., Fairfax, Va.

Katz, B.; Fermanian, T. W.; and Michalski, R. S. 1986. AgAssistant: An Experimental Expert System Builder for Agricultural Applications, UIUCDCS-F-87-978, Dept. of Computer Science, Univ. of Illinois.

Kerschberg, L., ed. 1988. *Expert Database Systems: Proceedings from the Second International Conference*, Fairfax, Va.: George Mason Univ.

Kerschberg, L., ed. 1987. *Expert Database Systems: Proceedings from the First International Conference.* Menlo Park, Calif.: Benjamin Cummings.

Kerschberg, L., ed. 1986. *Expert Database Systems: Proceedings from the First International Workshop.* Menlo Park, Calif.: Benjamin Cummings.

Kokar, M. M. 1986. Coper: A Methodology for Learning Invariant Functional Descriptions. In *Machine Learning: A Guide to Current Research*, eds. R. Michalski, T. Mitchell, and J. Carbonell, 151–154. Boston, Mass.: Kluwer.

Langley, P.; Bradshaw, G. L.; and Simon, H. A. 1983. Rediscovering Chemistry with the BACON System. In *Machine Learning: An Artificial Intelligence Approach*, Volume 1, eds. R. Michalski, T. Mitchell, J. Carbonell, 221–240. San Mateo, Calif.: Morgan Kaufmann.

Layman, T. C. 1979. A Pascal Program to Convert Extended Entry Decision Tables into Optimal Decision Trees, Internal Report, Dept. of Computer Science, Univ. of Illinois.

Michalski, R. S. 1983. Theory and Methodology of Inductive Learning. In *Machine Learning: An Artificial Intelligence Approach*, volume 1, eds. R. Michalski, T. Mitchell, and J. Carbonell, 83–134. San Mateo, Calif.: Morgan Kaufmann.

Michalski, R. S. 1978. Designing Extended Entry Decision Tables and Optimal Decision Trees Using Decision Diagrams, UIUCDCS-R-78-898, Dept. of Computer Science, Univ. of Illinois.

Michalski, R. S., and Baskin, A. B. 1983. Integrating Multiple Knowledge Representations and Learning Capabilities in an Expert System: The ADVISE System. In Proceedings of the Eighth International Joint Conference on Artificial Intelligence, 256–258. Menlo Park, Calif.: International Joint Conferences on Artificial Intelligence.

Michalski, R. S., and Larson, J. B. 1983. Incremental Generation of VL_1 Hypotheses: The Underlying Methodology and the Description of the Program AQ11, UIUCDCS-F-83-905, Dept. of Computer Science, Univ. of Illinois.

Michalski, R. S., and Larson, J. B. 1978. Selection of Most Representative Training Examples and Incremental Generation of VL1 Hypotheses: The Underlying Methodology and the Description of Programs ESEL and AQ11, 867, Dept. of Computer Science, Univ. of Illinois.

Michalski, R. S., and Stepp, R. E. 1983. Automated Construction of Classifications: Conceptual Clustering Versus Numerical Taxonomy. *IEEE Transactions on Pattern Analysis and Machine Intelligence*, PAMI-5(4):396–410.

Michalski, R. S.; Baskin, A. B.; and Spackman, K. A. 1982. A Logic-Based Approach to Conceptual Database Analysis. In Proceedings of the Sixth Annual Symposium on Computer

Applications in Medical Care (SCAMC- 6), 792-796. Washington, D.C.: George Washington Univ. Medical Center.

Michalski, R. S.; Stepp, R. E.; and Diday, E. 1981. A Recent Advance in Data Analysis: Clustering Objects into Classes Characterized by Conjunctive Concepts. In *Progress in Pattern Recognition*, volume 1, eds. L. N. Kanall and A. Rosenfeld, 33–56. New York: North Holland.

Michalski, R. S.; Baskin, A. B.; Uhrik, C.; and Channic, T. 1987. The ADVISE.1 Meta-Expert System: The General Design and a Technical Description, UIUCDCS-F-87-962, Dept. of Computer Science, Univ. of Illinois.

Michalski, R. S.; Iwanska, L.; Chen, K.; Ko, H.; and Haddawy, P. 1986. Machine Learning and Inference: An Overview of Programs and Examples of Their Performance, Artificial Intelligence Laboratory, Dept. of Computer Science, Univ. of Illinois.

Michalski, R. S.; Mozetic, I.; Hong, J.; and Lavrac, N. 1986. The AQ15 Inductive Learning System: An Overview and Experiments. UIUCDCS-R-86-1260, Dept. of Computer Science, Univ. of Illinois.

Reinke, R. E. 1984. Knowledge Acquisition and Refinement Tools for the ADVISE Meta-Expert System, Master's thesis, Dept. of Computer Science, Univ. of Illinois.

Spackman, K. A. 1983. QUIN: Integration of Inferential Operators within a Relational Database, ISG 83-13, UIUCDCS-F-83-917, Master's thesis, Dept. of Computer Science, Univ. of Illinois.

Stepp, R. E. 1984. Conjunctive Conceptual Clustering: A Methodology and Experimentation, Ph.D. diss., Dept. of Computer Science, Univ. of Illinois.

Stepp, R. E. 1983. A Description and User's Guide forCLUSTER/2, a Program for Conceptual Clustering, Dept. of Computer Science, Univ. of Illinois.

Żytkow, J. M. 1987. Combining Many Searches in the FAHRENHEIT Discovery System. In *Proceedings of the Fourth International Workshop on Machine Learning*, 281–287. San Mateo, Calif.: Morgan Kaufmann.

VII METHODOLOGY AND APPLICATION ISSUES

27 Automating the Discovery of Causal Relationships in a Medical Records Database

The POSCH AI Project

John M. Long, Erach A. Irani, James R. Slagle, and the POSCH Group
University of Minnesota

Abstract

The Program on the Surgical Control of the Hyperlipidemias (POSCH) has been experimenting with the use of AI as a way to more fully automate the analysis of its complex data. Expert systems have been built to analyze serial-graded exercise electrocardiography tests and serial coronary arteriography data. A back-propagation model was applied to these data with limited success. Ways of identifying structural relationships within the knowledge base are being studied. Some of the computational issues of the discovery problem for POSCH are presented.

27.1 An Expert System to Automate the Search for New Medical Knowledge

The use of AI, primarily in the form of expert decision support systems, is being widely explored in medicine. For those conducting large multicentered clinical studies and accumulating large numbers of patient records, AI has another promising possibility, that is, in the discovery and confirmation of causal relationships.

The Program on the Surgical Control of the Hyperlipidemias (POSCH) is a major national multiclinic randomized clinical trial designed to test the lipid-atherosclerosis hypotheses in a secondary prevention population (Buchwald et al. 1982). As an ancillary project, POSCH has inaugurated an experimental data analysis project using AI (Long, Slagle, Wick, et al. 1987). The database includes a total of 1400 variables, of which about 600 are computerized. They are collected for the ages from 7 to 14 years on 838 study participants. Although the database is fairly large, currently about 300 million characters, the large number of variables, as well as the complex relationships among them, is the real challenge of the project. The medical and statistical knowledge primarily consists of frames of observed data and calculated summaries. A frame characterizes each variable (for example, cholesterol), which contains a system of which it is a part (for example, lipid profile), component parts (for example, HDL, LDL, and VLDL), a range of normal values, related abnormal states, and the relative importance.

27.2 The POSCH AI Project

The initial motivation for the POSCH AI Project was to build a discovery system that can identify relationships that exist between and among the POSCH variables. This process

Table 27.1
Comparison of POSCH Study to RX Project.

	RX (Radix)	POSCH
Number of Patients	Large	838
Number of Variables	Nonstandard	1400
Number of Visits	Variable (up to 50)	8 to 15
Protocol	Nonrandomized	Randomized
Time of Visits	Variable	12 months
Data Elements	Variable	Standard
Total Size	Very large	Very large
Setting	Clinical	Clinical trial

entails building a system that can automate what biostatisticians do when faced with the analysis of a large database such as that in POSCH. The initial inspiration for the POSCH AI Project was the work of Robert Blum in his RX discovery project, later renamed Radix (Blum 1982; Walker and Blum 1986). His effort to build a discovery system to confirm causal relationships in a medical record database appears to be the first attempt to use this approach in medicine. The system used a discovery module to obtain its initial hypothesis. It combed through a selected subset of 50 patient records to produce a hypothesis such as A causes B. What it actually did was determine that A precedes B and is correlated to B. A study module designed a comprehensive study of the most promising hypotheses, as determined by the human researcher. A statistical module was used to test the hypothesis on the entire database. Newly discovered data were added to the knowledge base and used in future phases of the study. Later, in the Radix project, he and his co-workers used more advanced statistical methods (Walker and Blum 1986).

Much of the work required in the development of the original RX system had to deal with the fact that the data were not randomized and included many missing data elements. The frequency and timing of patient data were also variable. POSCH does not have these problems. POSCH data are collected using a standardized protocol that minimizes the amount of missing or noisy data. POSCH researchers must deal with many more variables than RX does as well as other issues. The differences are outlined in table 27.1.

Currently, our analysis staff uses conventional methods to examine all major POSCH variables (about 200). The major variables are those known to be related to the lipid hypothesis or to the partial ileal bypass surgery or known to have a potential effect on the patient. Because the designers of POSCH chose to collect many additional data items, it now appears that it will take the analysis staff many years to complete a comprehensive analysis of all these variables. The POSCH AI Project is an attempt to find a supplemental method for searching for causal relationships, especially among the minor variables, that might be missed simply because there are so many of them and because of limited staff.

The objectives of the POSCH AI project are to (1) develop an automated system, using AI in combination with more conventional techniques, that will assist an analysis staff in examining all the POSCH data, (2) identify an optimal subset of predictor variables for each of the POSCH end points (primary and secondary), and (3) use the automated system to examine POSCH data as a double check of the regular analyses.

27.2.1 Unifying Concepts

Some unifying concepts can be used to pull together the diverse variables in POSCH's database into fewer units. Logically formed clinical groupings already exist within the catalog of variables. Statistical clustering methods, perhaps in combination with clinical knowledge, could be used to produce a dozen or so groups into which all POSCH variables can be placed. The complexity of the problem could then be reduced by calculating or deriving an entity as a representative of each group.

27.2.2 Role of Statistics and Knowledge-Based Reasoning Systems

Standard statistical methods provide the basis for examining the database and describing and explaining the relationships that exist between and among the variables. It is desirable to use statistical techniques that are widely used and accepted for reporting relationships in the literature. The key to the success of the discovery system will be its ability to imitate what a biostatistician does in the discovery phases of his (her) work, which is a heuristic process. The heuristics often have no conventionally based scientific foundation and rely solely on the expert's experience. They represent that knowledge of an expert that goes beyond book knowledge; this knowledge is what makes the expert an expert. The heuristics and domain-specific knowledge of the POSCH database have to be used to limit the size of the search. Given the size of the database and the number and types of relationships that can exist in it, the problem of searching for all possible relationships existing in the database is NP-hard. The heuristics will be used to direct the search, so that searches likely to discover interesting relationships will be carried out. The domain-specific knowledge must represent the taxonomies of variables and relationships in the database. Incorrect domain-specific knowledge can lead to a relationship not being discovered until manual intervention takes place. Inappropriate domain knowledge can lead to a delay in discovering a relationship. Discovered knowledge about relationships can be incorporated in the taxonomy of relationships and can guide the search for more relationships.

Heuristics are especially important in the search and discovery phases of our system. It might not be possible to accurately place them in any conventional system of logic because we are trying to automate the creative phases of data analysis. Once the search and discovery phases are completed, the discovered relationships can be verified using more rigorous statistical techniques.

27.2.3 Database Issues

Another issue is finding the most efficient database structure to use to facilitate the needed logical manipulations of the data. Once identified, we must rebuild the database into this structure. This might simply mean that we should convert to some form of relational database. The system also needs a reasonably efficient query language that will allow the searching module to run efficiently.

Every care has been taken when collecting the data to guarantee that the data are as accurate as humanly possible. A rigid protocol specifies the collection of data. The importance of dealing with incorrect or missing or changing data is minimized.

Information in the database can change because newly discovered relationships can void previous relationships. For instance, if we discovered that A influences C, and B influences C, a discovery that A influences B might lead to a change in the model to indicate that A influences B, which, in turn, influences C, rather than both A and B influence C and A and B are independent of each other. Once such a discovery is made, previously discovered relationships involving A or B need to be reexamined.

27.3 Accomplishments

Two expert systems have been built to extract clinical data from the database. The first expert system, the exercise test analyzer (Eta), compares two graded exercise electrocardiography (ECG) tests taken several years apart. The evaluator of serial coronary angiograms (ESCA) compares the manual readings of a pair of coronary arteriograms. A back-propagation model was developed and compared with the expert system as well as a more standard statistical method, multiple linear regression.

With these accomplishments, a better understanding was gained of how well AI techniques fit into the domain for the type of data used at POSCH and other clinical trials. A method for discovery has not yet been implemented. Key features of the problem are being identified. In regard to the POSCH database, enough data are collected to make it likely that discovered relationships will have statistical significance. POSCH data is real world data and it is extremely clean for a real-world database. Currently, only limited sets of data, such as those used for testing Eta and ESCA, have been released.

The methods we develop at the POSCH AI Project will be suited for those applications that have little missing or incorrect data. This condition generally holds true for databases developed during clinical trials but does not hold for medical record databases collected in a normal clinical situation. An example of a medical database where these assumptions would not hold is the Aramis database used in the RX project.

27.3.1 An Expert System for Analyses of Serial-Graded Exercise Electrocardiography Tests

Our first expert system, Eta, was designed to compare the data from a pair of graded exercise ECG tests taken several years apart. Eta determines whether the patient's performance was better, unchanged, or worse over time using the scale shown in figure 27.3.1. This system can approximate the decision reached by a cardiologist evaluating the same data. Eta is only briefly described here because it was previously reported (Slagle et al. 1986a, 1986b; Long, Slagle, Leon, et al. 1987).

The expert system rules for the ECG system were developed using conventional knowledge engineering methods. The set of cases used were carefully selected to present a variety of typical situations and stimulate explanations by the clinician about what he was doing to solve the case. The clinical expert explained the factual knowledge he used from the scientific literature, often citing results of research performed by himself and others. He also used and explained the heuristics that he found helpful. The heuristics are based on experience rather than book knowledge.

The resulting expert system was tested on 100 cases that were used to validate the system. Each case consisted of a pair of tests taken by a POSCH patient two years apart. The cases were selected to be representative of a variety of situations. As a part of the validating process, the same cases were also evaluated by a panel of expert cardiologists. Because a more conventional way to automate this situation would be to use a statistical approach, we also developed a set of multiple linear regression equations as a third method of evaluation. All three methods used the seven-category scale shown in figure 27.3.1 to describe their conclusions. The evaluations were done by the cardiologists on the panel, the expert system Eta, and multiple regression equations. Based on each evaluation, it was concluded whether a patient's heart health was better or worse from the first to the second test. Although the equations worked, several variables used in the multiple regression equations had obscure clinical meanings, a matter of concern to POSCH clinicians.

Because of the strong element of subjective clinical judgment in these evaluations, the three methods for evaluating the test data were not necessarily expected to draw the same conclusions. For this reason, the evaluation methods were compared in two ways to judge how well they agreed. *Exact* agreement means that the same category on

```
'-3'  '-2'      '-1'      '0'      '1'      '2'     '3'
-----|-------|----------|--------|----------|--------|-------
much  worse  slightly     no    slightly   better   much
worse          worse    change   better             better
```

Figure 27.1
Scale for Evaluating Exercise Tests in Eta. The numeric scale is used as an abbreviated notation for the category of change; for example, "-3" would be entered on the form when the evaluation is "much worse."

Table 27.2
Average Agreement between Cardiologists and Compared to the Regression Equation and the Expert System (ES)

	Cardiologist vs Cardiologist	Cardiologist vs Equation	Card. vs E.S.
Exact	42.0%	34.0%	41.7%
Within One Category	76.0%	81.5%	83.5%

the seven-category scale was selected as the conclusion for both the evaluations being compared. Agreement *within one category* means that the two evaluations selected the same or immediately adjacent categories on the seven-category scale. The comparisons were made based on the percentage of agreement.

Table 27.2 summarizes the results. For exact agreement, the expert system agreed with the cardiologists about as well as cardiologists agreed between themselves and was better than the multiple regression equations. For agreement within one category, the expert system performed best, and the evaluations of the multiple regression equations were more in agreement with the cardiologists than the cardiologists were between themselves. After allowances for normal variation, it can be seen that even a relatively small and basic expert system can evaluate serial-graded exercise ECG test data about as well as either an individual cardiologist or the multiple regression equations.

27.3.2 An Expert System for Analysis of Serial Coronary Arteriograms

The next system built, ESCA, evaluates serial coronary arteriograms. Again, the details were previously reported, so only a summary is given here (Long et al. 1988). The general concept is the same as for the ECG system, but the medical aspects are far more complex. *Arteriography* (a procedure that photographs the pattern of blood flow in the coronary arteries) yields useful information about the condition of the coronary vessels. The technique involves injecting a contrast medium into the heart vessels that is opaque to X rays and taking a series of 35-mm X rays in rapid succession. A cine film strip is produced that shows how the blood flows in the arteries of the heart. By repeating this procedure from several angles, a cardiologist can tell which vessels have *stenosis* (narrowing of the artery) as well as the nature and extent of the stenosis. The key points are that the data are found on film and that expertise is required to extract and interpret these data.

Cases from the POSCH study were used to build and test the experimental system. Coronary arteriograms of participants in POSCH are taken at the time they enter the study and at 3, 5, and either 7 or 10 years later. An arteriography review panel of cardiologists and radiologists manually evaluates pairs of these serial coronary angiograms. The methods they use to evaluate these clinical data are subtle and require a considerable amount of clinical judgment. Specifically, a subpanel of two members from among the eight doctors on the arteriography review panel meets about once a month for two days to review 30 to 40 pairs of arteriograms. This task is extremely tedious for the doctors on the panel and logistically complex.

The subpanel review is conducted in a double-blinded fashion. The members know neither the identities of the participants nor the temporal sequence of the arteriograms. The film pairs are identified simply as film A and film B. Film A is evaluated, and all stenoses found are recorded. Film B is then evaluated for change from film A. In the final step of its evaluations, the subpanel carefully reviews all its findings and provides a global assessment of change using a scale similar to the one used for the ECG system. The total process requires about 20 minutes of the subpanel's time to review one pair of films, with the global assessment taking only a few minutes at the end.

The coronary vessels in the arteriogram appear in a tree-like branching structure wrapped around the heart muscle. What is visible in one frame of the cine film might be obscured in another. Stenoses near the branching point of arteries are especially difficult to estimate. One factor affecting visualization is the presence of collateral arteries (arteries at the ends of an adjacent branch of the system). When the normal blood flow in one branch of the system is blocked, collateral arteries sometimes open and extend their perfusion field, providing a blood supply to the affected muscle tissue. This ability of the heart to adjust, although amazing, can complicate the task of determining stenoses. Another factor that must be assessed by experts is whether the blockage is caused by a blood clot or stenosis.

Assessing the change in stenoses is further complicated by the fact that vessels tend to develop stenosis more quickly after coronary bypass grafts have been placed on them. Medical procedures such as *recanalizations* (opening the vessel by angioplasty) are also fairly common and complicate the evaluation.

Thus, many complex and interactive factors make assessing the percentage change in stenoses difficult. We chose to build ESCA to do the most clinically demanding part of the evaluation process. We chose to use trained technicians to review the film and locate and size lesions and then use their input and ESCA to approximate the global-assessment

Table 27.3
Average Agreement Rate of Subpanel (SP) compared to Expert System (ES).

	Subpanel vs Subpanel	Subpanel vs Expert System
Exact	38%	46%
Within One Category	92%	93%

process. This approach eliminates the need to use doctors. By using an automated film reader, further automation is possible, an idea POSCH is pursuing.

The knowledge base was built to perform the final clinically demanding task. Data elements from the consensus report (all previous steps) of the experts are used as the expert system's input and form the leaf (entry) nodes of the network. The top node represents the system's global assessment of the overall disease change. The interactions between the tree-like structure of arteries are not required at this point because the heart, as a pumping organ, is not evaluated. Thus, each artery can be treated independently. The change in each artery is assessed, and the individual changes are combined to obtain the overall assessment. The inference network, therefore, consists of a subnetwork that is evaluated 23 times, once for each of the 23 arterial segments for which data are supplied on the form, and a top-level network that merges the information passed up by the subnetworks.

The global-assessment expert system (ESCA) was applied to 200 POSCH cases. Terminology and comparison methods were similar to those used for the Eta system. The POSCH quality surveillance program showed that two different subpanel evaluations will agree exactly on a seven-category scale 38 percent of the time and agree within one category 92 percent of the time. The expert system's assessments of the set of 200 test cases agreed exactly with the panel 46 percent of the time and within one category of the panel's assessments in 93 percent of the cases. The system's performance is slightly better than that of the panel for the global assessment. The system does not consider many of the factors used by the subpanel members. For this reason, the results obtained by this system are somewhat better than expected. Table 27.3 summarizes these results.

27.3.3 Using Back Propagation for Discovering Relationships

One neural network algorithm, back propagation (Rumelhart, McClelland, and the PDP Research Group 1986), was tested and compared with a more conventional statistical method, multiple linear regression. One of the expectations of neural networks in general and back-propagation in particular is that once the network is trained, it can generalize to a test set. Networks trained by back-propagation can learn relationships such as exclusive-or, where the output is a function of both inputs. The hope was that a neural network trained with the back-propagation algorithm would learn the training set and generalize more accurately than multiple linear regression.

The neural network was trained on a sample of 125 cases drawn from the set of 200 validated cases previously used when developing an expert system for evaluating serial coronary arteriography data (Long et al. 1988). We then tested the network on the remaining 75 cases. The independent variables used were (1) the stenosis observed in an angiogram, called film A, and (2) the stenosis observed in another angiogram from the same patient, called film B. The dependent variable was the expert's assessment of change on the scale from much worse to much better, as previously described. During training, the independent variables were input to the network, and the network was trained to predict the dependent variable on the output. During testing, the independent variables were supplied as input, and the output of the network was compared to the assessment made by human experts.

In back propagation, units have to be arranged in layers. There is an input layer, an output layer, and zero or one or more hidden layers. Several network configurations were tested with varying performance.

The configurations were (1) no hidden layers; (2) one hidden layer, with 5, 7, 10, 15 or 20 units; (3) two hidden layers, with (3,3), (5,5), (5,7), (5,20), (7,5), (7,10), (7,15), (10,7), (15,7), or (15,15) units, where (i,j) stands for i units in the first layer and j units in the second layer; and (4) three hidden layers, with (3,3,3), (3,7,5), or (5,5,5) units, where (i,j,k) stands for i units in the first layer, j units in the second layer, and k units in the third layer.

The best results were obtained with the configuration using three hidden layers and three units in each layer. The data were fed to the net in another way, too, but this way did not prove to be better. In this way, the percent stenosis on film A and the change from film A to film B measured as that on film B minus that on film A were used as input. In all cases, nonvisualized segments were recorded as having zero-percent stenosis as a way of minimizing their effect. This same scheme was used for recording nonvisualized segments in the expert system ESCA.

The same 125 cases were used to develop a multiple linear regression equation. The equation was then used to predict the assessment for the same 75 test cases used with the neural network model. Results are summarized in table 27.4.

The best results of over 20 different configurations of the neural network used are given in table 27.4. In these setups, the networks were trained for 700 iterations. Additional details about the experiment are in Irani et al. (1989).

The results for the test set, the proper values to use for the comparison, show that the agreement rate for multiple linear regression is somewhat better than that for the neural network. The neural network agreed with the experts 39 percent and 84 percent, versus 44 percent and 93 percent for the standard statistical method. As shown in tables 27.3

Table 27.4
Comparison of Different Methods of Interpretation of Arteriographic Data

	Exact Agreement	Agreement Within 1 Category
Back Propagation vs. Panel		
Train	57%	98%
Test	39%	84%
Multiple Linear Regression vs. Panel		
Train	57%	98%
Test	44%	93%

and 27.4, results for the neural network are comparable to the expert panel for exact agreement (39 percent versus 38 percent) but worse (84 percent versus 93 percent) for comparison within one category.

Limitations of Using Back Propagation for Discovery Systems The limitations of using back propagation for discovery systems are substantial. First, the interaction among weights in back propagation is complex and distributed. It is not realistic to expect a researcher to supply the topology that would best represent the flow of influence.

Second, a completely connected network has too many weights to analyze. If we are supposed to make an a priori assumption about the layout of the network, we are making assumptions about the flow. By making these assumptions, we are supplying more domain-specific information than we would usually provide when using a statistical technique.

Third, the back propagation simulations take an excessive amount of computer time, more than eight hours to run on a SUN III. Ultimately, the runs for our experiments were done on several SUNs. The new generation of Risc workstations takes substantially less time. Regression takes a few minutes to analyze all 200 cases, and the expert system takes about one hour to evaluate all 200 cases. The expert system is in Lisp and can be significantly speeded up if recoded in C or Fortran.

Fourth, back propagation does not generate concise models of what happens in the real world. At best, in discovery systems, deriving the numeric relationships of the flow of influence between variables is tedious. Extracting symbolic information from the weights in back propagation is an even more difficult task at this stage because the information encoded in the weights is distributed.

Fifth, the ability of back propagation to generalize performance to the test set is unpredictable. Our application and other applications where statistical discovery is used consist of either numeric or symbolic data. Symbolic data can be numerically encoded. Statistical techniques seem better able to predict data and deliver more easily interpretable results. Incidentally, by their nature, expert systems are the closest to reality in their understanding.

Sixth, the necessity of running several configurations of the network makes back propagation more difficult to use. Running several configurations makes the research frustrating because comparisons have to be made to determine the best configurations. Neural network programs have not reached the state of maturity of statistical packages in terms of flexibility of supplying input, reporting results, and so on.

27.4 Structure Building Techniques

Current experimentation uses a hierarchical classifier (the maximum weight spanning tree) algorithm by Chow and Liu (1968). This algorithm organizes the input data in a hierarchy of attributes that can describe the structure of the data if certain assumptions are satisfied by the input data. The first level of the hierarchy is a set of variables that can be used to predict the variable of interest. The intent is to compare this classifier's performance using the first-level variable with back propagation and an expert system.

Acknowledgments

The Program on the Surgical Control of the Hyperlipidemias is funded by NHLBI Grant HL15265. Discussions with Dr. John P. Matts, chief biostatistician at POSCH, were instrumental in understanding the statistical issues involved in analyzing relationships in the POSCH database.

27.5 References

Blum, R. L. 1982. Discovery, Confirmation, and Incorporation of Causal Relationships from a Large Time-Oriented Clinical Database: The RX Project. *Computers and Biomedical Research* 15:165–187.

Buchwald, H.; Moore, R. B.; Matts, J. P.; Long, J. M.; et al. 1982. The Program on the Surgical Control of the Hyperlipidemias. *Surgery* 92(4): 654.

Chow, C. K., and Liu, C. N. 1968. Approximating Discrete Probability Distributions with Dependence Trees. *IEEE Transactions on Information Theory.* IT-14: 773–791.

Irani, E. A.; Matts, J. P.; Long, J. M.; Slagle, J. R.; and the POSCH group, 1989. Using Artificial Neural Nets for Statistical Discovery: Observations after Using Back Propagation, Expert Systems, and Multiple-Linear Regression on Clinical Trial Data. *Complex Systems* 3(3): 295–311.

Long, J. M.; Irani, E. A.; Hunter, D. W.; Slagle, J. R.; Matts, J. P.; et al. 1988. Using A Symbiotic Man/Machine Approach to Evaluating Visual Clinical Research Data. *Journal of*

Medical Systems, 12(5): 327–339.

Long, J. M.; Slagle, J. R.; Leon, A. S.; et al. 1987. An Example of Expert Systems Applied to Clinical Trials: Analysis of Serial Graded Exercise ECG Test Data. *Controlled Clinical Trials* 8: 136–145.

Long, J. M.; Slagle, J. R.; Wick, M. R.; Irani, E. A.; Matts, J. P.; and the POSCH Group, 1987. Use of Expert Systems in Medical Research Data Analysis: The POSCH AI Project. In Proceedings of the National Computer Conference, volume 56, 769–776.

Rumelhart, D. E.; McClelland, J. L.; and the PDP Research Group, 1986. *Parallel Distributed Processing: Explorations in the Microstructure of Cognition,* volume 1 and 2. Cambridge, Mass.: The MIT Press.

Slagle, J. R.; Long, J. M.; Wick, M. R.; Matts, J. P.; and Leon, A. S. 1986a. Expert Systems in Medical Studies - A New Twist. In Proceedings of the Symposium of the International Association of Optical Engineers, volume 635, 25–29. Bellingham, Wash.: International Society for Optical Engineering.

Slagle, J. R.; Long, J. M.; Wick, M. R.; Matts, J. P.; and Leon, A. S. 1986b. The ETA Project: A Case Study of Expert Systems for Analysis of Serial Clinical Trial Data. In Proceedings of MEDINFO '86, 155–159.

Walker, M. G.; and Blum, R. L. 1986. Towards Automated Discovery from Clinical Databases: The RADIX Project. In Proceedings of the Fifth Conference on Medical Informatics, volume 5, 32–36.

28 Discovery of Medical Diagnostic Information: An Overview of Methods and Results

Mary McLeish, P. Yao, M. Garg, and Tatiana Stirtzinger
University of Guelph

Abstract

A project involving the acquisition of knowledge from a large online database system of medical information was recently begun at the University of Guelph. A number of different methodologies were investigated, from machine learning and statistics to uncertainty management. This chapter outlines the results of using some of these methods and presents conclusions about their efficiency on certain domains.

28.1 Introduction

The University of Guelph hospital for veterinary medicine has had an extensive database system in place for a number of years to handle the usual admission and billing procedures. However, the system also stores a considerable amount of medical information on each patient, including bacteriology; clinical pathology; parasitology; radiology; and other patient information, such as age, sex, breed, presenting complaint, treatment procedures, diagnosis, and outcome. In the veterinary medical domain, follow-up information is particularly good for experimentation. Autopsies are always performed, and patients are extensively studied to determine the causes of any complaints. Our objective was to make use of these data to aid in the design of medical expert systems. Two prototype domains were chosen: equine colic and liver disease in small animals.

Initially, we experimented with several statistical and machine learning techniques (McLeish 1988; McLeish, Cecile, and Lopez-Suarez 1990), as discussed in Using Other Machine Learning Methods. We learned how difficult a sensible integration of these methodologies into one coherent system could be, although the methods could be used to complement each other in some situations.

The focus of the project as outlined in this chapter was on techniques that allow for the extraction of information from data followed by a refinement based on expert opinions. The reasons for this are several: Our data sets were not of the idealized types collected for full-scale epidemiological studies and were further complicated by missing data, the presence of different types of data (for example, discrete, continuous, nominal data), and reliance on some subjectively measured variables. The training set for the prototypes was not particularly large, especially when the missing data were considered. One of the methods chosen (evidence combination) was essentially a more elaborate form of the methods already used by the clinicians themselves. The Dempster-Shafer theory, in the presence of data, was applied to the liver disease domain in which the size of the data sets was smaller in relation to the number of outcomes. The next section describes these methods.

A parallel computing environment was used for most of the implementations. Implementation Issues describes some of these issues, including complexity, in more detail. The closing section presents some conclusions and future directions for the project.

28.2 Weight of Evidence and Belief Functions

This section describes and compares three methods for extracting information from data based on their application to two problems in veterinary medicine.

28.2.1 The Use of Weight of Evidence

The first domain (equine colic) provided a training set of 250 cases presented at the teaching hospital at Guelph. The initial problem was to identify surgical cases among the incoming colic complaints. Equine colic is a significant killer of horses, and unnecessary surgery is expensive and can be debilitating. Currently, a simple diagnostic chart is used, and symptoms are weighted according to importance (although this weighting scheme is not a function of a symptom's value). These weights are added according to medical and surgical possibilities, and whichever is largest is taken as an indication of the treatment required.

A more precise formulation that makes use of the data actually dates back to A. M. Turing. Good (1950, 1960) and Minsky and Selfridge (1961) subsequently investigated many of the properties and uses of Turing's formulation, which is expressed as

$$W(H:E) = \log(\frac{p(E|H)}{p(E|\bar{H})}) \quad \text{or} \quad W(H:E) = \log(\frac{O(H|E)}{O(H)}).$$

where $O(H)$ represents the odds of H, $p(H)/p(\bar{H})$.
Weight of evidence plays the following part in Bayesian inference:

$$\text{Prior log odds} + \sum_i \text{weight of evidence}_i = \text{posterior log odds.}$$

A weight of evidence that is highly negative implies that there is significant reason to believe in $\bar{H}$, and a positive $W(H:E)$ supports H. This formulation was most notably used in a decision support system called Gladys (Spiegelhalter, Franklin, and Bull 1989).

Two different implementations based on these basic ideas were put into place. Both methods made use of a fuzzy method to discretize some of the continuous variables.

Table 28.1
Input Data, Case No. 533954.

1	Rectal temperature		38.1	-0.258886
2	Pulse		72.	-0.1000831667
3	Respiratory rate		30.	-0.22545
4	Temp extremities	cool		0.507149
5	Peripheral pulse	reduced		0.83201
6	Mucous membrane	pale pink		0.167067
7	Cap refill time	less than 3 sec		-0.254991
8	Pain	intermittent severe pain		0.980933
9	Peristalsis	absent		0.959134
10	Abdominal distension	moderate		1.622711
11	Nasogastric tube GAS	slight		0.018617
12	Nasogastric tube fluid	none		-0.289182
13	Nasogastric tube PH		0.	0.
14	Rectal exam feces	decreased		-0.385611
15	Rectal exam abdomen	distended LH		0.847754
16	PCV		37.	-0.183532
17	TP		56.	-0.018787
18	Abdominocentesis app	serosanguinous		1.32813
19	Abdominocentesis TP		2.4	0.

Case number	= 533954
Medical score	= 1.5136
Surgical score	= 7.2635
Doctor's diagnosis	= Surgical
System's diagnosis	= Surgical
Expected accuracy	= 83%
Belief in results	= 88%

The clinicians provided (sometimes overlapping) membership functions, and a concept of fuzzy probabilities (Yager 1979) was used to incorporate the results into the model. Further details can be found in McLeish and Cecile (1990) and McLeish et al. (1989). The first version considered only individual symptoms (70) and was implemented in Q'Nail (Lisp/APL language), which can be run on an IBM PC (AT). A sample of input data and associated results is presented in table 28.1.

The expected accuracy was computed as a ratio of the highest score over the combined score (weight of evidence). The belief in the results is a type of second-order calculation that accounts for missing data and how significant the remaining information is. This system was run on a new data set of 52 cases. The system's overall accuracy was 97 percent; its negative predictive power, 87 percent. With only one exception, the wrongly diagnosed cases were close calls or had a low belief value. The physicians' performance level was about 75 percent in both categories.

The second method involved the use of attribute sets and was tested on a set of 368 cases (300 training, 68 test cases), which was a random amalgamation of old and new data. The most significant set of independent groups was found by a complicated search method involving tests for independence between symptom groups and a ranking of each group depending on a weighted average of its (1) weight of evidence, (2) error in the weight of evidence (tests for normality on the weights were carried out, and an error expression was borrowed from Spiegelhalter and Knill-Jones [1984]), and (3) the frequency of occurrence of the symptom group in the data set (a low frequency of occurrence strongly reduced the reliability).

This computationally intense methodology was feasible in real time only through the use of heuristic algorithms, even with an implementation on a Sequent parallel machine (8 CPUs). Two search methods were adopted (compare McLeish, Cecile, and Lopez-Suarez [1990]), and their performance was compared on ROC curves. Version 1 outperformed version 2. In version 1, chi-square tests were used to ensure two-way and three-way independence among all the pieces of evidence. Version 2 merely enforced a maximal overlapping condition on the evidence.

Logistic regression was run on the same data set (Matthews and Farewell 1985). The clinical data set was appropriately revised, splitting several nominal variables into new ones with binary outcomes. A 95 percent significance level was used. A major problem concerned missing data. If a key parameter in the regression model was missing, the equation was essentially meaningless. This reduced our test set from 68 to 38. The evidence combination scheme is less sensitive to missing data, essentially basing its prediction on all available information and not just a few key variables. Version 1 significantly outperformed the regression model on the 38 cases. See McLeish and Cecile (1990) and McLeish et al. (1989) for more details. A cut-off point for making a decision on the ROC curves could be chosen, making the accuracy of correctly predicted surgical cases 82 percent and that of medical cases, 78 percent.

28.2.2 Belief Functions for Liver Disease Diagnosis

This domain concerned the prebiopsy diagnosis of liver diseases in small animals, in particular, canine liver disease. Clinicians can accurately tell 75 percent of the time whether liver disease is present. They can predict the specific type of liver disease only about 15 percent of the time. The diagnostic process involves physical examination; laboratory tests; and other tests, often a biopsy or a necropsy. The cost of doing laboratory tests is about 20 times cheaper than the cost of performing a biopsy or necropsy, although providing the right answer might be too late to benefit the patient. There are risks in performing a biopsy; among them are the use of anesthetic, hemorrhage, infection and poor wound healing. The goal is to primarily use laboratory data to determine specific types of liver disease.

One study (Myers 1986) attempted to do this, but it used expert opinions to predict outcomes. Our study began by making use of the data collected by the hospital database to extract predictive information.

On the liver disease domain, the amount of data available was small compared to the number of outcomes and symptoms. With knowledge of the expert's inability to predict individual outcomes, it was decided to extract Shafer belief functions from data. *Belief functions* are strengths assigned to subsets of an outcome space rather than individual diseases. These belief functions were then modified by expert opinions. Modification was carried out after examining the values found from data, unlike the reserve procedure used in the probabilistic system in Spiegelhalter and Knill-Jones (1984).

Shafer (1976) mentions the question of extracting suitable mass functions from data and makes a suggestion. However, it is stated that the ideas given "are not implied by the general theory of evidence exposited in the preceding chapters. Rather, these assumptions must be regarded as conventions for establishing degrees of support, conventions that can be justified only by their general intuitive appeal and by their success in dealing with particular examples" (Shafer 1976). Several alternative methods have been tried and compared with those in Shafer (1976).

The interconnections between the variables in this domain are not well understood, and attempts at producing a network of causal relations resulted in a complicated structure of doubtful accuracy. The outcome space consisted of 30 different types of liver disease, and the laboratory tests produced 19 biochemical parameters and 21 hematologic parameters (all continuous variables, for example, ablumins, calcium, glucose, cholesterol, total protein, red blood cell, lymphocytes, reticulocytes). Initially, we only had 150 cases and solicited expert opinions to reduce the outcome space to a set of 14 classes based on the similarity of the lesions and the pathogenesis of liver disease. Examples of these classes are primary and metastic tumors, hepatocellular necrosis, hepatic fibrosis and cirrhosis, hepatic congestion, and hepatic atrophy and hypoplasia. Even on these 14 classes, the data sample was not large enough to be convincingly discriminatory. Because our intention was to solicit expert opinions to modify our statistically determined results, and these were also not always well defined on singleton classes, it was decided to use the belief function approach from the Dempster-Shafer theory. (In the equine domain, subsets of the small outcome space were meaningless, and substantially more data for each outcome were available). The problem formulation does not lend itself to the hierarchical or network approaches of Zarley, Hais, and Shafer (1988). Although tests of correlations between parameters were carried out, detailed hierarchies were not well known.

In the Dempster-Shafer theory, the frame of discernment θ is not the set over which a probability measure is defined. The power set, 2^θ, is the basic set on which judgments are made. The subtle distinction between a probability mass assigned to a singleton and a larger subset containing this singleton is not immediately achieved by considering the frequency of information occurrence. If different outcomes were well discriminated over some range of continuous variable (that is, a normal range for some medical symptom), values could easily be assigned. Unfortunately, plots of our 40 symptoms in the liver disease domain revealed this not to be the case, even with outcomes considered as members of 2^θ. The ranges of continuous variables to be considered as individual symptoms were specified by the experts. These regions could further be refined to produce a greater degree of discrimination, but the computational complexity of the domain was already so high that we decided to keep to the expert-defined ranges.

Method 1 Several ideas presented themselves about how to make use of data to assign mass and belief functions in such situations. One idea came from Shafer (1976), who defines a support function $S_x(A)$ by the following for all nonempty A:

$$S_x(A) = 1 - Pl_x(\bar{A}),$$

where the plausibility function

$$Pl_x(A) = \frac{(\max\ q_{\theta_i}(x), \theta_i \epsilon A)}{(\max\ q_{\theta_i}(x), \theta_i \epsilon \theta)}$$

and $\bar{A}$ stands for A complement.

Here, θ_i is an outcome, and x is a symptom. The functions $\{q_{\theta_i}\}$, $\theta_i \epsilon \theta$, are a statistical specification that obeys the rule that x renders $\theta_i \epsilon \theta$ more plausible than θ_i' whenever $q_{\theta_i}(x) > q_{\theta_{i'}}(x)$. Likelihood functions are possible choices for $\{q_{\theta_i}\}$ (Shafer 1976).

One can work out what the associated mass functions are (which is necessary for the method of implementation):

If $f_x(\theta_i)$ represents the frequency of occurrence of outcome θ_i given symptom x, and these outcomes are sorted in descending order by the f function for each x, then the nonzero mass functions are given by the formulas

$$\begin{aligned} m_x(\theta_1) &= \frac{f_x(\theta_1) - f_x(\theta_2)}{f_x(\theta_1)}, \\ m_x(\theta_1 \cdots \theta_j) &= \frac{f_x(\theta_j) - f_x(\theta_{j+1})}{f_x(\theta_1)}, \\ m_x(\theta_1 \cdots \theta_n) &= \frac{f_x(\theta_n)}{f_x(\theta_1)}, \end{aligned}$$

where $\theta = (\theta_1 \cdots \theta_n)$ and $f_x(\theta_i) \geq f_x(\theta_j)$, $i \leq j$.

Method 2 A search for a simple support function for each symptom was carried out by looking for individual symptoms or sets of symptoms with likelihoods greater than 0.5. Because the values were based on frequency data, only one singleton could have such a high value. If none had a suitably high value, then sets of size two were examined, and the pair with the highest value greater than 0.5 was chosen. The process continued to larger sets if necessary.

One problem concerned what to do with the remaining mass. Although the Dempster-Shafer theory would normally put it on θ, the remaining frequencies of occurrence were on the complement of the support subsets. Two methods were applied to the data: (1) Method 2A put the remaining mass on the complement set, excluding any singletons where proportions are zero. (2) Method 2B placed the remaining mass on θ.

An algorithm for the main part of method 2A (method 2B is similar) is as follows:

- Sort all the freq(A), where $A \subseteq \theta$, and A is a singleton, from the highest to the lowest values.
- From the highest to the lowest values, do the following:

```
- if freq (A) > 0.5 then
    * B ← A
    * m(B) ← freq(A)
- else
    while m(b) ≤ 0.5
    {to get total m(B) > 0.5}
    * B ← B∪A
    * m(B) ← M(B) + freq (A)
    * get the next freq(A)
- get the next lower freq(A), say freq(X) - if there is any
- while freq(X) equal to freq(A)
    {to include all the singletons in which the frequencies are the same}
    * B ← B∪X
    * m(B) ← m(B) + freq(X)
    * get the lower freq(X), and assign it to freq(X)
- while freq(X) > 0
    {collect all singletons in which the proportions are greater than zero}
    * C ← C∪X
    * m(C) ← m(C) + freq(X)
    * get the next lower freq(X), and assign it to freq(X)
- where B⊆ θ, A ⊂ θ, X ⊂ θ, A, X are singletons.
```

Table 28.2
Percentage Result Based on Methods of Acquiring BPAs from Data.

CATEGORY	Method 1	Method 2A	Method 2B
Precise Match	35.0	65.0	42.5
Imprecise Match	2.5	7.5	20.0
Nonmatch	62.5	27.5	37.5

28.2.3 Summary of Results

In this study, 30 different types of liver diseases were presented by 241 cases. The 30 groups were reclassified into 14 groups based on the similarity of the lesions and the pathogenesis of the liver disease. Forty new cases were used as test cases; the 241 cases were used as training cases. Before correlations were incorporated, 40 laboratory variables were used, further split into regions of normal, high, and low readings. The result from a run is called an *observed outcome set*, and the result from either a biopsy or necropsy is called an *expected outcome set.* Each comparison between the observed and expected outcome sets was categorized into one of the following: (1) a precise match (PM), where the singleton of the observed outcome was the same as the singleton of the expected outcome; (2) an imprecise match (IM), where the singleton of the expected outcome exists in the nonsingleton set of the observed outcomes; and (3) a nonmatch (NM), where no element of the observed outcome sets existed in the expected outcome set.

Later, the percentage of each category was calculated in terms of each methodology.

With respect to these categories, we preferred that each method have a high PM percentage and a low NM percentage. The IM could be in any range as long as it did not contribute to the NM category.

Table 28.2 shows that method 2A—the method that assigned the remaining BPNs to the remaining disease groups that have their singleton proportions greater than 0—provided a higher performance than method 2B—the method that assigned the remaining BPNs to θ. This happened because method 2A had a smaller number of liver disease groups in the second set of a given probability mass than did method 2B, which always had the total distinct number of liver disease groups. Thus, in method 2A, when all the evidences were combined, the common liver disease group had its evidence supported more than with method 2B. Furthermore, method 2A provided a high PM percentage, which was preferred in determining the effectiveness of different methods.

Method 1, which is the approach suggested by Shafer, turned out to have the worst performance. The NM percentage was about 25 percent to 35 percent higher than methods 2A and 2B, respectively. Because method 1 had the worst performance, the BPAs that were generated by method 1 were not modified by expert opinions.

To help eliminate highly correlated parameters and modify the data-derived belief values, further studies were carried out that incorporated expert opinions. Slightly better performance was obtained when the expert opinions were incorporated into the mass functions. Expert opinions also proved valuable in eliminating variables. The best performance was obtained when the experts were asked to refine the conclusions found by statistical tests.

An example of a sample output file generated by method 2A is given in table 28.3.

28.3 Using Other Machine Learning Methods

Other methods studied include the use of a machine learning method (PLS1 algorithm) on the pathology data, where some significant information was obtained (Rendell 1983) that was contrary to the results of earlier discriminant analyses. Quinlan's (1983) algorithm was run on a vastly decreased data set; the constraints imposed by the missing data were greatest when this method was applied. There were also problems handling the varied data types. Results are presented in McLeish (1988); McLeish and Cecile (1990); and McLeish et al. (1989).

Finally, Bayesian inductive inference (Cheeseman et al. 1988; McLeish, Cecile, and Lopez-Suarez 1990) was tried on all the data (clinical and pathological) together and then on the clinical data separately. This methodology used Bayes theorem to discover an optimal set of classes for a given set of examples. These classes can be used to make predictions or give insight into patterns that occur in a particular domain. Further details of results from this analysis can be found in McLeish, Cecile, and Lopez-Suarez (1990).

Although the classes can be used predictively, incoming cases can be classified according to the training set examples they are most like. If they are assigned to a class that is highly predictive of the types of outcomes under study, the information is valuable. Because the later runs of the Autoclass I program dropped the outcome information in doing the classifications, only some classes were particularly predictive of surgery–no surgery. However, the Bayesian method can also provide useful complementary information in many situations. If one considers a particular example analyzed by the symptom group combination-of-evidence method and looks at Bayesian classification, the case belongs to a class where 80.1 percent of the cases had a surgical lesion (a value close to the 80.4 percent chance of surgery predicted by evidence combination). The symptom group method calculated a p value of 80.1 percent. Both these findings would strongly encourage surgery.

On closer examination, in this class, only 19 percent of the cases lived, and only 15 per-

Table 28.3
Output File Using Method 2A.

Hospital Number: 147203
{Possible Outcomes} = Lower Probability – Upper Probability

{11 5 1 9 2 6} = 1.000000 – 1.000000
{11 5 1 2 6} = 0.999997 – 1.000000
{11 5 1 9 2} = 0.999907 – 1.000000
{11 5 1 2} = 0.999905 – 1.000000
{11 5 1 6} = 0.999554 – 1.000000
{11 5 1 9} = 0.999516 – 1.000000
{11 5 1} = 0.999516 – 1.000000
{11 1 9 2 6} = 0.994118 – 0.996828
{11 1 2 6} = 0.994117 – 0.996828
{11 1 9 2} = 0.994035 – 0.996828
{11 1 2} = 0.994035 – 0.996828
{11 1 6} = 0.993690 – 0.996828
{11 1 9} = 0.993656 – 0.996828
{11 1} = 0.993656 – 0.996828
{11 5} = 0.546105 – 0.672441
{11 2} = 0.542965 – 0.668876
{11} = 0.541891 – 0.668876
{5 1} = 0.331124 – 0.458035
{1} = 0.327560 – 0.453821
{5} = 0.003172 – 0.005882
{9} = 0.000000 – 0.000003
{6} = 0.000000 – 0.000093
{2} = 0.000000 – 0.000445

1 =	Primary and Metastatic Tumors	2 =	Hepatocellular Necrosis
3 =	Hepatic Congestion	4 =	Hepatic Failure
5 =	Hepatomegaly	6 =	Hepatic Fibrosis and Cirrhosis
7 =	Infectious Hepatocellular Necrosis	8 =	Traumatic Injury Hepatic
9 =	Hepatic Atrophy and Hyperplasia	10 =	Hepatic Fatty Infiltration
11 =	Steroid Hepatopathy	12 =	Hepatocellular Dissociation
13 =	Hepatic Encephalopathy	14 =	Hepatic Torsion

cent of the animals that had a lesion and were operated on actually survived. Pathology variables were particularly important for determining this class, and abdominal distension was only moderately significant (although the doctors rely heavily on this variable). Indeed, the doctors chose euthanasia for this case. The reasons for euthanasia are so varied, and our data set is so small that a regression analysis on this outcome would not be meaningful. In fact, in some of the publications by Cheeseman and his colleagues, it is suggested that Bayesian classification is useful for small training sets.

28.4 Implementation Issues

The methodology that searched for significant symptom groups was implemented on a Sequent parallel machine (eight processors) in the C programming language. A blackboard architecture was used to control this process and facilitate the parallelization of the problem. Considerable use was also made of the relational database management system ORACLE. Details of this implementation can be found in McLeish, Cecile, and Lopez-Suarez (1990). McLeish et al. (1989) describes how C and SQL (Oracle) can be used to implement a fuzzy relational database.

The liver disease domain problem was coded in C and also implemented on the Sequent machine. A relatively easy to use front end that allows for a variety of options is available to the user.

The data sets used for training purposes are available on diskettes for both domains. As more data become available, we redo our calculations of the weight of evidence and mass functions for the two domains. This revision can automatically be carried out at certain time intervals.

The complexity of uncertainty management methods is generally high (NP-complete) (see Maung and Paris, [1990]), and, in the case of Bayesian networks (Cooper 1990) is NP-hard. In the weight of evidence combination method, given a set of evidence $\{e_1 \cdots e_n\}$, one would like to know $p(H|E)$ for all possible instantiations of $e_1 \cdots e_n$. This usually requires a great number of samples for all but the simplest of domains, approximately $n((1+r)^m - 1)$, where r is the number of possible values in the tests, n is the number of hypotheses, and m is the number of tests. In our domain, roughly 8^{20} samples would be required! Our symptom group search involved a search in a space of this size, and although our heuristic methods reduced the complexity somewhat, the problem was still inherently exponential. The current implementation (with symptom groups restricted to certain fixed sizes) produces results in fewer than five minutes on the worst cases when run on a Sequent Symmetry machine (4386 CPUs). The majority of cases run in under a minute.

On the liver disease domain, the response time is faster when method 2A or 2B is used. The complexity is $0(2^n)$, where n represents the number of laboratory parameters for these methods. The complexity for method 1 is $0(2^{tn})$, where t is the number of outcomes. The current version is able to provide virtually instantaneous response time when a new case arrives.

28.5 General Conclusions

Perhaps the most significant conclusions from these studies are that different domains provide specific problems, and experimentation must be done to determine what is best suited in each situation. For the different domains, two particular conclusions were found: (1) for the first domain, the weight of evidence approach performed better than the other methods investigated and had several other advantages and (2) on the liver disease domain, a methodology was found for extracting belief functions from data, a method that was better than the others. On both domains, we were able to show that the use of statistical data provided generally better performance than the experts were able to give. This result would give support to the increased use of statistical data in (medical) expert systems.

Other conclusions were reached as well: Considering classical statistical methods along with methods from machine learning can be useful, rather than relying on only one of these methods to analyze data. The methodologies are based on different premises about the data, and some experimentation is necessary to determine which model best fits the data and which parameters are found to be important by one method and not another. Also, the use of uncertainty management schemes that involve all the parameters for which subjective values can be substituted or compared with statistically determined ones is a good overall approach and avoids the necessity of trying to integrate the results of classical statistical and machine learning methods with each other and with expert opinions.

As soon as data are present, many methodologies present themselves. Even within the medical domain, the appropriateness of the methodologies can change. It is a tricky and difficult task to decide which data analysis tools to use. Although many studies have already been carried out by biostatisticians, epidemiologists, and the like, these were sometimes not based on the actual tests taken by doctors in a local setting (and were not really carried out to provide the answers for individual case diagnosis). Because database systems capture more information about individual case histories online, diagnostic systems of the type we are proposing should become more prevalent.

Acknowledgments

This chapter was prepared in part while the first author was visiting the MRC Biostatistics Unit, Cambridge, England. The work was supported by NSERC grant A4515.

28.6 References

Cheeseman, P. C.; Kelly, J.; Self, M.; and Stutz, J. 1988. Automatic Bayesian Induction of Classes. In Proceedings of the Seventh National Conference on Artificial Intelligence, 607–611. Menlo Park, Calif.: American Association for Artificial Intelligence.

Cooper, G. F. 1990. The Computational Complexity of Probabilistic Inference Using Bayesian Belief Networks. *Journal of Artificial Intelligence.* Forthcoming.

Good, I. J. 1960. Weight of Evidence, Corroboration, Explanatory Power, Information, and the Utility of Experiments. *JRSS* B(22): 319–331.

Good, I. J. 1950. *Probability and Weighting of Evidence.* New York: Hafner.

McLeish, M. 1988. Exploring Knowledge Acquisition Tools for a Veterinary Medical Expert System. In Proceedings of the First International Conference of Industrial and Engineering Applications of Artificial Intelligence and Expert Systems, 778–788.

McLeish, M., and Cecile, M. 1990. Enhancing Medical Expert Systems with Knowledge Obtained from Statistical Data. *Annals of Mathematics and Artificial Intelligence Journal.* Forthcoming.

McLeish, M.; Cecile, M.; and Lopez-Suarez, A. 1990. Using a Blackboard Architecture in a Distributed DBMS Environment: An Expert System Application. Springer-Verlag Lectures Notes in Computer Science 420: 236–256.

McLeish, M.; Cecile, M.; Yao, P.; and Stirtzinger, T. 1989. Experiments Using Belief Functions and Weights of Evidence on Statistical Data and Expert Opinions, 253-264. In Proceedings of the Fifth Conference on Uncertainty Management.

Matthews, D., and Farewell, V. 1985. *Using and Understanding Statistics.* Karger.

Maung, I., and Paris, J. B. 1990. A Note on the Infeasibility of Some Inference Processes. *International Journal of Intelligent Systems.* Forthcoming.

Minsky, M., and Selfridge, O. G. 1961. Learning in Random Nets. In *Information Theory,* ed. Colin Cherry, 335–347. London: Butterworths.

Myers, J. 1986. The Computer as a Diagnostic Consultant with Emphasis on Use of Laboratory Data. *Clinical Chemistry* 32: 1714–1718.

Quinlan, R. 1983. Learning Efficient Classification Procedures and Their Application to Chess End Games. In *Machine Learning: An Artificial Intelligence Approach,* eds. R. Michalski, T. Mitchell, and J. Carbonell, 463–482. San Mateo, Calif.: Morgan Kaufmann.

Rendell, L. A. 1983. A New Basis for State-Space Learning Systems and a Successful Implementation. *Artificial Intelligence* 4: 369–392.

Shafer, G. 1976. *A Mathematical Theory of Evidence.* Princeton, N.J.: Princeton University Press.

Spiegelhalter, D. J., and Knill-Jones, R. B. 1984. Statistical and Knowledge-Based Approaches to Clinical Decision Support Systems. *JRSS* B(147):35–77.

Spiegelhalter, D.; Franklin, R.; and Bull, K. 1989. Assessment, Criticism, and Improvement of Imprecise Subjective Probabilities for a Medical Expert System. In Proceedings of the Fifth Uncertainty Management Workshop, 335–343.

Yager, R. 1979. A Note on Probabilities of Fuzzy Events. *Information Sciences* 18:113–129.

Zarley, D.; Hais, Y. -T.; Shafer, G. 1988. Evidential Reasoning Using DELIEF. In Proceedings of the Seventh National Conference on Artificial Intelligence, 205–209. Menlo Park, Calif.: American Association for Artificial Intelligence.

29 The Trade-Off Between Knowledge and Data In Knowledge Acquisition

Brian R. Gaines
University of Calgary

Abstract

The extraction of knowledge from databases through inductive methodologies has been recognized as a major research area central to the development and application of knowledge technologies. Such a machine learning approach to knowledge acquisition is often contrasted with expertise transfer approaches based on interviewing human experts in the relevant domain. This chapter provides a quantitative framework for knowledge acquisition that encompasses machine learning and expertise transfer as related paradigms within a single spectrum and shows that techniques supporting the development of practical knowledge-based systems generally lie between these extremes.

29.1 Introduction

There is currently a major paradigm split in knowledge-acquisition research and practice between techniques for the transfer of existing knowledge from human experts and those for the creation of new expertise through empirical induction (Gaines and Boose 1988; Boose and Gaines 1988). There is, however, a fundamental relation between the two paradigms in that existing expertise was at some time derived through empirical induction. There is also continuity between the two paradigms in that existing expertise might be partial, erroneous, and of various forms, such that it cannot completely replace empirical induction but can serve to guide and expedite it (Gaines 1987a).

Figure 29.1 makes these relations explicit. At the top, some world acts as a source from which data can be acquired. On the left, the acquisition is by a person who models the data and becomes an expert about some aspect of the world. In developing a knowledge-based system, such experts can be interviewed using expertise transfer tools (Boose 1986), and their knowledge (model of part of the world) can be transferred to a computer-based knowledge base. On the right, the acquisition loads a computer-based database. In developing a knowledge-based system, such a database can be modeled using empirical induction tools (Quinlan 1986), and the resultant knowledge (model of part of the world) can be transferred to a computer-based knowledge base.

This figure neatly captures the relation between *expertise transfer* and *empirical induction.* However, it overemphasizes the separation between the two approaches. On the left, the expert rarely makes available pure knowledge, that is, a minimal correct model

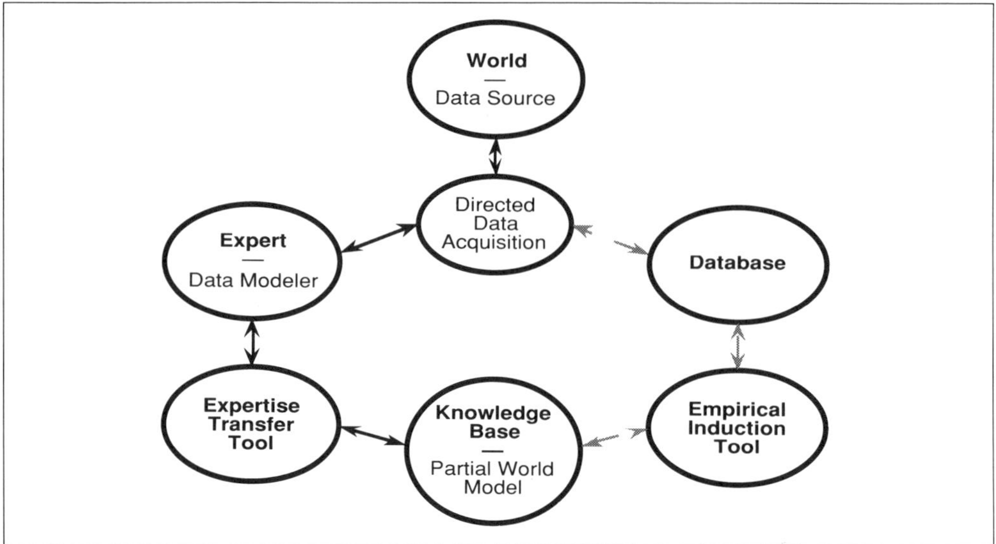

Figure 29.1
Expertise Transfer and Empirical Induction.

of part of the world. Experts provide a mixture of relevant and irrelevant viewpoints, correct and incorrect modeling rules, case histories with partially known outcomes, and so on. The current generation of expertise transfer and knowledge support systems, such as Aquinas (Boose and Bradshaw 1987) and KSS0 (Gaines and Shaw 1987), provide a wide range of tools to cope with, integrate, and clean up this variety of forms and qualities of knowledge. On the right, the database is not a complete or unselective collection of information about the world. It has been structured and collected by people for a purpose, and this structuring and collection already involves substantial expertise. Figure 29.1 emphasizes that the data used in both expertise and database formation are obtained by directed data acquisition. The provision of this direction is itself a task for experts.

Thus, an expert provides a mixture of knowledge, data, and *noise* (incorrect or irrelevant knowledge and data) and so does a database. There is much in common between the left- and right-hand paths in figure 29.1—both expertise transfer and empirical induction involve the extraction of knowledge from partial mixes of knowledge, data, and noise. The next section provides a qualitative analysis of the gradation of information between knowledge and data, and later sections provide quantitative measures of the resultant trade-off.

29.2 Levels of Expertise

Consider a practical knowledge-based system development in which both human experts and various sources of case histories are available, for example, Quinlan's development of thyroid diagnosis rules (Quinlan et al. 1987). The experts might know the following:

1. Minimal Rules: A complete, minimal set of correct decision rules

2. Adequate Rules: A set of decision rules that is complete in giving correct decisions but not minimal in containing redundant rules and references to irrelevant attributes

3. Critical Cases: A critical set of cases described in terms of a minimal set of relevant attributes with correct decisions

4. Source of Cases: A source of cases that contains such critical examples described in terms of a minimal set of relevant attributes with correct decisions

5. Irrelevant Attributes: A source of cases as in level 4 with correct decisions but described in terms of attributes among which are those relevant to the decision

6. Incorrect Decisions: A source of cases as in level 4 but with only a greater-than-chance probability of correct decisions

7. Irrelevant Attributes and Incorrect Decisions: A source of cases as in level 5 but with only a greater-than-chance probability of correct decisions.

These levels represent the sequence of decreasing knowledge on the part of the human expert. This sequence encompasses a range of situations met in practice and raises the question of how the amount of knowledge available from the expert affects the amount of data required for effective empirical induction. For level 1, no data are required for empirical induction because the correct answer is available. For level 7, the expert has provided little except access to a source of data from which the correct answer might be derived. How much data are required for an optimal empirical induction procedure to derive level 1 given level 7, and how much less data are required for levels 2 through 6?

The following sections report some studies that give quantitative answers to these questions. The studies are empirical rather than analytic, so it is not yet apparent how the answers generalize to arbitrary situations. However, they establish some baseline data that is interesting in its own right, a possible guide to practitioners of knowledge acquisition, and a test case for potential analytic estimates of the ratios involved.

29.3 Induct: Statistically Well-Founded Empirical Induction

Induct is part of a knowledge-acquisition tool KSS0 (Gaines 1987b) that uses entity-attribute grid techniques (Shaw 1980; Shaw and Gaines 1983; Boose 1984) to elicit relevant attributes and critical entities from experts and empirical induction based on these to build a knowledge base in terms of classes, objects, properties, values, and methods (rules). The tool also accepts rules entered by experts and entity-attribute data from databases so that its range of knowledge-data combinations encompasses all those listed in the previous section.

Cendrowska (1987) showed that empirical induction through decision trees and direct conversion to rules, even with pruning, leads to rule sets that test the values of irrelevant attributes and are much larger than is necessary. Her Prism algorithm goes from entity-attribute data direct to rules but does not address the problems of noisy data or missing values. Quinlan (1987) developed extended pruning techniques in ways that are effective in coping with noisy data but still involve decision tree production with problems of irrelevant attributes and missing values.

Induct extends the Prism algorithm to control direct rule generation through statistical tests that are effective in dealing with both noisy data and missing values. Figure 29.2 shows the basis for these statistical tests. Given a universe of entities, E, a target predicate, **Q**, and a set of possible test predicates of the form, **S**, on entities in E, construct a set of rules from which the target predicate can be inferred given the values of the test predicates.

For the purposes of the statistical analysis, the forms of **S** and **Q** do not matter. One can regard **S** as a *selector*, choosing those e out of some subset of E for which to assert **Q**(e), and can compare the selection process of the rule with that of random selection, asking, What is the probability that random selection of the same degree of generality would achieve the same accuracy or greater?

This probability is easily calculated: Let Q be the relevant entities in E for which **Q**(e) holds, S be the selected entities in E for which **S**(e) holds, and C be the correct entities in E for which both **S**(e) and **Q**(e) hold:

$$\mathrm{Q} \equiv \{\mathrm{e} : \mathrm{e} \in \mathrm{E} \wedge \mathbf{Q}(\mathrm{e})\}.$$

$$\mathrm{S} \equiv \{\mathrm{e} : \mathrm{e} \in \mathrm{E} \wedge \mathbf{S}(\mathrm{e})\}.$$

$$\mathrm{C} \equiv \{\mathrm{e} : \mathrm{e} \in \mathrm{E} \wedge \mathbf{S}(\mathrm{e}) \wedge \mathbf{Q}(\mathrm{e})\}.$$

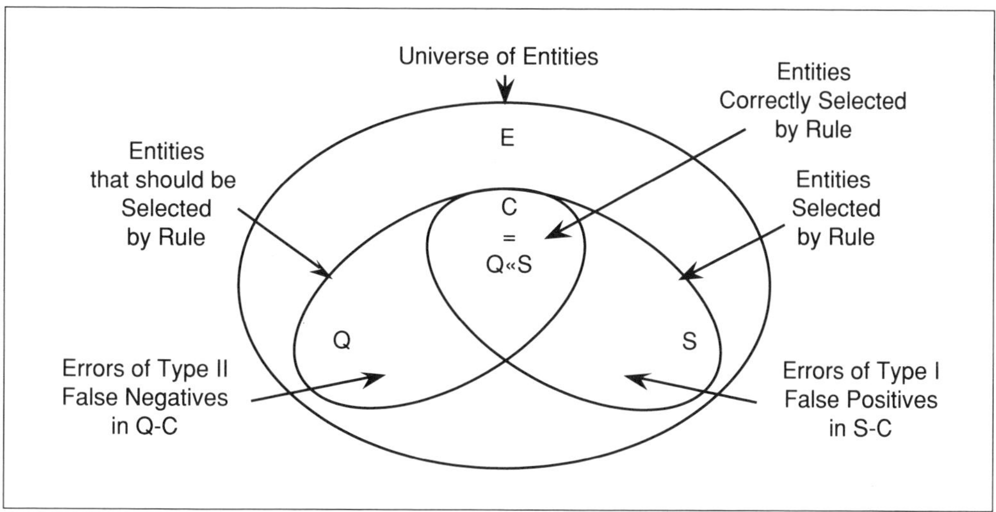

Figure 29.2
Problem of Empirical Induction.

Let the cardinalities of E, Q, S, and C be e, q, s, and c, respectively. The probability of selecting an entity from E for which **Q** holds at random is

$$p = q/e.$$

The probability of selecting s and getting c or more correct at random is

$$r = \sum_{i=c}^{s} C_{s,i}\ p^{i}(1-p)^{s-i}$$

The advantage of using r as a measure of the correctness of a rule is that it is easily understood—as the probability that the rule could be this good at random—and that it involves no assumptions about the problem, such as sampling distributions. Note that if $c = s$ (all correct), then $\log(r) = s \log(q/e)$, which seems to be the basis of information-theoretic measures.

As a rule is being generated, a criterion can be applied that selects the form of the rule most unlikely to have arisen through random selection. That is, if the addition of another clause improves the probability of the rule being correct but also increases the probability of it arising by chance, then the additional clause is not accepted. Even with deterministic data, this gives rise to rule sets showing default reasoning, and with noisy data, it is a powerful technique for preventing noise from leading to superstitious rules testing irrelevant attributes.

Results on Prob-Disj Data (3-term disjunct)		
	Error Rate (Type I + Type II)	
Data	ID3 to Pruned Rules	INDUCT
Sample	4.2 rules	3 rules
Test1	10.0%	10.0%
Test2	10.0%	10.0%

Results on Digits Data			
		Error Rate (Type I + Type II)	
Data	Rules	ID3 to Pruned Rules	INDUCT
Sample	10 16		31.05% 26.8%
Test1	10 16	31.3%	32.0% 29.0%
Test2	10 16	28.3%	31.4% 27.8%

Figure 29.3
Comparison of Induct and Optimally Pruned ID3

Missing values are taken into account by assuming that they might have any value. When the selection of an entity is tested, a missing value is assumed to have the required value for selection. In the statistics, a selection based on missing values is allowed to contribute to false positives but not to correct positives. This is useful in knowledge acquisition because it allows the expert to enter conjunctive rules as if they were entities with missing values. Induct then generates the same or an equivalent smaller rule set. It is reasonable to test the consistency of an inductive procedure by requiring the rule set produced by it to be fixed point if reentered as data.

29.4 Induct in Use

Induct has been tested on a wide range of data sets in the literature, together with many artificial data sets with known degrees of noise, missing values, and irrelevant attributes, and found to perform consistently at least as well as the previously published best results. For example, for Quinlan's (1987) noisy data sets, Prob-Disj (disjunction of three terms in three attributes, one irrelevant attribute, 10 percent noise) and Digits (seven-segment display, 10-percent noise in attributes, Bayes optimal solution 26 percent errors), the comparisons are shown in figure 29.3.

Cendrowska's (1987) contact lens data is a useful test set because it is well defined and previously analyzed, and it results in a range of rules of varying complexity, some of which are supported by a high proportion of the data set, and others of which are

Age	Prescription	Astigmatism	Tear Production	Lens
young	myope	not astigmatic	reduced	none
young	myope	not astigmatic	normal	soft
young	myope	astigmatic	reduced	none
young	myope	astigmatic	normal	hard
young	hypermetrope	not astigmatic	reduced	none
young	hypermetrope	not astigmatic	normal	soft
young	hypermetrope	astigmatic	reduced	none
young	hypermetrope	astigmatic	normal	hard
pre-presbyopic	myope	not astigmatic	reduced	none
pre-presbyopic	myope	not astigmatic	normal	soft
pre-presbyopic	myope	astigmatic	reduced	none
pre-presbyopic	myope	astigmatic	normal	hard
pre-presbyopic	hypermetrope	not astigmatic	reduced	none
pre-presbyopic	hypermetrope	not astigmatic	normal	soft
pre-presbyopic	hypermetrope	astigmatic	reduced	none
pre-presbyopic	hypermetrope	astigmatic	normal	none
presbyopic	myope	not astigmatic	reduced	none
presbyopic	myope	not astigmatic	normal	none
presbyopic	myope	astigmatic	reduced	none
presbyopic	myope	astigmatic	normal	hard
presbyopic	hypermetrope	not astigmatic	reduced	none
presbyopic	hypermetrope	not astigmatic	normal	soft
presbyopic	hypermetrope	astigmatic	reduced	none
presbyopic	hypermetrope	astigmatic	normal	none

Figure 29.4
Cendrowska's (1987) Contact Lens Data.

supported by only single cases. As shown in figure 29.4, the deterministic, complete data set involves 24 cases described in terms of three binary attributes, one ternary attribute, and one ternary decision attribute. Prism gives a solution based on nine rules, but using default logic, correct solutions with only five rules are available.

Figure 29.5 shows the nondefault solution generated by Induct operating in a similar mode to Prism. The two numbers following each rule are the estimates of probability of its being correct and the probability of its being ascribable to chance, respectively.

Figure 29.6 shows the Induct results when the "no increase in probability of rule being by chance" criterion is applied. The first three rules of Figure 29.5 have collapsed to one, which is less correct but also less likely to be the result of chance.

When the rules of figure 29.6 are used for default reasoning, the last four relating to the recommendation "none" collapse into an overall default of "none," and the second one of them also applies as an exception to the first rule relating to "soft." This gives the prioritized default set of five rules shown in figure 29.7—higher-priority rules supersede those of lower priority. These rules behave in their recommendations exactly as the nine rules in figure 29.5.

To present the default rules of figure 29.7 as "knowledge" for validation by an expert and be understood by users, it is better to put them into a frame-based knowledge

```
prescription=hypermetrope & astigmatism=not astigmatic & tear production=normal
   -> lens recommendation=soft 100% 0.904%
age=young & astigmatism=not astigmatic & tear production=normal
   -> lens recommendation=soft 100% 4.34%
age=pre-presbyopic & astigmatism=not astigmatic & tear production=normal
   -> lens recommendation=soft 100% 4.34%

prescription=myope & astigmatism=astigmatic & tear production=normal
   -> lens recommendation=hard 100% 0.463%
age=young & astigmatism=astigmatic & tear production=normal
   -> lens recommendation=hard 100% 2.78%

tear production=reduced -> lens recommendation=none 100% 0.355%
age=presbyopic & prescription=myope & astigmatism=not astigmatic
   -> lens recommendation=none 100% 39.1%
age=pre-presbyopic & prescription=hypermetrope & astigmatism=astigmatic
   -> lens recommendation=none 100% 39.1%
age=presbyopic & prescription=hypermetrope & astigmatism=astigmatic
   -> lens recommendation=none 100% 39.1%
```

Figure 29.5
Deterministic Decision Rules Derived from the Data Set of Figure 29.4.

```
astigmatism=not astigmatic & tear production=normal -> lens recommendation=soft
83.33% 0.195%

prescription=myope & astigmatism=astigmatic & tear production=normal
   -> lens recommendation=hard 100% 0.463%
age=young & astigmatism=astigmatic & tear production=normal
   -> lens recommendation=hard 100% 16.7%

tear production=reduced -> lens recommendation=none 100% 0.355%
age=presbyopic & prescription=myope & astigmatism=not astigmatic
   -> lens recommendation=none 100% 62.5%
age=pre-presbyopic & prescription=hypermetrope & astigmatism=astigmatic
   -> lens recommendation=none 100% 62.5%
age=presbyopic & prescription=hypermetrope & astigmatism=astigmatic
   -> lens recommendation=none 100% 62.5%
```

Figure 29.6
Alternative Decision Rules Derived from the Data Set of Figure 29.4.

```
-> lens recommendation=none Priority 1

prescription=myope & astigmatism=astigmatic & tear production=normal
   -> lens recommendation=hard Priority 2
age=young & astigmatism=astigmatic & tear production=normal
   -> lens recommendation=hard Priority 2

astigmatism=not astigmatic & tear production=normal
   -> lens recommendation=soft Priority 2
age=presbyopic & prescription=myope & astigmatism=not astigmatic
   & tear production=normal -> lens recommendation=none Priority 3
```

Figure 29.7
Default Decision Rules Based on Those of Figure 29.6.

representation system that computes their natural subsumption relations, such as Classic (Borgida et al. 1989). The left- and right-hand sides of the rules form concepts, and the subsumption relations between them allow the default rule structure to be easily visualized. Figure 29.8 shows the grapher output from KRS, a Classic-like knowledge representation server (Gaines 1990) based on the rules of figure 29.7. Subsumption relations are shown as black arrows and rules as gray arrows.

29.5 The Trade-Off between Knowledge and Data

After establishing that Induct behaves well as an empirical induction algorithm, in particular, having high noise rejection, it is possible to use it to quantitatively explore the trade-off between knowledge and data that was described in the introduction. The contact lens data was taken as a starting point for the reasons noted previously. The data of figure 29.4 are used as a kernel from which to generate corrupted data sets with varying probabilities of error and varying numbers of irrelevant attributes. As shown in figure 29.9, the generator selects an entity at random from the 24 cases, randomly changes the decision according to a prescribed probability, and adds a prescribed number of irrelevant binary attributes with random values. Induct is then run on the data set with 5000 items, 4999 items, and so on, until the data set fails to generate rules giving correct performance. This is done 10 times for different data sets generated with the same parameters to give estimates of the mean and standard deviation of the size of the data set required to generate correct performance for different forms and levels of distortion.

Figure 29.10 shows the results obtained to date with a variation from 6 to over 1000 data items being needed to cover the spectrum of knowledge availability previously specified in levels 1 through 7. It is interesting to note that high levels of noise can

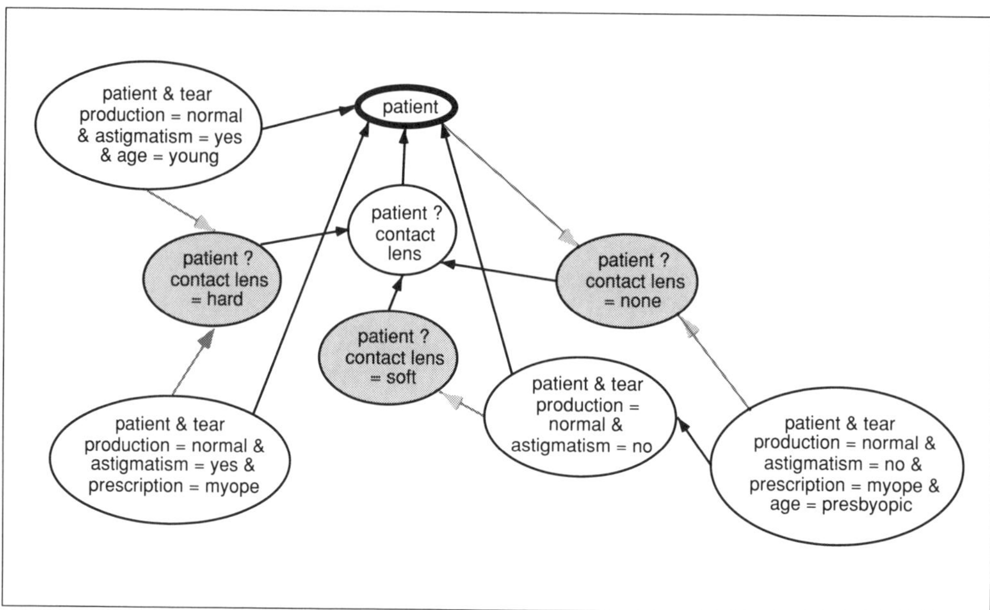

Figure 29.8
Conceptual Structure Generated from Default Rules.

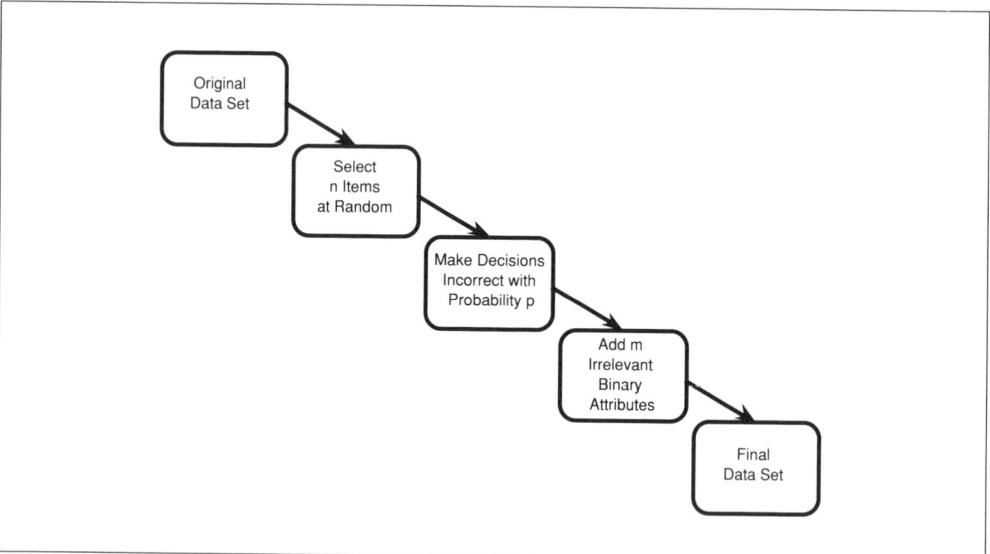

Figure 29.9
Data Set Generation for Empirical Studies of Knowledge-Data Trade-off.

Knowledge	*Data Required*	
	Mean	S.D.[1]
Exact rules	5	0
Critical cases	14	0
Correct cases	90	43
10% Errors	123	49
25% Errors	326	159
1 Irrelevant Att.[2]	160	77
2 Irrelevant Atts.	241	125
5 Irrelevant Atts.	641	352
10% Err.[3]+ 1 Irr.Att.[4]	1970	1046

1 S.D. = Standard deviation.
2 Alt. = Attribute.
3 Err. = Error.
4 Irr. Alt. = Irrelevant attribute.

Figure 29.10
Data-Knowledge Trade-Off.

be tolerated—the expert by no means has to be 100-percent correct, only better than chance. Noisy irrelevant attributes cause similar effects to noise in the decision, which seems to validate claims that knowledge-acquisition tools targeted on eliciting relevant attributes are in themselves worthwhile. There is strong interaction between errors and irrelevancy—much more data are required to eliminate both than either alone.

Figure 29.11 shows the same results used to define a measure of knowledge in terms of the logarithm of the data required to achieve it. The moral from figures 29.10 and 29.11 is not that expertise transfer is better than empirical induction, although the direct entry of overt knowledge is clearly highly ergonomic if it is available. It is rather that both techniques are capable of producing equivalent quality knowledge, and there is a continuum between them in which knowledge is traded for data. The knowledge of the database designer is implicit in the distinctions made and the data selected and can be made explicit through induction.

Figure 29.11 can be used to analyze the various knowledge acquisition techniques now in use:

Direct Entry of Knowledge: In terms of expertise transfer at the extreme bottom left, graphic editors providing direct access to semantic-network representations, allowing knowledge to be encoded in frames and rules, provide the most common development environment for knowledge-based systems. They are part of the application-programming support environment of most expert system shells, and the widespread availability of

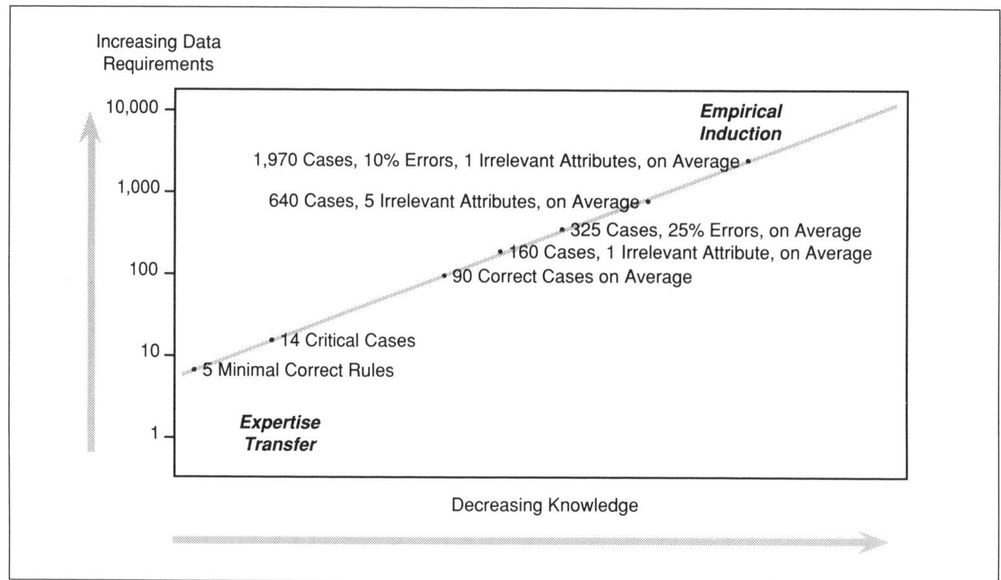

Figure 29.11
Knowledge-Data Trade-off in Expertise Transfer and Empirical Induction

modern graphic workstations has made it possible to provide excellent knowledge visualization environments. Examples are Mole (Eshelman et al. 1987); Knack (Klinker et al. 1987); Salt (Marcus 1987); Ontos (Monarch and Nirenburg 1987); Cognosys (Woodward 1990); Code (Skuce, Shenkang, and Beauville 1989); and techniques directly supporting domain ontologies, such as Kads (Breuker and Wielinga 1987).

Empirical Induction: In terms of empirical induction at the extreme top right, ID3 derivatives have long been commercially available. This chapter discussed some recent developments, such as C4.5, Prism, and Induct, and this book gives many more examples.

Repertory Grids: When the expert is not able to directly enter overt knowledge but is available for consultation, a variety of expertise transfer techniques that operate in the lower left region of figure 29.11. Most notable are *repertory grid techniques,* which attempt to elicit relevant distinctions and critical cases and build conceptual structures and rules using inductive tools to analyze these. Examples are Planet (Shaw and Gaines 1983), ETS (Boose 1984), Aquinas (Boose and Bradshaw 1987), Kriton (Diederich, Ruhmann, and May 1987), Kitten (Shaw and Gaines 1987), and KSS0 (Gaines and Shaw 1987).

Thus, the three major families of knowledge-acquisition tools currently in use are complementary alternatives that should be selected on the basis of appropriateness to the type, quality, and quantity of expertise and data available. Widely applicable tools have to be based on integrating the underlying methodologies to provide appropriate techniques for any particular situation. In large-scale system development, it might be expected that the nature and availability of expertise and data will vary within subdomains of the same problem.

29.6 Conclusions

In theoretical terms, the approach taken in this chapter seems to offer the possibility of developing a quantitative science of knowledge in terms of the amount of data reduction that knowledge buys us when carrying out empirical induction. This can be seen as a reasonably principled economic evaluation of the knowledge. The studies in this chapter are empirical using a particular situation. It should be possible to obtain some analytic results for more general cases.

In practical terms, the approach taken in this chapter integrates, into a coherent framework, many of the different approaches being taken to knowledge acquisition, from those based on expert interviews to those based on empirical induction. The trade-off data are a guide for practitioners to the appropriate approach and data requirements in their situations—it needs testing with other data sets, but this testing is now a matter of sheer number crunching. I hope the results in this chapter will encourage others to run similar experiments with their inductive methodologies and report the resulting trade-off plots. In design terms, the most important results obtained are that a single inductive algorithm is adequate to cover the complete spectrum of levels 1 through 7 of expertise, from rule simplification to noise reduction and relevancy determination, and that it is possible to generate an integrated system that ranges across this spectrum, from the transfer of expertise from experts to the creation of equivalent expertise through empirical induction.

What is particularly interesting about the trade-off graph in figure 29.11 is that it shows it is possible to commence with a wide variety of data sets of widely varying qualities and, with a single algorithm, arrive back at the concise, humanly understandable knowledge structure of figure 29.8. This is the basis of the concept of knowledge discovery from databases. Whether there is knowledge to be discovered in a database depends on the expertise of those who provided its structure and content.

Acknowledgments

Financial assistance for this work has been made available by the Natural Sciences and Engineering Research Council of Canada. I am grateful to many colleagues for discussions over the years that have influenced this chapter. In particular, I would like to thank John Boose, Jeff Bradshaw, Brent Krawchuk, Mildred Shaw, and Ross Quinlan for access to their research and many stimulating discussions. Brent Krawchuk originally discovered the optimum five-rule solution to the contact lens problem in his research on inductive methods.

References

Boose, J . H. 1986. *Expertise Transfer for Expert System Design.* New York: Elsevier.

Boose, J. H. 1984. Personal Construct Theory and the Transfer of Human Expertise. In *Proceedings of the Fourth National Conference on Artificial Intelligence*, 27–33. Menlo Park, Calif.: American Association for Artificial Intelligence.

Boose, J. H., and Bradshaw, J. M. 1987. Expertise Transfer and Complex Problems: Using AQUINAS as a Knowledge Acquisition Workbench for Knowledge-Based Systems. *International Journal of Man-Machine Studies* 26(1): 3–28.

Boose, J. H., and Gaines, B. R., eds., 1988. *Knowledge Acquisition Tools for Expert Systems.* London: Academic.

Borgida, A.; Brachman, R. J.; McGuiness, D. L.; and Resnick, L. A.1989. CLASSIC: A Structural Data Model for Objects. In Proceedings of 1989 ACM SIGMOD International Conference on the Management of Data, eds. J. Clifford, B. Lindsay, and D. Maier, 58–67. New York: Association for Computing Machinery.

Breuker, J., and Wielinga, B. 1987. Use of Models in the Interpretation of Verbal Data. In *Knowledge Elicitation for Expert Systems: A Practical Handbook*, ed. A. Kidd, 17–44. New York: Plenum.

Cendrowska, J. 1987. An Algorithm for Inducing Modular Rules. *International Journal of Man-Machine Studies* 27(4): 349–370.

Diederich, J.; Ruhmann, I.; and May, M. 1987. KRITON: A Knowledge Acquisition Tool for Expert Systems. *International Journal of Man-Machine Studies* 26(1): 29 40.

Eshelman, L.; Ehret, D.; McDermott, J.; and Tan, M. 1987. MOLE: A Tenacious Knowledge Acquisition Tool. *International Journal of Man-Machine Studies* 26(1): 41–54.

Gaines, B. R. 1990. An Architecture for Integrated Knowledge Acquisition Systems. In Proceedings of the Fifth AAAI Knowledge Acquisition for Knowledge-Based Systems Workshop, 8-1–8-22. Menlo Park, Calif.: American Association for Artificial Intelligence.

Gaines, B. R. 1987a. An Overview of Knowledge Acquisition and Transfer. *International Journal of Man-Machine Studies* 26(4):453–472.

Gaines, B. R. 1987b. Rapid Prototyping for Expert Systems. In *Intelligent Manufacturing: Proceedings from First International Conference on Expert Systems and the Leading Edge in Production Planning and Control*, ed. M. D. Oliff, 45–73. Menlo Park, Calif.: Benjamin Cummings.

Gaines, B. R., and Boose, J. H., eds. 1988. *Knowledge Acquisition for Knowledge-Based Systems*. London: Academic.

Gaines, B. R., and Shaw, M. L. G. 1987. Knowledge Support Systems. In *ACM MCC-University Research Symposium*, 47–66. MCC Corp., Austin, Tex.

Klinker, G.; Bentolila, J.; Genetet, S.; Grimes, M.; and McDermott, J. 1987. KNACK—Report-Driven Knowledge Acquisition. *International Journal of Man-Machine Studies* 26(1):65–79.

Marcus, S. 1987. Taking Backtracking with a Grain of SALT. *International Journal of Man-Machine Studies* 26(4):383–398.

Monarch, I. and Nirenburg, S. 1987. The Role of Ontology in Concept Acquisition for Knowledge-Based Systems. In Proceedings of the First European Workshop on Knowledge Acquisition for Knowledge-Based Systems (EKAW'87), Reading Univ., United Kingdom, September.

Quinlan, J. R. 1987. Simplifying Decision Trees. *International Journal of Man-Machine Studies* 27(3): 221–234.

Quinlan, J. R. 1986. Induction of Decision Trees. *Machine Learning* 1(1):81–106.

Quinlan, J. R.; Compton, P. J.; Horn, K. A.; and Lazarus, L. 1987. Inductive Knowledge Acquisition: a Case Study. In *Artificial Intelligence and Expert Systems*, ed. J. R. Quinlan, 157–173. Sydney: Addison-Wesley.

Shaw, M. L. G., 1980. *On Becoming a Personal Scientist*. London: Academic.

Shaw, M. L. G., and Gaines, B. R. 1987. KITTEN: Knowledge Initiation and Transfer Tools for Experts and Novices. *International Journal of Man-Machine Studies* 27:251–280.

Shaw, M. L. G., and Gaines, B. R. 1983. A Computer Aid to Knowledge Engineering. In Proceedings of British Computer Society Conference on Expert Systems, 263–271. London: British Computer Society.

Skuce, D.; Shenkang, W.; and Beauville, Y. 1989. A Generic Knowledge Acquisition Environment for Conceptual and Ontological Analysis. In Proceedings of the Fourth AAAI Knowledge Acquisition for Knowledge-Based Systems Workshop, 31-1–31-20. Menlo Park, Calif.: American Association for Artificial Intelligence.

Woodward, B. 1990. Knowledge Engineering at the Front-End: Defining the Domain. *Knowledge Acquisition* 2(1): 73–94.

30 Knowledge Discovery as a Threat to Database Security

Daniel E. O'Leary
University of Southern California

Abstract

This chapter investigates the affect of knowledge discovery from databases on the security of databases. First, it examines the current concern with database systems for security from knowledge discovery. Second, this chapter discusses some of the potential security risks associated with knowledge discovery. Third, some potential structure for the development of controls for such systems is examined. It is suggested that the technology itself and the voluntary or involuntary nature of the unauthorized disclosure form a basis for analysis. Fourth, the quality of database security in general is stressed as an important set of controls to secure against knowledge discovery. Finally, it is noted that any set of controls should be compared with the benefit derived from these controls. Security can be established; however, it is important not to forget that ease for the decision maker is one of the primary reasons for creating and maintaining the database.

30.1 Introduction

Knowledge acquisition is regularly referred to as a bottleneck in the development of expert systems and other knowledge-based systems. When accomplished through the use of a knowledge engineer and expert interaction, substantial time and resources are often required to develop the appropriate knowledge base. Even then, there is always this concern: Does the expert say what s/he does or do what s/he says? Based on articles that have appeared in, for example, the *Wall Street Journal*, it might be that experts do not always make decisions using the information that they say they use. At any rate, the implication from a security perspective is that knowledge possessed by experts is secure to a certain extent. In addition, the expert has at least some control over the flow of knowledge to others.

As a result of increasing efforts to induce knowledge from existing data and, thus, lessen dependence on expressed expert knowledge, there have been improvements in the technology of knowledge acquisition from data. Although such advances might yield a whole new class of data-derived expert systems, they also raise potential security difficulties. The intent and the practice of knowledge discovery as discussed in detail throughout this book suggest that those who have access to a database might be able to extract from it (by discovery) knowledge that the database owners would consider to be proprietary or secret. From the point of view of the database owner, such knowledge could be regarded as improperly acquired knowledge or unauthorized knowledge. (In the future, courts might deem it to be illegally acquired knowledge.) This gives rise to security concerns that are different from the concerns associated with traditional database security. These security risks and the corresponding controls are the focus of this chapter.

This chapter begins by demonstrating that knowledge acquisition from databases can be a major security problem by examining the consequences of unauthorized knowledge discovery. The Current Focus of Database Security section suggests that issues of knowledge acquisition from databases are not currently addressed. The fourth section, Security of Databases, examines current approaches to the security of database systems, including the use of knowledge discovery by these approaches. Methods and Limitations of Knowledge Discovery assesses some of the limitations of knowledge acquisition from data and then discusses the uses of these limitations as a basis for the development of controls. The next section suggests that the security concerns related to knowledge discovery from data can be investigated in terms of voluntary and involuntary disclosures and that the security controls associated with each might be different. Two subsequent sections treat some approaches to security with voluntary disclosures and examine the problems of involuntary disclosure. Finally, the last section offers a brief summary of the chapter and provides some extensions.

30.2 Consequences of Unauthorized Knowledge Discovery

Unauthorized knowledge discovery from a database can have several negative outcomes for the owner, depending on the contents of the particular database. These consequences derive primarily from an outside agent's ability to determine how the database is used in decision making.

First, given a database of characteristics and resulting decisions, an outsider might find that the owner's decisions are being made improperly or possibly illegally. For example, many applications gather information that is indirectly related to the characteristics of individual job applicants, and jobs can be granted or not granted on the basis of these characteristics. Typically, the name of an applicant contains a box for "Mr.," "Mrs.," or "Ms." Alternatively, names often indicate whether a person is male or female. If such information is captured in a database, then knowledge discovery techniques can be used to determine the relationship of the values to the ultimate disposition of applications. Although less offensive examples exist, this example does demonstrate the point: Knowledge discovery can be the basis for litigation or blackmail.

Second, the relationship between characteristics and decisions can be used by outsiders to develop unauthorized insights into decision making by database users. For example, auditors and judges are likely to base decisions on certain characteristics when determining whether a financial document should receive further attention or whether a guilty verdict should be issued. If an audit client has access to such a database, insights could be obtained to camouflage activity or change a decision. Auditor clients could then work around the rules established by auditors: If an auditor would audit a document only if it concerned an expenditure of more than $1000, then any illegal transaction would likely be for less than $1000. Further, cases could be constructed by attorneys so that judges would only see the appropriate responses. Thus, unauthorized or illegal knowledge acquisition can destroy established control relationships in various organizational settings.

Third, access to a database of decisions could provide insights that would allow the user to exploit future decision making. For example, transactions by a stockbroker could be anticipated if it were known which variables affected which decisions. Similarly, business strategies could be preempted by competitors who knew which decision variables were used. Thus, unauthorized knowledge acquisition can help to destroy a "level playing field."

These and, possibly, other consequences indicate the importance of considering knowledge discovery from databases as a major security issue. Unfortunately, maybe because of the relatively recent advent of knowledge-acquisition technology, current thinking about databases does not explicitly consider this issue in respect to security.

30.3 The Current Focus of Database Security

Ullman (1982) indicates that "we need to protect against both undesired modification or destruction of data and against unauthorized reading of data" (p. 355). With increasing knowledge discovery capabilities, a third type of protection is also deserving of attention: protection against undesired or unauthorized extraction of knowledge from data.

Protection against unauthorized extraction differs from protection against undesired modification because those interested in unauthorized knowledge acquisition would not likely change or destroy the data because it could lead to discovering the unauthorized knowledge extraction. Further, there is no reason to assume that protection against database changes or destruction will secure the system against all types of unauthorized knowledge acquisition.

Protection against unauthorized extraction also differs from protection against the reading of data. Legitimate users must be able to read the data; for example, they might need to read the data to accomplish their job responsibilities. However, at some point, they might be interested in unauthorized knowledge acquisition. Thus, eliminating the ability to read data might not be feasible in protecting against unauthorized knowledge acquisition because the threat might be posed by authorized personnel. This possibility suggests that additional security arrangements (controls) should be made to accommodate the need for protection against unauthorized knowledge extraction. This is not to understate the importance of general database security. In fact, as discussed later, general database security is an important control against unauthorized knowledge acquisition from data.

However, because knowledge acquisition is a different issue, it should be examined as its own source of control problems. As such, there are at least two sets of issues to examine. First, the technology associated with knowledge acquisition from data can be the source of limitations that can form the basis of some controls (Methods and Limitations of Knowledge Discovery: The Case of Rule Induction). Second, knowledge acquisition from data can be different from other database problems for a variety of reasons: For example, knowledge can be acquired from either voluntarily or involuntarily released data (Voluntary and Involuntary Disclosures).

30.4 Security of Databases: Alternative Approaches

The nature of the security risks discussed earlier suggests that once the damage is done, it might be too late to correct the problem of unauthorized knowledge acquisition. Although corrective steps such as litigation might be initiated, major efforts should be aimed at preventing and further detecting unauthorized knowledge acquisition.

To some extent, controls aimed at preventing unauthorized access can function as preventative controls against unwanted knowledge acquisition. Thus, some control is afforded by general database security that uses traditional methods, such as passwords and other approaches that are relatively new. In some cases, these new approaches use knowledge discovery to assist in the adaptive securing of the database system.

30.4.1 Views for Multilevel Database Security

Denning et al. (1987) develop a multilevel secure relational database model. This model has several critical aspects. First, they "explicitly allow the specification of derived data in a database schema so that the relationships between stored and derived data can be formally expressed" (p. 129). Second, they distinguish between views that retrieve data (access views) and views that classify data (classification constraints). Third, aggregation constraints serve to define and control the access to aggregates of information.

The design presented in Denning et al. (1987) is a sophisticated database security system to prevent unauthorized database access and change. Unfortunately, in published versions of this model, it does not appear that the system is designed to learn. Thus, the design does not include a knowledge-acquisition component. Further, the model does not appear to provide explicit concern for knowledge discovery from the database. Instead, the focus is on the protection of information and information about the information.

30.4.2 Intrusion-Detection Models

Intrusion-detection models are generally aimed at determining either when an unauthorized user is attempting to access the system or has entered the system or when an authorized user has exceeded the authorization level or is attempting to exceed the authorization level. Thus, the models are primarily preventative or detective. For example, if a user is trying to break into a system, then s/he would generate an abnormally high rate of password failures; the system would thus be alerted. The objective of of intrusion-detection systems (Denning 1987; Tenor 1988) is to detect a wide range of security violations, from unauthorized abuses by insiders to attempted break-ins by outsiders. These systems typically assume that the system or database is being exploited if use is abnormal.

This approach requires that a system can determine what is normal and abnormal use. Typically, these systems use a set of characteristics to define normal behavior profiles. The system then compares a user's actual behavior with these profiles to determine normality or abnormality. Based on its findings, it then takes some type of corrective action. Typically, these systems use both rule-based and statistical methods in their examination of user and system behavior. In addition, some (Tenor 1988) use a learning component designed to keep the system adaptive.

30.5 Methods and Limitations of Knowledge Discovery: The Case of Rule Induction

As previously noted, one of the potential variables in database security is the actual technology used in knowledge discovery. Limitations in the technology can form the basis for controls aimed to exploit these limitations. One of the primary approaches to knowledge discovery is *rule induction*, or learning from examples. Rule induction is the process of discovering decision-making rules from data. Rule induction from databases can be divided into at least two different categories: statistically oriented approaches (Quinlan 1983) and symbolic manipulation approaches (Mitchell 1977; Michalski and Chilausky 1980).

30.5.1 Limitations of Techniques

One of the primary limitations of any rule-induction system is the degree of nonstationarity in the database: Do the relationships in the data change over time? If the relationships change, then rules extracted from the data should also change.

There are also limitations associated with specific methods of rule induction (Goodman and Smyth 1988). First, statistical techniques cannot easily deal with incremental learning. Typically, given new information, a new decision tree must be designed each time the same data are examined. Second, although symbolic techniques typically include learning from new information as a basic mechanism, they do not handle noise in the data well.

30.5.2 Implications for Database Security

These and other limitations can form the basis for controls that assist in the development of databases that are more secure against knowledge discovery. First, consider the limitation of being nonstationary. Some types of decision-making information are secure if the process is nonstationary, depending on the type of security consequence (Consequences of Unauthorized Knowledge Discovery). Because of the ongoing change in such a system, competitors would rarely be able to obtain enough knowledge to build a system that could anticipate current decision-making rules for competitive advantage.

Although it might assist decision making, removing nonstationarity from data might have a negative affect on the security of this database. As a result, it is important to build smoothing approaches into specific application programs, rather than the databases, thus putting another level of security into the database.

In addition, in some situations, it might be beneficial to take steps to make the database appear to be nonstationary when it isn't. Such an approach might make it seem that the database is inappropriate for rule induction. Implementation of this feature could be placed in the application software used to access the database, which would protect the system when the offenders access the database directly. In other cases, however, the lack of stationarity might not provide a level of security because historical insights might be derived. These, too, can be evidence for, or point to, illegalities or anomalies in management.

Second, that incremental learning is difficult for statistical methods implies that nonstationarity increases the cost of unauthorized knowledge discovery and, thus, discourages such activity. If the database is frequently updated, and it is nonstationary, then it can be costly to update the discovered knowledge using statistical techniques. Alternatively, if the knowledge base is not frequently updated, and the database is nonstationary, then the knowledge discovery will often be outdated. However, if the database is stationary, then the frequency of updating will not likely have any impact on the data relationships that an intruder is trying to elicit, except that the intruder would not necessarily know whether the relationships are nonstationary. Thus, infrequent updates might discourage knowledge acquisition from data.

Third, as previously noted, symbolic techniques do not handle noise well. Thus, in some situations it might be appropriate to build noise into the database to establish system security, possibly by using false but identifiable records, or performing some form of operation on database elements to disguise the contents. The controls suggested by these limitations can be combined with others so that a collection of approaches is used to secure individual databases.

30.6 Voluntary and Involuntary Disclosures

Another major factor related to securing databases against unauthorized knowledge discovery is the nature of the ultimate disclosure of the data by the user: voluntary or involuntary. Whether the data are disclosed voluntarily or involuntarily can affect the security measures taken to mitigate the risks.

If the data are disclosed on a voluntary basis, perhaps to fulfill regulatory requirements (as is the case with accounting data disclosed to the Securities and Exchange Commission), it can be a signal to some group or subgroup of disclosees of some behavior of a firm or it might be explicit evidence of a firm's actions. In the first instance, it is assumed that the data have some meaning to the user. Typically, the extent and format of the data presentation are dictated. In the last two instances, the firm is dependent on the user to determine meaning from the data. Effectively, the user of the data must obtain some knowledge from it. The building of expert systems or knowledge-based systems is a relatively new type of voluntary data disclosure. Here, data are provided to a group of knowledge engineers or statisticians, and they are expected to find knowledge in the data.

If the data disclosure is involuntary, the disclosure can be accidental, or legitimate users might purposely obtain the data in an illegal manner. In any case, involuntary data disclosure can be used by the acquiring party to obtain insight into decision-making processes. Whether disclosure of data is involuntary or voluntary, if the data are used to build an expert system, the effect of the disclosure is limited to the extent to which technology exists for knowledge discovery from data.

30.6.1 Voluntary Disclosure

The voluntary disclosure of information is done for a number of reasons, which are largely beyond the scope of this chapter. However, a number of issues are of concern as a result of the voluntary nature of disclosure, particularly in those cases where regulatory concerns do not spell out disclosure requirements in detail, and substantial discretion is given to the discloser. First, the level of detail disclosed might provide the user of the data with too many insights and too much knowledge. Second, the voluntarily disclosured information can be assembled to determine undisclosed information. At least one system has been built to assist with these concerns, although it primarily deals with the second issue.

Rule-Based Systems: Edaas Edaas (expert disclosure analysis and avoidance system) is an expert system used by the Environmental Protection Agency (EPA). Edaas (Feinstein and Siems 1985) is designed to advise on the disclosure of confidential business information (CBI).

Chemical manufacturers, importers, and processors submit detailed information to EPA on thousands of chemical substances used in commerce. EPA has instituted security procedures to prevent the direct release of this information. However, if a request for information is not sensitive, then EPA tries to honor the request unless the information can be combined with other nonsensitive information to too closely estimate sensitive data protected under federal nondisclosure law. For example, this indirect disclosure could be used to estimate particular expenditures and, thus, might be used to estimate corporate strategies or research and development plans.

Edaas contains two separate knowledge bases, each represented in a different way. Rules are used to represent the specific law concerning information release. Another knowledge base contains known relationships between pieces of company-related CBI and non-CBI data.

Edaas includes about 60,000 chemicals in the database and has 30 categories of chemical data. For each class of chemical and category of data, there are approximately 11 rules; the system has about 200,000 rules. Clearly, the maintenance associated with such a large system of rules takes on monstrous proportions because an induction approach was not used.

Limitations of Rule-Based Approaches Systems such as Edaas suggest that rules for monitoring the security of databases could be developed. Unfortunately, such an approach might require a different set of rules for each database. Further, a rule-based approach can rapidly become outdated as new knowledge discovery techniques are elicited. Finally, such an approach can require substantial resources to develop and maintain such a system.

30.6.2 Involuntary Disclosure

As previously noted, one of the primary security concerns with illegal knowledge discovery lies in the involuntary disclosure of information. Control over such disclosure can take either a traditional or a nontraditional approach (for example, intrusion-detection methods).

Traditional Approaches As previously discussed, potentially important in establishing databases that are secure against knowledge discovery are traditional approaches, such as limiting physical or logical access using passwords or other vehicles (Denning et al. 1987) to establish hierarchical access to databases.

Use of Intrusion-Detection Models To date, no intrusion-detection models have been developed to protect databases against knowledge discovery intrusions. However, an intrusion-detection approach could be used to assist in this process.

Certain behavior might suggest that a user is going to try to extract knowledge from a database. For example, if a user is planning to induce knowledge from data, then one of the following approaches might be likely:

First, normal use of any database is unlikely to require examination of an entire record and its hierarchically related contents for a large number of records, yet such a database perusal would be one way to manually generate sufficient data for an induction program.

Second, a user interested in unauthorized induction can dump the database contents to hard copy for later use. In this case, the profiles developed from previous models would be useful. For example, Denning (1987) suggests that the leakage of data by a legitimate user can be detected by noting which users log onto the system at unusual times or route data to remote printers not normally used. In addition, the dumping of a database might be reason enough to arouse suspicion.

Third, a user could dump the data to a file for further processing. Because the database has the information in it, such large-scale dumping would be considered abnormal; thus, the security system could track and monitor such events.

Further, as is currently the case with some systems, not only should users be required to have authorization but also programs. An authorized user could not then use the database in conjunction with an induction program to tease knowledge from the database. Thus, unauthorized program use of a database would not be permitted, or it would be tracked by the system.

30.7 Summary and Extensions

This chapter examined the kinds of risks that might differentiate knowledge acquisition from databases from other security risks. Existing and potential opportunities for the security of database systems from knowledge acquisition were also studied.

Clearly, the sources of controls include general database security controls, primarily those aimed at the prevention and detection of unauthorized use. However, some additional controls can come from the technology of knowledge discovery. Limitations in the technology can be used against the technology.

Additionally, a useful structure for the overall set of controls is based on the voluntary or involuntary nature of the database disclosures. Systems can be developed to focus on the particular needs that derive from the voluntary or involuntary nature of the disclosures. AI-based systems and learning systems can be developed as controls.

In any case, a set of several controls is likely to result in the best security for the system. Unfortunately, some steps that ensure the security of the database might have a negative impact on decision makers. As a result, a cost-benefit analysis is clearly necessary.

30.8 References

Denning, D. 1987. An Intrusion-Detection Model. *IEEE Transactions on Software Engineering* SE-13(2).

Denning, D.; Akl, S.; Heckman, M.; Lunt, T.; Morgenstern, M.; Neumann, P.; and Schell, R. 1987. Views for Multilevel Database Security. *IEEE Transactions on Software Engineering* SE-13(2).

Feinstein, J., and Siems, J. 1985. EDDAS: An Experimental System at the U.S. Environmental Protection Agency for Avoiding Disclosure of Confidential Business Information. *Expert Systems* 2(2): 72–85.

Goodman, R. and Smyth, P. 1988a. Automated Rule Acquisition. Presented at the Third AAAI Knowledge Acquisition Workshop, St. Paul, Minn.

Michalski, R. and Chilausky, R. 1980. Learning from Being Told and Learning from Examples. *International Journal of Policy Analysis and Information Systems* 4: 125–161.

Mitchell, T. 1977. Version Spaces: A Candidate Elimination Approach to Rule Learning. In Proceedings of the Fifth International Joint Conference on Artificial Intelligence, 305–310. Menlo Park, Calif.: International Joint Conferences on Artificial Intelligence.

Quinlan, R. 1983. Learning Efficient Classification Procedures and Their Application to Chess Endgames. In *Machine Learning: An Artificial Intelligence Approach*, eds. R. Michalski, J. Carbonell, and T. Mitchell. San Mateo, Calif.: Morgan Kaufman.

Tenor, W. 1988. Expert Systems for Computer Security. *Expert Systems Review* 1(2).

Ullman, J. 1982. *Principles of Database Systems*. Rockville, Md.: Computer Science.

Index

Gregory Piatetsky-Shapiro

Dr. Gregory Piatetsky-Shapiro is a principal investigator of the Knowledge Discovery in Databases project at GTE Laboratories, Waltham, Massachusetts. He is working on developing an interactive discovery system that integrates multiple techniques, uses domain knowledge, and presents the results in a human-oriented way. Previously, he worked on intelligent interfaces to multiple heterogeneous databases, and on relational database systems for financial applications. Gregory's 1984 Ph.D. dissertation from New York University on "Self-Organizing Database Systems" has received NYU award for best dissertation in Sciences.

Gregory organized and chaired IJCAI-89 and AAAI-91 KDD workshops. He has over twenty publications in the areas of artificial intelligence and databases.

William Frawley

Dr. William Frawley has worked in the field of artificial intelligence since 1977. At the Schlumberger-Doll Research Center, he established the first industrial AI research team and was responsible for Gamma, a knowledge-based system for the interpretation of gamma ray spectra, and the Dipmeter Advisor, an expert system for subsurface geological interpretation. At the Mitre Corporation he was a member and leader of the Knowledge Based Systems Group which produced Knobs, a resource allocation and natural language system for tactical air mission planning.

At GTE Laboratories he established a machine learning research department and is currently the principal investigator of the Distributed Cooperating Learning Systems Project.